Exploring Java™

THE JAVA™ SERIES

Exploring Java™

Java™ Threads

Java™ Network Programming

Java™ Virtual Machine

Java™ AWT Reference

Java™ Language Reference

Java™ Fundamental Classes Reference

Database Programming with JDBC™ and Java™

Developing Java Beans™

Also from O'Reilly

Java™ in a Nutshell

Java™ in a Nutshell, Deluxe Edition

Java™ Examples in a Nutshell

Netscape IFC in a Nutshell

Exploring Java™

Second Edition

Patrick Niemeyer & Joshua Peck

O'REILLY™

Cambridge · *Köln* · *Paris* · *Sebastopol* · *Tokyo*

Exploring Java, Second Edition

by Patrick Niemeyer and Joshua Peck

Copyright © 1997, 1996 O'Reilly & Associates, Inc. All rights reserved.
Printed in the United States of America.

Published by O'Reilly & Associates, Inc., 101 Morris Street, Sebastopol, CA 95472.

Editors: Mike Loukides and Paula Ferguson

Production Editors: Mary Anne Weeks Mayo and Nancy Crumpton

Printing History:

May 1996:	First Edition
September 1997:	Second Edition

This book is printed on acid-free paper with 85% recycled content, 15% post-consumer waste. O'Reilly & Associates is committed to using paper with the highest recycled content available consistent with high quality.

ISBN: 1-56592-271-9 [4/99]

This book is dedicated to those who fight for our freedom of speech and its realization in a free and independent Internet.

Table of Contents

Preface

This book is about the Java™ language and programming environment. If you've been at all active on the Internet in the past few years, you've heard a lot about Java. It's one of the most exciting developments in the history of the Internet, rivaling the creation of the World Wide Web. Java became the darling of the Internet programming community as soon as the alpha version was released. Immediately, thousands of people were writing Java applets to add to their Web pages. Interest in Java only grew with time, and support for Java in Netscape Navigator guaranteed it would be a permanent part of the Net scene.

What, then, is Java? Java is a language for network programming that was developed by Sun Microsystems. It's already in widespread use for creating animated and interactive Web pages. However, this is only the start. The Java language and environment are rich enough to support entirely new kinds of applications, like dynamically extensible browsers and mobile agents. There are entirely new kinds of computer platforms being developed around Java (handheld devices and network computers) that download all their software over the network. In the coming years, we'll see what Java is capable of doing; fancy Web pages are fun and interesting, but they certainly aren't the end of the story. If Java is successful (and that isn't a foregone conclusion), it could change the way we think about computing in fundamental ways.

This book sets out to give you a head start on a lot of Java fundamentals. *Exploring Java* attempts to live up to its name by mapping out the Java language, its class libraries, programming techniques, and idioms. We'll dig deep into interesting areas, and at least scratch the surface of the rest. Other titles in the O'Reilly & Associates Java Series will pick up where we leave off and provide more comprehensive information on specific areas and applications of Java.

Whenever possible, we'll provide meaningful, realistic examples and avoid cataloging features. The examples are simple but hint at what can be done. We won't be developing the next great "killer Internet app" in these pages, but we hope to give you a starting point for many hours of experimentation and tinkering that will lead you to learn more on your own.

The Past Year

A lot has happened in the year since the first edition of this book. We're now up to release 1.1.3 of Java, which has many more features than the 1.0 release. Java 1.1 adds many, many new features, in addition to many extensions, to the features of Java 1.0. It's clear that Java is changing the way we think about computing in fundamental ways; we don't regret that prophecy at all. It's becoming more and more clear as time goes on that Java is central to the way software will be written in the future.

This second edition of *Exploring Java* tries to give you the flavor of Java 1.1. We have uncompromisingly rooted out all deprecated features from Java 1.0 in favor of the newer ways of doing things. For example, the chapters covering AWT all use the new Java 1.1 event model; we will mention the 1.0 event model only to describe the motivation for the new model and to illustrate some differences. The current tools are far superior to the old ones; we see no need for nostalgia.

There is a great deal of new material in this edition of the book. We have rearranged things a bit, adding seven new chapters. The new material expands coverage from the first edition and adds many completely new topics like Java Beans, RMI, and the new AWT event model. Java is growing by leaps and bounds; but as much as we want to cover it all, we have tried to keep this book to a size that's managable and readable.

Audience

This book is for computer professionals, students, technical people, and Finnish hackers. It's for everyone who has a need for hands-on experience with the Java language with an eye towards building real applications. This book could also be considered a crash course in object-oriented programming; as you learn about Java, you'll also learn a powerful and practical approach to object-oriented software development.

Superficially, Java looks like C or C++, so you'll be in the best position to use this book if you've some experience with one of these languages. If you do not, you might want to reference books like O'Reilly's *Practical C Programming* for a more thorough treatment of basic C syntax. However, don't make too much of the syntactic similarities between Java and C or C++. In many respects, Java acts like more dynamic languages such as Smalltalk and Lisp. Knowledge of another object-oriented programming language should certainly help, although you may have to change some ideas and unlearn a few habits. Java is considerably simpler than languages like C++ and Smalltalk.

Much of the interest in Java has centered around World Wide Web applets. Although we encourage you to take a broader view, you would have every right to be disappointed if we ignored the Web. Much of the book does discuss Java as a language for World Wide Web applications, so you should be familiar with the basic ideas behind Web browsers, servers, and Web documents.

Using This Book

This book divides roughly as follows:

- Chapters 1 and 2 provide a basic introduction to Java concepts and a tutorial to give you a jump start on Java programming.

- Chapter 3 discusses tools for developing with Java (the compiler, the interpreter, the JAR file package). It also covers important concepts such as embedding Java code in HTML support and object signing.

- Chapters 4 through 8 describe the Java language itself. Chapter 8 covers the language's thread facilities, which should be of particular interest to advanced programmers.

- Chapters 9 and 10 cover much of the core API. Chapter 9 describes basic utilities, and Chapter 10 covers I/O facilities.

- Chapters 11 and 12 cover Java networking, including sockets, URLs, and RMI.

- Chapters 13 through 17 cover the Abstract Window Toolkit (AWT), which provides graphics and graphical user interface (GUI) support.

- Chapter 18 covers the JavaBeans component architecture.

If you're like us, you don't read books from front to back. If you are really like us, you usually don't read the preface at all. However, on the off chance that you will see this in time, here are a few suggestions.

If you are an experienced programmer who has to learn Java in the next five minutes, you are probably looking for the examples. You might want to start by glancing at the tutorial in Chapter 2. If that doesn't float your boat, you should at least look at the information in Chapter 3, which tells you how to use the compiler and interpreter, and gives you the basics of a standalone Java application. This should get you started.

Chapters 11 and 12 are essential if you are interested in writing advanced networked applications. This is probably the most interesting and important part of Java. Unfortunately, we are still waiting for the major Web browsers to incoporate many of the important 1.1 features and for HotJava to fulfill all of its promise. Until then, you can still write useful standalone applications for the Net. Maybe you'll write the browser we're waiting for.

Chapters 13 through 18 discuss Java's graphics features and component architecture. You will want to read this carefully if you are interested in Java applications for the Web.

Getting Wired

There are many online sources for information about Java. Sun Microsystem's official web site for Java topics is *http://www.javasoft.com/*; look here for the latest news, updates, and Java releases. *www.javasoft.com* is where you'll find the Java Development Kit (JDK), which includes the compiler, the interpreter, and other tools. Another good source of Java information, including free applets, utility classes, and applications, is the Gamelan site, run by EarthWeb; its URL is *http://www.gamelan.com/*.

You should also visit O'Reilly & Associates' Java site at *http://www.oreilly.com/publishing/java/*. There you'll find information about other books in O'Reilly's Java Series, and a pointer to the home page for *Exploring Java*, *http://www.oreilly.com/catalog/expjava2/*, where you'll find the source code and examples for this book.

The *comp.lang.java* newsgroup can be a good source of information, announcements, and a place to ask intelligent questions.

Conventions Used in This Book

The font conventions used in this book are quite simple.

Italic is used for:

- UNIX pathnames, filenames, and program names
- Internet addresses, such as domain names and URLs
- New terms where they are defined

Boldface is used for:

- Names of GUI buttons and menus

`Typewriter Font` is used for:

- Anything that might appear in a Java program, including method names, variable names, and class names

- Command lines and options that should be typed verbatim on the screen

- Tags that might appear in an HTML document

In the main body of text, we always use a pair of empty parentheses after a method name to distinguish methods from variables and other creatures.

In the Java source listings, we follow the coding conventions most frequently used in the Java community. Class names begin with capital letters; variable and method names begin with lowercase. All the letters in the names of constants are capitalized. We don't use underscores to separate words in a long name; following common practice, we capitalize individual words (after the first) and run the words together. For example: `thisIsAVariable`, `thisIsAMethod()`, `ThisIsAClass`, and `THISISACONSTANT`.

Acknowledgments

Many people contributed to putting this book together under a schedule that became increasingly rushed as time passed. Thanks to their efforts, we gave birth to something we can all be proud of.

Foremost we would like to thank Tim O'Reilly for giving us the opportunity to write this book. Special thanks to Mike Loukides, the series editor, whose endless patience and experience got us through the difficult parts, and to Paula Ferguson, whose organizational and editing abilities got the material into its final form. Jonathan Knudsen helped us update Chapters 8 and 9. We could not have asked for a more skillful or responsive team of people with whom to work.

Particular thanks are due to our technical reviewers: Andrew Cohen, Eric Raymond, and Lisa Farley. Jim Farley (not related) reviewed some of the material we added for the second edition. All of them gave thorough reviews that were invaluable in assembling the final draft. Eric contributed many bits of text that eventually found their way into the book.

Speaking of borrowings, the original version of the glossary came from David Flanagan's book, *Java in a Nutshell*. We also borrowed the class hierarchy diagrams from David's book. These diagrams were based on similar diagrams by Charles L. Perkins. His original diagrams are available at *http://rendezvous.com/java/*.

Thanks also to Marc Wallace and Steven Burkett for reading the book in progress. As for the crowd in St. Louis: a special thanks to LeeAnn Langdon of the Library Ltd. and Kerri Bonasch. Deepest thanks to Victoria Doerr for her patience and love. Finally, thanks for the support of the "lunch" crowd: Karl "Gooch" Stiefvater, Bryan "Butter" O'Connor, Brian "Brian" Gottlieb, and the rest of the clan at Washington University.

Many people in O'Reilly's production and design groups contributed their blood, sweat, and tears to the project. Mary Anne Weeks Mayo was production editor and copy editor, and had the stress-filled job of working under a very tight deadline with chapters arriving asynchronously (which means at random and later than expected). Seth Maislin wrote the index, and Stephen Spainhour adapted David Flanagan's glossary for this book. Chris Reilley converted rough diagrams into professional technical illustrations. Erik Ray, Ellen Siever, and Lenny Muellner converted HTML files into SGML and made sure we could convert electrons into paper without mishap. Lenny also implemented a new design for this book, which was created by Nancy Priest. Hanna Dyer created the back cover; Edie Freedman designed the front cover.

For the Second Edition, Mary Anne Weeks Mayo and Nancy Crumpton served as production editors. Robert Romano created new figures and juggled several sets of other figures to produce those you see in this edition.

1

Yet Another Language?

The greatest challenges and most exciting opportunities for software developers today lie in harnessing the power of networks. Applications created today, whatever their intended scope or audience, will almost certainly be run on machines linked by a global network of computing resources. The increasing importance of networks is placing new demands on existing tools, and fueling the demand for a rapidly growing list of completely new kinds of applications.

We want software that works—consistently, anywhere, on any platform—and that plays well with other applications. We want dynamic applications that take advantage of a connected world, capable of accessing disparate and distributed information sources. We want truly distributed software that can be extended and upgraded seamlessly. We want intelligent applications—like autonomous agents that can roam the Net for us, ferreting out information and serving as electronic emissaries. We know, to some extent, what we want. So why don't we have it?

The problem has been that the tools for building these applications have fallen short. The requirements of speed and portability have been, for the most part, mutually exclusive, and security has largely been ignored or misunderstood. There are truly portable languages, but they are mostly bulky, interpreted, and slow. These languages are popular as much for their high level functionality as for their portability. And there are fast languages, but they usually provide speed by binding themselves to particular platforms, so they can meet the portability issue only half way. There are even a few recent safe languages, but they are primarily offshoots of the portable languages and suffer from the same problems.

Enter Java

The Java programming language, developed at Sun Microsystems under the guidance of Net luminaries James Gosling and Bill Joy, is designed to be a machine-independent programming language that is both safe enough to traverse networks and powerful enough to replace native executable code. Java addresses the issues raised here and may help us start building the kinds of applications we want.

Right now, most of the enthusiasm for Java stems from its capabilities for building embedded applications for the World Wide Web; these applications are called *applets*. This book will teach you how to build applets. But there is more to Java than applets, and we'll also try to show you the "more." The book will also show you how to use the tools of Java to accomplish real programming tasks, such as building networked applications and creating functional user interfaces. By the end of the book, you will be able to use these tools to build powerful Java applets and standalone applications.

Java's Origins

The seeds of Java were planted in 1990 by Sun Microsystems patriarch and chief researcher, Bill Joy. Since Sun's inception in the early '80s, it has steadily pushed one idea: "The network is the computer." At the time though, Sun was competing in a relatively small workstation market, while Microsoft was beginning its domination of the more mainstream, Intel-based PC world. When Sun missed the boat on the PC revolution, Joy retreated to Aspen, Colorado, to work on advanced research. He was committed to accomplishing complex tasks with simple software, and founded the aptly named Sun Aspen Smallworks.

Of the original members of the small team of programmers assembled in Aspen, James Gosling is the one who will be remembered as the father of Java. Gosling first made a name for himself in the early '80s as the author of Gosling Emacs, the first version of the popular Emacs editor that was written in C and ran under UNIX. Gosling Emacs became popular, but was soon eclipsed by a free version, GNU Emacs, written by Emacs's original designer. By that time, Gosling had moved on to design Sun's NeWS window system, which briefly contended with the X Window System for control of the UNIX graphic user interface (GUI) desktop in 1987. While some people would argue that NeWS was superior to X, NeWS lost out because Sun kept it proprietary and didn't publish source code, while the primary developers of X formed the X Consortium and took the opposite approach.

Designing NeWS taught Gosling the power of integrating an expressive language with a network-aware windowing GUI. It also taught Sun that the Internet programming community will refuse to accept proprietary standards, no matter how good they may be. The seeds of Java's remarkably permissive licensing scheme were sown by NeWS's failure. Gosling brought what he had learned to Bill Joy's nascent Aspen project, and in 1992, work on the project led to the founding of the Sun subsidiary, FirstPerson, Inc. Its mission was to lead Sun into the world of consumer electronics.

The FirstPerson team worked on developing software for information appliances, such as cellular phones and personal digital assistants (PDA). The goal was to enable the transfer of information and real-time applications over cheap infrared and packet-based networks. Memory and bandwidth limitations dictated small and efficient code. The nature of the applications also demanded they be safe and robust. Gosling and his teammates began programming in C++, but they soon found themselves confounded by a language that was too complex, unwieldy, and insecure for the task. They decided to start from scratch, and Gosling began working on something he dubbed "C++ minus minus."

With the floundering of the Apple Newton, it became apparent that the PDA's ship had not yet come in, so Sun shifted FirstPerson's efforts to interactive TV (ITV). The programming language of choice for ITV set-top boxes was the near ancestor of Java, a language called Oak. Even with its elegance and ability to provide safe interactivity, Oak could not salvage the lost cause of ITV. Customers didn't want it, and Sun soon abandoned the concept.

At that time, Joy and Gosling got together to decide on a new strategy for their language. It was 1993, and the explosion of interest in the Internet, and the World Wide Web in particular, presented a new opportunity. Oak was small, robust, architecture independent, and object oriented. As it happens, these are also the requirements for a universal, network-savvy programming language. Sun quickly changed focus, and with a little retooling, Oak became Java.

Future Buzz?

I don't think it's overdoing it to say that Java has caught on like wildfire. Even before its first official release, while Java was still a nonproduct, nearly every major industry player jumped on the Java bandwagon. Java licensees include Microsoft, Intel, IBM, and virtually all major hardware and software vendors.

As we begin looking at the Java architecture, you'll see that much of what is exciting about Java comes from the self-contained, virtual machine environment in which Java applications run. Java has been carefully designed so that this supporting architecture can be implemented either in software, for existing computer platforms, or in customized hardware, for new kinds of devices. Sun and other industry giants have announced their intentions to produce cheap, fast Java chips, the first of which should be available by the time you read this. Hardware implementations of Java could power inexpensive network terminals, PDAs, and other information appliances, to take advantage of transportable Java applications.

Many people see Java as part of a trend toward cheap, Net-based, "operating system-less" appliances that will extend the Net into more and more consumer-related areas. Only time will tell what people will do with Java, but it's probably worth at least a passing thought that the applet you write today might well be running on someone's wristwatch tomorrow. If that seems too futuristic, remember that you can already get a "smart card" (essentially a credit card) that has a Java interpreter embedded in it. Such a card could do everything from financial transactions (paying a hotel bill) to unlocking a door (the door to your hotel room) to rerouting phone calls (so your hotel room receives your business calls). The card is already here; it won't be long before the rest of the software has been built. A Java wristwatch is certainly not far away.

A Virtual Machine

Java is both a compiled and an interpreted language. Java source code is turned into simple binary instructions, much like ordinary microprocessor machine code. However, whereas C or C++ source is refined to native instructions for a particular model of processor, Java source is compiled into a universal format—instructions for a virtual machine.

Compiled Java byte-code, also called J-code, is executed by a Java run-time interpreter. The run-time system performs all the normal activities of a real processor, but it does so in a safe, virtual environment. It executes the stack-based instruction set and manages a storage heap. It creates and manipulates primitive data types, and loads and invokes newly referenced blocks of code. Most importantly, it does all this in accordance with a strictly defined open specification that can be implemented by anyone who wants to produce a Java-compliant virtual machine. Together, the virtual machine and language definition provide a complete specification. There are no features of Java left undefined or implementation dependent. For example, Java specifies the sizes of all its primitive data types, rather than leave it up to each implementation.

The Java interpreter is relatively lightweight and small; it can be implemented in whatever form is desirable for a particular platform. On most systems, the interpreter is written in a fast, natively compiled language like C or C++. The interpreter can be run as a separate application, or it can be embedded in another piece of software, such as a Web browser.

All of this means that Java code is implicitly portable. The same Java application can run on any platform that provides a Java run-time environment, as shown in Figure 1-1. You don't have to produce alternate versions of your application for different platforms, and you never have to distribute source code to end users.

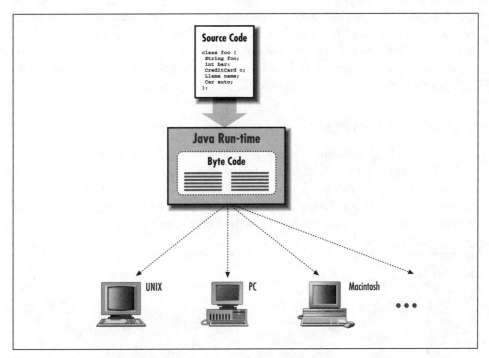

Figure 1–1: Java run-time environment

The fundamental unit of Java code is the *class*. As in other object-oriented languages, classes are application components that hold executable code and data. Compiled Java classes are distributed in a universal binary format that contains Java byte-code and other class information. Classes can be maintained discretely and stored in files or archives on a local system or on a network server. Classes are located and loaded dynamically at run-time, as they are needed by an application.

In addition to the platform-specific run-time system, Java has a number of fundamental classes that contain architecture-dependent methods. These *native methods* serve as Java's gateway to the real world. These methods are implemented in a native language on the host platform. They provide access to resources such as the network, the windowing system, and the host filesystem. The rest of Java is written entirely in Java, and is therefore portable. This includes fundamental Java utilities like the Java compiler and Sun's HotJava Web browser, which are also Java applications and are therefore immediately available on all Java platforms.

In general, interpreters are slow, but because the Java interpreter runs compiled byte-code, Java is a relatively fast interpreted language. More importantly, Java has also been designed so that software implementations of the run-time system can optimize their performance by compiling byte-code to native machine code on the fly. This is called "just in time" compilation. Sun claims that with just in time compilation, Java code can execute nearly as fast as native compiled code and maintain its transportability and security. The one performance hit that natively compiled Java code will always suffer is array bounds checking. But on the other hand, some of the basic design features of Java place more information in the hands of the compiler, which allows for certain kinds of optimizations not possible in C or C++.

Java Compared

Java is a new language, but it draws on many years of programming experience with other languages in its choice of features. So a lot can be said in comparing and contrasting Java with other languages. There are at least three pillars necessary to support a universal language for network programming today: portability, speed, and security. Figure 1-2 shows how Java compares to other languages.

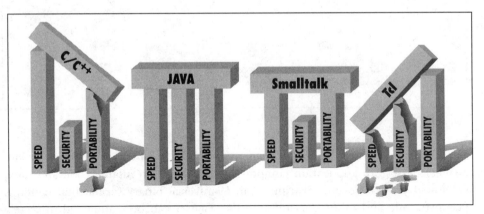

Figure 1–2: Programming languages compared

You may have heard that Java is a lot like C or C++, but that's really not true, except at a superficial level. When you first look at Java code, you'll see that the basic syntax looks a lot like C or C++. But that's where the similarities end. Java is by no means a direct descendant of C or a next generation C++. If you compare language features, you'll see that Java actually has more in common with languages like Smalltalk and Lisp. In fact, Java's implementation is about as far from native C as you can imagine.

The surface-level similarities to C and C++ are worth noting, however. Java borrows heavily from C and C++ syntax, so you'll see lots of familiar language constructs, including an abundance of curly braces and semicolons. Java also subscribes to the C philosophy that a good language should be compact; in other words, it should be sufficiently small and regular so that a programmer can hold all the language's capabilities in his or her head at once. As C is extensible with libraries, packages of Java classes can be added to the core language components.

C has been successful because it provides a reasonably featureful programming environment, with high performance and an acceptable degree of portability. Java also tries to balance functionality, speed, and portability, but it does so in a very different way. While C trades functionality to get portability, Java trades speed for portability. Java also addresses security issues, while C doesn't.

Java is an interpreted language, so it won't be as fast as a compiled language like C. But Java is fast enough, especially for interactive, network-based applications, where the application is often idle, waiting for the user to do something or waiting for data from the network. For situations where speed is critical, a Java implementation can optimize performance by compiling byte-code to native machine code on the fly.

Scripting languages, like Perl, Tcl/Tk, and Wksh, are becoming very popular, and for good reason. There's no reason a scripting language could not be suitable for safe, networked applications (e.g., Safe Tcl), but most scripting languages are not designed for serious, large-scale programming. The attraction to scripting languages is that they are dynamic; they are powerful tools for rapid prototyping. Some scripting languages, like awk and Perl, also provide powerful tools for text-processing tasks that more general purpose languages find unwieldy. Scripting languages are also highly portable.

One problem with scripting languages, however, is that they are rather casual about program structure and data typing. Most scripting languages (with a hesitant exception for Perl 5.0) are not object oriented. They also have vastly simplified type systems and generally don't provide for sophisticated scoping of variables and functions. These characteristics make them unsuitable for building large, modular applications. Speed is another problem with scripting languages; the high-level, fully interpreted nature of these languages often makes them quite slow.

Java offers some of the essential advantages of a scripting language, along with the added benefits of a lower-level language.

Incremental development with object-oriented components, combined with Java's simplicity, make it possible to develop applications rapidly and change them easily, with a short concept to implementation time. Java also comes with a large base of core classes for common tasks such as building GUIs and doing network communications. But along with these features, Java has the scalability and software-engineering advantages of more static languages. It provides a safe structure on which to build higher-level networked tools and languages.

As I've already said, Java is similar in design to languages like Smalltalk and Lisp. However, these languages are used mostly as research vehicles, rather than for developing large-scale systems. One reason is that they never developed a standard portable binding to operating-system services analogous to the C standard library or the Java core classes. Smalltalk is compiled to an interpreted byte-code format, and it can be dynamically compiled to native code on the fly, just like Java. But Java improves on the design by using a byte-code verifier to ensure the correctness of Java code. This verifier gives Java a performance advantage over Smalltalk because Java code requires fewer run-time checks. Java's byte-code verifier also helps with security issues, something that Smalltalk doesn't address. Smalltalk is a mature language though, and Java's designers took lessons from many of its features.

NOTE

> Don't confuse Java with JavaScript. JavaScript is an object-based scripting language being developed by Netscape and others. It currently serves as a glue and an "in the document" language for dynamic, interactive HTML-based applications. JavaScript draws its name from its intended integration with Java. You can currently interact with Java applets embedded in HTML using JavaScript. In the future we may see portable implementations of JavaScript that would promote it to the level of a general scripting language. For more information on JavaScript, check out Netscape's web site (*http://home.netscape.com/*).

Throughout the rest of this chapter, we'll take a bird's eye view of the Java language. I'll explain what's new and what's not so new about Java; how it differs from other languages, and why.

Safety of Design

You have no doubt heard a lot about the fact that Java is designed to be a safe language. But what do we mean by safe? Safe from what or whom? The security features that attract the most attention for Java are those features that make possible new types of dynamically portable software. Java provides several layers of protection from dangerously flawed code, as well as more mischievous things like viruses and trojan horses. In the next section, we'll take a look at how the Java virtual machine architecture assesses the safety of code before it's run, and how the Java class loader builds a wall around untrusted classes. These features provide the foundation for high-level security policies that allow or disallow various kinds of activities on an application-by-application basis.

In this section though, we'll look at some general features of the Java programming language. What is perhaps more important, although often overlooked in the security din, is the safety that Java provides by addressing common design and programming problems. Java is intended to be as safe as possible from the simple mistakes we make ourselves, as well as those we inherit from contractors and third-party software vendors. The goal with Java has been to keep the language simple, provide tools that have demonstrated their usefulness, and let users build more complicated facilities on top of the language when needed.

Syntactic Sweet 'n Low

Java is parsimonious in its features; simplicity rules. Compared to C, Java uses few automatic type coercions, and the ones that remain are simple and well-defined. Unlike C++, Java doesn't allow programmer-defined operator overloading. The string concatenation operator + is the only system-defined, overloaded operator in Java. All methods in Java are like C++ virtual methods, so overridden methods are dynamically selected at run-time.

Java doesn't have a preprocessor, so it doesn't have macros, #define statements, or conditional source compilation. These constructs exist in other languages primarily to support platform dependencies, so in that sense they should not be needed in Java. Another common use for conditional compilation is for debugging purposes. Debugging code can be included directly in your Java source code by making it conditional on a constant (i.e., static and final) variable. The Java compiler is smart enough to remove this code when it determines that it won't be called.

Java provides a well-defined package structure for organizing class files. The package system allows the compiler to handle most of the functionality of *make*. The compiler also works with compiled Java classes because all type information is preserved; there is no need for header files. All of this means that Java code requires little context to read. Indeed, you may sometimes find it faster to look at the Java source code than to refer to class documentation.

Java replaces some features that have been troublesome in other languages. For example, Java supports only a single inheritance class hierarchy, but allows multiple inheritance of interfaces. An interface, like an abstract class in C++, specifies the behavior of an object without defining its implementation, a powerful mechanism borrowed from Objective C. It allows a class to implement the behavior of the interface, without needing to be a subclass of the interface. Interfaces in Java eliminate the need for multiple inheritance of classes, without causing the problems associated with multiple inheritance. As you'll see in Chapter 4, Java is a simple, yet elegant, programming language.

Type Safety and Method Binding

One attribute of a language is the kind of type checking it uses. When we categorize a language as static or dynamic we are referring to the amount of information about variable types that is known at compile time versus what is determined while the application is running.

In a strictly statically typed language like C or C++, data types are etched in stone when the source code is compiled. The compiler benefits from having enough information to enforce usage rules, so that it can catch many kinds of errors before the code is executed. The code doesn't require run-time type checking, which is advantageous because it can be compiled to be small and fast. But statically typed languages are inflexible. They don't support high-level constructs like lists and collections as naturally as languages with dynamic type checking, and they make it impossible for an application to safely import new data types while it's running.

In contrast, a dynamic language like Smalltalk or Lisp has a run-time system that manages the types of objects and performs necessary type checking while an application is executing. These kinds of languages allow for more complex behavior, and are in many respects more powerful. However, they are also generally slower, less safe, and harder to debug.

The differences in languages have been likened to the differences between kinds of automobiles.[*] Statically typed languages like C++ are analogous to a sports car—reasonably safe and fast—but useful only if you're driving on a nicely paved road. Highly dynamic languages like Smalltalk are more like an offroad vehicle: they afford you more freedom, but can be somewhat unwieldy. It can be fun (and sometimes faster) to go roaring through the back woods, but you might also get stuck in a ditch or mauled by bears.

Another attribute of a language is the way it binds method calls to their definitions. In an early-binding language like C or C++, the definitions of methods are normally bound at compile-time, unless the programmer specifies otherwise. Smalltalk, on the other hand, is a late-binding language because it locates the definitions of methods dynamically at run-time. Early-binding is important for

---

[*] The credit for the car analogy goes to Marshall P. Cline, author of the C++ FAQ.

performance reasons; an application can run without the overhead incurred by searching method tables at run-time. But late-binding is more flexible. It's also necessary in an object-oriented language, where a subclass can override methods in its superclass, and only the run-time system can determine which method to run.

Java provides some of the benefits of both C++ and Smalltalk; it's a statically typed, late-binding language. Every object in Java has a well-defined type that is known at compile time. This means the Java compiler can do the same kind of static type checking and usage analysis as C++. As a result, you can't assign an object to the wrong type of reference or call nonexistent methods within it. The Java compiler goes even further and prevents you from messing up and trying to use uninitialized variables.

However, Java is fully run-time typed as well. The Java run-time system keeps track of all objects and makes it possible to determine their types and relationships during execution. This means you can inspect an object at run-time to determine what it is. Unlike C or C++, casts from one type of object to another are checked by the run-time system, and it's even possible to use completely new kinds of dynamically loaded objects with a level of type safety.

Since Java is a late-binding language, all methods are like virtual methods in C++. This makes it possible for a subclass to override methods in its superclass. But Java also allows you to gain the performance benefits of early-binding by declaring (with the `final` modifier) that certain methods can't be overridden by subclassing, removing the need for run-time lookup.

Incremental Development

Java carries all data-type and method-signature information with it from its source code to its compiled byte-code form. This means that Java classes can be developed incrementally. Your own Java classes can also be used safely with classes from other sources your compiler has never seen. In other words, you can write new code that references binary class files, without losing the type safety you gain from having the source code. The Java run-time system can load new classes while an application is running, thus providing the capabilities of a dynamic linker.

A common irritation with C++ is the "fragile base class" problem. In C++, the implementation of a base class can be effectively frozen by the fact that it has many derived classes; changing the base class may require recompilation of the derived classes. This is an especially difficult problem for developers of class libraries. Java avoids this problem by dynamically locating fields within classes. As long as a class maintains a valid form of its original structure, it can evolve without breaking other classes that are derived from it or that make use of it.

Dynamic Memory Management

Some of the most important differences between Java and C or C++ involve how Java manages memory. Java eliminates ad hoc pointers and adds garbage collection and true arrays to the language. These features eliminate many otherwise insurmountable problems with safety, portability, and optimization.

Garbage collection alone should save countless programmers from the single largest source of programming errors in C or C++: explicit memory allocation and deallocation. In addition to maintaining objects in memory, the Java run-time system keeps track of all references to those objects. When an object is no longer in use, Java automatically removes it from memory. You can simply throw away references to objects you no longer use and have confidence that the system will clean them up at an appropriate time. Sun's current implementation of Java uses a conservative, mark and sweep garbage collector that runs intermittently in the background, which means that most garbage collecting takes place between mouse clicks and keyboard hits. Once you get used to garbage collection, you won't go back. Being able to write air-tight C code that juggles memory without dropping any on the floor is an important skill, but once you become addicted to Java you can "realloc" some of those brain cells to new tasks.

You may hear people say that Java doesn't have pointers. Strictly speaking, this statement is true, but it's also misleading. What Java provides are *references*—a safe kind of pointer—and Java is rife with them. A reference is a strongly typed handle for an object. All objects in Java, with the exception of primitive numeric types, are accessed through references. If necessary, you can use references to build all the normal kinds of data structures you're accustomed to building with pointers, like linked lists, trees, and so forth. The only difference is that with references you have to do so in a type-safe way.

Another important difference between a reference and a pointer is that you can't do pointer arithmetic with references. A reference is an atomic thing; you can't manipulate the value of a reference except by assigning it to an object. References are passed by value, and you can't reference an object through more than a single level of indirection. The protection of references is one of the most fundamental aspects of Java security. It means that Java code has to play by the rules; it can't peek into places it shouldn't.

Unlike C or C++ pointers, Java references can point only to class types. There are no pointers to methods. People often complain about this missing feature, but you will find that most tasks that call for pointers to methods, such as callbacks, can be accomplished using interfaces and anonymous adapter classes instead.[*]

Finally, arrays in Java are true, first-class objects. They can be dynamically allocated and assigned like other objects. Arrays know their own size and type, and although you can't directly define array classes or subclass them, they do have a well-defined inheritance relationship based on the relationship of their base types. Having true arrays in the language alleviates much of the need for pointer arithmetic like that in C or C++.

Error Handling

Java's roots are in networked devices and embedded systems. For these applications, it's important to have robust and intelligent error management. Java has a powerful exception-handling mechanism, somewhat like that in newer implementations of C++. Exceptions provide a more natural and elegant way to handle errors. Exceptions allow you to separate error-handling code from normal code, which makes for cleaner, more readable applications.

When an exception occurs, it causes the flow of program execution to be transferred to a predesignated catcher block of code. The exception carries with it an object that contains information about the situation that caused the exception. The Java compiler requires that a method either declare the exceptions it can generate or catch and deal with them itself. This promotes error information to the same level of importance as argument and return typing. As a Java programmer, you know precisely what exceptional conditions you must deal with, and you have help from the compiler in writing correct software that doesn't leave them unhandled.

Multithreading

Applications today require a high degree of parallelism. Even a very single-minded application can have a complex user interface. As machines get faster, users become more sensitive to waiting for unrelated tasks that seize control of their time. Threads provide efficient multiprocessing and distribution of tasks. Java makes threads easy to use because support for them is built into the language.

Concurrency is nice, but there's more to programming with threads than just performing multiple tasks simultaneously. In many cases, threads need to be synchronized, which can be tricky without explicit language support. Java supports synchronization based on the monitor and condition model developed by C.A.R. Hoare—a sort of lock and key system for accessing resources. A keyword, synchronized, designates methods for safe, serialized access within an object. Only one

---

[*] Java 1.1 does have a Method class, which lets you have a reference to a method. You can use a Method object to construct a callback, but it's tricky.

synchronized method within the object may run at a given time. There are also simple, primitive methods for explicit waiting and signaling between threads interested in the same object.

Learning to program with threads is an important part of learning to program in Java. See Chapter 8 for a discussion of this topic. For complete coverage of threads, see *Java Threads*, by Scott Oaks and Henry Wong (O'Reilly & Associates).

Scalability

At the lowest level, Java programs consist of classes. Classes are intended to be small, modular components. They can be separated physically on different systems, retrieved dynamically, and even cached in various distribution schemes. Over classes, Java provides packages, a layer of structure that groups classes into functional units. Packages provide a naming convention for organizing classes and a second level of organizational control over the visibility of variables and methods in Java applications.

Within a package, a class is either publicly visible or protected from outside access. Packages form another type of scope that is closer to the application level. This lends itself to building reusable components that work together in a system. Packages also help in designing a scalable application that can grow without becoming a bird's nest of tightly coupled code dependency.

Safety of Implementation

It's one thing to create a language that prevents you from shooting yourself in the foot; it's quite another to create one that prevents others from shooting you in the foot.

Encapsulation is a technique for hiding data and behavior within a class; it's an important part of object-oriented design. It helps you write clean, modular software. In most languages, however, the visibility of data items is simply part of the relationship between the programmer and the compiler. It's a matter of semantics, not an assertion about the actual security of the data in the context of the running program's environment.

When Bjarne Stroustrup chose the keyword `private` to designate hidden members of classes in C++, he was probably thinking about shielding you from the messy details of a class developer's code, not the issues of shielding that developer's classes and objects from the onslaught of someone else's viruses and trojan horses. Arbitrary casting and pointer arithmetic in C or C++ make it trivial to violate access permissions on classes without breaking the rules of the language. Consider the following code:

```
// C++

class Finances {
    private:
        char creditCardNumber[16];
        ...
    };

main() {
    Finances finances;

    // Forge a pointer to peek inside the class
    char *cardno = (char *)&finances;
    printf("Card Number = %s\n", cardno);
}
```

In this little C++ drama, we have written some code that violates the encapsulation of the Finances class and pulls out some secret information. If this example seems unrealistic, consider how important it is to protect the foundation (system) classes of the run-time environment from similar kinds of attacks. If untrusted code can corrupt the components that provide access to real resources, such as the filesystem, the network, or the windowing system, it certainly has a chance at stealing your credit card numbers.

In Visual BASIC, it's also possible to compromise the system by peeking, poking, and, under DOS, installing interrupt handlers. Even some recent languages that have some commonalities with Java lack important security features. For example, the Apple Newton uses an object-oriented language called NewtonScript that is compiled into an interpreted byte-code format. However, NewtonScript has no concept of public and private members, so a Newton application has free reign to access any information it finds. General Magic's Telescript language is another example of a device-independent language that does not fully address security concerns.

If a Java application is to dynamically download code from an untrusted source on the Internet and run it alongside applications that might contain confidential information, protection has to extend very deep. The Java security model wraps three layers of protection around imported classes, as shown in Figure 1-3.

At the outside, application-level security decisions are made by a security manager. A security manager controls access to system resources like the filesystem, network ports, and the windowing environment. A security manager relies on the ability of a class loader to protect basic system classes. A class loader handles loading classes from the network. At the inner level, all system security ultimately rests on the Java verifier, which guarantees the integrity of incoming classes.

The Java byte-code verifier is an integral part of the Java run-time system. Class loaders and security managers, however, are implemented by applications that

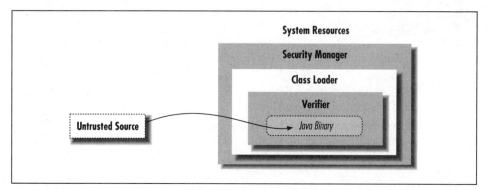

Figure 1–3: The Java security model

load applets, such as applet viewers and Web browsers. All these pieces need to be functioning properly to ensure security in the Java environment.*

The Verifier

Java's first line of defense is the byte-code *verifier*. The verifier reads byte-code before they are run and makes sure they are well-behaved and obey the basic rules of the Java language. A trusted Java compiler won't produce code that does otherwise. However, it's possible for a mischievous person to deliberately assemble bad code. It's the verifier's job to detect this.

Once code has been verified, it's considered safe from certain inadvertent or malicious errors. For example, verified code can't forge pointers or violate access permissions on objects. It can't perform illegal casts or use objects in ways other than they are intended. It can't even cause certain types of internal errors, such as overflowing or underflowing the operand stack. These fundamental guarantees underlie all of Java's security.

You might be wondering, isn't this kind of safety implicit in lots of interpreted languages? Well, while it's true that you shouldn't be able to corrupt the interpreter with bogus BASIC code, remember that the protection in most interpreted languages happens at a higher level. Those languages are likely to have heavyweight interpreters that do a great deal of run-time work, so they are necessarily slower and more cumbersome.

---

* You may have seen reports about various security flaws in Java. While these weaknesses are real, it's important to realize that they have been found in the implementations of various components, namely Sun's byte-code verifier and Netscape's class loader and security manager, not in the basic security model itself. One of the reasons Sun has released the source code for Java is to encourage people to search for weaknesses, so they can be removed.

By comparison, Java byte-code is a relatively light, low-level instruction set. The ability to statically verify the Java byte-code before execution lets the Java interpreter run at full speed with full safety, without expensive run-time checks. Of course, you are always going to pay the price of running an interpreter, but that's not a serious problem with the speed of modern CPUs. Java byte-code can also be compiled on the fly to native machine code, which has even less run-time overhead.

The verifier is a type of theorem prover. It steps through the Java byte-code and applies simple, inductive rules to determine certain aspects of how the byte-code will behave. This kind of analysis is possible because compiled Java byte-code has a lot more type information stored within it than other languages of this kind. The byte-code also has to obey a few extra rules that simplify its behavior. First, most byte-code instructions operate only on individual data types. For example, with stack operations, there are separate instructions for object references and for each of the numeric types in Java. Similarly, there is a different instruction for moving each type of value into and out of a local variable.

Second, the type of object resulting from any operation is always known in advance. There are no byte-code operations that consume values and produce more than one possible type of value as output. As a result, it's always possible to look at the next instruction and its operands, and know the type of value that will result.

Because an operation always produces a known type, by looking at the starting state, it's possible to determine the types of all items on the stack and in local variables at any point in the future. The collection of all this type information at any given time is called the *type state* of the stack; this is what Java tries to analyze before it runs an application. Java doesn't know anything about the actual values of stack and variable items at this time, just what kind of items they are. However, this is enough information to enforce the security rules and to insure that objects are not manipulated illegally.

To make it feasible to analyze the type state of the stack, Java places an additional restriction on how Java byte-code instructions are executed: all paths to the same point in the code have to arrive with exactly the same type state.* This restriction makes it possible for the verifier to trace each branch of the code just once and still know the type state at all points. Thus, the verifier can insure that instruction

---

* The implications of this rule are mainly of interest to compiler writers. The rule means that Java byte-code can't perform certain types of iterative actions within a single frame of execution. A common example would be looping and pushing values onto the stack. This is not allowed because the path of execution would return to the top of the loop with a potentially different type state on each pass, and there is no way that a static analysis of the code can determine whether it obeys the security rules.

types and stack value types always correspond, without actually following the execution of the code.

Class Loader

Java adds a second layer of security with a *class loader*. A class loader is responsible for bringing Java binary classes that contain byte-code into the interpreter. Every application that loads classes from the network must use a class loader to handle this task.

After a class has been loaded and passed through the verifier, it remains associated with its class loader. As a result, classes are effectively partitioned into separate namespaces based on their origin. When a class references another class, the request is served by its original class loader. This means that classes retrieved from a specific source can be restricted to interact only with other classes retrieved from that same location. For example, a Java-enabled Web browser can use a class loader to build a separate space for all the classes loaded from a given uniform resource locator (URL).

The search for classes always begins with the built-in Java system classes. These classes are loaded from the locations specified by the Java interpreter's class path (see Chapter 3). Classes in the class path are loaded by the system only once and can't be replaced. This means that it's impossible for an applet to replace fundamental system classes with its own versions that change their functionality.

Security Manager

Finally, a security manager is responsible for making application-level security decisions. A security manager is an object that can be installed by an application to restrict access to system resources. The security manager is consulted every time the application tries to access items like the filesystem, network ports, external processes, and the windowing environment, so the security manager can allow or deny the request.

A security manager is most useful for applications that run untrusted code as part of their normal operation. Since a Java-enabled Web browser can run applets that may be retrieved from untrusted sources on the Net, such a browser needs to install a security manager as one of its first actions. This security manager then restricts the kinds of access allowed after that point. This lets the application impose an effective level of trust before running an arbitrary piece of code. And once a security manager is installed, it can't be replaced.

A security manager can be as simple or complex as a particular application warrants. Sometimes it's sufficient simply to deny access to all resources or to general categories of services such as the filesystem or network. But it's also possible to make sophisticated decisions based on high-level information. For example, a Java-enabled Web browser could implement a security manager that lets users specify how much an applet is to be trusted or that allows or denies access to specific resources on a case-by-case basis. Of course, this assumes that the browser can determine which applets it ought to trust. We'll see how this problem is solved shortly.

The integrity of a security manager is based on the protection afforded by the lower levels of the Java security model. Without the guarantees provided by the verifier and the class loader, high-level assertions about the safety of system resources are meaningless. The safety provided by the Java byte-code verifier means that the interpreter can't be corrupted or subverted, and that Java code has to use components as they are intended. This, in turn, means that a class loader can guarantee that an application is using the core Java system classes and that these classes are the only means of accessing basic system resources. With these restrictions in place, it's possible to centralize control over those resources with a security manager.

Application and User Level Security

There's a fine line between having enough power to do something useful and having all the power to do anything you want. Java provides the foundation for a secure environment in which untrusted code can be quarantined, managed, and safely executed. However, unless you are content with keeping that code in a little black box and running it just for its own benefit, you will have to grant it access to at least some system resources so that it can be useful. Every kind of access carries with it certain risks and benefits. The advantages of granting an untrusted applet access to your windowing system, for example, are that it can display information and let you interact in a useful way. The associated risks are that the applet may instead display something worthless, annoying, or offensive. Since most people can accept that level of risk, graphical applets and the World Wide Web in general are possible.

At one extreme, the simple act of running an application gives it a resource, computation time, that it may put to good use or burn frivolously. It's difficult to prevent an untrusted application from wasting your time, or even attempting a "denial of service" attack. At the other extreme, a powerful, trusted application may justifiably deserve access to all sorts of system resources (e.g., the filesystem, process creation, network interfaces); a malicious application could wreak havoc with these resources. The message here is that important and sometimes complex security issues have to be addressed.

In some situations, it may be acceptable to simply ask the user to "okay" requests. Sun's HotJava Web browser can pop up a dialog box and ask the user's permission for an applet to access an otherwise restricted file. However, we can put only so much burden on our users. An experienced person will quickly grow tired of answering questions; an inexperienced user may not even be able to answer the questions. Is it okay for me to grant an applet access to something if I don't understand what that is?

Making decisions about what is dangerous and what is not can be difficult. Even ostensibly harmless access, like displaying a window, can become a threat when paired with the ability for an untrusted application to communicate from your host. The Java `SecurityManager` provides an option to flag windows created by an untrusted application with a special, recognizable border to prevent it from impersonating another application and perhaps tricking you into revealing your password or your secret recipe collection. There is also a grey area, in which an application can do devious things that aren't quite destructive. An applet that can mail a bug report can also mail-bomb your boss. The Java language provides the tools to implement whatever security policies you want. However, what these policies will be ultimately depends on who you are, what you are doing, and where you are doing it.

Signing Classes

Web browsers such as HotJava start by defining a few rules and some coarse levels of security that restrict where applets may come from and what system resources they may access. These rules are sufficient to keep the waving Duke applet from clutching your password file, but they aren't sufficient for applications you'd like to trust with sensitive information. To fully exploit the power of Java, we need to have some nontechnical basis on which to make reasonable decisions about what a program can be allowed to do. This nontechnical basis is "trust"; basically, you trust certain entities not to do anything that's harmful to you. For a home user, this may mean that you trust the "Bank of Boofa" to distribute applets that let you transfer funds between your accounts, or you may trust L.L. Bean to distribute an applet that debits your Visa account. For a company, that may mean that you trust applets originating behind your firewall, or perhaps applets from a few high-priority customers, to modify internal databases. In all of these cases, you don't need to know in detail what the program is going to do and give it permission for each operation. You only need to know that you trust your local bank.

This doesn't mean that there isn't a technical aspect to the problem of trust. Trusting your local bank when you walk up to the ATM machine means one thing; trusting some Web page that claims to come from your local bank means something else entirely. It would be very difficult to impersonate the ATM machine two blocks down the street (though it has been known to happen), but, depending on your position on the Net, it's not all that difficult to impersonate a web site, or to intercept data coming from a legitimate web site and substitute your own.

That's where cryptography comes in. Digital signatures, together with certificates, are techniques for verifying that data truly comes from the source it claims to have come from and hasn't been modified en route. If the Bank of Boofa signs its checkbook applet, your browser can verify that the applet actually came from the bank, not an imposter, and hasn't been modified. Therefore, you can tell your browser to trust applets that have the Bank of Boofa's signature. Java supports digital signatures; the details are covered in Chapter 3.

Java and the World Wide Web

Alice was beginning to get very tired of sitting by her sister on the bank, and of having nothing to do: once or twice she had peeped into the book her sister was reading, but it had no pictures or conversations in it, "and what is the use of a book," thought Alice, "without pictures or conversations?"

—*Alice in Wonderland*

The application-level safety features of Java make it possible to develop new kinds of applications not necessarily feasible before now. A Web browser that implements the Java run-time system can incorporate Java applets as executable content inside of documents. This means that Web pages can contain not only static hypertext information but also full-fledged interactive applications. The added potential for use of the WWW is enormous. A user can retrieve and use software simply by navigating with a Web browser. Formerly static information can be paired with portable software for interpreting and using the information. Instead of just providing some data for a spreadsheet, for example, a Web document might contain a fully functional spreadsheet application embedded within it that allows users to view and manipulate the information.

Applets

The term *applet* is used to mean a small, subordinate, or embeddable application. By embeddable, I mean it's designed to be run and used within the context of a larger system. In that sense, most programs are embedded within a computer's operating system. An operating system manages its native applications in a variety of ways: it starts, stops, suspends, and synchronizes applications; it provides them with certain standard resources; and it protects them from one another by partitioning their environments.

In this book, I'll be describing Java applets, which are Java applications meant to be embedded in and controlled by a larger application, such as a Java-enabled Web browser or an applet viewer. To include an applet as executable content in a Web document, you use a special HTML tag. The <applet> tag points to an applet and provides configuration information about the applet.

As far as the Web browser model is concerned, an applet is just another type of object to display. Browsers make a distinction between items presented inline and items anchored via hypertext links and made available by external means, such as a viewer or helper application. If you download an MPEG video clip, for instance, and your browser doesn't natively understand MPEG, it will look for a helper application (an MPEG player) to pass the information to. Java-enabled Web browsers generally execute applets inline, in the context of a particular document, as shown in Figure 1-4. However, less capable browsers could initially provide some support for Java applets through an external viewer.

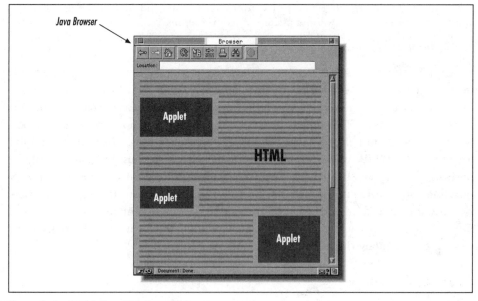

Figure 1–4: Applets in a Web document

A Java applet is a compiled Java program, composed of classes just like any Java program. While a simple applet may consist of only a single class, most large applets should be broken into many classes. Each class is stored in a separate class file. The class files for an applet are retrieved from the network as they are needed. A large applet doesn't need to retrieve all its parts or all its data before beginning to interact with the user. Well-designed applets can take advantage of multithreading to wait for certain resources in the background, while performing other activities.

An applet has a four-part life cycle. When an applet is initially loaded by a Web browser, it's asked to initialize itself. The applet is then informed each time it's displayed and each time it's no longer visible to the user. Finally, the applet is told when it's no longer needed, so that it can clean up after itself. During its lifetime, an applet may start and suspend itself, do work, communicate with other applications, and interact with the Web browser.

Applets are autonomous programs, but they are confined within the walls of a Web browser or applet viewer, and have to play by its rules. I'll be discussing the details of what applets can and can't do as we explore features of the Java language. However, under the most conservative security policies, an applet can interact only with the user and can only communicate over the network with the host from which it originated. Other types of activities, like accessing files or interacting directly with outside applications, are typically prevented by the security manager that is part of the Web browser or applet viewer. But aside from these restrictions, there is no fundamental difference between a Java applet and a standalone Java application.

New Kinds of Applications

Sun's HotJava Web browser is written entirely in Java. Because it's a Java application, HotJava is immediately available on any platform with the Java run-time system. This goes a long way towards the goal of a Web browser serving as a universal access point for resources on the Net. Netscape has also announced that a future version of their Communicator client software will be rewritten in Java.

In addition to displaying Java applets as executable content in Web pages, the HotJava application is uniquely customizable. HotJava can be dynamically extended with Java code from the Net. HotJava uses *protocol handlers* and *content handlers* to provide this functionality.[*] Protocol handlers and content handlers are classes in the Java API that let an application implement new types of URLs and interpret the objects retrieved from them. A Web browser that supports this functionality could load handlers from a remote location and effectively upgrade itself on the fly to use new protocols and access new kinds of information.

---

* Downloadable content and protocol handlers are not supported in HotJava 1.0 but are promised in a future release.

Like applets, content handlers and protocol handlers can be served by a web site, along with the information they interpret. As an example, consider the new Portable Network Graphics (PNG) format, a freely distributable alternative to GIF. By supplying a PNG content handler along with PNG images on our server, we give users the ability to use the new image format, just as they would a built-in format. We don't have to create a new standard and force every Web browser to support the new format. Instead, the first time a user loads a document referencing a PNG image from our site, the Web browser will realize it doesn't understand the object and will ask the server if it has a content handler for it. Since we've provided a content handler, the browser can load it and then use it to interpret and display the image dynamically.

In a similar manner, protocol handlers allow a Web browser to start speaking a new protocol with the server. This is especially useful for things like security protocols. If we invent a revolutionary new cryptographic protocol late one night, all we have to do is implement it in the form of a protocol handler and place it on our server. We can then start using URLs that point through our new protocol at objects on our server, and people can immediately begin using it.

These scenarios describe just a few things that safe, transportable code will allow. We will undoubtedly see many other new breeds of application we can't even begin to anticipate.

New Kinds of Media

When it was first released, Java quickly achieved a reputation for multimedia capabilities. Frankly, this wasn't really deserved. At that point, Java provided facilities for doing simple animations and playing audio. You could animate and play audio simultaneously, though you couldn't synchronize the two. Still, this was a significant advance for the Web, and people thought it was pretty impressive.

JavaSoft is now working on real media features, which go far beyond anything that has yet been seen on the Web. This includes CD-quality sound, 3D animation, media players that synchronize audio and video, speech synthesis and recognition, and more. These new features aren't yet in Java 1.1 but will make their way into Java over the next 18 months. In short, if you were impressed by Java 1.0, you haven't seen anything yet. Java's multimedia capabilities will be taking shape over the next two years.

New Software Development Models

For some time now, people have been using visual development environments to develop user interfaces. These environments let you generate applications by moving components around on the screen, connecting components to each other, and so on. In short, designing a user interface is a lot more like drawing a picture than like writing code.

For visual development environments to work well, you need to be able to create reusable software components. That's what Java Beans are all about. The JavaBeans architecture defines a way to package software as reusable building blocks. A graphical development tool can figure out a component's capabilities, customize the component, and connect it to other components to build applications. Java-Beans takes the idea of graphical development a step further. Beans aren't limited to visible, user interface components: you can have Beans that are entirely invisible and whose job is purely computational. For example, you could have a Bean that did database access; you could connect this to a Bean that let the user request information from the database; and you could use another Bean to display the result. Or you could have a set of Beans that implement the functions in a mathematical library; you could then do numerical analysis by connecting different functions to each other. In either case, you could "write" programs without writing a single line of code. Granted, someone would have to write the Beans in the first place; but that's a much smaller task, and we expect markets to develop for "off the shelf" Bean collections.

Before it can use a Bean, an application builder must find out the Bean's capabilities. There are a few ways it can do this; the simplest is called "reflection." To write a Bean that uses reflection, all you need to do is follow some well-defined conventions (design patterns) that let the graphical interface builder (or any other tool that wants to do the work) analyze the Bean.

If they need to, Beans can provide additional information using a process called *introspection*. But even without introspection, a graphical development tool can analyze a Bean, figure out what it can do, and let a user change the Bean's properties without writing any code.

Of course, once a development tool has customized a Bean and connected it to other Beans, it needs a way to save the result. A process called "serialization" lets a tool save the Bean's current state, along with any extra code it has written to stitch Beans together in an application.

Visual development tools that support Java Beans include IBM's upcoming VisualAge, Borland's JBuilder (*http://www.borland.com/*), Symantec's Visual Cafe (*http://www.symantec.com/*), and SunSoft's Java Workshop. By using a "bridge," Java Beans will be able to function inside other component environments, including ActiveX, OpenDoc, and LiveConnect. A beta version of the ActiveX bridge is currently available.

Java as a General Application Language

The Java applet API is a framework that allows Java-enabled Web browsers to manage and display embedded Java applications within WWW documents. However, Java is more than just a tool for building transportable multimedia applications. Java is a powerful, general purpose programming language that just happens to be safe and architecture independent. Standalone Java applications are not subject to the restrictions placed on applets; they can do all activities that software written in a language like C does.

Any software that implements the Java run-time system can run Java applications. Applications written in Java can be large or small, standalone or component-like, as in other languages. Java applets are different from other Java applications only in that they expect to be managed by a larger application. In this book, we will build examples of both applets and standalone Java applications. With the exception of the few things applets can't do, such as access files, all of the tools we examine in this book apply to both applets and standalone Java applications.

A Java Road Map

With everything that's going on, it's hard to keep track of what's available now, what's promised, and what has been around for some time. Here's a road map that imposes some order on Java's past, present, and future.

The Past: Java 1.0

Java 1.0 provided the basic framework for Java development: the language itself plus packages that let you write applets and simple applications. Although Java 1.0 is officially obsolete, it will be some time before vendors catch up with the new release.

The Present: Java 1.1

Java 1.1 is the current version of Java. It incorporates major improvements in the AWT package (Java's window facility). It also adds many completely new features, including:

JDBC
   A general facility for interacting with databases.

RMI
> Remote Method Invocation: a facility that lets you call methods that are provided by a server running somewhere else on the network.

JavaBeans
> Java's component architecture, which we discussed earlier.

Cryptographic security
> A facility for cryptography; this is the basis for signed classes, which we discussed earlier.

Internationalization
> The ability to write programs that adapt themselves to the language the user wants to use; the program automatically displays text in the appropriate language.

Java 1.1 incorporates many other improvements and new features, but these are the most important. As of May 1997, most Web browsers haven't yet incorporated Java 1.1, but they will as soon as possible. In this book, we'll try to give you a taste of as many features as possible; unfortunately for us, the Java environment has become so rich that it's impossible to cover everything in a single book.

The Future

We've mentioned a few of the things that are in the pipeline, including high quality audio, advanced 3D rendering, and speech synthesis. Other things to look forward to are class libraries for advanced 2D graphics (Java 2D), electronic commerce (JECF), managing network devices (Java Management), naming and directory services (JNDI), telephony (JTAPI), and writing network servers (Java Server). Beta versions of some of these facilities are available now.

We're also starting to see new kinds of computing devices that incorporate Java. Network computers that are based on Java and use the HotJava browser as their user interface are already available, as are "smart cards": credit card–like devices with a built-in Java processor. You can expect to see Java incorporated into PDAs, telephones, and many other devices.

Availability

By the time you read this book, you should have several choices for Java development environments and run-time systems. As this book goes to press, Sun's Java Development Kit (JDK) 1.1 is available for Solaris, Windows NT, and Windows 95. The JDK provides an interpreter and a compiler for building general purpose Java applications. A beta version of JDK 1.1 for the Macintosh will be available later in

1997. Visit Sun's Java web site at *http://www.javasoft.com/* for more information about the JDK. There are also a number of JDK ports for various platforms. Some of the most significant platforms are NetWare, HP-UX, OSF/1 (including Digital UNIX), Silicon Graphics' IRIX, IBM's AIX (among other IBM operating systems), and Linux. For more information, see the Web pages maintained by the vendor you're interested in. JavaSoft maintains a Web page summarizing porting efforts at *http://www.javasoft.com/products/jdk/jdk-ports.html*. Another good source for current information is the Java FAQ from the *comp.lang.java* newsgroup.

There are efforts under way to produce a free clone of Java, redistributable in source form. The Java Open Language Toolkit (JOLT) Project is working to assemble a high-quality Java implementation that will pass Sun's validation tests and earn a Java stamp. The JOLT Project Web page is accessible from *http://www.redhat.com/*.

The Netscape Navigator Web browser comes with its own implementation of the Java run-time system that runs Java applets. Microsoft's Internet Explorer also provides support for Java and appears to be ahead in supporting Java 1.1; both browsers should support 1.1 by the end of 1997. For more information about Navigator, check Netscape's web site, *http://home.netscape.com/*.

2

A First Applet

Before we turn our attention to the details of the language, let's take a crash course and jump right into some Java code. In this chapter, we'll build a contrived but friendly little applet that illustrates a number of techniques we use throughout the book. We'll take this opportunity to introduce general features of the Java language and of Java applets. However, many details won't be fleshed out here, but in subsequent chapters.

This chapter also serves as a brief introduction to the object-oriented and multi-threaded features of Java. If these concepts are new to you, you can take comfort in the knowledge that encountering them for the first time in Java should be a straightforward and pleasant experience. If you have worked with another object-oriented or multithreaded programming environment, clear your mind; you will especially appreciate Java's simplicity and elegance.

We can't stress enough the importance of experimentation as you learn new concepts. If you follow along with the online examples, be sure to take some time and compile them locally. Play with them; change their behavior, break them, fix them, and, as Java architect Arthur van Hoff would say: "Have fun!"

Hello Web!

In the tradition of all good introductory programming texts, we begin with Java's equivalent of the archetypal "Hello World" application. In the spirit of our new world, we'll call it "Hello Web!"

We'll take four passes at this example, adding features and introducing new concepts along the way. Here's a minimalist version:

```
public class HelloWeb extends java.applet.Applet {
    public void paint( java.awt.Graphics gc ) {
        gc.drawString("Hello Web!", 125, 95 );
    }
}
```

Place this text in a file called *HelloWeb.java.* Now compile this source:

```
% javac HelloWeb.java
```

This produces the Java byte-code binary class file *HelloWeb.class.*

We need an HTML document that contains the appropriate <APPLET> tag to display our example. Place the following text in a file called *HelloWeb.html* in the same directory as the binary class file:

```
<html>
<head>
</head>
<body>
    <applet code=HelloWeb width=300 height=200></applet>
</body>
</html>
```

Finally, you can point your Java-enabled Web browser at this document with a URL such as:

```
http://yourServer/wherever/HelloWeb.html
```

or

```
file:/wherever/HelloWeb.html
```

You should see the proclamation shown in Figure 2-1. Now congratulate yourself: you have written your first applet! Take a moment to bask in the glow of your monitor.

HelloWeb may be a small program, but there is actually quite a bit going on behind the scenes. Those five lines represent the tip of an iceberg. What lies under the surface are layers of functionality provided by the Java language and its foundation class libraries. In this chapter, we'll cover a lot of ground quickly in an effort to show you the big picture. We'll try to offer enough detail for a complete understanding of what is happening in each example without exhaustive explanations until the appropriate chapters. This holds for both elements of the Java language and the object-oriented concepts that apply to them. Later chapters will provide more detailed cataloging of Java's syntax, components, and object-oriented features.

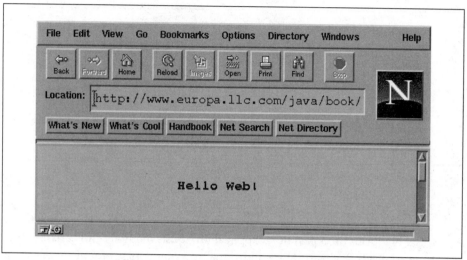

Figure 2–1: Hello Web! applet

Classes

The previous example defines a *class* named HelloWeb. Classes are the fundamental building blocks of most object-oriented languages. A class in Java is akin to the C++ concept of a class. Specifically, it's a group of data items (à la a C struct), with associated functions that perform operations on this data. The data items in a class are called *fields* or *variables*; the functions are called *methods*. A class might represent something concrete, like a button on a screen or the information in a spreadsheet, or it could be something more abstract, such as a sorting algorithm or possibly the sense of ennui in your MUD character. A hypothetical spreadsheet class might, for example, have variables that represent the values of its individual cells and methods that perform operations on those cells, such as "clear a row" or "compute values."

Our HelloWeb class is the container for our Java applet. It holds two general types of variables and methods: those we need for our specific applet's tasks and some special predesignated ones we provide to interact with the outside world. The Java run-time environment, in this case a Java-enabled Web browser, periodically calls methods in HelloWeb to pass us information and prod us to perform actions, as depicted in Figure 2-2. Our simple HelloWeb class defines a single method called paint(). The paint() method is called by Java when it's time for our application to draw itself on the screen.

You will see that the HelloWeb class derives some of its structure from another class called Applet. This is why we refer to HelloWeb as an applet.

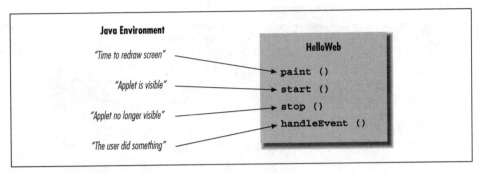

Figure 2–2: Method invocation in the Java environment

Class Instances and Objects

A class is a blueprint for a part of an application; it lists methods and variables that go into making up that part. Many individual working copies of a given class can exist while an application is active. These individual incarnations are called *instances* of the class. Two instances of a given class may contain different data, but they always have the same methods.

As an example, consider a Button class. There is only one Button class, but many actual working instances of buttons can be in an application. Furthermore, two Button instances might contain different data, perhaps giving each a different appearance or specifying a different message for each to send when pushed. In this sense, a class can be considered a mold for making the object it represents: something like a cookie cutter stamping out working instances of itself in the memory of the computer. As you'll see later, there's a bit more to it than that—a class can in fact share information among its instances—but this explanation suffices for now.

The term *object* is very general and in some other contexts is used almost interchangeably with class. Objects are the abstract entities all object-oriented languages refer to in one form or another. We will use object as a generic term for an instance of a class. We might, therefore, refer to an instance of the Button class as a Button, a Button object, or, indiscriminately, as an object.

A Java-enabled Web browser creates an instance of our HelloWeb class when we first use our applet. If we had included the HelloWeb applet tag in our HTML document twice (causing it to appear twice on the screen), the browser would create and manage two separate HelloWeb objects (two separate instances of the HelloWeb class).

Variables and Class Types

In Java, every class defines a new *type*. A variable can be of this type and then hold instances of that class. A variable could, for example, be of type Button and hold an instance of the Button class, or of type SpreadSheetCell and hold a Spread-SheetCell object, just as it could be any of the more familiar types such as int or float. In this way, by having variables containing complex objects, a class may use other classes as tools within itself. Using classes in this way is called *composition*. Our examples in this chapter are somewhat unrealistic in that we are building only a single class of our own. However, we will be using many classes as tools within our applet.

You have seen only one variable so far in our simple HelloWeb example. It's found in the declaration of our lonely paint() method:

```
public void paint( java.awt.Graphics gc ) {...}
```

Just like functions in C (and many other languages), a method in Java declares a list of variables that hold its arguments, and it specifies the types of those arguments. Our paint() method takes one argument named (somewhat tersely) gc, which is of type Graphics. When the paint() method is invoked, a Graphics object is assigned to gc, which we use in the body of the method. We'll say more about paint() and the Graphics class in a moment.

But first, a few words about variables. We have loosely referred to variables as holding objects. In reality, variables that have complex types (class types) don't so much contain objects as point to them. Class-type variables are *references* to objects. A reference is a pointer to, or another name for, an object.

Simply declaring a variable doesn't imply that any storage is allocated for that variable or that an instance of its type even exists anywhere. When a reference-type variable is first declared, if it's not assigned to an instance of a class, it doesn't point to anything. It's assigned the default value of null, meaning "no value." If you try to use a variable with a null value as if it were pointing to a real object, a run-time error (NullPointerException) occurs.

This discussion begs the question as to where to get an instance of a class to assign to a variable in the first place. The answer, as you will see later, is through the use of the new operator. In our first two passes at this example, we are dealing only with objects handed to us prefabricated from somewhere outside of our class. We examine object creation later in the chapter.

Inheritance

Java classes are arranged in a parent-child hierarchy, in which the parent and child are known as the *superclass* and *subclass*, respectively. In Java, every class has exactly one superclass (a single parent), but possibly many subclasses. Of course, a class's superclass probably has its own superclass.

The declaration of our class in the previous example uses the keyword `extends` to specify that `HelloWeb` is a subclass of the `Applet` class:

```
public class HelloWeb extends java.applet.Applet {...}
```

A subclass may be allowed to inherit some or all of the variables and methods of its superclass. Through *inheritance,* the subclass can use those members as if it has declared them itself. A subclass can add variables and methods of its own, and it can also override the meaning of inherited variables and methods. When we use a subclass, overridden variables and methods are hidden (replaced) by the subclass's own versions of them. In this way, inheritance provides a powerful mechanism whereby a subclass can refine or extend its superclass.

For example, the hypothetical spreadsheet class might be subclassed to produce a new scientific spreadsheet class with extra mathematical functions and special built-in constants. In this case, the source code for the scientific spreadsheet might declare methods for the added mathematical functions and variables for the special constants, but the new class automatically has all the variables and methods that constitute the normal functionality of a spreadsheet; they are inherited from the parent spreadsheet class. This means the scientific spreadsheet maintains its identity as a spreadsheet, and we can use it anywhere the simpler spreadsheet is used.

Our `HelloWeb` class is a subclass of the `Applet` class and inherits many variables and methods not explicitly declared in our source code. These members function in the same way as the ones we add or override.

Applet

The `Applet` class provides the framework for building applets. It contains methods that support the basic functionality for a Java application that is displayed and controlled by a Java-enabled Web browser or other Java-enabled software.

We override methods in the `Applet` class in a subclass to implement the behavior of our particular applet. This may sound restrictive, as if we are limited to some predefined set of routines, but that is not the case at all. Keep in mind that the methods we are talking about are means of getting information from the outside world. A realistic application might involve hundreds or even thousands of classes, with legions of methods and variables and multiple threads of execution. The vast majority of these are related to the particulars of our job. The inherited methods of the Applet class, and of other special components, serve as a framework on which to hang code that handles certain types of events and performs special tasks.

The paint() method is an important method of the Applet class; we override it to implement the way our particular applet displays itself on the screen. We don't override any of the other inherited members of Applet because they provide basic functionality and reasonable defaults for this (trivial) example. As HelloWeb grows, we'll delve deeper into the inherited members and override additional methods. Inherited members will allow us to get information from the user and give us more control over what our applet does. We will also add some arbitrary, application-specific methods and variables for the needs of HelloWeb.

If you want to verify for yourself what functionality the Applet class is providing our example, you can try out the world's least interesting applet: the Applet base class itself. Just use the class name java.applet.Applet in your HTML code, instead of HelloWeb:

```
<applet code=java.applet.Applet width=300 height=200></applet>
```

You should get a blank area of screen. We told you it's not very interesting.

Relationships and Finger Pointing

We can correctly refer to HelloWeb as an Applet because subclassing can be thought of as creating an "is a" relationship, in which the subclass is a kind of its superclass. HelloWeb is therefore a kind of Applet. When we refer to a kind of object, we mean any instance of that object's class or any of its subclasses. Later, we will look more closely at the Java class hierarchy and see that Applet is itself a subclass of the Panel class, which is further derived from a class called Container, and so on, as shown in Figure 2-3.

In this sense, an Applet is a kind of Panel, which is, itself, a kind of Container and each of these can ultimately be considered to be a kind of Component. You'll see later that it's from these classes that Applet inherits its basic graphical user interface functionality and the ability to have other graphical components embedded within it.

Component is a subclass of Object, so all of these classes are a kind of Object. As you'll see later, the Object class is at the top of the Java class hierarchy; Object doesn't have a superclass. Every other class in the Java API inherits behavior from Object, which defines a few basic methods, as you'll see in Chapter 7. The terminology here can become a bit muddled. We'll continue to use the word *object* (low-

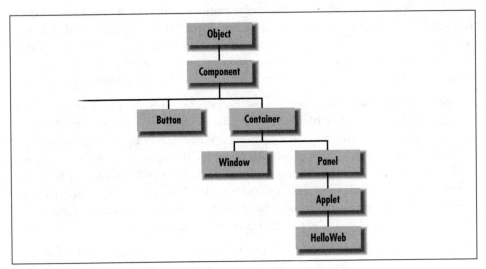

Figure 2–3: Part of the Java class hierarchy

ercase *o*) in a generic way to refer to an instance of any class; We'll use `Object` to refer specifically to that class.

Packages

In our previous example, the `Applet` class is referenced by its fully qualified name `java.applet.Applet`:

```
public class HelloWeb extends java.applet.Applet {...}
```

The prefix on the class name identifies it as belonging to the `java.applet` package. Packages provide a means for organizing Java classes. A *package* is a group of Java classes that are related by purpose or by application. Classes in the same package have special access privileges with respect to one another and may be designed to work together. Package names are hierarchical and are used somewhat like Internet domain and host names, to distinguish groups of classes by organization and application. Classes may be dynamically loaded over networks from arbitrary locations; within this context, packages provide a crude namespace of Java classes.*

---

* There are many efforts under way to find a general solution to the problem of locating resources in a globally distributed computing environment. The Uniform Resource Identifier Working Group of the IETF has proposed Uniform Resource Names (URNs). A URN would be a more abstract and persistent identifier that would be resolved to a URL through the use of a name service. We can imagine a day when there will exist a global namespace of trillions of persistent objects forming the infrastructure for all computing resources. Java provides an important evolutionary step in this direction.

java.applet identifies a particular package that contains classes related to applets. java.applet.Applet identifies a specific class, the Applet class, within that package. The java. hierarchy is special. Any package that begins with java. is part of the core Java API and is available on any platform that supports Java. Figure 2-4 illustrates some of the core Java packages, showing a representative class or two from each.

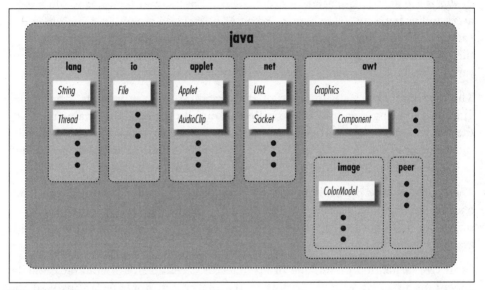

Figure 2–4: The core Java packages

Some notable core packages include: java.lang, which contains fundamental classes needed by the Java language itself; java.awt, which contains classes of the Java Abstract Window Toolkit; and java.net, which contains the networking classes.

A few classes contain methods that are not written in Java, but are instead part of the native Java implementation on a particular platform. Approximately 22 such classes are in the java package hierarchy; these are the only classes that have to be ported to a new platform. They form the basis for all interaction with the operating system. All other classes are built on or around these and are completely platform independent.

The paint() Method

The source for our HelloWeb class defines just one method, paint(), which overrides the paint() method from the Applet class:

```
public void paint( java.awt.Graphics gc ) {
    gc.drawString("Hello Web!", 125, 95 );
}
```

The paint() method is called by Java when it's time for our applet to draw itself on the screen. It takes a single argument, a Graphics object, and doesn't return any type of value (void) to its caller.

Modifiers are keywords placed before classes, variables, and methods to alter their accessibility, behavior, or semantics. paint() is declared as public, which means it can be invoked (called) by methods in classes other than HelloWeb. In this case, it's the Java windowing environment that is calling our paint() method. A method or variable declared as private is inaccessible from outside of its class.

The Graphics object, an instance of the Graphics class, represents a particular graphical drawing area and is also called a graphics context. It contains methods the applet calls to draw in this area, and variables that represent characteristics such as clipping or drawing modes. The particular Graphics object we are passed in the paint() method corresponds to our applet's area of the screen.

The Graphics class provides methods for rendering primitive shapes, images, and text. In HelloWeb, we invoke the drawString() method of our Graphics object to scrawl our message at the specified coordinates. (For a description of the methods available in the Graphics class, see Chapter 16.)

As in C++, a method or variable of an object is accessed in a hierarchical way by appending its name with a "." (dot) to the object that holds it. We invoked the drawString() method of the Graphics object (referenced by our gc variable) in this way:

```
gc.drawString( "Hello Web!", 125, 95 );
```

You may need to get used to the idea that our application is drawn by a method that is called by an outside agent at arbitrary times. How can we do anything useful with this? How do we control what gets done and when? These answers will be forthcoming. For now, just think about how you would structure applications that draw themselves on command.

Hello Web! II: The Sequel

Let's make our applet a little more interactive, shall we? The following improvement, HelloWeb2, allows us to drag the message around with the mouse. HelloWeb2

is also customizable. It takes the text of its message from a parameter of the
<APPLET> tag of the HTML document.

HelloWeb2 is a new applet—another subclass of the Applet class. In that sense, it's
a sibling of HelloWeb. Having just seen inheritance at work, you might wonder why
we aren't creating a subclass of HelloWeb and exploiting inheritance to build upon
our previous example and extend its functionality. Well, in this case, that would
not necessarily be an advantage, and for clarity we simply start over.* Here is Hel-
loWeb2:

```
import java.applet.Applet;
import java.awt.*;
import java.awt.event.*;
public class HelloWeb2 extends Applet implements MouseMotionListener {
    int messageX = 125, messageY = 95;
    String theMessage;

    public void init() {
        theMessage = getParameter("message");
        addMouseMotionListener(this);
    }

    public void paint( Graphics graphics ) {
        graphics.drawString( theMessage, messageX, messageY );
    }
    public void mouseDragged( MouseEvent e ) {
        messageX = e.getX();
        messageY = e.getY();
        repaint();
    }
    public void mouseMoved( MouseEvent e ) { }
}
```

Place the text of this example in a file called *HelloWeb2.java* and compile it as
before. You should get a new class file, *HelloWeb2.class*, as a result. We need to create a new <APPLET> tag for HelloWeb2. You can either create another HTML document (copy *HelloWeb.html* and modify it) or simply add a second <APPLET> tag to
the existing *HelloWeb.html* file. The <APPLET> tag for HelloWeb2 has to use a parameter; it should look like this:

```
<applet code=HelloWeb2 width=300 height=200>
<param name="message" value="Hello Web!" >
</applet>
```

Feel free to substitute your own salacious comment for the value of message.

---

* You are left to consider whether such a subclassing would even make sense. Should HelloWeb2 really
be a kind of HelloWeb? Are we looking for refinement or just code reuse?

Run this applet in your Java-enabled Web browser, and enjoy many hours of fun, dragging the text around with your mouse.

Import

So, what have we added? First you may notice that a few lines are now hovering above our class:

```
import java.applet.Applet;
import java.awt.*;
import java.awt.event.*;
public class HelloWeb2 extends Applet implements MouseMotionListener {
...
```

The import statement lists external classes to use in this file and tells the compiler where to look for them. In our first HelloWeb example, we designated the Applet class as the superclass of HelloWeb. Applet was not defined by us, and the compiler therefore had to look elsewhere for it. In that case, we referred to Applet by its fully qualified name, java.applet.Applet, which told the compiler that Applet belongs to the java.applet package so the compiler knew where to find it.

The import statement is really just a convenience; by importing java.applet.Applet in our newer example, we tell the compiler up front we are using this class and, thereafter in this file, we can simply refer to it as Applet. The second import statement makes use of the wildcard "*" to tell the compiler to import all of the classes in the java.awt package. But don't worry, the compiled code doesn't contain any excess baggage. Java doesn't do things like that. In fact, compiled Java classes don't contain other classes at all; they simply note their relationships. Our current example uses only the java.awt.Graphics class. However, we are anticipating using several more classes from this package in the upcoming examples. We also import all the classes from the package java.awt.event; these classes provide the Event objects that we use to communicate with the user. By listening for events, we find out when the user moved the mouse, clicked a button, and so on. Notice that importing java.awt.* doesn't automatically import the event package. The star only imports the classes in a particular package, not other packages.

The import statement may seem a bit like the C or C++ preprocessor #include statement, which injects header files into programs at the appropriate places. This is not true; there are no header files in Java. Unlike compiled C or C++ libraries, Java binary class files contain all necessary type information about the classes, methods, and variables they contain, obviating the need for prototyping.

Instance Variables

We have added some variables to our example:

```
public class HelloWeb2 extends Applet {
    int messageX = 125, messageY = 95;
    String theMessage;
    . . .
```

messageX and messageY are integers that hold the current coordinates of our movable message. They are initialized to default values, which should place a message of our length somewhere near the center of the applet. Java integers are always 32-bit signed numbers. There is no fretting about what architecture your code is running on; numeric types in Java are precisely defined. The variable theMessage is of type String and can hold instances of the String class.

You should note that these three variables are declared inside the braces of the class definition, but not inside any particular method in that class. These variables are called *instance variables* because they belong to the entire class, and copies of them appear in each separate instance of the class. Instance variables are always visible (usable) in any of the methods inside their class. Depending on their modifiers, they may also be accessible from outside the class.

Unless otherwise initialized, instance variables are set to a default value of 0 (zero), false, or null. Numeric types are set to zero, boolean variables are set to false, and class type variables always have their value set to null, which means "no value." Attempting to use an object with a null value results in a run-time error.

Instance variables differ from method arguments and other variables that are declared inside of a single method. The latter are called *local variables*. They are effectively private variables that can be seen only by code inside the method. Java doesn't initialize local variables, so you must assign values yourself. If you try to use a local variable that has not yet been assigned a value, your code will generate a compile-time error. Local variables live only as long as the method is executing and then disappear (which is fine since nothing outside of the method can see them anyway). Each time the method is invoked, its local variables are recreated and must be assigned values.

Methods

We have made some changes to our previously stodgy paint() method. All of the arguments in the call to drawString() are now variables.

Several new methods have appeared in our class. Like paint(), these are methods of the base Applet class we override to add our own functionality. init() is an important method of the Applet class. It's called once, when our applet is created, to give us an opportunity to do any work needed to set up shop. init() is a good place to allocate resources and perform other activities that need happen only once in the lifetime of the applet. A Java-enabled Web browser calls init() when it prepares to place the Applet on a page.

Our overridden init() method does two things: it sets the text of the theMessage instance variable, and it tells the system "Hey, I'm interested in anything that happens involving the mouse":

```
public void init() {
    theMessage = getParameter("message");
    addMouseMotionListener(this);
}
```

When an applet is instantiated, the parameters given in the <APPLET> tag of the HTML document are stored in a table and made available through the getParameter() method. Given the name of a parameter, this method returns the value as a String object. If the name is not found, it returns a null value.

So what, you may ask, is the type of the argument to the getParameter() method? It, too, is a String. With a little magic from the Java compiler, quoted strings in Java source code are turned into String objects. A bit of funny-business is going on here, but it's simply for convenience. (See Chapter 9 for a complete discussion of the String class.)

getParameter() is a public method we inherited from the Applet class. We can use it from any of our methods. Note that the getParameter() method is invoked directly by name; there is no object name prepended to it with a dot. If a method exists in our class or is inherited from a superclass, we can call it directly by name.

In addition, we can use a special read-only variable, called this, to explicitly refer to our object. A method can use this to refer to the instance of the object that holds it. The following two statements are therefore equivalent:

```
theMessage = getParameter("message");
```

or

```
theMessage = this.getParameter("message");
```

We'll always use the shorter form. We will need the this variable later when we have to pass a reference to our object to a method in another class. We often do this so that methods in another class can give us a call back later or can watch our public variables.

The other method that we call in init() is addMouseMotionListener(). This method is part of the event mechanism, which we discuss next.

Events

The last two methods of HelloWeb2 let us get information from the mouse. Each time the user performs an action, such as pressing a key on the keyboard, moving the mouse, or perhaps banging his or her head against a touch-sensitive screen, Java generates an *event*. An event represents an action that has occurred; it contains information about the action, such as its time and location. Most events are associated with a particular graphical user interface (GUI) component in an application. A keystroke, for instance, could correspond to a character being typed into a particular text entry field. Pressing a mouse button could cause a certain graphical button on the screen to activate. Even just moving the mouse within a certain area of the screen could be intended to trigger effects such as highlighting or changing the cursor to a special mouse cursor.

The way events work is one of the major changes between Java 1.0 and Java 1.1. We're going to talk about the Java 1.1 events only; they're a big improvement, and there's no sense in learning yesterday's news. In Java 1.1, there are many different event classes: MouseEvent, KeyEvent, ActionEvent, and many others. For the most part, the meaning of these events is fairly intuitive. A MouseEvent occurs when the user does something with the mouse, a KeyEvent occurs when the user types a key, and so on. ActionEvent is a little special; we'll see it at work later in this chapter in our third applet. For now, we'll focus on dealing with a MouseEvent.

The various GUI components in Java generate events. For example, if you click the mouse inside an applet, the applet generates a mouse event. (In the future, we will probably see events as a general-purpose way to communicate between Java objects; for the moment, let's limit ourselves to the simplest case.) In Java 1.1, any object can ask to receive the events generated by another component. We will call the object that wants to receive events a "listener." For example, to declare that a listener wants to receive a component's mouse motion events, you invoke that component's addMouseMotionListener() method. That's what our applet is doing in init(). In this case, the applet is calling its own addMouseMotionListener() method, with the argument this, meaning "I want to receive my own mouse motion events."

That's how we register to receive events. But how do we actually get them? That's what the two remaining methods in our applet are for. The mouseDragged() method is called automatically to receive the event generated whenever the user drags the mouse—that is, moves the mouse with any button pressed. The mouseMoved() method is called whenever the user moves the mouse over the area without pressing a button. Our mouseMoved() method is simple: it doesn't do anything. We're ignoring simple mouse motions.

mouseDragged() has a bit more meat to it. It is called repeatedly to give us updates on the position of the mouse. Here it is:

```
public void mouseDragged( MouseEvent e ) {
    messageX = e.getX();
    messageY = e.getY();
    repaint();
}
```

The first argument to mouseDragged() is a MouseEvent object, e, that contains all the information we need to know about this event. We ask the MouseEvent to tell us the x and y coordinates of the mouse's current position by calling its getX() and getY() methods. These are saved in the messageX and messageY instance variables. Now, having changed the coordinates for the message, we would like HelloWeb2 to redraw itself. We do this by calling repaint(), which asks the system to redraw the screen at a later time. We can't call paint() directly because we don't have a graphics context to pass to it.

The real beauty of this event model is that you only have to handle the kinds of events you want. If you don't care about keyboard events, you just don't register a listener for them; the user can type all he or she wants, and you won't be bothered. Java 1.1 doesn't go around asking potential recipients whether they might be interested in some event, as it did in older versions. If there are no listeners for a particular kind of event, Java won't even generate it. The result is that event handling in Java 1.1 is quite efficient.

We've danced around one question that may be bothering you by now: how does the system know to call mouseDragged() and mouseMoved()? And why do we have to supply a mouseMoved() method that doesn't do anything? The answer to these questions has to do with "interfaces." We'll discuss interfaces after clearing up some unfinished business with repaint().

The repaint() Method

We can use the repaint() method of the Applet class to request our applet be redrawn. repaint() causes the Java windowing system to schedule a call to our paint() method at the next possible time; Java supplies the necessary Graphics object, as shown in Figure 2-5.

This mode of operation isn't just an inconvenience brought about by not having the right graphics context handy at the moment. The foremost advantage to this mode of operation is that the repainting is handled by someone else, while we are free to go about our business. The Java system has a separate, dedicated thread of

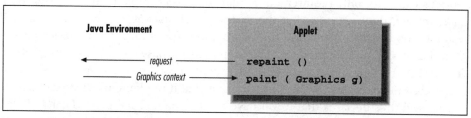

Figure 2–5: Invoking the repaint() method

execution that handles all repaint() requests. It can schedule and consolidate repaint() requests as necessary, which helps to prevent the windowing system from being overwhelmed during painting-intensive situations like scrolling. Another advantage is that all of the painting functionality can be kept in our paint() method; we aren't tempted to spread it throughout the application.

Interfaces

Now it's time to face up to the question we avoided earlier: how does the system know to call mouseDragged() when a mouse event occurs? Is it simply a matter of knowing that mouseDragged() is some magic name that our event handling method must have? Not quite; the answer to the question touches on the discussion of interfaces, which are one of the most important features of the Java language.

The first sign of an interface comes on the line of code that introduces the HelloWeb2 applet: we say that the applet implements MouseMotionListener. MouseMotionListener is an interface that the applet implements. Essentially, it's a list of methods that the applet must have; this particular interface requires our applet to have methods called mouseDragged() and mouseMoved(). The interface doesn't say what these methods have to do—and indeed, mouseMoved() doesn't do anything. It does say that the methods must take a MouseEvent as an argument and return void (i.e., no return value).

Another way of looking at an interface is as a contract between you, the code developer, and the compiler. By saying that your applet implements the MouseMotionListener interface, you're saying that these methods will be available for other parts of the system to call. If you don't provide them, the compiler will notice and give you an error message.

But that's not the only way interfaces impact this program. An interface also acts like a class. For example, a method could return a MouseMotionListener or take a MouseMotionListener as an argument. This means that you don't care about the object's class; the only requirement is that the object implement the given interface. In fact, that's exactly what the method addMouseMotionListener() does. If you look up the documentation for this method, you'll find that it takes a Mouse-MotionListener as an argument. The argument we pass is this, the applet itself. The fact that it's an applet is irrelevant—it could be a Cookie, an Aardvark, or any other class we dream up. What is important is that it implements MouseMotionListener, and thus declares that it will have the two named methods. That's why we need a mouseMoved() method, even though the one we supplied doesn't do anything: the MouseMotionListener interface says we have to have one.

In other languages, you'd handle this problem by passing a function pointer; for example, in C, the argument to addMouseMotionListener() might be a pointer to the function you want to have called when an event occurs. This technique is called a "callback." For a variety of reasons, the Java language has eliminated function pointers. Instead, we use interfaces to make contracts between classes and the compiler. (Some new features of the language make it easier to do something similar to a callback, but that's beyond the scope of this discussion.)

The Java distribution comes with many interfaces that define what classes have to do in various situations. It turns out that this idea of a contract between the compiler and a class is very important. There are many situations like the one we just saw, where you don't care what class something is, you just care that it has some capability, like listening for mouse events. Interfaces give you a way of acting on objects based on their capabilities, without knowing or caring about their actual type.

Furthermore, interfaces provide an important escape clause to the rule that any new class can extend only a single class (formally called "single inheritance"). They provide most of the advantages of multiple inheritance (a feature of languages like C++) without the confusion. A class in Java can extend only one class but can implement as many interfaces as it wants; our next applet will implement two interfaces, and the final example in this chapter will implement three. In many ways, interfaces are almost like classes but not quite. They can be used as data types, they can even extend other interfaces (but not classes), and can be inherited by classes (if class A implements interface B, subclasses of A also implement B). The crucial difference is that applets don't actually inherit methods from interfaces; the interfaces specify only the methods the applet must have.

Hello Web! III: The Button Strikes!

Well, now that we have those concepts under control, we can move on to some fun stuff. HelloWeb3 brings us a new graphical interface component: the Button. We add a Button component to our applet that changes the color of our text each time the button is pressed. Our new example is shown below:

```java
import java.applet.Applet;
import java.awt.*;
import java.awt.event.*;
public class HelloWeb3 extends Applet
    implements MouseMotionListener, ActionListener {
    int messageX = 125, messageY = 95;
    String theMessage;
    Button theButton;
    int colorIndex = 0;
    static Color[] someColors = {
        Color.black, Color.red, Color.green, Color.blue, Color.magenta};

    public void init() {
        theMessage = getParameter("message");
        theButton = new Button("Change Color");
        add(theButton);
        addMouseMotionListener(this);
        theButton.addActionListener(this);
    }

    public void paint( Graphics gc ) {
        gc.drawString( theMessage, messageX, messageY );
    }
    public void mouseDragged( MouseEvent e ) {
        messageX = e.getX();
        messageY = e.getY();
        repaint();
    }
    public void mouseMoved( MouseEvent e ) { }
    public void actionPerformed( ActionEvent e ) {
        if ( e.getSource() == theButton ) {
            changeColor();
        }
    }
    synchronized private void changeColor() {
        if ( ++colorIndex == someColors.length )
            colorIndex = 0;
        setForeground( currentColor() );
        repaint();
    }
    synchronized private Color currentColor() {
        return someColors[ colorIndex ];
    }
}
```

Create `HelloWeb3` just as the other applets and put an <APPLET> tag referencing it in an HTML document. An <APPLET> tag just like the one for `HelloWeb2` will do nicely. Run the example, and you should see the display shown in Figure 2-6. Drag the text. Each time you press the button the color should change. Call your friends! They should be duly impressed.

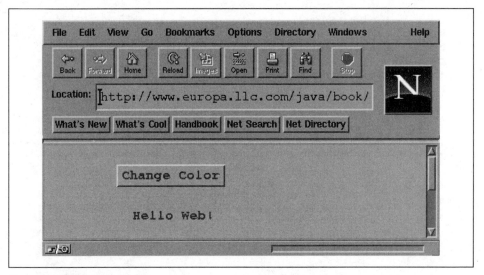

Figure 2–6: Hello Web! III

The New Operator

So what have we added this time? Well, for starters we have a new variable:

```
Button theButton;
```

The `theButton` variable is of type `Button` and is going to hold an instance of the `java.awt.Button` class. The `Button` class, as you might expect, represents a graphical button, which should look like other buttons in your windowing system.

Two additional lines in `init()` create the button and display it:

```
theButton = new Button("Change Color");
add(theButton);
```

The first line brings us to something new. The `new` keyword is used to create an instance of a class. Recall that the variable we have declared is just an empty reference and doesn't yet point to a real object—in this case, an instance of the `Button` class. This is a fundamental and important concept. We have dealt with objects previously in our examples. We have assigned them to variables, and we have called methods in them. So far, however, these objects have always been handed to us ready to go, and we have not had to explicitly create them ourselves. In the case of our paint() method, we were given a Graphics object with which to draw. The system created this instance of the Graphics class for our area of the screen and passed it to us in the parameter variable gc. Our theMessage variable is of type String, and we used it to hold a String that was returned by the getParameter() method. In each case, some other method instantiated (created a new instance of) the class for us.

The closest we came to actually instantiating an object was when we passed the name of the HTML <APPLET> parameter as an argument to the getParameter() method. In that case, we created a String object and passed it as the argument, but we did it in a rather sneaky fashion. As we mentioned previously, String objects have special status in the Java language. Because strings are used so frequently, the Java compiler creates an instance of the String class for us whenever it comes across quoted text in our source code. String objects are, in all other respects, normal objects.

The new operator provides the general mechanism for instantiating objects. It's the feature of the Java language that creates a new instance of a specified class. It arranges for Java to allocate storage for the object and then calls the constructor method of the objects' class to initialize it.

Constructors

A *constructor* is a special method that is called to set up a new instance of a class. When a new object is created, Java allocates storage for it, sets variables to their default values, and then calls the constructor method for the class to do whatever application-level setup is required.

A constructor method looks like a method with the same name as its class. For example, the constructor for the Button class is called Button(). Constructors don't have a return type; by definition they return an object of that class. But like other methods, constructors can take arguments. Their sole mission in life is to configure and initialize newly born class instances, possibly using whatever information is passed to them in parameters.

It's important to understand the difference between a constructor and a method like our init() method. Constructors are special methods of a class that help set up and initialize an instance of a class when it's first created. The init() method of the Applet class serves a very similar purpose; however, it's quite different. Constructors are a feature of the Java language. Every class, including Applet, has constructors. init(), however, is just a method of the Applet class like any other. It's an application-level phenomenon that happens to perform initialization.

An object is created by using the new operator with the constructor for the class and any necessary arguments. The resulting object instance is returned as a value. In our example, we create a new instance of Button and assign it to our theButton variable:

```
theButton = new Button("Change Color");
```

This Button constructor takes a String as an argument and, as it turns out, uses it to set the label of the button on the screen. A class could also, of course, provide methods that allow us to configure an object manually after it's created or to change its configuration at a later time. Many classes do both; the constructor simply takes its arguments and passes them to the appropriate methods. The Button class, for example, has a public method, setLabel(), that allows us to set a Button's label at any time. Constructors with parameters are therefore a convenience that allows a sort of shorthand to set up a new object.

Method Overloading

We said this Button constructor because there could be more than one. A class can have multiple constructors, each taking different parameters and possibly using them to do different kinds of setup. When there are multiple constructors for a class, Java chooses the correct one based on the types of arguments that are passed to it. We call the Button constructor and pass it a String argument, so Java locates the constructor method of the Button class that takes a single String argument and uses it to set up the object. This is called *method overloading*. All methods in Java, not just constructors, can be overloaded; this is one aspect of the object-oriented programming principle of polymorphism.

A constructor method that takes no arguments is called the *default constructor*. As you'll see in Chapter 5, default constructors play a special role in the initialization of inherited class members.

Garbage Collection

We've told you how to create a new object with the new operator, but we haven't said anything about how to get rid of an object when you are done with it. If you are a C programmer, you're probably wondering why not. The reason is that you don't have to do anything to get rid of objects when you are done with them.

The Java run-time system uses a *garbage collection* mechanism to deal with objects no longer in use. The garbage collector sweeps up objects not referenced by any variables and removes them from memory. Garbage collection is one of the most important features of Java. It frees you from the error-prone task of having to worry about details of memory allocation and deallocation.

Components

We have used the terms *component* and *container* somewhat loosely to describe graphical elements of Java applications. However, you may recall from Figure 2-3 that these terms are the names of actual classes in the `java.awt` package.

`Component` is a base class from which all of Java's GUI components are derived. It contains variables that represent the location, shape, general appearance, and status of the object, as well as methods for basic painting and event handling. The familiar `paint()` method we have been using in our example is actually inherited from the `Component` class. `Applet` is, of course, a kind of `Component` and inherits all of its public members, just as other (perhaps simpler) types of GUI components do.

The `Button` class is also derived from `Component` and therefore shares this functionality. This means that the developer of the `Button` class had methods like `paint()` available with which to implement the behavior of the `Button` object, just as we did when creating our applet. What's exciting is that we are perfectly free to further subclass components like `Button` and override their behavior to create our own special types of user-interface components.

Both `Button` and `Applet` are, in this respect, equivalent types of things. However, the `Applet` class is further derived from a class called `Container`, which gives it the added ability to hold other components and manage them.

Containers

A `Button` object is a simple GUI component. It makes sense only in the context of some larger application. The `Container` class is an extended type of `Component` that maintains a list of child components and helps to group them. The `Container` causes its children to be displayed and arranges them on the screen according to a particular scheme. A `Container` also commonly arranges to receive events related to its child components. This gives us a great deal of flexibility in managing interface components. We could, for example, create a smart button by subclassing the `Button` class and overriding certain methods to deal with the action of being pressed. Alternatively, we could simply have the `Button`'s container note when the `Button` is pressed and handle the event appropriately. In the interest of keeping our examples contained in a single class, we are using the gestalt view and letting our `Button`'s container, `HelloWeb3`, deal with its events.

Remember that a `Container` is a `Component` too and, as such, can be placed alongside other `Component` objects in other `Container`s, in a hierarchical fashion, as shown in Figure 2-7. Our `HelloWeb3` applet is a kind of `Container` and can therefore hold and manage other Java AWT components and containers like buttons, sliders, text fields, and panels.

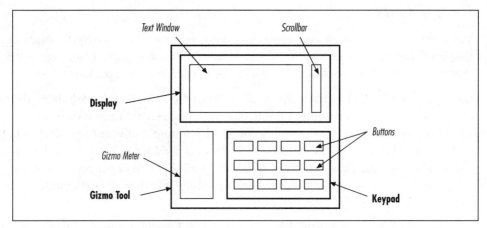

Figure 2–7: A hypothetical layout of Java containers and components

In Figure 2-7, the italicized items are components, and the bold items are containers. The keypad is implemented as a container object that manages a number of keys. The keypad itself is contained in the `GizmoTool` container object.

Layout

After creating the `Button` object, we'd like to stick it in our applet. To do so, we invoke the `add()` method of `Applet`, passing the `Button` object as a parameter:

```
add(theButton);
```

`add()` is a method inherited by our `Applet` from the `Container` class. It appends our `Button` to the list of components `HelloWeb3` manages. Thereafter, `HelloWeb3` is responsible for the `Button`: the applet causes the button to be displayed, it determines where in our part of the screen the button should be placed, and it receives events when the button is pushed.

Java uses an object called a `LayoutManager` to determine the precise location in `HelloWeb3`'s screen area the `Button` is displayed. A `LayoutManager` object embodies a particular scheme for arranging components on the screen and adjusting their sizes. You'll learn more about layout managers in Chapter 15. There are several standard layout managers to choose from, and we can, of course, create new ones. In our case, we have not specified a layout manager, so we get the default one, which means our button appears centered at the top of the applet.

Subclassing and Subtypes

If you look up the add() method of the Container class, you'll see that it takes a Component object as an argument. But in our example we've given it a Button object. What's going on?

Well, if you check the inheritance diagram in Figure 2-3 again, you'll see that Button is a subclass of the Component class. Because a subclass is a kind of its superclass and has, at minimum, the same public methods and variables, we can use an instance of a subclass anywhere we use an instance of its superclass. This is a very important concept, and it's a second aspect of the object-oriented principle of polymorphism. Button is a kind of Component, and any method that expects a Component as an argument will accept a Button.

More Events and Interfaces

Now that we have a Button, we need some way to communicate with it: that is, to get the events it generates. We could just listen for mouse clicks within the button and act accordingly. But that would be doing the Button's job and we would be giving up the advantages of using a prebuilt component. Instead, a Button generates a special kind of event called an ActionEvent when someone actually uses it. To receive these events, we have added another method to our class:

```
public void actionPerformed( ActionEvent e ) {
    if ( e.getSource() == theButton ) {
        changeColor();
    }
}
```

If you understood the previous applet, you shouldn't be surprised to see that Hel-loWeb3 now declares that it implements the ActionListener interface, in addition to MouseMotionListener. ActionListener requires us to implement an action-Performed() method, which is called whenever an ActionEvent occurs. You also shouldn't be surprised to see that we added a line to init(), registering the applet as a listener for the button's action events: this is the call to theBut-ton.addActionListener(this).

The actionPerformed() method takes care of any action events that arise. First, it checks to make sure that the event's source (the component generating the event) is what we think it should be: theButton, the only button we've put in the applet. This may seem superfluous; after all, what else could possibly generate an action event? In this applet, nothing. But it's a good idea to check, because another applet may have several buttons, and you may need to figure out which one is meant. Or you may add a second button to this applet later, and you don't want the applet to break something. To check this, we call the getSource() method of the ActionEvent object, e. Then we use the == operator to make sure that the event source matches theButton. Remember that in Java, == is a test for identity, not equality; it is true if the event source and theButton are the same object. The distinction between equality and identity is important. We would consider two String objects to be equal if they have the same characters in the same sequence. However, they might not be the same object. In Chapter 7, we'll look at the equals() method, which tests for equivalence. Once we establish that the event e comes from the right button, we call our changeColor() method, and we're finished.

You may be wondering why we don't have to change mouseDragged() now that we have a Button in our applet. The rationale is that the coordinates of the event are all that matter for this method. We are not particularly concerned if the event happens to fall within an area of the screen occupied by another component. This means that you can drag the text right through the Button and even lose it behind the Button if you aren't careful: try it and see!

Color Commentary

To support HelloWeb3's colorful side we have added a couple of new variables and two helpful methods. We create and initialize an array of Color objects representing the colors through which we cycle when the button is pressed. We also declare an integer variable that serves as an index to this array, specifying the current color:

```
Color[] someColors = {
    Color.black, Color.red, Color.green, Color.blue, Color.magenta };
int colorIndex;
```

A number of things are going on here. First let's look at the Color objects we are putting into the array. Instances of the java.awt.Color class represent colors and are used by all classes in the java.awt package that deal with color graphics. Notice that we are referencing variables such as Color.black and Color.red. These look like normal references to an object's instance variables; however, Color is not an object, it's a class. What is the meaning of this?

Static Members

If you recall our discussion of classes and instances, we hinted then that a class can contain methods and variables that are shared among all instances of the class. These shared members are called *static variables* and *static methods*. The most common use of static variables in a class is to hold predefined constants or unchanging objects all of the instances can use.

There are two advantages to this approach. The more obvious advantage is that static members take up space only in the class; the members are not replicated in each instance. The second advantage is that static members can be accessed even if no instances of the class exist. A hypothetical Component class might have a static variable called defaultColor. Some other class that has to deal with this component, such as a special container, might want to know the default color of such a component, even if there aren't any around at the moment. Since defaultColor is a static variable, the container could get this information directly from the class.

An instance of the Color class represents a color. For convenience, the Color class contains some static, predefined color objects with friendly names like green, red, and (our favorite) magenta. Color.green is thus a predefined Color object that is set to a green color. In this case, these static members of Color are not changeable, so they are effectively constants and can be optimized as such by the compiler. Constant static members make up for the lack of a #define construct in Java. The alternative to using these predefined colors is to create a color manually by specifying its red, green, blue (RGB) components using a Color class constructor.

Arrays

Next, we turn our attention to the array. We have declared a variable called some-Colors, which is an array of Color objects. Arrays are syntactically supported by the Java language; however, they are true, first-class objects. This means that an array is, itself, a type of object that knows how to hold an indexed list of some other type of object. An array is indexed by integers; when you index an array, the resulting value is the object in the corresponding slot in the array. Our code uses the col-orIndex variable to index someColors. It's also possible to have an array of simple primitive types, rather than objects.

When we declare an array, we can initialize it by using the familiar C-like curly brace construct. Specifying a comma-separated list of elements inside of curly braces is a convenience that instructs the compiler to create an instance of the array with those elements and assign it to our variable. Alternatively, we could have just declared our someColors variable and, later, allocated an array object for it and assigned individual elements to that array's slots. See Chapter 5 for a complete discussion of arrays.

Our Color Methods

So, we now have an array of Color objects and a variable with which to index them. What do we do with them? Well, we have declared two private methods that do the actual work for us. The private modifier on these methods specifies that they can be called only by other methods in the same instance of the class. They are not visible outside of the object. We declare members to be private to hide the detailed inner workings of a class from the outside world. This is called *encapsulation* and is another tenet of object-oriented design, as well as good programming practice. Private methods are also often created as helper functions for use solely within the class implementation.

The first method, currentColor(), is simply a convenience routine that returns the Color object representing the current text color. It returns the Color object in the someColors array at the index specified by our colorIndex variable:

```
synchronized private Color currentColor() {
    return someColors[ colorIndex ];
}
```

We could just as readily have used the expression someColors[colorIndex] everywhere we use currentColor(); however, creating methods to wrap common tasks is another way of shielding ourselves from the details of our class. In an alternative implementation, we might have shuffled off details of all color-related code into a separate class. We could have created a class that takes an array of colors in its constructor and then provided two methods: one to ask for the current color and one to cycle to the next color (just some food for thought).

The second method, changeColor(), is responsible for incrementing the colorIndex variable to point to the next Color in the array. changeColor() is called from our action() method whenever the button is pressed:

```
synchronized private void changeColor() {
    if ( ++colorIndex == someColors.length )
        colorIndex = 0;
    setForeground( currentColor() );
    repaint();
}
```

We increment colorIndex and compare it to the length of the someColors array. All array objects have a variable called length that specifies the number of elements in the array. If we have reached the end of the array, we reset our index to zero and start over. After changing the currently selected color, we do two things. First, we call the applet's setForeground() method, which changes the color used to draw text in the applet and the color of the button's label. Then we call repaint() to cause the applet to be redrawn with the new color for the draggable message.

So, what is the synchronized keyword that appears in front of our currentColor() and changeColor() methods? Synchronization has to do with threads, which we'll examine in the next section. For now, all you need know is that the synchronized keyword indicates these two methods can never be running at the same time. They must always run one after the other.

The reason is that in changeColor() we increment colorIndex before testing its value. That means that for some brief period of time while Java is running through our code, colorIndex can have a value that is past the end of our array. If our currentColor() method happened to run at that same moment, we would see a run-time "array out of bounds" error. There are, of course, ways in which we could fudge around the problem in this case, but this simple example is representative of more general synchronization issues we need to address. In the next section, you'll see that Java makes dealing with these problems easy through language-level synchronization support.

Hello Web! IV: Netscape's Revenge

We have explored quite a few features of Java with the first three versions of the HelloWeb applet. But until now, our applet has been rather passive; it has waited patiently for events to come its way and responded to the whims of the user. Now our applet is going to take some initiative—HelloWeb4 will blink! The code for our latest version is shown below:

```java
import java.applet.Applet;
import java.awt.*;
import java.awt.event.*;
public class HelloWeb4 extends Applet
    implements MouseMotionListener, ActionListener, Runnable {
    int messageX = 125, messageY = 95;
    String theMessage;
    Button theButton;
    int colorIndex = 0;
    static Color[] someColors = {
        Color.black, Color.red, Color.green, Color.blue, Color.magenta};
    Thread blinkThread;
    boolean blinkState;
    public void init() {
        theMessage = getParameter("message");
        theButton = new Button("Change Color");
        add(theButton);
        addMouseMotionListener(this);
        theButton.addActionListener(this);
    }

    public void paint( Graphics graphics ) {
        graphics.setColor( blinkState ? Color.white : currentColor() );
        graphics.drawString( theMessage, messageX, messageY );
    }
    public void mouseDragged( MouseEvent e ) {
        messageX = e.getX();
```

```
            messageY = e.getY();
            repaint();
        }
    public void mouseMoved( MouseEvent e ) { }
    public void actionPerformed( ActionEvent e ) {
        if ( e.getSource() == theButton ) {
            changeColor();
        }
    }
    synchronized private void changeColor() {
        if ( ++colorIndex == someColors.length )
            colorIndex = 0;
        theButton.setForeground( currentColor() );
        repaint();
    }
    synchronized private Color currentColor() {
        return someColors[ colorIndex ];
    }
    public void run() {
        while ( true ) {
            blinkState = !blinkState;
            repaint();
            try {
                Thread.sleep(500);
            } catch (Exception e ) {
                // Handle error condition here...
            }
        }
    }
    public void start() {
        if ( blinkThread == null ) {
            blinkThread = new Thread(this);
            blinkThread.start();
        }
    }
    public void stop() {
        if ( blinkThread != null ) {
            blinkThread.stop();
            blinkThread = null;
        }
    }
}
```

If you create HelloWeb4 as you have the other applets and then run it in a Java-enabled Web browser, you'll see that the text does in fact blink. Our apologies if you don't like blinking text—we're not overly fond of it either—but it does make for a simple, instructive example.

Threads

All the changes we've made in HelloWeb4 have to do with setting up a separate thread of execution to make the text of our applet blink. Java is a *multithreaded* language, which means there can be many threads running at the same time. A *thread* is a separate flow of control within a program. Conceptually, threads are similar to processes, except that unlike processes, multiple threads share the same address space, which means that they can share variables and methods (but they have their own local variables). Threads are also quite lightweight in comparison to processes, so it's conceivable for a single application to be running hundreds of threads concurrently.

Multithreading provides a way for an application to handle many different tasks at the same time. It's easy to imagine multiple things going on at the same time in an application like a Web browser. The user could be listening to an audio clip while scrolling an image, and in the background the browser is downloading an image. Multithreading is especially useful in GUI-based applications, as it can improve the interactive performance of these applications.

Unfortunately for us, programming with multiple threads can be quite a headache. The difficulty lies in making sure routines are implemented so they can be run by multiple concurrent threads. If a routine changes the value of a state variable, for example, then only one thread can be executing the routine at a time. Later in this section, we'll examine briefly the issue of coordinating multiple thread's access to shared data. In other languages, synchronization of threads can be an extremely complex and error-prone endeavor. You'll see that Java gives you a few simple tools that help you deal with many of these problems. Java threads can be started, stopped, suspended, and prioritized. Threads are preemptive, so a higher priority thread can interrupt a lower priority thread when vying for processor time. See Chapter 8 for a complete discussion of threads.

The Java run-time system creates and manages a number of threads. We've already mentioned the AWT thread, which manages repaint() requests and event processing for GUI components that belong to the java.awt package. A Java-enabled Web browser typically has at least one separate thread of execution it uses to manage the applets it displays. Until now, our example has done most of its work from methods of the Applet class, which means that it has been borrowing time from these threads. Methods like mouseDragged() and actionPerformed() are invoked by the AWT thread and run on its time. Similarly, our init() method is called by a thread in the Web browser. This means we are somewhat limited in the amount of processing we do within these methods. If we were, for instance, to go into an endless loop in our init() method, our applet would never appear, as it would never finish initializing. If we want an applet to perform any extensive processing, such as animation, a lengthy calculation, or communication, we should create separate threads for these tasks.

The Thread Class

As you might have guessed, threads are created and controlled as `Thread` objects. We have added a new instance variable, `blinkThread`, to our example to hold the `Thread` that handles our blinking activity:

```
Thread blinkThread;
```

An instance of the `Thread` class corresponds to a single thread. It contains methods to start, control, and stop the thread's execution. Our basic plan is to create a `Thread` object to handle our blinking code. We call the `Thread`'s `start()` method to begin execution. Once the thread starts, it continues to run until we call the `Thread`'s `stop()` method to terminate it.

But Java doesn't allow pointers to methods, so how do we tell the thread which method to run? Well, the `Thread` object is rather picky; it always expects to execute a method called `run()` to perform the action of the thread. The `run()` method can, however, with a little persuasion, be located in any class we desire.

We specify the location of the `run()` method in one of two ways. First, the `Thread` class itself has a method called `run()`. One way to execute some Java code in a separate thread is to subclass `Thread` and override its `run()` method to do our bidding. In this case, we simply create an instance of this subclass and call its `start()` method.

It's not always desirable or possible to create a subclass of `Thread` to contain our `run()` method. In this case, we need to tell the `Thread` which object contains the `run()` method it should execute. The `Thread` class has a constructor that takes an object reference as its argument. If we create a `Thread` object using this constructor and call its `start()` method, the `Thread` executes the `run()` method of the target object, rather than its own. In order to accomplish this, Java needs to have a guarantee that the object we are passing it does indeed contain a compatible `run()` method. We already know how to make such a guarantee: we use an interface. Java provides an interface named `Runnable` that must be implemented by any class that wants to become a `Thread`.

The Runnable Interface

The second technique we described for creating a `Thread` object involved passing an object that implements the `Runnable` interface to the `Thread` constructor. The

Runnable interface specifies that the object contains a run() method that takes no arguments and returns no value. This method is called automatically when the system needs to start the thread.

Sticking with our technique for implementing our applet in a single class, we have opted to add the run() method for blinkThread to our HelloWeb4 class. This means that HelloWeb4 needs to implement the Runnable interface. We indicate that the class implements the interface in our class declaration:

```
public class HelloWeb4 extends Applet
    implements MouseMotionListener, ActionListener, Runnable {...}
```

At compile time, the Java compiler checks to make sure we abide by this statement. We have carried through by adding an appropriate run() method to our applet. Our run() method has the task of changing the color of our text a couple of times a second. It's a very short routine, but We're going to delay looking at it until we tie up some loose ends in dealing with the Thread itself.

start() and stop()

Now that we know how to create a Thread to execute our applet's run() method, we need to figure out where to do it. The start() and stop() methods of the Applet class are similar to init(). The start() method is called when an applet is first displayed. If the user then leaves the Web document or scrolls the applet off the screen, the stop() method is invoked. If the user subsequently returns, the start() method is called again, and so on. Unlike init(), start() and stop() can be called repeatedly during the lifetime of an applet.

The start() and stop() methods of the Applet class have absolutely nothing to do with the Thread object, except that they are a good place for an applet to start and stop a thread. An applet is responsible for managing the threads that it creates. It would be considered rude for an applet to continue such tasks as animation, making noise, or performing extensive calculations long after it's no longer visible on the screen. It's common practice, therefore, to start a thread when an applet becomes visible and stop it when the applet is no longer visible.

Here's the start() method from HelloWeb4:

```
public void start() {
    if ( blinkThread == null ) {
        blinkThread = new Thread(this);
        blinkThread.start();
    }
}
```

The method first checks to see if an object is assigned to blinkThread; recall that an uninitialized instance variable has a default value of null. If not, the method creates a new instance of Thread, passing the target object that contains the run() method to the constructor. Since HelloWeb4 contains our run() method, we pass the special variable this to the constructor to let the thread know where to find the run() method it should run. this always refers to our object. Finally, after creating the new Thread, we call its start() method to begin execution.

Our stop() method takes the complementary position:

```
public void stop() {
    if ( blinkThread != null ) {
        blinkThread.stop();
        blinkThread = null;
    }
}
```

This method checks to see if blinkThread is empty. If not, it calls the thread's stop() method to terminate its execution. By setting the value of blinkThread back to null, we have eliminated all references to the thread object we created in the start() method, so the garbage collector can dispose of the object.

run()

Our run() method does its job by setting the value of the variable blinkState. We have added blinkState, a boolean value, to represent whether we are currently blinking on or off:

```
boolean blinkState;
```

The setColor() line of our paint() method has been modified slightly to handle blinking. The call to setColor() now draws the text in white when blinkState is true:

```
gc.setColor( blinkState ? Color.white : currentColor() );
```

Here we are being somewhat terse and using the C-like ternary operator to return one of two alternate color values based on the value of blinkState.

Finally, we come to the run() method itself:

```
public void run() {
    while ( true ) {
        blinkState = !blinkState;
        repaint();
        try {
            Thread.sleep(500);
        }
        catch (InterruptedException e ) {
        }
```

```
        }
     }
```

At its outermost level, run() uses an infinite while loop. This means the method will run continuously until the thread is terminated by a call to the controlling Thread object's stop() method.

The body of the loop does three things on each pass:

- Flips the value of blinkState to its opposite value using the not operator, !.

- Calls repaint() so that our paint() method can have an opportunity to redraw the text in accordance with blinkState.

- Uses a try/catch statement to trap for an error in our call to the sleep() method of the Thread class. sleep() is a static method of the Thread class. The method can be invoked from anywhere and has the effect of putting the current thread to sleep for the specified number of milliseconds. The effect here is to give us approximately two blinks per second.

Exceptions

The try/catch statement in Java is used to handle special conditions called *exceptions*. An exception is a message that is sent, normally in response to an error, during the execution of a statement or a method. When an exceptional condition arises, an object is created that contains information about the particular problem or condition. Exceptions act somewhat like events. Java stops execution at the place where the exception occurred, and the exception object is said to be *thrown* by that section of code. Like events, an exception must be delivered somewhere and handled. The section of code that receives the exception object is said to *catch* the exception. An exception causes the execution of the instigating section of code to abruptly stop and transfers control to the code that receives the exception object.

The try/catch construct allows you to catch exceptions for a section of code. If an exception is caused by a statement inside of a try clause, Java attempts to deliver the exception to the appropriate catch clause. A catch clause looks like a method declaration with one argument and no return type. If Java finds a catch clause with an argument type that matches the type of the exception, that catch clause is invoked. A try clause can have multiple catch clauses with different argument types; Java chooses the appropriate one in a way that is analogous to the selection of overloaded methods.

If there is no try/catch clause surrounding the code, or a matching catch clause is not found, the exception is thrown up the call stack to the calling method. If the exception is not caught there, it's thrown up another level, and so on until the exception is handled. This provides a very flexible error-handling mechanism, so that exceptions in deeply nested calls can bubble up to the surface of the call stack for handling. As a programmer, you need to know what exceptions a particular statement can generate, so methods in Java are required to declare the exceptions they can throw. If a method doesn't handle an exception itself, it must specify that it can throw that exception, so that the calling method knows that it may have to handle it. See Chapter 4, for a complete discussion of exceptions and the try/catch clause.

So, why do we need a try/catch clause around our sleep() call? What kind of exception can Thread's sleep() method throw and why do we care about it, when we don't seem to check for exceptions anywhere else? Under some circumstances, Thread's sleep() method can throw an InterruptedException, indicating that it was interrupted by another thread. Since the run() method specified in the Runnable interface doesn't declare it can throw an InterruptedException, we must catch it ourselves, or the compiler will complain. The try/catch statement in our example has an empty catch clause, which means that it handles the exception by ignoring it. In this case, our thread's functionality is so simple it doesn't matter if it's interrupted. All of the other methods we have used either handle their own exceptions or throw only general-purpose exceptions that are assumed to be possible everywhere and don't need to be explicitly declared.

A Word About Synchronization

At any given time, there can be a number of threads running in the Java interpreter. Unless we explicitly coordinate them, these threads will be executing methods without any regard for what the other threads are doing. Problems can arise when these methods share the same data. If one method is changing the value of some variables at the same time that another method is reading these variables, it's possible that the reading thread might catch things in the middle and get some variables with old values and some with new. Depending on the application, this situation could cause a critical error.

In our HelloWeb examples, both our paint() and mouseDragged() methods access the messageX and messageY variables. Without knowing the implementation of our particular Java environment, we have to assume that these methods could conceivably be called by different threads and run concurrently. paint() could be called while mouseDragged() is in the midst of updating messageX and messageY. At that point, the data is in an inconsistent state and if paint() gets lucky, it could get the new x value with the old y value. Fortunately, in this case, we probably would not even notice if this were to happen in our application. We did, however, see another case, in our `changeColor()` and `currentColor()` methods, where there is the potential for a more serious "out of bounds" error to occur.

The `synchronized` modifier tells Java to acquire a *lock* for the class that contains the method before executing that method. Only one method can have the lock on a class at any given time, which means that only one synchronized method in that class can be running at a time. This allows a method to alter data and leave it in a consistent state before a concurrently running method is allowed to access it. When the method is done, it releases the lock on the class.

Unlike synchronization in other languages, the `synchronized` keyword in Java provides locking at the language level. This means there is no way that you can forget to unlock a class. Even if the method throws an exception or the thread is terminated, Java will release the lock. This feature makes programming with threads in Java much easier than in other languages. See Chapter 8 for more details on coordinating threads and shared data.

Whew! Now it's time to say goodbye to `HelloWeb`. We hope that you have developed a feel for the major features of the Java language, and that this will help you as you go on to explore the details of programming with Java.

3

Tools of the Trade

You have many options for Java development environments. By the time you read this book, fancy graphical development tools should even be available. The examples in this book were developed using the Solaris version of the Java Development Kit (JDK), so I'm going to describe those tools here. When I refer to the compiler or interpreter, I'll be referring to the command-line versions of these tools, so the book is decidedly biased toward those of you who are working in a UNIX or DOS-like environment with a shell and filesystem. However, the basic features I'll be describing for Sun's Java interpreter and compiler should be applicable to other Java environments as well.

In this chapter, I'll describe the tools you'll need to compile and run Java applications. I'll also cover the HTML <APPLET> tag and other information you'll need to know to incorporate Java applets in your Web pages.

Roughly the last half of the chapter discusses how to pack Java class files into Java archives (JAR files). In itself, this topic is simple enough; but JAR files give you the ability to "sign" classes, and to give greater privileges to classes with a signature that you trust. This capability requires a detour into cryptography, certificate authorities, and related concepts. While there's a lot to digest, signed classes are among the most important recent extensions to Java.

The Java Interpreter

A Java interpreter is software that implements the Java virtual machine and runs Java applications. It can be a separate piece of software like the one that comes with the JDK, or part of a larger application like the Netscape Navigator Web browser. It's likely that the interpreter itself is written in a native, compiled language for your particular platform. Other tools, like Java compilers and development environments, can (and one could argue, should) be written in Java.

The Java interpreter performs all of the activities of the Java run-time system. It loads Java class files and interprets the compiled byte-code. It verifies compiled classes that are loaded from untrusted sources. In an implementation that supports dynamic, or "just in time," compilation, the interpreter also serves as a specialized compiler that turns Java byte-code into native machine instructions.

Throughout the rest of this book, we'll be building both standalone Java programs and applets. Both are kinds of Java applications run by a Java interpreter. The difference is that a standalone Java application has all of its parts; it's a complete program that runs independently. An applet is more like an embeddable program module; it relies on *appletviewer* or a Web browser for support. Although Java applets are, of course, compiled Java code, the Java interpreter can't directly run them because they are used as part of a larger application. To run an applet, you can use a Web browser like Sun's HotJava or Netscape Navigator, or *appletviewer* that comes with Sun's Java Development Kit. All of Sun's tools, including HotJava, are written entirely in Java. Both HotJava and *appletviewer* are standalone Java applications run directly by the Java interpreter; these programs implement the additional structure needed to run Java applets.

Sun's Java interpreter is called *java*. To start a standalone application with it, you specify an initial class to be loaded. You can also specify options to the interpreter, as well as any command-line arguments that are needed for the application:

```
% java [interpreter options] class name [program arguments]
```

The class should be specified as a fully qualified class name including the class package, if any. Note, however, that you don't include the *.class* file extension. Here are a few examples:

```
% java animals.birds.BigBird
% java test
```

java searches for the class in the current *class path*, which is a list of locations where packages of classes are stored. I'll discuss the class path in detail in the next section, but for now you should know that you can set the class path with the –class-path option.

There are a few other interpreter options you may find useful. The –cs or –check-source option tells *java* to check the modification times on the specified class file and its corresponding source file. If the class file is out of date, it's automatically recompiled from the source. The –verify, –noverify, and –verifyremote options control the byte-code verification process. By default, *java* runs the byte-code verifier only on classes loaded from an untrusted source; this is the –verifyremote option. If you specify –verify, the byte-code verifier is run on all classes; –noverify means that the verifier is never run.

Once the class is loaded, *java* follows a very C-like convention and looks to see if the class contains a method called main(). If it finds an appropriate main() method, the interpreter starts the application by executing that method. From there, the application can start additional threads, reference other classes, and create its user interface or other structures, as shown in Figure 3-1.

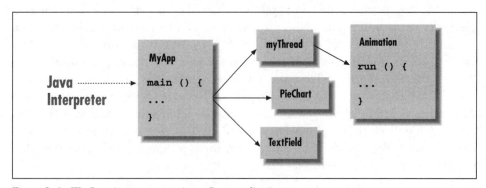

Figure 3–1: The Java interpreter starting a Java application

In order to run, main() must have the right *method signature*. A method signature is a collection of information about the method, as in a C prototype or a forward function declaration in other languages. It includes the method's name, type, and visibility, as well as its arguments and return type. In this case, main() must be a public, static method that takes an array of String objects as its argument and does not return any value (void):

```
public static void main ( String [] myArgs )
```

Because main() is a public and static method, it can be accessed directly from another class using the name of the class that contains it. We'll discuss the implications of visibility modifiers such as public and the meaning of static in Chapters 4 through 6.

The main() method's single argument, the array of String objects, holds the command-line arguments passed to *java*. As in C, the name that we give the parameter doesn't matter; only the type is important. Unlike C, the content of myArgs is a true array. There's no need for an argument count parameter, because myArgs knows how many arguments it contains and can happily provide that information:

```
int argc = myArgs.length;
```

Java also differs from C in another respect here: myArgs[0] is the first command-line argument, not the name of the application. If you're accustomed to parsing C command-line arguments, you'll need to be careful not to trip over this difference.

The Java virtual machine continues to run until the main() method of its initial class file has returned, and until any threads that it started are complete. Special threads designated as "daemon" threads are silently killed when the rest of the application has completed.

The Class Path

The concept of a path should be familiar to anyone who has worked on a DOS or UNIX platform. It's a piece of environment information that provides an application with a list of places to look for some resource. The most common example is a path for executable programs. In a UNIX shell, the PATH environment variable is a colon-separated list of directories that are searched, in order, when the user types the name of a command. The Java CLASSPATH environment variable, similarly, is a list of locations that can be searched for packages containing Java class files. Both the Java interpreter and the Java compiler use CLASSPATH when searching for files on the local host platform.

Classes loaded from the local host via the class path have special features. For example, the Java interpreter loads classes in the class path just once; after a core class has been loaded, it can't be modified or replaced. The interpreter can also be told to trust classes in the class path and to load them without passing them through the byte-code verification process. This is important because certain kinds of optimizations on Java virtual machine instructions can produce valid byte-code that, nonetheless, can't pass the verification process. Byte-code that is precompiled on the native host is an extreme example.

The class path is a list of locations where Java class packages are found. A location can be a path such as a directory name or the name of a class archive file. Java supports archives of class files in its own Java archive (JAR) format, and in the uncompressed ZIP format. JAR and ZIP are really the same format, but JAR files can carry extra information about their contents. JAR files are created with the *jar* utility that's part of the JDK; many tools for creating ZIP archives are publicly available. Java automatically looks inside archives and retrieves classes, which then allows large groups of classes to be distributed in a single file.

The precise means and format for setting the class path varies from system to system. On a UNIX system, you set the CLASSPATH environment variable with a colon-separated list of directories and class archive files:

```
CLASSPATH=/usr/lib/java/classes.zip:/home/vicky/Java/classes:\
/home/vicky/Java/utils/classutils.jar:/home/josh/oldstuff/foo.zip:.
```

On a DOS/Windows system, the CLASSPATH environment variable is set with a semi-colon-separated list of directories and class archive files:

```
set CLASSPATH=C:\tools\java\classes.zip;D:\users\vicky\Java\classes;.
```

The first example above, for UNIX, specifies a class path with four locations: a ZIP archive in */usr/lib/java*, a directory in the user's home, another ZIP file in another user's directory, and the current directory, which is always specified with a dot (.). The last component of the class path, the current directory, is useful when tinkering with classes, but as a general rule, it's bad practice to put the current directory in any kind of path.

The Java interpreter searches each of these four locations in order to find classes. *java* expects to find class files in a directory hierarchy or in a directory within a ZIP archive that maps to the fully qualified name of the class. The components of a class-package name become the components of a pathname. Given the above class path, the first time we reference a class with the fully qualified name of ani-mals.birds.BigBird, for example, *java* begins the search with the *classes.zip* archive in */usr/lib/java*. It looks for a class archived under the path *animals/birds/BigBird*. If *java* does not find the class there, it looks for the class in */home/vicky/Java/classes/animals/birds/BigBird*. If it's not found there, *java* moves on to the archive file specified next in the class path, and so on.

For some applications, like the Java interpreter *java* and the Java compiler *javac*, the class path can also be specified with the –classpath option:

```
% javac -classpath /pkg/jdk/lib/classes.zip:/home/pat/mystuff:. Foo.java
```

If you don't specify the CLASSPATH environment variable or the –classpath option, *java* uses the following default class path:

```
.:$JDK_HOME/classes:$JDK_HOME/lib/classes.zip          UNIX systems
.;%JDK_HOME%\classes;$%JDK_HOME%\lib\classes.zip       Windows systems
```

In this path, $JAVA is the main Java directory on your system. Notice that the current directory (.) is the first location in the default class path; this means the files in your current directory are always available. If you change the class path and don't include the current directory, these files will no longer be accessible.

The Java Compiler

In this section, I'm going to say a few words about *javac*, the Java compiler that is supplied as part of Sun's JDK. (If you are happily working in another development environment, you may want to skip ahead to the next section.) The *javac* compiler is written entirely in Java, so it's available for any platform that supports the Java run-time system. The ability to support its own development environments is an important stage in a language's development. Java makes this bootstrapping automatic by supplying a ready-to-run compiler at the same cost as porting the interpreter.

javac turns Java source code into a compiled class that contains Java virtual machine byte-code. By convention, source files are named with a *.java* extension; the resulting class files have a *.class* extension. *javac* considers a file to be a single compilation unit. As you'll see in Chapter 6, classes in a given compilation unit share certain features like package and import statements.

javac allows you one public class per file and insists the file have the same name as the class. If the filename and class name don't match, *javac* issues a compilation error. A single file can contain multiple classes, as long as only one of the classes is public. You should avoid packing lots of classes into a single file. The compiler lets you include extra non-public classes in a *.java* file, so that you can implement a class that is tightly coupled to another class without a lot of hassle. But you should do this only if the public class in the file is the only one that ever uses the additional classes. In this case you might also consider using inner classes (see Chapter 6).

Now for an example. The source code for the following class should be placed in a file called *BigBird.java*:

```
package animals.birds;

public class BigBird extends Bird {
    ...
}
```

We can then compile it with:

```
% javac BigBird.java
```

Unlike the Java interpreter, which takes a class name as its argument, *javac* requires an actual filename to process. The above command produces the class file *BigBird.class* and stores it in the same directory as the source file. While it's useful to have the class file in the same directory as the source when you are working on a simple example, for most real applications you'll need to store the class file in an appropriate place in the class path.

You can use the −d option to *javac* to specify an alternate directory for storing the class files it generates. The specified directory is used as the root of the class hierarchy, so *.class* files are placed in this directory or in a subdirectory below it, depending on the package name of the class. For example, we can use the following command to put our *BigBird.class* file in an appropriate location:

```
% javac -d /home/vicky/Java/classes BigBird.java
```

When you use the −d option, *javac* automatically creates any directories needed to store the class file in the appropriate place. In the above command, the *Big-Bird.class* file is stored in */home/vicky/Java/classes/animals/birds*.

You can specify multiple *.java* files in a single *javac* command; the compiler simply creates a class file for each source file. But you don't need to list source files for other classes your class references, as long as the other classes have already been compiled. During compilation, Java resolves other class references using the class path. If our class refers to other classes in `animals.birds` or other packages, the appropriate paths should be listed in the class path at compile time, so that *javac* can find the appropriate class files. You either make sure that the CLASSPATH environment variable is set or use the −classpath option to *javac*.

The Java compiler is more intelligent than your average compiler and replaces some of the functionality of a *make* utility. For example, *javac* compares the modification times of the source and class files for all referenced classes and recompiles them as necessary. A compiled Java class remembers the source file from which it was compiled, so as long as the source file is in the same directory as the class file, *javac* can recompile the source if necessary. If, in the above example, class BigBird references another class, `animals.furry.Grover`, *javac* looks for the source *Grover.java* in an `animals.furry` package and recompiles it if necessary to bring the *Grover.class* class file up to date.

By default however, *javac* only checks source files that are referenced directly from other source files. This means that if you have an out-of-date class file that is referenced only by an up-to-date class file, it may not be noticed and recompiled. You can force *javac* to walk the entire graph of objects using the −depend option. But be warned, this can add a lot of time to your compile. And this technique still won't help if you want to keep class libraries or other collections of classes up to date even if they aren't being referenced at all. For that you should consider a *make* utility.

Finally, it's important to note that *javac* can do its job and compile an application even if only the compiled versions of referenced classes are available. You don't need source code for all of your objects. Java class files contain all the data type and method signature information source files do, so compiling against binary class files is as type safe (and exception safe) as compiling with Java source code.

The Applet Tag

Applets are embedded in HTML documents with the `<APPLET>` tag. The `<APPLET>` tag resembles the HTML `<IMG>` image tag.[*] It contains attributes that identify the applet to be displayed and, optionally, give the Web browser hints about how it should be displayed. The standard image tag sizing and alignment attributes, such as `height` and `width`, can be used inside the applet tag. Unlike images, however, applets have both an opening `<APPLET>` and a closing `</APPLET>` tag. Sandwiched between these can be any number of `<param>` tags that contain application-specific parameters to be passed to the applet itself:

```
<applet attribute [ attribute ] ... >
[<param parameter >]
[<param parameter >]
...
</applet>
```

Attributes

Attributes are name=value pairs that are interpreted by a Web browser or *appletviewer*. (Many HTML tags besides `<APPLET>` have attributes.) Attributes of the `<APPLET>` tag specify general features that apply to all applets, such as size and alignment. The definition of the `<APPLET>` tag lists a fixed set of recognized attributes; specifying an incorrect or nonexistent attribute should be considered an HTML error.

Three attributes are required in the `<APPLET>` tag. Two of these attributes specify the space the applet occupies on the screen: not surprisingly, they're named `width` and `height`. The third required attribute may be either `code` or `object`; you must supply one of these attributes, and you can't specify both. The `code` attribute specifies the class file from which the applet is loaded; the `object` attribute specifies a serialized representation of an applet. Most often, you'll use the `code` attribute; the tools for creating serialized applets aren't quite there yet. (Serializing an applet, or any Java class, means saving it, perhaps after customizing it, for use later. You can use *appletviewer* to create serialized applets, but that feature isn't really useful yet. Serialized applets will become interesting when the next generation of integrated development environments for Java are available.)

The following is an HTML fragment for a hypothetical, simple clock applet that takes no parameters and requires no special HTML layout:

---

[*] If you are not familiar with HTML or other markup languages, you may want to refer to *HTML: The Definitive Guide*, from O'Reilly & Associates, for a complete reference on HTML and structured Web documents.

```
<applet code=AnalogClock width=100 height=100></applet>
```

The HTML file that contains this <APPLET> tag must be stored in the same directory as the AnalogClock.class class file. The applet tag is not sensitive to spacing, so the above is therefore equivalent to:

```
<applet
    code=AnalogClock
    width=100
    height=100>
</applet>
```

You can use whatever form seems appropriate.

Parameters

Parameters are analogous to command-line arguments; they provide a way to pass information to an applet. Each <param> tag contains a name and a value that are passed as strings to the applet:

```
<param name = parameter_name value = parameter_value>
```

Parameters provide a means of embedding application-specific data and configuration information within an HTML document.[*] Our AnalogClock applet, for example, might accept a parameter that selects between local and universal time:

```
<applet code=AnalogClock width=100 height=100>
    <param name=zone value=GMT>
</applet>
```

Presumably, this AnalogClock applet is designed to look for a parameter named zone with a possible value of GMT.

Parameter names and values can be quoted to contain spaces and other special characters. We could therefore be more verbose and use a parameter value like the following:

```
<param name=zone value="Greenwich Mean Time">
```

The parameters a given applet expects are determined by the developer of that applet. There is no fixed set of parameter names or values; it's up to the applet to interpret the parameter name/value pairs that are passed to it. Any number of parameters can be specified, and the applet may choose to use or ignore them as it sees fit. The applet might also consider parameters to be either optional or required and act accordingly.

---

[*] If you are wondering why the applet's parameters are specified in yet another type of tag, here's the reason. In the original alpha release of Java, applet parameters were included inside of a single <app> tag along with formatting attributes. However, this format was not SGML-compliant, so the <param> tag was added.

¿Habla Applet?

Web browsers ignore tags they don't understand; if the Web browser doesn't interpret the <APPLET> or <PARAM> tags, they should disappear and any HTML between
the <APPLET> and </APPLET> tags should appear normally.

By convention, Java-enabled Web browsers do the opposite and ignore any extra
HTML between the <APPLET> and </APPLET> tags. This means we can place some
alternate HTML inside the <APPLET> tag, which is then displayed only by Web
browsers that can't run the applet.

For our AnalogClock example, we could display a small text explanation and an
image of the clock applet as a teaser:

```
<applet code=AnalogClock width=100 height=100>
    <param name=zone value=GMT>
    <strong>If you see this you don't have a Java-enabled Web
    browser. Here's a picture of what you are missing.</strong>
    <img src="clockface.gif">
</applet>
```

The Complete Applet Tag

We can now spell out the full-blown <APPLET> tag:

```
<applet
    code = class name      —or
    object = serialized applet name
    width = pixels wide
    height = pixels high
    [ codebase = location URL ]
    [ archive = comma separated list of archives files ]
    [ name = instance name ]
    [ alt = alternate text ]
    [ align = alignment style ]
    [ vspace = vertical pad pixels ]
    [ hspace = horizontal pad pixels ]
>
[ <param name = parameter name value = parameter value> ]
[ <param name = parameter name value = parameter value> ]
...
[ HTML for non Java aware browsers ]
</applet>
```

Either the code attribute or the object attribute must be present to specify the
applet to run. The code attribute specifies the applet's class file; you'll see this most
frequently. The object attribute specifies a serialized (pickled) representation of
an applet. When you use the object attribute to load an applet, the applet's
init() method is not called. However, the serialized applet's start() method is
called.

The width, height, align, vspace, and hspace attributes have the same meanings as those of the <IMG> tag and determine the preferred size, alignment, and padding, respectively. The width and height attributes are required.

The codebase attribute specifies the directory in which the applet's class file (or archive file) is located. If this attribute isn't present, the browser looks in the same directory as the HTML file. The archive attribute specifies a list of JAR or ZIP files in which the applet's class file is located. To put two or more files in the list, separate the filenames by commas; for example, the attribute below tells the browser to search three archives for the applet:

```
archive=Part1.jar,Part2.jar,Utilities.jar
```

The archive attribute must be present if you have packaged your applet in one of these archives. When searching for classes, a browser checks the files listed in the archives attribute before searching any other locations on the server.

The alt attribute specifies alternate text that is displayed by browsers that understand the <APPLET> tag and its attributes, but can't actually run applets. This attribute can also describe the applet, since in this case any alternate HTML between <APPLET> and </applet> is ignored.

The name attribute specifies an instance name for the executing applet. This is a name specified as a unique label for each copy of an applet on a particular HTML page. For example, if we include our clock twice on the same page (using two applet tags), we could give each instance a unique name to differentiate them:

```
<applet code=AnalogClock name="bigClock" width=300 height=300></applet>
<applet code=AnalogClock name="smallClock" width=50 height=50></applet>
```

Applets use instance names to recognize and communicate with other applets on the same page. We could, for instance, create a "clock setter" applet that knows how to set the time on an AnalogClock applet and pass it the instance name of a particular target clock on this page as a parameter. This might look something like:

```
<applet code=ClockSetter>
    <param name=clockToSet value="bigClock">
</applet>
```

Loading Class Files

The code attribute of the <APPLET> tag should specify the name of an applet. This is either a simple class name, or a package path and class name. For now, let's look at simple class names; I'll discuss packages in a moment. By default, the Java runtime system looks for the class file in the same location as the HTML document that contains it. This location is known as the base URL for the document.

Consider an HTML document, *clock.html*, that contains our clock applet example:

```
<applet code=AnalogClock width=100 height=100></applet>
```

Let's say we retrieve the document at the following URL:

```
http://www.time.ch/documents/clock.html
```

Java tries to retrieve the applet class file from the same base location:

```
http://www.time.ch/documents/AnalogClock.class
```

The codebase attribute of the <APPLET> tag can be used to specify an alternative base URL for the class file search. Let's say our HTML document now specifies codebase, as in the following example:

```
<applet
    codebase=http://www.joes.ch/stuff/
    code=AnalogClock
    width=100
    height=100>
</applet>
```

Java now looks for the applet class file at:

```
http://www.joes.ch/stuff/AnalogClock.class
```

Packages

Packages are groups of Java classes. A package name is a little like an Internet host-name, in that they both use a hierarchical, dot-separated naming convention. A Java class file can be identified by its full name by prefixing the class name with the package name. We might therefore have a package called time for time-related Java classes, and perhaps a subordinate package called time.clock to hold classes related to one or more clock applications.

In addition to providing a naming scheme, packages can be used to locate classes stored at a particular location. Before a class file is retrieved from a server, its package-name component is translated by the client into a relative path name under the base URL of the document. The components of a class package name are simply turned into the components of a path name, just like with classes on your local system.

Let's suppose that our AnalogClock has been placed into the time.clock package and now has the fully qualified name of time.clock.AnalogClock. Our simple <APPLET> tag would now look like:

```
<applet code=time.clock.AnalogClock width=100 height=100></applet>
```

Let's say the *clock.html* document is once again retrieved from:

```
http://www.time.ch/documents/clock.html
```

Java now looks for the class file in the following location:

```
http://www.time.ch/documents/time/clock/AnalogClock.class
```

The same is true when specifying an alternative codebase:

```
<applet
    codebase=http://www.joes.ch/stuff/
    code=time.clock.AnalogClock
    width=100
    height=100>
</applet>
```

Java now tries to find the class in the corresponding path under the new base URL:

```
http://www.joes.ch/stuff/time/clock/AnalogClock.class
```

One possible package-naming convention proposes that Internet host and domain names be incorporated as part of package names to form a unique identifier for classes produced by a given organization. If a company with the domain name foobar.com produced our AnalogClock class, they might distribute it in a package called com.foobar.time.clock. The fully qualified name of the AnalogClock class would then be com.foobar.time.clock.AnalogClock. This would presumably be a unique name stored on an arbitrary server. A future version of the Java class loader might use this to automatically search for classes on remote hosts.

Perhaps soon we'll run Sun's latest and greatest Web browser directly from its source with:

```
% java com.sun.java.hotjava.HotJava
```

The OBJECT Tag

The <APPLET> tag that we described in the previous section is currently the standard for embedding Java applets into HTML, but many other kinds of embeddable objects, in addition to applets, are on the Web. There are new multimedia types like audio, video, and VRML, and there are browser plug-ins that also need to be recognized in Web documents. It is logical that as the Web matures, HTML standards will come to adopt a more generic (less Java-specific) method for embedding objects like Java applets into Web documents.

The universal <OBJECT> tag[*] that is being defined by the World Wide Web Consortium (W3C) in cooperation with Sun, Netscape, Microsoft, and others is the

---

[*] The <OBJECT> tag is currently defined by the W3C draft: "Inserting Objects into HTML." See *http://www.w3.org/TR/*.

ordained successor to the <APPLET> tag. The <OBJECT> tag supersedes <APPLET>, along with Netscape's <EMBED> tag, Microsoft's <DYNSRC> tag, and even the generic HTML <IMG> element tag. It unifies syntax for embedding all kinds of multimedia objects into HTML.

The <OBJECT> tag has many similarities with the <APPLET> tag. We'll just give a few brief examples here. These work in the latest versions of Netscape Commmunicator and Sun's HotJava browser and *appletviewer.*

As simple applet is embedded like so:

```
<object classid="java:time.clock.AnalogClock" codebase="time1.jar,time2.jar"
        height=100 width=100>
</object>
```

The classid attribute specifies the object's class, like the code attribute of the <APPLET> tag. But the classid attribute also requires a colon-separated prefix specifying what kind of object code it is. For an applet this is "java:". As with the <APPLET> tag, the optional codebase attribute can be used to specify a URL for loading class files. But the <OBJECT> tag's codebase attribute can also take the place of the <APPLET> tag's archive atttribute. In the above we have specified two JAR files to be loaded with our applet.

As with the <APPLET> tag, you can place HTML for backward compatability inside the opening and closing <OBJECT> tags. A browser that doesn't recognize the <OBJECT> tag will ignore it and use the HTML inside.

```
<object classid="java:time.clock.AnalogClock" codebase="time.jar"
    height=100 width=100>
<applet code=time.clock.AnalogClock archive="time.jar"
    height=100 width=100>
<h3>You're browser does not support Java</h3>
<img src="whatyouremissing.gif">
</applet>
</object>
```

You can also use the <OBJECT> tag to load a serialized Java object. This feature is especially important for support of Java Beans.

```
<object codebase="time.jar"
    data="time/clock/AnalogClock.ser"
    type="application/x-java-serialized-object">
</object>
```

The above uses the data attribute to specify a serialized Java object in the JAR file. In this case a serialized Java object is treated more as a data type than an application. type specifies the MIME type of the object.

Viewing Applets

Sun's JDK comes with an applet-viewer program aptly called *appletviewer*. To use *appletviewer*, specify the URL of the document on the command line. For example, to view our `AnalogClock` at the URL shown above, use the following command:

```
% appletviewer http://www.time.ch/documents/clock.html
```

appletviewer retrieves all applets in the specified document and displays each one in a separate window. *appletviewer* is not a Web browser; it doesn't attempt to display HTML. It's primarily a convenience for testing and debugging applets. If the document doesn't contain <APPLET> tags, *appletviewer* does nothing.

Packaging: Java Archive (JAR) Files

JAR files are Java's suitcases. They are the standard and portable way to pack up all of the parts of your Java application into a compact bundle for distribution or installation. You can put whatever you want into a JAR file: Java class files, serialized objects, data files, images, sounds, etc. As we'll see, a JAR file can carry one or more digital signatures that attest to the integrity and authenticity of that data. A signature can be attached to the file as a whole or to individual items in the file.

The Java run-time environment understands JAR files and can load class files directly from an archive. So you can pack your application's classes in a JAR and place it in your CLASSPATH. You can do the equivalent for applets by listing the JAR file in the ARCHIVES attribute of the HTML <APPLET> tag. Other types of files (data, images, etc.) contained in your JAR file can be retrieved using the getResource() methods. (described in Chapter 10). Therefore, your code doesn't have to know whether any resource is a plain file or a member of a JAR archive. Whether a given class or data file is resident in a JAR file, located separately in the local class path, or accessible at the server of a remotely loaded applet, you can always refer to it in a standard way, and let Java's class loader resolve the location.

Compression

Items stored in JAR files may be compressed with ZLIB[*] compression. JAR files are completely compatible with the ZIP archives familiar to Windows users. You could even use tools like *pkzip* to create and maintain simple JAR files. But *jar*, the Java archive utility, can do a bit more.

Compression makes downloading classes over a network much faster. A quick survey of the JDK distribution shows that a typical class file shrinks by about 40 percent when it is compressed. Text files such as arbitrary HTML or ASCII containing

---

* See *http://www.cdrom.com/pub/infozip/zlib/* and RFC 1950.

English words often compress by as much as 75 percent—to one quarter of their original size. (On the other hand, image files don't get smaller when compressed; both of the common image formats have compression built in.)

Compression is not the only advantage that a JAR file has for transporting files over a slow network. For an application with many components, the amount of time it takes to transport all of the parts may be less significant than the time involved in setting up the connections and making the requests for them. This is especially important for applets loaded via the Web. As it is widely implemented today, your Web browser has to make a separate HTTP request for each class or data file. An applet comprised of 100 classes, for example, would require at least 100 separate trips to the Web server to gather all its parts. By placing all of these classes in a JAR file, they can be downloaded together, in a single transaction. Eliminating the overhead of making HTTP requests is likely to be a big savings, since individual class files tend to be small, and a complex applet could easily require many of them.

The jar Utility

The *jar* utility provided with the JDK is a simple tool for creating and reading JAR files. Its user interface isn't friendly; it mimics the UNIX *tar* (tape archive) command.* If you're familiar with *tar*, you'll recognize the incantations in Table 3-1

Table 3–1: Common jar Commands

jar -cvf *jarFile path* [*path*] [...]	Create *jarFile* containing path(s)
jar -tvf *jarFile* [*path*] [...]	List the contents of *jarFile*, optionally show just path(s)
jar -xvf *jarFile* [*path*] [...]	Extract the contents of *jarFile*, optionally extract just path(s)

In these commands, the letters c, t, and x tell *jar* whether it is creating an archive, listing an archive's contents, or extracting files from an archive. The f means that the next argument will be the name of the JAR file on which to operate. The v tells jar to be more verbose when displaying information about files. In verbose mode you can get information about file sizes, modification times, and compression ratios. If you don't want this information, you can omit the v.

Anything left over on the command line (i.e., anything aside from the letters telling *jar* what to do and the file on which *jar* should operate) is taken as a file-name. If you're creating an archive, the files and directories you list are placed in

---

* Although I'm discussing the rather ugly *jar* utility, you shouldn't find it surprising that people are already creating alternatives. One nice free tool that's available is MoaJar; it is available from *http://www.opengroup.org/RI/DMO/moajar/index.html.* Check it out.

it. If you're extracting, the filenames you give are extracted from the archive (if you don't list any files, *jar* extracts everything in the archive).

For example, let's say we have just completed our new game: spaceblaster. All the files associated with the game are in three directories. The Java classes themselves are in the *spaceblaster/game* directory; *spaceblaster/images* contains the game's images; and *spaceblaster/docs* contains associated game data. We can pack all of this in an archive with this command:

```
% jar cvf spaceblaster.jar spaceblaster
```

Because we requested verbose output, *jar* tells us what it is doing:

```
adding:  spaceblaster/ (in=0) (out=0) (stored 0%)
adding:  spaceblaster/game/ (in=0) (out=0) (stored 0%)
adding:  spaceblaster/game/Game.class (in=8035) (out=3936) (deflated 51%)
adding:  spaceblaster/game/Planetoid.class (in=6254) (out=3288) (deflated 47%)
adding:  spaceblaster/game/SpaceShip.class (in=2295) (out=1280) (deflated 44%)
adding:  spaceblaster/images/ (in=0) (out=0) (stored 0%)
adding:  spaceblaster/images/spaceship.gif (in=6174) (out=5936) (deflated 3%)
adding:  spaceblaster/images/planetoid.gif (in=23444) (out=23454) (deflated 0%)
adding:  spaceblaster/docs/ (in=0) (out=0) (stored 0%)
adding:  spaceblaster/docs/help1.html (in=3592) (out=1545) (deflated 56%)
adding:  spaceblaster/docs/help2.html (in=3148) (out=1535) (deflated 51%)
```

jar creates the file *spaceblaster.jar* and adds the directory *spaceblaster*, in turn adding the directories and files within *spaceblaster* to the archive. In verbose mode, *jar* reports the savings gained by compressing the files in the archive.

Now that we have an archive, we can unpack it with the command:

```
% jar xvf spaceblaster.jar
```

Likewise, we can extract an individual file or directory with:

```
% jar xvf spaceblaster.jar filename
```

You normally don't have to unpack a JAR file to use its contents; Java knows how to extract files from archives automatically. We can list the contents of our JAR with the command:

```
% jar tvf spaceblaster.jar
```

Here's the output; it lists all the files, their sizes, and creation times:

```
1074 Thu May 15 12:18:54 PDT 1997 META-INF/MANIFEST.MF
   0 Thu May 15 12:09:24 PDT 1997 spaceblaster/
   0 Thu May 15 11:59:32 PDT 1997 spaceblaster/game/
8035 Thu May 15 12:14:08 PDT 1997 spaceblaster/game/Game.class
6254 Thu May 15 12:15:18 PDT 1997 spaceblaster/game/Planetoid.class
2295 Thu May 15 12:15:26 PDT 1997 spaceblaster/game/SpaceShip.class
   0 Thu May 15 12:17:00 PDT 1997 spaceblaster/images/
6174 Thu May 15 12:16:54 PDT 1997 spaceblaster/images/spaceship.gif
```

```
23444 Thu May 15 12:16:58 PDT 1997 spaceblaster/images/planetoid.gif
    0 Thu May 15 12:10:02 PDT 1997 spaceblaster/docs/
 3592 Thu May 15 12:10:16 PDT 1997 spaceblaster/docs/help1.html
 3148 Thu May 15 12:10:02 PDT 1997 spaceblaster/docs/help2.html
```

Note that something odd has appeared. *jar* has added a directory called *META-INF* to our archive; it contains one file: *MANIFEST.MF*. The *META-INF* directory holds files describing the contents of the JAR. The *MANIFEST.MF* file that *jar* has added is an automatically generated packing list naming the files in the archive along with cryptographic "checksums" for each.

JAR manifests

The manifest is a text file containing a section of *keyword: value* lines describing each item in the archive. The beginning of our manifest file looks like this:

```
Manifest-Version: 1.0

Name: spaceblaster/game/Game.class
Digest-Algorithms: SHA MD5
SHA-Digest: D5Vi4UV+O+XprdFYaUt0bCv2GDo=
MD5-Digest: 9/W62mC4th6G/x8tTnP2Ng==

Name: spaceblaster/game/Planetoid.class
Digest-Algorithms: SHA MD5
SHA-Digest: SuSUd6pYAASO5JiIGlBrWYzLGVk=
MD5-Digest: KN/4cLDxAxDk/INKHi2emA==

...
```

The first line is simply a version number. Following it are groups of lines describing each item. The first line tells you the item's name; in this case, I'm showing you the lines describing the files *Game.class* and *Planetoid.class*. The remaining lines in each section describe various attributes of the item. In this case, the `Digest-Algorithms` line specifies that the manifest provides message digests (similar to checksums) in two forms: SHA and MD5.[*] This is followed by the actual message digest for the item, computed using these two algorithms. As we'll discuss in the next section, the *META-INF* directory and manifest file can also hold digital signature information for items in the archive. We'll talk more about this in the next section.

You can add your own information to the manifest descriptions by specifing a supplimentary manifest file when you create the archive. This is a good place to store other simple kinds of attribute information about the files in the archive; perhaps version or authorship info.

---

[*] SHA and MD5 stand for Secure Hashing Algorithm and Message Digest 5. That's all you really need to know about them; an explanation of these algorithms is way beyond the scope of this book.

For example, we can create a file with the following name:value pairs:

```
Name: spaceblaster/images/planetoid.gif
RevisionNumber: 42.7
Artist-Temperment: moody
```

To add this information to the manifest in our archive, place it in a file called *myManifest.mf* and give the following *jar* command:

```
% jar -cvmf myManifest.mf spaceblaster.jar spaceblaster
```

We've added an additional option to the command, m, which specifies that *jar* should read additional manifest information from the file given on the command line. How does *jar* know which file is which? Because m is before f, it expects to find the manifest information before the name of the *jar* file it will create. If you think that's awkward, you're right; get the names in the wrong order, and *jar* will do the wrong thing. That's another good reason to look into the MoaJar program I mentioned earlier.

What can we do with the revision and temperament information we've so cleverly included in the JAR file? Unfortunately, nothing, except for unpacking the archive and reading the manifest. However, if you were writing your own JAR utility or some kind of resource loader, you could include code to look at the manifest, check for your private keywords, and act accordingly—perhaps darkening the display if the artist's temperament is "moody." At present, only one keyword is defined, aside from the ones we've seen already: Java-Bean. The value of this keyword should be true if the item is a Java Bean; this information is used by the BeanBox and other utilities that work with Java Beans (see Chapter 18).

Code and Data Signing

Digital signatures provide a way to authenticate documents and other data. They solve one of the Internet's biggest problems: given that you've received a message from Ms. X, how do you know that the message really came from Ms. X and not an imposter? Just as important for Java, let's say that you've downloaded a great new applet written by your favorite author, Pat Niemeyer, and you'd like to grant it some additional privileges, so that it can do something cool for you. You trust that this particular author wouldn't intentionally distribute something harmful. But how do you know that the author really is who he says he is? And what if you downloaded the applet from a third party location, like an archive? How can you be sure that someone hasn't modified the applet since the author wrote it? With Java's default security manager, such an applet can't do anything serious, but when we're talking about configuring your browser to grant additional privileges to applets coming from trusted sites, you would be in for trouble—if it weren't for digital signatures.

Like their inky analogs, digital signatures associate a name with an item in a way that is difficult to forge. In reality, a digital signature is actually much more difficult to forge than a traditional signature. Furthermore, digital signatures provide another benefit: they allow you to authenticate a document, proving that it hasn't been altered in transit. In other words, you know who the sender is, and that the data you received is exactly what the sender sent. Some malicious person can't clip out a digital signature, modify the original document (or applet), and attach the old signature to the result. And he can't generate a new signature—at least, he can't generate a signature claiming that the document came from its original sender. (He could, of course, attach his own signature—but that would be like signing the stick up note you hand to the bank teller.)

Digital signatures are based on public-key cryptography, which is beyond the scope of this book. However, the basics are important and interesting.* In a public-key system, there are two pieces of information: a public key (as you might have guessed) and a private one. They have a special, asymmetric relationship, such that a message encrypted with one key can only be decrypted with the other key. Furthermore, if you only know one key, it is very difficult to compute the other. Therefore, if I give you my public key, you can send me messages that only I can read. No one else, including you, has enough information to go through the process of decrypting the encoded message, so it's safe to send it over untrusted networks. Furthermore, I can (and probably will) give my public key to anyone in the world, since the public key only lets people send me messages; it doesn't let them read my messages.

Digital signatures are based on the reverse process. If I encrypt something with my private key, anyone can use my public key to read the message. That may not sound very useful, since I already said that I'd give my public key away to anyone who wants it. But in this case, we're not trying to keep the message secret, we're trying to prove that I'm the only one who could have sent the message. And that's exactly what we've done. No one else has my private key, so no one else can send a message that can be decrypted with my public key. Therefore, only the real me could have sent the message.

I've simplified the process in one crucial way. Encrypting a large message with complex algorithms takes a long time, even with fast computers. And some public key algorithms just aren't suitable for encrypting large amounts of data for other reasons as well. For digital signatures then, we don't usually encrypt the entire message. First, we use a standard algorithm to create a "hash" or "message digest." We've already seen a message digest; they're the special SHA and MD5 values that *jar* puts into the manifest. To produce the signature, we then encrypt the

---

* See Bruce Schneier's encyclopedic *Applied Cryptography* (John Wiley & Sons).

(relatively small) message digest with the private key. The recipient can then decrypt the signature with the public key and check whether or not the resulting message digest matches the message he received. If it does, the recipient knows that the message hasn't been altered and that the sender is who he claims to be.

Digital signatures can be used to authenticate Java class files and other types of data sent over the network. The author of an object signs the data with his or her digital signature, and we use the author's public key to authenticate that signature after we retrieve it. We don't have to communicate with anyone in order to verify the authenticity of the data. We don't even have to make sure that the communications by which we received the data are secure. We simply check the signature after the data arrives. If it is valid, we know that we have the authentic data and that it has not been tampered with . . . or do we?

Well, there is a larger problem that digital signatures alone don't solve: verifying identity. If the signature checks out, we know that only the person (or entity) that published the public key could have sent the data. But how do we know that the public key really belongs to whomever we think it does? How do we associate an identity with that public key in the first place? We've made it more difficult to counterfeit a message, but it's not impossible. A forger could conceivably create a counterfeit Java class, sign it with his own private key, and try to trick you into believing that his public key is that of the real author or the trusted web site. In this case, you'll download the bad applet, then use the wrong public key to verify the applet, and be tricked into thinking that there's nothing wrong. This is where *certificates* and *certificate authorities* come into play.

Certificates

A certificate is a document that lists a name and a public key. By a name, we mean some real world information describing a person or entity. For example, a certificate might contain your full name and address, or the name of a company and the location of its headquarters. We'll consider the combination of a name and a public key in this way to make up an *identity*. If we have valid information for a particular identity, we can verify data that the identity has signed.

A certificate is signed with the digital signature of a certificate authority—the entity that issued the certificate. The certificate is, in effect, a proclamation by the certificate authority that the identity listed is valid—in other words, that the listed public key really does belong to the entity named. If we decide to trust the certificate authority, we can then believe the identities contained in the certificates it issues are valid. The certificate acts as a sort of electronic ID card, backed up by the credentials of the certificate authority. Of course, we no longer issue certificates on fancy vellum scrolls, as shown in Figure 3-2; the format for modern certificates is described by a standard called X.509.

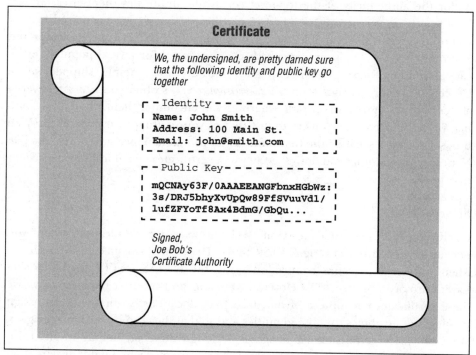

Certificate

We, the undersigned, are pretty darned sure that the following identity and public key go together

```
┌ ─ Identity ─ ─ ─ ─ ─ ─ ─ ─ ─ ┐
│ Name: John Smith              │
│ Address: 100 Main St.         │
│ Email: john@smith.com         │
└ ─ ─ ─ ─ ─ ─ ─ ─ ─ ─ ─ ─ ─ ─ ┘

┌ ─ Public Key ─ ─ ─ ─ ─ ─ ─ ─ ┐
│                               │
│ mQCNAy63F/0AAAEEANGFbnxHGbWz: │
│ 3s/DRJ5bhyXvUpQw89FfSVuuVdl/  │
│ 1ufZFYoTf8Ax4BdmG/GbQu...     │
└ ─ ─ ─ ─ ─ ─ ─ ─ ─ ─ ─ ─ ─ ─ ┘
```

Signed,
Joe Bob's
Certificate Authority

Figure 3–2: An old-fashioned certificate

Certificate authority (CA) certificates

This is all well and good, but the original problem remains: in order to verify the authenticity of a certificate, we need to verify its signature. Now, to do that, we need to know the certificate authority's public key; rather than solving the problem, we simply seem to have shifted the problem to a new front. If a counterfeiter could substitute her public key for the public key of one entity, she might be able to do the same for the certificate authority. But shifting the problem helps quite a bit. We have reduced the number of public keys that we need to know from an unlimited number (all of the identities we might ever encounter) to a very small number: one for each certificate authority. We have chained our trust of the identity to the trust of the certificate authority's identity. Chaining can be allowed to extend further, to an arbitrary depth, allowing certificate authorities to back up lower certificate authorities, and so on. At some point, of course, the chain has to stop, and that usually happens with a "self-signed" or *certificate authority certificate*, that is, a certificate that is issued by the certificate authority for itself, containing its own public key. "What good is that?" you might ask.

As for the authenticity of the top-level certificate authorities themselves, we will have to rely on very strong, well-known certificates that we have acquired by very secure or perhaps very tangible means. Web browsers, like Netscape Navigator and Microsoft Internet Explorer, come with CA certificates for several popular certificate authorities. Netscape Navigator and MSIE are, for example, shipped with a CA certificate for Verisign (*http://www.verisign.com/*), so that you can safely verify any certificates signed by Verisign, wherever you encounter them. So, if all is working, we've reduced the problem to just that of your getting your copy of the Web browser software securely the first time. As far as maintenance goes, browsers like Netscape Navigator let you download new CA certificates dynamically, using secure transports.

Site certificates

Certificates are presented to your Web browser for verification when you encounter signed objects (signed JAR files). They are also issued by Web servers when you make a secure connection using the HTTPS (HTTP Secure Socket Layer) protocol. Browsers like HotJava, Netscape, and Internet Explorer may save these certificates encountered from third party locations, so that you can assign privileges or attributes to those identities and so that they can be recognized again. We'll call these certificates *site certificates*—though they may belong to any third party, like a person or an organization. For example, you might declare that objects signed by a certain site are allowed to write local files. The browser then saves that site's certificate, marking it with the privileges (writing local files) that it should grant.

User (signer) certificates

Finally, you, the user, can have your own identity and your own certificates to validate your identity. Browsers like Netscape Navigator store *user certificates* that can be used to identify you to third parties. A user certificate is associated with a private key—the private key that goes with the public key in the certificate. When you use a private key to sign an object, the corresponding certificate is shipped as part of the signature. Remember, the recipient needs the public key in your certificate to validate your signature. The certificate says on whose authority the recipient should trust that public key.

So, where do you get private keys, public keys, and certificates validating your public keys? Well, as for the keys, you generate those yourself. No other party should ever have access to your private key, much less generate it for you. After you generate a public and private key pair, using a utility like *javakey*, you send your public key to the certificate authority to request that they certify you. The CA can make you jump through whatever hoops are necessary; when they are satisfied that you are who you say you are, they grant you a certificate.

In Netscape Navigator, this entire process can be accomplished by the user, within the browser, using the KEYGEN extension to HTML. You can then use Netscape tools to sign JAR files, send secure email, etc. HotJava is not quite as slick. The JDK supplies a utility called *javakey* for managing keys, certificates, and signing JAR files. We'll discuss that in detail in the next section.

Signed JAR Files and javakey

javakey is a utility for managing a database of identities. With it, you can generate or import key pairs and certificates, and use these keys and certificates to sign JAR files.

For a variety of reasons, including antiquated cryptography export control laws in the U.S. and patents on various cryptographic algorithms, JavaSoft was forced to separate the security API itself from the packages that actually implement encryption algorithms.* The packages that implement cryptography are called "provider" packages; Sun's security provider package comes with the JDK by default. Other packages can be installed to provide additional or alternate implementations of the cryptographic alogrithms. By default, *javakey* uses the implementations found in Sun's provider package, though it can use other packages if any are available.

The user interface to *javakey* is awkward, to say the least. It's a good bet that someone will implement a key management utility with a more friendly graphical interface; it wouldn't be surprising if this utility was built into HotJava. Therefore, we won't spend a great deal of time discussing the details of *javakey*; it's more important to understand the concepts.

What about Netscape and Internet Explorer?

Netscape's Navigator 4.0 has extensive support for signed JAR files. Netscape has extended the core Java security model to create a *capabilities-based* model in which signed objects request permission for specific operations. (These are the kinds of features found in the U.S. government's C2 security specification.) Because Netscape's extensions are not part of the core Java API, we won't go into them here. Netscape says that it is possible to write code that will function in both Netscape's security model and the basic Java model.

Unfortunately, there are currently incompatabilities between the Netscape and Java digital signature implementations. The largest obstacle is that Netscape supports Version 3 of X.509 certificates, while Java currently supports Version 1 only.

---

* See the JCE (Java Cryptography Extensions), which are available to U.S. citizens from *http://java.sun.com/products/jdk/1.1/jce/*.

Support for X.509 v3 certificates is promised in JDK 1.2. Future releases of
Netscape Navigator, HotJava, and others should be able to share certificates and
signed JAR files.

Microsoft has plans for Java object-signing capabilities in Internet Explorer 4.0.
They too are planning to extend Java's security model.

The TestWrite example

Before we dive into the muck, let's take a look at an example, just to prove that you
can actually sign objects with the current releases of the JDK and HotJava. In the
process of discussing the example, we'll point out some things that are lacking.

Make sure that HotJava's security is set to the default level, and navigate to
http://www.ooi.com/exploringjava/examples/jar/unsigned/testwrite.html. You'll see the
applet shown in Figure 3-3.

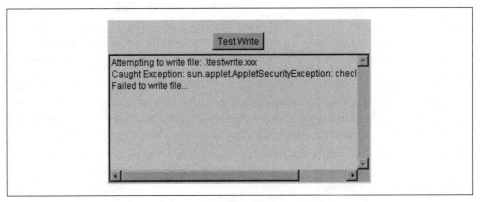

Figure 3–3: An unsigned applet violating security policy

When you push the button, this applet attempts to write a harmless file on the
local host. Give it a try. If you do have HotJava's security at the default level, a dialog will pop up, asking if you'd like to authorize the write operation. Feel free to
click No. The applet should fail with a security exception and display a message.
Had you clicked Yes, the action would have been authorized for this session, but
the next time you came across this applet, you would have to authorize the write
operation again.

At this point you can navigate to a Web page that displays the same applet:
http://www.ooi.com/exploringjava/examples/jar/signed/testwrite.html. The only difference is that I've wrapped the applet in a JAR file that I have signed, with a key and
certificate that I generated using *javakey.* When it loads the applet's JAR file,

HotJava also retrieves the signature. However, nothing has changed for the applet just yet. When you click the button, you still get a dialog asking if you want to allow the write operation. If you say Yes, HotJava allows the applet to write. As before, the permission is good for this session only; if you run across the applet again, you'll be asked to authorize the write operation.

But now that an identity is associated with the applet, we can do more. Select the Security Preferences page from the HotJava menu, and go to the Advanced Security section. You should see my certificate in the list, as shown in Figure 3-4.

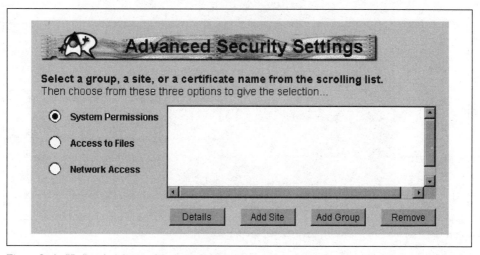

Figure 3–4: HotJava's Advanced Security Settings menu

Pat Niemeyer, O'Reilly & Associates, Java Author

This is where we need to be in order to grant this applet greater (or lesser) permissions based on my signature. But there is a problem. HotJava doesn't recognize the certificate authority that signed my certificate. That's because I signed my own certificate (I've decided to be my own certificate authority of one, for now). What can we do? Well, in Netscape or a future version of HotJava, we might have a means to download my certificate and use it as a new certificate authority. Or I might simply get a certificate signed by a more popular authority than myself.

For now, you can verify my certificate by hand. We'll do this not only to get through this example, but because it presents a useful analogy to the process of certification. By selecting my certificate and clicking the Details button, HotJava presents you with a dialog showing my certificate's information, which is shown in Figure 3-5.

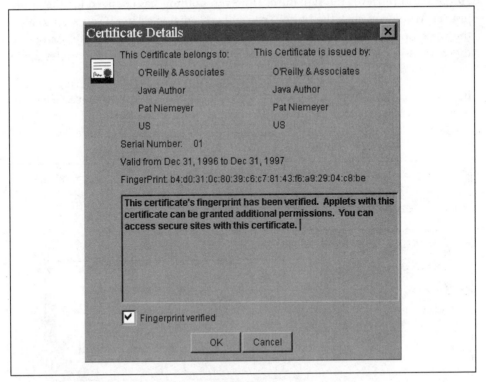

Figure 3–5: A modern certificate, as displayed by HotJava

The "thumbprint" that HotJava displays should match this:

```
b4:d0:31:0c:80:39:c6:c7:81:43:f6:a9:29:04:c8:be
```

If everything looks good, you can click on the box to accept my certificate. By doing so, you are saying that you accept my identity, and believe that I have in fact signed certificates that match this thumbprint. You have effectively chained your trust to this printed page rather than an online certificate authority. You can be reasonably sure that no one has gone to the effort of issuing counterfeit O'Reilly books.

You can now assign greater privileges to this applet. For example, you can allow it to write files. HotJava stores the certificate and marks it with whatever permissions you have decided to grant.[*] The next time you visit this page (or find this applet anywhere else on the Web!), it will be allowed to write the file.

---

[*] HotJava 1.0 stores its site certificates in the user's *.hotjava/security* directory. It does not add these certificates to the Java system identity database. In Java 1.2, the certificate database will be separated from the system's identity database.

So, how did I create my certificate and sign the JAR file? Let's move on.

The Identity Database

The Sun security provider package implements an identity database that holds a set of identities along with their public keys, private keys, and certificates. The identities in this database are visible to Java. We'll discuss what that means in a bit, but for the most part, we'll only use this database as a repository while we create and work with our identity locally.

An identity can be a person, an organization, or perhaps a logical part of an organization. Before it can be used, an identity must have a public key and at least one certificate validating its public key. *javakey* refers to entities in the local database by IDs or handles. These names are arbitrary and are not used outside of the local database. Identities that have a private key stored locally in the database, along with their public key, can be used to sign JAR files. These identities are also called *signers.*

The default location for the identity database is the file: *identitydb.obj* in the user's home directory. On a single user system, the Java installation directory is used instead of the user's home directory.[*] As an option, the system administrator can take control of the database and put it in a unique location systemwide. You can control the location by setting the `identity.database` property in the *java.security* properties file (located in the *lib/security* directory of the JDK installation):

```
identity.database=/etc/identitydb.obj
```

If you are going to maintain any private keys in the identity database (if you will have any signers), you must take special care to keep the *identities.obj* file safe (and not publicly readable). Private keys must be kept private.

Using javakey

We can create an identity in the database with the *javakey* command below:

```
% javakey -cs sarah
```

The –c option tells *javakey* to create a new identity. The s says that this identity is to be a signer: that is, it will be capable of signing JAR files using its private key. You can leave off the s if you are creating an identity that will only be used locally and won't be used to sign files. The argument, sarah, is the name I'm assigning to the new identity. I could have used a longer name by quoting it; however, since this ID is only used as a convenient way to access the local database, the name doesn't

---

[*] Beware if you have both the JDK and HotJava installed in separate locations on a single user system, such as a PC running Windows. You will have to inform HotJava where to find the JDK package using the JDK_HOME environment variable.

really matter.

Once we've created an ID, we can display it with the command:

```
% javakey -li sarah
```

Or we can list the entire contents of the database:

```
% javakey -ld
```

Public and private keys

So far, we've created an identity but haven't created any keys for it. Since we're on our way to signing JAR files, the next thing we need to do is create a key pair for our signer. We can create a key pair with the command:

```
% javakey -gk sarah DSA 1024
```

The gk option tells *javakey* to generate a key. The first argument, sarah, is the ID for which we are going to generate keys. The next argument, DSA, is the algorithm for which we are going to generate the keys. The current release of Java only supports one: DSA, the Digital Signature Algorithm, which is a U.S. government standard for signing. The final argument is the key length in bits. For most algorithms, larger key sizes provide stronger encryption. DSA supports keys of either 512 or 1024 bits. You should use the latter, unless you have a specific reason to do otherwise. It's not clear what a valid reason would be for using the smaller key size, particularly in the context of signed applets.

javakey generates the keys and places them in the database. To retrieve the public key we have generated, give the command:

```
% javakey -ek sarah sarah.public
```

The -ek option tells *javakey* to export the key belonging to the named identity. The next argument, *sarah.public*, is the name of the file into which *javakey* places the public key it retrieves. Obviously, we could have picked any filename we wanted. Once you've exported a key, you can move the file to another system and import it into another key database.

To retrieve both public and private keys, give the command below; the third argument, *sarah.private*, is the name of the file in which *javakey* stores the private key. Be careful about exporting any private key. It should never be stored in an unsecure or publicly readable location.

```
% javakey -ek sarah sarah.public sarah.private
```

If we previously generated a public key for this identity, and have placed that key in the file *sarah.public*, we can import the public key into the identity database with the command:

```
% javakey -ik sarah sarah.public
```

The key file must be in the X.509 format used by *javakey*. If you also have a private key in the file *sarah.private*, you can import the key pair with the command:

```
% javakey -ikp sarah sarah.public sarah.private
```

Certificates

Now that we have keys, we want a certificate in which to wrap our public key for distribution. Ideally, at this point, we'd send a public key to a trusted certificate authority and receive a certificate in return. A number of different and incompatible standards for certificates are available. Currently, *javakey* understands and generates only X.509 Version 1 certificates; it should soon be able to work with X.509 Version 3 certificates. Once you have received a compatible certificate from a certificate authority or some other source you trust, you can import the certificate from a file with the command:

```
% javakey -ic sarah sarah.x509
```

The file *sarah.x509* contains the certificate for the identity sarah in X.509 format. If you want this identity to be able to sign files, you should have already placed the matching private key in the database.

To demonstrate the features of *javakey*, we will serve as our own authority (as we did in the example) and create our own self-signed certificate. To create a certificate we have to make a "directives" file. It might look something like this:

```
issuer.name=sarah
subject.name=sarah
subject.real.name=Sarah Burcham
subject.org.unit=Student
subject.org=Washington University
subject.country=US
start.date=1 Jan 1997
end.date=1 Jan 1998
serial.number=1001
```

This file includes all the information necessary to generate a certificate. The first piece of information, `issuer.name`, specifies the *javakey* ID of the identity that is creating the certificate. This identity must be a signer and must have public and private keys initialized. In this case we are signing our own certificate, so we don't have to have a certificate to back up our signature.

The next few lines describe the subject of the certificate (i.e., the person for whom we're issuing the certificate). It includes a "real world" name and organization information. The type of information in these fields is defined by X.500 standards;

it is also the subject of much debate and extension activity. This information is very important because a certificate is useless if the receiver does not know exactly what it proports to be certifying.

The start and end dates describe the period in which the certificate is valid. An invalid certificate should not be honored.

Finally, the `serial.number` directive should be a unique number assigned by the issuer (signer). You should never issue two certificates with the same serial number. We've picked an an arbitrary number—1001—here for a reason. Whenever *javakey* imports or creates a certificate for an identity, it assigns its own, internal (sequential), number to that certificate. (In our case, *javakey*'s serial number is probably "1", because this is the first certificate associated with this identity.) This can be confusing. *javakey*'s certificate numbers are like its identity names; they are used for reference only within *javakey*. We will use the number that *javakey* has assigned later, when we want to use a certificate to sign a JAR file. The serial number included in the directive file, however, is a real world piece of information that may be referenced outside of *javakey*'s database.

Signing JARs

If we have a signer identity, initialized with its private and public keys, and at least one certificate, we are ready to sign JAR files. We start by creating another directives file that specifies what identity we are using to sign the JAR file and some other parameters. This file contains at least four pieces of information; it might look like this:

```
signer=sarah
cert=1
chain=0
signature.file=sarahSig
```

The `signer` directive specifies the identity that will be used to generate the signature. `cert` is the *javakey* certificate number of the certificate that will be included with the digital signature—not the serial number that we assigned when creating this certificate. To see *javakey*'s certificate numbers, use the *javakey -li* or *-ld* commands.

In the current release of the JDK, the `chain` directive is unimplemented; its value should be set to 0. In the future, this directive will allow you to specify a depth of certificate chaining: the maximum number of intermediate certificates that may be used to authenticate this signature.

Finally, the `signature.file` directive specifies the name of the signature file to be placed in the signed JAR. The file is stored in the *META-INF* directory, along with the manifest. Signature filenames should be eight characters or less, and case is not significant. *javakey* adds the extension *.SF* to the filename you give.

Now we're ready to sign a JAR file. Place the four directives into a file called *sarah.sdirs*, and give the command:

```
javakey -gs sarah.sdirs foo.jar
```

If we now list the archive, we will see that *javakey* has added two files to the *META-INF* directory: *SARAHSIG.SF* and *SARAHSIG.DSA*. *SARAHSIG.SF* is the signature file—it is like the manifest file for this particular signature. It lists the objects that were signed and the signature algorithms. *SARAHSIG.DSA* is the actual binary signature in PKCS format.

Where We've Been

We've covered a lot of territory in the past few pages. Here's a summary of what we can and can't do. We can:

- Use *javakey* to create an identity, and create public and private keys for that identity.

- Use *javakey* to create a self-signed certificate for that identity, or import a certificate that has been issued by a certificate authority, containing the public key we generated.

- Use *javakey* to sign a JAR file.

- Tell HotJava (by hand) what certificates it should trust, and what permissions to grant to each identity.

Unfortunately, we can't do any of this automatically. We can't just tell HotJava, "I trust John Doe" and have HotJava try to look up a verifiable certificate for John Doe. Furthermore, we are personally responsible for the security of our *javakey* database. This is a major hole: it's important that private keys remain private; but anyone who walks up to my computer can use *javakey* to retrieve information about any identity that I have issued. It's easy to imagine that a future version of HotJava will make it much easier to work with signed classes. The other problem, keeping secrets secret, is much more difficult.

4

The Java Language

In this chapter, we'll introduce the framework of the Java language and some of its fundamental tools. We're not going to try to provide a full language reference here. Instead, we'll lay out the basic structures of Java with special attention to how it differs from other languages. For example, we'll take a close look at arrays in Java, because they are significantly different from those in some other languages. We won't, on the other hand, spend much time explaining basic language constructs like loops and control structures. Nor will we we talk much about Java's object oriented side here, as that's covered in detail in Chapters 5 through 7.

As always, we'll try to provide meaningful examples to illustrate how to use Java in everyday programming tasks.

Text Encoding

Java is a language for the Internet. Since the people of the Net speak and write in many different human languages, Java must be able to handle a number of languages as well. One of the ways in which Java supports international access is through Unicode character encoding. Unicode uses a 16-bit character encoding; it's a worldwide standard that supports the scripts (character sets) of most languages.[*]

Java source code can be written using the Unicode character encoding and stored either in its full form or with ASCII-encoded Unicode character values. This makes Java a friendly language for non-English speaking programmers who can use their native alphabet for class, method, and variable names in Java code.

---

[*] For more information about Unicode, see the following URL: *http://www.unicode.org/*. Ironically, one of the scripts listed as "obsolete and archaic" and not currently supported by the Unicode standard is Javanese—a historical language of the people of the Island of Java.

The Java char type and String objects also support Unicode. But if you're concerned about having to labor with two-byte characters, you can relax. The String API makes the character encoding transparent to you. Unicode is also ASCII-friendly; the first 256 characters are identical to the first 256 characters in the ISO8859-1 (Latin-1) encoding and if you stick with these values, there's really no distinction between the two.

Most platforms can't display all currently defined Unicode characters. As a result, Java programs can be written with special Unicode escape sequences. A Unicode character can be represented with the escape sequence:

    \uxxxx

xxxx is a sequence of one to four hexadecimal digits. The escape sequence indicates an ASCII-encoded Unicode character. This is also the form Java uses to output a Unicode character in an environment that doesn't otherwise support them.

Java stores and manipulates characters and strings internally as Unicode values. Java also comes with classes to read and write Unicode-formatted character streams.

Comments

Java supports both C-style block comments delimited by /* and */ and C++-style line comments indicated by //:

```
/*  This is a
        multiline
            comment.    */

// This is a single line comment
// and so // is this
```

As in C, block comments can't be nested. Single-line comments are delimited by the end of a line; extra // indicators inside a single line have no effect. Line comments are useful for short comments within methods because you can still wrap block comments around large chunks of code during development.

By convention, a block comment beginning with /** indicates a special "doc comment." A doc comment is commentary that is extracted by automated documentation generators, such as Sun's *javadoc* program that comes with the Java Development Kit. A doc comment is terminated by the next */, just as with a regular block comment. Leading spacing up to a * on each line is ignored; lines beginning with @ are interpreted as special tags for the documentation generator:

```
/**
 * I think this class is possibly the most amazing thing you will
 * ever see. Let me tell you about my own personal vision and
 * motivation in creating it.
 * <p>
 * It all began when I was a small child, growing up on the
 * streets of Idaho. Potatoes were the rage, and life was good...
 *
 * @see PotatoPeeler
 * @see PotatoMasher
 * @author John 'Spuds' Smith
 * @version 1.00, 19 Dec 1996
 */
```

javadoc creates HTML class documentation by reading the source code and the embedded comments. The author and version information is presented in the output, and the @see tags make hypertext links to the appropriate class documentation. The compiler also looks at the doc comments; in particular, it is interested in the @deprecated tag, which means that the method has been declared obsolete and should be avoided in new programs. The compiler generates a warning message whenever it sees a deprecated feature in your code.

Doc comments can appear above class, method, and variable definitions, but some tags may not be applicable to all. For example, a variable declaration can contain only a @see tag. Table 4-1 summarizes the tags used in doc comments.

Table 4–1: Doc Comment Tags

Tag	Description	Applies to
@see	Associated class name	Class, method, or variable
@author	Author name	Class
@version	Version string	Class
@param	Parameter name and description	Method
@return	Description of return value	Method
@exception	Exception name and description	Method
@deprecated	Declares an item obsolete	Class, method, or variable

Types

The type system of a programming language describes how its data elements (variables and constants) are associated with actual storage. In a statically typed language, such as C or C++, the type of a data element is a simple, unchanging attribute that often corresponds directly to some underlying hardware phenomenon, like a register value or a pointer indirection. In a more dynamic language like Smalltalk or Lisp, variables can be assigned arbitrary elements and can effectively change their type throughout their lifetime. A considerable amount of overhead goes into validating what happens in these languages at run-time. Scripting languages like Perl and Tcl achieve ease of use by providing drastically simplified type systems in which only certain data elements can be stored in variables, and values are unified into a common representation such as strings.

Java combines the best features of both statically and dynamically typed languages. As in a statically typed language, every variable and programming element in Java has a type that is known at compile-time, so the interpreter doesn't normally have to check the type validity of assignments while the code is executing. Unlike C or C++ though, Java also maintains run-time information about objects and uses this to allow safe run-time polymorphism.

Java data types fall into two categories. *Primitive types* represent simple values that have built-in functionality in the language; they are fixed elements like literal constants and numeric expressions. *Reference types* (or class types) include objects and arrays; they are called reference types because they are passed "by reference" as I'll explain shortly.

Primitive Types

Numbers, characters, and boolean values are fundamental elements in Java. Unlike some other (perhaps more pure) object-oriented languages, they are not objects. For those situations where it's desirable to treat a primitive value as an object, Java provides "wrapper" classes (see Chapter 9). One major advantage of treating primitive values as such is that the Java compiler can more readily optimize their usage.

Another advantage of working with the Java virtual-machine architecture is that primitive types are precisely defined. For example, you never have to worry about the size of an int on a particular platform; it's always a 32-bit, signed, two's complement number. Table 4-2 summarizes Java's primitive types.

Table 4–2: Java Primitive Data Types

Type	Definition
boolean	true or false
char	16-bit Unicode character
byte	8-bit signed two's complement integer
short	16-bit signed two's complement integer
int	32-bit signed two's complement integer
long	64-bit signed two's complement integer

Table 4–2: Java Primitive Data Types (continued)

Type	Definition
float	32-bit IEEE 754 floating-point value
double	64-bit IEEE 754 floating-point value

If you think the primitive types look like an idealization of C scalar types on a byte-oriented 32-bit machine, you're absolutely right. That's how they're supposed to look. The 16-bit characters were forced by Unicode, and generic pointers were deleted for other reasons, but the syntax and semantics of Java primitive types are meant to fit a C programmer's mental habits. You'll probably find this saves you a lot of mental effort in learning the language.

Declaration and initialization

Variables are declared inside of methods or classes in C style. For example:

```
int foo;
double d1, d2;
boolean isFun;
```

Variables can optionally be initialized with an appropriate expression when they are declared:

```
int foo = 42;
double d1 = 3.14, d2 = 2 * 3.14;
boolean isFun = true;
```

Variables that are declared as instance variables in a class are set to default values if they are not initialized. In this case, they act much like static variables in C or C++. Numeric types default to the appropriate flavor of zero, characters are set to the null character "\0," and boolean variables have the value false. Local variables declared in methods, on the other hand, must be explicitly initialized before they can be used.

Integer literals

Integer literals can be specified in octal (base 8), decimal (base 10), or hexadecimal (base 16). A decimal integer is specified by a sequence of digits beginning with one of the characters 1–9:

```
int i = 1230;
```

Octal numbers are distinguished from decimal by a leading zero:

```
int i = 01230;              // i = 664 decimal
```

As in C, a hexadecimal number is denoted by the leading characters 0x or 0X (zero "x"), followed by digits and the characters a–f or A–F, which represent the decimal values 10–15 respectively:

```
int i = 0xFFFF;             // i = 65535 decimal
```

Integer literals are of type int unless they are suffixed with an L, denoting that they are to be produced as a long value:

```
long l = 13L;
long l = 13;                // equivalent–13 is converted from type int
```

(The lowercase character l ("el") is also acceptable, but should be avoided because it often looks like the numeral 1.)

When a numeric type is used in an assignment or an expression involving a type with a larger range, it can be promoted to the larger type. For example, in the second line of the above example, the number 13 has the default type of int, but it's promoted to type long for assignment to the long variable. Certain other numeric and comparison operations also cause this kind of arithmetic promotion. A numeric value can never be assigned to a type with a smaller range without an explicit (C-style) cast, however:

```
int i = 13;
byte b = i;                 // Compile time error–explicit cast needed
byte b = (byte) i;          // Okay
```

Conversions from floating point to integer types always require an explicit cast because of the potential loss of precision.

Floating-point literals

Floating-point values can be specified in decimal or scientific notation. Floating-point literals are of type double unless they are suffixed with an f denoting that they are to be produced as a float value:

```
double d = 8.31;
double e = 3.00e+8;
float f = 8.31F;
float g = 3.00e+8F;
```

Character literals

A literal character value can be specified either as a single-quoted character or as an escaped ASCII or Unicode sequence:

```
char a = 'a';
char newline = '\n';
char smiley = '\u263a';
```

Reference Types

In C, you can make a new, complex data type by creating a structure. In Java (and other object-oriented languages), you instead create a class that defines a new type in the language. For instance, if we create a new class called Foo in Java, we are also implicitly creating a new type called Foo. The type of an item governs how it's used and where it's assigned. An item of type Foo can, in general, be assigned to a variable of type Foo or passed as an argument to a method that accepts a Foo value.

In an object-oriented language like Java, a type is not necessarily just a simple attribute. Reference types are related in the same way as the classes they represent. Classes exist in a hierarchy, where a subclass is a specialized kind of its parent class. The corresponding types have a similar relationship, where the type of the child class is considered a subtype of the parent class. Because child classes always extend their parents and have, at a minimum, the same functionality, an object of the child's type can be used in place of an object of the parent's type. For example, if I create a new class, Bar, that extends Foo, there is a new type Bar that is considered a subtype of Foo. Objects of type Bar can then be used anywhere an object of type Foo could be used; an object of type Bar is said to be assignable to a variable of type Foo. This is called *subtype polymorphism* and is one of the primary features of an object-oriented language. We'll look more closely at classes and objects in Chapter 5.

Primitive types in Java are used and passed "by value." In other words, when a primitive value is assigned or passed as an argument to a method, it's simply copied. Reference types, on the other hand, are always accessed "by reference." A *reference* is simply a handle or a name for an object. What a variable of a reference type holds is a reference to an object of its type (or of a subtype). A reference is like a pointer in C or C++, except that its type is strictly enforced and the reference value itself is a primitive entity that can't be examined directly. A reference value can't be created or changed other than through assignment to an appropriate object. When references are assigned or passed to methods, they are copied by value. You can think of a reference as a pointer type that is automatically dereferenced whenever it's mentioned.

Let's run through an example. We specify a variable of type Foo, called myFoo, and assign it an appropriate object:

```
Foo myFoo = new Foo();
Foo anotherFoo = myFoo;
```

myFoo is a reference type variable that holds a reference to the newly constructed Foo object. For now, don't worry about the details of creating an object; we'll cover that in Chapter 5. We designate a second Foo type variable, anotherFoo, and assign it to the same object. There are now two identical references: myFoo and another-Foo. If we change things in the state of the Foo object itself, we will see the same effect by looking at it with either reference. The comparable code in C++ would be:

```
// C++
Foo& myFoo = *(new Foo());
Foo& anotherFoo = myFoo;
```

We can pass one of the variables to a method, as in:

```
myMethod( myFoo );
```

An important, but sometimes confusing, distinction to make at this point is that the reference itself is passed by value. That is, the argument passed to the method (a local variable from the method's point of view) is actually a third copy of the reference. The method can alter the state of the Foo object itself through that reference, but it can't change the caller's notion of the reference to myFoo. That is, the method can't change the caller's myFoo to point to a different Foo object. For the times we want a method to change a reference for us, we have to pass a reference to the object that contains it.

Reference types always point to objects, and objects are always defined by classes. However, two special kinds of reference types specify the type of object they point to in a slightly different way. Arrays in Java have a special place in the type system. They are a special kind of object automatically created to hold a number of some other type of object, known as the base type. Declaring an array-type reference implicitly creates the new class type, as you'll see in the next section.

Interfaces are a bit sneakier. An interface defines a set of methods and a corresponding type. Any object that implements all methods of the interface can be treated as an object of that type. Variables and method arguments can be declared to be of interface types, just like class types, and any object that implements the interface can be assigned to them. This allows Java to cross the lines of the class hierarchy in a type safe way.

A Word About Strings

Strings in Java are objects; they are therefore a reference type. `String` objects do, however, have some special help from the Java compiler that makes them look more primitive. Literal string values in Java source code are turned into `String` objects by the compiler. They can be used directly, passed as arguments to methods, or assigned to `String` type variables:

```
System.out.println( "Hello World..." );
String s = "I am the walrus...";
String t = "John said: \"I am the walrus...\"";
```

The + and += operators in Java are overloaded to provide string concatenation; these are currently the only overloaded operators in the language.

```
String quote = "Four score and " + "seven years ago,";
String more = quote + " our" + " fathers" +  " brought...";
```

Java builds a single `String` object from the concatenated strings and provides it as the result of the expression. We will discuss the `String` class in Chapter 9.

Statements and Expressions

Although the method declaration syntax of Java is quite different from that of C++, Java statement and expression syntax is like that of C. Again, the intention was to make the low-level details of Java easily accessible to C programmers, so that they can concentrate on learning the parts of the language that are really different. Java *statements* appear inside of methods and class and variable initializers; they describe all activities of a Java program. Variable declarations and initializations like those in the previous section are statements, as are the basic language structures like conditionals and loops. *Expressions* are statements that produce a result that can be used as part of another statement. Method calls, object allocations, and, of course, mathematical expressions are examples of expressions.

One of the tenets of Java is to keep things simple and consistent. To that end, when there are no other constraints, evaluations and initializations in Java always occur in the order in which they appear in the code—from left to right. We'll see this rule used in the evaluation of assignment expressions, method calls, and array indexes, to name a few cases. In some other languages, the order of evaluation is more complicated or even implementation dependent. Java removes this element of danger by precisely and simply defining how the code is evaluated. This doesn't, however, mean you should start writing obscure and convoluted statements. Relying on the order of evaluation of expressions is a bad programming habit, even when it works. It produces code that is hard to read and harder to modify. Real programmers, however, are not made of stone, and you may catch me doing this once or twice when I can't resist the urge to write terse code.

Statements

As in C or C++, statements and expressions in Java appear within a *code block*. A code block is syntactically just a number of statements surrounded by an open curly brace ({) and a close curly brace (}). The statements in a code block can contain variable declarations:

```
{
    int size = 5;
    setName("Max");
    ...
}
```

Methods, which look like C functions, are in a sense code blocks that take parameters and can be called by name:

```
setUpDog( String name ) {
    int size = 5;
    setName( name );
    ...
}
```

Variable declarations are limited in scope to their enclosing code block. That is, they can't be seen outside of the nearest set of braces:

```
{
    int i = 5;
}

i = 6;          // compile time error, no such variable i
```

In this way, code blocks can be used to arbitrarily group other statements and variables. The most common use of code blocks, however, is to define a group of statements for use in a conditional or iterative statement.

Since a code block is itself collectively treated as a statement, we define a conditional like an if/else clause as follows:

```
if ( condition )
    statement;
[ else
    statement; ]
```

Thus, if/else in Java has the familiar functionality of taking either of the forms:

```
if ( condition )
    statement;
```

or:

```
if ( condition )  {
    [ statement; ]
    [ statement; ]
    [ ... ]
}
```

Here the *condition* is a `boolean` expression. In the second form, the statement is a code block, and all of its enclosed statements are executed if the conditional succeeds. Any variables declared within that block are visible only to the statements within the successful branch of the condition. Like the `if`/`else` conditional, most of the remaining Java statements are concerned with controlling the flow of execution. They act for the most part like their namesakes in C or C++.

The `do` and `while` iterative statements have the familiar functionality, except that their conditional test is also a `boolean` expression. You can't use an integer expression or a reference type; in other words you must explicitly test your value. In other words, while `i==0` is legitimate, `i` is not, unless `i` is `boolean`. Here are the forms of these two statements:

```
while ( conditional )
    statement;

do
    statement;
while ( conditional );
```

The `for` statement also looks like it does in C:

```
for ( initialization; conditional; incrementor )
    statement;
```

The variable initialization expression can declare a new variable; this variable is limited to the scope of the `for` statement:

```
for (int i = 0; i < 100; i++ ) {
    System.out.println( i )
    int j = i;
    ...
}
```

Java doesn't support the C comma operator, which groups multiple expressions into a single expression. However, you can use multiple, comma-separated expressions in the initialization and increment sections of the `for` loop. For example:

```
for (int i = 0, j = 10; i < j; i++, j-- ) {
    ...
}
```

The Java `switch` statement takes an integer type (or an argument that can be promoted to an integer type) and selects among a number of alternative case branches:*

```
switch ( int_expression ) {
    case int_expression :
        statement;
    [ case int_expression
        statement;
    ...
    default :
        statement;  ]
}
```

No two of the case expressions can evaluate to the same value. As in C, an optional `default` case can be specified to catch unmatched conditions. Normally, the special statement `break` is used to terminate a branch of the `switch`:

```
switch ( retVal ) {
    case myClass.GOOD :
        // something good
        break;
    case myClass.BAD :
        // something bad
        break;
    default :
        // neither one
        break;
}
```

The Java `break` statement and its friend `continue` perform unconditional jumps out of a loop or conditional statement. They differ from the corresponding statements in C by taking an optional label as an argument. Enclosing statements, like code blocks and iterators, can be labeled with identifier statements:

```
one:
    while ( condition ) {
        ...
        two:
            while ( condition ) {
                ...
                // break or continue point
            }
        // after two
    }
// after one
```

In the above example, a `break` or `continue` without argument at the indicated position would have the normal, C-style effect. A `break` would cause processing to

---

* An object-based `switch` statement is desirable and could find its way into the language someday.

resume at the point labeled "after two"; a continue would immediately cause the two loop to return to its condition test.

The statement break two at the indicated point would have the same effect as an ordinary break, but break one would break two levels and resume at the point labeled "after one." Similarly, continue two would serve as a normal continue, but continue one would return to the test of the one loop. Multilevel break and continue statements remove much of the need for the evil goto statement in C and C++.

There are a few Java statements we aren't going to discuss right now. The try, catch, and finally statements are used in exception handling, as we'll discuss later in this chapter. The synchronized statement in Java is used to coordinate access to statements among multiple threads of execution; see Chapter 8 for a discussion of thread synchronization.

On a final note, I should mention that the Java compiler flags "unreachable" statements as compile-time errors. Of course, when I say unreachable, I mean those statements the compiler determines won't be called by a static look at compile-time.

Expressions

As I said earlier, expressions are statements that produce a result when they are evaluated. The value of an expression can be a numeric type, as in an arithmetic expression; a reference type, as in an object allocation; or the special type void, which results from a call to a method that doesn't return a value. In the last case, the expression is evaluated only for its side effects (i.e., the work it does aside from producing a value). The type of an expression is known at compile-time. The value produced at run-time is either of this type or, in the case of a reference type, a compatible (assignable) type.

Operators

Java supports almost all standard C operators. These operators also have the same precedence in Java as they do in C, as you can see in Table 4-3.

Table 4–3: Java Operators

Precedence	Operator	Operand Type	Description
1	++, −	Arithmetic	Increment and decrement
1	+, −	Arithmetic	Unary plus and minus
1	~	Integral	Bitwise complement
1	!	Boolean	Logical complement
1	(type)	Any	Cast

Table 4–3: Java Operators (continued)

Precedence	Operator	Operand Type	Description
2	`*, /, %`	Arithmetic	Multiplication, division, remainder
3	`+, -`	Arithmetic	Addition and subtraction
3	`+`	String	String concatenation
4	`<<`	Integral	Left shift
4	`>>`	Integral	Right shift with sign extension
4	`>>>`	Integral	Right shift with no extension
5	`<, <=, >, >=`	Arithmetic	Numeric comparison
5	`instanceof`	Object	Type comparison
6	`==, !=`	Primitive	Equality and inequality of value
6	`==, !=`	Object	Equality and inequality of reference
7	`&`	Integral	Bitwise AND
7	`&`	Boolean	Boolean AND
8	`^`	Integral	Bitwise XOR
8	`^`	Boolean	Boolean XOR
9	`|`	Integral	Bitwise OR
9	`|`	Boolean	Boolean OR
10	`&&`	Boolean	Conditional AND
11	`||`	Boolean	Conditional OR
12	`?:`	NA	Conditional ternary operator
13	`=`	Any	Assignment
13	`*=, /=, %=, +=, -=, <<=, >>=, >>>=, &=, ^=, |=`	Any	Assignment with operation

There are a few operators missing from the standard C collection. For example, Java doesn't support the comma operator for combining expressions, although the `for` statement allows you to use it in the initialization and increment sections. Java doesn't allow direct pointer manipulation, so it does not support the reference (`*`), dereference (`&`), and `sizeof` operators.

Java also adds some new operators. As we've seen, the + operator can be used with `String` values to perform string concatenation. Because all integral types in Java are signed values, the `>>` operator performs a right-shift operation with sign extension. The `>>>` operator treats the operand as an unsigned number and performs a right shift with no extension. The `new` operator is used to create objects; we will discuss it in detail shortly.

Assignment

While variable initialization (i.e., declaration and assignment together) is considered a statement, variable assignment alone is an expression:

```
int i, j;
i = 5;                          // expression
```

Normally, we rely on assignment for its side effects alone, but, as in C, an assignment can be used as a value in another part of an expression:

```
j = ( i = 5 );
```

Again, relying on order of evaluation extensively (in this case, using compound assignments in complex expressions) can make code very obscure and hard to read. Do so at your own peril.

null

The expression null can be assigned to any reference type. It has the meaning of "no reference." A null reference can't be used to select a method or variable and attempting to do so generates a NullPointerException at run-time.

Variable access

Using the dot (.) to access a variable in an object is a type of expression that results in the value of the variable accessed. This can be either a numeric type or a reference type:

```
int i;
String s;
i = myObject.length;
s = myObject.name;
```

A reference type expression can be used in further evaluations, by selecting variables or calling methods within it:

```
int len = myObject.name.length();
int initialLen = myObject.name.substring(5, 10).length();
```

Here we have found the length of our name variable by invoking the length() method of the String object. In the second case, we took an intermediate step and asked for a substring of the name string. The substring method of the String class also returns a String reference, for which we ask the length.

Method invocation

A method invocation is basically a function call, or, in other words, an expression that results in a value, the type of which is the return type of the method. Thus far, we have seen methods invoked via their name:

```
System.out.println( "Hello World..." );
int myLength = myString.length();
```

Selecting which method to invoke is more complicated than it appears because Java allows method overloading and overriding; the details are discussed in Chapter 5.

Like the result of any expression, the result of a method invocation can be used in further evaluations, as we saw above. Whether to allocate intermediate variables and make it absolutely clear what your code is doing or to opt for brevity where it's appropriate is a matter of coding style.

Object creation

Objects in Java are allocated with the new operator:

```
Object o = new Object();
```

The argument to new is a *constructor* that specifies the type of object and any required parameters to create it. The return type of the expression is a reference type for the created object.

We'll look at object creation in detail in Chapter 5. For now, I just want to point out that object creation is a type of expression, and that the resulting object reference can be used in general expressions. In fact, because the binding of new is "tighter" than that of the dot-field selector, you can easily allocate a new object and invoke a method in it for the resulting expression:

```
int hours = new Date().getHours();
```

The Date class is a utility class that represents the current time. Here we create a new instance of Date with the new operator and call its getHours() method to retrieve the current hour as an integer value. The Date object reference lives long enough to service the method call and is then cut loose and garbage collected at some point in the future.

Calling methods in object references in this way is, again, a matter of style. It would certainly be clearer to allocate an intermediate variable of type Date to hold the new object and then call its getHours() method. However, some of us still find the need to be terse in our code.

instanceof

The instanceof operator can be used to determine the type of an object at runtime. instanceof returns a boolean value that indicates whether an object is an instance of a particular class or a subclass of that class:

```
Boolean b;
String str = "foo";
b = ( str instanceof String );      // true
```

```
b = ( str instanceof Object );    // also true
b = ( str instanceof Date );      // false—not a Date or subclass
```

instanceof also correctly reports if an object is of the type of an arry or a specified interface:

```
if ( foo instanceof byte[] )
    . . .
```

It is also important to note that the value null is not considered an instance of any object. So the following test will return false, no matter what the declared type of the variable:

```
String s = null;
if ( s instanceof String )
    // won't happen
```

Exceptions

> Do, or do not. . . . There is no try.
>
> —Yoda (*The Empire Strikes Back*)

Java's roots are in embedded systems—software that runs inside specialized devices like hand-held computers, cellular phones, and fancy toasters. In those kinds of applications, it's especially important that software errors be handled properly. Most users would agree that it's unacceptable for their phone to simply crash or for their toast (and perhaps their house) to burn because their software failed. Given that we can't eliminate the possibility of software errors, a step in the right direction is to at least try to recognize and deal with the application-level errors that we can anticipate in a methodical and systematic way.

Dealing with errors in a language like C is the responsibility of the programmer. There is no help from the language itself in identifying error types, and there are no tools for dealing with them easily. In C and C++, a routine generally indicates a failure by returning an "unreasonable" value (e.g., the idiomatic –1 or null). As the programmer, you must know what constitutes a bad result, and what it means. It's often awkward to work around the limitations of passing error values in the normal path of data flow.[*] An even worse problem is that certain types of errors can legitimately occur almost anywhere, and it's prohibitive and unreasonable to explicitly test for them at every point in the software.

Java offers an elegant solution to these problems with exception handling. (Java exception handling is similar to, but not quite the same as, exception handling in

---

[*] The somewhat obscure setjmp() and longjmp() statements in C can save a point in the execution of code and later return to it unconditionally from a deeply buried location. In a limited sense, this is the functionality of exceptions in Java.

C++.) An *exception* indicates an unusual condition or an error condition. Program control becomes unconditionally transferred or thrown to a specially designated section of code where it's caught and handled. In this way, error handling is somewhat orthogonal to the normal flow of the program. We don't have to have special return values for all our methods; errors are handled by a separate mechanism. Control can be passed long distance from a deeply nested routine and handled in a single location when that is desirable, or an error can be handled immediately at its source. There are still some methods that return –1 as a special value, but these are generally limited to situations where we are expecting a special value.[*]

A Java method is required to specify the exceptions it can throw (i.e., the ones that it doesn't catch itself); this means that the compiler can make sure we handle them. In this way, the information about what errors a method can produce is promoted to the same level of importance as its argument and return types. You may still decide to punt and ignore obvious errors, but in Java you must do so explicitly.

Exceptions and Error Classes

Exceptions are represented by instances of the class java.lang.Exception and its subclasses. Subclasses of Exception can hold specialized information (and possibly behavior) for different kinds of exceptional conditions. However, more often they are simply "logical" subclasses that exist only to serve as a new exception type. Figure 4-1 shows the subclasses of Exception in the java.lang package. It should give you a feel for how exceptions are organized. Most other packages define their own exception types, which usually are subclasses of Exception itself, or of RuntimeException. The most important exception in the other packages is IOException, which belongs to java.io. IOException has many subclasses for typical I/O problems (like FileNotFoundException) and networking problems (like SocketException); network exceptions belong to the java.net package. Another important descendant of IOException is RemoteException, which belongs to the java.rmi package and is used when problems arise during remote method invocation (RMI). Throughout this book we'll mention the exceptions you need to be aware of as we run into them.

An Exception object is created by the code at the point where the error condition arises. It can hold whatever information is necessary to describe the exceptional condition, including a full stack trace for debugging. The exception object is passed, along with the flow of control, to the handling block of code. This is where the terms "throw" and "catch" come from: the Exception object is thrown from one point in the code and caught by the other, where execution resumes.

---

[*] For example, the getHeight() method of the Image class returns –1 if the height isn't known yet. No error has occurred; the height will be available in the future. In this situation, throwing an exception would be inappropriate.

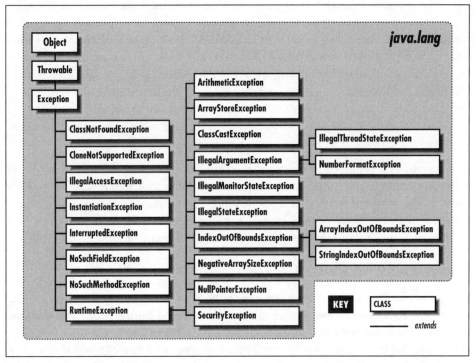

Figure 4–1: java.lang Exception classes

The Java API also defines the java.lang.Error class for unrecoverable errors. The
subclasses of Error in the java.lang package are shown in Figure 4-2. Although a
few other packages define their own subclasses of Error, subclasses of Error are
much less common (and less important) than subclasses of Exception. You
needn't worry about these errors (i.e., you do not have to catch them); they normally indicate linkage problems or virtual machine errors. An error of this kind
usually causes the Java interpreter to display a message and exit.

Exception Handling

The try/catch guarding statements wrap a block of code and catch designated
types of exceptions that occur within it:

```
try {
    readFromFile("foo");
    ...
}
catch ( Exception e ) {
    // Handle error
```

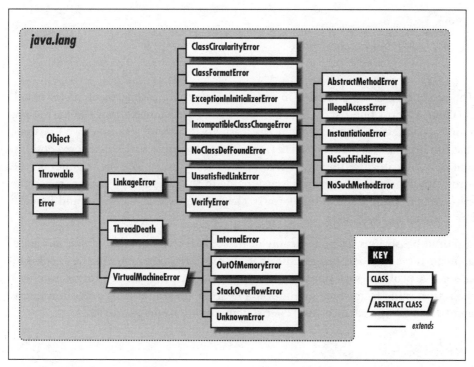

Figure 4–2: java.lang Error classes

```
        System.out.println( "Exception while reading file: " + e );
        ...
    }
```

In the above example, exceptions that occur within the body of the `try` statement are directed to the `catch` clause for possible handling. The `catch` clause acts like a method; it specifies an argument of the type of exception it wants to handle, and, if it's invoked, the `Exception` object is passed into its body as an argument. Here we receive the object in the variable `e` and print it along with a message.

A `try` statement can have multiple `catch` clauses that specify different specific types (subclasses) of `Exception`:

```
try {
    readFromFile("foo");
    ...
}
catch ( FileNotFoundException e ) {
    // Handle file not found
    ...
}
catch ( IOException e ) {
    // Handle read error
```

```
        ...
    }
    catch ( Exception e ) {
        // Handle all other errors
        ...
    }
```

The catch clauses are evaluated in order, and the first possible (assignable) match is taken. At most one catch clause is executed, which means that the exceptions should be listed from most specific to least. In the above example, we'll assume that the hypothetical readFromFile() can throw two different kinds of exceptions: one that indicates the file is not found; the other indicates a more general read error. Any subclass of Exception is assignable to the parent type Exception, so the third catch clause acts like the default clause in a switch statement and handles any remaining possibilities.

It should be obvious, but one beauty of the try/catch statement is that any statement in the try block can assume that all previous statements in the block succeeded. A problem won't arise suddenly because a programmer forgot to check the return value from some method. If an earlier statement fails, execution jumps immediately to the catch clause; later statements are never executed.

Bubbling Up

What if we hadn't caught the exception? Where would it have gone? Well, if there is no enclosing try/catch statement, the exception pops to the top of the method in which it appeared and is, in turn, thrown from that method. In this way, the exception bubbles up until it's caught, or until it pops out of the top of the program, terminating it with a run-time error message. There's a bit more to it than that because, in this case, the compiler would have reminded us to deal with it, but we'll get back to that in a moment.

Let's look at another example. In Figure 4-3, the method getContent() invokes the method openConnection() from within a try/catch statement. openConnection(), in turn, invokes the method sendRequest(), which calls the method write() to send some data.

In this figure, the second call to write() throws an IOException. Since sendRequest() doesn't contain a try/catch statement to handle the exception, it's thrown again, from the point that it was called in the method openConnection(). Since openConnection() doesn't catch the exception either, it's thrown once more. Finally it's caught by the try statement in getContent() and handled by its catch clause.

Since an exception can bubble up quite a distance before it is caught and handled, we may need a way to determine exactly where it was thrown. All exceptions can

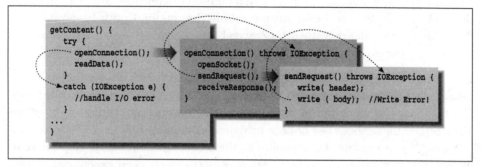

Figure 4–3: Exception propagation

dump a *stack trace* that lists their method of origin and all of the nested method calls that it took to arrive there, using the `printStackTrace()` method.

```
try {
    // complex task
} catch ( Exception e ) {
    // dump information about exactly where the exception occurred
    e.printStackTrack( System.err );
    ...
}
```

Checked and Unchecked Exceptions

I mentioned earlier that Java makes us be explicit about our error handling. But Java is programmer-friendly, and it's not possible to require that every conceivable type of error be handled in every situation. So Java exceptions are divided into two categories: *checked exceptions* and *unchecked exceptions.* Most application-level exceptions are checked, which means that any method that throws one, either by generating it itself (as we'll discuss below) or by passively ignoring one that occurs within it, must declare that it can throw that type of exception in a special `throws` clause in its method declaration. We haven't yet talked in detail about declaring methods; we'll cover that in Chapter 5. For now all you need know is that methods have to declare the checked exceptions they can throw or allow to be thrown.

Again in Figure 4-3, notice that the methods `openConnection()` and `sendRequest()` both specify that they can throw an `IOException`. If we had to throw multiple types of exceptions, we could declare them separated with commas:

```
void readFile( String s ) throws IOException, InterruptedException {
    ...
}
```

The throws clause tells the compiler that a method is a possible source of that type of checked exception and that anyone calling that method must be prepared to deal with it. The caller may use a try/catch block to catch it, or it may declare that it can throw the exception itself.

In contrast, exceptions that are subclasses of either the class java.lang.RuntimeException or the class java.lang.Error are unchecked. See Figure 4-1 for the subclasses of RuntimeException. (Subclasses of Error are generally reserved for serious class linkage or virtual machine problems.) It's not a compile-time error to ignore the possibility of these exceptions; methods don't have to declare they can throw them. In all other respects, unchecked exceptions behave the same as other exceptions. We are free to catch them if we wish; we simply aren't required to.

Checked and unchecked exceptions can be summarized as follows:

Checked exceptions
  Exceptions a reasonable application should try to handle gracefully.

Unchecked exception (run-time exceptions or errors)
  Problems from which we would not expect our software to recover.

Checked exceptions include application-level problems like missing files and unavailable hosts. As good programmers (and upstanding citizens), we should design software to recover gracefully from these kinds of conditions. Unchecked exceptions include problems such as "out of memory" and "array index out of bounds." While these may indicate application-level programming errors, they can occur almost anywhere and usually aren't easy to recover from. Fortunately, because there are unchecked exceptions, you don't have to wrap every one of your array-index operations in a try/catch statement.

Throwing Exceptions

We can throw our own exceptions: either instances of Exception or one of its existing subclasses, or our own specialized exception classes. All we have to do is create an instance of the Exception and throw it with the throw statement:

```
throw new Exception();
```

Execution stops and is transferred to the nearest enclosing try/catch statement. (There is little point in keeping a reference to the Exception object we've created here.) An alternative constructor lets us specify a string with an error message:

```
throw new Exception("Something really bad happened");
```

By convention, all types of Exception have a String constructor like this. The String message above is somewhat facetious and vague. Normally you won't be throwing a plain old `Exception`, but a more specific subclass. For example:

```
public void checkRead( String s ) {
    if ( new File(s).isAbsolute() || (s.indexOf("..") != -1) )
        throw new SecurityException(



            "Access to file : "+ s +" denied.");
}
```

In the above, we partially implement a method to check for an illegal path. If we find one, we throw a `SecurityException`, with some information about the transgression.

Of course, we could include whatever other information is useful in our own specialized subclasses of `Exception`. Often, though, just having a new type of exception is good enough, because it's sufficient to help direct the flow of control. For example, if we are building a parser, we might want to make our own kind of exception to indicate a particular kind of failure:

```
class ParseException extends Exception {
    ParseException() {
        super();
    }
    ParseException( String desc ) {
        super( desc ) };
}
```

See Chapter 5 for a full description of classes and class constructors. The body of our exception class here simply allows a `ParseException` to be created in the conventional ways that we have created exceptions above. Now that we have our new exception type, we can guard like this:

```
// Somewhere in our code
...
try {
    parseStream( input );
} catch ( ParseException pe ) {
    // Bad input...
} catch ( IOException ioe ) {
    // Low level communications problem
}
```

As you can see, although our new exception doesn't currently hold any specialized information about the problem (it certainly could), it does let us distinguish a parse error from an arbitrary communications error in the same chunk of code.

Re-throwing exceptions

Sometimes you'll want to take some action based on an exception and then turn around and throw a new exception in its place. For example, suppose that we want to handle an IOException by freeing up some resources before allowing the failure to pass on to the rest of the application. You can do this in the obvious way, by simply catching the exception and then throwing it again or throwing a new one.

Try Creep

The try statement imposes a condition on the statements they guard. It says that if an exception occurs within it, the remaining statements will be abandoned. This has consequences for local variable initialization. If the compiler can't determine whether a local variable assignment we placed inside a try/catch block will happen, it won't let us use the variable:

```
void myMethod() {
    int foo;

    try {
        foo = getResults();
    }
    catch ( Exception e ) {
        ...
    }

    int bar = foo;  // Compile time error—foo may not have been initialized
```

In the above example, we can't use foo in the indicated place because there's a chance it was never assigned a value. One obvious option is to move the assignment inside the try statement:

```
try {
    foo = getResults();



    int bar = foo;  // Okay because we only get here
                    // if previous assignment succeeds
}
catch ( Exception e ) {
    ...
}
```

Sometimes this works just fine. However, now we have the same problem if we want to use bar later in myMethod(). If we're not careful, we might end up pulling everything into the try statement. The situation changes if we transfer control out of the method in the catch clause:

```
try {
    foo = getResults();
}
catch ( Exception e ) {
    ...
    return;
}

int bar = foo;   // Okay because we only get here
                 // if previous assignment succeeds
```

Your code will dictate its own needs; you should just be aware of the options.

The finally Clause

What if we have some clean up to do before we exit our method from one of the catch clauses? To avoid duplicating the code in each catch branch and to make the cleanup more explicit, Java supplies the finally clause. A finally clause can be added after a try and any associated catch clauses. Any statements in the body of the finally clause are guaranteed to be executed, no matter why control leaves the try body:

```
try {
    // Do something here
}
catch ( FileNotFoundException e ) {
    ...
}
catch ( IOException e ) {
    ...
}
catch ( Exception e ) {
    ...
}
finally {
    // Cleanup here
}
```

In the above example the statements at the cleanup point will be executed eventually, no matter how control leaves the try. If control transfers to one of the catch clauses, the statements in finally are executed after the catch completes. If none of the catch clauses handles the exception, the finally statements are executed before the exception propagates to the next level.

If the statements in the try execute cleanly, or even if we perform a return, break, or continue, the statements in the finally clause are executed. To perform cleanup operations, we can even use try and finally without any catch clauses:

```
try {
    // Do something here
    return;
```

```
    }
    finally {
        System.out.println("Whoo-hoo!");
    }
```

Exceptions that occur in a catch or finally clause are handled normally; the search for an enclosing try/catch begins outside the offending try statement.

Performance issues

We mentioned at the beginning of this section that there are methods in the core Java APIs that will still return "out of bound" values like -1 or null, instead of throwing Exceptions. Why is this? Well, for some it is simple a matter of convenience; where a special value is easily discernible, we may not want to have to wrap those methods in try/catch blocks. But there is also a performance issue.

Because of the way the Java virtual machine is implemented, guarding against an exception being thrown (using a try) is free. It doesn't add any overhead to the execution of your code. However, throwing an exception is not free. When an exception is thrown, Java has to locate the appropriate try/catch block and perform other time-consuming activities at run-time.

The result is that you should throw exceptions only in truly "exceptional" circumstances and try to avoid using them for expected conditions, when performance is an issue. For example, if you have a loop, it may be better to perform a small test on each pass and avoid throwing the exception, rather than throwing it frequently. On the other hand, if the exception is only thrown one in a gazillion times, you may want to eliminate the overhead of the test code and not worry about the cost of throwing that exception.

Arrays

An array is a special type of object that can hold an ordered collection of elements. The type of the elements of the array is called the *base type* of the array; the number of elements it holds is a fixed attribute called its *length*. Java supports arrays of all numeric and reference types.

The basic syntax of arrays looks much like that of C or C++. We create an array of a specified length and access the elements with the special index operator, []. Unlike other languages, however, arrays in Java are true, first-class objects, which means they are real objects within the Java language. An array is an instance of a special Java array class and has a corresponding type in the type system. This means that to use an array, as with any other object, we first declare a variable of the appropriate type and then use the new operator to create an instance of it.

Array objects differ from other objects in Java in three respects:

- Java implicitly creates a special array class for us whenever we declare an array type variable. It's not strictly necessary to know about this process in order to use arrays, but it helps in understanding their structure and their relationship to other objects in Java.

- Java lets us use the special [] operator to access array elements, so that arrays look as we expect. We could implement our own classes that act like arrays, but because Java doesn't have user-defined operator overloading, we would have to settle for having methods like get() and put() instead of using the special [] notation.

- Java provides a corresponding special form of the new operator that lets us construct an instance of an array and specify its length with the [] notation.

Array Types

An array type variable is denoted by a base type followed by empty brackets []. Alternatively, Java accepts a C-style declaration, with the brackets placed after the array name. The following are equivalent:

```
int [] arrayOfInts;
int arrayOfInts [];
```

In each case, arrayOfInts is declared as an array of integers. The size of the array is not yet an issue, because we are declaring only the array type variable. We have not yet created an actual instance of the array class, with its associated storage. It's not even possible to specify the length of an array as part of its type.

An array of objects can be created in the same way:

```
String [] someStrings;
Button someButtons [];
```

Array Creation and Initialization

Having declared an array type variable, we can now use the new operator to create an instance of the array. After the new operator, we specify the base type of the array and its length, with a bracketed integer expression:

```
arrayOfInts = new int [42];
someStrings = new String [ number + 2 ];
```

We can, of course, combine the steps of declaring and allocating the array:

```
double [] someNumbers = new double [20];
Component widgets [] = new Component [12];
```

As in C, array indices start with zero. Thus, the first element of someNumbers[] is 0 and the last element is 19. After creation, the array elements are initialized to the default values for their type. For numeric types, this means the elements are initially zero:

```
int [] grades = new int [30];
grades[0] = 99;
grades[1] = 72;
// grades[2] == 0
```

The elements of an array of objects are references to the objects, not actual instances of the objects. The default value of each element is therefore null, until we assign instances of appropriate objects:

```
String names [] = new String [4];
names [0] = new String();
names [1] = "Boofa";
names [2] = someObject.toString();
// names[3] == null
```

This is an important distinction that can cause confusion. In many other languages, the act of creating an array is the same as allocating storage for its elements. In Java, an array of objects actually contains only reference variables and those variables, have the value null until they are assigned to real objects.* Figure 4-4 illustrates the names array of the previous example.

names is a variable of type String[] (i.e., a string array). The String[] object can be thought of as containing four String type variables. We have assigned String objects to the first three array elements. The fourth has the default value null.

Java supports the C-style curly braces {} construct for creating an array and initializing its elements when it is declared:

```
int [] primes = { 1, 2, 3, 5, 7, 7+4 };    // primes[2] == 3
```

An array object of the proper type and length is implicitly created and the values of the comma-separated list of expressions are assigned to its elements.

We can use the {} syntax with an array of objects. In this case, each of the expressions must evaluate to an object that can be assigned to a variable of the base type of the array, or the value null. Here are some examples:

---

* The analog in C or C++ would be an array of pointers to objects. However, pointers in C or C++ are themselves two- or four-byte values. Allocating an array of pointers is, in actuality, allocating the storage for some number of those pointer objects. An array of references is conceptually similar, although references are not themselves objects. We can't manipulate references or parts of references other than by assignment, and their storage requirements (or lack thereof) are not part of the high-level language specification.

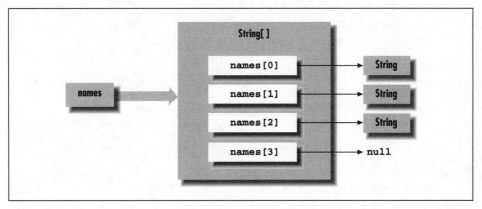

Figure 4–4: The names array

```
String [] verbs = { "run", "jump", someWord.toString() };
Button [] controls = { stopButton, new Button("Forwards"),
    new Button("Backwards") };
// all types are subtypes of Object
Object [] objects = { stopButton, "A word", null };
```

You should create and initialize arrays in whatever manner is appropriate for your application. The following are equivalent:

```
Button [] threeButtons = new Button [3];
Button [] threeButtons = { null, null, null };
```

Using Arrays

The size of an array object is available in the public variable `length`:

```
char [] alphabet = new char [26];
int alphaLen = alphabet.length;              // alphaLen == 26

String [] musketeers = { "one", "two", "three" };
int num = musketeers.length;                 // num == 3
```

`length` is the only accessible field of an array; it is a variable, not a method.

Array access in Java is just like array access in C; you access an element by putting an integer-valued expression between brackets after the name of the array. The following example creates an array of `Button` objects called `keyPad` and then fills the array with `Button` objects:

```
Button [] keyPad = new Button [ 10 ];
for ( int i=0; i < keyPad.length; i++ )
    keyPad[ i ] = new Button( Integer.toString( i ) );
```

Attempting to access an element that is outside the range of the array generates an `ArrayIndexOutOfBoundsException`. This is a type of `RuntimeException`, so you can either catch it and handle it yourself, or ignore it, as we already discussed:

```
String [] states = new String [50];

try {
    states[0] = "California";
    states[1] = "Oregon";
    ...
    states[50] = "McDonald's Land";  // Error—array out of bounds
}
catch ( ArrayIndexOutOfBoundsException err ) {
    System.out.println( "Handled error: " + err.getMessage() );
}
```

It's a common task to copy a range of elements from one array into another. Java supplies the `arraycopy()` method for this purpose; it's a utility method of the `System` class:

```
System.arraycopy( source, sourceStart, destination, destStart, length );
```

The example below doubles the size of the `names` array from an earlier example:

```
String [] tmpVar = new String [ 2 * names.length ];
System.arraycopy( names, 0, tmpVar, 0, names.length );
names = tmpVar;
```

A new array, twice the size of `names`, is allocated and assigned to a temporary variable `tmpVar`. `arraycopy()` is used to copy the elements of `names` to the new array. Finally, the new array is assigned to `names`. If there are no remaining references to the old array object after `names` has been copied, it will be garbage collected on the next pass.

Anonymous Arrays

You often want to create "throw-away" arrays: arrays that are only used in one place and never referenced anywhere else. Such arrays don't need to have a name, because you never need to refer to them again in that context. For example, you may want to create a collection of objects to pass as an argument to some method. It's easy enough to create a normal, named array—but if you don't actually work with the array (if you use the array only as a holder for some collection), you shouldn't have to. Java makes it easy to create "anonymous" (i.e., unnamed) arrays.

Let's say you need to call a method named `setPets()`, which takes an array of `Animal` objects as arguments. `Cat` and `Dog` are subclasses of `Animal`. Here's how to call `setPets()` using an anonymous array:

```
Dog pokey = new Dog ("gray");
Cat squiggles = new Cat ("black");
Cat jasmine = new Cat ("orange");
setPets ( new Animal [] { pokey, squiggles, jasmine });
```

The syntax looks just like the initialization of an array in a variable declaration. We implicitly define the size of the array and fill in its elements using the curly brace notation. However, since this is not a variable declaration, we have to explicitly use the new operator to create the array object.

You can use anonymous arrays to simulate variable length argument lists (often called VARARGS), a feature of many programming languages that Java doesn't provide. The advantage of anonymous arrays over variable length argument lists is that the former allow stricter type checking; the compiler always knows exactly what arguments are expected, and therefore it can verify that method calls are correct.

Multidimensional Arrays

Java supports multidimensional arrays in the form of arrays of array type objects. You create a multidimensional array with C-like syntax, using multiple bracket pairs, one for each dimension. You also use this syntax to access elements at various positions within the array. Here's an example of a multidimensional array that represents a chess board:

```
ChessPiece [][] chessBoard;
chessBoard = new ChessPiece [8][8];
chessBoard[0][0] = new ChessPiece( "Rook" );
chessBoard[1][0] = new ChessPiece( "Pawn" );
...
```

Here chessBoard is declared as a variable of type ChessPiece[][] (i.e., an array of ChessPiece arrays). This declaration implicitly creates the type ChessPiece[] as well. The example illustrates the special form of the new operator used to create a multidimensional array. It creates an array of ChessPiece[] objects and then, in turn, creates each array of ChessPiece objects. We then index chessBoard to specify values for particular ChessPiece elements. (We'll neglect the color of the pieces here.)

Of course, you can create arrays with more than two dimensions. Here's a slightly impractical example:

```
Color [][][] rgbCube = new Color [256][256][256];
rgbCube[0][0][0] = Color.black;
rgbCube[255][255][0] = Color.yellow;
...
```

As in C, we can specify the initial index of a multidimensional array to get an array type object with fewer dimensions. In our example, the variable chessBoard is of type `ChessPiece[][]`. The expression `chessBoard[0]` is valid and refers to the first element of `chessBoard`, which is of type `ChessPiece[]`. For example, we can create a row for our chess board:

```
ChessPiece [] startRow =  {
    new ChessPiece("Rook"), new ChessPiece("Knight"),
    new ChessPiece("Bishop"), new ChessPiece("King"),
    new ChessPiece("Queen"), new ChessPiece("Bishop"),
    new ChessPiece("Knight"), new ChessPiece("Rook")
};

chessBoard[0] = startRow;
```

We don't necessarily have to specify the dimension sizes of a multidimensional array with a single `new` operation. The syntax of the `new` operator lets us leave the sizes of some dimensions unspecified. The size of at least the first dimension (the most significant dimension of the array) has to be specified, but the sizes of any number of the less significant array dimensions may be left undefined. We can assign appropriate array type values later.

We can create a checkerboard of `boolean` values (which is not quite sufficient for a real game of checkers) using this technique:

```
boolean [][] checkerBoard;
checkerBoard = new boolean [8][];
```

Here, `checkerBoard` is declared and created, but its elements, the eight `boolean[]` objects of the next level, are left empty. Thus, for example, `checkerBoard[0]` is `null` until we explicitly create an array and assign it, as follows:

```
checkerBoard[0] = new boolean [8];
checkerBoard[1] = new boolean [8];
...
checkerBoard[7] = new boolean [8];
```

The code of the previous two examples is equivalent to:

```
boolean [][] checkerBoard = new boolean [8][8];
```

One reason we might want to leave dimensions of an array unspecified is so that we can store arrays given to us by another method.

Note that since the length of the array is not part of its type, the arrays in the checkerboard do not necessarily have to be of the same length. Here's a defective (but perfectly legal) checkerboard:

```
checkerBoard[2] = new boolean [3];
checkerBoard[3] = new boolean [10];
```

Since Java implements multidimensional arrays as arrays of arrays, multidimensional arrays do not have to be rectangular. For example, here's how you could create and initialize a triangular array:

```
int [][] triangle = new int [5][];
for (int i = 0; i < triangle.length; i++) {
    triangle[i] = new int [i + 1];
    for (int j = 0; j < i + 1; j++)
        triangle[i][j] = i + j;
}
```

Inside Arrays

I said earlier that arrays are instances of special array classes in the Java language. If arrays have classes, where do they fit into the class hierarchy and how are they related? These are good questions; however, we need to talk more about the object-oriented aspects of Java before I can answer them. For now, take it on faith that arrays fit into the class hierarchy.

5

In this chapter:
• *Classes*
• *Methods*
• *Object Creation*
• *Object Destruction*

Objects in Java

In this chapter, we'll get to the heart of Java and explore the object-oriented aspects of the language. Object-oriented design is the art of decomposing an application into some number of objects—self-contained application components that work together. The goal is to break the problem down into a number of smaller problems that are simpler and easier to understand. Ideally, the components can be implemented directly as objects in the Java language. And if things are truly ideal, the components correspond to well-known objects that already exist, so they don't have to be created at all.

An object design methodology is a system or a set of rules created to help you identify objects in your application domain and pick the real ones from the noise. In other words, such a methodology helps you factor your application into a good set of reusable objects. The problem is that though it wants to be a science, good object-oriented design is still pretty much an art form. While you can learn from the various off-the-shelf design methodologies, none of them will help you in all situations. The truth is that experience pays.

I won't try to push you into a particular methodology here; there are shelves full of books to do that.[*] Instead, I'll provide a few hints to get you started. Here are some general design guidelines, which should be taken with a liberal amount of salt and common sense:

---

[*] Once you have some experience with basic object-oriented concepts, you might want to take a look at *Design Patterns: Elements of Reusable Object Oriented Software* by Gamma, Helm, Johnson, Vlissides (Addison Wesley). This book catalogs useful object-oriented designs that have been refined over the years by experience. Many appear in the design of the Java APIs.

- Think of an object in terms of its interface, not its implementation. It's perfectly fine for an object's internals to be unfathomably complex, as long as its "public face" is easy to understand.

- Hide and abstract as much of your implementation as possible. Avoid public variables in your objects, with the possible exception of constants. Instead define "accessor" methods to set and return values (even if they are simple types). Later, when you need to, you'll be able to modify and extend the behavior of your objects without breaking other classes that rely on them.

- Specialize objects only when you have to. When you use an object in its existing form, as a piece of a new object, you are composing objects. When you change or refine the behavior of an object, you are using inheritance. You should try to reuse objects by composition rather than inheritance whenever possible because when you compose objects you are taking full advantage of existing tools. Inheritance involves breaking down the barrier of an object and should be done only when there's a real advantage. Ask yourself if you really need to inherit the whole public interface of an object (do you want to be a "kind" of that object), or if you can just delegate certain jobs to the object and use it by composition.

- Minimize relationships between objects and try to organize related objects in packages. To enhance your code's reusability, write it as if there *is* a tomorrow. Find what one object needs to know about another to get its job done and try to minimize the coupling between them.

Classes

Classes are the building blocks of a Java application. A *class* can contain methods, variables, initialization code, and, as we'll discuss later on, even other classes. It serves as a blueprint for making class *instances*, which are run-time objects that implement the class structure. You declare a class with the class keyword. Methods and variables of the class appear inside the braces of the class declaration:

```
class Pendulum {
    float mass;
    float length = 1.0;
    int cycles;

    float position ( float time ) {
        ...
    }
    ...
}
```

The above class, Pendulum, contains three variables: mass, length, and cycles. It also defines a method called position() that takes a float value as an argument and returns a float value. Variables and method declarations can appear in any order, but variable initializers can't use forward references to uninitialized variables.

Once we've defined the Pendulum class, we can create a Pendulum object (an instance of that class) as follows:

```
Pendulum p;
p = new Pendulum();
```

Recall that our declaration of the variable p does not create a Pendulum object; it simply creates a variable that refers to an object of type Pendulum. We still have to create the object dynamically, using the new keyword. Now that we've created a Pendulum object, we can access its variables and methods, as we've already seen many times:

```
p.mass = 5.0;
float pos = p.position( 1.0 );
```

Variables defined in a class are called *instance variables*. Every object has its own set of instance variables; the values of these variables in one object can differ from the values in another object. If you don't initialize an instance variable when you declare it, it's given a default value appropriate for its type.

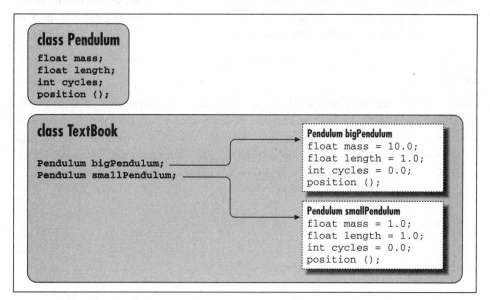

Figure 5–1: Instances of the Pendulum class

In Figure 5-1, we have a hypothetical TextBook application that uses two instances of Pendulum through the reference type variables bigPendulum and smallPendulum.

Each of these Pendulum objects has its own copy of mass, length, and cycles.

As with variables, methods defined in a class are *instance methods*. An instance method is associated with an instance of the class, but each instance doesn't really have its own copy of the method. Instead, there's just one copy of the method, but it operates on the values of the instance variables of a particular object. As you'll see later when we talk about subclassing, there's more to learn about method selection.

Accessing Members

Inside of a class, we can access instance variables and call instance methods of the class directly by name. Here's an example that expands upon our Pendulum:

```
class Pendulum {
    ...
    void resetEverything() {
        cycles = 0;
        mass = 1.0;
        ...
        float startingPosition = position( 0.0 );
    }
    ...
}
```

Other classes access members of an object through a reference, using the C-style dot notation:

```
class TextBook {
    ...
    void showPendulum() {
        Pendulum bob = new Pendulum();
        ...
        int i = bob.cycles;
        bob.resetEverything();
        bob.mass = 1.01;
        ...
    }
    ...
}
```

Here we have created a second class, TextBook, that uses a Pendulum object. It creates an instance in showPendulum() and then invokes methods and accesses variables of the object through the reference bob.

Several factors affect whether class members can be accessed from outside the class. You can use the visibility modifiers, public, private, and protected to restrict access; classes can also be placed into packages that affect their scope. The private modifier, for example, designates a variable or method for use only by other members inside the class itself. In the previous example, we could change the declaration of our variable cycles to private:

```
class Pendulum {
    ...
    private int cycles;
    ...
```

Now we can't access cycles from TextBook:

```
class TextBook {
    ...
    void showPendulum() {
        ...
        int i = bob.cycles;          // Compile time error
```

If we need to access cycles, we might add a getCycles() method to the Pendulum class. We'll look at access modifiers and how they affect the scope of variables and methods in detail later.

Static Members

Instance variables and methods are associated with and accessed through a particular object. In contrast, members that are declared with the static modifier live in the class and are shared by all instances of the class. Variables declared with the static modifier are called *static variables* or *class variables*; similarly, these kinds of methods are called *static methods* or *class methods*.

We can add a static variable to our Pendulum example:

```
class Pendulum {
    ...
    static float gravAccel = 9.80;
    ...
```

We have declared the new float variable gravAccel as static. That means if we change its value in any instance of a Pendulum, the value changes for all Pendulum objects, as shown in Figure 5-2.

Static members can be accessed like instance members. Inside our Pendulum class, we can refer to gravAccel by name, like an instance variable:

```
class Pendulum {
    ...
    float getWeight () {
        return mass * gravAccel;
    }
    ...
}
```

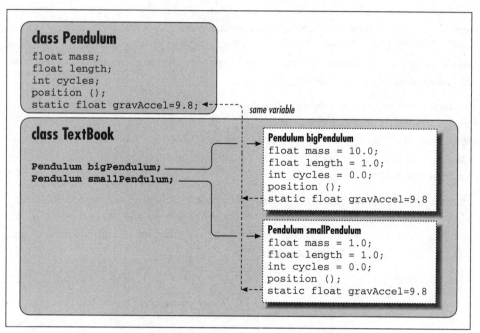

Figure 5–2: Static variables shared by all instances of a class

However, since static members exist in the class itself, independent of any instance, we can also access them directly through the class. We don't need a Pendulum object to set the variable gravAccel; instead we can use the class name as a reference:

```
Pendulum.gravAccel = 8.76;
```

This changes the value of gravAccel for any current or future instances. Why would we want to change the value of gravAccel? Well, perhaps we want to explore how pendulums would work on different planets. Static variables are also very useful for other kinds of data shared among classes at run-time. For instance, you can create methods to register your objects so that they can communicate, or you can count references to them.

We can use static variables to define constant values. In this case, we use the static modifier along with the final modifier. So, if we cared only about pendulums under the influence of the Earth's gravitational pull, we could change Pendulum as follows:

```
class Pendulum {
    ...
    static final float EARTH_G = 9.80;
    ...
```

We have followed a common convention and named our constant with capital letters; C programmers should recognize the capitalization convention, which resembles C #define statements. Now the value of EARTH_G is a constant; it can be accessed by any instance of Pendulum (or anywhere, for that matter), but its value can't be changed at run-time.

It's important to use the combination of static and final only for things that are really constant. That's because the compiler is allowed to "inline" static and final values within classes that reference them. This is probably okay for constants like PI, which aren't likely to change for a while, but may not be ideal for other kinds of identifiers.

Static members are useful as flags and identifiers, which can be accessed from anywhere. They are especially useful for values needed in the construction of an instance itself. In our example, we might declare a number of static values to represent various kinds of Pendulum objects:

```
class Pendulum {
    ...
    static int SIMPLE = 0, ONE_SPRING = 1, TWO_SPRING = 2;
    ...
```

We might then use these flags in a method that sets the type of a Pendulum or, more likely, in a special constructor, as we'll discuss shortly:

```
Pendulum pendy = new Pendulum();
pendy.setType( Pendulum.ONE_SPRING );
```

Remember, inside the Pendulum class, we can use static members directly by name as well:

```
class Pendulum {
    ...
    void resetEverything() {
        setType ( SIMPLE );
        ...
    }
    ...
}
```

Methods

Methods appear inside class bodies. They contain local variable declarations and other Java statements that are executed by a calling thread when the method is invoked. Method declarations in Java look like ANSI C-style function declarations with two restrictions:

- A method in Java always specifies a return type (there's no default). The returned value can be a primitive numeric type, a reference type, or the type void, which indicates no returned value.

- A method always has a fixed number of arguments. The combination of method overloading and true arrays removes most of the need for a variable number of arguments. These techniques are type-safe and easier to use than C's variable argument list mechanism.

Here's a simple example:

```
class Bird {
    int xPos, yPos;

    double fly ( int x, int y ) {
        double distance = Math.sqrt( x*x + y*y );
        flap( distance );
        xPos = x;
        yPos = y;
        return distance;
    }
    ...
}
```

In this example, the class Bird defines a method, fly(), that takes as arguments two integers: x and y. It returns a double type value as a result.

Local Variables

The fly() method declares a local variable called distance that it uses to compute the distance flown. A local variable is temporary; it exists only within the scope of its method. Local variables are allocated and initialized when a method is invoked; they are normally destroyed when the method returns. They can't be referenced from outside the method itself. If the method is executing concurrently in different threads, each thread has its own copies of the method's local variables. A method's arguments also serve as local variables within the scope of the method.

An object created within a method and assigned to a local variable may or may not persist after the method has returned. As with all objects in Java, it depends on whether any references to the object remain. If an object is created, assigned to a local variable, and never used anywhere else, that object will no longer be referenced when the local variable is destroyed, so garbage collection will remove the object. If, however, we assign the object to an instance variable, pass it as an argument to another method, or pass it back as a return value, it may be saved by another variable holding its reference. We'll discuss object creation and garbage collection in more detail shortly.

Shadowing

If a local variable and an instance variable have the same name, the local variable *shadows* or hides the name of the instance variable within the scope of the method. In the following example, the local variables xPos and yPos hide the instance variables of the same name:

```
class Bird {
    int xPos, yPos;
    int xNest, yNest;
    ...
    double flyToNest() {
        int xPos = xNest;
        int yPos = yNest:
        return ( fly( xPos, yPos ) );
    }
    ...
}
```

When we set the values of the local variables in flyToNest(), it has no effect on the values of the instance variables.

this

The special reference this refers to the current object. You can use it any time you need to refer explicitly to the current object instance. At times you don't need to use this because the reference to the current object is implicit; this is the case with using instance variables and methods inside of a class. But we can use this to refer explicitly to instance variables in the object, even if they are shadowed.

The following example shows how we can use this to allow argument names that shadow instance variable names. This is a fairly common technique, as it saves your having to deliberately make up alternate names. Here's how we could implement our fly() method with shadowed variables:

```
class Bird {
    int xPos, yPos;

    double fly ( int xPos, int yPos ) {
        double distance = Math.sqrt( xPos*xPos + yPos*yPos );
        flap( distance );
        this.xPos = xPos;
        this.yPos = yPos;
        return distance;
    }
    ...
}
```

In this example, the expression this.xPos refers to the instance variable xPos and assigns it the value of the local variable xPos, which would otherwise hide its name.

The only reason we need to use this in the above example is because we've used argument names that hide our instance variables, and we want to refer to the instance variables.

Static Methods

Static methods (class methods), like static variables, belong to the class and not to an individual instance of the class. What does this mean? Well, foremost, a static method lives outside of any particular class instance. It can be invoked by name, through the class name, without any objects around. Because it is not bound to a particular object instance, a static method can only directly access other static members of classes. It can't directly see any instance variables or call any instance methods, because to do so we'd have to ask, "on which instance?" Static methods can be called from instances, just like instance methods, but the important thing is that they can also be used independently.

Our fly() method uses a static method: Math.sqrt(). This method is defined by the java.lang.Math class; we'll explore this class in detail in Chapter 9. For now, the important thing to note is that Math is the name of a class and not an instance of a Math object (you can't even make an instance of Math). Because static methods can be invoked wherever the class name is available, class methods are closer to normal C-style functions. Static methods are particularly useful for utility methods that perform work that might be useful either independently of instances of the class or in creating instances of the class.

For example, in our Bird class we can enumerate all types of birds that can be created:

```
class Bird {
    ...
    static String [] getBirdTypes( ) {
        String [] types;
        // Create list...
        return types;
    }
    ...
}
```

Here we've defined a static method getBirdTypes() that returns an array of strings containing bird names. We can use getBirdTypes() from within an instance of Bird, just like an instance method. However, we can also call it from other classes, using the Bird class name as a reference:

```
String [] names = Bird.getBirdTypes();
```

Perhaps a special version of the Bird class constructor accepts the name of a bird type. We could use this list to decide what kind of bird to create.

Local Variable Initialization

In the flyToNest() example, we made a point of initializing the local variables
xPos and yPos. Unlike instance variables, local variables must be initialized before
they can be used. It's a compile-time error to try to access a local variable without
first assigning it a value:

```
void myMethod() {
    int foo = 42;
    int bar;

    // bar += 1;        // Compile time error, bar uninitialized

    bar = 99;
    bar += 1;           // ok here
}
```

Notice that this doesn't imply local variables have to be initialized when declared,
just that the first time they are referenced must be in an assignment. More subtle
possibilities arise when making assignments inside of conditionals:

```
void myMethod {
    int foo;

    if ( someCondition ) {
        foo = 42;
        ...
    }
    foo += 1;               // Compile time error; foo may not have been initialized
}
```

In the above example, foo is initialized only if someCondition is true. The compiler doesn't let you make this wager, so it flags the use of foo as an error. We
could correct this situation in several ways. We could initialize the variable to a
default value in advance or move the usage inside of the conditional. We could
also make sure the path of execution doesn't reach the uninitialized variable
through some other means, depending on what makes sense for our particular
application. For example, we could return from the method abruptly:

```
int foo;
...
if ( someCondition ) {
    foo = 42;
    ...
} else
    return;

foo += 1;
```

In this case, there's no chance of reaching foo in an unused state and the compiler
allows the use of foo after the conditional.

Why is Java so picky about local variables? One of the most common (and insidious) sources of error in C or C++ is forgetting to initialize local variables, so Java tries to help us out. If it didn't, Java would suffer the same potential irregularities as C or C++.[*]

Argument Passing and References

Let's consider what happens when you pass arguments to a method. All primitive data types (e.g., int, char, float) are passed by value. Now you're probably used to the idea that reference types (i.e., any kind of object, including arrays and strings) are used through references. An important distinction is that the references themselves (the pointers to these objects) are actually primitive types, and are passed by value too.

Consider the following piece of code:

```
// somewhere
    int i = 0;
    SomeKindOfObject obj = new SomeKindOfObject();
    myMethod( i, obj );
    ...
void myMethod(int j, SomeKindOfObject o) {
    ...
}
```

The first chunk of code calls myMethod(), passing it two arguments. The first argument, i, is passed by value; when the method is called, the value of i is copied into the method's parameter j. If myMethod() changes the value of i, it's changing only its copy of the local variable.

In the same way, a copy of the reference to obj is placed into the reference variable o of myMethod(). Both references refer to the same object, of course, and any changes made through either reference affect the actual (single) object instance, but there are two copies of the pointer. If we change the value of, say, o.size, the change is visible through either reference. However, if myMethod() changes the reference o itself—to point to another object—it's affecting only its copy. In this sense, passing the reference is like passing a pointer in C and *unlike* passing by reference in C++.

What if myMethod() needs to modify the calling method's notion of the obj reference as well (i.e., make obj point to a different object)? The easy way to do that is to wrap obj inside some kind of object. A good candidate would be to wrap the

---

[*] As with malloc'ed storage in C or C++, Java objects and their instance variables are allocated on a heap, which allows them default values once, when they are created. Local variables, however, are allocated on the Java virtual machine stack. As with the stack in C and C++, failing to initialize these could mean successive method calls could receive garbage values, and program execution might be inconsistent or implementation dependent.

object up as the lone element in an array:

```
SomeKindOfObject [] wrapper = { obj };
```

All parties could then refer to the object as wrapper[0] and would have the ability to change the reference. This is not very asthetically pleasing, but it does illustrate that what is needed is the level of indirection. Another possibility is to use this to pass a reference to the calling object.

Let's look at another piece of code that could be from an implementation of a linked list:

```
class Element {
    public Element nextElement;

    void addToList( List list ) {
        list.addToList( this );
    }
}

class List {
    void addToList( Element element ) {
        ...
        element.nextElement = getNextElement();
    }
}
```

Every element in a linked list contains a pointer to the next element in the list. In this code, the Element class represents one element; it includes a method for adding itself to the list. The List class itself contains a method for adding an arbitrary Element to the list. The method addToList() calls addToList() with the argument this (which is, of course, an Element). addToList() can use the this reference to modify the Element's nextElement instance variable. The same technique can be used in conjunction with interfaces to implement callbacks for arbitrary method invocations.

Method Overloading

Method overloading is the ability to define multiple methods with the same name in a class; when the method is invoked, the compiler picks the correct one based on the arguments passed to the method. This implies, of course, that overloaded methods must have different numbers or types of arguments. In a later section we'll look at method overriding, which occurs when we declare methods with identical signatures in different classes.

Method overloading is a powerful and useful feature. It's another form of polymorphism (ad-hoc polymorphism). The idea is to create methods that act in the same way on different types of arguments and have what appears to be a single method that operates on any of the types. The Java PrintStream's print() method is a good example of method overloading in action. As you've probably deduced by now, you can print a string representation of just about anything using the expression:

```
System.out.print( argument )
```

The variable out is a reference to an object (a PrintStream) that defines nine different versions of the print() method. They take, respectively, arguments of the following types: Object, String, char[], char, int, long, float, double, and boolean.

```
class PrintStream {
    void print( Object arg ) { ... }
    void print( String arg ) { ... }
    void print( char [] arg ) { ... }
    ...
}
```

You can invoke the print() method with any of these types as an argument, and it's printed in an appropriate way. In a language without method overloading, this would require something more cumbersome, such as a separate method for printing each type of object. Then it would be your responsibility to remember what method to use for each data type.

In the above example, print() has been overloaded to support two reference types: Object and String. What if we try to call print() with some other reference type? Say, perhaps, a Date object? The answer is that since Date is a subclass of Object, the Object method is selected. When there's not an exact type match, the compiler searches for an acceptable, assignable match. Since Date, like all classes, is a subclass of Object, a Date object can be assigned to a variable of type Object. It's therefore an acceptable match, and the Object method is selected.

What if there's more than one possible match? Say, for example, we tried to print a subclass of String called MyString. (The String class is final, so it can't be subclassed, but allow me this brief transgression for purposes of explanation.) MyString is assignable to either String or to Object. Here the compiler makes a determination as to which match is "better" and selects that method. In this case, it's the String method.

The intuitive explanation is that the String class is closer to MyString in the inheritance hierarchy. It is a *more specific* match. A more rigorous way of specifying it would be to say that a given method is more specific than another method if the argument types of the first method are all assignable to the argument types of the second method. In this case, the String method is more specific to a subclass of String than the Object method because type String is assignable to type Object. The reverse is not true.

If you're paying close attention, you may have noticed I said that the compiler resolves overloaded methods. Method overloading is not something that happens at run-time; this is an important distinction. It means that the selected method is chosen once, when the code is compiled. Once the overloaded method is selected, the choice is fixed until the code is recompiled, even if the class containing the called method is later revised and an even more specific overloaded method is added. This is in contrast to overridden (virtual) methods, which are located at run-time and can be found even if they didn't exist when the calling class was compiled. We'll talk about method overriding later in the chapter.

One last note about overloading. In earlier chapters, we've pointed out that Java doesn't support programmer-defined overloaded operators, and that + is the only system-defined overloaded operator. If you've been wondering what an overloaded operator is, I can finally clear up that mystery. In a language like C++, you can customize operators such as + and * to work with objects that you create. For example, you could create a class Complex that implements complex numbers, and then overload methods corresponding to + and * to add and multiply Complex objects. Some people argue that operator overloading makes for elegant and readable programs, while others say it's just "syntactic sugar" that makes for obfuscated code. The Java designers clearly espoused the latter opinion when they chose not to support programmer-defined overloaded operators.

Object Creation

Objects in Java are allocated from a system heap space, much like malloc'ed storage in C or C++. Unlike C or C++, however, we needn't manage that memory ourselves. Java takes care of memory allocation and deallocation for you. Java explicitly allocates storage for an object when you create it with the new keyword. More importantly, objects are removed by garbage collection when they're no longer referenced.

Constructors

You allocate an object by specifying the new operator with an object *constructor*. A constructor is a special method with the same name as its class and no return type. It's called when a new class instance is created, which gives the class an opportunity to set up the object for use. Constructors, like other methods, can accept arguments and can be overloaded (they are not, however, inherited like other methods; we'll discuss inheritance later).

```
class Date {
    long time;

    Date() {
        time = currentTime();
    }

    Date( String date ) {
        time = parseDate( date );
    }
    ...
}
```

In the above example, the class Date has two constructors. The first takes no arguments; it's known as the default constructor. Default constructors play a special role in that, if we don't define any constructors for a class, an empty default constructor is supplied for us. The default constructor is what gets called whenever you create an object by calling its constructor with no arguments. Here we have implemented the default constructor so that it sets the instance variable time by calling a hypothetical method: currentTime(), which resembles the functionality of the real java.util.Date class.

The second constructor takes a String argument. Presumably, this String contains a string representation of the time that can be parsed to set the time variable.

Given the constructors above, we create a Date object in the following ways:

```
Date now = new Date();
Date christmas = new Date("Dec 25, 1997");
```

In each case, Java chooses the appropriate constructor at compile-time based on the rules for overloaded method selection.

If we later remove all references to an allocated object, it'll be garbage collected, as we'll discuss shortly:

```
christmas = null;          // fair game for the garbage collector
```

Setting the above reference to null means it's no longer pointing to the "Dec 25, 1997" object. Unless that object is referenced by another variable, it's now inaccessible and can be garbage collected. Actually, setting christmas to any other value would have the same results, but using the value null is a clear way to indicate that christmas no longer has a useful value.

A few more notes about constructors. Constructors can't be abstract, synchronized, or final. Constructors can, however, be declared with the visibility modifiers public, private, or protected, to control their accessibility. We'll talk in detail about visibility modifiers later in the chapter.

Working with Overloaded Constructors

A constructor can refer to another constructor in the same class or the immediate superclass using special forms of the this and super references. We'll discuss the first case here, and return to that of the superclass constructor again after we have talked more about subclassing and inheritance.

A constructor can invoke another, overloaded constructor in its class using the reference this() with appropriate arguments to select the desired constructor. If a constructor calls another constructor, it must do so as its first statement:

```
class Car {
    String model;
    int doors;

    Car( String m, int d ) {
        model = m;
        doors = d;
        // other, complicated setup
        ...
    }

    Car( String m ) {
        this( m, 4 );
    }
    ...
}
```

In the example above, the class Car has two overloaded constructors. The first, more explicit one, accepts arguments specifying the car's model and its number of doors and uses them to set up the object. We have also provided a simpler constructor that takes just the model as an argument and, in turn, calls the first constructor with a default value of four doors. The advantage of this approach is that you can have a single constructor do all the complicated setup work; other auxiliary constructors simply feed the appropriate arguments to that constructor.

The important point is the call to this(), which must appear as the first statement our second constructor. The syntax is restricted in this way because there's a need to identify a clear chain of command in the calling of constructors. At one end of the chain, Java invokes the constructor of the superclass (if we don't do it explicitly) to ensure that inherited members are initialized properly before we proceed. There's also a point in the chain, just after the constructor of the superclass is invoked, where the initializers of the current class's instance variables are evaluated. Before that point, we can't even reference the instance variables of our class. We'll explain this situation again in complete detail after we have talked about inheritance.

For now, all you need to know is that you can invoke a second constructor only as the first statement of another constructor. In addition, you can't do anything at that point other than pass along arguments of the current constructor. For example, the following code is illegal and causes a compile-time error:

```
Car( String m ) {
    int doors = determineDoors();
    this( m, doors );   // Error—constructor call must be first statement
}
```

The simple model name constructor can't do any additional setup before calling the more explicit constructor. It can't even refer to an instance member for a constant value:

```
class Car {
    ...
    final int default_doors = 4;
    ...

    Car( String m ) {
        this( m, default_doors ); // Error—referencing
                                  // uninitialized variable

    }
    ...
}
```

The instance variable `defaultDoors` above is not initialized until a later point in the chain of constructor calls, so the compiler doesn't let us access it yet. Fortunately, we can solve this particular problem by making the identifier `static` as well:

```
class Car {
    ...
    static final int DEFAULT_DOORS = 4;
    ...

    Car( String m ) {
        this( m, DEFAULT_DOORS );  // Okay now
    }
    ...
}
```

The `static` members of our class have been initialized for some time (since the class was first loaded), so it's safe to access them.

Static and Nonstatic Code Blocks

It's possible to declare a code block (some statements within curly braces) directly within the scope of a class. This code block doesn't belong to any method; instead, it's executed once, at the time the object is constructed, or, in the case of a code block marked `static`, at the time the class is loaded.

Nonstatic code blocks can be thought of as an extension of instance variable initialization. They are called at the time the instance variable's initializers are evaluated (after superclass construction), in the order they appear in the Java source:

```
class MyClass {
    Properties myProps = new Properties();
    // set up myProps
    {
        myProps.put("foo", "bar");
        myProps.put("boo", "gee");
    }
    int a = 5;
        ...
```

You can use static code blocks to initialize static class members. So the static members of a class can have complex initialization just like objects:

```
class ColorWheel {
    static Hashtable colors = new Hashtable();

    // set up colors
    static {
        colors.put("Red", Color.red );
        colors.put("Green", Color.green );
        colors.put("Blue", Color.blue );
        ...
    }
    ...
}
```

The class ColorWheel provides a variable colors that maps the names of colors to Color objects in a Hashtable. The first time the class ColorWheel is referenced and loaded, the static components of ColorWheel are evaluated, in the order they appear in the source. In this case, the static code block simply adds elements to the colors Hashtable.

Object Destruction

Now that we've seen how to create objects, it's time to talk about their destruction. If you're accustomed to programming in C or C++, you've probably spent time hunting down memory leaks in your code. Java takes care of object destruction for you; you don't have to worry about memory leaks, and you can concentrate on more important programming tasks.

Garbage Collection

Java uses a technique known as *garbage collection* to remove objects that are no longer needed. The garbage collector is Java's grim reaper. It lingers, usually in a low priority thread, stalking objects and awaiting their demise. It finds them, watches them, and periodically counts references to them to see when their time has come. When all references to an object are gone, and it's no longer accessible, the garbage-collection mechanism reclaims it and returns the space to the available pool of resources.

There are many different algorithms for garbage collection; the Java virtual machine architecture doesn't specify a particular scheme. It's worth noting, though, that current implementations of Java use a conservative mark and sweep system. Under this scheme, Java first walks through the tree of all accessible object references and marks them as alive. Then Java scans the heap looking for identifiable objects that aren't so marked. Java finds objects on the heap because they are stored in a characteristic way and have a particular signature of bits in their handles unlikely to be reproduced naturally. This kind of algorithm doesn't suffer from the problem of cyclic references, where detached objects can mutually reference each other and appear alive.

By default, the Java virtual machine is configured to run the garbage collector in a low-priority thread, so that the garbage collector runs periodically to collect stray objects. With the *java* interpreter that comes with the JDK, you can turn off garbage collection by using the –noasyncgc command-line option. If you do this, the garbage collector will be run only if it's requested explicitly or if the Java virtual machine runs out of memory.

A Java application can prompt the garbage collector to make a sweep explicitly by invoking the System.gc() method. An extremely time-sensitive Java application might use this to its advantage by running in an interpreter with asynchronous garbage collection deactivated and scheduling its own cleanup periods. This issue is necessarily implementation dependent, however, because on different platforms, garbage collection may be implemented in different ways. On some systems it may be continuously running in hardware.

Finalization

Before an object is removed by garbage collection, its finalize() method is invoked to give it a last opportunity to clean up its act and free other kinds of resources it may be holding. While the garbage collector can reclaim memory resources, it may not take care of things like closing files and terminating network connections gracefully or efficiently. That's what the finalize() method is for.

An object's `finalize()` method is called once and only once before the object is garbage collected. However, there's no guarantee when that will happen. Garbage collection may never run on a system that is not short of memory. It is also interesting to note that finalization and collection occur in two distinct phases of the garbage-collection process. First items are finalized; then they are collected. It is therefore possible that finalization could (intentionally or unintentionally) create a lingering reference to the object in question, postponing its garbage collection. The object could, of course, be subject to collection later, if the reference goes away, but its `finalize()` method would not be called again.

The `finalize()` methods of superclasses are not invoked automatically for you. If you need to chain together the finalization of your parent classes, you should invoke the `finalize()` method of your superclass, using `super.finalize()`. We discuss inheritance and overridden methods in Chapter 6.

Relationships Between Classes

So far, we know how to create a Java class, and to create objects, which are instances of a class. But an object by itself isn't very interesting—no more interesting than, say, a table knife. You can marvel at a table knife's perfection, but you can't really do anything with it until you have some other pieces of cutlery and food to use the cutlery on. The same is true of objects and classes in Java: they're interesting by themselves, but what's really important comes from relationships that you establish between them.

That's what we'll cover in this chapter. In particular, we'll be looking at several kinds of relationships:

- Inheritance relationships—how a class inherits methods and variables from its parent class.

- Interfaces—how to declare that a class supports certain behavior and define a type to refer to that behavior.

- Packaging—how to organize objects into logical groups.

- Inner classes—a generalization of classes that lets you nest a class definition inside of another class.

Subclassing and Inheritance

Classes in Java exist in a class hierarchy. A class in Java can be declared as a *subclass* of another class using the `extends` keyword. A subclass *inherits* variables and methods from its *superclass* and uses them as if they're declared within the subclass itself:

```
class Animal {
    float weight;
    ...
```

```
        void eat() {
            ...
        }
        ...
    }

    class Mammal extends Animal {
        int heartRate;
        // inherits weight
        ...
        void breathe() {
            ...
        }
        // inherits eat()
    }
```

In the above example, an object of type Mammal has both the instance variable
weight and the method eat(). They are inherited from Animal.

A class can extend only one other class. To use the proper terminology, Java allows
single inheritance of class implementation. Later we'll talk about interfaces, which
take the place of *multiple inheritance* as it's primarily used in C++.

A subclass can, of course, be further subclassed. Normally, subclassing specializes
or refines a class by adding variables and methods:

```
    class Cat extends Mammal {
        boolean longHair;
        // inherits weight and heartRate
        ...
        void purr() {
            ...
        }
        // inherits eat() and breathe()
    }
```

The Cat class is a type of Mammal that is ultimately a type of Animal. Cat objects
inherit all the characteristics of Mammal objects and, in turn, Animal objects. Cat
also provides additional behavior in the form of the purr() method and the long-
Hair variable. We can denote the class relationship in a diagram, as shown in Figure 6-1.

A subclass inherits all members of its superclass not designated as private. As we'll
discuss shortly, other levels of visibility affect what inherited members of the class
can be seen from outside of the class and its subclasses, but at a minimum, a subclass always has the same set of visible members as its parent. For this reason, the
type of a subclass can be considered a subtype of its parent, and instances of the
subtype can be used anywhere instances of the supertype are allowed. Consider the
following example:

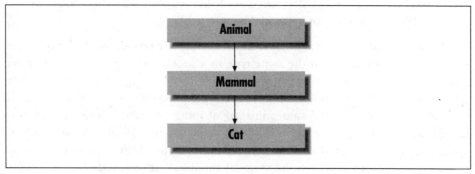

Figure 6–1: A class hierarchy

```
Cat simon = new Cat();
Animal creature = simon;
```

The Cat simon in the above example can be assigned to the Animal type variable creature because Cat is a subtype of Animal.

Shadowed Variables

In the section on methods in Chapter 5, we saw that a local variable of the same name as an instance variable hides the instance variable. Similarly, an instance variable in a subclass can shadow an instance variable of the same name in its parent class, as shown in Figure 6-2.

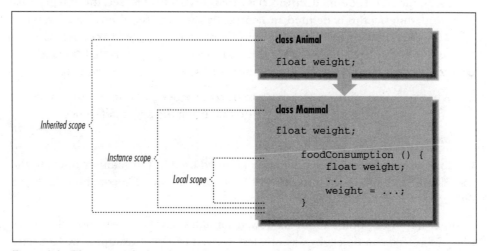

Figure 6–2: The scope of shadowed variables

In Figure 6-2, the variable weight is declared in three places: as a local variable in the method foodConsumption() of the class Mammal, as an instance variable of the class Mammal, and as an instance variable of the class Animal. The actual variable selected depends on the scope in which we are working.

In the above example, all variables were of the same type. About the only reason for declaring a variable with the same type in a subclass is to provide an alternate initializer. A more important use of shadowed variables involves changing their types. We could, for example, shadow an int variable with a double variable in a subclass that needs decimal values instead of integer values. We do this without changing the existing code because, as its name suggests, when we shadow variables, we don't replace them but instead mask them. Both variables still exist; methods of the superclass see the original variable, and methods of the subclass see the new version. The determination of what variables the various methods see is static and happens at compile-time.

Here's a simple example:

```
class IntegerCalculator {
    int sum;
    ...
}

class DecimalCalculator extends IntegerCalculator {
    double sum;
    ...
}
```

In this example, we override the instance variable sum to change its type from int to double.* Methods defined in the class IntegerCalculator see the integer variable sum, while methods defined in DecimalCalculator see the decimal variable sum. However, both variables actually exist for a given instance of DecimalCalculator, and they can have independent values. In fact, any methods that DecimalCalculator inherits from IntegerCalculator actually see the integer variable sum.

Since both variables exist in DecimalCalculator, we need to reference the variable inherited from IntegerCalculator. We do that using the super reference:

```
int s = super.sum;
```

Inside of DecimalCalculator, the super keyword used in this manner refers to the sum variable defined in the superclass. I'll explain the use of super more fully in a bit.

Another important point about shadowed variables has to do with how they work when we refer to an object by way of a less derived type. For example, we can refer to a DecimalCalculator object as an IntegerCalculator. If we do so and then

---

* Note that a better way to design our calculators would be to have an abstract Calculator class with two subclasses: IntegerCalculator and DecimalCalculator.

access the variable sum, we get the integer variable, not the decimal one:

```
DecimalCalculator dc = new DecimalCalculator();
IntegerCalculator ic = dc;

int s = ic.sum;                    // Accesses IntegerCalculator sum
```

After this detailed explanation, you may still be wondering what shadowed variables are good for. Well, to be honest, the usefulness of shadowed variables is limited, but it's important to understand the concepts before we talk about doing the same thing with methods. We'll see a different and more dynamic type of behavior with method shadowing, or more correctly, *method overriding*.

Overriding Methods

In Chapter 5, we saw we could declare overloaded methods (i.e., methods with the same name but a different number or type of arguments) within a class. Overloaded method selection works the way we described on all methods available to a class, including inherited ones. This means that a subclass can define some overloaded methods that augment the overloaded methods provided by a superclass.

But a subclass does more than that; it can define a method that has exactly the *same* method signature (arguments and return type) as a method in its superclass. In that case, the method in the subclass *overrides* the method in the superclass and effectively replaces its implementation, as shown in Figure 6-3. Overriding methods to change the behavior of objects is another form of polymorphism (sub-type polymorphism): the one most people think of when they talk about the power of object-oriented languages.

In Figure 6-3, Mammal overrides the reproduce() method of Animal, perhaps to specialize the method for the peculiar behavior of Mammals giving live birth.[*] The Cat object's sleeping behavior is overridden to be different from that of a general Animal, perhaps to accommodate cat naps. The Cat class also adds the more unique behaviors of purring and hunting mice.

From what you've seen so far, overridden methods probably look like they shadow methods in superclasses, just as variables do. But overridden methods are actually more powerful than that. An overridden method in Java acts like a virtual method in C++. When there are multiple implementations of a method in the inheritance hierarchy of an object, the one in the most derived class always overrides the others, even if we refer to the object by way of a less derived type. In other words, if we have a Cat instance assigned to a variable of the more general

---

* We'll ignore the platypus, which is an obscure nonovoviviparous mammal.

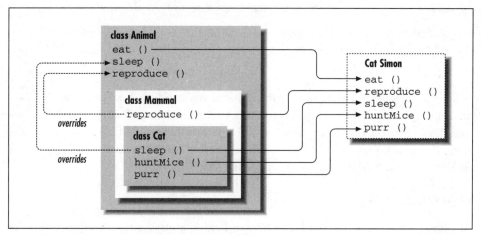

Figure 6–3: Method overriding

type `Animal` and we call its `sleep()` method, we get the `sleep()` method implemented in the `Cat` class, not the one in `Animal`:

```
Cat simon = new Cat();
Animal creature = simon;

creature.sleep();        // Accesses Cat sleep();
```

In other respects, the variable `creature` looks like an `Animal`. For example, access
to a shadowed variable would find the implementation in the `Animal` class, not the
`Cat` class. However, because methods are virtual, the appropriate method in the
`Cat` class can be located, even though we are dealing with an `Animal` object. This
means we can deal with specialized objects as if they were more general types of
objects and still take advantage of their specialized implementations of behavior.

Much of what you'll be doing when you're writing a Java applet or application is
overriding methods defined by various classes in the Java API. For example, think
back to the applets we developed in the tutorial in Chapter 2. Almost all of the
methods we implemented for those applets were overridden methods. Recall that
we created a subclass of `Applet` for each of the examples. Then we overrode
`init()` to set up our applet and `paint()` to draw our applet.

A common programming error in Java (at least for me) is to miss and accidentally
overload a method when trying to override it. Any difference in the number or
type of arguments or the return type of a method produces two overloaded methods instead of a single, overridden method. Make it a habit to look twice when
overriding methods.

Overridden methods and dynamic binding

In a previous section, we mentioned that overloaded methods are selected by the compiler at compile-time. Overridden methods, on the other hand, are selected dynamically at run-time. Even if we create an instance of a subclass our code has never seen before (perhaps a new object type loaded from the network), any overriding methods that it contains will be located and invoked at run-time to replace those that existed when we last compiled our code.

In contrast, if we load a new class that implements an additional, more specific overloaded method, our code will continue to use the implementation it discovered at compile-time. Another effect of this is that casting (i.e., explicitly telling the compiler to treat an object as one of its assignable types) affects the selection of overloaded methods, but not overridden methods.

Static method binding

static methods do not belong to any object instance; they are accessed directly through a class name, so they are not dynamically selected at run-time like instance methods. That is why static methods are called "static"—they are always bound at compile-time.

A static method in a superclass can be shadowed by another static method in a subclass, as long as the original method was not declared final. However, you can't override a static method with a nonstatic method. In other words, you can't change a static method into an instance method in a subclass.

Dynamic method selection and performance

When Java has to search dynamically for overridden methods in subclasses, there's a small performance penalty. In languages like C++, the default is for methods to act like shadowed variables, so you have to declare explicitly the methods you want to be virtual. Java is more dynamic, and by default, all instance methods are virtual. In Java you can, however, go the other direction and declare explicitly that an instance method can't be overridden, so that it will not be subject to dynamic binding and will not suffer in terms of performance. This is done with the final modifier. We have seen final used with variables to effectively make them constants. When final is applied to a method, it means that that method can't be overridden (its implementation is constant). final can also be applied to an entire class, which means the class can't be subclassed.

Compiler optimizations

When *javac,* the Java compiler, is run with the -O switch, it performs certain optimizations. It can inline `final` methods to improve performance (while slightly
increasing the size of the resulting class file). `private` methods, which are effectively `final`, can also be inlined, and `final` classes may also benefit from more
powerful optimizations.

Another kind of optimization allows you to include debugging code in your Java
source without penalty. Java doesn't have a preprocessor to explicitly control what
source is included, but you can get some of the same effects by making a block of
code conditional on a constant (i.e., `static` and `final`) variable. The Java compiler is smart enough to remove this code when it determines that it won't be
called. For example:

```
static final boolean DEBUG = false;
...
static void debug (String message) {
    if (DEBUG) {
        System.err.println(message);
        // do other stuff
        ...
    }
}
```

If we compile the above code using the -O switch, the compiler will recognize that
the condition on the `DEBUG` variable is always false, and the body of the `debug()`
method will be optimized away. But that's not all—since `debug()` itself is also
`final` it can be inlined, and an empty inlined method generates no code at all. So
when we compile with `DEBUG` set to `false`, calls to the `debug()` method will generate no residual code at all.

Method selection revisited

By now you should have a good, intuitive idea as to how methods are selected from
the pool of potentially overloaded and overridden method names of a class. If,
however, you are dying for a dry definition, I'll provide one now. If you are satisfied with your understanding, you may wish to skip this little exercise in logic.

In a previous section, I offered an inductive rule for overloaded method resolution. It said that a method is considered more specific than another if its arguments are polymorphically assignable to the arguments of the second method. We
can now expand this rule to include the resolution of overridden methods by
adding the following condition: to be more specific than another method, the type
of the class containing the method must also be assignable to the type of the class
holding the second method.

What does that mean? Well, the only classes whose types are assignable are classes in the same inheritance hierarchy. So, what we're talking about now is the set of all methods of the same name in a class or any of its parent or child classes. Since subclass types are assignable to superclass types, but not vice versa, the resolution is pushed, in the way that we expect, down the chain, towards the subclasses. This effectively adds a second dimension to the search, in which resolution is pushed down the inheritance tree towards more refined classes and, simultaneously, towards the most specific overloaded method within a given class.

Exceptions and overridden methods

When we talked about exception handling in Chapter 4, we didn't mention an important restriction that applies when you override a method. When you override a method, the new method (the overriding method) must adhere to the throws clause of the method it overrides. In other words, if an overridden method declares that it can throw an exception, the overriding method must also specify that it can throw the same kind of exception, or a subtype of that exception. By allowing the exception to be a subtype of the one specified by the parent, the overriding method can refine the type of exception thrown to go along with its new behavior. For example:

```
// A more refined exception
class MeatInedibleException extends InedibleException { ...
}

class Animal {
    void eat( Food f ) throws InedibleException { ...
}
class Herbivore extends Animal {
    void eat( Food f ) throws InedibleException {
        if ( f instanceof Meat )
            throw new MeatInedibleException();
        ....
    }
}
```

In this code, Animal specifies that it can throw an InedibleException from its eat() method. Herbivore is a subclass of Animal, so its eat() method must also be able to throw an InedibleException. However, Herbivore's eat() method actually throws a more specific exception: MeatInedibleException. It can do this because MeatInedibleException is a subtype of InedibleException (remember that exceptions are classes too). Our calling code's catch clause can therefore be more specific:

```
Animal creature = ...
try {
    creature.eat( food );
} catch ( MeatInedibleException ) {
```

```
        // creature can't eat this food because it's meat
    } catch ( InedibleException ) {
        // creature can't eat this food
    }
```

However, if we don't care why the food is inedible, we're free to catch InedibleException alone, because a MeatInedibleException is also an InedibleException.

this and super

The special references this and super allow you to refer to the members of the current object instance or those of the superclass, respectively. We have seen this used elsewhere to pass a reference to the current object and to refer to shadowed instance variables. The reference super does the same for the parents of a class. You can use it to refer to members of a superclass that have been shadowed or overridden. A common arrangement is for an overridden method in a subclass to do some preliminary work and then defer to the method of the superclass to finish the job.

```
    class Animal {
        void eat( Food f ) throws InedibleException {
            // consume food
        }
    }

    class Herbivore extends Animal {
        void eat( Food f ) throws InedibleException {
            // check if edible
            ...
            super.eat( f );
        }
    }
```

In the above example, our Herbivore class overrides the Animal eat() method to first do some checking on the food object. After doing its job it simply calls the (otherwise overridden) implementation of eat() in its superclass, using super.

super prompts a search for the method or variable to begin in the scope of the immediate superclass rather than the current class. The inherited method or variable found may reside in the immediate superclass, or in a more distant one. The usage of the super reference when applied to overridden methods of a superclass is special; it tells the method resolution system to stop the dynamic method search at the superclass, instead of in the most derived class (as it otherwise does). Without super, there would be no way to access overridden methods.

Casting

As in C++, a *cast* explicitly tells the compiler to change the apparent type of an object reference. Unlike in C++, casts in Java are checked both at compile-time and at run-time to make sure they are legal. Attempting to cast an object to an incompatible type at run-time results in a ClassCastException. Only casts between objects in the same inheritance hierarchy (and as we'll see later, to appropriate interfaces) are legal in Java and pass the scrutiny of the compiler and the run-time system.

Casts in Java affect only the treatment of references; they never change the form of the actual object. This is an important rule to keep in mind. You never change the object pointed to by a reference by casting it; you change only the compiler's (or run-time system's) notion of it.

A cast can be used to *narrow* the type of a reference—to make it more specific. Often, we'll do this when we have to retrieve an object from a more general type of collection or when it has been previously used as a less derived type. (The prototypical example is using an object in a Vector or Hashtable, as you'll see in Chapter 9.) Continuing with our Cat example:

```
Animal creature = ...
Cat simon = ...

creature = simon;        // Okay
// simon = creature;      // Compile time error, incompatible type
simon = (Cat)creature;    // Okay
```

We can't reassign the reference in creature to the variable simon even though we know it holds an instance of a Cat (Simon). We have to perform the indicated cast. This is also called *downcasting* the reference.

Note that an implicit cast was performed when we went the other way to *widen* the reference simon to type Animal during the first assignment. In this case, an explicit cast would have been legal, but superfluous.

If casting seems complicated, here's a simple way to think about it. Basically, you can't lie about what an object is. If you have a Cat object, you can cast it to a less derived type (i.e., a type above it in the class hierarchy) such as Animal or even Object, since all Java classes are a subclass of Object. If you have an Object you know is a Cat, you can downcast the Object to be an Animal or a Cat. However, if you aren't sure if the Object is a Cat or a Dog at run-time, you should check it with instanceof before you perform the cast. If you get the cast wrong, Java throws a ClassCastException.

As I mentioned earlier, casting can affect the selection of compile-time items like variables and overloaded methods, but not the selection of overridden methods. Figure 6-4 shows the difference. As shown in the top half of the diagram, casting the reference `simon` to type `Animal` (widening it) affects the selection of the shadowed variable `weight` within it. However, as the lower half of the diagram indicates, the cast doesn't affect the selection of the overridden method `sleep()`.

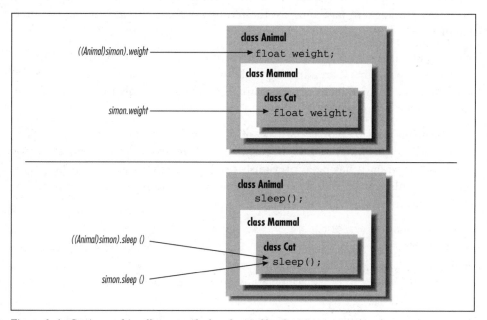

Figure 6–4: Casting and its effect on method and variable selection

Using Superclass Constructors

When we talked earlier about constructors, we discussed how the special statement `this()` invokes an overloaded constructor upon entry to another constructor. Similarly, the statement `super()` explicitly invokes the constructor of a superclass. Of course, we also talked about how Java makes a chain of constructor calls that includes the superclass's constructor, so why use `super()` explicitly? When Java makes an implicit call to the superclass constructor, it calls the default constructor. So, if we want to invoke a superclass constructor that takes arguments, we have to do so explicitly using `super()`.

If we are going to call a superclass constructor with `super()`, it must be the first statement of our constructor, just as `this()` must be the first call we make in an overloaded constructor. Here's a simple example:

```
class Person {
    Person ( String name ) {
        //  setup based on name
        ...
    }
    ...
}

class Doctor extends Person {
    Doctor ( String name, String specialty ) {
        super( name );
        // setup based on specialty
        ...
    }
    ...
}
```

In this example, we use super() to take advantage of the implementation of the superclass constructor and avoid duplicating the code to set up the object based on its name. In fact, because the class Person doesn't define a default (no arguments) constructor, we have no choice but to call super() explicitly. Otherwise, the compiler would complain that it couldn't find an appropriate default constructor to call. Said another way, if you subclass a class that has only constructors that take arguments, you have to invoke one of the superclass's constructors explicitly from your subclass constructor.

Instance variables of the class are initialized upon return from the superclass constructor, whether that's due to an explicit call via super() or an implicit call to the default superclass constructor.

We can now give the full story of how constructors are chained together and when instance variable initialization occurs. The rule has three parts and is applied repeatedly for each successive constructor invoked.

- If the first statement of a constructor is an ordinary statement—i.e., not a call to this() or super()—Java inserts an implicit call to super() to invoke the default constructor of the superclass. Upon returning from that call, Java initializes the instance variables of the current class and proceeds to execute the statements of the current constructor.

- If the first statement of a constructor is a call to a superclass constructor via super(), Java invokes the selected superclass constructor. Upon its return, Java initializes the current class's instance variables and proceeds with the statements of the current constructor.

- If the first statement of a constructor is a call to an overloaded constructor via this(), Java invokes the selected constructor and upon its return simply proceeds with the statements of the current constructor. The call to the superclass's constructor has happened within the overloaded constructor, either explicitly or implicitly, so the initialization of instance variables has already occurred.

Abstract Methods and Classes

A method in Java can be declared with the abstract modifier to indicate that it's just a prototype. An abstract method has no body; it's simply a signature definition followed by a semicolon. You can't directly use a class that contains an abstract method; you must instead create a subclass that implements the abstract method's body.

```
abstract void vaporMethod( String name );
```

In Java, a class that contains one or more abstract methods must be explicitly declared as an abstract class, also using the abstract modifier:

```
abstract class vaporClass {
    ...
    abstract void vaporMethod( String name );
    ...
}
```

An abstract class can contain other, nonabstract methods and ordinary variable declarations; however, it can't be instantiated. To be used, it must be subclassed and its abstract methods must be overridden with methods that implement a body. Not all abstract methods have to be implemented in a single subclass, but a subclass that doesn't override all its superclass's abstract methods with actual, concrete implementations must also be declared abstract.

Abstract classes provide a framework for classes that are to be "filled in" by the implementor. The java.io.InputStream class, for example, has a single abstract method called read(). Various subclasses of InputStream implement read() in their own ways to read from their own sources. The rest of the InputStream class, however, provides extended functionality built on the simple read() method. A subclass of InputStream inherits these nonabstract methods that provide functionality based on the simple read() method that the subclass implements.

It's often desirable to specify the prototypes for a set of methods and provide no implementation. In Java, this is called an *interface*. An interface defines a set of methods a class must implement (i.e., the behavior of a class). A class in Java can simply say that it *implements* an interface and go about implementing those methods. A class that implements an interface doesn't have to inherit from any particular part of the inheritance hierarchy or use a particular implementation.

Interfaces

Interfaces are kind of like Boy Scout or Girl Scout merit badges. When a scout has learned to build a bird house, he can walk around wearing a little patch with a picture of one on his sleeve. This says to the world, "I know how to build a bird house." Similarly, an *interface* is a list of methods that define some set of behavior for an object. Any class that implements each of the methods listed in the interface can declare that it implements the interface and wear, as its merit badge, an extra type—the interface's type.

Interface types act like class types. You can declare variables to be of an interface type, you can declare arguments of methods to accept interface types, and you can even specify that the return type of a method is an interface type. In each of these cases, what is meant is that any object that implements the interface (i.e., wears the right merit badge) can fill that spot. In this sense, interfaces are orthogonal to the class hierarchy. They cut across the boundaries of what kind of object an item is and deal with it only in terms of what it can do. A class implements as many interfaces as it desires. In this way, interfaces in Java replace the need for multiple inheritance (and all of its messy side effects).

An interface looks like a purely abstract class (i.e., a class with only abstract methods). You define an interface with the interface keyword and list its methods with no bodies:

```
interface Driveable {
    boolean startEngine();
    void stopEngine();
    float accelerate( float acc );
    boolean turn( Direction dir );
}
```

The example above defines an interface called Driveable with four methods. It's acceptable, but not necessary, to declare the methods in an interface with the abstract modifier; we haven't done that here. More importantly, the methods of an interface are always considered public, and you can optionally declare them as so. Why public? Well, the user of the interface wouldn't necessarily be able to see them otherwise.

Interfaces define capabilities, so it's common to name interfaces after their capabilities. Driveable, Runnable, and Updateable are good interface names. Any class that implements all the methods can then declare it implements the interface by using a special implements clause in its class definition:

```
class Automobile implements Driveable {
    ...
    public boolean startEngine() {
        if ( notTooCold )
            engineRunning = true;
        ...
    }

    public void stopEngine() {
        engineRunning = false;
    }

    public float accelerate( float acc ) {
        ...
    }

    public boolean turn( Direction dir ) {
        ...
    }
    ...
}
```

The class Automobile implements the methods of the Driveable interface and
declares itself Driveable using an implements clause.

As shown in Figure 6-5, another class, such as LawnMower, can also implement the
Driveable interface. The figure illustrates the Driveable interface being implemented by two different classes. While it's possible that both Automobile and Lawnmower could derive from some primitive kind of vehicle, they don't have to in this
scenario. This is a significant advantage of interfaces over standard multiple inheritance as implemented in C++.

After declaring the interface, we have a new type, Driveable. We can declare variables of type Driveable and assign them any instance of a Driveable object:

```
Automobile auto = new Automobile();
Lawnmower mower = new Lawnmower();
Driveable vehicle;

vehicle = auto;
vehicle.startEngine();
vehicle.stopEngine();
...
vehicle = mower;
vehicle.startEngine();
vehicle.stopEngine();
```

Both Automobile and Lawnmower implement Driveable and can be considered of
that type.

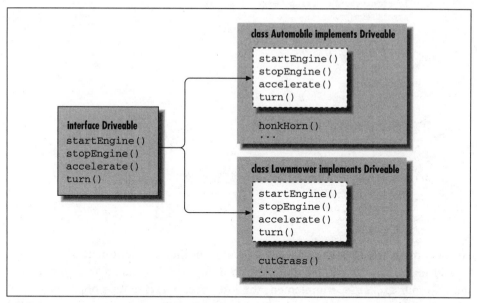

Figure 6–5: Implementing the Driveable interface

Interfaces as Callbacks

Interfaces can be used to implement callbacks in Java. A *callback* is a situation where you'd like to pass a reference to some behavior and have another object invoke it later. In C or C++, this is prime territory for function pointers; in Java, we'll use interfaces instead.

Consider two classes: a TickerTape class that displays data and a TextSource class that provides an information feed. We'd like our TextSource to send any new text data. We could have TextSource store a reference to a TickerTape object, but then we could never use our TextSource to send data to any other kind of object. Instead, we'd have to proliferate subclasses of TextSource that dealt with different types. A more elegant solution is to have TextSource store a reference to an interface type, TextUpdateable:

```
interface TextUpdateable {
    receiveText( String text );
}

class TickerTape implements TextUpdateable {
    TextSource source;

    init() {
        source = new TextSource( this );
        ...
    }
```

```
        public receiveText( String text ) {
            scrollText( text ):
        }
        ...
    }

class TextSource {
    TextUpdateable receiver;

    TextSource( TextUpdateable r ) {
        receiver = r;
    }

    private sendText( String s ) {
        receiver.receiveText( s );
    }
    ...
    }
```

The only thing TextSource really cares about is finding the right method to invoke
to send text. Thus, we can list that method in an interface called TextUpdateable
and have our TickerTape implement the interface. A TickerTape object can then
be used anywhere we need something of the type TextUpdateable. In this case, the
TextSource constructor takes a TextUpdateable object and stores the reference in
an instance variable of type TextUpdateable. Our TickerTape object simply passes
a reference to itself as the callback for text updates, and the source can invoke its
receiveText() method as necessary.

Interface Variables

Although interfaces allow us to specify behavior without implementation, there's
one exception. An interface can contain constant variable identifiers; these identifiers appear in any class that implements the interface. This feature allows predefined parameters that can be used with the methods:

```
interface Scaleable {
    static final int BIG = 0, MEDIUM = 1, SMALL = 2;

    void setScale( int size );
}
```

The Scaleable interface defines three integers: BIG, MEDIUM, and SMALL. All variables defined in interfaces are implicitly final and static; we don't have to use
the modifiers but, for clarity, we recommend you do. A class that implements
Scaleable sees these variables:

```
class Box implements Scaleable {

    public void setScale( int size ) {
        switch( size ) {
```

```
            case BIG:
                ...
            case MEDIUM:
                ...
            case SMALL:
                ...
        }
    }
    ...
}
```

Empty interfaces

Sometimes, interfaces are created just to hold constants; anyone who implements the interfaces can see the constant names, much as if they were included by a C/C++ include file. This is a somewhat degenerate, but acceptable, use of interfaces.

Sometimes completely empty interfaces serve as a marker that a class has some special property. The `java.io.Serializeable` interface is a good example. Classes that implement `Serializable` don't add any methods or variables. Their additional type simply identifies them to Java as classes that want to be able to be serialized.

Subinterfaces

An interface can extend another interface, just as a class can extend another class. Such an interface is called a *subinterface*:

```
interface DynamicallyScaleable extends Scaleable {
    void changeScale( int size );
}
```

The interface `DynamicallyScaleable` extends our previous `Scaleable` interface and adds an additional method. A class that implements `DynamicallyScaleable` must implement all methods of both interfaces.

Interfaces can't specify that they implement other interfaces because interfaces never include any method implementations. However, interfaces are allowed to extend other interfaces. In fact, an interface is allowed to extend as many interfaces as it wants (multiple inheritance of interface)—unlike classes, which can only extend a single class. If you want to extend two or more interfaces, list them after the `extends` keyword, separated by commas:

```
interface DynamicallyScaleable extends Scaleable, SomethingElseable {
    ...
```

Packages and Compilation Units

A *package* is a name for a group of related classes and interfaces. In Chapter 3, we discussed how Java uses package names to locate classes during compilation and at run-time. In this sense, packages are somewhat like libraries; they organize and manage sets of classes. Packages provide more than just source code-level organization though. They also create an additional level of scope for their classes and the variables and methods within them. We'll talk about the visibility of classes in this section. In the next section, we'll discuss the effect that packages have on access to variables and methods between classes.

Compilation Units

The source code for a Java class is called a *compilation unit*. A compilation unit normally contains a single class definition and is named for that class. The definition of a class named MyClass, for instance, should appear in a file named *MyClass.java*. For most of us, a compilation unit is just a file with a *.java* extension, but in an integrated development environment, it could be an arbitrary entity. For brevity here, we'll refer to a compilation unit simply as a file.

The division of classes into their own compilation units is important because the Java compiler assumes much of the responsibility of a *make* utility. The compiler relies on the names of source files to find and compile dependent classes. It's possible (and common) to put more than one class definition into a single file, but there are some restrictions we'll discuss shortly.

A class is declared to belong to a particular package with the package statement. The package statement must appear as the first statement in a compilation unit. There can be only one package statement, and it applies to the entire file:

```
package mytools.text;

class TextComponent {
    ...
}
```

In the above example, the class TextComponent is placed in the package mytools.text.

A Word About Package Names

Package names are constructed in a hierarchical way, using a dot-separated naming convention. Package-name components construct a unique path for the compiler and run-time systems to locate files; however, they don't affect the contents directly in any other way. There is no such thing as a subpackage (the package name space is really flat, not hierarchical) and packages under a particular part of a package hierarchy are related only by association. For example, if we create another package called mytools.text.poetry (presumably for text classes specialized in some way to work with poetry), those classes would not be considered part of the mytools.text package and would have no special access to its members. In this sense, the package-naming convention can be misleading.

Class Visibility

By default, a class is accessible only to other classes within its package. This means that the class TextComponent is available only to other classes in the mytools.text package. To be visible elsewhere, a class must be declared as public:

```
package mytools.text;

public class TextEditor {
    ...
}
```

The class TextEditor can now be referenced anywhere. There can be only a single public class defined in a compilation unit; the file must be named for that class.

By hiding unimportant or extraneous classes, a package builds a subsystem that has a well-defined interface to the rest of the world. Public classes provide a facade for the operation of the system and the details of its inner workings can remain hidden, as shown in Figure 6-6. In this sense, packages hide classes in the way classes hide private members.

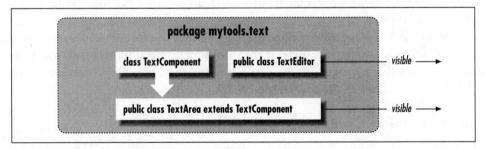

Figure 6–6: Class visibility and packages

Figure 6-6 shows part of the hypothetical mytools.text package. The classes TextArea and TextEditor are declared public and can be used elsewhere in an application. The class TextComponent is part of the implementation of TextArea and is not accessible from outside of the package.

Importing Classes

Classes within a package can refer to each other by their simple names. However, to locate a class in another package, we have to supply a qualifier. Continuing with the above example, an application refers directly to our editor class by its fully qualified name of mytools.text.TextEditor. But we'd quickly grow tired of typing such long class names, so Java gives us the import statement. One or more import statements can appear at the top of a compilation unit, beneath the package statement. The import statements list the full names of classes to be used within the file. Like a package statement, import statements apply to the entire compilation unit. Here's how you might use an import statement:

```
package somewhere.else;

import mytools.text.TextEditor;

class MyClass {
    TextEditor editBoy;
    ...
}
```

As shown in the example above, once a class is imported, it can be referenced by its simple name throughout the code. It's also possible to import all of the classes in a package using the * notation:

```
import mytools.text.*;
```

Now we can refer to all public classes in the mytools.text package by their simple names.

Obviously, there can be a problem with importing classes that have conflicting names. If two different packages contain classes that use the same name, you just have to fall back to using fully qualified names to refer to those classes. Other than the potential for naming conflicts, there's no penalty for importing classes. Java doesn't carry extra baggage into the compiled class files. In other words, Java class files don't contain other class definitions, they only reference them.

The Unnamed Package

A class that is defined in a compilation unit that doesn't specify a package falls into the large, amorphous unnamed package. Classes in this nameless package can refer to each other by their simple names. Their path at compile- and run-time is considered to be the current directory, so package-less classes are useful for experimentation, testing, and brevity in providing examples for books about Java.

Variable and Method Visibility

One of the most important aspects of object-oriented design is data hiding, or *encapsulation*. By treating an object in some respects as a "black box" and ignoring the details of its implementation, we can write stronger, simpler code with components that can be easily reused.

Basic Access Modifiers

By default, the variables and methods of a class are accessible to members of the class itself and other classes in the same package. To borrow from C++ terminology, classes in the same package are *friendly*. We'll call this the default level of visibility. As you'll see as we go on, the default visibility lies in the middle of the range of restrictiveness that can be specified.

The modifiers `public` and `private`, on the other hand, define the extremes. As we mentioned earlier, methods and variables declared as `private` are accessible only within their class. At the other end of the spectrum, members declared as `public` are always accessible, from any class in any package. Of course, the class that contains the methods must also be `public`, as we just discussed. The `public` members of a class should define its most general functionality—what the black box is supposed to do. Figure 6-7 illustrates the four simplest levels of visibility.

Figure 6-7 continues with the example from the previous section. Public members in `TextArea` are accessible from anywhere. Private members are not visible from outside the class. The default visibility allows access by other classes in the package.

The `protected` modifier allows special access permissions for subclasses. Contrary to how it might sound, `protected` is slightly less restrictive than the default level of accessibility. In addition to the default access afforded classes in the same package, `protected` members are visible to subclasses of the class, even if they are defined in a different package. If you are a C++ programmer and so used to more restrictive meanings, this may rub you the wrong way. [*]

Table 6-1 summarizes the levels of visibility available in Java; it runs generally from most restrictive to least. Methods and variables are always visible within a class, so the table doesn't address those.

---

[*] Early on, the Java language allowed for certain combinations of modifiers, one of which was `private protected`. The meaning of private protected was to limit visibility strictly to subclasses (and remove package access). This was later deemed confusing and overly complex and is no longer supported.

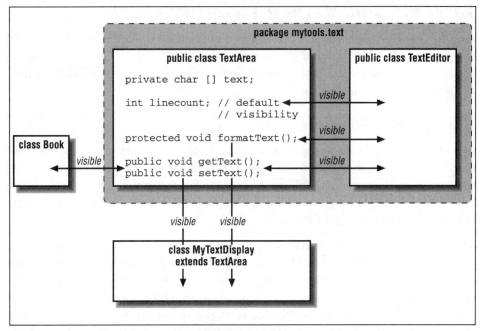

Figure 6–7: Private, default, protected, and public visibility

Table 6–1: Visibility Modifiers

Modifier	Visibility
private	None
none (default)	Classes in the package
protected	Classes in package and subclasses inside or outside the package
public	All classes

Subclasses and Visibility

Subclasses add two important (but unrelated) complications to the topic of visibility. First, when you override methods in a subclass, the overriding method must be at least as visible as the overridden method. While it is possible to take a private method and override it with a public method in a subclass, the reverse is not possible; you can't override a public method with a private method. This restriction makes sense if you realize that subtypes have to be usable as instances of their supertype (e.g., a Mammal is a subclass of Animal and therefore must be usable as an Animal). If we could override a method with a less visible method, we would have a problem: our Mammal might not be able to do all the things an Animal can.

However, we can reduce the visibility of a variable because it simply results in a shadowed variable. As with all shadowed variables, the two variables are distinct and can have separate visibilities in different classes.

Second, the protected variables of a class are visible to its subclasses, but only in objects of the subclass's type or its subtypes. In other words, a subclass can see a protected variable from its superclass as an inherited variable, but it can't access the variable in a separate instance of the superclass itself. This can be confusing because we often forget that visibility modifiers don't restrict access between instances of the same class in the same way that they restrict access between instances of different classes. Two instances of the same type of object can normally access all of each other's members, including private ones. Said another way: two instances of Cat can access all of each other's variables and methods (including private ones), but a Cat can't access a protected member in an instance of Animal unless the compiler can prove that the Animal is a Cat.

Interfaces and Visibility

Interfaces behave like classes within packages. An interface can be declared public to make it visible outside of its package. Under the default visibility, an interface is visible only inside of its package. There can be only one public interface declared in a compilation unit.

Inside Arrays

At the end of Chapter 4, we mentioned that arrays have a place in the Java class hierarchy, but we didn't give you any details. Now that we've discussed the object-oriented aspects of Java, we can give you the whole story.

Array classes live in a parallel Java class hierarchy under the Object class. If a class is a direct subclass of Object, then an array class for that base type also exists as a direct subclass of Object. Arrays of more derived classes are subclasses of the corresponding array classes. For example, consider the following class types:

```
class Animal { ... }
class Bird extends Animal { ... }
class Penguin extends Bird { ... }
```

Figure 6-8 illustrates the class hierarchy for arrays of these classes. Arrays of the same dimension are related to one another in the same manner as their base type classes. In our example, Bird is a subclass of Animal, which means that the Bird[] type is a subtype of Animal[]. In the same way a Bird object can be used in place of an Animal object, a Bird[] array can be assigned to an Animal[] array:

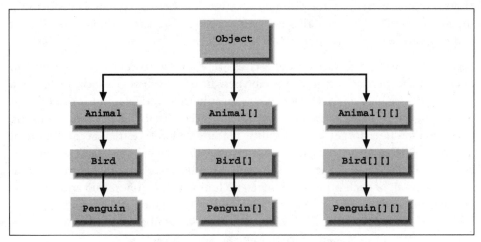

Figure 6–8: Arrays in the Java class hierarchy

```
Animal [][] animals;
Bird [][] birds = new Bird [10][10];
birds[0][0] = new Bird();

// make animals and birds reference the same array object
animals = birds;
System.out.println( animals[0][0] );                    // prints Bird
```

Because arrays are part of the class hierarchy, we can use instanceof to check the type of an array:

```
if ( birds instanceof Animal[][] )                    // yes
```

An array is a subtype of Object and can therefore be assigned to Object type variables:

```
Object something;
something = animals;
```

Since Java knows the actual type of all objects, you can also cast back if appropriate:

```
animals = (Animal [][])something;
```

Under unusual circumstances, Java may not be able to check the types of objects you place into arrays at compile-time. In those cases, it's possible to receive an ArrayStoreException if you try to assign the wrong type of object to an array element. Consider the following:

```
class Dog { ... }
class Poodle extends Dog { ... }
class Chihuahua extends Dog { ... }
```

```
Dog [] dogs;
Poodle [] poodles = new Poodle [10];

dogs = poodles;

dogs[3] = new Chihuahua();       // Run-time error, ArrayStoreException
```

Both Poodle and Chihuahua are subclasses of Dog, so an array of Poodle objects can therefore be assigned to an array of Dog objects, as I described previously. The problem is that an object assignable to an element of an array of type Dog[] may not be assignable to an element of an array of type Poodle. A Chihuahua object, for instance, can be assigned to a Dog element because it's a subtype of Dog, but not to a Poodle element.[*]

Inner Classes

Java 1.1 adds to the language a large heap of syntactic sugar called *inner classes*. Simply put, classes in Java can be declared at any level of scope. That is, you can declare a class within any set of curly braces (i.e., almost anywhere that you could put any other Java statement), and its visibility is limited to that scope in the same way that the name of a variable or method would be. Inner classes are a powerful and aesthetically pleasing facility for structuring code. Their even sweeter cousins, *anonymous inner classes*, are another powerful shorthand that make it seem like you can create classes dynamically within Java's statically typed environment.

However, if you delve into the inner workings of Java, inner classes are not quite as aesthetically pleasing or dynamic. We said that they are syntactic sugar; this means that they let you leverage the compiler by writing a few lines of code that trigger a lot of behind-the-scenes work somewhere between the compiler's front end and the byte-code. Inner classes rely on code generation; they are a feature of the Java language, but not of the Java virtual machine. As a programmer you may never need be aware of this; you can simply rely on inner classes like any other language construct. However, you should know a little about how inner classes work, to better understand the results and a few potential side effects.

To this point, all of our classes have been *top level* classes. We have declared them, free standing, at the package level. Inner classes are essentially nested classes, like this:

---

[*] In some sense this could be considered a hole in the Java type system. It doesn't occur elsewhere in Java, only with arrays. This is because array objects exhibit *covariance* in overriding their assignment and extraction methods. Covariance allows array subclasses to override methods with arguments or return values that are subtypes of the overridden methods, where the methods would normally be overloaded or prohibited. This allows array subclasses to operate on their base types with type safety, but also means that subclasses have different capabilities than their parents, leading to the problem shown above.

```
Class Animal {
    Class Brain {
        ...
    }
}
```

Here the class Brain is an inner class: it is a class declared inside the scope of class Animal. Although the details of what that means require a fair bit of explanation, we'll start by saying that the Java language tries to make the meaning, as much as possible, the same as for the other Java entities (methods and variables) living at that level of scope. For example, let's add a method to the Animal class:

```
Class Animal {
    Class Brain {
        ...
    }
    void performBehavior() { ... }
}
```

Both the inner class Brain and the method performBehavior() are within the scope of Animal. Therefore, anywhere within Animal we can refer to Brain and performBehavior() directly, by name. Within Animal we can call the constructor for Brain (new Brain()) to get a Brain object, or invoke performBehavior() to carry out that method's function. But neither Brain nor performBehavior() are accessible outside of the class Animal without some additional qualification.

Within the body of the Brain class and the body of the performBehavior() method, we have direct access to all of the other methods and variables of the Animal class. So, just as the performBehavior() method could work with the Brain class and create instances of Brain, code within the Brain class can invoke the performBehavior() method of Animal as well as work with any other methods and variables declared in Animal.

That last bit has important consequences. From within Brain we can invoke the method performBehavior(); that is, from within an instance of Brain we can invoke the performBehavior() method of an instance of Animal. Well, which instance of Animal? If we have several Animal objects around (say, a few Cats and Dogs), we need to know whose performBehavior() method we are calling. What does it mean for a class definition to be "inside" another class definition? The answer is that a Brain object always lives within a single instance of Animal: the one that it was told about when it was created. We'll call the object that contains any instance of Brain its *enclosing instance*.

A Brain object cannot live outside of an enclosing instance of an Animal object. Anywhere you see an instance of Brain, it will be tethered to an instance of Animal. Although it is possible to construct a Brain object from elsewhere (i.e., another class), Brain always requires an enclosing instance of Animal to "hold" it. We'll also say now that if Brain is to be referred to from outside of Animal, it acts something like an Animal.Brain class. And just as with the performBehavior() method, modifiers can be applied to restrict its visibility. There is even an interpretation of the static modifier, which we'll talk about a bit later. However, the details are somewhat boring and not immediately useful, so you should consult a full language reference for more info (like O'Reilly's *Java Language Reference*, Second Edition). Before we get too far afield, let's turn to a more compelling example.

A particularly important use of inner classes is to make *adapter classes*. An adapter class is a "helper" class that ties one class to another in a very specific way. Using adapter classes, you can write your classes more naturally, without having to anticipate every conceivable user's needs in advance. Instead, you provide adapter classes that marry your class to a particular interface. As an example, let's say that we have an EmployeeList object:

```
public class EmployeeList {
    private Employee [] employees = ... ;
    ...
}
```

EmployeeList holds information about a set of employees, representing some view of our database. Let's say that we would like to have EmployeeList provide its elements as an enumeration. An enumeration is a simple interface to a set of objects that looks like this:

```
// the java.util.Enumeration interface
public interface Enumeration {
    boolean hasMoreElements();
    Object nextElement();
}
```

It lets us iterate through its elements, asking for the next one and testing to see if more remain. The enumeration is a good candidate for an adapter class because it is an interface that our EmployeeList can't readily implement itself. That's because an enumeration is a "one way," disposable view of our data. It isn't intended to be reset and used again, and therefore should be kept separate from the Employee-List itself. This is crying out for a simple class to provide the enumeration capability. But what should that class look like?

Well, before we knew about inner classes, our only recourse would have been to make a new "top level" class. We would probably feel obliged to call it EmployeeListEnumeration:

```
class EmployeeListEnumeration implements Enumeration {
    // lots of knowledge about EmployeeList
    ...
}
```

Here we have a comment representing the machinery that the EmployeeList-Enumeration requires. Think for just a second about what you'd have to do to implement that machinery. The resulting class would be completely coupled to the EmployeeList and unusable in other situations. Worse, to function it must have access to the inner workings of EmployeeList. We would have to allow Employee-ListEnumeration access to the private array in EmployeeList, exposing this data more widely than it should be. This is less than ideal.

This sounds like a job for inner classes. We already said that EmployeeList-Enumeration was useless without the EmployeeList; this sounds a lot like the "lives inside" relationship we described earlier. Furthermore, an inner class lets us avoid the encapsulation problem, because it can access all the members of its enclosing instance. Therefore, if we use an inner class to implement the enumeration, the array employees can remain private, invisible outside the EmployeeList. So let's just shove that helper class inside the scope of our EmployeeList:

```
public class EmployeeList {
    private Employee [] employees = ... ;

    // ...

    class Enumerator implements java.util.Enumeration {
        int element = 0;
        boolean hasMoreElements() {
            return  element < employees.length ;
        }
        Object nextElement() {
            if ( hasMoreElements() )
                return employees[ element++ ];
            else
                throw new NoSuchElementException();
        }
    }
}
```

Now EmployeeList can provide an accessor method like the following to let other classes work with the list:

```
    ...
    Enumeration getEnumeration() {
        return new Enumerator();
    }
```

One effect of the move is that we are free to be a little more familiar in the naming of our enumeration class. Since it is no longer a top level class, we can give it a name that is appropriate only within the EmployeeList. In this case, we've named it Enumerator to emphasize what it does—but we don't need a name like Employ-eeEnumerator that shows the relationship to the EmployeeList class because that's implicit. We've also filled in the guts of the Enumerator class. As you can see, now that it is inside the scope of EmployeeList, Enumerator has direct access to its private members, so it can directly access the employees array. This greatly simplifies the code and maintains the compile-time safety.

Before we move on, we should note that inner classes can have constructors, even though we didn't need one in this example. They are in all respects real classes.

Inner Classes Within Methods

Inner classes may also be declared within the body of a method. Returning to the Animal class, we could put Brain inside the performBehavior() method if we decided that the class was useful only inside of that method:

```
Class Animal {
    void performBehavior() {
        Class Brain {
            . . .
        }
    }
}
```

In this situation, the rules governing what Brain can see are the same as in our earlier example. The body of Brain can see anything in the scope of performBehavior() and, of course, above it. This includes local variables of performBehavior(), and its arguments. This raises a few questions.

performBehavior() is a method, and methods have limited lifetimes. When they exit, their local variables normally disappear into the stacky abyss. But an instance of Brain (like any object) lives on as long as it is referenced. So Java makes sure that any local variables used by instances of Brain created within an invocation of performBehavior() also live on. Furthermore, all of the instances of Brain that we make within a single invocation of performBehavior() will see the same local variables.

Static inner classes

We mentioned earlier that the inner class Brain of the class Animal could in some ways be considered an Animal.Brain class. That is, it is possible to work with a Brain from outside the Animal class, using just such a qualified name:

Animal.Brain. But given that our Animal.Brain class always requires an instance of an Animal as its enclosing instance, some explicit setup is needed.*

But there is another situation where we might use inner classes by name. An inner class that lives within the body of a top level class (not within a method or another inner class) can be declared static. For example:

```
class Animal {
    static class MigrationPattern {
        ...
}
    ...
}
```

A static inner class such as this acts just like a new top level class called Animal.MigrationPattern; we can use it without regard to any enclosing instances. Although this seems strange, it is not inconsistent since a static member never has an object instance associated with it. The requirement that the inner class be defined directly inside a top level class ensures that an enclosing instance won't be needed. If we have permission, we can create an instance of the class using the qualified name:

```
Animal.MigrationPattern stlToSanFrancisco = new Animal.MigrationPattern();
```

As you see, the effect is that Animal acts something like a mini-package, holding the MigrationPattern class. We can use all of the standard visibility modifiers on inner classes, so a static inner class could be private, protected, default, or publicly visible.

Anonymous inner classes

Now we get to the best part. As a general rule, the more deeply encapsulated and limited in scope our classes are, the more freedom we have in naming them. We saw this in our enumeration example. This is not just a purely aesthetic issue. Naming is an important part of writing readable and maintainable code. We generally want to give things the most concise and meaningful names possible. A corollary to this is that we prefer to avoid doling out names for purely ephemeral objects that are going to be used only once.

Anonymous inner classes are an extension of the syntax of the new operation. When you create an anonymous inner class, you combine the class's declaration with the allocation of an instance of that class. After the new operator, you specify either the name of a class or an interface, followed by a class body. The class body

---

* Specifically, we would have to follow a design pattern and pass a reference to the enclosing instance of Animal into the Animal.Brain constructor. See a language reference for more information. We don't expect you to run into this situation very often.

becomes an inner class, which either extends the specified class or, in the case of an interface, is expected to implement the specified interface. A single instance of the class is created and returned as the value.

For example, we could do away with the declaration of the `Enumerator` class in the `EmployeeList` example by using an anonymous inner class in the `getEnumera-tion()` method:

```
...

Enumeration getEnumeration() {

    return new Enumeration() {
        int element = 0;
        boolean hasMoreElements() {
            return  element < employees.length ;
        }
        Object nextElement() {
            if ( hasMoreElements() )
                return employees[ element++ ];
            else
                throw new NoSuchElementException();
        }
    };
}
```

Here we have simply moved the guts of `Enumerator` into the body of an anonymous inner class. The call to `new` implicitly constructs the class and returns an instance of the class as its result. Note the extent of the curly braces and the semicolon at the end. It is a single statement.

But the code above certainly does not improve readability. Inner classes are best used when you want to implement a few lines of code, when the verbiage and conspicuousness of declaring a separate class detracts from the task at hand. Here's a better example. Suppose that we want to start a new thread to execute the `performBehavior()` method of our `Animal`:

```
new Thread ( new Runnable() {
    public void run() {  performBehavior();  }
} ).start();
```

Here we have gone over to the terse side. We've allocated and started a new `Thread`, providing an anonymous inner class that implements the `Runnable` interface by calling our `performBehavior()` method. The effect is similar to using a method pointer in some other language; the inner class effectively substitutes the method we want called (`performBehavior()`) for the method the system wants to call (run()). However, the inner class allows the compiler to check type consistency, which would be difficult (if not impossible) with a true method pointer. At the same time, our anonymous adapter class with its three lines of code is much more efficient and readable than creating a new, top level adapter class named AnimalBehaviorThreadAdapter.

While we're getting a bit ahead of the story, anonymous adapter classes are a perfect fit for event handling (which we'll cover fully in Chapter 13). Skipping a lot of explanation, let's say you want the method handleClicks() to be called whenever the user clicks the mouse. You would write code like this:

```
addMouseListener(new MouseAdapter() {
    public void mouseClicked(MouseEvent e) { handleClicks(e); }
});
```

In this case, the anonymous class extends the AWT's MouseAdapter class by overriding its mouseClicked() method to call our method. A lot is going on in a very small space, but the result is clean, readable code. You get to assign method names that are meaningful to you, while allowing Java to do its job of type checking.

this and scoping

Sometimes an inner class may want to get a handle on its "parent" enclosing instance. It might want to pass a reference to its parent, or to refer to one of the parent's variables or methods that has been hidden by one of its own. For example:

```
class Animal {
    int size;
    class Brain {
        int size;
    }
}
```

Here, as far as Brain is concerned, the variable size in Animal is hidden by its own version.

Normally an object refers to itself using the special this reference (implicitly or explicitly). But what is the meaning of this for an object with one or more enclosing instances? The answer is that an inner class has multiple this references. You can specify which this you want by prepending the name of the class. So, for instance (no pun intended), we can get a reference to our Animal from within Brain like so:

```
    ...
class Brain {
    Animal ourAnimal = Animal.this;
        ...
```

Similarly, we could refer to the `size` variable in `Animal`:

```
...
class Brain {
    int animalSize = Animal.this.size;
    ...
```

How do inner classes really work?

Finally, we'll get our hands dirty and take a look at what's really going on when we use an inner class. We've said that the compiler is doing all of the things that we had hoped to forget about. Let's see what's actually happening. Try compiling our simple example:

```
class Animal {
    class Brain {
    }
}
```

(Oh, come on, do it. . . .) What you'll find is that the compiler generates two *.class* files: *Animal.class* and *Animal$Brain.class*.

The second file is the class file for our inner class. Yes, as we feared, inner classes are really just compiler magic. The compiler has created the inner class for us as a normal, top level class and named it by combining the class names with a dollar sign. The dollar sign is a valid character in class names, but is intended for use only by automated tools. (Please don't start naming your classes with dollar signs.) Had our class been more deeply nested, the intervening inner class names would have been attached in the same way to generate a unique top level name.

Now take a look at it using the *javap* utility:

```
% javap 'Animal$Brain'
class Animal$Brain extends java.lang.Object
{
    Animal$Brain(Animal);
}
```

You'll see that the compiler has given our inner class a constructor that takes a reference to an `Animal` as an argument. This is how the real inner class gets the handle on its enclosing instance.

The worst thing about these additional class files is that you need to know they are there. Utilities like *jar* don't automatically find them; when you are invoking a utility like *jar*, you need to specify these files explicitly, or use a wild card that finds them.

Security Implications

Given what we just saw above—that the inner class really does exist as an automatically generated top level class—how does it get access to private variables? The answer, unfortunately, is that the compiler is forced to break the encapsulation of your object and insert accessor methods so that the inner class can reach them. The accessor methods will be given package level access, so your object is still safe within its package walls, but it is conceivable that this difference could be meaningful if people were allowed to create new classes within your package.

The visibility modifiers on inner classes also have some problems. Current implementations of the virtual machine do not implement the notion of a private or protected class within a package, so giving your inner class anything other than public or default visibility is only a compile-time guarantee. It is difficult to conceive of how these security issues could be abused, but it is interesting to note that Java is straining a bit to stay within its original design.

7

In this chapter:
- *The Object Class*
- *The Class Class*
- *Reflection*

Working with Objects and Classes

In the previous two chapters, we came to know Java objects and then their interrelationships. We have now climbed the scaffolding of the Java class hierarchy and reached the top. In this chapter we'll talk about the Object class itself, which is the "grandmother" of all classes in Java. We'll also describe the even more fundamental Class class (the class named "Class") that represents Java classes in the Java virtual machine. We'll discuss what you can do with these objects in their own right. Finally, this will lead us to a more general topic: the reflection interface, which lets a Java program inspect and interact with objects on the fly.

The Object Class

java.lang.Object is the ancestor of all objects; it's the primordial class from which all other classes are ultimately derived. Methods defined in Object are therefore very important because they appear in every instance of any class, throughout all of Java. At last count, there were nine public methods in Object. Five of these are versions of wait() and notify() that are used to synchronize threads on object instances, as we'll discuss in Chapter 8. The remaining four methods are used for basic comparison, conversion, and administration.

Every object has a toString() method that is called when it's to be represented as a text value. PrintStream objects use toString() to print data, as discussed in Chapter 10. toString() is also used when an object is referenced in a string concatenation. Here are some examples:

```
MyObj myObject = new MyObj();
Answer theAnswer = new Answer();

System.out.println( myObject );
String s = "The answer is: " + theAnswer ;
```

To be friendly, a new kind of object should override toString() and implement its own version that provides appropriate printing functionality. Two other methods, equals() and hashCode(), may also require specialization when you create a new class.

Equality

equals() determines whether two objects are equivalent. Precisely what that means for a particular class is something that you'll have to decide for yourself. Two String objects, for example, are considered equivalent if they hold precisely the same characters in the same sequence:

```
String userName = "Joe";
...
if ( userName.equals( suspectName ) )
    arrest( userName );
```

Using equals() is *not* the same as:

```
// if ( userName == suspectName )        // Wrong!
```

The above code tests to see if the two String objects are the same object, which is sufficient but not necessary for them to be equivalent objects.

A class should override the equals() method if it needs to implement its own notion of equality. If you have no need to compare objects of a particular class, you don't need to override equals().

Watch out for accidentally overloading equals() when you mean to override it. equals() takes an Object as an argument and returns a boolean value. While you'll probably want to check only if an object is equivalent to an object of its own type, in order to properly override equals(), the method should accept a generic Object as its argument. Here's an example of implementing equals():

```
class Sneakers extends Shoes {
    public boolean equals( Object arg ) {
        if ( (arg != null) && (arg instanceof Sneakers) ) {
            // compare arg with this object to check equivalence
            // If comparison is okay...
            return true;
        }
        return false;
    }
    ...
}
```

A Sneakers object can now be properly compared by any current or future Java classes. If we had instead used a Sneakers type object as the argument to equals(), all would be well for classes that reference our objects as Sneakers, but methods that simply use Shoes would not see the overloaded method and would compare Sneakers against other Sneakers improperly.

Hashcodes

The hashCode() method returns an integer that is a hashcode for the object. A hashcode is like a signature or checksum for an object; it's a random-looking identifying number that is usually generated from the contents of the object. The hashcode should always be different for instances of the class that contain different data, but should normally be the same for instances that compare "equal" with the equals() method. Hashcodes are used in the process of storing objects in a Hashtable, or a similar kind of collection. The hashcode helps the Hashtable optimize its storage of objects by serving as an identifier for distributing them into storage evenly, and locating them quickly later.

The default implementation of hashCode() in Object assigns each object instance a unique number. If you don't override this method when you create a subclass, each instance of your class will have a unique hashcode. This is sufficient for some objects. However, if your classes have a notion of equivalent objects (if you have overriden equals()) and you want equal objects to serve as equivalent keys in a Hashtable, then you should override hashCode() so that your equivalent objects generate the same hashcode value.

Cloning Objects

Objects can use the clone() method of the Object class to make copies of themselves. A copied object will be a new object instance, separate from the original. It may or may not contain the same state as the original—that is, under the control of the object type being copied. Just as important, the decision as to whether the object allows itself to be cloned at all is up to the object.

The Java Object class provides the mechanism to make a simple copy of an object including all of its state—a bitwise copy. But by default this capability is turned off. (We'll hit upon why in a moment.) To make itself cloneable an object must implement the java.lang.Cloneable interface. This is a flag indicating to Java that the object wants to cooperate in being cloned. If the object isn't cloneable, the clone() method throws a CloneNotSupportedException.

clone() is a protected method, so by default it can only be called by an object on itself, an object in the same package, or another object of the same type or a supertype. If we want to make an object cloneable by everyone, we have to override its clone() method and make it public.

Here is a simple, cloneable class—Sheep:

```
import java.util.Hashtable;

public class Sheep implements Cloneable {
    Hashtable flock = new Hashtable();

    public Object clone() {
        try {
            return super.clone();
        } catch (CloneNotSupportedException e ) {
            throw new Error("This should never happen!");
        }
    }
}
```

Sheep has one instance variable, a Hashtable called flock (which the sheep uses to
keep track of its fellow sheep). Our class implements the Cloneable interface, indicating that it is okay to copy Sheep and it has overridden the clone() method to
make it public. Our clone() simply returns the object created by the superclass's
clone—a copy of our Sheep. Unfortunately, the compiler is not smart enough to
figure out that the object we're cloning will never throw the Clone-
NotSupportedException, so we have to guard against it anyway. Our sheep is now
cloneable. We can make copies like so:

```
Sheep one = new Sheep();
Sheep anotherOne = (Sheep)one.clone();
```

We now have two sheep instead of one. The equals() method would tell us that
the sheep are equivalent, but == tells us that they aren't equal—that is, they are
two distinct objects. Java has made a "shallow" copy of our Sheep. What's so shallow
about it? Java has simply copied the bits of our variables. That means that the
flock instance variable in each of our Sheep still holds the same information—
that is, both sheep have a reference to the same Hashtable. The situation looks
like that shown in Figure 7-1.

This may or may not be what you intended. If we instead want our Sheep to have
separate copies of all of its variables (or something in between), we can take control ourselves. In the following example, DeepSheep, we implement a "deep" copy,
duplicating our own flock variable:

```
public class DeepSheep implements Cloneable {
    Hashtable flock = new Hashtable();

    public Object clone() {
        try {
            DeepSheep copy = (DeepSheep)super.clone();
            copy.flock = (Hashtable)flock.clone();
            return copy;
        } catch (CloneNotSupportedException e ) {
```

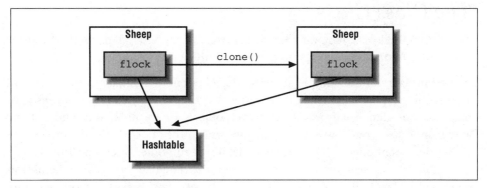

Figure 7–1: Bitwise (Shallow) copy

```
        throw new Error("This should never happen!");
    }
  }
}
```

Our `clone()` method now clones the `Hashtable` as well. Now, when a `DeepSheep` is cloned, the situation looks more like that shown in Figure 7-2.

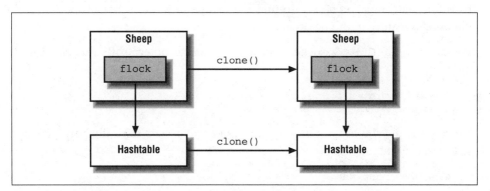

Figure 7–2: Deep copy

Each `DeepSheep` now has its own hashtable. You can see now why objects are not cloneable by default. It would make no sense to assume that all objects can be sensibly duplicated with a shallow copy. Likewise, it makes no sense to assume that a deep copy is necessary, or even correct. In this case, we probably don't need a deep copy; the flock contains the same members no matter which sheep you're looking at, so there's no need to copy the `Hashtable`. But the decision depends on the object itself and its requirements.

The Class Class

The last method of `Object` we need to discuss is `getClass()`. This method returns a reference to the `Class` object that produced the object instance.

A good measure of the complexity of an object-oriented language is the degree of abstraction of its class structures. We know that every object in Java is an instance of a class, but what exactly is a class? In C++, objects are formulated by and instantiated from classes, but classes are really just artifacts of the compiler. Thus, you see classes only mentioned in C++ source code, not at run-time. By comparison, classes in Smalltalk are real, run-time entities in the language that are themselves described by "meta-classes" and "meta-class classes." Java strikes a happy medium between these two languages with what is, effectively, a two-tiered system that uses `Class` objects.

Classes in Java source code are represented at run-time by instances of the `java.lang.Class` class. There's a `Class` object for every class you use; this `Class` object is responsible for producing instances for its class. This may sound overwhelming, but you don't have to worry about any of it unless you are interested in loading new kinds of classes dynamically at run-time. The `Class` object is also the basis for "reflecting" on a class to find out its methods and other properties; we'll discuss this feature in the next section.

We can get the `Class` associated with a particular object with the `getClass()` method:

```
String myString = "Foo!"
Class c = myString.getClass();
```

We can also get the `Class` reference for a particular class statically, using the special `.class` notation:

```
Class c = String.class;
```

The `.class` reference looks like a static field that exists in every class. However, it is really resolved by the compiler.

One thing we can do with the `Class` object is to ask for the name of the object's class:

```
String s = "Boofa!";
Class strClass = s.getClass();
System.out.println( strClass.getName() ); // prints "java.lang.String"
```

Another thing that we can do with a `Class` is to ask it to produce a new instance of its type of object. Continuing with the above example:

```
try {
    String s2 = (String)strClass.newInstance();
}
catch ( InstantiationException e ) { ... }
catch ( IllegalAccessException e ) { ... }
```

newInstance() has a return type of Object, so we have to cast it to a reference of the appropriate type. A couple of problems can occur here. An InstantiationException indicates we're trying to instantiate an abstract class or an interface. IllegalAccessException is a more general exception that indicates we can't access a constructor for the object. Note that newInstance() can create only an instance of a class that has an accessible default constructor. There's no way for us to pass any arguments to a constructor.

All this becomes more meaningful when we add the capability to look up a Class by name. forName() is a static method of Class that returns a Class object given its name as a String:

```
try {
    Class sneakersClass = Class.forName("Sneakers");
}
catch ( ClassNotFoundException e ) { ... }
```

A ClassNotFoundException is thrown if the class can't be located.

Combining the above tools, we have the power to load new kinds of classes dynamically. When combined with the power of interfaces, we can use new data types by name in our applications:

```
interface Typewriter {
    void typeLine( String s );
    ...
}

class Printer implements Typewriter {
    ...
}

class MyApplication {
    ...
    String outputDeviceName = "Printer";

    try {
        Class newClass = Class.forName( outputDeviceName );
        Typewriter device = (Typewriter)newClass.newInstance();
        ...
        device.typeLine("Hello...");
    }
    catch ( Exception e ) {
}
```

Reflection

In this section we'll take a look at the Java reflection API, supported by the classes in the `java.lang.reflect` package. As its name suggests, reflection is the ability for a programming language to examine itself. Reflection lets Java code look at an object (more precisely, the class of the object) and determine its structure. Within the limits imposed by the security manager, you can find out what constructors, methods, and fields a class has, and their attributes. You can even change the value of fields, dynamically invoke methods, and construct new objects, much as if Java had primitive pointers to variables and methods.

We don't have room here to fully cover the reflection API. As you might expect, the `reflect` package is complex and rich in details. But reflection has been designed so that you can do a lot with relatively little effort; 20 percent of the effort will give you 80 percent of the fun.

The reflection API is used by Java Beans to determine the capabilities of objects at run-time. It's also used at a lower level by object serialization to tear apart and build objects for transport over streams or into persistent storage. Obviously, the power to pick apart objects and see their internals must be zealously guarded by the security manager. Your code is not allowed to do anything with the reflection API that it couldn't do with static Java code. In short, reflection is a powerful tool, but it isn't a loophole. An object can't use it to find out about data fields that it wouldn't normally be able to access (for example, another object's private fields), and you can't use it to modify any data inappropriately.

The three primary features of a class are its fields (variables), methods, and constructors. For purposes of describing or accessing an object, these three features are represented by the classes in the reflection API: the `java.lang.reflect.Field`, `java.lang.reflect.Method`, and `java.lang.reflect.Constructor` classes represent the fields, methods, and constructors of a class. To get one of these objects, we use the class's `Class`.

Table 7-1 shows that the `Class` class provides two pairs of methods for getting at each type of feature. One pair allows access to a class's public features (including those inherited from its superclasses), while the other pair allows access to any public or nonpublic item declared within the class (but not features that are inherited), subject to security considerations. For example, `getFields()` returns an array of `Field` objects representing all of a class's public variables, including those it inherits. `getDeclaredFields()` returns an array representing all the variables declared in the class, regardless of their access modifiers (not including variables the security manager won't let you see), but not including inherited variables. (For constructors, the distinction between "all constructors" and "declared constructors" is meaningful, so getConstructors() and getDeclaredConstructors() differ only in that the former returns public constructors, while the latter returns all the class's constructors.) Each pair of methods includes a method for listing all of the items at once (for example, getFields()), and a method for looking up a particular item by name and (for methods and constructors) signature (for example, get-Field(), which takes the field name as an argument).

Table 7–1: Methods for Analyzing a Class

Method	Description
`Field [] getFields();`	Get the public variables, including inherited ones.
`Field getField(String name);`	Get the specified public variable, which may be inherited.
`Field [] getDeclaredFields();`	Get all public and nonpublic variables declared in this class (not including those inherited from superclasses).
`Field getDeclaredField(String name);`	Get the specified variable, public or nonpublic, declared in this class (inherited variables not considered).
`Method [] getMethods();`	Get the public methods, including inherited ones.
`Method getMethod(String name,` `Class [] argumentTypes);`	Get the specified public method, whose arguments match the types listed in argumentTypes. The method may be inherited.
`Method [] getDeclaredMethods();`	Get all public and nonpublic methods declared in this class (not including those inherited from superclasses).
`Method getDeclaredMethod(String name,` `Class [] argumentTypes);`	Get the specified method, public or nonpublic, whose arguments match the types listed in argumentTypes, and which is declared in this class (inherited methods not considered).
`Constructor [] getConstructors();`	Get the public constructors of this class.
`Constructor getConstructor(` `Class [] argumentTypes);`	Get the specified public constructor of this class, whose arguments match the types listed in argumentTypes.
`Constructor [] getDeclaredConstructors();`	Get all public and nonpublic constructors of this class.
`Constructor getDeclaredConstructor(` `Class [] argumentTypes);`	Get the specified constructor, public or nonpublic, whose arguments match the types listed in argumentTypes.

As a quick example, we'll show how easy it is to list all of the public methods of the java.util.Calendar class:

```
Method [] methods = Calendar.class.getMethods();
for (int i=0; i < methods.length; i++)
    System.out.println( methods[i] );
```

Here we have used the .class notation to get a reference to the Class of Calendar. Remember the discussion of the Class class—the reflection methods don't belong to the Calendar class itself; they belong to the java.lang.Class object that describes the Calendar class. If we wanted to start from an instance of Calendar (or, say, an unknown object), we could have used the getClass() method of the object instead:

```
Method [] methods = myUnknownObject.getClass().getMethods();
```

Security

Access to the reflection API is governed by a security manager. A fully trusted application has access to all of the above functionality—it can gain access to members of classes at the level of restriction normally granted code within its scope. There is currently no "special" access granted by the reflection API. It is possible that in the future, the full power of the reflection API will be available to completely trusted code such as debuggers; right now, user code can only see what it could have seen at compile-time. Untrusted code (for example, an unsigned applet) has the normal level of access to classes loaded from its own origin (classes sharing its classloader), but can only rely on the ability to access the public members of public classes coming from the rest of the system.

Accessing Fields

The class java.lang.reflect.Field is used to represent static variables and instance variables. Field has a full set of accessor methods for all of the base types (for example, getInt() and setInt(), getBoolean() and setBoolean()), and get() and set() methods for accessing members that are object references.

For example, given the following class:

```
class BankAccount {
    public int balance;
}
```

with the reflection API we can read and modify the value of the public integer
field balance:

```
BankAccount myBankAccount = ...;
...
try {
    Field balanceField = BankAccount.class.getField("balance");
    int balance = balanceField.getInt( myBankAccount );   // read it
    balanceField.setInt( myBankAccount, 42 );             // change it
} catch ( NoSuchFieldException e ) {
    // There is no "balance" field in this class
} catch ( IllegalAccessException e2) {
    // We don't have permission to access the field.
}
```

The various methods of Field take a reference to the particular object instance
that we want to access. In the code above, the getField() method returns a Field
object that represents the balance of the BankAccount class; this object doesn't
refer to any specific BankAccount. Therefore, to read or modify any specific
BankAccount, we call getInt() and setInt() with a reference to myBankAccount,
which is the account we want to work with. As you can see, an exception occurs if
we ask for access to a field that doesn't exist, or if we don't have the proper permission to read or write the field. If we make balance a private field, we can still look
up the Field object that describes it, but we won't be able to read or write its value.

Therefore, we aren't doing anything that we couldn't have done with static code at
compile-time; as long as balance is a public member of a class that we can access,
we can write code to read and modify its value. What's important is that we're
accessing balance at run-time, and could use this technique to examine the balance field in a class that was dynamically loaded.

Accessing Methods

The class java.lang.reflect.Method represents a static or instance method. Subject to the normal security rules, a Method object's invoke() method can be used to
call the underlying object's method with specified arguments. Yes, Java has something like a method pointer!

As an example, we'll write a Java application called invoke that takes as command-
line arguments the name of a Java class and the name of a method to invoke. For
simplicity, we'll assume that the method is static and takes no arguments:

```
import java.lang.reflect.*;
class invoke {
    public static void main( String [] args ) {
        try {
            Class c = Class.forName( args[0] );
            Method m = c.getMethod( args[1], new Class [] { } );
            Object ret = m.invoke( null, null );
```

```
                System.out.println( "Invoked static method: " + args[1] +
                       " of class: " + args[0] + " with no args\nResults: " + ret );
            } catch ( ClassNotFoundException e ) {
                // Class.forName() can't find the class
            } catch ( NoSuchMethodException e2 ) {
                // that method doesn't exist
            } catch ( IllegalAccessException e3 ) {
                // we don't have permission to invoke that method
            } catch ( InvocationTargetException e4 ) {
                // an exception ocurred while invoking that method
                System.out.println("Method threw an: " + e4.getTargetException() );
            }
        }
    }
```

We can run invoke to fetch the value of the system clock:

```
% java invoke java.lang.System currentTimeMillis
Invoked static method: currentTimeMillis of class: java.lang.System with no args
Results: 861129235818
```

Turning to the code, our first task is to look up the specified Class by name. To do so, we call the forName() method with the name of the desired class (the first command-line argument). We then ask for the specified method by its name. get-Method() has two arguments: the first is the method name (the second command-line argument), and the second is an array of Class objects that specifies the method's signature. (Remember that any method may be overloaded; you must specify the signature to make it clear which version you want.) Since our simple program calls only methods with no arguments, we create an anonymous empty array of Class objects. Had we wanted to invoke a method that takes arguments, we would have passed an array of the classes of their respective types, in the proper order. For primitive types we would have used the necessary wrappers. The classes of primitive types are represented by the static TYPE fields of their respective wrappers; for example, use Integer.TYPE for the class of a primitive integer.

Once we have the Method object, we call its invoke() method. This calls our target method and returns the result as an Object. (To do anything nontrivial with this object, you have to cast it to something more specific. Presumably, since you're calling the method, you know what kind of object to expect.) If the returned value is a primitive type like int or boolean, it will be wrapped in the standard wrapper class for its type. (Wrappers for primitive types are discussed in Chapter 9.) If the method returns void, invoke() returns a Void object. (This is why a wrapper class is needed for void; we need a class to represent void return values.)

The first argument to invoke() is the object on which we would like to invoke the method. If the method is static, there is no object, so we set the first argument to null. That's the case in our example. The second argument is an array of objects to be passed as arguments to the methods. The types of these should match the types specified in the call to getMethod(). Because we're calling a method with no arguments, we can pass null for the second argument to invoke(). As with the return value, the types of primitive arguments are expected to be wrapped in wrapper classes. The reflection API automatically unpacks them for the method invocation.

The exceptions shown in the code above occur if we cannot find or don't have permission to access the method. Additionally, an InvocationTargetException occurs if the method being invoked throws some kind of exception itself. You can find out what it threw by calling the getTargetException() method of InvocationTarget-Exception.

Accessing Constructors

The java.lang.reflect.Constructor class represents an object constructor. You can use it, subject to the security manager, to create a new instance of an object, with arguments. Although you can load new classes dynamically and create instances of them with Class.forName() and Class.newInstance(), you cannot specify arguments with those methods.

Here we'll create an instance of java.util.Date, passing a string argument to the constructor:

```
try {
    Constructor c = Date.class.getConstructor( new Class [] { String.class } );
    Object o = c.newInstance( new Object [] { "Jan 1, 1997" } );
    Date d = (Date)o;
    System.out.println(d);
} catch ( NoSuchMethodException e ) {
    // getConstructor() couldn't find the constructor we described
} catch ( InstantiationException e2 ) {
    // the class is abstract
} catch ( IllegalAccessException e3 ) {
    // we don't have permission to create an instance
} catch ( InvocationTargetException e4 ) {
    // the construct threw an exception
}
```

The story is much the same as with a method invocation; after all, a constructor is really no more than a method with some strange properties. We look up the appropriate constructor for our Date class—the one that takes a single String as its argument—by passing getConstructor() an array containing the String class as its only element. (If the constructor required more arguments, we would put additional objects in the array, representing the classes of each argument.) We can then invoke newInstance(), passing it a corresponding array of argument objects. Again, to pass primitive types, we would wrap them in their wrapper types first. Finally, we cast the resulting object to a Date and print it.

The same exceptions seen in the previous example apply here, including the possible IllegalArgumentException. In addition, newInstance() throws an Instanti-ationException if the class is abstract and cannot be instantiated.

What about arrays?

The reflection API allows you to create and inspect arrays of base types using the java.lang.reflect.Array class. The process is very much the same as with the other classes, so we won't cover it here. For more information, look in your favorite language reference.

What is reflection good for?

We've already said that reflection is used by the serialization process. In Chapter 18 we'll learn how it is used by JavaBeans to dynamically discover capabilities and features of Java Bean objects. But these are somewhat behind-the-scenes applications. What can reflection do for us in everyday situations?

Well, we could use reflection to go about acting as if Java had dynamic method invocation and other useful capabilities; in Chapter 18, we'll develop a dynamic adapter class using reflection. But as a general coding practice, dynamic method invocation is a very bad idea. One of the primary features of Java is its strong typing and safety. You abandon much of that when you take a dip in the reflecting pool.

More appropriately, you can use reflection in situations where you need to work with objects that you can't know about in advance. Reflection puts Java on a higher plane of programming languages, opening up possibilities for new kinds of applications. As we hinted earlier, one of the most important uses for reflection will be in integrating Java with scripting languages. With reflection one could write an interpreter in Java that could access the full Java API, create objects, invoke methods, modify variables and do all of the other things that a Java program can do at compile-time, while it is running. The invoke example from a few pages back should give you a brief hint about how to write this interpreter.

8

Threads

Threads have been around for some time, but few programmers have actually worked with them. There is even some debate over whether or not the average programmer can use threads effectively. In Java, working with threads can be easy and productive. In fact, threads provide the only way to effectively handle a number of tasks. So it's important that you become familiar with threads early in your exploration of Java.

Threads are integral to the way Java works. We've already seen that an applet's paint() method isn't called by the applet itself, but by another thread within the interpreter. At any given time, there may be many such background threads, performing activities in parallel with your application. In fact, it's easy to get a half dozen or more threads running in an applet without even trying, simply by requesting images, updating the screen, playing audio, and so on. But these things happen behind the scenes; you don't normally have to worry about them. In this chapter, we'll talk about writing applications that create and use their own threads explicitly.

Introducing Threads

Conceptually, a thread is a flow of control within a program. A thread is similar to the more familiar notion of a process, except that multiple threads within the same application share much of the same state—in particular, they run in the same address space. It's not unlike a golf course, which can be used by many players at the same time. Sharing the same address space means that threads share instance variables, but not local variables, just like players share the golf course, but not personal things like clubs and balls.

Multiple threads in an application have the same problems as the players sharing a golf course: in a word, synchronization. Just as you can't have two sets of players blindly playing the same green at the same time, you can't have several threads trying to access the same variables without some kind of coordination. Someone is bound to get hurt. A thread can reserve the right to use an object until it's finished with its task, just as a golf party gets exclusive rights to the green until it's done. And a thread that is more important can raise its priority, asserting its right to play through.

The devil is in the details, of course, and those details have historically made threads difficult to use. Java makes creating, controlling, and coordinating threads simple. When creating a new thread is the best way to accomplish some task, it should be as easy as adding a new component to your application.

It is common to stumble over threads when you first look at them, because creating a thread exercises many of your new Java skills all at once. You can avoid confusion by remembering there are always two players involved in running a thread: a Java language object that represents the thread itself and an arbitrary target object that contains the method the thread is to execute. Later, you will see that it is possible to play some sleight of hand and combine these two roles, but that special case just changes the packaging, not the relationship.

The Thread Class and the Runnable Interface

A new thread is born when we create an instance of the java.lang.Thread class. The Thread object represents a real thread in the Java interpreter and serves as a handle for controlling and synchronizing its execution. With it, we can start the thread, stop the thread, or suspend it temporarily. The constructor for the Thread class accepts information about where the thread should begin its execution. Conceptually, we would like to simply tell it what method to run, but since there are no pointers to methods in Java, we can't specify one directly. Instead, we have to take a short detour and use the Runnable interface to create an object that contains a "runnable" method.

An object that wants to serve as the target of a Thread can declare that it has an appropriate executable method by implementing the java.lang.Runnable interface. Runnable defines a single, general-purpose method:

```
public interface Runnable {
    abstract public void run();
}
```

Every thread begins its life by executing a run() method in a particular object. run() is a rather mundane method that can hold an arbitrary body of code. It is public, takes no arguments, has no return value, and is not allowed to throw any exceptions.

Any class that contains an appropriate run() method can declare that it implements the Runnable interface. An instance of this class is then a runnable object that can serve as the target of a new Thread. If you don't want to put the run() method directly in your object, you can always make an adapter class that serves as the Runnable for you. The adapter's run() method can call any method it wants to start the thread.

Creating and starting threads

A newly born Thread remains idle until we give it a figurative slap on the bottom by calling its start() method. The thread then wakes up and proceeds to execute the run() method of its target object. start() can be called only once in the lifetime of a Thread. Once a thread starts, it continues running until the target object's run() method completes, or we call the thread's stop() method to kill the thread permanently. A little later, we will look at some other methods you can use to control the thread's progress while it is running.

Now let's look at an example. The following class, Animation, implements a run() method to drive its drawing loop:

```
class Animation implements Runnable {
    ...
    public void run() {

        while ( true ) {
            // Draw Frames
            ...
        }
    }
}
```

To use it, we create a Thread object with an instance of Animation as its target object, and invoke its start() method. We can perform these steps explicitly, as in the following:

```
Animation happy = new Animation("Mr. Happy");
Thread myThread = new Thread( happy );
myThread.start();
...
```

Here we have created an instance of our Animation class and passed it as the argument to the constructor for myThread. When we call the start() method, myThread begins to execute Animation's run() method. Let the show begin!

The above situation is not terribly object oriented. More often, we want an object to handle its own threads, as shown in Figure 8-1, which depicts a Runnable object that creates and starts its own Thread. We'll show our Animation class performing these actions in its constructor:

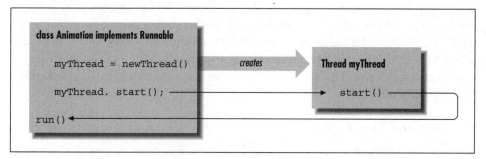

Figure 8–1: Interaction between Animation and its thread

```
class Animation implements Runnable {

    Thread myThread;

    Animation (String name) {
        myThread = new Thread( this );
        myThread.start();
    }
    ...
```

In this case, the argument we pass to the Thread constructor is this, the current object instance. We keep the Thread reference in the instance variable myThread, in case we want to stop the show, or exercise some other kind of control.

A natural born thread

The Runnable interface lets us make an arbitrary object the target of a thread, as we did above. This is the most important, general usage of the Thread class. In most situations where you need to use threads, you'll create a class that implements the Runnable interface. I'd be remiss, however, if I didn't show you the other technique for creating a thread. Another design option is to make our target class a subclass of a type that is already runnable. The Thread class itself implements the Runnable interface; it has its own run() method we can override to make it do something useful:

```
class Animation extends Thread {
    ...

    public void run() {
        while (true ) {
            // Draw Frames
            ...
        }
    }
}
```

The skeleton of our Animation class above looks much the same as before, except that our class is now a kind of Thread. To go along with this scheme, the default constructor of the Thread class makes itself the default target. That is, by default, the Thread executes its own run() method when we call the start() method, as shown in Figure 8-2. Now our subclass can just override the run() method in the Thread class (Thread simply defines an empty run() method).

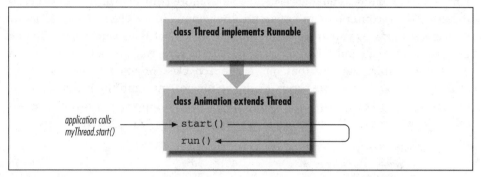

Figure 8–2: Animation as a subclass of Thread

Now we create an instance of Animation and call its start() method:

```
Animation bouncy = new Animation("Bouncy");
bouncy.start();
```

Alternatively, we can have the Animation object start itself when it is created, as before:

```
class Animation extends Thread {

    Animation (String name) {
        start();
    }
    ...
```

Here our Animation object just calls its own start() method when an instance is created. (It's better form to start and stop our objects explicitly after they're created.)

Subclassing Thread seems like a convenient way to bundle a Thread and its target run() method. However, this approach often isn't the best design. If you subclass Thread to implement a thread, you are saying you need a new type of object that is a kind of Thread. While there is something unnaturally satisfying about taking an object that's primarily concerned with performing a task and making it a type of Thread, the actual situations where you'll want to create a subclass of Thread should be rather rare. In most cases, it will be more natural to let the requirements of your program dictate the class structure. If you find you're subclassing Thread left and right, you may want to examine whether you are falling into the design trap of making objects that are simply glorified functions.

Using an adapter

Finally, we can build an adapter class to give us more control over how to structure the code. It is convenient to create an anonymous inner class that implements Runnable and invokes an arbitrary method in our object. This almost gives the feel of starting a thread and telling it what method to run, as if we had method pointers. For example, suppose that our Animation class provides a method called startAnimating() that does setup, loads the images, etc., and then starts a thread to perform the actual animation loop. The animation loop is in a private method called drawFrames(). We could use an an adapter to run drawFrames() for us:

```
class Animation {

    public void startAnimating() {
        // Do setup, load images, etc.
        ...

        // Start a drawing thread
        myThread = new Thread ( new Runnable() {
            public void run() { drawFrames(); }
        } );
        myThread.start();
    }

    private void drawFrames() {
        // do animation ...
    }
}
```

In this code, the anonymous inner class implementing Runnable is generated for us by the compiler. We create a Thread with this anonymous class as its target and have its run() method call our drawFrames() method. We have avoided implementing a generic run() method in our application code, but at the expense of generating an extra class.

Controlling Threads

We have seen the start() method used to bring a newly created Thread to life. Five other methods, listed below, let us control a Thread's execution: stop(), suspend(), resume(), sleep() and interrupt(). None of these methods take any arguments; they all operate on the thread object on which they are called.

- The stop() method complements start(); it destroys the thread. start() and stop() can be called only once in the life of a Thread.

- By contrast, the suspend() and resume() methods can be used to arbitrarily pause and then restart the execution of a Thread.

- The sleep() method causes a thread to wait for a designated period of time.

- The interrupt() method can be used to wake up a thread that is sleeping or is otherwise blocked on a long I/O operation.[*]

For simple tasks, it is often easy enough to throw away a thread when we want to stop it and simply create a new one when want to proceed again. suspend() and resume() can be used in situations where the Thread's setup is very expensive. For example, if creating the thread involves opening a socket and setting up some elaborate communication, it probably makes more sense to use suspend() and resume() with this thread.

We often need to tell a thread to wait, or "sleep," for a fixed period of time. While a thread is asleep, or otherwise blocked on input of some kind, it doesn't consume CPU time or compete with other threads for processing. For this we can either call the thread's sleep() method or use a convenience method of the Thread class. Thread.sleep() is a static method that causes the currently executing thread to delay for a specified number of milliseconds:

```
try {
    Thread.sleep( 1000 );
    // Thread.currentThread().sleep( 1000 );
}
catch ( InterruptedException e ) {
    // Someone woke us up prematurely
}
```

The call to Thread.sleep() is equivalent to the "commented out" call below it that calls sleep() explicitly on the currently executing thread. In any form, sleep() throws an InterruptedException if it is interrupted by another Thread. To interrupt a thread, call its interrupt() method. As you see in the code above, the thread can catch this exception and take the opportunity to perform some action, or perhaps just go back to sleep.

Finally, if you need to coordinate your activities with another thread by waiting for the other thread to complete its task, you can use the join() method. Calling a thread's join() method causes the caller to block until the thread dies. Alternatively, you can poll the thread by calling join() with a number of milliseconds to wait. Later we'll look at a much more general and powerful mechanism for coordinating the activities of threads: wait() and notify().

---

[*] interrupt() does not work in versions of Java prior to 1.1.

A Thread's Life

A Thread continues to execute until one of the following things happens:

- It returns from its target run() method

- It's interrupted by an uncaught exception

- Its stop() method is called

So what happens if the run() method for a thread never terminates, and the application that started the thread never calls its stop() method? The answer is that the thread lives on, even after the application that created it has finished. This means we have to be aware of how our threads eventually terminate, or an application can end up leaving orphaned threads that unnecessarily consume resources.

In many cases, we really want to create background threads that do simple, periodic tasks in an application. The setDaemon() method can be used to mark a Thread as a daemon thread that should be killed and discarded when no other application threads remain. Normally, the Java interpreter continues to run until all threads have completed. But when daemon threads are the only threads still alive, the interpreter will exit.

Here's a devilish example using daemon threads:

```
class Devil extends Thread {

    Devil() {
        setDaemon( true );
        start();
    }

    public void run() {
        // Perform evil tasks
        ...
    }
}
```

In the above example, the Devil thread sets its daemon status when it is created. If any Devil threads remain when our application is otherwise complete, Java kills them for us. We don't have to worry about cleaning them up.

Daemon threads are primarily useful in standalone Java applications and in the implementation of the Java system itself, but not in applets. Since an applet runs inside of another Java application, any daemon threads it creates could continue to live until the controlling application exits—probably not the desired effect. A browser or an application can use ThreadGroups to control all of the threads created by an application and clean them up if necessary.

Threading Applets

Applets are embeddable Java applications that are expected to be able to start and stop themselves on command. Unlike threads, applets can be started and stopped any number of times. A Java-enabled Web browser normally starts an applet when the applet is displayed and stops it when the user moves to another page or scrolls the applet out of view. We would like an applet to cease its nonessential activity when it is stopped and resume it when started again.

In this section, we will build UpdateApplet, a simple base class for an Applet that maintains a Thread to automatically update its display at regular intervals. UpdateApplet handles the basic starting and stopping behavior for us, as shown below:

```
public class UpdateApplet extends java.applet.Applet
    implements Runnable {

    private Thread updateThread;
    int updateInterval = 1000;

    public void run() {
        while ( true ) {
            try {
                Thread.sleep( updateInterval );
            } catch (InterruptedException e ) { }

            repaint();
        }
    }

    public void start() {
        if ( updateThread == null ) {
            updateThread = new Thread(this);
            updateThread.start();
        }
    }
    public void stop() {
        if ( updateThread != null ) {
            updateThread.stop();
            updateThread = null;
        }
    }
}
```

UpdateApplet is a Runnable object that alternately sleeps and calls its repaint() method. It has two other public methods: start() and stop(). These are methods of the Applet class we are overriding; do not confuse them with the similarly named methods of the Thread class. These start() and stop() methods are called by the Java environment to tell the applet when it should and should not be running.

UpdateApplet illustrates an environmentally friendly way to deal with threads in a simple applet. UpdateApplet kills its thread each time the applet is stopped and recreates it if the applet is restarted. When UpdateApplet's start() method is called, we first check to make sure there is no currently executing updateThread. We then create one to begin our execution. When our applet is subsequently stopped, we kill the thread by invoking its stop() method and throw away the reference by setting it to null. Setting updateThread to null serves both to allow the garbage collector to clean up the dead Thread object, and to indicate to Update-Applet's start() method that the thread is gone.

In truth, an Applet's start() and stop() methods are guaranteed to be called in sequence. As a result, we shouldn't have to check for the existence of updateThread in start() (it should always be null). However, it's good programming practice to perform the test. If we didn't, and for some reason stop() were to fail at its job, we might inadvertently start a lot of threads.

With UpdateApplet doing all of the work for us, we can now create the world's simplest clock applet with just a few lines of code, given below. Figure 8-3 shows our Clock. (This might be a good one to run on your Java wristwatch.)

```
public class Clock extends UpdateApplet {
    public void paint( java.awt.Graphics g ) {
        g.drawString( new java.util.Date().toString(), 10, 25 );
    }
}
```

Mon Apr 22 09:37:51 MDT 1996

Figure 8–3: The clock applet

The java.util.Date().toString() sequence simply creates a string that contains the current time.

Our Clock applet provides a good example of a simple thread; we don't mind throwing it away and subsequently rebuilding it if the user should happen to wander on and off of our Web page a few times. But what if the task that our thread handles isn't so simple? What if, for instance, we have to open a socket and establish a connection with another system? One solution is to use Thread's suspend() and resume() methods, as I'll show you in a moment.

Now if you've been wondering why we've been using stop() to kill the thread, rather than using the suspend() and resume() methods all along, here's the explanation you've been waiting for. The problem with applets is that we have no control over how a user navigates Web pages. For example, say a user scrolls our applet out of view, and we use suspend() to suspend the applet. Now we have no way of ensuring that the user will bring the applet back into view before moving on to another page. And actually, the same situation would occur if the user simply moves on to another page and never comes back.

If we call suspend(), we'd really like to make sure we call resume() at a later date, or we'll end up leaving the thread hanging in permanent suspense. But we have no way of knowing if the applet will ever be restarted, so just putting a call to resume() in the applet's start() method won't work. Leaving the suspended thread around forever might not hurt us, but it's not good programming practice to be wasteful. What we need is a way to guarantee we can clean up our mess if the applet is never used again. What to do?

There is a solution for this dilemma, but in many cases, like with our simple Clock, it's just easier to use stop(), with a subsequent call to start() if necessary. In cases where it is expensive to set up and tear down a thread, we could make the following modifications to UpdateApplet:

```
public void start() {
    if ( updateThread == null ) {
        updateThread = new Thread(this);
        updateThread.start();
    }
    else
        updateThread.resume();
}

public void stop() {
    updateThread.suspend();
}

public void destroy() {
    if ( updateThread != null ) {
        updateThread.stop();
        updateThread = null;
    }
}
```

These modifications change UpdateApplet so that it suspends and restarts its updateThread, rather than killing and recreating it. The new start() method creates the thread and calls start() if updateThread is null; otherwise it assumes that the thread has been suspended, so it calls resume(). The applet's stop() method simply suspends the thread by calling suspend().

What's new here is the destroy() method. This is another method that Update-
Applet inherits from the Applet class. The method is called by the Java environment when the applet is going to be removed (often from a cache). It provides a
place where we can free up any resources the applet is holding. This is the perfect
place to cut the suspense and clean up after our thread. In our destroy() method,
we check to see that the thread exists, and if it does, we call stop() to kill it and set
its reference to null.

Synchronization

Every thread has a life of its own. Normally, a thread goes about its business without any regard for what other threads in the application are doing. Threads may
be time-sliced, which means they can run in arbitrary spurts and bursts as directed
by the operating system. On a multiprocessor system, it is even possible for many
different threads to be running simultaneously on different CPUs. This section is
about coordinating the activities of two or more threads, so they can work together
and not collide in their use of the same address space.

Java provides a few simple structures for synchronizing the activities of threads.
They are all based on the concept of *monitors*, a widely used synchronization
scheme developed by C.A.R. Hoare. You don't have to know the details about how
monitors work to be able to use them, but it may help you to have a picture in
mind.

A monitor is essentially a lock. The lock is attached to a resource that many
threads may need to access, but that should be accessed by only one thread at a
time. It's not unlike a public restroom at a gas station. If the resource is not being
used, the thread can acquire the lock and access the resource. By the same token,
if the restroom is unlocked, you can enter and lock the door. When the thread is
done, it relinquishes the lock, just as you unlock the door and leave it open for the
next person. However, if another thread already has the lock for the resource, all
other threads have to wait until the current thread finishes and releases the lock,
just as if the restroom is locked when you arrive, you have to wait until the current
occupant is done and unlocks the door.

Fortunately, Java makes the process of synchronizing access to resources quite easy.
The language handles setting up and acquiring locks; all you have to do is specify
which resources require locks.

Serializing Access to Methods

The most common need for synchronization among threads in Java is to serialize their access to some resource (an object). In other words, to make sure that only one thread at a time can perform certain activities that manipulate the object. In Java, every object has a lock associated with it. To be more specific, every class and every instance of a class has its own lock. The synchronized keyword marks places where a thread must acquire the lock before proceeding.

For example, say we implemented a SpeechSynthesizer class that contains a say() method. We don't want multiple threads calling say() at the same time or we wouldn't be able to understand anything being said. So we mark the say() method as synchronized, which means that a thread has to acquire the lock on the Speech-Synthesizer object before it can speak:

```
class SpeechSynthesizer {

    synchronized void say( String words ) {
        // Speak
    }
}
```

Because say() is an instance method, a thread has to acquire the lock on the particular SpeechSynthesizer instance it is using before it can invoke the say() method. When say() has completed, it gives up the lock, which allows the next waiting thread to acquire the lock and run the method. Note that it doesn't matter whether the thread is owned by the SpeechSynthesizer itself or some other object; every thread has to acquire the same lock, that of the SpeechSynthesizer instance. If say() were a class (static) method instead of an instance method, we could still mark it as synchronized. But in this case as there is no instance object involved, the lock would be on the class object itself.

Often, you want to synchronize multiple methods of the same class, so that only one of the methods modifies or examines parts of the class at a time. All static synchronized methods in a class use the same class object lock. By the same token, all instance methods in a class use the same instance object lock. In this way, Java can guarantee that only one of a set of synchronized methods is running at a time. For example, a SpreadSheet class might contain a number of instance variables that represent cell values, as well as some methods that manipulate the cells in a row:

```
class SpreadSheet {

    int cellA1, cellA2, cellA3;

    synchronized int sumRow() {
        return cellA1 + cellA2 + cellA3;
    }
```

```
    synchronized void setRow( int a1, int a2, int a3 ) {
        cellA1 = a1;
        cellA2 = a2;
        cellA3 = a3;
    }
    ...
}
```

In this example, both methods setRow() and sumRow() access the cell values. You can see that problems might arise if one thread were changing the values of the variables in setRow() at the same moment another thread was reading the values in sumRow(). To prevent this, we have marked both methods as synchronized. When threads are synchronized, only one will be run at a time. If a thread is in the middle of executing setRow() when another thread calls sumRow(), the second thread waits until the first one is done executing setRow() before it gets to run sumRow(). This synchronization allows us to preserve the consistency of the SpreadSheet. And the best part is that all of this locking and waiting is handled by Java; it's transparent to the programmer.

In addition to synchronizing entire methods, the synchronized keyword can be used in a special construct to guard arbitrary blocks of code. In this form it also takes an explicit argument that specifies the object for which it is to acquire a lock:

```
    synchronized ( myObject ) {
        // Functionality that needs to be synced
        ...
    }
```

The code block above can appear in any method. When it is reached, the thread has to acquire the lock on myObject before proceeding. In this way, we can have methods (or parts of methods) in different classes synchronized the same as methods in the same class.

A synchronized method is, therefore, equivalent to a method with its statements synchronized on the current object. Thus:

```
    synchronized void myMethod () {
        ...
    }
```

is equivalent to:

```
    void myMethod () {
        synchronized ( this ) {
            ...
        }
    }
```

Accessing instance variables

In the SpreadSheet example, we guarded access to a set of instance variables with a sychronized method, which we did mainly so that we wouldn't change one of the variables while someone was reading the rest of them. We wanted to keep them coordinated. But what about individual variable types? Do they need to be synchronized? Normally the answer is no. Almost all operations on primitives and object reference types in Java happen "atomically": they are handled by the virtual machine in one step, with no opportunity for two threads to collide. You can't be in the middle of changing a reference and be only "part way" done when another thread looks at the reference. But watch out—I did say "almost." If you read the Java virtual machine specification carefully, you will see that the double and long primitive types are not guaranteed to be handled automatically. Both of these types represent 64-bit values. The problem has to do with how the Java Virtual Machine's stack handles them. It is possible that this specification will be beefed up in the future. But for now, if you have any fears, synchronize access to your double and long instance variables through "accessor" methods.

wait() and notify()

With the synchronized keyword, we can serialize the execution of complete methods and blocks of code. The wait() and notify() methods of the Object class extend this capability. Every object in Java is a subclass of Object, so every object inherits these methods. By using wait() and notify(), a thread can effectively give up its hold on a lock at an arbitrary point, and then wait for another thread to give it back before continuing.[*] All of the coordinated activity still happens inside of synchronized blocks, and still only one thread is executing at a given time.

By executing wait() from a synchronized block, a thread gives up its hold on the lock and goes to sleep. A thread might do this if it needs to wait for something to happen in another part of the application, as you'll see shortly. Later, when the necessary event happens, the thread that is running it calls notify() from a block synchronized on the same object. Now the first thread wakes up and begins trying to acquire the lock again.

When the first thread manages to reacquire the lock, it continues from the point it left off. However, the thread that waited may not get the lock immediately (or perhaps ever). It depends on when the second thread eventually releases the lock, and which thread manages to snag it next. Note also that the first thread won't wake up from the wait() unless another thread calls notify(). There is an overloaded version of wait(), however, that allows us to specify a timeout period. If

---

[*] In actuality they don't really pass the lock around; the lock becomes available and, as we'll describe, a thread that is scheduled to run acquires it.

another thread doesn't call `notify()` in the specified period, the waiting thread automatically wakes up.

Let's look at a simple scenario to see what's going on. In the following example, we'll assume there are three threads—one waiting to execute each of the three synchronized methods of the `MyThing` class. We'll call them the `waiter`, `notifier`, and `related` threads, respectively. Here's a code fragment to illustrate:

```
class MyThing {

    synchronized void waiterMethod() {
        // Do some stuff

        // Now we need to wait for notifier to do something
        wait();

        // Continue where we left off
    }

    synchronized void notifierMethod() {
        // Do some stuff

        // Notify waiter that we've done it
        notify();

        // Do more things
    }

    synchronized void relatedMethod() {
        // Do some related stuff
    }
}
```

Let's assume `waiter` gets through the gate first and begins executing `waiterMethod()`. The two other threads are initially blocked, trying to acquire the lock for the `MyThing` object. When `waiter` executes the `wait()` method, it relinquishes its hold on the lock and goes to sleep. Now there are now two viable threads waiting for the lock. Which thread gets it depends on several factors, including chance and the priorities of the threads. (We'll discuss thread scheduling in the next section.)

Let's say that `notifier` is the next thread to acquire the lock, so it begins to run. `waiter` continues to sleep and `related` languishes, waiting for its turn. When `notifier` executes the call to `notify()`, Java prods the `waiter` thread, effectively telling it something has changed. `waiter` then wakes up and rejoins `related` in vying for the `MyThing` lock. Note that it doesn't actually receive the lock; it just changes from saying "leave me alone" to "I want the lock."

At this point, notifier still owns the lock and continues to hold it until it leaves its synchronized method (or perhaps executes a wait() itself). When it finally completes, the other two methods get to fight over the lock. waiter would like to continue executing waiterMethod() from the point it left off, while related, which has been patient, would like to get started. We'll let you choose your own ending for the story.

For each call to notify(), Java wakes up just one method that is asleep in a wait() call. If there are multiple threads waiting, Java picks a thread on an arbitrary basis, which may be implementation dependant. The Object class also provides a notifyAll() call to wake up all waiting threads. In most cases, you'll probably want to use notifyAll() rather than notify(). Keep in mind that notify() really means "Hey, something related to this object has changed. The condition you are waiting for may have changed, so check it again." In general, there is no reason to assume only one thread at a time is interested in the change or able to act upon it. Different threads might look upon whatever has changed in different ways.

Often, our waiter thread is waiting for a particular condition to change and we will want to sit in a loop like the following:

```
...
while ( condition != true )
    wait();
...
```

Other synchronized threads call notify() or notifyAll() when they have modified the environment so that waiter can check the condition again. Using "wait conditions" like this is the civilized alternative to polling and sleeping, as you'll see in the following section.

The Message Passer

Now we'll illustrate a classic interaction between two threads: a Producer and a Consumer. A producer thread creates messages and places them into a queue, while a consumer reads them out and displays them. To be realistic, we'll give the queue a maximum depth. And to make things really interesting, we'll have our consumer thread be lazy and run much slower than the producer. This means that Producer occasionally has to stop and wait for Consumer to catch up. The example below shows the Producer and Consumer classes:

```
import java.util.Vector;

class Producer extends Thread {
    static final int MAXQUEUE = 5;
    private Vector messages = new Vector();

    public void run() {
```

```
            try {
                while ( true ) {
                    putMessage();
                    sleep( 1000 );
                }
            }
            catch( InterruptedException e ) { }
        }

    private synchronized void putMessage() throws InterruptedException {

        while ( messages.size() == MAXQUEUE )
            wait();
        messages.addElement( new java.util.Date().toString() );
        notify();
    }

    // Called by Consumer
    public synchronized String getMessage() throws InterruptedException {
        notify();
        while ( messages.size() == 0 )
            wait();
        String message = (String)messages.firstElement();
        messages.removeElement( message );
        return message;
    }
}

class Consumer extends Thread {
    Producer producer;

    Consumer(Producer p) {
        producer = p;
    }

    public void run() {
        try {
            while ( true ) {
                String message = producer.getMessage();
                System.out.println("Got message: " + message);
                sleep( 2000 );
            }
        }
        catch( InterruptedException e ) { }
    }

    public static void main(String args[]) {
        Producer producer = new Producer();
```

```
        producer.start();
        new Consumer( producer ).start();
    }
}
```

For convenience, we have included a main() method in the Consumer class that runs the complete example. It creates a Consumer that is tied to a Producer and starts the two classes. You can run the example as follows:

```
% java Consumer
```

The output is the time-stamp messages created by the Producer:

```
Got message: Sun Dec 19 03:35:55 CST 1996
Got message: Sun Dec 19 03:35:56 CST 1996
Got message: Sun Dec 19 03:35:57 CST 1996
...
```

The time stamps initially show a spacing of one second, although they appear every two seconds. Our Producer runs faster than our Consumer. Producer would like to generate a new message every second, while Consumer gets around to reading and displaying a message only every two seconds. Can you see how long it will take the message queue to fill up? What will happen when it does?

Let's look at the code. We are using a few new tools here. Producer and Consumer are subclasses of Thread. It would have been a better design decision to have Producer and Consumer implement the Runnable interface, but we took the slightly easier path and subclassed Thread. You should find it fairly simple to use the other technique; you might try it as an exercise.

The Producer and Consumer classes pass messages through an instance of a java.util.Vector object. We haven't discussed the Vector class yet, but you can think of this one as a queue where we add and remove elements in first-in, first-out order.

The important activity is in the synchronized methods: putMessage() and getMessage(). Although one of the methods is used by the Producer thread and the other by the Consumer thread, they both live in the Producer class because they have to be synchronized on the same object to work together. Here they both implicitly use the Producer object's lock. If the queue is empty, the Consumer blocks in a call in the Producer, waiting for another message.

Another design option would implement the getMessage() method in the Consumer class and use a synchronized code block to synchronize explicitly on the Producer object. In either case, synchronizing on the Producer is important because it allows us to have multiple Consumer objects that feed on the same Producer.

putMessage()'s job is to add a new message to the queue. It can't do this if the queue is already full, so it first checks the number of elements in messages. If there is room, it stuffs in another time stamp. If the queue is at its limit, however, putMessage() has to wait until there's space. In this situation, putMessage() executes a wait() and relies on the consumer to call notify() to wake it up after a message has been read. Here we have putMessage() testing the condition in a loop. In this simple example, the test probably isn't necessary; we could assume that when putMessage() wakes up, there is a free spot. However, this test is another example of good programming practice. Before it finishes, putMessage() calls notify() itself to prod any Consumer that might be waiting on an empty queue.

getMessage() retrieves a message for the Consumer. It enters a loop like the Producer's, waiting for the queue to have at least one element before proceeding. If the queue is empty, it executes a wait() and expects the producer to call notify() when more items are available. Notice that getMessage() makes its own unconditional call to notify(). This is a somewhat lazy way of keeping the Producer on its toes, so that the queue should generally be full. Alternatively, getMessage() might test to see if the queue had fallen below a low water mark before waking up the producer.

Now let's add another Consumer to the scenario, just to make things really interesting. Most of the necessary changes are in the Consumer class; the example below shows the code for the modified class:

```
class Consumer extends Thread {
    Producer producer;
    String name;

    Consumer(String name, Producer producer) {
        this.producer = producer;
        this.name = name;
    }

    public void run() {
        try {
            while ( true ) {
                String message = producer.getMessage();
                System.out.println(name + " got message: " + message);
                sleep( 2000 );
            }
        }
        catch( InterruptedException e ) { }
    }
```

```
public static void main(String args[]) {
    Producer producer = new Producer();
    producer.start();

    // Start two this time
    new Consumer( "One", producer ).start();
    new Consumer( "Two", producer ).start();
}
}
```

The Consumer constructor now takes a string name, to identify each consumer. The run() method uses this name in the call to println() to identify which consumer received the message.

The only modification to make in the Producer code is to change the call to notify() in putMessage() to a call to notifyAll(). Now, instead of the consumer and producer playing tag with the queue, we can have many players waiting on the condition of the queue to change. We might have a number of consumers waiting for a message, or we might have the producer waiting for a consumer to take a message. Whenever the condition of the queue changes, we prod all of the waiting methods to reevaluate the situation by calling notifyAll(). Note, however, that we don't need to change the call to notify() in getMessage(). If a Consumer thread is waiting for a message to appear in the queue, it's not possible for the Producer to be simultaneously waiting because the queue is full.

Here is some sample output when there are two consumers running, as in the main() method shown above:

```
One got message: Wed Mar 20 20:00:01 CST 1996
Two got message: Wed Mar 20 20:00:02 CST 1996
One got message: Wed Mar 20 20:00:03 CST 1996
Two got message: Wed Mar 20 20:00:04 CST 1996
One got message: Wed Mar 20 20:00:05 CST 1996
Two got message: Wed Mar 20 20:00:06 CST 1996
One got message: Wed Mar 20 20:00:07 CST 1996
Two got message: Wed Mar 20 20:00:08 CST 1996
...
```

We see nice, orderly alternation between the two consumers, as a result of the calls to sleep() in the various methods. Interesting things would happen, however, if we were to remove all of the calls to sleep() and let things run at full speed. The threads would compete and their behavior would depend on whether or not the system is using time slicing. On a time-sliced system, there should be a fairly random distribution between the two consumers, while on a nontime-sliced system, a single consumer could monopolize the messages. And since you're probably wondering about time slicing, let's talk about thread priority and scheduling.

Scheduling and Priority

Java makes few guarantees about how it schedules threads. Almost all of Java's thread scheduling is left up to the Java implementation and, to some extent, the application. Although it might have made sense (and would certainly have made many developers happier) if Java's developers had specified a scheduling algorithm, a single scheduling algorithm isn't necessarily suitable for all of the roles that Java can play. Instead, JavaSoft decided that it is better for you to write robust code that works whatever the scheduling algorithm, and let the implemenation tune the algorithm for whatever is best.

Therefore, the priority rules that we'll describe next are carefully worded in the Java language specification to be a general guideline for thread scheduling. You should be able to rely on this behavior overall (statistically), but it is not a good idea to write code that relies on very specific features of the scheduler to work properly. You should instead use the control and synchronization tools that we have described in this chapter to coordinate your threads.*

Every thread has a priority value. If, at any time, a thread of a higher priority than the current thread becomes runnable, it preempts the lower priority thread and begins executing. By default, threads at the same priority are scheduled round robin, which means once a thread starts to run, it continues until it does one of the following:

Sleeps
   Calls `Thread.sleep()` or `wait()`

Waits for lock
   Waits for a lock in order to run a synchronized method

Blocks on I/O
   Blocks, for example, in a `read()` or an `accept()` call

Explicitly yields control
   Calls `yield()`

Terminates
   Completes its target method or is terminated by a `stop()` call

This situation looks something like what's shown in Figure 8-4.

---

* *Java Threads*, by Scott Oaks and Henry Wong (O'Reilly), includes a detailed discussion of synchronization, scheduling, and other thread-related issues.

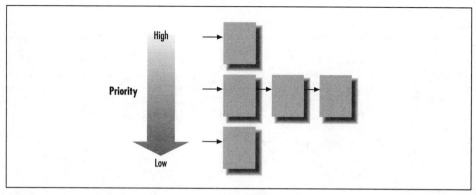

Figure 8–4: Priority preemptive, round-robin scheduling

Time Slicing

In addition to prioritization, many systems implement *time slicing* of threads.[*]

In a time-sliced system, thread processing is chopped up, so that each thread runs for a short period of time before the context is switched to the next thread, as shown in Figure 8-5.

Higher priority threads still preempt lower priority threads in this scheme. The addition of time slicing mixes up the processing among threads of the same priority; on a multiprocessor machine, threads may even be run simultaneously. This can introduce a difference in behavior for applications that don't use threads and synchronization properly.

Since Java doesn't guarantee time slicing, you shouldn't write code that relies on this type of scheduling; any software you write needs to function under the default round-robin scheduling. If you're wondering what your particular flavor of Java does, try the following experiment:

```
class Thready {
    public static void main( String args [] ) {
        new MyThread("Foo").start();
        new MyThread("Bar").start();
    }
}

class MyThread extends Thread {
    String message;
```

---

[*] As of Java Release 1.0, Sun's Java Interpreter for the Windows 95 and Windows NT platforms uses time slicing, as does the Netscape Navigator Java environment. Sun's Java 1.0 for the Solaris UNIX platforms doesn't.

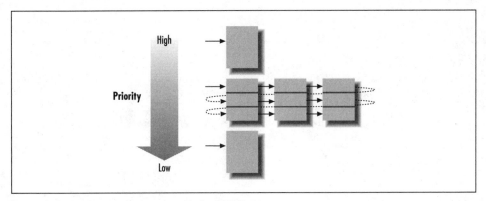

Figure 8–5: Priority preemptive, time-sliced scheduling

```
MyThread ( String message ) {
    this.message = message;
}

public void run() {
    while ( true )
        System.out.println( message );
}
}
```

The Thready class starts up two MyThread objects. Thready is a thread that goes into a hard loop (very bad form) and prints its message. Since we don't specify a priority for either thread, they both inherit the priority of their creator, so they have the same priority. When you run this example, you will see how your Java implementation does its scheduling. Under a round-robin scheme, only "Foo" should be printed; "Bar" never appears. In a time-slicing implementation, you should occasionally see the "Foo" and "Bar" messages alternate.

Priorities

Now let's change the priority of the second thread:

```
class Thready {
    public static void main( String args [] ) {
        new MyThread("Foo").start();
        Thread bar = new MyThread("Bar");
        bar.setPriority( Thread.NORM_PRIORITY + 1 );
        bar.start();
    }
}
```

As you might expect, this changes how our example behaves. Now you may see a few "Foo" messages, but "Bar" should quickly take over and not relinquish control, regardless of the scheduling policy.

Here we have used the setPriority() method of the Thread class to adjust our thread's priority. The Thread class defines three standard priority values, as shown in Table 8-1.

Table 8–1: Thread Priority Values

Value	Definition
MIN_PRIORITY	Minimum priority
NORM_PRIORITY	Normal priority
MAX_PRIORITY	Maximum priority

If you need to change the priority of a thread, you should use one of these values or a close relative value. But let me warn you against using MAX_PRIORITY or a close relative value; if you elevate many threads to this priority level, priority will quickly become meaningless. A slight increase in priority should be enough for most needs. For example, specifying NORM_PRIORITY + 1 in our example is enough to beat out our other thread.

Yielding

Whenever a thread sleeps, waits, or blocks on I/O, it gives up its time slot, and another thread is scheduled. So as long as you don't write methods that use hard loops, all threads should get their due. However, a Thread can also give up its time voluntarily with the yield() call. We can change our previous example to include a yield() on each iteration:

```
class MyThread extends Thread {
    ...

    public void run() {
        while ( true ) {
            System.out.println( message );
            yield();
        }
    }
}
```

Now you should see "Foo" and "Bar" messages alternating one for one. If you have threads that perform very intensive calculations, or otherwise eat a lot of CPU time, you might want to find an appropriate place for them to yield control occasionally. Alternatively, you might want to drop the priority of your intensive thread, so that more important processing can proceed around it.

Native Threads

I mentioned the possibility that different threads could run on different processors. This would be an ideal Java implementation. Unfortunately, most implementations don't even allow multiple threads to run in parallel with other processes running on the same machine. The most common implementations of threads today effectively simulate threading for an individual process like the Java virtual machine. One feature that you might want to look for in the future is called *native threads*. This means that Java is able to use the real (native) threading mechanism of the host environment, which should perform better and, ideally, could allow multi-processor operation.

Thread Groups

The ThreadGroup class allows us to deal with threads "wholesale": we can use it to arrange threads in groups and deal with the groups as a whole. A ThreadGroup can contain other ThreadGroups, in addition to Threads, so our arrangements can be hierarchical. Thread groups are particularly useful when we want to start a task that might create many threads of its own. By assigning the task a thread group, we can later identify and control all of the task's threads. ThreadGroups are also the subject of restrictions that can be imposed by the Java security manager. So we can restrict a thread's behavior according to its thread group. For example, we can forbid threads in a thread group from interacting with threads in other thread groups. This is one way that Web browsers can prevent threads started by Java applets from stopping important system threads.

When we create a Thread, it normally becomes part of the ThreadGroup that the currently running thread belongs to. To create a new ThreadGroup of our own, we can call the constructor:

```
ThreadGroup myTaskGroup = new ThreadGroup("My Task Group");
```

The ThreadGroup constructor takes a name, which a debugger can use to help you identify the group. (You can also assign names to the threads themselves.) Once we have a group, we can put threads in the group by supplying the ThreadGroup object as an argument to the Thread constructor:

```
Thread myTask = new Thread( myTaskGroup, taskPerformer );
```

Here, myTaskGroup is the thread group, and taskPerformer is the object that performs the task; of course, it must implement Runnable. Any additional threads that myTask creates will also belong to the myTaskGroup thread group.

Working with the ThreadGroup

Creating thread groups isn't interesting unless you can do things to them. The ThreadGroup class exists so that you can control threads in batches. It has methods that parallel the basic Thread control methods. For example, we can stop all of the threads in a group by calling the group's stop() method. ThreadGroups also have suspend() and resume() methods that operate on all of the threads they contain. You can also mark a ThreadGroup as a "daemon"; a daemon thread group is automatically removed when all of its children are gone. If a thread group isn't a daemon, you have to call destroy() to remove it when it is empty.

We can set the maximum priority for any thread in a ThreadGroup by calling setMaximumPriority(). Thereafter, no threads can be created with a priority higher than the maximum; threads that change their priority can't set their new priority higher than the maximum.

Finally, you can get a list of all of the threads in a group. The method activeCount() tells you how many threads are in the group; the method enumerate() gives you a list of them. The argument to enumerate() is an array of Threads, which enumerate() fills in with the group's threads. (Use activeCount() to make an array of the right size.) Both activeCount() and enumerate() operate recursively on all thread groups that the group contains.

9

In this chapter:
- *Strings*
- *Math Utilities*
- *Dates*
- *Vectors and Hashtables*
- *Properties*
- *The Security Manager*
- *Internationalization*

Basic Utility Classes

If you've been reading this book sequentially, you've read all about the core Java language constructs, including the object-oriented aspects of the language and the use of threads. Now it's time to shift gears and talk about the Java Application Programming Interface (API), the collection of classes that comes with every Java implementation. The Java API encompasses all the public methods and variables in the classes that make up the core Java packages. Table 9-1 lists the most important packages in the API and shows which chapters in this book discuss each of the packages.

Table 9–1: Packages of the Java API

Package	Contents	Chapter
java.lang	Basic language classes	4, 5, 6, 7, 8
java.lang.reflect	Reflection	7
java.io	Input and output	10
java.util	Utilities and collections classes	9
java.text	International text classes	9
java.net	Sockets and URLs	11, 12
java.applet	The applet API	13
java.awt	The Abstract Window Toolkit	13, 14, 15, 16, 17
java.awt.event	AWT event classes	13, 14
java.awt.image	AWT image-processing classes	17
java.beans	Java Beans API	18
java.rmi	RMI classes	11

As you can see in Table 9-1, we've already examined some of the classes in java.lang in earlier chapters on the core language constructs. Starting with this chapter, we'll throw open the Java toolbox and begin examining the rest of the classes in the API.

We'll begin our exploration with some of the fundamental language classes in java.lang, including strings and math utilities. Figure 9-1 shows the class hierarchy of the java.lang package.

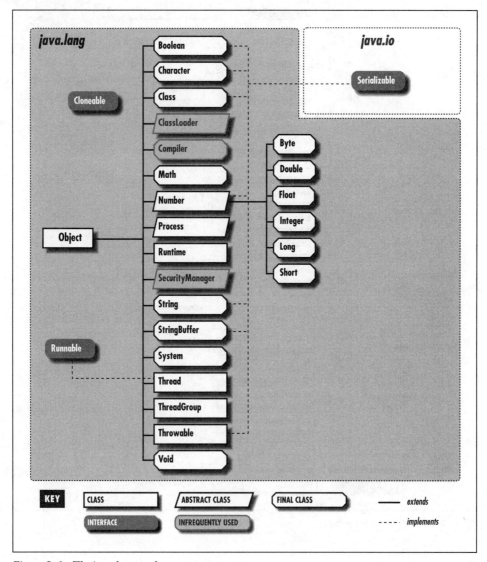

Figure 9–1: The java.lang package

We'll cover some of the classes in java.util, such as classes that support date and time values, random numbers, vectors, and hashtables. Figure 9-2 shows the class hierarchy of the java.util package.

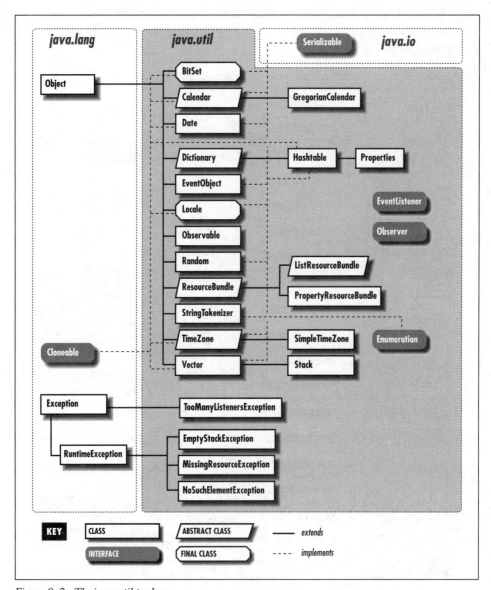

Figure 9–2: The java.util package

Strings

In this section, we take a closer look at the Java String class (or more specifically, java.lang.String). Because strings are used so extensively throughout Java (or any programming language, for that matter), the Java String class has quite a bit of functionality. We'll test drive most of the important features, but before you go off and write a complex parser or regular expression library, you should refer to a Java class reference manual for additional details.

Strings are immutable; once you create a String object, you can't change its value. Operations that would otherwise change the characters or the length of a string instead return a new String object that copies the needed parts of the original. Because of this feature, strings can be safely shared. Java makes an effort to consolidate identical strings and string literals in the same class into a shared string pool.

String Constructors

To create a string, assign a double-quoted constant to a String variable:

```
String quote = "To be or not to be";
```

Java automatically converts the string literal into a String object. If you're a C or C++ programmer, you may be wondering if quote is null-terminated. This question doesn't make any sense with Java strings. The String class actually uses a Java character array internally. It's private to the String class, so you can't get at the characters and change them. As always, arrays in Java are real objects that know their own length, so String objects in Java don't require special terminators (not even internally). If you need to know the length of a String, use the length() method:

```
int length = quote.length();
```

Strings can take advantage of the only overloaded operator in Java, the + operator, for string concatenation. The following code produces equivalent strings:

```
String name = "John " + "Smith";
String name = "John ".concat("Smith");
```

Literal strings can't span lines in Java source files, but we can concatenate lines to produce the same effect:

```
String poem =
    "'Twas brillig, and the slithy toves\n" +
    "   Did gyre and gimble in the wabe;\n" +
    "All mimsy were the borogoves,\n" +
    "   And the mome raths outgrabe.\n";
```

Of course, embedding lengthy text in source code should now be a thing of the past, given that we can retrieve a String from anywhere on the planet via a URL. In Chapter 12, we'll see how to do things like:

```
String poem =
    (String) new URL
        ("http://server/~dodgson/jabberwocky.txt").getContent();
```

In addition to making strings from literal expressions, we can construct a `String` from an array of characters:

```
char [] data = { 'L', 'e', 'm', 'm', 'i', 'n', 'g' };
String lemming = new String( data );
```

Or from an array of bytes:

```
byte [] data = { 97, 98, 99 };
String abc = new String(data, "8859_5");
```

The second argument to the `String` constructor for byte arrays is the name of an encoding scheme. It's used to convert the given bytes to the string's Unicode characters. Unless you know something about Unicode, you can use the form of the constructor that accepts a byte array only; the default encoding scheme will be used.

Strings from Things

We can get the string representation of most things with the static `String.valueOf()` method. Various overloaded versions of this method give us string values for all of the primitive types:

```
String one = String.valueOf( 1 );
String two = String.valueOf( 2.0f );
String notTrue = String.valueOf( false );
```

All objects in Java have a `toString()` method, inherited from the `Object` class. For class-type references, `String.valueOf()` invokes the object's `toString()` method to get its string representation. If the reference is `null`, the result is the literal string "null":

```
String date = String.valueOf( new Date() );
System.out.println( date );
// Sun Dec 19 05:45:34 CST 1999

date = null;
System.out.println( date );
// null
```

Things from Strings

Producing primitives like numbers from `String` objects is not a function of the `String` class. For that we need the primitive wrapper classes; they are described in the next section on the `Math` utilities. The wrapper classes provide `valueOf()` methods that produce an object from a `String`, as well as corresponding methods to retrieve the value in various primitive forms. Two examples are:

```
int i = Integer.valueOf("123").intValue();
double d = Double.valueOf("123.0").doubleValue();
```

In the above code, the `Integer.valueOf()` call yields an `Integer` object that represents the value 123. An `Integer` object can provide its primitive value in the form of an int with the `intValue()` method.

Although the techniques above may work for simple cases, they will not work internationally. Let's pretend for a moment that we are programming Java in the rolling hills of Tuscany. We would follow the local customs for representing numbers and write code like the following:

```
double d = Double.valueOf("1.234,56").doubleValue();          // oops!
```

Unfortunately, this code throws a `NumberFormatException`. The `java.text` package, which we'll discuss later, contains the tools we need to generate and parse strings in different countries and languages.

The `charAt()` method of the `String` class lets us get at the characters of a `String` in an array-like fashion:

```
String s = "Newton";

for ( int i = 0; i < s.length(); i++ )    System.out.println( s.charAt( i ) );
```

This code prints the characters of the string one at a time. Alternately, we can get the characters all at once with `toCharArray()`. Here's a way to save typing a bunch of single quotes:

```
char [] abcs = "abcdefghijklmnopqrstuvwxyz".toCharArray();
```

Comparisons

Just as in C, you can't compare strings for equality with "==" because as in C, strings are actually references. If your Java compiler doesn't happen to coalesce multiple instances of the same string literal to a single string pool item, even the expression `"foo" == "foo"` will return `false`. Comparisons with <, >, <=, and >= don't work at all, because Java can't convert references to integers.

Use the `equals()` method to compare strings:

```
String one = "Foo";

char [] c = { 'F', 'o', 'o' };
String two = new String ( c );

if ( one.equals( two ) )                 // yes
```

An alternate version, `equalsIgnoreCase()`, can be used to check the equivalence of strings in a case-insensitive way:

```
String one = "FOO";
String two = "foo";

if ( one.equalsIgnoreCase( two ) )        // yes
```

The compareTo() method compares the lexical value of the String against another String. It returns an integer that is less than, equal to, or greater than zero, just like the C routine strcmp():

```
String abc = "abc";
String def = "def";
String num = "123";

if ( abc.compareTo( def ) < 0 )           // yes
if ( abc.compareTo( abc ) == 0 )          // yes
if ( abc.compareTo( num ) > 0 )           // yes
```

On some systems, the behavior of lexical comparison is complex, and obscure alternative character sets exist. Java avoids this problem by comparing characters strictly by their position in the Unicode specification.

In Java 1.1, the java.text package provides a sophisticated set of classes for comparing strings, even in different languages. German, for example, has vowels with umlauts (those funny dots) over them and a weird looking beta character that represents a double *s*. How should we sort these? Although the rules for sorting these characters are precisely defined, you can't assume that the lexical comparison we used above works correctly for languages other than English. Fortunately, the Collator class takes care of these complex sorting problems.

In the following example, we use a Collator designed to compare German strings. (We'll talk about Locales in a later section.) You can obtain a default Collator by calling the Collator.getInstance() method that has no arguments. Once you have an appropriate Collator instance, you can use its compare() method, which returns values just like String's compareTo() method. The following code creates two strings for the German translations of "fun" and "later," using Unicode constants for these two special characters. It then compares them, using a Collator for the German locale; the result is that "later" (später) sorts before "fun" (spaß).

```
String fun = "Spa\u00df";
String later = "sp\u00e4ter";
Collator german = Collator.getInstance(Locale.GERMAN);
if (german.compare(later, fun) < 0)       // yes
```

Using collators is essential if you're working with languages other than English. In Spanish, for example, *ll* and *ch* are treated as separate characters and alphabetized separately. A collator handles cases like these automatically.

Searching

The String class provides several methods for finding substrings within a string. The startsWith() and endsWith() methods compare an argument String with the beginning and end of the String, respectively:

```
String url = "http://foo.bar.com/";
if ( url.startsWith("http:") )
    // do HTTP
```

Overloaded versions of indexOf() search for the first occurrence of a character or substring:

```
int i = abcs.indexOf( 'p' );         // i = 15
int i = abcs.indexOf( "def" );       // i = 3
```

Correspondingly, overloaded versions of lastIndexOf() search for the last occurrence of a character or substring.

Editing

A number of methods operate on the String and return a new String as a result. While this is useful, you should be aware that creating lots of strings in this manner can affect performance. If you need to modify a string often, you should use the StringBuffer class, as I'll discuss shortly.

trim() is a useful method that removes leading and trailing white space (i.e., carriage return, newline, and tab) from the String:

```
String abc = "    abc    ";
abc = abc.trim();                    // "abc"
```

In the above example, we have thrown away the original String (with excess white space), so it will be garbage collected.

The toUpperCase() and toLowerCase() methods return a new String of the appropriate case:

```
String foo = "FOO".toLowerCase();
String FOO = foo.toUpperCase();
```

substring() returns a specified range of characters. The starting index is inclusive; the ending is exclusive:

```
String abcs = "abcdefghijklmnopqrstuvwxyz";
String cde = abcs.substring(2, 5);   // "cde"
```

String Method Summary

Many people complain when they discover the Java `String` class is `final` (i.e., it can't be subclassed). There is a lot of functionality in `String`, and it would be nice to be able to modify its behavior directly. Unfortunately, there is also a serious need to optimize and rely on the performance of `String` objects. The Java compiler can optimize `final` classes by inlining methods when appropriate. The implementation of `final` classes can also be trusted by classes that work closely together, allowing for special cooperative optimizations. If you want to make a new string class that uses basic `String` functionality, use a `String` object in your class and provide methods that delegate method calls to the appropriate `String` methods.

Table 9-2 summarizes the methods provided by the `String` class.

Table 9–2: String Methods

Method	Functionality
`charAt()`	Gets at a particular character in the string
`compareTo()`	Compares the string with another string
`concat()`	Concatenates the string with another string
`copyValueOf()`	Returns a string equivalent to the specified character array
`endsWith()`	Checks if the string ends with a suffix
`equals()`	Compares the string with another string
`equalsIgnoreCase()`	Compares the string with another string and ignores case
`getBytes()`	Copies characters from the string into a byte array
`getChars()`	Copies characters from the string into a character array
`hashCode()`	Returns a hashcode for the string
`indexOf()`	Searches for the first occurrence of a character or substring in the string
`intern()`	Fetches a unique instance of the string from a global shared string pool
`lastIndexOf()`	Searches for the last occurrence of a character or substring in a string
`length()`	Returns the length of the string
`regionMatches()`	Checks whether a region of the string matches the specified region of another string
`replace()`	Replaces all occurrences of a character in the string with another character
`startsWith()`	Checks if the string starts with a prefix
`substring()`	Returns a substring from the string
`toCharArray()`	Returns the array of characters from the string
`toLowerCase()`	Converts the string to uppercase
`toString()`	Converts the string to a string

Table 9–2: String Methods (continued)

Method	Functionality
toUpperCase()	Converts the string to lowercase
trim()	Removes the leading and trailing white space from the string
valueOf()	Returns a string representation of a value

java.lang.StringBuffer

The java.lang.StringBuffer class is a growable buffer for characters. It's an efficient alternative to code like the following:

```
String ball = "Hello";
ball = ball + " there.";
ball = ball + " How are you?";
```

The above example repeatedly produces new String objects. This means that the character array must be copied over and over, which can adversely affect performance. A more economical alternative is to use a StringBuffer object and its append() method:

```
StringBuffer ball = new StringBuffer("Hello");
ball.append(" there.");
ball.append(" How are you?");
```

The StringBuffer class actually provides a number of overloaded append() methods, for appending various types of data to the buffer.

We can get a String from the StringBuffer with its toString() method:

```
String message = ball.toString();
```

StringBuffer also provides a number of overloaded insert() methods for inserting various types of data at a particular location in the string buffer.

The String and StringBuffer classes cooperate, so that even in this last operation, no copy has to be made. The string data is shared between the objects, unless and until we try to change it in the StringBuffer.

So, when should you use a StringBuffer instead of a String? If you need to keep adding characters to a string, use a StringBuffer; it's designed to efficiently handle such modifications. You'll still have to convert the StringBuffer to a String when you need to use any of the methods in the String class. You can print a StringBuffer directly using System.out.println() because println() calls the toString() for you.

Another thing you should know about StringBuffer methods is that they are thread-safe, just like all public methods in the Java API. This means that any time you modify a StringBuffer, you don't have to worry about another thread coming along and messing up the string while you are modifying it. If you recall our discussion of synchronization in Chapter 8, you know that being thread-safe means that only one thread at a time can change the state of a StringBuffer instance.

On a final note, I mentioned earlier that strings take advantage of the single overloaded operator in Java, +, for concatenation. You might be interested to know that the compiler uses a StringBuffer to implement concatenation. Consider the following expression:

```
String foo = "To " + "be " + "or";
```

This is equivalent to:

```
String foo = new
    StringBuffer().append("To ").append("be ").append("or").toString();
```

This kind of chaining of expressions is one of the things operator overloading hides in other languages.

java.util.StringTokenizer

A common programming task involves parsing a string of text into words or "tokens" that are separated by some set of delimiter characters. The java.util.StringTokenizer class is a utility that does just this. The following example reads words from the string text:

```
String text = "Now is the time for all good men (and women)...";
StringTokenizer st = new StringTokenizer( text );

while ( st.hasMoreTokens() )  {
    String word = st.nextToken();
    ...
}
```

First, we create a new StringTokenizer from the String. We invoke the hasMore-Tokens() and nextToken() methods to loop over the words of the text. By default, we use white space (i.e., carriage return, newline, and tab) as delimiters.

The StringTokenizer implements the java.util.Enumeration interface, which means that StringTokenizer also implements two more general methods for accessing elements: hasMoreElements() and nextElement(). These methods are defined by the Enumeration interface; they provide a standard way of returning a sequence of values, as we'll discuss a bit later. The advantage of nextToken() is that it returns a `String`, while `nextElement()` returns an `Object`. The `Enumeration` interface is implemented by many items that return sequences or collections of objects, as you'll see when we talk about hashtables and vectors later in the chapter. Those of you who have used the C `strtok()` function should appreciate how useful this object-oriented equivalent is.

You can also specify your own set of delimiter characters in the `StringTokenizer` constructor, using another `String` argument to the constructor. Any combination of the specified characters is treated as the equivalent of white space for tokenizing:

```
text = "http://foo.bar.com/";
tok = new StringTokenizer( text, "/:" );

if ( tok.countTokens() < 2 )            // bad URL

String protocol = tok.nextToken();   // protocol = "http"
String host = tok.nextToken();       // host = "foo.bar.com"
```

The example above parses a URL specification to get at the protocol and host components. The characters "/" and ":" are used as separators. The `countTokens()` method provides a fast way to see how many tokens will be returned by `nextToken()`, without actually creating the `String` objects.

An overloaded form of `nextToken()` accepts a string that defines a new delimiter set for that and subsequent reads. And finally, the `StringTokenizer` constructor accepts a flag that specifies that separator characters are to be returned individually as tokens themselves. By default, the token separators are not returned.

Math Utilities

Java supports integer and floating-point arithmetic directly. Higher-level math operations are supported through the `java.lang.Math` class. Java provides wrapper classes for all primitive data types, so you can treat them as objects if necessary. Java also provides the `java.util.Random` class for generating random numbers.

Java handles errors in integer arithmetic by throwing an `ArithmeticException`:

```
int zero = 0;

try {
    int i = 72 / zero;
}
catch ( ArithmeticException e ) {        // division by zero
}
```

To generate the error in the above example, we created the intermediate variable zero. The compiler is somewhat crafty and would have caught us if we had blatantly tried to perform a division by zero.

Floating-point arithmetic expressions, on the other hand, don't throw exceptions. Instead, they take on the special out-of-range values shown in Table 9-3.

Table 9–3: Special Floating-Point Values

Value	Mathematical Representation
POSITIVE_INFINITY	1.0/0.0
NEGATIVE_INFINITY	-1.0/0.0
NaN	0.0/0.0

The following example generates an infinite result:

```
double zero = 0.0;
double d = 1.0/zero;

if ( d == Double.POSITIVE_INFINITY )
    System.out.println( "Division by zero" );
```

The special value NaN indicates the result is "not a number." The value NaN has the special distinction of not being equal to itself (NaN != NaN). Use Float.isNaN() or Double.isNaN() to test for NaN.

java.lang.Math

The java.lang.Math class provides Java's math library. All its methods are static and used directly; you can't instantiate a Math object. We use this kind of degenerate class when we really want methods to approximate normal functions in C. While this tactic defies the principles of object-oriented design, it makes sense in this case, as it provides a means of grouping some related utility functions in a single class. Table 9-4 summarizes the methods in java.lang.Math.

Table 9–4: Methods in java.lang.Math

Method	Argument Type(s)	Functionality
Math.abs(a)	int, long, float, double	Absolute value
Math.acos(a)	double	Arc cosine
Math.asin(a)	double	Arc sine
Math.atan(a)	double	Arc tangent
Math.atan2(a,b)	double	Converts rectangular to polar coordinates
Math.ceil(a)	double	Smallest whole number greater than or equal to a

Table 9–4: Methods in java.lang.Math (continued)

Method	Argument Type(s)	Functionality
Math.cos(a)	double	Cosine
Math.exp(a)	double	Exponential number to the power of a
Math.floor(a)	double	Largest whole number less than or equal to a
Math.log(a)	double	Natural logarithm of a
Math.max(a, b)	int, long, float, double	Maximum
Math.min(a, b)	int, long, float, double	Minimum
Math.pow(a, b)	double	a to the power of b
Math.random()	None	Random number generator
Math.rint(a)	double	Converts double value to integral value in double format
Math.round(a)	float, double	Rounds
Math.sin(a)	double	Sine
Math.sqrt(a)	double	Square root
Math.tan(a)	double	Tangent

log(), pow(), and sqrt() can throw an ArithmeticException. abs(), max(), and min() are overloaded for all the scalar values, int, long, float, or double, and return the corresponding type. Versions of Math.round() accept either float or double and return int or long respectively. The rest of the methods operate on and return double values:

```
double irrational = Math.sqrt( 2.0 );
int bigger = Math.max( 3, 4 );
long one = Math.round( 1.125798 );
```

For convenience, Math also contains the static final double values E and PI:

```
double circumference = diameter * Math.PI;
```

java.math

If a long or a double just isn't big enough for you, the java.math package provides two classes, BigInteger and BigDecimal, that support arbitrary-precision numbers. These are full-featured classes with a bevy of methods for performing arbitrary-precision math. In the following example, we use BigDecimal to add two numbers:

```
try {
    BigDecimal twentyone = new BigDecimal("21");
    BigDecimal seven = new BigDecimal("7");
    BigDecimal sum = twentyone.add(seven);

    int twentyeight = sum.intValue();
```

```
    }
    catch (NumberFormatException nfe) { }
    catch (ArithmeticException ae) { }
```

Wrappers for Primitive Types

In languages like Smalltalk, numbers and other simple types are objects, which makes for an elegant language design, but has trade-offs in efficiency and complexity. By contrast, there is a schism in the Java world between class types (i.e., objects) and primitive types (i.e., numbers, characters, and boolean values). Java accepts this trade-off simply for efficiency reasons. When you're crunching numbers you want your computations to be lightweight; having to use objects for primitive types would seriously affect performance. For the times you want to treat values as objects, Java supplies a wrapper class for each of the primitive types, as shown in Table 9-5.

Table 9–5: Primitive Type Wrappers

Primitive	Wrapper
void	java.lang.Void
boolean	java.lang.Boolean
char	java.lang.Character
byte	java.lang.Byte
short	java.lang.Short
int	java.lang.Integer
long	java.lang.Long
float	java.lang.Float
double	java.lang.Double

An instance of a wrapper class encapsulates a single value of its corresponding type. It's an immutable object that serves as a container to hold the value and let us retrieve it later. You can construct a wrapper object from a primitive value or from a String representation of the value. The following code is equivalent:

```
    Float pi = new Float( 3.14 );
    Float pi = new Float( "3.14" );
```

Wrapper classes throw a NumberFormatException when there is an error in parsing from a string:

```
    try {
        Double bogus = new Double( "huh?" );
    }
    catch ( NumberFormatException e ) {      // bad number
    }
```

You should arrange to catch this exception if you want to deal with it. Otherwise, since it's a subclass of RuntimeException, it will propagate up the call stack and eventually cause a run-time error if not caught.

Sometimes you'll use the wrapper classes simply to parse the `String` representation of a number:

```
String sheep = getParameter("sheep");
int n = new Integer( sheep ).intValue();
```

Here we are retrieving the value of the `sheep` parameter. This value is returned as a `String`, so we need to convert it to a numeric value before we can use it. Every wrapper class provides methods to get primitive values out of the wrapper; we are using `intValue()` to retrieve an `int` out of `Integer`. Since parsing a `String` representation of a number is such a common thing to do, the `Integer` and `Long` classes also provide the `static` methods `Integer.parseInt()` and `Long.parseLong()` that read a `String` and return the appropriate type. So the second line above is equivalent to:

```
int n = Integer.parseInt( sheep );
```

All wrappers provide access to their values in various forms. You can retrieve scalar values with the methods `doubleValue()`, `floatValue()`, `longValue()`, and `intValue()`:

```
Double size = new Double ( 32.76 );

double d = size.doubleValue();
float f = size.floatValue();
long l = size.longValue();
int i = size.intValue();
```

The code above is equivalent to the primitive `double` value cast to the various types. For convenience, you can cast between the wrapper classes like `Double` class and the primitive data types.

Another common use of wrappers occurs when we have to treat a primitive value as an object in order to place it in a list or other structure that operates on objects. As you'll see shortly, a `Vector` is an extensible array of `Objects`. We can use wrappers to hold numbers in a `Vector`, along with other objects:

```
Vector myNumbers = new Vector();

Integer thirtyThree = new Integer( 33 );
myNumbers.addElement( thirtyThree );
```

Here we have created an `Integer` wrapper so that we can insert the number into the `Vector` using `addElement()`. Later, when we are taking elements back out of the `Vector`, we can get the number back out of the `Integer` as follows:

```
Integer theNumber = (Integer)myNumbers.firstElement();
int n = theNumber.intValue();                // n = 33
```

Random Numbers

You can use the `java.util.Random` class to generate random values. It's a pseudo-random number generator that can be initialized with a 48-bit seed.* The default constructor uses the current time as a seed, but if you want a repeatable sequence, specify your own seed with:

```
long seed = mySeed;
Random rnums = new Random( seed );
```

This code creates a random-number generator. Once you have a generator, you can ask for random values of various types using the methods listed in Table 9-6.

Table 9–6: Random Number Methods

Method	Range
nextInt()	-2147483648 to 2147483647
nextLong()	-9223372036854775808 to 9223372036854775807
nextFloat()	-1.0 to 1.0
nextDouble()	-1.0 to 1.0

By default, the values are uniformly distributed. You can use the `nextGaussian()` method to create a Gaussian distribution of `double` values, with a mean of 0.0 and a standard deviation of 1.0.

The `static` method `Math.random()` retrieves a random `double` value. This method initializes a `private` random-number generator in the `Math` class, using the default `Random` constructor. So every call to `Math.random()` corresponds to a call to `nextDouble()` on that random number generator.

Dates

Working with dates and times without the proper tools can be a chore.† Java 1.1 gives you three classes that do all the hard work for you. The `java.util.Date` class encapsulates a point in time. The `java.util.GregorianCalendar` class, which descends from the abstract `java.util.Calendar`, translates between a point in time and calendar fields like month, day, and year. Finally, the

---

* The generator uses a linear congruential formula. See *The Art of Computer Programming*, Volume 2, "Semi-numerical Algorithms," by Donald Knuth (Addison-Wesley).

† For a wealth of information about time and world time-keeping conventions, see the web site *http://tycho.usno.navy.mil/*, the U.S. Navy Directorate of Time. For a fascinating history of the Gregorian and Julian calendars, try *http://www.magnet.ch/serendipity/hermetic/cal_stud/cal_art.htm*.

`java.text.DateFormat` class knows how to generate and parse string representations of dates and times. In Java 1.0.2, the `Date` class performed all three functions. In Java 1.1, most of its methods have been deprecated, so that the only purpose of the `Date` class is to represent a point in time.

The separation of the `Date` class and the `GregorianCalendar` class is analogous to having a class representing temperature and a class that translates that temperature to Celsius units. Conceivably, we could define other subclasses of `Calendar`, say `JulianCalendar` or `LunarCalendar`.

The default `GregorianCalendar` constructor creates an object that represents the current time, as determined by the system clock:

```
GregorianCalendar now = new GregorianCalendar();
```

Other constructors accept values to initialize the calendar. In the first statement below, we construct an object representing August 9, 1996; the second statement specifies both a date and a time, yielding an object that represents 9:01 a.m., April 8, 1997.

```
GregorianCalendar daphne =
    new GregorianCalendar(1996, Calendar.AUGUST, 9);
GregorianCalendar sometime =
    new GregorianCalendar(1997, Calendar.APRIL, 8, 9, 1); // 9:01 AM
```

We can also create a `GregorianCalendar` by setting specific fields using the `set()` method. The `Calendar` class contains a torrent of constants representing both calendar fields and field values. The first argument to the `set()` method is a field constant; the second argument is the new value for the field.

```
GregorianCalendar kristen = new GregorianCalendar();
kristen.set(Calendar.YEAR, 1972);
kristen.set(Calendar.MONTH, Calendar.MAY);
kristen.set(Calendar.DATE, 20);
```

A `GregorianCalendar` is created in the default time zone. Setting the time zone of the calendar is as easy as obtaining the desired `TimeZone` and giving it to the `GregorianCalendar`:

```
GregorianCalendar smokey = new GregorianCalendar();
smokey.setTimeZone(TimeZone.getTimeZone("MST"));
```

To create a string representing a point in time, use the `DateFormat` class. Although `DateFormat` itself is abstract, it has several factory methods that return useful `DateFormat` subclass instances. To get a default `DateFormat`, simply call `getInstance()`:

```
DateFormat plain = DateFormat.getInstance();
String now = plain.format(new Date());     // 4/9/97 6:06 AM
```

Those of you who don't live on the West coast of North America will notice that the example above produces a result that is not quite right. DateFormat instances stubbornly insist on using Pacific Standard Time, so you have to tell them what time zone you're in:

```
DateFormat plain = DateFormat.getInstance();
plain.setTimeZone(TimeZone.getDefault());
String now = plain.format(new Date());    // 4/9/97 9:06 AM
```

You can generate a date string or a time string, or both, using the getDateInstance(), getTimeInstance(), and getDateTimeInstance() factory methods. The argument to these methods describes what level of detail you'd like to see. DateFormat defines four constants representing detail levels: they are SHORT, MEDIUM, LONG, and FULL. There is also a DEFAULT, which is the same as MEDIUM. The code below creates three DateFormat instances: one to format a date, one to format a time, and one to format a date and time together. Note that getDateTimeInstance() requires two arguments: the first specifies how to format the date, the second says how to format the time:

```
DateFormat df = DateFormat.getDateInstance(DateFormat.DEFAULT);     // 09-Apr-97
DateFormat tf = DateFormat.getTimeInstance(DateFormat.DEFAULT);     // 9:18:27 AM
DateFormat dtf = // Wednesday, April 09, 1997 9:18:27 o'clock AM EDT
    DateFormat.getDateTimeInstance(DateFormat.FULL, DateFormat.FULL);
```

Formatting dates and times for other countries is just as easy. Overloaded factory methods accept a Locale argument:

```
DateFormat df =      // 9 avr. 97
    DateFormat.getDateInstance(DateFormat.DEFAULT, Locale.FRANCE);
DateFormat tf =      // 9:27:49
    DateFormat.getTimeInstance(DateFormat.DEFAULT, Locale.GERMANY);
DateFormat dtf =     // mercoledi 9 aprile 1997 9.27.49 GMT-04:00
    DateFormat.getDateTimeInstance(DateFormat.FULL, DateFormat.FULL, Locale.ITALY);
```

To parse a string representing a date, we use the parse() method of the DateFormat class. The result is a Date object. The parsing algorithms are finicky, so it's safest to parse dates and times that are in the same format that is produced by the DateFormat. The parse() method throws a ParseException if it doesn't understand the string you give it. All the calls to parse() below succeed except the last; we don't supply a time zone, but the format for the time is LONG. Other exceptions are occasionally thrown from the parse() method. To cover all the bases, catch NullPointerExceptions and StringIndexOutOfBoundsExceptions also.

```
try {
  Date d;
  DateFormat df;
```

```
    df = DateFormat.getDateTimeInstance(DateFormat.FULL, DateFormat.FULL);
    d = df.parse("Wednesday, April 09, 1997 2:22:22 o'clock PM EST");

    df = DateFormat.getDateTimeInstance(DateFormat.MEDIUM, DateFormat.MEDIUM);
    d = df.parse("09-Apr-97 2:22:22 PM");

    df = DateFormat.getDateTimeInstance(DateFormat.LONG, DateFormat.LONG);
    d = df.parse("April 09, 1997 2:22:22 PM EST");
    d = df.parse("09-Apr-97 2:22:22 PM");//ParseException; detail level mismatch
  }
  catch (Exception e) {}
```

The Year 2000 Problem

There's been a lot of talk lately about the *millenium bug*. This refers to the expected failure of some software in the year 2000, when programs that use two digits to represent years "roll over" and interpret "00" as 1900 instead of 2000. Java is mostly safe from this error. The Date class has no specific field for year and is thus immune to this problem. Internally, Java keeps track of time in milliseconds since some base date, which is fundamentally safe; the field used to hold the current count won't overflow for a very long time. The only time you could run into this error in Java is when you use a DateFormat to parse a date string with a two-digit year. Two-digit years are automatically prefixed with 19 for the current century. My advice is to use a four-digit year when you expect to parse a date string.

Vectors and Hashtables

Vectors and hashtables are *collection classes*. Each stores a group of objects according to a particular retrieval scheme. Aside from that, they are not particularly closely related things. A *hashtable* is a dictionary; it stores and retrieves objects by a key value. A *vector*, on the other hand, holds an ordered collection of elements. It's essentially a dynamic array. Both of these, however, have more subtle characteristics in common. First, they are two of the most useful aspects of the core Java distribution. Second, they both take full advantage of Java's dynamic nature at the expense of some of its more static type safety.

If you work with dictionaries or associative arrays in other languages, you should understand how useful these classes are. If you are someone who has worked in C or another static language, you should find collections to be truly magical. They are part of what makes Java powerful and dynamic. Being able to work with lists of objects and make associations between them is an abstraction from the details of the types. It lets you think about the problems at a higher level and saves you from having to reproduce common structures every time you need them.

java.util.Vector

A Vector is a dynamic array; it can grow to accommodate new items. You can also insert and remove elements at arbitrary positions within it. As with other mutable objects in Java, Vector is thread-safe. The Vector class works directly with the type Object, so we can use Vectors with instances of any class.* We can even put different kinds of Objects in a Vector together; the Vector doesn't know the difference.

As you might guess, this is where things get tricky. To do anything useful with an Object after we take it back out of a Vector, we have to cast it back (narrow) it to its original type. This can be done with safety in Java because the cast is checked at run-time. Java throws a ClassCastException if we try to cast an object to the wrong type. However, this need for casting means that your code must remember types or methodically test them with instanceof. That is the price we pay for having a completely dynamic collection class that operates on all types.

You might wonder if you can subclass Vector to produce a class that looks like a Vector, but that works on just one type of element in a type-safe way. Unfortunately, the answer is no. We could override Vector's methods to make a Vector that rejects the wrong type of element at run-time, but this does not provide any new compile-time, static type safety. In C++, templates provide a safe mechanism for parameterizing types by restricting the types of objects used at compile-time. The keyword generic is a reserved word in Java. This means that it's possible that future versions might support C++-style templates, using generic to allow statically checked parameterized types.

We can construct a Vector with default characteristics and add elements to it using addElement() and insertElementAt():

```
Vector things = new Vector();

String one = "one";
String two = "two";
String three = "three";

things.addElement( one );
things.addElement( three );
things.insertElementAt( two, 1 );
```

things now contains three String objects in the order "one," "two," and "three." We can retrieve objects by their position with elementAt(), firstElement(), and lastElement():

---

* In C++, where classes don't derive from a single Object class that supplies a base type and common methods, the elements of a collection would usually be derived from some common collectable class. This forces the use of multiple inheritance and brings its associated problems.

```
String s1 = (String)things.firstElement();      // "one"
String s3 = (String)things.lastElement();       // "three"
String s2 = (String)things.elementAt(1);        // "two"
```

We have to cast each `Object` back to a `String` in order to assign it a `String` reference. `ClassCastException` is a type of `RuntimeException`, so we can neglect to guard for the exception if we are feeling confident about the type we are retrieving. Often, as in this example, you'll just have one type of object in the `Vector`. If we were unsure about the types of objects we were retrieving, we would want to be prepared to catch the `ClassCastException` or test the type explicitly with the `instanceof` operator.

We can search for an item in a `Vector` with the `indexOf()` method:

```
int i = things.indexOf( three );                // i = 2
```

`indexOf()` returns a value of `-1` if the object is not found. As a convenience, we can also use `contains()` simply to test for the presence of the object.

Finally, `removeElement()` removes a specified `Object` from the `Vector`:

```
things.removeElement( two );
```

The element formerly at position three now becomes the second element.

The `size()` method reports the number of objects currently in the `Vector`. You might think of using this to loop through all elements of a `Vector`, using `elementAt()` to get at each element. This works just fine, but there is a more general way to operate on a complete set of elements like those in a `Vector`.

java.util.Enumeration

The `java.util.Enumeration` interface can be used by any sort of set to provide serial access to its elements. An object that implements the `Enumeration` interface presents two methods: `nextElement()` and `hasMoreElements()`. `nextElement()` returns an `Object` type, so it can be used with any kind of collection. As with taking objects from a `Vector`, you need to know or determine what the objects are and cast them to the appropriate types before using them.

`Enumeration` is useful because it is a general interface for any kind of object that wants to provide "one shot" sequential access to its elements. All you have to do is provide a `hasMoreElements()` test and a `nextElement()` iterator and declare that your class implements `java.util.Enumeration`. Another advantage of an `Enumeration` is that you don't have to provide all values up front; you can provide each value as it's requested with `nextElement()`.

An Enumeration does not guarantee the order in which elements are returned, however, so if order is important you don't want to use an Enumeration. You can iterate through the elements in an Enumeration only once; there is no way to reset it to the beginning or move backwards through the elements.

A Vector returns an Enumeration of its contents when we call the elements() method:

```
Enumeration e = myVector.elements();

while ( e.hasMoreElements() ) {
    String s = (String)e.nextElement();
    System.out.println( s ):
}
```

The above code loops three times and calls nextElement() to fetch our strings. The actual type of object returned by elements() is a VectorEnumeration, but we don't have to worry about that. We can always refer to an Enumeration simply by its interface.

Note that Vector does not implement the Enumeration interface. If it did, that would put a serious limitation on Vector because we could cycle through the elements in it only once. That's clearly not the purpose of a Vector, which is why Vector instead provides a method that returns an Enumeration.

java.util.Hashtable

As I said earlier, a hashtable is a dictionary, similar to an associative array. A hashtable stores and retrieves elements with key values; they are very useful for things like caches and minimalist databases. When you store a value in a hashtable, you associate a key with that value. When you need to look up the value, the hashtable retrieves it efficiently using the key. The name hashtable itself refers to how the indexing and storage of elements is performed, as we'll discuss shortly. First I want to talk about how to use a hashtable.

The java.util.Hashtable class implements a hashtable that, like Vector, operates on the type Object. A Hashtable stores an element of type Object and associates it with a key, also of type Object. In this way, we can index arbitrary types of elements using arbitrary types as keys. As with Vector, casting is generally required to narrow objects back to their original type after pulling them out of a hashtable.

A Hashtable is quite easy to use. We can use the put() method to store items:

```
Hashtable dates = new Hashtable();

dates.put( "christmas", new GregorianCalendar( 1997, Calendar.DECEMBER, 25 ) );
dates.put( "independence", new GregorianCalendar( 1997, Calendar.JULY, 4 ) );
dates.put( "groundhog", new GregorianCalendar( 1997, Calendar.FEBRUARY, 2 ) );
```

First we create a new `Hashtable`. Then we add three `GregorianCalendar` objects to the hashtable, using `String` objects as keys. The key is the first argument to `put()`; the value is the second. Only one value can be stored per key. If we try to store a second object under a key that already exists in the `Hashtable`, the old element is booted out and replaced by the new one. The return value of the `put()` method is normally `null`, but if the call to `put()` results in replacing an element, the method instead returns the old stored `Object`.

We can now use the `get()` method to retrieve each of the above dates by name, using the `String` key by which it was indexed:

```
GregorianCalendar g = (GregorianCalendar)dates.get( "christmas" );
```

The `get()` method returns a `null` value if no element exists for the given key. The cast is required to narrow the returned object back to type `GregorianCalendar`. I hope you can see the advantage of using a `Hashtable` over a regular array. Each value is indexed by a key instead of a simple number, so unlike a simple array, we don't have to remember where each `GregorianCalendar` is stored.

Once we've put a value in a `Hashtable`, we can take it back out with the `remove()` method, again using the key to access the value:

```
dates.remove("christmas");
```

We can test for the existence of a key with `containsKey()`:

```
if ( dates.containsKey( "groundhog" ) ) {    // yes
```

Just like with a `Vector`, we're dealing with a set of items. Actually, we're dealing with two sets: keys and values. The `Hashtable` class has two methods, `keys()` and `elements()`, for getting at these sets. The `keys()` method returns an `Enumeration` of the keys for all of the elements in the `Hashtable`. We can use this `Enumeration` to loop through all of the keys:

```
for (Enumeration e = dates.keys(); e.hasMoreElements(); ) {
    String key = (String)e.nextElement();
    ...
}
```

Similarly, `elements()` provides an `Enumeration` of the elements themselves.

Hashcodes and key values

If you've used a hashtable before, you've probably guessed that there's more going on behind the scenes than we've let on. An element in a hashtable is not associated with a key strictly by the key's identity, but rather by the key's contents. This allows keys that are equivalent to access the same object. By "equivalent," we mean those objects that compare true with equals(). So, if you store an object in a Hashtable using another object as a key, you can use any object that equals() tells you is equivalent to retrieve the stored object.

It's easy to see why equivalence is important if you remember our discussion of strings. It is easy to create two String objects that have the same text in them but which come from different sources in Java. In this case, the == operator will tell you that the objects are different, but the equals() method of the String class will tell you that they are equivalent. Because they are equivalent, if we store an object in a Hashtable using one of the String objects as a key, we can retrieve it using the other.

Okay, since Hashtables have a notion of equivalent keys, what does the hashcode do? The hashcode is like a fingerprint of the object's data content. The Hashtable uses the hashcode to store the objects so that they can be retrieved efficiently. The hashcode is nothing more than a number (an integer) that is a function of the data. The number always turns out the same for identical data, but the hashing function is intentionally designed to generate as random a number as possible for different combinations of data. That is, a very small change in the data should produce a big difference in the number. It is unlikely that two similar data sets will produce the same hashcode.

A Hashtable really just keeps a number of lists of objects, but it puts objects into the lists based on their hashcode. So when it wants to find the object again, it can look at the hashcode and know immediately how to get to the appropriate list. The Hashtable still might end up with a number of objects to examine, but the list should be short. For each object it finds, it does the following comparison to see if the key matches:

```
if ((keyHashcode == storedKeyHashcode) && key.equals(storedKey))
    return object;
```

There is no prescribed way to generate hashcodes. The only requirement is that they be somewhat randomly distributed and reproducible (based on the data). This means that two objects that are not the same could end up with the same hashcode by accident. This is unlikely (there are 2^{32} possible integer values), but it doesn't cause a problem because the Hashtable ultimately checks the actual keys, as well as the hashcodes, to see if they are equal. Therefore, even if two objects have the same hashcode, they can still co-exist in the hashtable.

Here's an interesting example. In Java 1.1, the hashCode() method for the String class does not take into account all characters in the string. Instead, it samples a representative few, in order to save time. Knowing how it works, we can construct two Strings that are obviously not equivalent but nonetheless have the same hashcode. We can show that they can still serve as unique keys in a Hashtable:

```
String
    s1 = "xxxxxxxxxxxxxxxx",
    s2 = "x1x2x3x4x5x6x7x8";
System.out.println( s1.hashCode());
System.out.println( s2.hashCode());   // Identical in 1.1

Hashtable h = new Hashtable();
h.put(s1, new Integer(1));
h.put(s2, new Integer(2));
System.out.println( h.get(s1) );      // gets integer 1
System.out.println( h.get(s2) );      // gets integer 2
```

Hashcodes are computed by an object's hashCode() method, which is inherited from the Object class if it isn't overridden. The default hashCode() method simply assigns each object instance a unique number to be used as a hashcode. If a class does not override this method, each instance of the class will have a unique hashcode. This goes along well with the default implementation of equals() in Object, which only compares objects for identity using ==. You're probably used to overriding equals() in any classes for which equivalence is meaningful. Likewise, if you want equivalent objects to serve as equivalent keys, you need to override the hashCode() method as well to return identical hashcode values. To do this, you need to create some suitably complex and arbitrary function of the contents of your object. The only criterion for the function is that it should be almost certain to return different values for objects with different data, but the same value for objects with identical data.

java.util.Dictionary

java.util.Dictionary is the abstract superclass of Hashtable. It lays out the basic get(), put(), and remove() functionality for dictionary-style collections. You could derive other types of dictionaries from this class. For example, you could implement a dictionary with a different storage format, such as a binary tree.

Properties

The java.util.Properties class is a specialized hashtable for strings. Java uses the Properties object to replace the environment variables used in other programming environments. You can use a Properties table to hold arbitrary configuration information for an application in an easily accessible format. The Properties object can also load and store information using streams (see Chapter 10 for information on streams).

Any string values can be stored as key/value pairs in a Properties table. However, the convention is to use a dot-separated naming hierarchy to group property names into logical structures, as is done with X resources on UNIX systems.[*] The java.lang.System class provides system-environment information in this way, through a system Properties table I'll describe shortly.

Create an empty Properties table and add String key/value pairs just as with any Hashtable:

```
Properties props = new Properties();
props.put("myApp.xsize", "52");
props.put("myApp.ysize", "79");
```

Thereafter, you can retrieve values with the getProperty() method:

```
String xsize = props.getProperty( "myApp.xsize" );
```

If the named property doesn't exist, getProperty() returns null. You can get an Enumeration of the property names with the propertyNames() method:

```
for ( Enumeration e = props.propertyNames(); e.hasMoreElements; ) {
    String name = e.nextElement();
    ...
}
```

Default Values

When you create a Properties table, you can specify a second table for default property values:

```
Properties defaults;
...
Properties props = new Properties( defaults );
```

Now when you call getProperty(), the method searches the default table if it doesn't find the named property in the current table. An alternative version of getProperty() also accepts a default value; this value is returned if the property is not found in the current list or in the default list:

```
String xsize = props.getProperty( "myApp.xsize", "50" );
```

Loading and Storing

You can save a Properties table to an OutputStream using the save() method. The property information is output in flat ASCII format. Continuing with the above example, output the property information to System.out as follows:

---

* Unfortunately, this is just a naming convention right now, so you can't access logical groups of properties as you can with X resources.

```
props.save( System.out, "Application Parameters" );
```

`System.out` is a standard output stream similar to C's `stdout`. We could also save the information to a file by using a `FileOutputStream` as the first argument to `save()`. The second argument to `save()` is a `String` that is used as a header for the data. The above code outputs something like the following to `System.out`:

```
#Application Parameters
#Mon Feb 12 09:24:23 CST 1997
myApp.ysize=79
myApp.xsize=52
```

The `load()` method reads the previously saved contents of a `Properties` object from an `InputStream`:

```
FileInputStream fin;
...
Properties props = new Properties()
props.load( fin );
```

The `list()` method is useful for debugging. It prints the contents to an `Output-Stream` in a format that is more human-readable but not retrievable by `load()` (it truncates long lines with a " ... ").

System Properties

The `java.lang.System` class provides access to basic system environment information through the `static System.getProperty()` method. This method returns a `Properties` table that contains system properties. System properties take the place of environment variables in other programming environments. Table 9-7 summarizes system properties that are guaranteed to be defined in any Java environment.

Table 9–7: System Properties

System Property	Meaning
java.vendor	Vendor-specific string
java.vendor.url	URL of vendor
java.version	Java version
java.home	Java installation directory
java.class.version	Java class version
java.class.path	The class path
os.name	Operating-system name
os.arch	Operating-system architecture
os.version	Operating-system version
file.separator	File separator (such as "/" or "\")
path.separator	Path separator (such as ":" or ";")
line.separator	Line separator (such as "\n" or "\r\n")

Table 9–7: System Properties (continued)

System Property	Meaning
user.name	User account name
user.home	User's home directory
user.dir	Current working directory

Applets are, by current Web browser conventions, prevented from reading the following properties: `java.home`, `java.class.path`, `user.name`, `user.home`, and `user.dir`. As you'll see in the next section, these restrictions are implemented by a `SecurityManager` object.

Your application can set system properties with the static method `System.setProperty()`. You can also set system properties when you run the Java interpreter, using the –D option:

```
%java -Dfoo=bar -Dcat=Boojum MyApp
```

Since it is common to use system properties to provide parameters like numbers and colors, Java provides some convenience routines for retrieving property values and parsing them into their appropriate types. The classes `Boolean`, `Integer`, `Long`, and `Color` each come with a "get" method that looks up and parses a system property. For example, `Integer.getInteger("foo")` looks for a system property called foo and returns it as an `Integer`. `Color.getColor("foo")` would parse the property as an RGB value and return a `Color` object.

Observers and Observables

The `java.util.Observer` interface and `java.util.Observable` class are relatively small utilities, but they provide a peek at a fundamental design pattern. The concept of observers and observables is part of the MVC (Model View Controller) framework. It is an abstraction that lets a number of client objects (the observers) be notified whenever a certain object or resource (the observable) changes in some way. We will see this pattern used extensively in Java's event mechanism and in the AWT image producer model.

The basic idea behind observers and observables is that the `Observable` object has a method that an `Observer` calls to register its interest. When a change happens, the `Observable` sends a notification by calling a method in each of the `Observers`. The observers implement the `Observer` interface, which specifies the method (`update()`) to invoke.

In the following example, we create a `MessageBoard` object that holds a `String` message. `MessageBoard` extends `Observable`, from which it inherits the mechanism for registering and notifying observers; all the `MessageBoard` has to do is call `notifyObservers()` with the new message as an argument whenever the message changes. To observe the `MessageBoard`, we have `Student` objects that implement the `Observer` interface so that they can be notified when the message changes.

```
import java.util.*;

public class MessageBoard extends Observable {
    private String message;

    public String getMessage() {
        return message;
    }
    public void changeMessage( String message ) {
        this.message = message;
        setChanged();
        notifyObservers( message );
    }
    public static void main( String [] args ) {
        MessageBoard board = new MessageBoard();
        Student bob = new Student();
        Student joe = new Student();
        board.addObserver( bob );
        board.addObserver( joe );
        board.changeMessage("More Homework!");
    }
}

class Student implements Observer {
    public void update(Observable o, Object arg) {
        System.out.println( "Message board changed: " + arg );
    }
}
```

Our `MessageBoard` object extends `Observable`, which provides a method called `addObserver()`. Each of our `Student` objects registers itself using this method and receives updates via its `update()` method. When a new message string is set, using the `MessageBoard`'s `changeMessage()` method, the `Observable` calls the `setChanged()` and `notifyObservers()` methods to notify the observers. `notifyObservers()` can take as an argument an `Object` to pass along as an indication of the change. This object, in this case, the `String` containing the new message, is passed to the observer's `update()` method.

The `main()` method of `MessageBoard` creates a `MessageBoard` and registers two `Student` objects with it. Then it changes the message. When you run the code, you should see each `Student` object print the message as it is notified.

You can imagine how you could implement the observer/observable relationship yourself using a Vector to hold the list of observers. These classes are not so much of value in and of themselves, as for what they represent. In Chapter 13 and beyond, we'll see that the AWT event model extends this design patttern to use strongly typed notification objects and observers; these are events and event listeners.

The Security Manager

A Java application's access to system resources, such as the display, the filesystem, threads, external processes, and the network, can be controlled at a single point with a *security manager*. The class that implements this functionality in the Java API is the java.lang.SecurityManager class.

An instance of the SecurityManager class can be installed once, and only once, in the life of the Java run-time environment. Thereafter, every access to a fundamental system resource is filtered through specific methods of the SecurityManager object by the core Java packages. By installing a specialized SecurityManager, we can implement arbitrarily complex (or simple) security policies for allowing access to individual resources.

When the Java run-time system starts executing, it's in a wide-open state until a SecurityManager is installed. The "null" security manager grants all requests, so the Java virtual environment can perform any activity with the same level of access as other programs running under the user's authority. If the application that is running needs to ensure a secure environment, it can install a SecurityManager with the static System.setSecurityManager() method. For example, a Java-enabled Web browser like Netscape Navigator installs a SecurityManager before it runs any Java applets.

java.lang.SecurityManager must be subclassed to be used. This class does not actually contain any abstract methods; it's abstract as an indication that its default implementation is not very useful. By default, each security method in SecurityManager is implemented to provide the strictest level of security. In other words, the default SecurityManager simply rejects all requests.

The following example, MyApp, installs a trivial subclass of SecurityManager as one of its first activities:

```
class FascistSecurityManager extends SecurityManager { }

public class MyApp {
    public static void main( Strings [] args ) {
        System.setSecurityManager( new FascistSecurityManager() );
        // No access to files, network, windows, etc.
        ...
```

```
        }
    }
```

In the above scenario, MyApp does little aside from reading from System.in and writing to System.out. Any attempt to read or write files, access the network, or even open a window, results in a SecurityException being thrown.

After this draconian SecurityManager is installed, it's impossible to change the SecurityManager in any way. The security of this feature is not dependent on the SecurityManager; you can't replace or modify the SecurityManager under any circumstances. The upshot of this is that you have to install one that handles all your needs up front.

To do something more useful, we can override the methods that are consulted for access to various kinds of resources. Table 9-8 lists some of the more important access methods. You should not normally have to call these methods yourself, although you could. They are called by the core Java classes before granting particular types of access.

Table 9–8: SecurityManager Methods

Method	Can I ...
checkAccess(Thread g)	Access this thread?
checkExit(int status)	Execute a System.exit()?
checkExec(String cmd)	exec() this process?
checkRead(String file)	Read a file?
checkWrite(String file)	Write a file?
checkDelete(String file)	Delete a file?
checkConnect(String host, int port)	Connect a socket to a host?
checkListen(int port)	Create a server socket?
checkAccept(String host, int port)	Accept this connection?
checkPropertyAccess(String key)	Access this system property?
checkTopLevelWindow(Object window)	Create this new top-level window?

All these methods, with the exception of checkTopLevelWindow(), simply return to grant access. If access is not granted, they throw a SecurityException. checkTopLevelWindow() returns a boolean value. A value of true indicates the access is granted; a value of false indicates the access is granted with the restriction that the new window should provide a warning border that serves to identify it as an untrusted window.

Let's implement a silly SecurityManager that allows only files beginning with the name *foo* to be read:

```
class  FooFileSecurityManager extends SecurityManager {

    public void checkRead( String s ) {
        if ( !s.startsWith("foo") )
            throw new SecurityException("Access to non-foo file: " +
                s + " not allowed." );
    }
}
```

Once the `FooFileSecurityManager` is installed, any attempt to read a filename other than *foo** from any class will fail and cause a `SecurityException` to be thrown. All other security methods are inherited from `SecurityManager`, so they are left at their default restrictiveness.

As we've shown, security managers can make their decisions about what to allow and disallow based on any kind of criterion. One very powerful facility that the `SecurityManager` class provides is the `classDepth()` method. `classDepth()` takes as an argument the name of a Java class; it returns an integer indicating the depth of that class if it is present on the Java stack. The depth indicates the number of nested method invocations that occurred between the call to `classDepth()` and the last method invocation from the given class. This can be used to determine what class required the security check. For example, if a class shows a depth of 1, the security check must have been caused by a method in that class—there are no method calls intervening between the last call to that class and the call requiring the check. You could allow or refuse an operation based on the knowledge that it came from a specific class.

All restrictions placed on applets by an applet-viewer application are enforced through a `SecurityManager`, which allows untrusted code loaded from over the network to be executed safely. The `AppletSecurityManager` is responsible for applying the various rules for untrusted applets and allowing user configured access to trusted (signed) applets.

Internationalization

In order to deliver on the promise "write once, run anywhere," the engineers at Java designed the famous Java Virtual Machine. True, your program will run anywhere there is a JVM, but what about users in other countries? Will they have to know English to use your application? Java 1.1 answers that question with a resounding "no," backed up by various classes that are designed to make it easy for you to write a "global" application. In this section we'll talk about the concepts of internationalization and the classes that support them.

java.util.Locale

Internationalization programming revolves around the `Locale` class. The class itself is very simple; it encapsulates a country code, a language code, and a rarely used variant code. Commonly used languages and countries are defined as constants in the `Locale` class. (It's ironic that these names are all in English.) You can retrieve the codes or readable names, as follows:

```
Locale l = Locale.ITALIAN;
System.out.println(l.getCountry());          // IT
System.out.println(l.getDisplayCountry());   // Italy
System.out.println(l.getLanguage());         // it
System.out.println(l.getDisplayLanguage());  // Italian
```

The country codes comply with ISO 639. A complete list of country codes is at *http://www.ics.uci.edu/pub/ietf/http/related/iso639.txt*. The language codes comply with ISO 3166. A complete list of language codes is at *http://www.chemie.fu-berlin.de/diverse/doc/ISO_3166.html*. There is no official set of variant codes; they are designated as vendor-specific or platform-specific.

Various classes throughout the Java API use a `Locale` to decide how to represent themselves. We have already seen how the `DateFormat` class uses `Locales` to determine how to format and parse strings.

Resource Bundles

If you're writing an internationalized program, you want all the text that is displayed by your application to be in the correct language. Given what you have just learned about `Locale`, you could print out different messages by testing the `Locale`. This gets cumbersome quickly, however, because the messages for all `Locales` are embedded in your source code. `ResourceBundle` and its subclasses offer a cleaner, more flexible solution.

A `ResourceBundle` is a collection of objects that your application can access by name, much like a `Hashtable` with `String` keys. The same `ResourceBundle` may be defined for many different `Locales`. To get a particular `ResourceBundle`, call the factory method `ResourceBundle.getBundle()`, which accepts the name of a `ResourceBundle` and a `Locale`. The following example gets a `ResourceBundle` for two `Locales`, retrieves a string message from it, and prints the message. We'll define the `ResourceBundles` later to make this example work.

```
import java.util.*;
public class Hello {
  public static void main(String[] args) {
    ResourceBundle bun;
    bun = ResourceBundle.getBundle("Message", Locale.ITALY);
    System.out.println(bun.getString("HelloMessage"));
```

```
      bun = ResourceBundle.getBundle("Message", Locale.US);
      System.out.println(bun.getString("HelloMessage"));
    }
  }
```

The getBundle() method throws the run-time exception MissingResourceException if an appropriate ResourceBundle cannot be located.

Locales are defined in three ways. They can be standalone classes, in which case they will be either subclasses of ListResourceBundle or direct subclasses of ResourceBundle. They can also be defined by a property file, in which case they will be represented at run-time by a PropertyResourceBundle object. When you call ResourceBundle.getBundle(), either a matching class is returned or an instance of PropertyResourceBundle corresponding to a matching property file. The algorithm used by getBundle() is based on appending the country and language codes of the requested Locale to the name of the resource. Specifically, it searches for resources using this order:

```
name_language_country_variant
name_language_country
name_language
name
name_default-language_default-country_default-variant
name_default-language_default-country
name_default-language
```

In the example above, when we try to get the ResourceBundle named Message, specific to Locale.ITALY, it searches for the following names (no variant codes are in the Locales we are using):

```
Message_it_IT
Message_it
Message
Message_en_US
Message_en
```

Let's define the Message_it_IT ResourceBundle now, using a subclass of ListResourceBundle:

```
import java.util.*;
public class Message_it_IT extends ListResourceBundle {
  public Object[][] getContents() {
    return contents;
  }

  static final Object[][] contents = {
    {"HelloMessage", "Buon giorno, world!"},
    {"OtherMessage", "Ciao."},
  };
}
```

ListResourceBundle makes it easy to define a ResourceBundle class; all we have to do is override the getContents() method.

Now let's define a ResourceBundle for Locale.US. This time, we'll make a property file. Save the following data in a file called *Message_en_US.properties*:

```
HelloMessage=Hello, world!
OtherMessage=Bye.
```

So what happens if somebody runs your program in Locale.FRANCE, and no ResourceBundle is defined for that Locale? To avoid a run-time Missing-ResourceException, it's a good idea to define a default ResourceBundle. So in our example, you could change the name of the property file to Message.properties. That way, if a language-specific or country-specific ResourceBundle cannot be found, your application can still run.

java.text

The java.text package includes, among other things, a set of classes designed for generating and parsing string representations of objects. We have already seen one of these classes, DateFormat. In this section we'll talk about the other format classes, NumberFormat, ChoiceFormat, and MessageFormat.

The NumberFormat class can be used to format and parse currency, percents, or plain old numbers. Like DateFormat, NumberFormat is an abstract class. However, it has several useful factory methods. For example, to generate currency strings, use getCurrencyInstance():

```
double salary = 1234.56;
String here =      // $1,234.56
    NumberFormat.getCurrencyInstance().format(salary);
String italy =     // L 1.234,56
    NumberFormat.getCurrencyInstance(Locale.ITALY).format(salary);
```

The first statement generates an American salary, with a dollar sign, a comma to separate thousands, and a period as a decimal point. The second statement presents the same string in Italian, with a lire sign, a period to separate thousands, and a comma as a decimal point. Remember that the NumberFormat worries about format only; it doesn't attempt to do currency conversion. (Among other things, that would require access to a dynamically updated table and exchange rates—a good opportunity for a Java Bean but too much to ask of a simple formatter.)

Likewise, getPercentInstance() returns a formatter you can use for generating and parsing percents. If you do not specify a Locale when calling a getInstance() method, the default Locale is used:

```
NumberFormat pf = NumberFormat.getPercentInstance();
System.out.println(pf.format(progress)); // 44%
try {
  System.out.println(pf.parse("77.2%")); // 0.772
}
catch (ParseException e) {}
```

And if you just want to generate and parse plain old numbers, use a `NumberFormat` returned by `getInstance()` or its equivalent, `getNumberInstance()`:

```
NumberFormat guiseppe = NumberFormat.getInstance(Locale.ITALY);
NumberFormat joe = NumberFormat.getInstance();// defaults to Locale.US
try {
  double theValue = guiseppe.parse("34.663,252").doubleValue();
  System.out.println(joe.format(theValue));          // 34,663.252
}
catch (ParseException e) {}
```

We use `guiseppe` to parse a number in Italian format (periods separate thousands, comma is the decimal point). The return type of `parse()` is `Number`, so we use the `doubleValue()` method to retrieve the value of the `Number` as a `double`. Then we use `joe` to format the number correctly for the default (U.S.) locale.

Here's a list of the factory methods for text formatters in the `java.text` package:

```
DateFormat.getDateInstance()
DateFormat.getDateInstance(int style)
DateFormat.getDateInstance(int style, Locale aLocale)
DateFormat.getDateTimeInstance()
DateFormat.getDateTimeInstance(int dateStyle, int timeStyle)
DateFormat.getDateTimeInstance(int dateStyle, int timeStyle,
    Locale aLocale)
DateFormat.getInstance()
DateFormat.getTimeInstance()
DateFormat.getTimeInstance(int style)
DateFormat.getTimeInstance(int style, Locale aLocale)
NumberFormat.getCurrencyInstance()
NumberFormat.getCurrencyInstance(Locale inLocale)
NumberFormat.getInstance()
NumberFormat.getInstance(Locale inLocale)
NumberFormat.getNumberInstance()
NumberFormat.getNumberInstance(Locale inLocale)
NumberFormat.getPercentInstance()
NumberFormat.getPercentInstance(Locale inLocale)
```

Thus far we've seen how to format dates and numbers as text. Now we'll take a look at a class, `ChoiceFormat`, that maps numerical ranges to text. `ChoiceFormat` is constructed by specifying the numerical ranges and the strings that correspond to them. One constructor accepts an array of `doubles` and an array of `Strings`, where each string corresponds to the range running from the matching number up through the next number:

```
double[] limits = {0, 20, 40};
String[] labels = {"young", "less young", "old"};
ChoiceFormat cf = new ChoiceFormat(limits, labels);
System.out.println(cf.format(12)); // young
System.out.println(cf.format(26)); // less young
```

You can specify both the limits and the labels using a special string in another ChoiceFormat constructor:

```
ChoiceFormat cf = new ChoiceFormat("0#young|20#less young|40#old");
System.out.println(cf.format(40)); // old
System.out.println(cf.format(50)); // old
```

The limit and value pairs are separated by pipe characters (|—also known as a "vertical bar"), while the number sign serves to separate each limit from its corresponding value.

To complete our discussion of the formatting classes, we'll take a look at another class, MessageFormat, that helps you construct human-readable messages. To construct a MessageFormat, pass it a *pattern string*. A pattern string is a lot like the string you feed to printf() in C, although the syntax is different. Arguments are delineated by curly brackets and may include information about how they should be formatted. Each argument consists of a number, an optional type, and an optional style. These are summarized in Table 9-9.

Table 9-9: MessageFormat Arguments

Type	Styles
choice	*pattern*
date	short, medium, long, full, *pattern*
number	integer, percent, currency, *pattern*
time	short, medium, long, full, *pattern*

Let's use an example to clarify all of this:

```
MessageFormat mf = new MessageFormat("You have {0} messages.");
Object[] arguments = {"no"};
System.out.println(mf.format(arguments)); // You have no messages.
```

We start by constructing a MessageFormat object; the argument to the constructor is the pattern on which messages will be based. The special incantation {0} means "in this position, substitute element 0 from the array passed as an argument to the format() method." Thus, we construct a MessageFormat object with a pattern, which is a template on which messages are based. When we generate a message, by calling format(), we pass in values to fill the blank spaces in the template. In this case, we pass the array arguments[] to mf.format; this substitutes arguments[0], yielding the result "You have no messages."

Let's try this example again, except we'll show how to format a number and a date instead of a string argument:

```
MessageFormat mf = new MessageFormat(
    "You have {0, number, integer} messages on {1, date, long}.");
Object[] arguments = {new Integer(93), new Date()};
System.out.println(mf.format(arguments));
    // You have 93 messages on April 10, 1997.
```

In this example, we need to fill in two spaces in the template, and therefore we need two elements in the arguments[] array. Element 0 must be a number and is formatted as an integer. Element 1 must be a Date and will be printed in the long format. When we call format(), the arguments[] array supplies these two values.

This is still sloppy. What if there is only one message? To make this grammatically correct, we can embed a ChoiceFormat-style pattern string in our MessageFormat pattern string:

```
MessageFormat mf = new MessageFormat(
    "You have {0, number, integer} message{0, choice, 0#s|1#|2#s}.");
Object[] arguments = {new Integer(1)};
System.out.println(mf.format(arguments)); // You have 1 message.
```

In this case, we use element 0 of arguments[] twice: once to supply the number of messages, and once to provide input to the ChoiceFormat pattern. The pattern says to add an *s* if argument 0 has the value zero or is two or more.

Finally, a few words on how to be clever. If you want to write international programs, you can use resource bundles to supply the strings for your MessageFormat objects. This way, you can automatically format messages that are in the appropriate language with dates and other language-dependent fields handled appropriately.

In this context, it's helpful to realize that messages don't need to read elements from the array in order. In English, you would say "Disk C has 123 files"; in some other language, you might say "123 files are on Disk C." You could implement both messages with the same set of arguments:

```
MessageFormat m1 = new MessageFormat(
    "Disk {0} has {1, number, integer} files.");
MessageFormat m2 = new MessageFormat(
    "{1, number, integer} files are on disk {0}.");
Object[] arguments = {"C", new Integer(123)};
```

In real life, the code could be even more compact; you'd only use a single MessageFormat object, initialized with a string taken from a resource bundle.

10

Input/Output Facilities

In this chapter, we'll continue our exploration of the Java API by looking at many of the classes in the `java.io` package. Figure 10-1 shows the class hierarchy of the `java.io` package.

We'll start by looking at the stream classes in `java.io`; these classes are all subclasses of the basic `InputStream`, `OutputStream`, `Reader`, and `Writer` classes. Then we'll examine the `File` class and discuss how you can interact with the filesystem using classes in `java.io`. Finally, we'll take a quick look at the data compression classes provided in `java.util.zip`.

Streams

All fundamental I/O in Java is based on *streams*. A stream represents a flow of data, or a channel of communication with (at least conceptually) a writer at one end and a reader at the other. When you are working with terminal input and output, reading or writing files, or communicating through sockets in Java, you are using a stream of one type or another. So that you can see the forest without being distracted by the trees, I'll start by summarizing the different types of streams:

InputStream/OutputStream

Abstract classes that define the basic functionality for reading or writing an unstructured sequence of bytes. All other byte streams in Java are built on top of the basic `InputStream` and `OutputStream`.

Reader/Writer

Abstract classes that define the basic functionality for reading or writing an unstructured sequence of characters. All other character streams in Java are built on top of `Reader` and `Writer`.

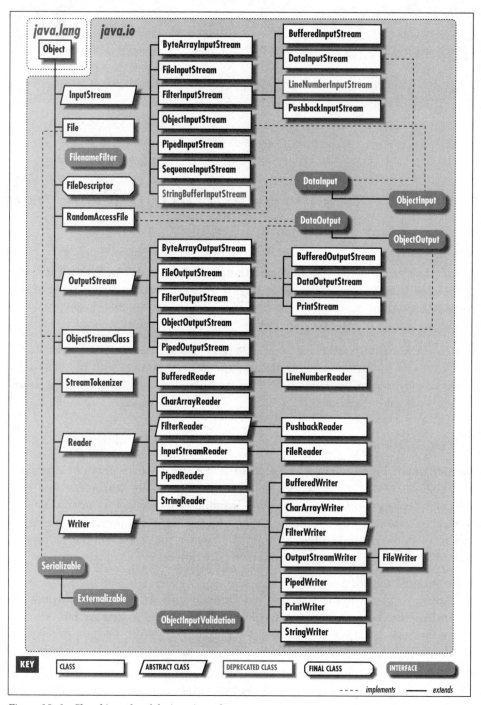

Figure 10–1: Class hierarchy of the java.io package

InputStreamReader/OutputStreamWriter
"Bridge" classes that convert bytes to characters and vice versa.

DataInputStream/DataOutputStream
Specialized stream filters that add the ability to read and write simple data types like numeric primitives and String objects.

ObjectInputStream/ObjectOutputStream
Specialized stream filters that are capable of writing serialized Java objects and reconstructing them.

BufferedInputStream/BufferedOutputStream/BufferedReader/
BufferedWriter
Specialized streams that add buffering for additional efficiency.

PrintWriter
A specialized character stream that makes it simple to print text.

PipedInputStream/PipedOutputStream /PipedReader/PipedWriter
"Double-ended" streams that always occur in pairs. Data written into a Piped-OutputStream or PipedWriter is read from its corresponding PipedInput-Stream or PipedReader.

FileInputStream/FileOutputStream /FileReader/FileWriter
Implementations of InputStream, OutputStream, Reader, and Writer that read from and write to files on the local filesystem.

Streams in Java are one-way streets. The java.io input and output classes represent the ends of a simple stream, as shown in Figure 10-2. For bidirectional conversations, we use one of each type of stream.

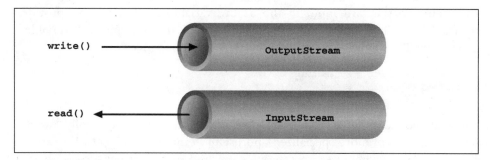

Figure 10–2: Basic input and output stream functionality

InputStream and OutputStream are abstract classes that define the lowest-level interface for all byte streams. They contain methods for reading or writing an unstructured flow of byte-level data. Because these classes are abstract, you can never create a "pure" input or output stream. Java implements subclasses of these for activities like reading and writing files and communicating with sockets. Because all byte streams inherit the structure of InputStream or OutputStream, the various kinds of byte streams can be used interchangeably. For example, a method often takes an InputStream as an argument. This means the method accepts any subclass of InputStream. Specialized types of streams can also be layered to provide features, such as buffering or handling larger data types.

In Java 1.1, new classes based around Reader and Writer were added to the java.io package. Reader and Writer are very much like InputStream and Output-Stream, except that they deal with characters instead of bytes. As true character streams, these classes correctly handle Unicode characters, which was not always the case with the byte streams. However, some sort of bridge is needed between these character streams and the byte streams of physical devices like disks and networks. InputStreamReader and OutputStreamWriter are special classes that use an *encoding scheme* to translate between character and byte streams.

We'll discuss all of the interesting stream types in this section, with the exception of FileInputStream, FileOutputStream, FileReader, and FileWriter. We'll postpone the discussion of file streams until the next section, where we'll cover issues involved with accessing the filesystem in Java.

Terminal I/O

The prototypical example of an InputStream object is the standard input of a Java application. Like stdin in C or cin in C++, this object reads data from the program's environment, which is usually a terminal window or a command pipe. The java.lang.System class, a general repository for system-related resources, provides a reference to standard input in the static variable in. System also provides objects for standard output and standard error in the out and err variables, respectively. The following example shows the correspondence:

```
InputStream stdin = System.in;
OutputStream stdout = System.out;
OutputStream stderr = System.err;
```

This example hides the fact that System.out and System.err aren't really Output-Stream objects, but more specialized and useful PrintStream objects. I'll explain these later, but for now we can reference out and err as OutputStream objects, since they are a kind of OutputStream by inheritance.

We can read a single byte at a time from standard input with the InputStream's read() method. If you look closely at the API, you'll see that the read() method of the base InputStream class is actually an abstract method. What lies behind System.in is an implementation of InputStream, so it's valid to call read() for this stream:

```
try {
    int val = System.in.read();
    ...
}
catch ( IOException e ) {
}
```

As is the convention in C, `read()` provides a byte of information, but its return type is `int`. A return value of −1 indicates a normal end of stream has been reached; you'll need to test for this condition when using the simple `read()` method. If an error occurs during the read, an `IOException` is thrown. All basic input and output stream commands can throw an `IOException`, so you should arrange to catch and handle them as appropriate.

To retrieve the value as a byte, perform the cast:

```
byte b = (byte) val;
```

Of course, you'll need to check for the end-of-stream condition before you perform the cast. An overloaded form of `read()` fills a byte array with as much data as possible up to the limit of the array size and returns the number of bytes read:

```
byte [] bity = new byte [1024];
int got = System.in.read( bity );
```

We can also check the number of bytes available for reading on an `InputStream` with the `available()` method. Once we have that information, we can create an array of exactly the right size:

```
int waiting = System.in.available();
if ( waiting > 0 ) {
    byte [] data = new byte [ waiting ];
    System.in.read( data );
    ...
}
```

`InputStream` provides the `skip()` method as a way of jumping over a number of bytes. Depending on the implementation of the stream and if you aren't interested in the intermediate data, skipping bytes may be more efficient than reading them. The `close()` method shuts down the stream and frees up any associated system resources. It's a good idea to close a stream when you are done using it.

Character Streams

The `InputStream` and `OutputStream` subclasses of Java 1.0.2 included methods for reading and writing strings, but most of them operated by assuming that a 16-bit Unicode character was equivalent to an 8-bit byte in the stream. This only works for Latin-1 (ISO 8859-1) characters, so the character stream classes Reader and Writer were introduced in Java 1.1. Two special classes, InputStreamReader and OutputStreamWriter, bridge the gap between the world of character streams and the world of byte streams. These are character streams that are wrapped around an underlying byte stream. An encoding scheme is used to convert between bytes and characters. An encoding scheme name can be specified in the constructor of InputStreamReader or OutputStreamWriter. Another constructor simply accepts the underlying stream and uses the system's default encoding scheme. For example, let's parse a human-readable string from the standard input into an integer. We'll assume that the bytes coming from System.in use the system's default encoding scheme:

```
try {
    InputStreamReader converter = new InputStreamReader(System.in);
    BufferedReader in = new BufferedReader(converter);

    String text = in.readLine();
    int i = NumberFormat.getInstance().parse(text).intValue();
}
catch ( IOException e ) { }
catch ( ParseException pe ) { }
```

First, we wrap an InputStreamReader around System.in. This object converts the incoming bytes of System.in to characters using the default encoding scheme. Then, we wrap a BufferedReader around the InputStreamReader. BufferedReader gives us the readLine() method, which we can use to convert a full line of text into a String. The string is then parsed into an integer using the techniques described in Chapter 9.

We could have programmed the previous example using only byte streams, and it would have worked for users in the United States, at least. So why go to the extra trouble of using character streams? Character streams were introduced in Java 1.1 to correctly support Unicode strings. Unicode was designed to support almost all of the written languages of the world. If you want to write a program that works in any part of the world, in any language, you definitely want to use streams that don't mangle Unicode.

So how do you decide when you need a byte stream and when you need a character stream? If you want to read or write character strings, use some variety of Reader or Writer. Otherwise, a byte stream should suffice. Let's say, for example, that you want to read strings from a file that was written by a Java 1.0.2 application. In this case, you could simply create a FileReader, which will convert the bytes in the file to characters using the system's default encoding scheme. If you have a file in a specific encoding scheme, you can create an InputStreamReader with that encoding scheme and read characters from it. Another example comes from the Internet. Web servers serve files as byte streams. If you want to read Unicode strings from a file with a particular encoding scheme, you'll need an appropriate InputStreamReader wrapped around the socket's InputStream.

Stream Wrappers

What if we want to do more than read and write a mess of bytes or characters? Many of the InputStream, OutputStream, Reader, and Writer classes wrap other streams and add new features. A filtered stream takes another stream in its constructor; it delegates calls to the underlying stream while doing some additional processing of its own.

In Java 1.0.2, all wrapper streams were subclasses of FilterInputStream and FilterOutputStream. The character stream classes introduced in Java 1.1 break this pattern, but they operate in the same way. For example, BufferedInputStream extends FilterInputStream in the byte world, but BufferedReader extends Reader in the character world. It doesn't really matter—both classes accept a stream in their constructor and perform buffering. Like the byte stream classes, the character stream classes include the abstract FilterReader and FilterWriter classes, which simply pass all method calls to an underlying stream.

The FilterInputStream, FilterOutputStream, FilterReader, and FilterWriter classes themselves aren't useful; they must be subclassed and specialized to create a new type of filtering operation. For example, specialized wrapper streams like DataInputStream and DataOutputStream provide additional methods for reading and writing primitive data types.

As we said, when you create an instance of a filtered stream, you specify another stream in the constructor. The specialized stream wraps an additional layer of functionality around the other stream, as shown in Figure 10-3. Because filtered streams themselves are subclasses of the fundamental stream types, filtered streams can be layered on top of each other to provide different combinations of features. For example, you could wrap a PushbackReader around a LineNumberReader that was wrapped around a FileReader.

Data streams

DataInputStream and DataOutputStream are filtered streams that let you read or write strings and primitive data types that comprise more than a single byte. DataInputStream and DataOutputStream implement the DataInput and DataOutput interfaces, respectively. These interfaces define the methods required for streams that read and write strings and Java primitive types in a machine-independent manner.

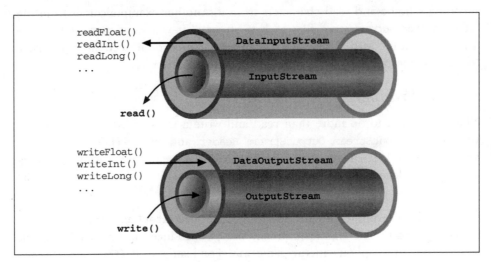

Figure 10–3: Layered streams

You can construct a `DataInputStream` from an `InputStream` and then use a method like `readDouble()` to read a primitive data type:

```
DataInputStream dis = new DataInputStream( System.in );
double d = dis.readDouble();
```

The above example wraps the standard input stream in a `DataInputStream` and uses it to read a double value. `readDouble()` reads bytes from the stream and constructs a `double` from them. All `DataInputStream` methods that read primitive types also read binary information.

The `DataOutputStream` class provides write methods that correspond to the read methods in `DataInputStream`. For example, `writeInt()` writes an integer in binary format to the underlying output stream.

The `readUTF()` and `writeUTF()` methods of `DataInputStream` and `DataOutput-Stream` read and write a Java `String` of Unicode characters using the UTF-8 "transformation format." UTF-8 is an ASCII-compatible encoding of Unicode characters commonly used for the transmission and storage of Unicode text.[*]

We can use a `DataInputStream` with any kind of input stream, whether it be from a file, a socket, or standard input. The same applies to using a `DataOutputStream`, or, for that matter, any other specialized streams in `java.io`.

---

[*] Check out the URL *http://www.stonehand.com/unicode/standard/utf8.html* for more information on UTF-8.

Buffered streams

The `BufferedInputStream`, `BufferedOutputStream`, `BufferedReader`, and `BufferedWriter` classes add a data buffer of a specified size to the stream path. A buffer can increase efficiency by reducing the number of physical read or write operations that correspond to `read()` or `write()` method calls. You create a buffered stream with an appropriate input or output stream and a buffer size. Furthermore, you can wrap another stream around a buffered stream so that it benefits from the buffering. Here's a simple buffered input stream:

```
BufferedInputStream bis = new BufferedInputStream(myInputStream, 4096);
...
bis.read();
```

In this example, we specify a buffer size of 4096 bytes. If we leave off the size of the buffer in the constructor, a reasonably sized one is chosen for us. On our first call to `read()`, `bis` tries to fill the entire 4096-byte buffer with data. Thereafter, calls to `read()` retrieve data from the buffer until it's empty.

A `BufferedOutputStream` works in a similar way. Calls to `write()` store the data in a buffer; data is actually written only when the buffer fills up. You can also use the `flush()` method to wring out the contents of a `BufferedOutputStream` before the buffer is full.

Some input streams like `BufferedInputStream` support the ability to mark a location in the data and later reset the stream to that position. The `mark()` method sets the return point in the stream. It takes an integer value that specifies the number of bytes that can be read before the stream gives up and forgets about the mark. The `reset()` method returns the stream to the marked point; any data read after the call to `mark()` is read again.

This functionality is especially useful when you are reading the stream in a parser. You may occasionally fail to parse a structure and so must try something else. In this situation, you can have your parser generate an error (a homemade `ParseException`) and then reset the stream to the point before it began parsing the structure:

```
BufferedInputStream input;
...
try {
    input.mark( MAX_DATA_STRUCTURE_SIZE );
    return( parseDataStructure( input ) );
}
catch ( ParseException e ) {
    input.reset();
    ...
}
```

The BufferedReader and BufferedWriter classes work just like their byte-based counterparts, but operate on characters instead of bytes.

Print streams

Another useful wrapper stream is java.io.PrintWriter. This class provides a suite of overloaded print() methods that turn their arguments into strings and push them out the stream. A complementary set of println() methods adds a newline to the end of the strings. PrintWriter is the more capable big brother of the PrintStream byte stream. PrintWriter is an unusual character stream because it can wrap either an OutputStream or another Writer. The System.out and System.err streams are PrintStream objects; you have already seen such streams strewn throughout this book:

```
System.out.print("Hello world...\n");
System.out.println("Hello world...");
System.out.println( "The answer is: " + 17 );
System.out.println( 3.14 );
```

In Java 1.1, the PrintStream class has been enhanced to translate characters to bytes using the system's default encoding scheme. Although PrintStream is not deprecated in Java 1.1, its constructors are. For all new development, use a PrintWriter instead of a PrintStream. Because a PrintWriter can wrap an OutputStream, the two classes are interchangeable.

When you create a PrintWriter object, you can pass an additional boolean value to the constructor. If this value is true, the PrintWriter automatically performs a flush() on the underlying OutputStream or Writer each time it sends a newline:

```
boolean autoFlush = true;
PrintWriter p = new PrintWriter( myOutputStream, autoFlush );
```

When this technique is used with a buffered output stream, it corresponds to the behavior of terminals that send data line by line.

Unlike methods in other stream classes, the methods of PrintWriter and PrintStream do not throw IOExceptions. Instead, if we are interested, we can check for errors with the checkError() method:

```
System.out.println( reallyLongString );
if ( System.out.checkError() )                    // Uh oh
```

Pipes

Normally, our applications are directly involved with one side of a given stream at a time. PipedInputStream and PipedOutputStream (or PipedReader and

PipedWriter), however, let us create two sides of a stream and connect them together, as shown in Figure 10-4. This provides a stream of communication between threads, for example.

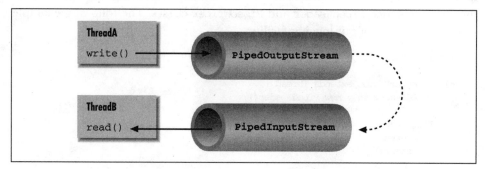

Figure 10–4: Piped streams

To create a pipe, we use both a PipedInputStream and a PipedOutputStream. We can simply choose a side and then construct the other side using the first as an argument:

```
PipedInputStream pin = new PipedInputStream();
PipedOutputStream pout = new PipedOutputStream( pin );
```

Alternatively:

```
PipedOutputStream pout = new PipedOutputStream( );
PipedInputStream pin = new PipedInputStream( pout );
```

In each of these examples, the effect is to produce an input stream, pin, and an output stream, pout, that are connected. Data written to pout can then be read by pin. It is also possible to create the PipedInputStream and the PipedOutputStream separately, and then connect them with the connect() method.

We can do exactly the same thing in the character-based world, using PipedReader and PipedWriter in place of PipedInputStream and PipedOutputStream.

Once the two ends of the pipe are connected, use the two streams as you would other input and output streams. You can use read() to read data from the Piped-InputStream (or PipedReader) and write() to write data to the PipedOutput-Stream (or PipedWriter). If the internal buffer of the pipe fills up, the writer blocks and waits until space is available. Conversely, if the pipe is empty, the reader blocks and waits until some data is available.

One advantage to using piped streams is that they provide stream functionality in our code, without compelling us to build new, specialized streams. For example,

we can use pipes to create a simple logging facility for our application. We can
send messages to the logging facility through an ordinary PrintWriter, and then it
can do whatever processing or buffering is required before sending the messages
off to their ultimate location. Because we are dealing with string messages, we use
the character-based PipedReader and PipedWriter classes. The following example
shows the skeleton of our logging facility:

```
import java.io.*;

class LoggerDaemon extends Thread {
    PipedReader in = new PipedReader();

    LoggerDaemon() {
        setDaemon( true );
        start();
    }

    public void run() {
        BufferedReader din = new BufferedReader( in );
        String s;

        try {
            while ( (s = din.readLine()) != null ) {
                // process line of data
                // ...
            }
        }
        catch (IOException e ) { }
    }

    PrintWriter getWriter() throws IOException {
        return new PrintWriter( new PipedWriter( in ) );
    }
}

class myApplication {
    public static void main ( String [] args ) throws IOException {
        PrintWriter out = new LoggerDaemon().getWriter();

        out.println("Application starting...");
        // ...
        out.println("Warning: does not compute!");
        // ...
    }
}
```

LoggerDaemon is a daemon thread, so it will die when our application exits. LoggerDaemon reads strings from its end of the pipe, the PipedReader in. LoggerDaemon also provides a method, getWriter(), that returns a PipedWriter that is
connected to its input stream. Simply create a new LoggerDaemon and fetch the
output stream to begin sending messages.

In order to read strings with the readLine() method, LoggerDaemon wraps a BufferedReader around its PipedReader. For convenience, it also presents its PipedWriter as a PrintWriter, rather than a simple Writer.

One advantage of implementing LoggerDaemon with pipes is that we can log messages as easily as we write text to a terminal or any other stream. In other words, we can use all our normal tools and techniques. Another advantage is that the processing happens in another thread, so we can go about our business while the processing takes place.

There is nothing stopping us from connecting more than two piped streams. For example, we could chain multiple pipes together to perform a series of filtering operations.

Strings to Streams and Back

The StringReader class is another useful stream class. The stream is created from a String; StringReader essentially wraps stream functionality around a String. Here's how to use a StringReader:

```
String data = "There once was a man from Nantucket...";
StringReader sr = new StringReader( data );

char T = (char)sr.read();
char h = (char)sr.read();
char e = (char)sr.read();
```

Note that you will still have to catch IOExceptions thrown by some of the StringReader's methods.

The StringReader class is useful when you want to read data in a String as if it were coming from a stream, such as a file, pipe, or socket. For example, suppose you create a parser that expects to read tokens from a stream. But you want to provide a method that also parses a big string. You can easily add one using StringReader.

Turning things around, the StringWriter class lets us write to a character string through an output stream. The internal string grows as necessary to accommodate the data. In the following example, we create a StringWriter and wrap it in a PrintWriter for convenience:

```
StringWriter buffer = new StringWriter();
PrintWriter out = new PrintWriter( buffer );

out.println("A moose once bit my sister.");
out.println("No, really!");

String results = buffer.toString();
```

First we print a few lines to the output stream, to give it some data, then retrieve the results as a string with the toString() method. Alternately, we could get the results as a StringBuffer with the getBuffer() method.

The StringWriter class is useful if you want to capture the output of something that normally sends output to a stream, such as a file or the console. A Print-Writer wrapped around a StringWriter competes with StringBuffer as the easiest way to construct large strings piece by piece. While using a StringBuffer is more efficient, PrintWriter provides more functionality than the normal append() method used by StringBuffer.

rot13InputStream

Before we leave streams, let's try our hand at making one of our own. I mentioned earlier that specialized stream wrappers are built on top of the FilterInputStream and FilterOutputStream classes. It's quite easy to create our own subclass of FilterInputStream that can be wrapped around other streams to add new functionality.

The following example, rot13InputStream, performs a *rot13* operation on the bytes that it reads. *rot13* is a trivial algorithm that shifts alphanumeric letters to make them not quite human-readable; it's cute because it's symmetric. That is, to "un-rot13" some text, simply *rot13* it again. We'll use the rot13InputStream class again in the crypt protocol handler example in Chapter 12, so we've put the class in the exploringjava.io package to facilitate reuse. Here's our rot13InputStream class:

```
package example.io;
import java.io.*;

public class rot13InputStream extends FilterInputStream {

    public rot13InputStream ( InputStream i ) {
        super( i );
    }

    public int read() throws IOException {
        return rot13( in.read() );
    }

    private int rot13 ( int c ) {
        if ( (c >= 'A') && (c <= 'Z') )
            c=(((c-'A')+13)%26)+'A';
        if ( (c >= 'a') && (c <= 'z') )
            c=(((c-'a')+13)%26)+'a';
        return c;
    }
}
```

The FilterInputStream needs to be initialized with an InputStream; this is the stream to be filtered. We provide an appropriate constructor for the rot-13InputStream class and invoke the parent constructor with a call to super(). FilterInputStream contains a protected instance variable, in, where it stores the stream reference and makes it available to the rest of our class.

The primary feature of a FilterInputStream is that it overrides the normal InputStream methods to delegate calls to the InputStream in the variable in. So, for instance, a call to read() simply turns around and calls read() on in to fetch a byte. An instance of FilterInputStream itself could be instantiated from an InputStream; it would pass its method calls on to that stream and serve as a pass-through filter. To make things interesting, we can override methods of the Filter-InputStream class and do extra work on the data as it passes through.

In our example, we have overridden the read() method to fetch bytes from the underlying InputStream, in, and then performed the *rot13* shift on the data before returning it. Note that the rot13() method shifts alphabetic characters, while simply passing all other values, including the end of stream value (-1). Our subclass now acts like a *rot13* filter. All other normal functionality of an InputStream, like skip() and available(), is unmodified, so calls to these methods are answered by the underlying InputStream.

Strictly speaking, rot13InputStream only works on an ASCII byte stream, since the underlying algorithm is based on the Roman alphabet. A more generalized character-scrambling algorithm would have to be based on FilterReader to handle Unicode correctly. (Anyone want to try *rot32768?*).

Files

Unless otherwise restricted, a Java application can read and write to the host filesystem with the same level of access as the user who runs the Java interpreter. Java applets and other kinds of networked applications can, of course, be restricted by the SecurityManager and cut off from these services. We'll discuss applet access at the end of this section. First, let's take a look at the tools for basic file access.

Working with files in Java is still somewhat problematic. The host filesystem lies outside of Java's virtual environment, in the real world, and can therefore still suffer from architecture and implementation differences. Java tries to mask some of these differences by providing information to help an application tailor itself to the local environment; I'll mention these areas as they occur.

java.io.File

The java.io.File class encapsulates access to information about a file or directory entry in the filesystem. It gets attribute information about a file, lists the
entries in a directory, and performs basic filesystem operations like removing a file
or making a directory. While the File object handles these tasks, it doesn't provide
direct access for reading and writing file data; there are specialized streams for
that purpose.

File constructors

You can create an instance of File from a String pathname:

```
File fooFile = new File( "/tmp/foo.txt" );
File barDir = new File( "/tmp/bar" );
```

You can also create a file with a relative path:

```
File f = new File( "foo" );
```

In this case, Java works relative to the current directory of the Java interpreter. You
can determine the current directory by checking the user.dir property in the
System Properties list (System.getProperty("user.dir")).

An overloaded version of the File constructor lets you specify the directory path
and filename as separate String objects:

```
File fooFile = new File( "/tmp", "foo.txt" );
```

With yet another variation, you can specify the directory with a File object and the
filename with a String:

```
File tmpDir = new File( "/tmp" );
File fooFile = new File ( tmpDir, "foo.txt" );
```

None of the File constructors throw any exceptions. This means the object is created whether or not the file or directory actually exists; it isn't an error to create a
File object for an nonexistent file. You can use the exists() method to find out
whether the file or directory exists.

Path localization

One of the reasons that working with files in Java is problematic is that pathnames
are expected to follow the conventions of the local filesystem. Java's designers
intend to provide an abstraction that deals with most system-dependent filename

features, such as the file separator, path separator, device specifier, and root directory. Unfortunately, not all of these features are implemented in the current version.

On some systems, Java can compensate for differences such as the direction of the file separator slashes in the above string. For example, in the current implementation on Windows platforms, Java accepts paths with either forward slashes or backslashes. However, under Solaris, Java accepts only paths with forward slashes.

Your best bet is to make sure you follow the filename conventions of the host filesystem. If your application is just opening and saving files at the user's request, you should be able to handle that functionality with the `java.awt.FileDialog` class. This class encapsulates a graphical file–selection dialog box. The methods of the `FileDialog` take care of system-dependent filename features for you.

If your application needs to deal with files on its own behalf, however, things get a little more complicated. The `File` class contains a few `static` variables to make this task easier. `File.separator` defines a `String` that specifies the file separator on the local host (e.g., "/" on UNIX and Macintosh systems and "\" on Windows systems), while `File.separatorChar` provides the same information in character form. `File.pathSeparator` defines a `String` that separates items in a path (e.g., ":" on UNIX systems and ";" on Macintosh and Windows systems); `File.pathSeparatorChar` provides the information in character form.

You can use this system-dependent information in several ways. Probably the simplest way to localize pathnames is to pick a convention you use internally, say "/", and do a `String` replace to substitute for the localized separator character:

```
// We'll use forward slash as our standard
String path = "mail/1995/june/merle";
path = path.replace('/', File.separatorChar);
File mailbox = new File( path );
```

Alternately, you could work with the components of a pathname and build the local pathname when you need it:

```
String [] path = { "mail", "1995", "june", "merle" };

StringBuffer sb = new StringBuffer(path[0]);
for (int i=1; i< path.length; i++)
    sb.append( File.separator + path[i] );
File mailbox = new File( sb.toString() );
```

One thing to remember is that Java interprets the backslash character (\) as an escape character when used in a `String`. To get a backslash in a `String`, you have to use "\\".

File methods

Once we have a valid `File` object, we can use it to ask for information about the file itself and to perform standard operations on it. A number of methods let us ask certain questions about the `File`. For example, `isFile()` returns `true` if the `File` represents a file, while `isDirectory()` returns `true` if it's a directory. `isAbsolute()` indicates whether the `File` has an absolute or relative path specification.

The components of the `File` pathname are available through the following methods: `getName()`, `getPath()`, `getAbsolutePath()`, and `getParent()`. `getName()` returns a `String` for the filename without any directory information; `getPath()` returns the directory information without the filename. If the `File` has an absolute path specification, `getAbsolutePath()` returns that path. Otherwise it returns the relative path appended to the current working directory. `getParent()` returns the parent directory of the `File`.

Interestingly, the string returned by `getPath()` or `getAbsolutePath()` may not be the same case as the actual name of the file. You can retrieve the case-correct version of the file's path using `getCanonicalPath()`. In Windows 95, for example, you can create a `File` object whose `getAbsolutePath()` is `C:\Autoexec.bat` but whose `getCanonicalPath()` is `C:\AUTOEXEC.BAT`.

We can get the modification time of a file or directory with `lastModified()`. This time value is not useful as an absolute time; you should use it only to compare two modification times. We can also get the size of the file in bytes with `length()`. Here's a fragment of code that prints some information about a file:

```
File fooFile = new File( "/tmp/boofa" );

String type = fooFile.isFile() ? "File " : "Directory ";
String name = fooFile.getName();
long len = fooFile.length();
System.out.println(type + name + ", " + len + " bytes " );
```

If the `File` object corresponds to a directory, we can list the files in the directory with the `list()` method:

```
String [] files = fooFile.list();
```

`list()` returns an array of `String` objects that contains filenames. (You might expect that `list()` would return an `Enumeration` instead of an array, but it doesn't.)

If the `File` refers to a nonexistent directory, we can create the directory with `mkdir()` or `mkdirs()`. `mkdir()` creates a single directory; `mkdirs()` creates all of the directories in a `File` specification. Use `renameTo()` to rename a file or directory and delete() to delete a file or directory. Note that File doesn't provide a method to create a file; creation is handled with a FileOutputStream as we'll discuss in a moment.

Table 10-1 summarizes the methods provided by the File class.

Table 10–1: File Methods

Method	Return type	Description
canRead()	boolean	Is the file (or directory) readable?
canWrite()	boolean	Is the file (or directory) writable?
delete()	boolean	Deletes the file (or directory)
exists()	boolean	Does the file (or directory) exist?
getAbsolutePath()	String	Returns the absolute path of the file (or directory)
getCanonicalPath()	String	Returns the absolute, case-correct path of the file (or directory)
getName()	String	Returns the name of the file (or directory)
getParent()	String	Returns the name of the parent directory of the file (or directory)
getPath()	String	Returns the path of the file (or directory)
isAbsolute()	boolean	Is the filename (or directory name) absolute?
isDirectory()	boolean	Is the item a directory?
isFile()	boolean	Is the item a file?
lastModified()	long	Returns the last modification time of the file (or directory)
length()	long	Returns the length of the file
list()	String []	Returns a list of files in the directory
mkdir()	boolean	Creates the directory
mkdirs()	boolean	Creates all directories in the path
renameTo(File dest)	boolean	Renames the file (or directory)

File Streams

Java provides two specialized streams for reading and writing files in the filesystem: FileInputStream and FileOutputStream. These streams provide the basic InputStream and OutputStream functionality applied to reading and writing the contents of files. They can be combined with the filtered streams described earlier to work with files in the same way we do other stream communications.

Because FileInputStream is a subclass of InputStream, it inherits all standard InputStream functionality for reading the contents of a file. FileInputStream provides only a low-level interface to reading data, however, so you'll typically wrap another stream like a DataInputStream around the FileInputStream.

You can create a `FileInputStream` from a `String` pathname or a `File` object:

```
FileInputStream foois = new FileInputStream( fooFile );
FileInputStream passwdis = new FileInputStream( "/etc/passwd" );
```

When you create a `FileInputStream`, Java attempts to open the specified file. Thus, the `FileInputStream` constructors can throw a `FileNotFoundException` if the specified file doesn't exist, or an `IOException` if some other I/O error occurs. You should be sure to catch and handle these exceptions in your code. When the stream is first created, its `available()` method and the `File` object's `length()` method should return the same value. Be sure to call the `close()` method when you are done with the file.

To read characters from a file, you can wrap an `InputStreamReader` around a `FileInputStream`. If you want to use the default character encoding scheme, you can use the `FileReader` class instead, which is provided as a convenience. File-Reader works just like `FileInputStream`, except that it reads characters instead of bytes and wraps a `Reader` instead of an `InputStream`.

The following class, `ListIt`, is a small utility that displays the contents of a file or directory to standard output:

```java
import java.io.*;

class ListIt {
    public static void main ( String args[] ) throws Exception {
        File file =  new File( args[0] );

        if ( !file.exists() || !file.canRead() ) {
            System.out.println( "Can't read " + file );
            return;
        }

        if ( file.isDirectory() ) {
            String [] files = file.list();
            for (int i=0; i< files.length; i++)
                System.out.println( files[i] );
        }
        else
            try {
                FileReader fr = new FileReader ( file );
                BufferedReader in = new BufferedReader( fr );
                String line;
                while ((line = in.readLine()) != null)
                    System.out.println(line);
            }
            catch ( FileNotFoundException e ) {
                System.out.println( "File Disappeared" );
            }
    }
}
```

```
        }
```

ListIt constructs a `File` object from its first command-line argument and tests the `File` to see if it exists and is readable. If the `File` is a directory, `ListIt` prints the names of the files in the directory. Otherwise, `ListIt` reads and prints the file.

`FileOutputStream` is a subclass of `OutputStream`, so it inherits all the standard `OutputStream` functionality for writing to a file. Just like `FileInputStream` though, `FileOutputStream` provides only a low-level interface to writing data. You'll typically wrap another stream like a `DataOutputStream` or a `PrintStream` around the `FileOutputStream` to provide higher level functionality. You can create a `FileOutputStream` from a `String` pathname or a `File` object. Unlike `FileInputStream`, however, the `FileOutputStream` constructors don't throw a `FileNotFoundException`. If the specified file doesn't exist, the `FileOutputStream` creates the file. The `FileOutputStream` constructors can throw an `IOException` if some other I/O error occurs, so you still need to handle this exception.

If the specified file does exist, the `FileOutputStream` opens it for writing. When you actually call a `write()` method, the new data overwrites the current contents of the file. If you need to append data to an existing file, you should use a different constructor that accepts an append flag, as shown here:

```
FileInputStream foois = new FileOutputStream( fooFile, true);
FileInputStream passwdis = new FileOutputStream( "/etc/passwd", true);
```

Another way to append files is with a `RandomAccessFile`, as I'll discuss shortly.

To write characters (instead of bytes) to a file, you can wrap an `OutputStreamWriter` around a `FileOutputStream`. If you want to use the default character-encoding scheme, you can use the `FileWriter` class instead, which is provided as a convenience. `FileWriter` works just like `FileOutputStream`, except that it writes characters instead of bytes and wraps a `Writer` instead of an `OutputStream`.

The following example reads a line of data from standard input and writes it to the file */tmp/foo.txt*:

```
String s = new BufferedReader( new InputStreamReader( System.in ) ).readLine();

File out = new File( "/tmp/foo.txt" );
FileWriter fw = new FileWriter ( out );
PrintWriter pw = new PrintWriter( fw, true )
pw.println( s );
```

Notice how we have wrapped a `PrintWriter` around the `FileWriter` to facilitate writing the data. To be a good filesystem citizen, you need to call the `close()` method when you are done with the `FileWriter`.

java.io.RandomAccessFile

The `java.io.RandomAccessFile` class provides the ability to read and write data from or to any specified location in a file. `RandomAccessFile` implements both the `DataInput` and `DataOutput` interfaces, so you can use it to read and write strings and Java primitive types. In other words, `RandomAccessFile` defines the same methods for reading and writing data as `DataInputStream` and `DataOutputStream`. However, because the class provides random, rather than sequential, access to file data, it's not a subclass of either `InputStream` or `OutputStream`.

You can create a `RandomAccessFile` from a `String` pathname or a `File` object. The constructor also takes a second `String` argument that specifies the mode of the file. Use "r" for a read-only file or "rw" for a read-write file. Here's how to create a simple database to keep track of user information:

```
try {
    RandomAccessFile users = new RandomAccessFile( "Users", "rw" );
    ...
}
catch (IOException e) {
}
```

When you create a `RandomAccessFile` in read-only mode, Java tries to open the specified file. If the file doesn't exist, `RandomAccessFile` throws an `IOException`. If, however, you are creating a `RandomAccessFile` in read-write mode, the object creates the file if it doesn't exist. The constructor can still throw an `IOException` if some other I/O error occurs, so you still need to handle this exception.

After you have created a `RandomAccessFile`, call any of the normal reading and writing methods, just as you would with a `DataInputStream` or `DataOutputStream`. If you try to write to a read-only file, the write method throws an `IOException`.

What makes a `RandomAccessFile` special is the `seek()` method. This method takes a `long` value and uses it to set the location for reading and writing in the file. You can use the `getFilePointer()` method to get the current location. If you need to append data on the end of the file, use `length()` to determine that location. You can write or seek beyond the end of a file, but you can't read beyond the end of a file. The read methods throws a `EOFException` if you try to do this.

Here's an example of writing some data to our user database:

```
users.seek( userNum * RECORDSIZE );
users.writeUTF( userName );
users.writeInt( userID );
```

One caveat to notice with this example is that we need to be sure that the `String` length for userName, along with any data that comes after it, fits within the boundaries of the record size.

Applets and Files

For security reasons, untrusted applets are not permitted to read and write to arbitrary places in the filesystem. The ability of an applet to read and write files, as with any kind of system resource, is under the control of a SecurityManager object. A SecurityManager is installed by the application that is running the applet, such as *appletviewer* or a Java-enabled Web browser. All filesystem access must first pass the scrutiny of the SecurityManager. With that in mind, applet-viewer applications are free to implement their own schemes for what, if any, access an applet may have.

For example, Sun's HotJava Web browser allows even untrusted applets to have access to specific files designated by the user in an access-control list. Netscape Navigator, on the other hand, currently doesn't allow untrusted applets any access to the filesystem. In both cases trusted applets can be given arbitrary access to the filesystem, just like a standalone Java application.

It isn't unusual to want an applet to maintain some kind of state information on the system where it's running. But for a Java applet that is restricted from access to the local filesystem, the only option is to store data over the network on its server. Although, at the moment, the Web is a relatively static, read-only environment, applets have at their disposal powerful, general means for communicating data over networks. The only limitation is that, by convention, an applet's network communication is restricted to the server that launched it. This limits the options for where the data will reside.

Currently, the only way for a Java program to send data to a server is through a network socket or tools like RMI which run over sockets.[*] In Chapter 11 we'll take a detailed look at building networked applications with sockets. With the tools described in that chapter, it's possible to build powerful client/server applications.

Loading Class Resources

We often have data files and other objects that we want our programs to use. Java provides many ways to access these resources. In a standalone application, we can simply open files and read the bytes. In both standalone applications and applets, we can construct URLs to well-known locations. The problem with these methods is that we have to know where our application lives in order to find our data. This is not always as easy as it seems. What is needed is a universal way to access resources associated with our classes. The Java Class class's getResource() method provides just this.

---

[*] Sun has promised that a future release of Java will include NFS support for the Java File class. This would allow applets and applications to read and write network mounted files as if they were local.

What does getResource() do for us? To construct a URL to a file, we normally have to figure out a home directory for our code and construct a path relative to that. In an applet, we could use getCodeBase() or getDocumentBase() to find the base URL, and use that base to create the URL for the resource we want. But these methods don't help a standalone application—and there's no reason that a standalone application and an applet shouldn't be able to share classes anyway. To solve this problem, the Class getResource() method provides a standard way to get objects relative to a given class file. getResource() returns a special URL that uses the class's class loader. This means that no matter where the class came from—a Web server, the local filesystem, or even a JAR file—we can simply ask for an object, get a URL for the object, and use the URL to access the object.

getResource() takes as an argument a slash-separated (/) pathname for the resource and returns a URL. There are two kinds of paths: absolute and relative. An absolute path begins with a slash. For example: */foo/bar/blah.txt*. In this case, the search for the object begins at the top of the classpath. If there is a directory *foo/bar* in the classpath, getResource() searches that directory for the *blah.txt* file. A relative URL does not begin with a slash. In this case, the search begins at the location of the class file, whether it is local, on a remote server, or in a JAR file (either local or remote). So if we were calling getResource() on a classloader that loaded a class in the foo.bar package, we could refer to the file as *blah.txt*. In this case, the class itself would be loaded from the directory *foo/bar* somewhere on the classpath, and we'd expect to find the file in the same directory.

For example, here's an application that looks up some resources:

```
package mypackage;

import java.net.URL;

class FindResources {
    public static void main( String [] args ) throws IOException {

        // Absolute from the classpath
        URL url = FindResources.class.getResource("/mypackage/foo.txt");
            ...
        // Relative to the class location
        url = FindResources.class.getResource("foo.txt");
            ...
        // Another relative document
        url = FindResources.class.getResource("docs/bar.txt");
            ...
    }
}
```

The FindResources class belongs to the mypackage package, so its class file will live in a *mypackage* directory somewhere on the classpath. FindResources locates the document *foo.txt* using an absolute and then a relative URL. At the end,

FindResources uses a relative path to reach a document in the *mypackage/docs* directory. In each case we refer to the FindResources's Class object using the static .class notation. Alternatively, if we had an instance of the object, we could use its getClass() method to reach the class.

For an applet, the search is similar but occurs on the host from which the applet was loaded. getResource() first checks any JAR files loaded with the applet, and then searches the normal remote applet classpath, constructed relative to the applet's codebase URL.

getResource() returns a URL for whatever type of object you reference. This could be a text file or properties file that you will want to read as a stream, or it might be an image or sound file, or some other object. If you want the data as a stream, the Class class also provides a getResourceAsStream() method. In the case of an image, you'd probably hand the URL over to the getImage() method for loading.

Serialization

Using streams and files, you can write an application that saves and loads its data to a disk drive. Java 1.1 provides an even more powerful mechanism called *object serialization* that does a lot of the work for you. In its simplest form, object serialization is an automatic way to save and load the state of an object. However, object serialization has depths that we cannot plumb within the scope of this book, including complete control over the serialization process and interesting conundrums like class versioning.

Basically, any class that implements the Serializable interface can be saved and restored from a stream. Special stream subclasses, ObjectInputStream and ObjectOutputStream, are used to serialize primitive types and objects. Subclasses of Serializable classes are also serializable. The default serialization mechanism saves the value of an object's nonstatic and nontransient member variables.

One of the tricky things about serialization is that when an object is serialized, any object references it contains are also serialized. Serialization can capture entire "graphs" of interconnected objects and put them back together on the receiving end. We'll see this in an upcoming example. The implication is that any object we serialize must only contain references to Serializable objects. There are ways around this problem, like marking nonserializable members as transient or overriding the default serialization mechanisms. The transient modifier can be applied to any instance variable to indicate that its contents are not useful outside of the current context and should never be saved.

In the following example, we create a Hashtable and write it to a disk file called *h.ser*:

```java
import java.io.*;
import java.util.*;
public class Save {
  public static void main(String[] args) {
    Hashtable h = new Hashtable();
    h.put("string", "Gabriel Garcia Marquez");
    h.put("int", new Integer(26));
    h.put("double", new Double(Math.PI));

    try {
      FileOutputStream fileOut = new FileOutputStream("h.ser");
      ObjectOutputStream out = new ObjectOutputStream(fileOut);
      out.writeObject(h);
    }
    catch (Exception e) {
      System.out.println(e);
    }
  }
}
```

First we construct a Hashtable with a few elements in it. Then, in the three lines of code inside the try block, we write the Hashtable to a file called *h.ser*, using the writeObject() method of ObjectOutputStream. The ObjectOutputStream class is a lot like the DataOutputStream class, except that it includes the powerful writeObject() method. The Hashtable object is serializable because it implements the Serializable interface.

The Hashtable we created has internal references to the items it contains. Thus, these components are automatically serialized along with the Hashtable. We'll see this in the next example when we deserialize the Hashtable:

```java
import java.io.*;
import java.util.*;
public class Load {
  public static void main(String[] args) {
    try {
      FileInputStream fileIn = new FileInputStream("h.ser");
      ObjectInputStream in = new ObjectInputStream(fileIn);
      Hashtable h = (Hashtable)in.readObject();
      System.out.println(h.toString());
    }
    catch (Exception e) {
      System.out.println(e);
    }
  }
}
```

In this example, we read the Hashtable from the *h.ser* file, using the readObject() method of ObjectInputStream. The ObjectInputStream class is a lot like DataInputStream, except it includes the readObject() method. The return type of readObject() is Object, so we need to cast it to a Hashtable. Finally, we print out the contents of the Hashtable using its toString() method.

We'll see more examples of serialization at work in Chapter 18 when we discuss JavaBeans. There we'll see that it is even possible to serialize graphical AWT components in mid-use and bring them back to life later.

Data Compression

Java 1.1 includes a new package, java.util.zip, that contains classes you can use for data compression. In this section we'll talk about how to use the classes. We'll also present two useful example programs that build on what you have just learned about streams and files.

The classes in the java.util.zip package support two widespread compression formats: GZIP and ZIP. Both of these are based on the ZLIB compression algorithm, which is discussed in RFC 1950, RFC 1951, and RFC 1952. These documents are available at *ftp://ds.internic.net/rfc/*. We don't recommend reading these documents unless you want to implement your own compression algorithm or otherwise extend the functionality of the java.util.zip package.

Compressing Data

The java.util.zip class provides two FilterOutputStream subclasses to write compressed data to a stream. To write compressed data in the GZIP format, simply wrap a GZIPOutputStream around an underlying stream and write to it. The following is a complete example that shows how to compress a file using the GZIP format:

```java
import java.io.*;
import java.util.zip.*;
public class GZip {
  public static int sChunk = 8192;
  public static void main(String[] args) {
    if (args.length != 1) {
      System.out.println("Usage: GZip source");
      return;
    }
    // Create output stream.
    String zipname = args[0] + ".gz";
    GZIPOutputStream zipout;
    try {
      FileOutputStream out = new FileOutputStream(zipname);
      zipout = new GZIPOutputStream(out);
    }
    catch (IOException e) {
      System.out.println("Couldn't create " + zipname + ".");
      return;
    }
    byte[] buffer = new byte[sChunk];
    // Compress the file.
```

```
  try {
    FileInputStream in = new FileInputStream(args[0]);
    int length;
    while ((length = in.read(buffer, 0, sChunk)) != -1)
      zipout.write(buffer, 0, length);
    in.close();
  }
  catch (IOException e) {
    System.out.println("Couldn't compress " + args[0] + ".");
  }
  try { zipout.close(); }
  catch (IOException e) {}
  }
}
```

First we check to make sure we have a command-line argument representing a file-name. Then we construct a GZIPOutputStream wrapped around a FileOutput-Stream representing the given filename with the *.gz* suffix appended. With this in place, we open the source file. We read chunks of data from it and write them into the GZIPOutputStream. Finally, we clean up by closing our open streams.

Writing data to a ZIP file is a little more involved but still quite manageable. While a GZIP file contains only one compressed file, a ZIP file is actually an archive of files, some (or all) of which may be compressed. Each item in the ZIP file is repre-sented by a ZipEntry object. When writing to a ZipOutputStream, you'll need to call putNextEntry() before writing the data for each item. The following example shows how to create a ZipOutputStream. You'll notice it's just like creating a GZIPOutputStream:

```
ZipOutputStream zipout;
try {
  FileOutputStream out = new FileOutputStream("archive.zip");
  zipout = new ZipOutputStream(out);
}
catch (IOException e) {}
```

Let's say we have two files we want to write into this archive. Before we begin writ-ing we need to call putNextEntry(). We'll create a simple entry with just a name. There are other fields in ZipEntry that you can set, but most of the time you won't need to bother with them.

```
try {
  ZipEntry entry = new ZipEntry("First");
  zipout.putNextEntry(entry);
}
catch (IOException e) {}
```

At this point you can write the contents of the first file into the archive. When you're ready to write the second file into the archive, you simply call putNextEn-try() again:

```
try {
  ZipEntry entry = new ZipEntry("Second");
  zipout.putNextEntry(entry);
}
catch (IOException e) {}
```

Decompressing Data

To decompress data, you can use one of the two FilterInputStream subclasses provided in java.util.zip. To decompress data in the GZIP format, simply wrap a GZIPInputStream around an underlying stream and read from it. The following is a complete example that shows how to decompress a GZIP file:

```
import java.io.*;
import java.util.zip.*;
public class GUnzip {
  public static int sChunk = 8192;
  public static void main(String[] args) {
    if (args.length != 1) {
      System.out.println("Usage: GUnzip source");
      return;
    }
    // Create input stream.
    String zipname, source;
    if (args[0].endsWith(".gz")) {
      zipname = args[0];
      source = args[0].substring(0, args[0].length() - 3);
    }
    else {
      zipname = args[0] + ".gz";
      source = args[0];
    }
    GZIPInputStream zipin;
    try {
      FileInputStream in = new FileInputStream(zipname);
      zipin = new GZIPInputStream(in);
    }
    catch (IOException e) {
      System.out.println("Couldn't open " + zipname + ".");
      return;
    }
    byte[] buffer = new byte[sChunk];
    // Decompress the file.
    try {
      FileOutputStream out = new FileOutputStream(source);
      int length;
      while ((length = zipin.read(buffer, 0, sChunk)) != -1)
        out.write(buffer, 0, length);
      out.close();
    }
    catch (IOException e) {
      System.out.println("Couldn't decompress " + args[0] + ".");
    }
```

```
    try { zipin.close(); }
    catch (IOException e) {}
  }
}
```

First we check to make sure we have a command-line argument representing a file-name. If the argument ends with .gz, we figure out what the filename for the uncompressed file should be. Otherwise, we just use the given argument and assume the compressed file has the .gz suffix. Then we construct a GZIPInput-Stream wrapped around a FileInputStream representing the compressed file. With this in place, we open the target file. We read chunks of data from the GZIP-InputStream and write them into the target file. Finally, we clean up by closing our open streams.

Again, the ZIP archive presents a little more complexity than the GZIP file. When reading from a ZipInputStream, you should call getNextEntry() before reading each item. When getNextEntry() returns null, there are no more items to read. The following example shows how to create a ZipInputStream. You'll notice it's just like creating a GZIPInputStream:

```
ZipInputStream zipin;
try {
  FileInputStream in = new FileInputStream("archive.zip");
  zipin = new ZipInputStream(in);
}
catch (IOException e) {}
```

Suppose we want to read two files from this archive. Before we begin reading we need to call getNextEntry(). At the least, the entry will give us a name of the item we are reading from the archive:

```
try {
  ZipEntry first = zipin.getNextEntry();
}
catch (IOException e) {}
```

At this point you can read the contents of the first item in the archive. When you come to the end of the item, the read() method will return -1. Now you can call getNextEntry() again to read the second item from the archive:

```
try {
  ZipEntry second = zipin.getNextEntry();
}
catch (IOException e) {}
```

If you call getNextEntry() and it returns null, there are no more items, and you have reached the end of the archive.

11

Network Programming with Sockets and RMI

The network is the soul of Java. Most of what is new and exciting about Java centers around the potential for new kinds of dynamic, networked applications. This chapter discusses the java.net package, which contains classes for communications and working with networked resources. These classes fall into two categories: the sockets API and classes for working with Uniform Resource Locators (URLs). Figure 11-1 shows all of the classes in java.net.

Java's sockets interface provides access to the standard network protocols used for communications between hosts on the Internet. Sockets are the mechanism underlying all other kinds of portable networked communications. Your processes can use sockets to communicate with a server or peer applications on the Net, but you have to implement your own application-level protocols for handling and interpreting the data. Higher-level features, like remote method calls and distributed objects, are implemented over sockets.

In this chapter, we'll try to provide some practical and realistic examples of Java network programming using sockets and remote method invocation (RMI). In the next chapter, we'll look at URLs, content handlers, and protocol handlers.

Sockets

Sockets are a low-level programming interface for networked communications. They send streams of data between applications that may or may not be on the same host. Sockets originated in BSD UNIX and are, in other languages, hairy and complicated things with lots of small parts that can break off and choke little children. The reason for this is that most socket APIs can be used with almost any kind of underlying network protocol. Since the protocols that transport data across the

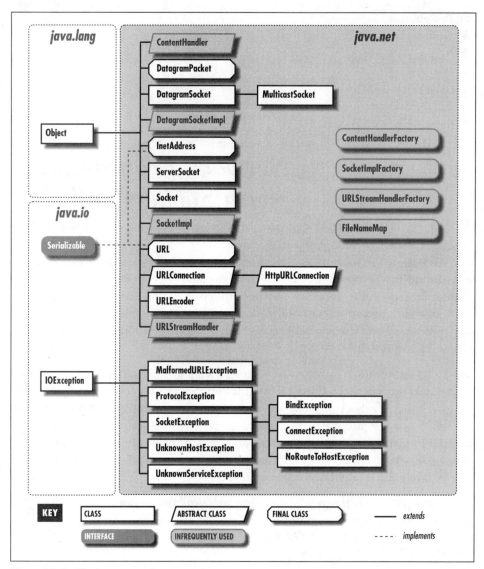

Figure 11–1: The java.net package

network can have radically different features, the socket interface can be quite complex.[*]

---

* For a discussion of sockets in general, see *UNIX Network Programming*, by Richard Stevens (Prentice-Hall). For a complete discussion of network programming in Java, see *Java Network Programming* by Elliotte Rusty Harold (O'Reilly).

Java supports a simplified object-oriented interface to sockets that makes network communications considerably easier. If you have done network programming using sockets in C or another structured language, you should be pleasantly surprised at how simple things can be when objects encapsulate the gory details. If this is the first time you've come across sockets, you'll find that talking to another application can be as simple as reading a file or getting user input. Most forms of I/O in Java, including network I/O, use the stream classes described in Chapter 10. Streams provide a unified I/O interface; reading or writing across the Internet is similar to reading or writing a file on the local system.

Java provides different kinds of sockets to support three different distinct classes of underlying protocols. In this first section, we'll look at Java's Socket class, which uses a *connection-oriented* protocol. A connection-oriented protocol gives you the equivalent of a telephone conversation; after establishing a connection, two applications can send data back and forth; the connection stays in place even when no one is talking. The protocol ensures that no data is lost and that it always arrives in order. In the next section we'll look at the DatagramSocket class, which uses a *connectionless* protocol. A connectionless protocol is more like the postal service. Applications can send short messages to each other, but no attempt is made to keep the connection open between messages, to keep the messages in order, or even to guarantee that they arrive. A MulticastSocket is a variation of a Datagram-Socket that can be used to send data to multiple recipients (multicasting); we don't discuss multicasting in this book.

In theory, just about any protocol family can be used underneath the socket layer: Novell's IPX, Apple's AppleTalk, even the old ChaosNet protocols. But this isn't a theoretical world. In practice, there's only one protocol family people care about on the Internet, and only one protocol family Java supports: the Internet protocols, IP. The Socket class speaks TCP, and the DatagramSocket class speaks UDP, both standard Internet protocols. These protocols are available on any system that is connected to the Internet.

Clients and Servers

When writing network applications, it's common to talk about clients and servers. The distinction is increasingly vague, but the side that initiates the conversation is usually the *client*. The side that accepts the request to talk is usually the *server*. In the case where there are two peer applications using sockets to talk, the distinction is less important, but for simplicity we'll use the above definition.

For our purposes, the most important difference between a client and a server is that a client can create a socket to initiate a conversation with a server application at any time, while a server must prepare to listen for incoming conversations in advance. The `java.net.Socket` class represents a single side of a socket connection on either the client or server. In addition, the server uses the `java.net.ServerSocket` class to wait for connections from clients. An application acting as a server creates a `ServerSocket` object and waits, blocked in a call to its `accept()` method, until a connection arrives. When it does, the `accept()` method creates a `Socket` object the server uses to communicate with the client. A server carries on multiple conversations at once; there is only a single `ServerSocket`, but one active `Socket` object for each client, as shown in Figure 11-2.

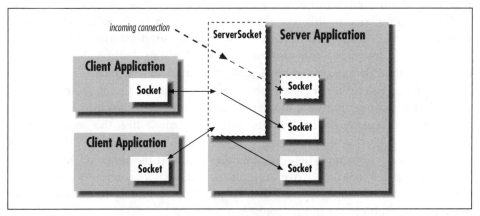

Figure 11–2: Clients and servers, Sockets and ServerSockets

A client needs two pieces of information to locate and connect to another server on the Internet: a hostname (used to find the host's network address) and a port number. The port number is an identifier that differentiates between multiple clients or servers on the same host. A server application listens on a prearranged port while waiting for connections. Clients select the port number assigned to the service they want to access. If you think of the host computers as hotels and the applications as guests, then the ports are like the guests' room numbers. For one guest to call another, he or she must know the other party's hotel name and room number.

Clients

A client application opens a connection to a server by constructing a `Socket` that specifies the hostname and port number of the desired server:

```
try {
    Socket sock = new Socket("wupost.wustl.edu", 25);
}
catch ( UnknownHostException e ) {
    System.out.println("Can't find host.");
```

```
    }
    catch ( IOException e ) {
        System.out.println("Error connecting to host.");
    }
```

This code fragment attempts to connect a `Socket` to port 25 (the SMTP mail service) of the host *wupost.wustl.edu*. The client handles the possibility that the hostname can't be resolved (`UnknownHostException`) and that it might not be able to connect to it (`IOException`). As an alternative to using a hostname, you can provide a string version of the host's IP address:

```
    Socket sock = new Socket("128.252.120.1", 25);     // wupost.wustl.edu
```

Once a connection is made, input and output streams can be retrieved with the `Socket getInputStream()` and `getOutputStream()` methods. The following (rather arbitrary and strange) code sends and receives some data with the streams.

```
    try {
        Socket server = new Socket("foo.bar.com", 1234);
        InputStream in = server.getInputStream();
        OutputStream out = server.getOutputStream();

        // Write a byte
        out.write(42);

        // Write a newline or carriage return delimited string
        PrintWriter pout = new PrintWriter( out, true );
        pout.println("Hello!");

        // Read a byte
        Byte back = in.read();

        // Read a newline or carriage return delimited string
        BufferedReader bin = new BufferedReader( new InputStreamReader( in ) );
        String response = bin.readLine();

        // Send a serialized Java object
        ObjectOutputStream oout = new ObjectOutputStream( out );
        oout.writeObject( new java.util.Date() );
        oout.flush();

        server.close();
    }
    catch (IOException e ) { }
```

In the exchange above, the client first creates a `Socket` for communicating with the server. The `Socket` constructor specifies the server's hostname (*foo.bar.com*) and a prearranged port number (1234). Once the connection is established, the client writes a single byte to the server using the `OutputStream`'s `write()` method. It then wraps a `PrintWriter` around the `OutputStream` in order to send text more easily. Next, it performs the complementary operations, reading a byte from the server using `InputStream`'s `read()` and then creating a `DataInputStream` from which to get a string of text. Finally, we do something really funky and send a serialized Java object to the server, using an `ObjectOutputStream`. (We'll talk in depth about sending serialized objects later in this chapter.) The client then terminates the connection with the `close()` method. All these operations have the potential to generate `IOExceptions`; the catch clause is where our application would deal with these.

Servers

After a connection is established, a server application uses the same kind of `Socket` object for its side of the communications. However, to accept a connection from a client, it must first create a `ServerSocket`, bound to the correct port. Let's recreate the previous conversation from the server's point of view:

```
// Meanwhile, on foo.bar.com...
try {
    ServerSocket listener = new ServerSocket( 1234 );

    while ( !finished ) {
        Socket client = listener.accept();    // wait for connection

        InputStream in = client.getInputStream();
        OutputStream out = client.getOutputStream();

        // Read a byte
        Byte someByte = in.read();

        // Read a newline or carriage return delimited string
        BufferedReader bin = new BufferedReader( new InputStreamReader( in ) );
        String someString = bin.readLine();

        // Write a byte
        out.write(43);

        // Say goodbye
        PrintWriter pout = new PrintWriter( out, true );
        pout.println("Goodbye!");

        // Read a serialized Java object
        ObjectInputStream oin = new ObjectInputStream( in );
        Date date = (Date)oin.readObject();

        client.close();
    }
```

```
        listener.close();
    }
    catch (IOException e ) { }
```

First, our server creates a `ServerSocket` attached to port 1234. On some systems there are rules about what ports an application can use. Port numbers below 1024 are usually reserved for system processes and standard, well-known services, so we pick a port number outside of this range. The `ServerSocket` need be created only once. Thereafter we can accept as many connections as arrive.

Next we enter a loop, waiting for the `accept()` method of the `ServerSocket` to return an active `Socket` connection from a client. When a connection has been established, we perform the server side of our dialog, then close the connection and return to the top of the loop to wait for another connection. Finally, when the server application wants to stop listening for connections altogether, it calls the `close()` method of the `ServerSocket`.*

As you can see, this server is single-threaded; it handles one connection at a time; it doesn't call `accept()` to listen for a new connection until it's finished with the current connection. A more realistic server would have a loop that accepts connections concurrently and passes them off to their own threads for processing. (Our tiny HTTP daemon in a later section will do just this.)

Sockets and security

The examples above presuppose the client has permission to connect to the server, and that the server is allowed to listen on the specified socket. This is not always the case. Specifically, applets and other applications run under the auspices of a `SecurityManager` that can impose arbitrary restrictions on what hosts they may or may not talk to, and whether they can listen for connections. The security policy imposed by the current version of Netscape Navigator allows untrusted applets to open socket connections only to the host that served them. That is, they can talk back only to the server from which their class files were retrieved. Untrusted applets are not allowed to open server sockets themselves.

Now, this doesn't mean that an untrusted applet can't cooperate with its server to communicate with anyone, anywhere. A server could run a proxy that lets the applet communicate indirectly with anyone it likes. What the current security policy prevents is malicious applets roaming around inside corporate firewalls. It places the burden of security on the originating server, and not the client machine. Restricting access to the originating server limits the usefulness of

---

* A somewhat obscure security feature in TCP/IP specifies that if a server socket actively closes a connection while a client is connected, it may not be able to bind (attach itself) to the same port on the server host again for a period of time (the maximum time to live of a packet on the network). It's possible to turn off this feature, and it's likely that your Java implementation will have done so.

"trojan" applications that do annoying things from the client side. You won't let your proxy mail-bomb people, because you'll be blamed.

The DateAtHost Client

Many networked workstations run a time service that dispenses their local clock time on a well-known port. This was a precursor of NTP, the more general Network Time Protocol. In the next example, DateAtHost, we'll make a specialized subclass of java.util.Date that fetches the time from a remote host instead of initializing itself from the local clock. (See Chapter 9 for a complete discussion of the Date class.)

DateAtHost connects to the time service (port 37) and reads four bytes representing the time on the remote host. These four bytes are interpreted as an integer representing the number of seconds since the turn of the century. DateAtHost converts this to Java's variant of the absolute time (milliseconds since January 1, 1970, a date that should be familiar to UNIX users) and then uses the remote host's time to initialize itself:

```
import java.net.Socket;
import java.io.*;

public class DateAtHost extends java.util.Date {
    static int timePort = 37;
    static final long offset = 2208988800L;   //  Seconds from century to
                                               //   Jan 1, 1970 00:00 GMT

    public DateAtHost( String host ) throws IOException {
        this( host, timePort );
    }

    public DateAtHost( String host, int port ) throws IOException {
        Socket server = new Socket( host, port );
        DataInputStream din = new DataInputStream( server.getInputStream() );
        int time = din.readInt();
        server.close();

        setTime( (((1L << 32) + time) - offset) * 1000 );
    }
}
```

That's all there is to it. It's not very long, even with a few frills. We have supplied two possible constructors for DateAtHost. Normally we'll use the first, which simply takes the name of the remote host as an argument. The second, overloaded constructor specifies the hostname and the port number of the remote time service. (If the time service were running on a nonstandard port, we would use the second constructor to specify the alternate port number.) This second constructor does the work of making the connection and setting the time. The first constructor simply invokes the second (using the `this()` construct) with the default port as an argument. Supplying simplified constructors that invoke their siblings with default arguments is a common and useful technique.

The second constructor opens a socket to the specified port on the remote host. It creates a `DataInputStream` to wrap the input stream and then reads a 4-byte integer using the `readInt()` method. It's no coincidence that the bytes are in the right order. Java's `DataInputStream` and `DataOutputStream` classes work with the bytes of integer types in *network byte order* (most significant to least significant). The time protocol (and other standard network protocols that deal with binary data) also uses the network byte order, so we don't need to call any conversion routines. (Explicit data conversions would probably be necessary if we were using a nonstandard protocol, especially when talking to a non-Java client or server.) After reading the data, we're finished with the socket, so we close it, terminating the connection to the server. Finally, the constructor initializes the rest of the object by calling `Date`'s `setTime()` method with the calculated time value.[*]

The `DateAtHost` class can work with a time retrieved from a remote host almost as easily as `Date` is used with the time on the local host. The only additional overhead is that we have to deal with the possible `IOException` that can be thrown by the `DateAtHost` constructor:

```
try {
    Date d = new DateAtHost( "sura.net" );
    System.out.println( "The time over there is: " + d );
    int hours = d.getHours();
    int minutes = d.getMinutes();
    ...
}
catch ( IOException e ) { }
```

This example fetches the time at the host *sura.net* and prints its value. It then looks at some components of the time using the `getHours()` and `getMinutes()` methods of the `Date` class.

The TinyHttpd Server

Have you ever wanted your very own Web server? Well, you're in luck. In this section, we're going to build `TinyHttpd`, a minimal but functional HTTP daemon. `TinyHttpd` listens on a specified port and services simple HTTP "get file" requests. They look something like this:

---

[*] The conversion first creates a long value, which is the unsigned equivalent of the integer time. It subtracts an offset to make the time relative to the epoch (January 1, 1970) rather than the century, and multiples by 1000 to convert to milliseconds.

```
GET /path/filename [optional stuff]
```

Your Web browser sends one or more requests as lines for each document it
retrieves. Upon reading a request, the server tries to open the specified file and
send its contents. If that document contains references to images or other items to
be displayed inline, the browser continues with additional GET requests. For best
performance (especially in a time-slicing environment), TinyHttpd services each
request in its own thread. Therefore, TinyHttpd can service several requests concurrently.

Over and above the limitations imposed by its simplicity, TinyHttpd suffers from
the limitations imposed by the fickleness of filesystem access. It's important to
remember that file pathnames are still architecture dependent—as is the concept
of a filesystem to begin with. This example should work, as-is, on UNIX and DOS-
like systems, but may require some customizations to account for differences on
other platforms. It's possible to write more elaborate code that uses the environ-
mental information provided by Java to tailor itself to the local system. (Chapter 10
gives some hints about how.)

WARNING

The next example will serve files from your host without protection. Don't
try this at work.

Now, without further ado, here's TinyHttpd:

```
import java.net.*;
import java.io.*;
import java.util.*;

public class TinyHttpd {
    public static void main( String argv[] ) throws IOException {
        ServerSocket ss = new ServerSocket( Integer.parseInt(argv[0]) );
        while ( true )
            new TinyHttpdConnection( ss.accept() ).start();
    }
}

class TinyHttpdConnection extends Thread {
    Socket client;
    TinyHttpdConnection ( Socket client ) throws SocketException {
        this.client = client;
        setPriority( NORM_PRIORITY - 1 );
    }

    public void run() {
        try {
            BufferedReader in = new BufferedReader(
                new InputStreamReader(client.getInputStream(), "8859_1") );
            OutputStream out = client.getOutputStream();
```

```
        PrintWriter pout = new PrintWriter(
            new OutputStreamWriter(out, "8859_1"), true );
        String request = in.readLine();
        System.out.println( "Request: "+request );

        StringTokenizer st = new StringTokenizer( request );
        if ( (st.countTokens() >= 2) && st.nextToken().equals("GET") ) {
            if ( (request = st.nextToken()).startsWith("/") )
                request = request.substring( 1 );
            if ( request.endsWith("/") || request.equals("") )
                request = request + "index.html";
            try {
                FileInputStream fis = new FileInputStream ( request );
                byte [] data = new byte [ fis.available() ];
                fis.read( data );
                out.write( data );
                out.flush();
            } catch ( FileNotFoundException e ) {
                pout.println( "404 Object Not Found" ); }
        } else
            pout.println( "400 Bad Request" );
        client.close();
    } catch ( IOException e ) {
        System.out.println( "I/O error " + e ); }
    }
}
```

Compile TinyHttpd and place it in your class path. Go to a directory with some interesting documents and start the daemon, specifying an unused port number as an argument. For example:

```
% java TinyHttpd 1234
```

You should now be able to use your Web browser to retrieve files from your host. You'll have to specify the nonstandard port number in the URL. For example, if your hostname is *foo.bar.com*, and you started the server as above, you could reference a file as in:

```
http://foo.bar.com:1234/welcome.html
```

TinyHttpd looks for files relative to its current directory, so the pathnames you provide should be relative to that location. Retrieved some files? All righty then, let's take a closer look.

TinyHttpd is comprised of two classes. The public TinyHttpd class contains the main() method of our standalone application. It begins by creating a Server-Socket, attached to the specified port. It then loops, waiting for client connections and creating instances of the second class, a TinyHttpdConnection thread, to service each request. The while loop waits for the ServerSocket accept() method to return a new Socket for each client connection. The Socket is passed as an argument to construct the TinyHttpdConnection thread that handles it.

TinyHttpdConnection is a subclass of Thread. It lives long enough to process one client connection and then dies. TinyHttpdConnection's constructor does two things. After saving the Socket argument for its caller, it adjusts its priority. By lowering its priority to NORM_PRIORITY-1 (just below the default priority), we ensure that the threads servicing established connections won't block TinyHttpd's main thread from accepting new requests. (On a time-slicing system, this is less important.) After our object is constructed, its start() method is invoked to bring the run() method to life.

The body of TinyHttpdConnection's run() method is where all the magic happens. First, we fetch an OutputStream for talking back to our client. The second line reads the GET request from the InputStream into the variable req. This request is a single newline-terminated String that looks like the GET request we described earlier. For this we use a BufferedInputStream wrapped around an InputStream-Reader. We'll say more about the InputStreamReader in a moment.

We then parse the contents of req to extract a filename. The next few lines are a brief exercise in string manipulation. We create a StringTokenizer and make sure there are at least two tokens. Using nextToken(), we take the first token and make sure it's the word GET. (If both conditions aren't met, we have an error.) Then we take the next token (which should be a filename), assign it to req, and check whether it begins with "/". If so, we use substring() to strip the first character, giving us a filename relative to the current directory. If it doesn't begin with "/", the filename is already relative to the current directory. Finally, we check to see if the requested filename looks like a directory name (i.e., ends in slash) or is empty. In these cases, we append the familiar default filename *index.html*.

Once we have the filename, we try to open the specified file and load its contents into a large byte array. If all goes well, we write the data out to the client on the OutputStream. If we can't parse the request or the file doesn't exist, we wrap our OutputStream with a PrintStream to make it easier to send a textual message. Then we return an appropriate HTTP error message. Finally, we close the socket and return from run(), removing our Thread.

Do French Web servers speak French?

In TinyHttpd, we explicitly created the InputStreamReader for our BufferedRead and the OutputStreamWriter for our PrintWriter. We do this so that we can specify the character encoding to use when converting from text to bytes. If we didn't specify, we'd get the default character encoding for the local system. For many purposes that's correct, but in this case we are speaking a well-defined protocol. The RFC for HTTP specifies that Web clients and servers should use the ISO 8859-1 character encoding, which is, for our purposes, just ASCII. We specify this encoding explicitly when we construct the InputStreamReader and OutputStreamWriter.

Taming the daemon

The biggest problem with TinyHttpd is that there are no restrictions on the files it
can access. With a little trickery, the daemon will happily send any file in your
filesystem to the client. It would be nice if we could restrict TinyHttpd to files that
are in the current directory, or a subdirectory. To make the daemon safer, let's add
a security manager. We discussed the general framework for security managers in
Chapter 9. Normally, a security manager is used to prevent Java code downloaded
over the Net from doing anything suspicious. However, a security manager will
serve nicely to restrict file access in a self-contained application.

Here's the code for the security manager class:

```
import java.io.*;

class TinyHttpdSecurityManager extends SecurityManager {

    public void checkAccess(Thread g) { };
    public void checkListen(int port) { };
    public void checkLink(String lib) { };
    public void checkPropertyAccess(String key) { };
    public void checkAccept(String host, int port) { };
    public void checkWrite(FileDescriptor fd) { };
    public void checkRead(FileDescriptor fd) { };

    public void checkRead( String s ) {
        if ( new File(s).isAbsolute() || (s.indexOf("..") != -1) )
            throw new SecurityException("Access to file : "+s+" denied.");
    }
}
```

The heart of this security manager is the checkRead() method. It checks two
things: it makes sure that the pathname we've been given isn't an absolute path,
which could name any file in the filesystem; and it makes sure the pathname
doesn't have a double dot (..) in it, which refers to the parent of the current
directory. With these two restrictions, we can be sure (at least on a UNIX or DOS-
like filesystem) that we have restricted access to only subdirectories of the current
directory. If the pathname is absolute or contains "..", checkRead() throws a
SecurityException.

The other do-nothing method implementations—e.g., checkAccess()—allow the
daemon to do its work without interference from the security manager. If we don't
install a security manager, the application runs with no restrictions. However, as
soon as we install any security manager, we inherit implementations of many
"check" routines. The default implementations won't let you do anything; they just
throw a security exception as soon as they are called. We have to open holes so the

daemon can do its own work; it still has to accept connections, listen on sockets, create threads, read property lists, etc. Therefore, we override the default checks with routines that allow these things.

Now you're thinking, isn't that overly permissive? Not for this application; after all, TinyHttpd never tries to load foreign classes from the Net. The only code we are executing is our own, and it's assumed we won't do anything dangerous. If we were planning to execute untrusted code, the security manager would have to be more careful about what to permit.

Now that we have a security manager, we must modify TinyHttpd to use it. Two changes are necessary: we must install the security manager and catch the security exceptions it generates. To install the security manager, add the following code at the beginning of TinyHttpd's main() method:

```
System.setSecurityManager( new TinyHttpdSecurityManager() );
```

To catch the security exception, add the following catch clause after FileNot-FoundException's catch clause:

```
catch ( SecurityException e )
    pout.println( "403 Forbidden" );
```

Now the daemon can't access anything that isn't within the current directory or a subdirectory. If it tries to, the security manager throws an exception and prevents access to the file. The daemon then returns a standard HTTP error message to the client.

TinyHttpd still has room for improvement. First, it consumes a lot of memory by allocating a huge array to read the entire contents of the file all at once. A more realistic implementation would use a buffer and send large amounts of data in several passes. TinyHttpd also fails to deal with simple things like directories. It wouldn't be hard to add a few lines of code to read a directory and generate linked HTML listings like most Web servers do.

Socket Options

The Java sockets API is a simplified interface to the general socket mechanisms. In a C environment, where all of the gory details of the network are visible to you, a lot of complex and sometimes esoteric options can be set on sockets to govern the behavior of the underlying protocols. Java gives us access to a few of the important ones. We'll refer to them by their C names so that you can recognize them in other networking books.

SO_TIMEOUT

The SO_TIMEOUT option sets a timer on I/O methods of a socket that block so that you don't have to wait forever if they don't complete successfully. This works for operations like accept() on server sockets and read() or write() on all sockets. If the timer expires before the operation would complete, an InterruptedIO-Exception is thrown. You can catch the exception and continue to use the socket normally. You set the timer by calling the setSoTimeout() method of the Socket class with the timeout period, in milliseconds, as an int argument. This works for regular Sockets and ServerSockets (TCP) and DatagramSockets (UDP), which we'll discuss in the next section.

To find out the current timeout value, call getSoTimeout().

TCP_NODELAY

This option turns off a feature of TCP called Nagle's algorithm, which tries to prevent certain interactive applications from flooding the network with very tiny packets. Turn this off if you have a fast network and you want all packets sent as soon as possible. The Socket setTcpNoDelay() method takes a boolean argument specifying whether the delay is on or off.

To find out whether the TCP_NODELAY option is enabled, call getTcpNoDelay(), which returns a boolean.

SO_LINGER

This option controls what happens to any unsent data when you perform a close() on an active socket connection. Normally the system tries to deliver any network buffered data and close the connection gracefully. The setSoLinger() method of the Socket class takes two arguments: a boolean that enables or disables the option, and an int that sets the "linger" value, in milliseconds. If you set the linger value to 0, any unsent data is discarded, and the TCP connection is aborted (terminated with a reset).

To find out the current linger value, call getSoLinger().

Proxies and Firewalls

Many networks are behind firewalls that prevent applications from opening direct socket connections to the outside network. Instead, they provide a service called SOCKS (named for sockets) that serves as a proxy server for socket connections, giving the administrators more control over what connections are allowed.

Java has built-in support for SOCKS. All you have to do is set some system properties in your application (in an applet, this should be already taken care of for you since you wouldn't have authority to set properties). Here's a list of the properties that configure Java to use a proxy server:

`http.proxySet`
> A `boolean` (`true` or `false`) indicating whether to use the proxy

`http.proxyHost`
> The proxy server name

`http.proxyPort`
> The proxy port number

You can set these properties on the command line using the Java interpreter's `-D` option or by calling the `System.setProperty()` method. The command below runs `MyProgram` using the proxy server at *foo.bar.com* on port 1234:

```
% java -Dhttp.proxySet=true -Dhttp.proxyServer=foo.bar.com
    -Dhttp.proxyPort=1234 MyProgram
```

In Java 1.0.2 the names didn't have the *http.* prefix. Java version 1.1 and later checks for the new names and then the old names. If the firewall does not allow any outside socket connections, your applet or application may still be able to communicate with the outside world by using HTTP to send and receive data. See Chapter 12 for an example of how to perform an HTTP POST from an applet.

Datagram Sockets

`TinyHttpd` used a `Socket` to create a connection to the client using the TCP protocol. In that example, TCP itself took care of data integrity; we didn't have to worry about data arriving out of order or incorrect. Now we'll take a walk on the wild side. We'll build an applet that uses a `java.net.DatagramSocket`, which uses the UDP protocol. A datagram is sort of like a "data telegram": it's a discrete chunk of data transmitted in one packet. Unlike the previous example, where we could get a convenient `OutputStream` from our `Socket` and write the data as if writing to a file, with a `DatagramSocket` we have to work one datagram at a time. (Of course, the TCP protocol was taking our `OutputStream` and slicing the data into packets, but we didn't have to worry about those details.)

UDP doesn't guarantee that the data will get through. If the data do get through, it may not arrive in the right order; it's even possible for duplicate datagrams to arrive. Using UDP is something like cutting the pages out of the encyclopedia, putting them into separate envelopes, and mailing them to your friend. If your friend wants to read the encyclopedia, it's his or her job to put the pages in order. If some pages got lost in the mail, your friend has to send you a letter asking for replacements.

Obviously, you wouldn't use UDP to send a huge amount of data. But it's significantly more efficient than TCP, particularly if you don't care about the order in which messages arrive, or whether the data arrive at all. For example, in a database lookup, the client can send a query; the server's response itself constitutes an acknowledgment. If the response doesn't arrive within a certain time, the client can send another query. It shouldn't be hard for the client to match responses to its original queries. Some important applications that use UDP are the Domain Name System (DNS) and Sun's Network Filesystem (NFS).

The HeartBeat Applet

In this section we'll build a simple applet, HeartBeat, that sends a datagram to its server each time it's started and stopped. We'll also build a simple standalone server application, Pulse, that receives these datagrams and prints them. By tracking the output, you could have a crude measure of who is currently looking at your Web page at any given time. This is an ideal application for UDP: we don't want the overhead of a TCP socket, and if datagrams get lost, it's no big deal.

First, the HeartBeat applet:

```
import java.net.*;
import java.io.*;

public class HeartBeat extends java.applet.Applet {
    String myHost;
    int myPort;

    public void init() {
        myHost = getCodeBase().getHost();
        myPort = Integer.parseInt( getParameter("myPort") );
    }

    private void sendMessage( String message ) {
        try {
            byte [] data = message.getBytes();
            InetAddress addr = InetAddress.getByName( myHost );
            DatagramPacket pack =
                new DatagramPacket(data, data.length, addr, myPort );
            DatagramSocket ds = new DatagramSocket();
            ds.send( pack );
            ds.close();
        } catch ( IOException e ) {
            System.out.println( e );  // Error creating socket
        }
    }
```

```
    public void start() {
        sendMessage("Arrived");
    }
    public void stop() {
        sendMessage("Departed");
    }
}
```

Compile the applet and include it in an HTML document with an <APPLET> tag:

```
<applet height=10 width=10 code=HeartBeat>
    <param name="myPort" value="1234">
</applet>
```

The myPort parameter should specify the port number on which our server application listens for data.

Next, the server-side application, Pulse:

```
import java.net.*;
import java.io.*;

public class Pulse {
    public static void main( String [] argv ) throws IOException {
        DatagramSocket s = new DatagramSocket( Integer.parseInt(argv[0]) );

        while ( true ) {
            DatagramPacket packet = new DatagramPacket(new byte [1024], 1024);
            s.receive( packet );
            String message = new String( packet.getData() );
            System.out.println( "Heartbeat from: " +
                    packet.getAddress().getHostName() + " - " + message );
        }
    }
}
```

Compile Pulse and run it on your Web server, specifying a port number as an argument:

```
% java Pulse 1234
```

The port number should be the same as the one you used in the myPort parameter of the <APPLET> tag for HeartBeat.

Now, pull up the Web page in your browser. You won't see anything there (a better application might do something visual as well), but you should get a blip from the Pulse application. Leave the page and return to it a few times. Each time the applet is started or stopped, it sends a message:

```
Heartbeat from: foo.bar.com - Arrived
Heartbeat from: foo.bar.com - Departed
Heartbeat from: foo.bar.com - Arrived
```

```
Heartbeat from: foo.bar.com - Departed
  ...
```

Cool, eh? Just remember the datagrams are not guaranteed to arrive (although it's unlikely you'll see them fail), and it's possible that you could miss an arrival or a departure. Now let's look at the code.

HeartBeat

HeartBeat overrides the init(), start(), and stop() methods of the Applet class, and implements one private method of its own, sendMessage(), that sends a datagram. HeartBeat begins its life in init(), where it determines the destination for its messages. It uses the Applet getCodeBase() and getHost() methods to find the name of its originating host and fetches the correct port number from the myPort parameter of the HTML tag. After init() has finished, the start() and stop() methods are called whenever the applet is started or stopped. These methods merely call sendMessage() with the appropriate message.

sendMessage() is responsible for sending a String message to the server as a datagram. It takes the text as an argument, constructs a datagram packet containing the message, and then sends the datagram. All of the datagram information is packed into a java.net.DatagramPacket object, including the destination and port number. The DatagramPacket is like an addressed envelope, stuffed with our bytes. After the DatagramPacket is created, sendMessage() simply has to open a DatagramSocket and send it.

The first five lines of sendMessage() build the DatagramPacket:

```
try {
    byte [] data = message.getBytes();
    InetAddress addr = InetAddress.getByName( myHost );
    DatagramPacket pack =
        new DatagramPacket(data, data.length, addr, myPort );
```

First, the contents of message are placed into an array of bytes called data. Next a java.net.InetAddress object is created from the name myHost. An InetAddress simply holds the network address information for a host in a special format. We get an InetAddress object for our host by using the static getByName() method of the InetAddress class. (We can't construct an InetAddress object directly.) Finally, we call the DatagramPacket constructor with four arguments: the byte array containing our data, the length of the data, the destination address object, and the port number.

The remaining lines construct a default client DatagramSocket and call its send() method to transmit the DatagramPacket; after sending the datagram, we close the socket:

```
DatagramSocket ds = new DatagramSocket();
ds.send( pack );
ds.close();
```

Two operations throw a type of IOException: the InetAddress.getByName() lookup and the DatagramSocket send(). InetAddress.getByName() can throw an UnknownHostException, which is a type of IOException that indicates that the host name can't be resolved. If send() throws an IOException, it implies a serious client side problem in talking to the network. We need to catch these exceptions; our catch block simply prints a message telling us that something went wrong. If we get one of these exceptions, we can assume the datagram never arrived. However, we can't assume the converse. Even if we don't get an exception, we still don't know that the host is actually accessible or that the data actually arrived; with a DatagramSocket, we never find out.

Pulse

The Pulse server corresponds to the HeartBeat applet. First, it creates a Datagram-Socket to listen on our prearranged port. This time, we specify a port number in the constructor; we get the port number from the command line as a string (argv[0]) and convert it to an integer with Integer.parseInt(). Note the difference between this call to the constructor and the call in HeartBeat. In the server, we need to listen for incoming datagrams on a prearranged port, so we need to specify the port when creating the DatagramSocket. In the client, we only need to send datagrams, so we don't have to specify the port in advance; we build the port number into the DatagramPacket itself.

Second, Pulse creates an empty DatagramPacket of a fixed size to receive an incoming datagram. This alternative constructor for DatagramPacket takes a byte array and a length as arguments. As much data as possible is stored in the byte array when it's received. (A practical limit on the size of a UDP datagram is 8K.) Finally, Pulse calls the DatagramSocket's receive() method to wait for a packet to arrive. When a packet arrives, its contents are printed.

As you can see, working with DatagramSocket is slightly more tedious than working with Sockets. With datagrams, it's harder to spackle over the messiness of the socket interface. However, the Java API rather slavishly follows the UNIX interface, and that doesn't help. I don't see any reason why we have to prepare a datagram to hand to receive() (at least for the current functionality); receive() ought to create an appropriate object on its own and hand it to us, saving us the effort of building the datagram in advance and unpacking the data from it afterwards. It's easy to imagine other conveniences; perhaps we'll have them in a future release.

Simple Serialized Object Protocols

Earlier in this chapter we showed a hypothetical conversation in which a client and server exchanged some primitive data and a serialized Java object. Passing an object between two programs may not have seemed like a big deal at the time, but in the context of Java as a portable byte-code language, it has profound implications. In this section we'll show how a protocol can be built using serialized Java objects.

Before we move on, it's worth considering network protocols. Most programmers would consider working with sockets to be "low level" and unfriendly. Even though Java makes sockets much much easier to use than many other languages, sockets still only provide an unstructured flow of bytes between their endpoints. If you want to do serious communications using sockets, the first thing you have to do is come up with a protocol that defines the data you'll be sending and receiving. The most complex part of that protocol usually involves how to marshall (package) your data for transfer over the Net and unpack it on the other side.

As we've seen, Java's `DataInputStream` and `DataOutputStream` classes solve this problem for simple data types. We can read and write numbers, `Strings`, and Java primitives in a recognizable format that can be understood on any other Java platform. But to do real work we need to be able to put simple types together into larger structures. Java object serialization solves this problem elegantly, by allowing us to send our data just as we use it, as the state of Java objects. Serialization can pack up entire graphs of interconnected objects and put them back together at a later time, possibly in another context.

A Simple Object-Based Server

In the following example, a client will send a serialized object to the server, and the server will respond in kind. The client object represents a request, and the server object represents a response. The conversation ends when the client closes the connection. It's hard to imagine a simpler protocol. All the hairy details are taken care of by object serialization, so we can keep them out of our design.

To start we'll define a class, `Request`, to serve as a base class for the various kinds of requests we make to the server. Using a common base class is a convenient way to identify the object as a type of request. In a real application, we might also use it to hold basic information like client names and passwords, time stamps, serial numbers, etc. In our example, `Request` can be an empty class that exists so others can extend it:

```
public class Request implements java.io.Serializable { }
```

Request implements Serializable, so all of its subclasses will be serializable by default. Next we'll create some specific kinds of Requests. The first, DateRequest, is also a trivial class. We'll use it to ask the server to send us a java.util.Date object as a response:

```
public class DateRequest extends Request { }
```

Next, we'll create a generic WorkRequest object. The client sends a WorkRequest to get the server to perform work for it. The server calls the request object's execute() method and returns the resulting object as a response:

```
public class WorkRequest extends Request {
    public Object execute() { return null; }
}
```

For our application, we'll subclass WorkRequest to create MyCalculation, which adds code that performs a specific calculation; in this case, we'll just square a number:

```
public class MyCalculation extends WorkRequest {
    int n;

    public MyCalculation( int n ) {
        this.n = n;
    }
    public Object execute() {
        return new Integer( n * n );
    }
}
```

As far as data is concerned, MyCalculation really doesn't do much; it only transports an integer value for us. Keep in mind that a request object could hold lots of data, including references to many other objects in complex structures like arrays or linked lists.

Now that we have our protocol, we need the server. The Server class below looks a lot like the TinyHttpd server that we developed earlier in this chapter:

```
import java.net.*;
import java.io.*;

public class Server {
    public static void main( String argv[] ) throws IOException {
        ServerSocket ss = new ServerSocket( Integer.parseInt(argv[0]) );
        while ( true )
            new ServerConnection( ss.accept() ).start();
    }
}

class ServerConnection extends Thread {
    Socket client;
```

```
            ServerConnection ( Socket client ) throws SocketException {
                this.client = client;
                setPriority( NORM_PRIORITY - 1 );
            }

            public void run() {
                try {
                    ObjectInputStream in =
                        new ObjectInputStream( client.getInputStream() );
                    ObjectOutputStream out =
                        new ObjectOutputStream( client.getOutputStream() );
                    while ( true ) {
                        out.writeObject( processRequest( in.readObject() ) );
                        out.flush();
                    }
                } catch ( EOFException e3 ) { // Normal EOF
                    try {
                        client.close();
                    } catch ( IOException e ) { }
                } catch ( IOException e ) {
                    System.out.println( "I/O error " + e ); // I/O error
                } catch ( ClassNotFoundException e2 ) {
                    System.out.println( e2 ); // Unknown type of request object
                }
            }

            private Object processRequest( Object request ) {
                if ( request instanceof DateRequest )
                    return new java.util.Date();
                else if ( request instanceof WorkRequest )
                    return ((WorkRequest)request).execute();
                else
                    return null;
            }
        }
```

The Server services each request in a separate thread. For each connection, the run() method creates an ObjectInputStream and an ObjectOutputStream, which the server uses to receive the request and send the response. The processRequest() method decides what the request means and comes up with the response. To figure out what kind of request we have, we use the instanceof operator to look at the object's type.

Finally, we get to our Client, which is even simpler:

```
        import java.net.*;
        import java.io.*;

        public class Client {
            public static void main( String argv[] ) {
                try {
                    Socket server =
                        new Socket( argv[0], Integer.parseInt(argv[1]) );
```

```
            ObjectOutputStream out =
                new ObjectOutputStream( server.getOutputStream() );
            ObjectInputStream in =
                new ObjectInputStream( server.getInputStream() );

            out.writeObject( new DateRequest() );
            out.flush();
            System.out.println( in.readObject() );

            out.writeObject( new MyCalculation( 2 ) );
            out.flush();
            System.out.println( in.readObject() );

            server.close();
        } catch ( IOException e ) {
            System.out.println( "I/O error " + e ); // I/O error
        } catch ( ClassNotFoundException e2 ) {
            System.out.println( e2 ); // Unknown type of response object
        }
    }
}
```

Just like the server, Client creates the pair of object streams. It sends a
DateRequest and prints the response; it then sends a MyCalculation object and
prints the response. Finally, it closes the connection. On both the client and the
server, we call the flush() method after each call to writeObject(). This method
forces the system to send any buffered data, and is important because it ensures
that the other side sees the entire request before we wait for a response. When the
client closes the connection, our server catches the EOFException that is thrown
and ends the session. Alternatively, our client could write a special object, perhaps
null, to end the session; the server could watch for this item in its main loop.

The order in which we construct the object streams is important. We create the
output streams first because the constructor of an ObjectInputStream tries to read
a header from the stream to make sure that the InputStream really is an object
stream. If we tried to create both of our input streams first, we would deadlock
waiting for the other side to write the headers.

Finally, we can run the example. Run the Server, giving it a port number as an
argument:

```
% java Server 1234
```

Then run the Client, telling it the server's hostname and port number:

```
% java Client flatland 1234
```

You should see the following result:

```
Fri Jul 11 14:25:25 PDT 1997
4
```

All right, the result isn't that impressive, but it's easy to imagine more substantial applications. Imagine that you needed to perform some complex computation on many large data sets. This might take days on your PC, but you just happen to have a supercomputer in the back room. Using a protocol like the one we've just developed, it's simple to transfer the data to the supercomputer, perform the computation, and return the results.

Limitations

There is one catch in this scenario: both the client and server need access to the necessary classes. That is, all of the `Request` classes—including `MyCalculation`, which is really the property of the `Client`—have to be in the class path of both the client and the server. Given that Java is portable, can't we just ship the byte-code along with the serialized object data? After all, we transport Java classes between Java applications all the time when we run applets. We can, but with a bit more work. We could create this solution on our own, using a network classloader to load the classes for us. But we don't have to: Java's RMI facility automates that for us. The ability to send serialized data and classes over the network makes Java a powerful tool for developing advanced applications.

Remote Method Invocation

The most fundamental means of interobject communication in Java is method invocation. Mechanisms like the Java event model are built on simple method invocations between objects that share a virtual machine. Therefore, when we want to communicate between virtual machines on different hosts, it's natural to want a mechanism with similar capabilities and semantics. Java's Remote Method Invocation mechanism does just that. It lets us get a reference to an object on a remote host and use it as if it were in our own virtual machine. RMI lets us invoke methods on remote objects, passing real objects as arguments and getting real objects as returned values.

Remote invocation is nothing new. For many years C programmers have used remote procedure calls (RPC) to execute a C function on a remote host and return the results. The primary difference between RPC and RMI is that RPC, being an offshoot of the C language, is primarily concerned with data structures. It's relatively easy to pack up data and ship it around, but for Java, that's not enough. In Java we don't work with simple data structures; we work with objects, which contain both data and methods for working on the data. Not only do we have to be able to ship the state of an object over the wire (the data), but the recipient has to be able to interact with the object after receiving it.

It should be no surprise that RMI uses object serialization, which allows us to send graphs of objects (objects and all of the connected objects that they reference). When necessary, RMI uses dynamic class loading and the security manager to transport Java classes safely. The real breakthrough of RMI is that it's possible to ship both code and data around the Net.

Remote and Non-Remote Objects

Before an object can be used with RMI, it must be serializable. But that's not sufficient. Remote objects in RMI are real distributed objects. As their name suggests, a remote object can refer to an object on a different machine; it can also refer to an object on the local host. The term *remote* means that the object is used through a special kind of object reference that can be passed over the network. Like normal Java objects, remote objects are passed by reference. Regardless of where the reference is used, the method invocation occurs at the original object, which still lives on its original host. If a server returns a reference to a remote object to you, you can call the object's methods; the actual method invocations will happen on the remote object's server. If a client creates a remote object and passes a reference to a server, the server can use the reference to invoke methods on the original object on the client side.

Non-remote objects are simpler. They are just normal serializable objects. The catch is that when you pass a non-remote object over the network it is simply copied. So references to the object on one host are not the same as those on the remote host. This is acceptable for many simple kinds of objects, especially objects that cannot be modified.

Stubs and skeletons

No, we're not talking about a gruesome horror movie. Stubs and skeletons are used in the implementation of remote objects. When you invoke a method on a remote object (which could be on a different host), you are actually calling some local code that serves as a proxy for that object. This is the *stub*. (It is called a *stub* because it is something like a truncated placeholder for the object.) The *skeleton* is another proxy that lives with the real object on its original host. It receives remote method invocations from the stub and passes them to the object.

You never have to work with stubs or skeletons directly; they are hidden from you (in the closet). Stubs and skeletons for your remote objects are created by running the *rmic* (RMI compiler) utility. After compiling your Java source files normally, you run *rmic*.

Remote interfaces

So far we've been referring to remote objects as objects (and they are, of course). But to be more specific, remote objects are objects that implement a special remote interface that specifies which of the object's methods can be invoked remotely. The remote interface must extend the java.rmi.Remote interface. Your remote object must implement its remote interface; so does the stub object that is automatically generated for you. In the rest of your code, you should refer to the remote object using its interface—not the object's actual class. Because both the real object and stub implement the remote interface, they are equivalent as far as we are concerned; we never have to worry about whether we have a reference to a stub or an actual implementation of the object locally. This "type equivalence" means that we can use normal language features like casting with remote objects.

All methods in the remote interface must declare that they can throw the exception java.rmi.RemoteException. This exception (actually, one of many subclasses to RemoteException) is thrown when any kind of networking error happens: for example, the server could crash, the network could fail, or you could be requesting an object that for some reason isn't available.

Here's a simple example of the remote interface that defines the behavior of MyRemoteObject; we'll give it two methods that can be invoked remotely, both of which return some kind of Widget object:

```
public interface MyRemoteObject
        extends java.rmi.Remote {
    public Widget doSomething() throws java.rmi.RemoteException;
    public Widget doSomethingElse() throws java.rmi.RemoteException;
}
```

UnicastRemoteObject

The actual implementation of a remote object (not the interface we discussed previously) must extend java.rmi.server.UnicastRemoteObject. This is the RMI equivalent to the familiar Object class. It provides implementations of equals(), hashcode(), and toString() that make sense for remote objects. It also "exports" the object by preparing the Java run-time system to accept network connections for this object. It's possible to do this work yourself, but it isn't necessary.

Here's a remote object class that matches the MyRemoteObject interface; we haven't supplied implementation for the two methods or the constructor:

```
public class RemoteObjectImpl
        implements MyRemoteObject
        extends java.rmi.UnicastRemoteObject {
    public RemoteObjectImpl() throws java.rmi.RemoteException {...}
    public Widget doSomething() throws java.rmi.RemoteException {...}
    public Widget doSomethingElse() throws java.rmi.RemoteException {...}
```

```
// other non-public methods
...
}
```

This class can have as many additional methods as it needs; presumably, most of them will be private, but that isn't strictly necessary. We have to supply a constructor explicitly, even if the constructor does nothing, because the constructor (like any method) can throw a RemoteException; we therefore can't use the default constructor.

The name UnicastRemoteObject begs the question, "what other kinds of remote objects are there?" Right now, none. It's possible that JavaSoft will develop remote objects using other protocols or multicast techniques in the future.

The RMI registry

The registry is the RMI phone book. You use the registry to look up a reference to a registered remote object on another host. We've already described how remote references can be passed back and forth by remote method calls. But the registry is needed to bootstrap the process; the client needs some way of looking up some initial object.

The registry is implemented by a class called Naming and an application called *rmiregistry*, which must be running before you start a Java program that uses the registry. To use the registry, create an instance of a remote object and have it bind itself to a particular name in the registry. (Remote objects that bind themselves to the registry usually provide a main() method for this purpose.) The name can be anything you choose; it takes the form of a slash (/) separated path. When a client object wants to find your object, it constructs a special URL with the rmi: protocol, the hostname, and the object name. On the client, the RMI Naming class then talks to the registry and returns the remote object reference.

Which objects need to register themselves with the registry? Certainly, any object that the client has no other way of finding. A call to a remote method can return another remote object without using the registry. Likewise, a call to a remote method can have another remote object as its argument, without requiring the registry. You could design your system so that only one object registers itself, and then serves as a factory for any other remote objects you need. In other words, it wouldn't be hard to build a simple object request "bouncer" (I won't say "broker") that returns references to various objects. Why avoid using the registry? The current RMI registry is not very sophisticated, and lookups tend to be slow. It is not intended to be a general purpose directory service but simply to bootstrap RMI communications. It wouldn't be surprising if JavaSoft releases a much improved registry in the future, but that's not the one we have now.

The Example

The first thing we'll implement using RMI is a duplication of the simple serialized object protocol from the previous section. We'll make a remote RMI object called `Server` on which we can invoke methods to get a `Date` object or execute a `WorkRequest` object. First, we'll define our `Remote` interface:

```
import java.rmi.*;
import java.util.*;

public interface Server extends java.rmi.Remote {

    Date getDate() throws java.rmi.RemoteException;
    Object execute( WorkRequest work ) throws java.rmi.RemoteException;
}
```

The `Server` interface extends the `java.rmi.Remote` interface, which identifies objects that implement it as remote objects. We supply two methods that take the place of our old protocol: `getDate()` and `execute()`.

Next, we'll implement this interface in a class called `MyServer` that holds the bodies of these methods. (In this example, we're not using the convention of adding `Impl` to the interface name to create the actual object name. Using this convention, the name of the server would be `ServerImpl`.)

```
public class MyServer
    extends java.rmi.server.UnicastRemoteObject implements Server {

    public MyServer() throws RemoteException { }

    // Implement the Server interface

    public Date getDate() throws RemoteException {
        return new Date();
    }
    public Object execute( WorkRequest work ) throws RemoteException {
        return work.execute();
    }

    public static void main(String args[]) {
        System.setSecurityManager(new RMISecurityManager());
        try {
            Server server = new MyServer();
            Naming.rebind("NiftyServer", server);
        } catch (java.io.IOException e) {
            // Problem registering server
        }
    }
}
```

`MyServer` extends `java.rmi.UnicastRemoteObject`, so when we create an instance of `MyServer` it will automatically be exported and start listening to the network. We start by providing a constructor that throws RemoteException. This exception accommodates errors that might occur in exporting an instance. We can't use the default constructor provided by the compiler, because the automatically generated constructor won't throw the exception. Next, MyServer implements the methods of the remote Server interface. These methods are straightforward.

The last method in this class is main(). This method lets the object set itself up as a server. main() starts by installing a special security manager, RMISecurityManager. This is a special security manager that watches any stub classes loaded over the network by RMI. It prevents someone from handing you a misbehaving stub, in addition to performing the other functions of a security manager. main() creates an instance of the MyServer object and then calls the static method Naming.rebind() to register the object with the registry. The arguments to rebind() are the name of the remote object in the registry (NiftyServer), which clients will use to look up the object, and reference to the server object itself. We could have called bind() instead, but rebind() is less prone to problems: if there's already a NiftyServer registered, rebind() replaces it.

We wouldn't need the main() method or this Naming business if we weren't expecting clients to use the registry to find the server. That is, we could omit main() and still use this object as a remote object. We would be limited to passing the object in method invocations or returning it from method invocations—but in many situations (not ours) those aren't big limitations.

Now we need our client:

```
public class MyClient {

    public static void main(String [] args) throws RemoteException {
        System.setSecurityManager(new RMISecurityManager());
        new MyClient( args[0] );
    }

    public MyClient(String host) {
        try {
            Server server = (Server)
                Naming.lookup("rmi://"+host+"/NiftyServer");
            System.out.println( server.getDate() );
            System.out.println( server.execute( new MyCalculation(2) ) );
        } catch (java.io.IOException e) {
                        // I/O Error or bad URL
        } catch (NotBoundException e) {
                        // NiftyServer isn't registered
        }
    }
}
```

When we run MyClient, we pass it the hostname of the server on which the registry is running. The main() method installs the RMISecurityManager and then creates an instance of the `MyClient` object, passing the hostname from the command line as an argument to the constructor.

The constructor for `MyClient` uses the hostname to construct a URL for the object. The URL will look something like this: *rmi://hostname/NiftyServer*, where `Nifty-Server` is the name under which we registered our `Server`. We pass the URL to the static `Naming.lookup()` method. If all goes well, we get back a reference to a `Server`! Of course, the registry has no idea what kind of object it will return; `lookup()` therefore returns an `Object`, which we cast to `Server`.

Compile all of the code. Then run RMI compiler to make the stub and skeleton files for `MyServer`:

```
% rmic MyServer
```

Let's run the code. For the first pass, we'll assume that you have all of the class files, including the stubs and skeletons generated by *rmic*, available in the class path on both the client and server machines. (You can run this example on a single host to test it if you want.) Make sure your class path is correct and then start the registry; then start the server:

```
% rmiregistry &
% java MyServer
```

On a Windows system, run *rmiregistry* in another window by preceding it with the *start* command. Finally, on the client machine, run `MyClient`, passing the hostname of the server:

```
% java MyClient myhost
```

The client should print the date and the number four, which the server graciously calculated.

Dynamic class loading

Before running the example, we told you to distribute all the class files to both the client and server machines. However, RMI was designed to ship classes, in addition to data, around the network; you shouldn't have to distribute all the classes in advance. Let's go a step further, and have RMI load classes for us, as needed.

First, we need to tell RMI where to find any other classes it needs. We can use the system property `java.rmi.server.codebase` to specify a URL on an HTTP server when we run our client or server. This URL specifies the base directory in which RMI will begin its search for classes. When RMI sends a serialized object (i.e., an object's data) to some client, it also sends this URL. If the recipient needs the class file in addition to the data, it fetches the file via HTTP. To be more precise: if the object needed is a remote object, the recipient fetches the desired class's stub, which was created by *rmic.* Remember that stubs are stand-ins for the objects themselves; their job is to talk to the object, which remains on the server. If the object needed doesn't implement the Remote interface, the recipient fetches the object's class file itself, and uses the object locally. Therefore, we don't have to distribute class files; we can let clients download them as necessary. In Figure 11-3, we see MyClient going to the registry to get a reference to the Server object. Then MyClient dynamically downloads the stub class for MyServer from the HTTP daemon running on the server host.

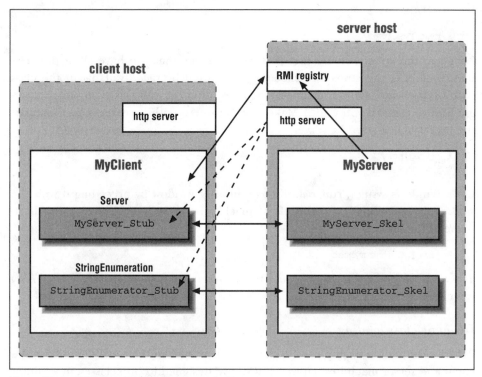

Figure 11–3: RMI clients load classes dynamically

We can now split our class files between the server and client machines. For example, we could withhold the MyCalculation class from the server, since it really belongs to the client. Instead, we can make the MyCalculation class available via an HTTP daemon on some machine (probably our client's) and specify the URL when we run MyClient:

```
% java -Djava.rmi.server.codebase='http://myserver/foo/' MyClient
```

In this case we would expect that MyCalculation would be accessible at the URL *http://myserver/foo/MyCalculation.class.*

Passing remote object references

So far, we haven't done anything that we couldn't have done with the simple object protocol. We only used one remote object, `MyServer`, and we got its reference from the RMI registry. Now we'll extend our example to pass some remote references between the client and server. We'll add two methods to our remote `Server` interface:

```
public interface Server extends java.rmi.Remote {

    ...

    StringEnumeration getList() throws java.rmi.RemoteException;

    void asyncExecute( WorkRequest work, WorkListener listener )
            throws java.rmi.RemoteException;
}
```

`getList()` retrieves a new kind of object from the server: a `StringEnumeration`. The `StringEnumeration` is a simple list of strings, with some methods for accessing the strings in order. We will make it a remote object so that implementations of `StringEnumeration` can stay on the server.

Next we'll spice up our work request feature by adding an `asyncExecute()` method. `asyncExecute()` lets us hand off a `WorkRequest` object as before, but it does the calulation on its own time. The return type for `asyncExecute()` is `void`, because it doesn't actually return a value; we get the result later. With the request, our client passes a reference to a `WorkListener` object that is to be notified when the `WorkRequest` is done. We'll have our client implement `WorkListener` itself.

Because this is to be a remote object, our interface must extend `Remote`, and its methods must throw `RemoteExceptions`:

```
public interface StringEnumeration extends Remote {
    public boolean hasMoreItems() throws RemoteException;
    public String nextItem() throws RemoteException;
}
```

Next, we provide a simple implementation of `StringEnumeration`, called `String-Enumerator`:

```
public class StringEnumerator
    extends java.rmi.server.UnicastRemoteObject implements StringEnumeration {

    String [] list;
    int index = 0;

    public StringEnumerator( String [] list ) throws RemoteException {
        this.list = list;
    }
    public boolean hasMoreItems() throws RemoteException {
        return index < list.length;
```

```
    }
    public String nextItem() throws RemoteException {
        return list[index++];
    }
}
```

The `StringEnumerator` extends `UnicastRemoteObject`. Its methods are simple: it can give you the next string in the list, and it can tell you whether there are any strings that you haven't seen yet.

Next, we'll define the `WorkListener` remote interface. This is the interface that defines how an object should listen for a completed `WorkRequest`. It has one method, `workCompleted()`, which the server that is executing a `WorkRequest` calls when the job is done:

```
public interface WorkListener extends Remote {
    public void workCompleted( WorkRequest request, Object result )
            throws RemoteException;
}
```

Next, let's add the new features to `MyServer`. We need to add implementations of the `getList()` and `asyncExecute()` methods, which we just added to the `Server` interface:

```
public class MyServer
    extends java.rmi.server.UnicastRemoteObject implements Server {

        ...

    public StringEnumeration getList() throws RemoteException {
        return new StringEnumerator(
            new String [] { "Foo", "Bar", "Gee" } );
    }
    public void asyncExecute( WorkRequest request , WorkListener listener )
        throws java.rmi.RemoteException {

        Object result = request.execute();
        listener.workCompleted( request, result );
    }
}
```

`getList()` just returns a `StringEnumerator` with some stuff in it. `asyncExecute()` calls a `WorkRequest`'s `execute()` method and notifies the listener when it's done. (Our implementation of `asyncExecute()` is a little cheesy. If we were forming a more complex calculation we would want to start a thread to do the calculation, and return immediately from `asyncExecute()`, so the client won't block. The thread would call `workCompleted()` at a later time, when the computation was done. In this simple example, it would take longer to start the thread than to perform the calculation.)

We have to modify `MyClient` to implement the remote `WorkListener` interface. This turns `MyClient` into a remote object, so we must make it a

UnicastRemoteObject. We also add the workCompleted() method that the Work-
Listener interface requires:

```
public class MyClient extends java.rmi.server.UnicastRemoteObject
        implements WorkListener {

    ...
    public void workCompleted( WorkRequest request, Object result )
        throws RemoteException {
        System.out.println("Async work result = " + result);
    }
}
```

Finally, we want MyClient to exercise the new features. Add these lines after the
calls to getDate() and execute():

```
// MyClient constructor
...
StringEnumeration se = server.getList();
while ( se.hasMoreItems() )
    System.out.println( se.nextItem() );

server.asyncExecute( new MyCalculation(100), this );
```

We use getList() to get the enumeration from the server, then loop, printing the
strings. We also call asyncExecute() to perform another calculation; this time, we
square the number 100. The second argument to asyncExecute() is the WorkLis-
tener to notify when the data is ready; we pass a reference to ourself (this).

Now all we have to do is compile everything and run *rmic* to make the stubs for all
our remote objects:

```
rmic MyClient MyServer StringEnumerator
```

Restart the RMI registry and MyServer on your server, and run the client somewhere. You should get the following:

```
Fri Jul 11 23:57:19 PDT 1997
4
Foo
Bar
Gee
Async work result = 10000
```

Alternatives to RMI

Java supports one important alternative to RMI, called CORBA (Common Object
Request Broker Architecture). We won't say much about CORBA, but you should
know it exists. CORBA is a standard developed by the Object Management Group

(OMG), of which Sun Microsystems is one of the founding members. Its major advantage is that it works cross language: a Java program can use CORBA to talk to objects written in other languages, like C or C++. This is a considerable advantage if you want to build a Java front end for an older program that you can't afford to reimplement. CORBA also provides some other services that aren't yet available in Java. CORBA's major disadvantage is that it's complex. JavaSoft has announced that they will be making efforts to integrate RMI and CORBA, but it's too early to see where these efforts will lead.

12

Working with URLs

A URL points to an object on the Internet. It's a collection of information that identifies an item, tells you where to find it, and specifies a method for communicating with it or retrieving it from its source. A URL refers to any kind of information source. It might point to static data, such as a file on a local filesystem, a Web server, or an FTP archive; or it can point to a more dynamic object such as a news article on a news spool or a record in a WAIS database. URLs can even refer to less tangible resources such as Telnet sessions and mailing addresses.

The Java URL classes provide an API for accessing well-defined networked resources, like documents and applications on servers. The classes use an extensible set of prefabricated protocol and content handlers to perform the necessary communication and data conversion for accessing URL resources. With URLs, an application can fetch a complete file or database record from a server on the network with just a few lines of code. Applications like Web browsers, which deal with networked content, use the URL class to simplify the task of network programming. They also take advantage of the dynamic nature of Java, which allows handlers for new types of URLs to be added on the fly. As new types of servers and new formats for content evolve, additional URL handlers can be supplied to retrieve and interpret the data without modifying the original application.

A URL is usually presented as a string of text, like an address.* Since there are many different ways to locate an item on the Net, and different mediums and transports require different kinds of information, there are different formats for different kinds of URLs. The most common form specifies three things: a network

---

* The term URL was coined by the Uniform Resource Identifier (URI) working group of the IETF to distinguish URLs from the more general notion of Uniform Resource Names or URNs. URLs are really just static addresses, whereas URNs would be more persistent and abstract identifiers used to resolve the location of an object anywhere on the Net. URLs are defined in RFC 1738 and RFC 1808.

host or server, the name of the item and its location on that host, and a protocol by which the host should communicate:

```
protocol://hostname/location/item
```

protocol is an identifier such as "http," "ftp," or "gopher"; *hostname* is an Internet hostname; and the *location* and *item* components form a path that identifies the object on that host. Variants of this form allow extra information to be packed into the URL, specifying things like port numbers for the communications protocol and fragment identifiers that reference parts inside the object.

We sometimes speak of a URL that is relative to a base URL. In that case we are using the base URL as a starting point and supplying additional information. For example, the base URL might point to a directory on a Web server; a relative URL might name a particular file in that directory.

The URL Class

A URL is represented by an instance of the `java.net.URL` class. A URL object manages all information in a URL string and provides methods for retrieving the object it identifies. We can construct a URL object from a URL specification string or from its component parts:

```
try {
    URL aDoc = new URL( "http://foo.bar.com/documents/homepage.html" );
    URL sameDoc = new URL("http","foo.bar.com","documents/homepage.html");
}
catch ( MalformedURLException e ) { }
```

The two URL objects above point to the same network resource, the *homepage.html* document on the server *foo.bar.com*. Whether or not the resource actually exists and is available isn't known until we try to access it. At this point, the URL object just contains data about the object's location and how to access it. No connection to the server has been made. We can examine the URL's components with the get-Protocol(), getHost(), and getFile() methods. We can also compare it to another URL with the sameFile() method. sameFile() determines if two URLs point to the same resource. It can be fooled, but sameFile does more than compare the URLs for equality; it takes into account the possibility that one server may have several names, and other factors.

When a URL is created, its specification is parsed to identify the protocol component. If the protocol doesn't make sense, or if Java can't find a protocol handler for it, the URL constructor throws a MalformedURLException. A protocol handler is a Java class that implements the communications protocol for accessing the URL resource. For example, given an "http" URL, Java prepares to use the HTTP protocol handler to retrieve documents from the specified server.

Stream Data

The lowest level way to get data back from URL is to ask for an InputStream from the URL by calling openStream(). Currently, if you're writing an applet that will be running under Netscape or Internet Explorer, this is about your only choice. It's particularly useful if you want to receive continuous updates from a dynamic information source. The drawback is that you have to parse the contents of the object yourself. Not all types of URLs support the openStream() method; you'll get an UnknownServiceException if yours doesn't.

The following code prints the contents of an HTML file:

```
try {
    URL url = new URL("http://server/index.html");

    BufferedReader bin = new BufferedReader (
        new InputStreamReader( url.openStream() ));

    String line;
    while ( (line = bin.readLine()) != null )
        System.out.println( line );
} catch (Exception e) { }
```

We ask for an InputStream with openStream() and wrap it in a BufferedReader to read the lines of text. Because we specify the "http" protocol in the URL, we still require the services of an HTTP protocol handler. As we'll discuss later, that raises some questions about what handlers we have available. This example partially works around those issues because no content handler is involved; we read the data and interpret it as a content handler would. However, there are even more limitations on what applets can do right now. For the time being, if you construct URLs relative to the applet's codeBase(), you should be able to use them in applets as in the above example. This should guarantee that the needed protocol is available and accessible to the applet. (If you are just trying to get data associated with an applet, there are better ways; see the discussion of getResource() in Chapter 10.)

Getting the Content as an Object

openStream() operates at a lower level than the more general content-handling mechanism implemented by the URL class. We showed it first because, until some things are settled, you'll be limited as to when you can use URLs in their more powerful role. When a proper content handler is available to Java, you'll be able to retrieve the object the URL addresses as a complete object, by calling the URL's get-Content() method. (Currently, this only works if you supply one with your

application or install one in the local classpath for HotJava, as we'll discuss later.)
getContent() initiates a connection to the host, fetches the data for you, determines the MIME (Multipurpose Internet Mail Extensions) type of the contents,
and invokes a content handler to turn the bytes into a Java object. MIME is a standard that was developed to facilitate multimedia email, but it has become widely
used as a general way to specify how to treat data; Java uses MIME to help it pick
the right content handler.

For example, given the URL *http://foo.bar.com/index.html*, a call to getContent()
would use the HTTP protocol handler to retrieve data and an HTML content handler to turn the data into an appropriate document object. A URL that points to a
plain-text file might use a text-content handler that returns a String object. Similarly, a GIF file might be turned into an Image object using a GIF content handler.
If we accessed the GIF file using an "ftp" URL, Java would use the same content
handler but would use the FTP protocol handler to receive the data.

getContent() returns the output of the content handler. Now we're faced with a
problem: exactly what did we get? Since the content handler has to be able to
return almost anything, the return type of getContent() is Object. In a moment
we'll describe how we could ask the protocol handler about the object's MIME
type, which it discovered. Based on this, and whatever other knowledge we have
about the kind of object we are expecting, we can cast the Object to its appropriate, more specific type. For example, if we expect a String, we'll cast the result of
getContent() to a String:

```
try {
    String content = (String)myURL.getContent();
} catch ( ClassCastException e ) { ... }
```

If we're wrong about the type, we'll get a ClassCastException. As an alternative,
we could check the type of the returned object using the instanceof operator:

```
if ( content instanceof String ) {
    String s = (String)content;
    ...
```

Various kinds of errors can occur when trying to retrieve the data. For example,
getContent() can throw an IOException if there is a communications error. Other
kinds of errors can occur at the application level: some knowledge of how the
application-specific content and protocol handlers deal with errors is necessary.

One problem that could arise is that a content handler for the data's MIME type
wouldn't be available. In this case, getContent() just invokes an "unknown type"
handler and returns the data as a raw InputStream. A sophisticated application
might specialize this behavior to try to decide what to do with the data on its own.

In some situations we may also need knowledge of the protocol handler. For example, consider a URL that refers to a nonexistent file on an HTTP server. When requested, the server probably returns a valid HTML document that contains the familiar "404 Not Found" message. In a naive implementation, an HTML content handler might be invoked to interpret this message and return it as it would any other HTML document. To check the validity of protocol-specific operations like this, we may need to talk to the protocol handler.

The openStream() and getContent() methods both implicitly create the connection to the remote URL object. When the connection is set up, the protocol handler is consulted to create a URLConnection object. The URLConnection manages the protocol-specific communications. We can get a URLConnection for our URL with the openConnection() method. One of the things we can do with the URLConnection is ask for the object's content type. For example:

```
URLConnection connection = myURL.openConnection();
String mimeType = connection.getContentType();
...
Object contents = myURL.getContents();
```

We can also get protocol-specific information. Different protocols provide different types of URLConnection objects. The HttpURLConnection object, for instance, can interpret the "404 Not Found" message and tell us about the problem. We'll examine URLConnections further when we start writing protocol handlers.

Web Browsers and Handlers

The content- and protocol-handler mechanisms we've introduced can be used by any application that accesses data via URLs. This mechanism is extremely flexible; to handle a URL, you need only the appropriate protocol and content handlers. One obvious application is for Java-based Web browsers that can handle new and specialized kinds of URLs. Furthermore, Java's ability to load new classes over the Net means that, in theory, the handlers don't even need to be a part of the browser. Content and protocol handlers could be downloaded over the Net, from the same site that supplies the data, and used by the browser. If you wanted to supply some completely new data type, using a completely new protocol, you could make your data file plus a content handler and a protocol handler available on your Web server; anyone using a Web browser supporting Java could automatically get the appropriate handlers whenever they access your data. In short, Java lets you build dynamically extensible Web applications. Instead of gigantic do-everything software, you can build a lightweight scaffold that dynamically incorporates extensions as needed. Figure 12-1 shows the conceptual operation of a downloadable content handler in a Web browser; Figure 12-2 does the same for a protocol handler.

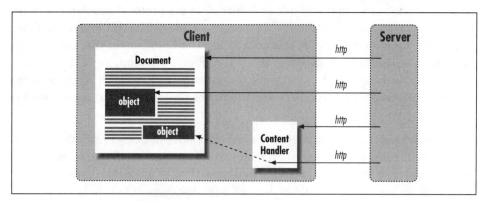

Figure 12–1: A content handler at work

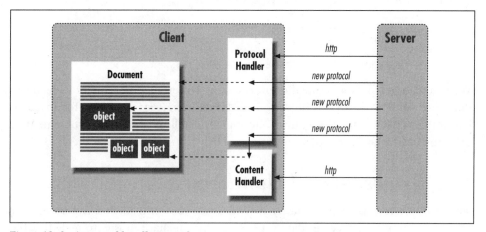

Figure 12–2: A protocol handler at work

Sun's HotJava was the first browser to begin to provide these features. When Hot-Java encounters a type of content or a protocol it doesn't understand, it searches its classpath for an appropriate handler class. HotJava is built from the ground up on content and protocol handlers. Even document formats like HTML aren't privileged and built into the browser. HTML documents use the same content- and protocol-handler mechanisms as other data types—which means that HotJava could support other document formats easily. Furthermore, you can (at least in theory) use protocol and content handlers as powerful tools for creating applications, as JavaSoft has demonstrated with HotJava. Essentially, you use the protocol handler to manage a new class of URL, specific to your application—for example, a "sale" URL to manage a point-of-sale application.

Unfortunately, a few nasty flies are stuck in this ointment. Although content and protocol handlers are part of the Java API and they're an intrinsic part of the mechanism for working with URLs, specific content and protocol handlers aren't part of the API. The standard Java classes don't, for example, include content handlers for HTML, GIF, MPEG, or other common data types. Sun's JDK and all of the other Java environments do come with handlers, but these are installed on an application-level basis.

There are two real issues here:

- There isn't a standard that says that certain types of handlers have to be provided in each environment along with the core Java API. Instead we have to rely on the application to decide what kinds of data types it needs. This makes sense but is frustrating when it should be reasonable to expect certain basic types to be covered in all environments.

- There isn't any standard that tells you what kind of object the content handler should return. It's common sense that GIF data should be turned into an Image object, but at the moment, that's an application-level decision. If you're writing your own application and your own content handlers, that isn't an issue: you can make any decision you want. But if you're writing content handlers that are to be used by arbitrary applications (like HotJava), you need to know what they expect.

Furthermore, downloadable handlers are not part of HotJava 1.0. (We've been waiting a long time.) You can install them locally, as for all Java applications, but HotJava will not yet retrieve them from a remote host. And other browsers like Netscape Navigator and Internet Explorer do not directly support handlers at all. You can install them locally for use in your own applets, as with HotJava, but you cannot use them to extend the capabilities of the browser. Netscape and Internet Explorer are currently classic monolithic applications: knowledge about certain kinds of objects, like HTML and GIF files, is built in. These browsers can be extended via a plug-in mechanism, but plug-ins aren't portable and can't be downloaded dynamically over the Net. (Microsoft's ActiveX controls can be downloaded, but most are written in Visual Basic, which has serious security problems.) If you're writing applets for use in Netscape or Internet Explorer now, about all you can do is use the openStream() method to get a raw input stream from which to read data. Netscape, at least, has promised that a future release of Navigator will be written in Java. We hope then that we'll see more universal support for the power of handlers.

Writing a Content Handler

getContent() invokes a content handler whenever it's called to retrieve an object at some URL. The content handler must read the flat stream of data produced by the URL's protocol handler (the data read from the remote source), and construct a well-defined Java object from it. By "flat," I mean that the data stream the content handler receives has no artifacts left over from retrieving the data and processing the protocol. It's the protocol handler's job to fetch and decode the data before passing it along. The protocol handler's output is your data, pure and simple.

The roles of content and protocol handlers do not overlap. The content handler doesn't care how the data arrives, or what form it takes. It's concerned only with what kind of object it's supposed to create. For example, if a particular protocol involves sending an object over the network in a compressed format, the protocol handler should do whatever is necessary to unpack it before passing the data on to the content handler. The same content handler can then be used again with a completely different protocol handler to construct the *same* type of object received via a *different* transport mechanism.

Let's look at an example. The following lines construct a URL that points to a GIF file on an FTP archive and attempt to retrieve its contents:

```
try {
    URL url = new URL ("ftp://ftp.wustl.edu/graphics/gif/a/apple.gif");
    Image img = (Image)url.getContent();
    ...
```

When we construct the URL object, Java looks at the first part of the URL string (i.e., everything prior to the colon) to determine the protocol and locate a protocol handler. In this case, it locates the FTP protocol handler, which is used to open a connection to the host and transfer data for the specified file.

After making the connection, the URL object asks the protocol handler to identify the resource's MIME type. The handler can try to resolve the MIME type through a variety of means, but in this case, it might just look at the filename extension (*.gif*) and determine that the MIME type of the data is image/gif. Here, "image/gif" is a string that denotes that the content falls into the category of images and is, more specifically, a GIF image. The protocol handler then looks for the content handler responsible for the image/gif type and uses it to construct the right kind of object from the data. The content handler returns an Image object, which getContent() returns to us as an Object. As we've seen before, we cast this Object back to its real type, an Image, so we can work with it.

In an upcoming section, we'll build a simple content handler. To keep things as simple as possible, our example will produce text as output; the URL's getContent() method will return this as a String object.

Locating Content Handlers

When Java searches for a class, it translates package names into filesystem pathnames. This applies to locating content-handler classes as well as other kinds of classes. For example, on a UNIX- or DOS-based system, a class in a package named foo.bar.handlers would live in a directory with *foo/bar/handlers/* as part of its pathname. To allow Java to find handler classes for arbitrary new MIME types, content handlers are organized into packages corresponding to the basic MIME type categories. The handler classes themselves are then named after the specific MIME type. This allows Java to map MIME types directly to class names. The only remaining piece of information Java needs is a list of packages in which the handlers might reside. To supply this information, use the system properties java.content.handler.pkgs and java.protocol.handler.pkgs. In these properties, you can use a vertical bar (|) to separate different packages in a list.[*]

We'll put our content handlers in the exploringjava.contenthandlers package. According to the scheme for naming content handlers, a handler for the image/gif MIME type is called gif and placed in a package called exploringjava.contenthandlers.image. The fully qualified name of the class would then be exploringjava.contenthandlers.image.gif, and it would be located in the file *exploringjava/contenthandlers/image/gif.class*, somewhere in the local class path or, perhaps someday, on a server. Likewise, a content handler for the video/mpeg MIME type would be called mpeg, and an *mpeg.class* file would be located in a *exploringjava/contenthandlers/video/* directory somewhere in the class path.

Many MIME type names include a dash (-), which is illegal in a class name. You should convert dashes and other illegal characters into underscores (_) when building Java class and package names. Also note that there are no capital letters in the class names. This violates the coding convention used in most Java source files, in which class names start with capital letters. However, capitalization is not significant in MIME type names, so it's simpler to name the handler classes accordingly.

---

[*] This method for locating handlers is completely different from the method I described in the first edition. Evidently, my educated guesses about how HotJava would develop weren't good enough. The method I described in the first edition will still work for your own applications.

The application/x-tar Handler

In this section, we'll build a simple content handler that reads and interprets *tar* (tape archive) files. *tar* is an archival format widely used in the UNIX-world to hold collections of files, along with their basic type and attribute information.[*] A *tar* file is similar to a ZIP file, except that it's not compressed. Files in the archive are stored sequentially, in flat text or binary with no special encoding. In practice, *tar* files are usually compressed for storage using an application like UNIX *compress* or GNU *gzip* and then named with a filename extension like *.tar.gz* or *.tgz*.

Most Web browsers, upon retrieving a *tar* file, prompt the user with a **File Save** dialog. The assumption is that if you are retrieving an archive, you probably want to save it for later unpacking and use. We would like to implement a *tar* content handler that allows an application to read the contents of the archive and give us a listing of the files that it contains. In itself, this would not be the most useful thing in the world, because we would be left with the dilemma of how to get at the archive's contents. However, a more complete implementation of our content handler, used in conjunction with an application like a Web browser, could generate HTML output or pop up a dialog that lets us select and save individual files within the archive.

Some code that fetches a *.tar* file and lists its contents might look like this:

```
try {
    URL listing =
        new URL("http://somewhere.an.edu/lynx/lynx2html.tar");
    String s = (String)listing.getContents();
    System.out.println( s );
    ...
```

Our handler will produce a listing similar to the UNIX *tar* application's output:

```
Tape Archive Listing:

0      Tue Sep 28 18:12:47 CDT 1993 lynx2html/
14773  Tue Sep 28 18:01:55 CDT 1993 lynx2html/lynx2html.c
470    Tue Sep 28 18:13:24 CDT 1993 lynx2html/Makefile
172    Thu Apr 01 15:05:43 CST 1993 lynx2html/lynxgate
3656   Wed Mar 03 15:40:20 CST 1993 lynx2html/install.csh
490    Thu Apr 01 14:55:04 CST 1993 lynx2html/new_globals.c
...
```

Our handler will dissect the file to read the contents and generate the listing. The URL's getContent() method will return that information to an application as a String object.

---

[*] There are several slightly different versions of the *tar* format. This content handler understands the most widely used variant.

First we must decide what to call our content handler and where to put it. The MIME-type hierarchy classifies the *tar* format as an "application type extension." Its proper MIME type is then application/x-tar. Therefore, our handler belongs in the exploringjava.contenthandlers.application package and goes into the class file *exploringjava/contenthandlers/application/x_tar.class*. Note that the name of our class is x_tar, rather than x-tar; you'll remember the dash is illegal in a class name so, by convention, we convert it to an underscore.

Here's the code for the content handler; compile it and put it in *exploringjava/contenthandlers/application/*, somewhere in your class path:

```
package exploringjava.contenthandlers.application;

import java.net.*;
import java.io.*;
import java.util.Date;

public class x_tar extends ContentHandler {
    static int
        RECORDLEN = 512,
        NAMEOFF = 0, NAMELEN = 100,
        SIZEOFF = 124, SIZELEN = 12,
        MTIMEOFF = 136, MTIMELEN = 12;

    public Object getContent(URLConnection uc) throws IOException {
        InputStream is = uc.getInputStream();
        StringBuffer output = new StringBuffer( "Tape Archive Listing:\n\n" );
        byte [] header = new byte[RECORDLEN];
        int count = 0;

        while ( (is.read(header) == RECORDLEN) && (header[NAMEOFF] != 0) ) {

            String name = new String(header, NAMEOFF, NAMELEN, "8859_1").trim();
            String s = new String(header, SIZEOFF, SIZELEN, "8859_1").trim();
            int size = Integer.parseInt(s, 8);
            s = new String(header, MTIMEOFF, MTIMELEN, "8859_1").trim();
            long l = Integer.parseInt(s, 8);
            Date mtime = new Date( l*1000 );

            output.append( size + " " + mtime + " " + name + "\n" );

            count += is.skip( size ) + RECORDLEN;
            if ( count % RECORDLEN != 0 )
                count += is.skip ( RECORDLEN - count % RECORDLEN);
        }

        if ( count == 0 )
            output.append("Not a valid TAR file\n");

        return( output.toString() );
    }
}
```

The ContentHandler class

Our x_tar handler is a subclass of the abstract class java.net.ContentHandler. Its
job is to implement one method: getContent(), which takes as an argument a special "protocol connection" object and returns a constructed Java Object. The get-
Content() method of the URL class ultimately uses this getContent() method when
we ask for the contents of the URL.

The code looks formidable, but most of it's involved with processing the details of
the *tar* format. If we remove these details, there isn't much left:

```
public class x_tar extends ContentHandler {

    public Object getContent( URLConnection uc ) throws IOException {
        // get input stream
        InputStream is = uc.getInputStream();

        // read stream and construct object
        // ...

        // return the constructed object
        return( output.toString() );
    }
}
```

That's really all there is to a content handler; it's relatively simple.

The URLConnection

The java.net.URLConnection object that getContent() receives represents the
protocol handler's connection to the remote resource. It provides a number of
methods for examining information about the URL resource, such as header and
type fields, and for determining the kinds of operations the protocol supports.
However, its most important method is getInputStream(), which returns an
InputStream from the protocol handler. Reading this InputStream gives you the
raw data for the object the URL addresses. In our case, reading the InputStream
feeds x_tar the bytes of the *tar* file it's to process.

Constructing the object

The majority of our getContent() method is devoted to interpreting the stream of
bytes of the *tar* file and building our output object: the String that lists the contents of the *tar* file. Again, this means that this example involves the particulars of
reading *tar* files, so you shouldn't fret too much about the details.

After requesting an InputStream from the URLConnection, x_tar loops, gathering
information about each file. Each archived item is preceded by a header that

contains attribute and length fields. x_tar interprets each header and then skips over the remaining portion of the item. To parse the header, we use the String constructor to read a fixed number of characters from the byte array header[]. To convert these bytes into a Java String properly, we specify the character encoding used by Web servers: 8859_1, which (for the most part) is equivalent to ASCII. Once we have a file's name, size, and time stamp, we accumulate the results (the file listings) in a StringBuffer—one line per file. When the listing is complete, getContent() returns the StringBuffer as a String object.

The main while loop continues as long as it's able to read another header record, and as long as the record's "name" field isn't full of ASCII null values. (The *tar* file format calls for the end of the archive to be padded with an empty header record, although most *tar* implementations don't seem to do this.) The while loop retrieves the name, size, and modification times as character strings from fields in the header. The most common *tar* format stores its numeric values in octal, as fixed-length ASCII strings. We extract the strings and use Integer.parseInt() to parse them.

After reading and parsing the header, x_tar skips over the data portion of the file and updates the variable count, which keeps track of the offset into the archive. The two lines following the initial skip account for *tar*'s "blocking" of the data records. In other words, if the data portion of a file doesn't fit precisely into an integral number of blocks of RECORDLEN bytes, *tar* adds padding to make it fit.

Whew. Well, as I said, the details of parsing *tar* files are not really our main concern here. But x_tar does illustrate a few tricks of data manipulation in Java.

It may surprise you that we didn't have to provide a constructor; our content handler relies on its default constructor. We don't need to provide a constructor because there isn't anything for it to do. Java doesn't pass the class any argument information when it creates an instance of it. You might suspect that the URLConnection object would be a natural thing to provide at that point. However, when you are calling the constructor of a class that is loaded at run-time, you can't easily pass it any arguments.

Using our new handler

When we began this discussion of content handlers, we showed a brief example of how our x_tar content handler would work for us. You can try that code snippet now with your favorite *tar* file by setting the java.content.handler.pkgs system property to exploringjava.contenthandlers and making sure that package is in your class path.

To make things more exciting, try setting the property in your HotJava properties file. (The HotJava properties file usually resides in a *.hotjava* directory in your home directory or in the HotJava installation directory on a Windows machine.) Make sure that the class path is set before you start HotJava. Once HotJava is running, go to the **Preferences** menu, and select **Viewer Applications**. Find the type **TAR archive**, and set its **Action** to **View in HotJava**. This tells HotJava to try to use a content handler to display the data in the browser. Now, drive HotJava to a URL that contains a *tar* file. The result should look something like that shown in Figure 12-3.

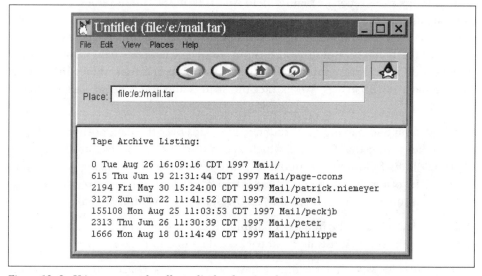

Figure 12–3: Using a content handler to display data in a browser

We've just extended our copy of HotJava to understand *tar* files! In the next section, we'll turn the tables and look at protocol handlers. There we'll be building URLConnection objects; someone else will have the pleasure of reconstituting the data.

Writing a Protocol Handler

A URL object uses a protocol handler to establish a connection with a server and perform whatever protocol is necessary to retrieve data. For example, an HTTP protocol handler knows how to talk to an HTTP server and retrieve a document; an FTP protocol handler knows how to talk to an FTP server and retrieve a file. All types of URLs use protocol handlers to access their objects. Even the lowly "file" type URLs use a special "file" protocol handler that retrieves files from the local filesystem. The data a protocol handler retrieves is then fed to an appropriate content handler for interpretation.

While we refer to a protocol handler as a single entity, it really has two parts: a java.net.URLStreamHandler and a java.net.URLConnection. These are both abstract classes we will subclass to create our protocol handler. (Note that these are abstract classes, not interfaces. Although they contain abstract methods we are required to implement, they also contain many utility methods we can use or override.) The URL looks up an appropriate URLStreamHandler, based on the protocol component of the URL. The URLStreamHandler then finishes parsing the URL and creates a URLConnection when it's time to communicate with the server. The URLConnection represents a single connection with a server, and implements the communication protocol itself.

Locating Protocol Handlers

Protocol handlers are organized in a package hierarchy similar to content handlers. But unlike content handlers, which are grouped into packages by the MIME types of the objects that they handle, protocol handlers are given individual packages. Both parts of the protocol handler (the URLStreamHandler class and the URLConnection class) are located in a package named for the protocol they support.

For example, if we wrote an FTP protocol handler, we might put it in an exploringjava.protocolhandlers.ftp package. The URLStreamHandler is placed in this package and given the name Handler; all URLStreamHandlers are named Handler and distinguished by the package in which they reside. The URLConnection portion of the protocol handler is placed in the same package and can be given any name. There is no need for a naming convention because the corresponding URLStreamHandler is responsible for creating the URLConnection objects it uses.

As with content handlers, Java locates packages containing protocol handlers using the java.protocol.handler.pkgs system property. The value of this property is a list of package names; if more than one package is in the list, use a vertical bar (|) to separate them. For our example, we will set this property to include exploringjava.protocolhandlers.

URLs, Stream Handlers, and Connections

The URL, URLStreamHandler, URLConnection, and ContentHandler classes work together closely. Before diving into an example, let's take a step back, look at the parts a little more, and see how these things communicate. Figure 12-4 shows how these components relate to each other.

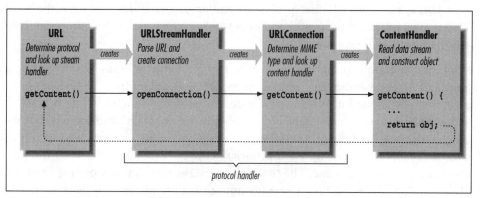

Figure 12–4: The protocol handler machinery

We begin with the URL object, which points to the resource we'd like to retrieve. The URLStreamHandler helps the URL class parse the URL specification string for its particular protocol. For example, consider the following call to the URL constructor:

```
URL url = new URL("protocol://foo.bar.com/file.ext");
```

The URL class parses only the protocol component; later, a call to the URL class's getContent() or openStream() method starts the machinery in motion. The URL class locates the appropriate protocol handler by looking in the protocol-package hierarchy. It then creates an instance of the appropriate URLStreamHandler class.

The URLStreamHandler is responsible for parsing the rest of the URL string, including hostname and filename, and possibly an alternative port designation. This allows different protocols to have their own variations on the format of the URL specification string. Note that this step is skipped when a URL is constructed with the "protocol," "host," and "file" components specified explicitly. If the protocol is straightforward, its URLStreamHandler class can let Java do the parsing and accept the default behavior. For this illustration, we'll assume that the URL string requires no special parsing. (If we use a nonstandard URL with a strange format, we're responsible for parsing it ourselves, as I'll show shortly.)

The URL object next invokes the handler's openConnection() method, prompting the handler to create a new URLConnection to the resource. The URLConnection performs whatever communications are necessary to talk to the resource and begins to fetch data for the object. At that time, it also determines the MIME type of the incoming object data and prepares an InputStream to hand to the appropriate content handler. This InputStream must send "pure" data with all traces of the protocol removed.

The URLConnection also locates an appropriate content handler in the content-handler package hierarchy. The URLConnection creates an instance of a content handler; to put the content handler to work, the URLConnection's getContent() method calls the content handler's getContent() method. If this sounds confusing, it is: we have three getContent() methods calling each other in a chain. The newly created ContentHandler object then acquires the stream of incoming data for the object by calling the URLConnection's getInputStream() method. (Recall that we acquired an InputStream in our x_tar content handler.) The content handler reads the stream and constructs an object from the data. This object is then returned up the getContent() chain: from the content handler, the URLConnection, and finally the URL itself. Now our application has the desired object in its greedy little hands.

To summarize, we create a protocol handler by implementing a URLStreamHandler class that creates specialized URLConnection objects to handle our protocol. The URLConnection objects implement the getInputStream() method, which provides data to a content handler for construction of an object. The base URLConnection class implements many of the methods we need; therefore, our URLConnection needs only to provide the methods that generate the data stream and return the MIME type of the object data.

Okay. If you're not thoroughly confused by all that terminology (or even if you are), let's move on to the example. It should help to pin down what all these classes are doing.

The crypt Handler

In this section, we'll build a *crypt* protocol handler. It parses URLs of the form:

```
crypt:type://hostname[:port]/location/item
```

type is an identifier that specifies what kind of encryption to use. The protocol itself is a simplified version of HTTP; we'll implement the GET command and no more. I added the *type* identifier to the URL to show how to parse a nonstandard URL specification. Once the handler has figured out the encryption type, it dynamically loads a class that implements the chosen encryption algorithm and uses it to retrieve the data. Obviously, we don't have room to implement a full-blown public-key encryption algorithm, so we'll use the rot13InputStream class from Chapter 10. It should be apparent how the example can be extended by plugging in a more powerful encryption class.

The Encryption class

First, we'll lay out our plug-in encryption class. We'll define an abstract class called CryptInputStream that provides some essentials for our plug-in encrypted

protocol. From the `CryptInputStream` we'll create a subclass called
`rot13CryptInputStream`, that implements our particular kind of encryption:

```
package exploringjava.protocolhandlers.crypt;

import java.io.*;

abstract class CryptInputStream extends InputStream {
    InputStream in;
    OutputStream out;
    abstract public void set( InputStream in, OutputStream out );
}

class rot13CryptInputStream extends CryptInputStream {

    public void set( InputStream in, OutputStream out ) {
        this.in = new exploringjava.io.rot13InputStream( in );
    }
    public int read() throws IOException {
        return in.read();
    }
}
```

Our `CryptInputStream` class defines a method called `set()` that passes in the
`InputStream` it's to translate. Our `URLConnection` calls `set()` after creating an
instance of the encryption class. We need a `set()` method because we want to load
the encryption class dynamically, and we aren't allowed to pass arguments to the
constructor of a class when it's dynamically loaded. (We noticed this same issue in
our content handler previously.) In the encryption class, we also provide for the
possibility of an `OutputStream`. A more complex kind of encryption might use the
`OutputStream` to transfer public-key information. Needless to say, *rot13* doesn't, so
we'll ignore the `OutputStream` here.

The implementation of `rot13CryptInputStream` is very simple. `set()` just takes the
`InputStream` it receives and wraps it with the `rot13InputStream` filter. `read()` reads
filtered data from the `InputStream`, throwing an exception if `set()` hasn't been
called.

The URLStreamHandler

Next we'll build our `URLStreamHandler` class. The class name is `Handler`; it extends
the abstract `URLStreamHandler` class. This is the class the Java `URL` looks up by converting the protocol name (*crypt*) into a package name. Remember that Java
expects this class to be named `Handler`, and to live in a package named for the protocol type.

```
package exploringjava.protocolhandlers.crypt;

import java.io.*;
```

```
import java.net.*;

public class Handler extends URLStreamHandler {

    protected void parseURL(URL url, String spec, int start, int end) {
        int slash = spec.indexOf('/');
        String crypType = spec.substring(start, slash-1);
        super.parseURL(url, spec, slash, end);
        setURL( url, "crypt:"+crypType, url.getHost(),
            url.getPort(), url.getFile(), url.getRef() );
    }

    protected URLConnection openConnection(URL url) throws IOException {
        String crypType = url.getProtocol().substring(6);
        return new CryptURLConnection( url, crypType );
    }
}
```

Java creates an instance of our URLStreamHandler when we create a URL specifying the *crypt* protocol. Handler has two jobs: to assist in parsing the URL specification strings and to create CryptURLConnection objects when it's time to open a connection to the host.

Our parseURL() method overrides the parseURL() method in the URLStreamHandler class. It's called whenever the URL constructor sees a URL requesting the *crypt* protocol. For example:

```
URL url = new URL("crypt:rot13://foo.bar.com/file.txt");
```

parseURL() is passed a reference to the URL object, the URL specification string, and starting and ending indexes that show what portion of the URL string we're expected to parse. The URL class has already identified the simple protocol name; otherwise, it wouldn't have found our protocol handler. Our version of parseURL() retrieves our *type* identifier from the specification and stores it temporarily in the variable cryptype. To find the encryption type, we take everything between the starting index we were given and the character preceding the first slash in the URL string (i.e., everything up to the colon in ://). We then defer to the superclass parseURL() method to complete the job of parsing the URL after that point. We call super.parseURL() with the new start index, so that it points to the character just after the type specifier. This tells the superclass parseURL() that we've already parsed everything prior to the first slash, and it's responsible for the rest. Finally we use the utility method setURL() to put together the final URL. Most everything has already been set correctly for us, but we need to call setURL() to add our special type to the protocol identifier. We'll need this information later when someone wants to open the URL connection.

Before going on, we'll note two other possibilities. If we hadn't hacked the URL string for our own purposes by adding a type specifier, we'd be dealing with a standard URL specification. In this case, we wouldn't need to override parseURL(); the default implementation would have been sufficient. It could have sliced the URL into host, port, and filename components normally. On the other hand, if we had created a completely bizarre URL format, we would need to parse the entire string. There would be no point calling super.parseURL(); instead, we'd have called the URLStreamHandler's protected method setURL() to pass the URL's components back to the URL object.

The other method in our Handler class is openConnection(). After the URL has been completely parsed, the URL object calls openConnection() to set up the data transfer. openConnection() calls the constructor for our URLConnection with appropriate arguments. In this case, our URLConnection object is named Crypt-URLConnection, and the constructor requires the URL and the encryption type as arguments. parseURL() put the encryption type in the protocol identifier of the URL. We recognize this and pass the information along. openConnection() returns the reference to our URLConnection, which the URL object uses to drive the rest of the process.

The URLConnection

Finally, we reach the real guts of our protocol handler, the URLConnection class. This is the class that opens the socket, talks to the server on the remote host, and implements the protocol itself. This class doesn't have to be public, so you can put it in the same file as the Handler class we just defined. We call our class Crypt-URLConnection; it extends the abstract URLConnection class. Unlike ContentHandler and StreamURLConnection, whose names are defined by convention, we can call this class anything we want; the only class that needs to know about the URLConnection is the URLStreamHandler, which we wrote ourselves.

```
class CryptURLConnection extends URLConnection {
    static int defaultPort = 80;
    CryptInputStream cis;

    public String getContentType() {
        return guessContentTypeFromName( url.getFile() );
    }

    CryptURLConnection ( URL url, String crypType ) throws IOException {
        super( url );
        try {
            String classname = "exploringjava.protocolhandlers.crypt."
                + crypType + "CryptInputStream";
            cis = (CryptInputStream)Class.forName(classname).newInstance();
        } catch ( Exception e ) {
            throw new IOException("Crypt Class Not Found: "+e);
```

```
            }
        }

    public void connect() throws IOException {
        int port = ( url.getPort() == -1 ) ? defaultPort : url.getPort();
        Socket s = new Socket( url.getHost(), port );

        // Send the filename in plaintext
        OutputStream server = s.getOutputStream();
        new PrintWriter( new OutputStreamWriter( server, "8859_1" ), true
            ).println( "GET " + url.getFile() );

        // Initialize the CryptInputStream
        cis.set( s.getInputStream(), server );
        connected = true;
    }

    public InputStream getInputStream() throws IOException {
        if (!connected)
            connect();
        return ( cis );
    }
}
```

The constructor for our CryptURLConnection class takes as arguments the destination URL and the name of an encryption type. We pass the URL on to the constructor of our superclass, which saves it in a protected url instance variable. We could have saved the URL ourselves, but calling our parent's constructor shields us from possible changes or enhancements to the base class. We use crypType to construct the name of an encryption class, using the convention that the encryption class is in the same package as the protocol handler (i.e., exploring-java.protocolhandlers.crypt); its name is the encryption type followed by the suffix CryptInputStream.

Once we have a name, we need to create an instance of the encryption class. To do so, we use the static method Class.forName() to turn the name into a Class object and newInstance() to load and instantiate the class. (This is how Java loads the content and protocol handlers themselves.) newInstance() returns an Object; we need to cast it to something more specific before we can work with it. Therefore, we cast it to our CryptInputStream class, the abstract class that rot13CryptInputStream extends. If we implement any additional encryption types as extensions to CryptInputStream and name them appropriately, they will fit into our protocol handler without modification.

We do the rest of our setup in the connect() method of the URLConnection. There, we make sure we have an encryption class and open a Socket to the appropriate port on the remote host. getPort() returns –1 if the URL doesn't specify a port explicitly; in that case we use the default port for an HTTP connection (port 80). We ask for an OutputStream on the socket, assemble a GET command using the getFile() method to discover the filename specified by the URL, and send our request by writing it into the OutputStream. (For convenience, we wrap the OutputStream with a PrintWriter and call println() to send the message.) We then initialize the CryptInputStream class by calling its set() method and passing it an InputStream from the Socket and the OutputStream.

The last thing connect() does is set the boolean variable connected to true. connected is a protected variable inherited from the URLConnection class. We need to track the state of our connection because connect() is a public method. It's called by the URLConnection's getInputStream() method, but it could also be called by other classes. Since we don't want to start a connection if one already exists, we check connected first.

In a more sophisticated protocol handler, connect() would also be responsible for dealing with any protocol headers that come back from the server. In particular, it would probably stash any important information it can deduce from the headers (e.g., MIME type, content length, time stamp) in instance variables, where it's available to other methods. At a minimum, connect() strips the headers from the data so the content handler won't see them. I'm being lazy and assuming that we'll connect to a minimal server, like the modified TinyHttpd daemon I discuss below, which doesn't bother with any headers.

The bulk of the work has been done; a few details remain. The URLConnection's getContent() method needs to figure out which content handler to invoke for this URL. In order to compute the content handler's name, getContent() needs to know the resource's MIME type. To find out, it calls the URLConnection's getContentType() method, which returns the MIME type as a String. Our protocol handler overrides getContentType(), providing our own implementation.

The URLConnection class provides a number of tools to help determine the MIME type. It's possible that the MIME type is conveyed explicitly in a protocol header; in this case, a more sophisticated version of connect() would have stored the MIME type in a convenient location for us. Some servers don't bother to insert the appropriate headers, though, so you can use the method guessContentTypeFrom-Name() to examine filename extensions, like *.gif* or *.html*, and map them to MIME types. In the worst case, you can use guessContentTypeFromStream() to intuit the MIME type from the raw data. The Java developers call this method "a disgusting hack" that shouldn't be needed, but that is unfortunately necessary in a world where HTTP servers lie about content types and extensions are often nonstandard. We'll take the easy way out and use the guessContentTypeFromName() utility of the URLConnection class to determine the MIME type from the filename extension of the URL we are retrieving.

Once the URLConnection has found a content handler, it calls the content handler's getContent() method. The content handler then needs to get an Input-Stream from which to read the data. To find an InputStream, it calls the URLConnection's getInputStream() method. getInputStream() returns an InputStream from which its caller can read the data after protocol processing is finished. It checks whether a connection is already established; if not, it calls connect() to make the connection. Then it returns a reference to our CryptInputStream.

A final note on getting the content type: the URLConnection's default getContent-Type() calls getHeaderField(), which is presumably supposed to extract the named field from the protocol headers (it would probably spit back information connect() had stored away). But the default implementation of getHeaderField() just returns null; we would have to override it to make it do anything interesting. Several other connection attributes use this mechanism, so in a more general implementation, we'd probably override getHeaderField() rather than getContentType() directly.

Trying it out

Let's try out our new protocol! Compile all of the classes and put them in the exploringjava.protocolhandlers package somewhere in your class path. Now set the java.protocol.handler.pkgs system property in HotJava to include exploringjava.protocolhandlers. Type a "crypt" style URL for a text document; you should see something like that shown in Figure 12-5.

This example would be more interesting if we had a *rot13* server. Since the *crypt* protocol is nothing more than HTTP with some encryption added, we can make a *rot13* server by modifying one line of the TinyHttpd server we developed earlier, so that it spews its files in *rot13*. Just change the line that reads the data from the file; replace this line:

```
f.read( data );
```

with a line that reads through a rot13InputStream:

```
new example.io.rot13InputStream( f ).read( data );
```

We'll assume you placed the rot13InputStream example in a package called exploringjava.io, and that it's somewhere in your class path. Now recompile and run the server. It automatically encodes the files before sending them; our sample application decodes them on the other end.

We hope that this example and the rest of this chapter have given you some food for thought. Content and protocol handlers are among the most exciting ideas in

Figure 12–5: The crypt protocol handler at work

Java. It's unfortunate that we have to wait for future releases of HotJava and Netscape to take full advantage of them. In the meantime, you can experiment and implement your own applications.

Talking to CGI Programs

CGI stands for Common Gateway Interface; it is an API for writing applications (often scripts) that can be run by a Web server to service a particular range of URLs. CGIs can perform dynamic activities like automatically generating Web documents. More important, they can accept data sent from the browser; they are most frequently used to process forms. The name=value pairs of the form fields are encoded by the browser in a special format and sent to the application using one of two methods. The first method, called GET, places the user's input directly into the URL and requests the corresponding document. The server recognizes that the first part of the URL refers to a CGI program and invokes it, passing along the information encoded in the URL as a string parameter. The second method for submitting data to a server is called POST. In this method, the browser uses the HTTP POST command to ask the server to accept the encoded data and pass it to the CGI program as a stream. Most CGI programs use utilities that shield them from the details of receiving the data and decoding it. But because of common limitations, the POST method is more suitable for sending large amounts of data.

In Java, we can create a URL that refers to a CGI program and send it data using either the GET or POST methods. Why would we want to talk to a CGI? Well, they are currently the most widely used technique for building advanced Web applications. Other techniques, like opening a socket or writing a Java servlet, are coming on strong, but CGI has been in widespread use for several years. Another important reason for using CGI is that many firewalls block socket connections entirely. But all firewalls that allow Web access have to let us use GET and POST to talk to CGIs. So CGI programs can be used as a last resort communications mechanism between applets and servers.

Using the GET Method

Using the GET method is pretty easy. All we have to do is create a URL pointing to a CGI program and use a simple convention to tack on the encoded name=value pairs that make up our data. For example, the following code snippet opens a URL to a CGI program called *login.cgi* on the server *myhost* and passes it two name=value pairs. It also prints whatever text the CGI sends back:

```
URL url = new URL(
    "http://myhost/cgi-bin/login.cgi?Name=Pat&Password=foobar");

BufferedReader bin = new BufferedReader (
    new InputStreamReader( url.openStream() ));

String line;
while ( (line = bin.readLine()) != null )
    System.out.println( line );
```

To form the new URL, we start with the URL of *login.cgi*; we add a question mark (?), which marks the beginning of the data, followed by the first name=value pair. We can add as many pairs as we want, separated by ampersand (&) characters. The rest of our code opens the stream and reads back the data. Remember that creating a URL doesn't actually open the connection. In this case, the URL connection was made implicitly when we called openStream(). Although we are assuming here that our CGI sends back text, it could send anything. We could use the getContentType() method of the URL to check the MIME type of any returned data, and try to retrieve the data as an object using getContent().

Finally, it's important to point out that we have skipped a step here. This example works because our name=value pairs happen to be simple text. If any "nonprintable" or special characters (including "?" or "&") are in the data itself, they have to be encoded first. The java.net.URLEncoder class provides a utility for encoding the data. We'll show how to use it in the next example.

Using the POST Method

Let's create an applet that acts like a simple form. It presents two text fields, Name and Password, and a Post button that sends the data to a specified URL:

```java
import java.net.*;
import java.io.*;
import java.awt.*;
import java.awt.event.*;

public class Post extends java.applet.Applet implements ActionListener {
    TextField nameField, passwordField;

    GridBagConstraints constraints = new GridBagConstraints();
    void addGB( Component component, int x, int y  ) {
        constraints.gridx = x;   constraints.gridy = y;
        add ( component, constraints );
    }
    public void init() {
        Button postButton = new Button("Post");
        postButton.addActionListener( this );
        setLayout( new GridBagLayout() );
        addGB( new Label("Name:"),              0,0 );
        addGB( nameField = new TextField(20),   1,0 );
        addGB( new Label("Password:"),          0,1 );
        addGB( passwordField = new TextField(20),1,1 );
        Panel p = new Panel();
        p.add ( postButton );
        constraints.gridwidth = 2;
        addGB( p, 0,2 );
    }
    public void actionPerformed(ActionEvent e) {
        postData();
    }

    private void postData() {
        StringBuffer sb = new StringBuffer();
        sb.append( URLEncoder.encode("Name") + "=" );
        sb.append( URLEncoder.encode(nameField.getText()) );
        sb.append( "&" + URLEncoder.encode("Password") + "=" );
        sb.append( URLEncoder.encode(passwordField.getText()) );
        String formData = sb.toString();
        try {
            URL url = new URL( getParameter("postURL") );
            HttpURLConnection urlcon = (HttpURLConnection)url.openConnection();
            urlcon.setRequestMethod("POST");
            urlcon.setRequestProperty("Content-type",
                "application/x-www-form-urlencoded");
            urlcon.setDoOutput(true);
            urlcon.setDoInput(true);
            PrintWriter pout = new PrintWriter( new OutputStreamWriter(
                urlcon.getOutputStream(), "8859_1"), true );
            pout.print( formData );
            pout.flush();
```

```
                // read results...
                if ( urlcon.getResponseCode() != HttpURLConnection.HTTP_OK ) {
                    System.out.println("Bad post...");
                    return;
                }
                InputStream in = urlcon.getInputStream();
                // ...

            } catch (MalformedURLException e) {
                System.out.println("Bad postURL");
            } catch (IOException e2) {
                System.out.println("I/O error: "+e2);
            }
        }
    }
```

To use this applet, you must specify the URL of your CGI program by using the "postURL" HTML parameter. For example:

```
<param name="postURL" value="http://myhost/cgi-bin/post-login.cgi" >
```

The beginning of the applet creates the form; there's nothing here that won't be obvious after you've read the chapters on AWT. All the magic happens in the private postData() method. First we create a StringBuffer and use it to append name=value pairs, separated by ampersands. (We don't need the initial question mark when we're using the POST method.) Each pair is first encoded using the static URLEncoder.encode() method. We ran the name fields through the encoder as well as the value fields, even though we know from the first example that they contain no special characters, and we didn't have to.

Next we set up the connection to the CGI program. In our previous example, we didn't have to do anything special to send the data, because the request was made by the Web browser for us. Here, we have to carry some of the weight of talking to the remote Web server. Fortunately, the HttpURLConnection object does most of the work for us; we just have to tell it that we want to do a POST to the URL and the type of data we are sending. We ask for the URLConnection object using the URL's openConnection() method. We know that we are using HTTP, so we should be able to cast it to an HttpURLConnection type, which has the support we need.

Next we use setRequestMethod() to tell the connection we want to POST. We also use setRequestProperty() to set the "Content-Type" field of our HTTP request to the appropriate type—in this case, the proper MIME type for encoded form data. (This helps the CGI sort out what we're sending.) Finally, we use the setDoOutput() and setDoInput() methods to tell the connection that we want to send and receive stream data. We get an output stream from the connection with getOutputStream() and create a PrintWriter so we can easily write our encoded data.

After we post the data, we call getResponseCode() to check the HTTP response code from the server to see if it indicates the POST was successful. Other response codes (defined as constants in HttpURLConnection) indicate various failures. At the end, we indicate where we could read back the response. I haven't implemented anything; you can add your own code if you want.

Although form-encoded data is the most common, other types of communications are possible. We could have used the input and output streams to exchange arbitrary data with the CGI.

What About HTTPS?

HTTPS is the standard HTTP protocol run over SSL (Secure Socket Layer) sockets, which use public-key encryption techniques to encrypt the data sent. Most browsers currently come with built-in support for HTTPS (or raw SSL sockets). Therefore, if the server supports HTTPS, you can use the browser to send and receive secure data simply by specifying the *https:* protocol in your URLs.

13

The Abstract Window Toolkit

The Abstract Window Toolkit (AWT), or "another window toolkit," as some people affectionately call it, provides a large collection of classes for building graphical user interfaces (GUIs) in Java. With AWT, you can create windows, draw, work with images, and use components like buttons, scrollbars, and pull-down menus in a platform-independent way. The `java.awt` package contains the AWT GUI classes. The `java.awt.image` package provides some additional tools for working with images.

AWT is the largest and most complicated part of the standard Java distribution, so it shouldn't be any surprise that we'll take several chapters (five, to be precise) to discuss it. Here's the lay of the land:

- Chapter 13 covers the basic concepts you need to understand how AWT builds user interfaces.

- In Chapter 14, we discuss the basic components from which user interfaces are built: lists, text fields, checkboxes, and so on.

- Chapter 15 discusses layout managers, which are responsible for arranging components within a display.

- Chapter 16 discusses the fundamentals of drawing, including simple image displays.

- Chapter 17, the last chapter to discuss AWT in detail, covers the image generation and processing tools that are in the `java.awt.image` package. We'll throw in audio for good measure.

We can't cover the full functionality of AWT in this book; if you want complete coverage, see the *Java AWT Reference* (O'Reilly). Instead, we'll cover the basics of the tools you are most likely to use and show some examples of what can be done with some of the more advanced features. Figure 13-1 shows the user interface portion of the java.awt package.

As its name suggests, AWT is an abstraction. Its classes and functionality are the same for all Java implementations, so Java applications built with AWT should work in the same way on all platforms. You could choose to write your code under Windows NT/95, and then run it on an X Window System or a Macintosh. To achieve platform independence, AWT uses interchangeable toolkits that interact with the host windowing system to display user interface components, thus shielding your application code from the details of the environment it's running in. Let's say you ask AWT to create a button. When your application or applet runs, a toolkit appropriate to the host environment renders the button appropriately: on Windows, you can get a button that looks like other Windows buttons; on a Macintosh, you can get a Mac button; and so on.

Working with user interface components in AWT is meant to be easy. While the low-level (possibly native) GUI toolkits may be complex, you won't have to work with them directly unless you want to port AWT to a new platform or provide an alternative "look and feel" for the built-in components. When building a user interface for your application, you'll be working with prefabricated components. It's easy to assemble a collection of user interface components (buttons, text areas, etc.) and arrange them inside containers to build complex layouts. You can also use simple components as building blocks for making entirely new kinds of interface gadgets that are completely portable and reusable.

AWT uses layout managers to arrange components inside containers and control their sizing and positioning. Layout managers define a strategy for arranging components instead of relying on absolute positioning. For example, you can define a user interface with a collection of buttons and text areas and be reasonably confident it will always display correctly. It doesn't matter that Windows, UNIX, and the Macintosh render your buttons and text areas differently; the layout manager should still position them sensibly with respect to each other.

Unfortunately, the reality is that most of the complaints about Java center around AWT. AWT is very different from what many people are used to and (at least for now) lacks some of the advanced features other GUI environments provide. It's also true that most of the bugs in current implementations of Java lie in the AWT toolkits. As bugs are fixed and developers become accustomed to AWT, we would expect the number of complaints to diminish. Java 1.1 is a substantial improvement over previous versions, but there are some rough edges. JavaSoft has released an early version of Swing, which is Java's next generation user interface and part of the larger JFC (Java Foundation Classes). Swing includes many new components, plus support for customizable look-and-feel. It's worth playing with Swing, but we can't cover it in this edition.

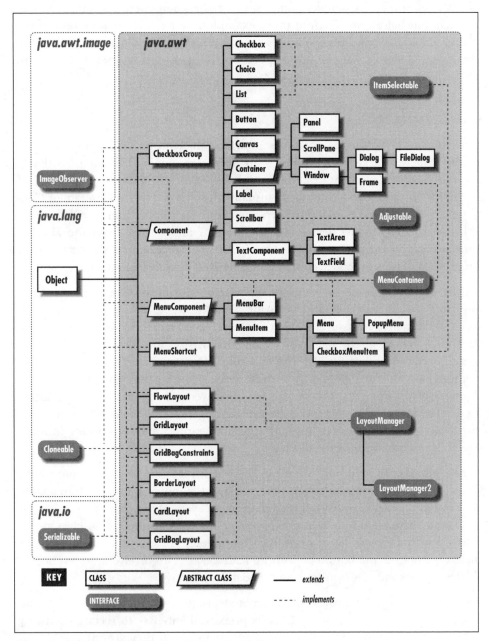

Figure 13–1: User interface classes of the java.awt package

Chapter 14 contains examples using most of the components in the java.awt package. But before we dive into those examples, we need to spend a bit of time talking about the concepts AWT uses for creating and handling user interfaces. This material should get you up to speed on GUI concepts and on how they are used in Java.

Components

A component is the fundamental user interface object in Java. Everything you see on the display in a Java application is an AWT component. This includes things like windows, drawing canvases, buttons, checkboxes, scrollbars, lists, menus, and text fields. To be used, a component usually must be placed in a container. Container objects group components, arrange them for display, and associate them with a particular display device. All components are derived from the abstract java.awt.Component class, as you saw in Figure 13-1. For example, the Button class is a subclass of the Component class, which is derived directly from Object.

For the sake of simplicity, we can split the functionality of the Component class into two categories: appearance and behavior. The Component class contains methods and variables that control an object's general appearance. This includes basic attributes such as whether it's visible, its current size and location, and certain common graphical defaults like font and color. The Component class also contains methods implemented by specific subclasses to produce the actual graphics the object displays. When a component is first displayed, it's associated with a particular display device. The Component class encapsulates access to its display area on that device. This includes methods for accessing graphics and for working with off-screen drawing buffers for the display.

By a "component's behavior," we mean the way it responds to user-driven events. When the user performs an action (like pressing the mouse button) within a component's display area, an AWT thread delivers an event object that describes "what happened." The event is delivered to objects that have registered themselves as "listeners" for that type of event from that component. For example, when the user clicks on a button, the button delivers an ActionEvent. To receive those events, an object registers with the button as an ActionListener.

Events are delivered by invoking designated event-handler methods within the receiving object (the "listener"). Objects prepare themselves to receive events by implementing methods for the types of events in which they are interested and then registering as listeners with the sources of the events. Specific types of events cover different categories of component and user interaction. For example,

MouseEvents describe activities of the mouse within a component's area, KeyEvents describe key presses, and functionally higher level events such as ActionEvents indicate that a user interface component has done its job.

Although events are crucial to the workings of AWT, they aren't limited to building user interfaces. Events are an important interobject communications mechanism that may be used by completely nongraphical parts of an application as well. They are particularly important in the context of Java Beans, which use events as an extremely general notification mechanism. We will describe events thoroughly in this chapter because they are so fundamental to the way in which user interfaces function in Java, but it's good to keep the bigger picture in mind.

Containers often take on certain responsibilities for the components that they hold. Instead of every component handling events for its own bit of the user interface, a container may register itself or another object to receive the events for its child components and "glue" those events to the correct application logic.

A component informs its container when it does something that might affect other components in the container, such as changing its size or visibility. The container can then tell the layout manager that it is time to rearrange the child components.

Containers in Java are themselves a kind of component. Because all components share this structure, container objects can manage and arrange Component objects without knowing what they are and what they are doing. Components can be swapped and replaced with new versions easily and combined into composite user interface objects that can be treated as individual components. This lends itself well to building larger, reusable user interface items.

Peers

We have just described a nice system in which components govern their own appearance, and events are delivered to objects that are "listening" to those components. Unfortunately, getting data out to a display medium and receiving events from input devices involve crossing the line from Java to the real world. The real world is a nasty place full of architecture dependence, local peculiarities, and strange physical devices like mice, trackballs, and '69 Buicks.

At some level, our components will have to talk to objects that contain native methods to interact with the host operating environment. To keep this interaction as clean and well-defined as possible, Java uses a set of *peer* interfaces. The peer interface makes it possible for a pure Java-language AWT component to use a corresponding real component—the peer object—in the native environment. You won't generally deal directly with peer interfaces or the objects behind them; peer handling is encapsulated within the Component class. It's important to understand the architecture, though, because it imposes some limitations on what you can do with components.

For example, when a component such as a Button is first created and displayed on the screen, code in the Component class asks an AWT Toolkit class to create a corresponding peer object, as shown in Figure 13-2. The Toolkit is a *factory* that knows how to create objects in the native display system; Java uses this factory design pattern to provide an abstraction that separates the implementation of component objects from their functionality. The Toolkit object contains methods for making instances of each type of component peer. (As a developer, you will probably never work with a native user interface directly.) Toolkits can be swapped and replaced to provide new implementations of the components without affecting the rest of Java.

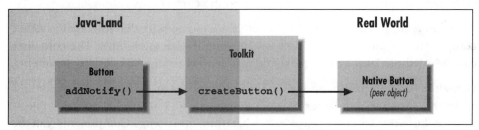

Figure 13–2: A toolkit creating a peer object

Figure 13-2 shows a Toolkit producing a peer object for a Button. When you add a button to a container, the container calls the Button's addNotify() method. In turn, addNotify() calls the Toolkit's createButton() method to make the Button's peer object in the real display system. Thereafter, the Component class keeps a reference to the peer object and delegates calls to its methods.

The java.awt.peer package, shown in Figure 13-3, parallels the java.awt package and contains an interface for each type of component. For example, the Button component has a ButtonPeer interface, which defines the capabilities of a button.

The peer objects themselves can be built in whatever way is necessary, using a combination of Java and native code. (We will discuss the implementation of peers a bit more in the AWT performance section of this chapter.) A Java-land button doesn't know or care how the real-world button is implemented or what additional capabilities it may have; it knows only about the existence of the methods defined in the ButtonPeer interface. Figure 13-4 shows a call to the setLabel() method of a Button object, which results in a call to the corresponding setLabel() method of the native button object.

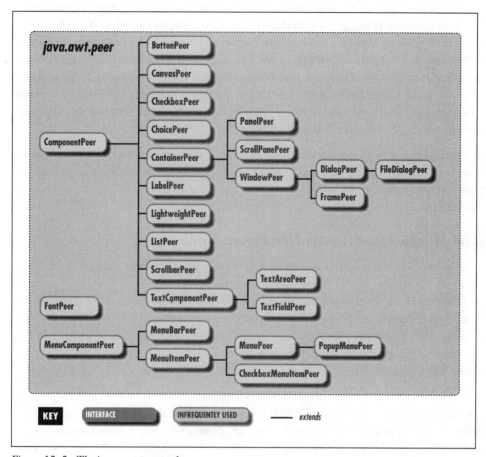

Figure 13–3: The java.awt.peer package

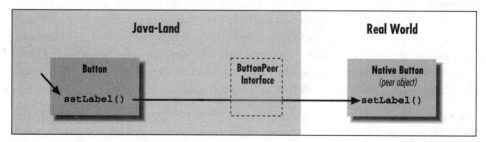

Figure 13–4: Invoking a method in the peer interface

In this case, the only action a button peer must be able to perform is to set its label text; setLabel() is the only method in the ButtonPeer interface. How the native button acts, responds to user input, etc., is entirely up to it. It might turn green when pressed or make a "ka-chunk" sound. The component in Java-land has no control over these aspects of the native button's behavior—and this has important implications. This abstraction allows AWT to use native components from whatever platform it resides on. However, it also means that a lot of a component's functionality is locked away where we can't get to it. We'll see that we can usually intercept events before the peer object has a chance to act on them, but we usually can't change much of the object's basic behavior.

A component gets its peer when it's added to a container. Containers are associated with display devices through Toolkit objects, and thus control the process of peer creation. We'll talk more about the ramifications of this when we discuss addNotify() later.

The Model/View/Controller Framework

Before we continue our discussion of GUI concepts, I want to make a brief aside and talk about the Model/View/Controller (MVC) framework. MVC is a method of building reusable components that logically separates the structure, representation, and behavior of a component into separate pieces. MVC is primarily concerned with building user interface components, but the basic ideas can be applied to many design issues; its principles can be seen throughout Java. Java doesn't implement all of MVC, whose origins are in Smalltalk, but MVC's influence is apparent throughout the language.

The fundamental idea behind MVC is the separation of the data model for an item from its presentation. For example, we can draw different representations (e.g., bar graphs, pie charts) of the data in a spreadsheet. The data is the "model"; the particular representation is the "view." A single model can have many views that show different representations of the data. The behavior of a user interface component usually changes its model and affects how the component is rendered as a view. If we were to create a button component, for example, its data model could be as simple as a boolean value for whether it's up or down. The behavior for handling mouse-press events would alter the model, and the display would examine that data when it draws the on-screen representation.

The way in which AWT objects communicate, by passing events from sources to listeners, is part of this MVC concept of separation. Event listeners are "observers," and event sources are "observables." When an observable changes or performs a function, it notifies all of its observers of the activity. In Chapter 9 we described the Observer class and Observable interface of the java.util package. AWT doesn't use these classes directly, but it does use exactly the same design pattern for handling event sources and listeners.

This model of operation is also central to the way in which Java works with graphics, as you'll see in Chapter 17. Image information from a producer, such as a graphics engine or video stream, is distributed to consumers that can represent different views of the data. Consumers register with a producer and receive updates as the image is created or when the image has changed.

The factory concept used by the `Toolkit` objects is related to MVC; factories use Java interfaces to separate the implementation of an object from its behavior. An object that implements an interface doesn't have to fit into a particular class structure; it needs only to provide the methods defined by the interface. Thus, an AWT `Toolkit` is a factory that produces native user interface components that correspond to Java components. The native components don't need to match AWT's class structure, provided they implement the appropriate interface.

Painting and Updating

Components can be asked to draw themselves at any time. In a more procedural programming environment, you might expect a component to be involved in drawing only when first created or when it changes its appearance. In Java, components act in a way that is more closely tied to the underlying behavior of the display environment. For example, when you obscure a component with a window and then re-expose it, an AWT thread asks the component to redraw itself.

AWT asks a component to draw itself by calling its `paint()` method. `paint()` may be called at any time, but in practice, it's called when the object is first made visible, whenever it changes its appearance, and whenever some tragedy in the display system messes up its area. Because `paint()` can't make any assumptions about why it was called, it must redraw the component's entire display.

However, redrawing the whole component is unnecessary if only a small part changes, especially in an anticipated way. In this case, you'd like to specify what part of the component has changed, and redraw that part alone. Painting a large portion of the screen is time consuming and can cause flickering that is especially annoying if you're redrawing the object frequently, as is the case with animation. When a component realizes it needs to redraw itself, it should ask AWT to schedule a call to its `update()` method. `update()` can do drawing of its own, but it often simply defines a clipping region—by calling `clipRect()`—on its graphics context; to limit the extent of the painted area and then calls `paint()` explicitly. A simple component doesn't have to implement its own `update()` method, but that doesn't mean the method doesn't exist. In this case, the component gets a default version of `update()` that simply clears the component's area and calls `paint()`.

A component never calls its update() method directly. Instead, when a component requires redrawing, it schedules a call to update() by invoking repaint(). The repaint() method asks AWT to schedule the component for repainting. At some point in the future, a call to update() occurs. AWT is allowed to manage these requests in whatever way is most efficient. If there are too many requests to handle, or if there are multiple requests for the same component, AWT can reschedule a number of repaint requests into a single call to update(). This means that you can't predict exactly when update() will be called in response to a repaint(); all you can expect is that it happens at least once, after you request it.

Calling repaint() is normally an implicit request to be updated as soon as possible. Another form of repaint() allows you to specify a time period within which you would like an update, giving the system more flexibility in scheduling the request. An application can use this method to govern its refresh rate. For example, the rate at which you render frames for an animation might vary, depending on other factors (like the complexity of the image). You could impose an effective maximum frame rate by calling repaint() with a time (the inverse of the frame rate) as an argument. If you then happen to make more than one repaint request within that time period, AWT is not obliged to physically repaint for each one. It can simply condense them to carry out a single update within the time you have specified.

Both paint() and update() take a single argument: a Graphics object. The Graphics object represents the component's graphics context. It corresponds to the area of the screen on which the component can draw and provides the methods for performing primitive drawing and image manipulation. We'll look at the Graphics class in detail in Chapter 16.

All components paint and update themselves using this mechanism. However, you really care about it only when doing your own drawing, and in practice, you should be drawing only on a Canvas, Panel, Applet, or your own subclasses of Component. Other kinds of objects, like buttons and scrollbars, have lots of behavior built into their peers. You may be able to draw on one of these objects, but unless you specifically catch the appropriate events and redraw (which could get complicated), your handiwork is likely to disappear.

Canvases, Panels, and lightweight components are "blank slates" on which to implement your own behavior and appearance. For example, by itself, the AWT Canvas has no outward appearance; it takes up space and has a background color, but otherwise, it's empty. By subclassing Canvas and adding your own code, you can create a more complicated object like a graph or a flying toaster. A lightweight component is even "emptier" than that. It doesn't have a real Toolkit peer for its implementation; you get to specify all of the behavior and appearance yourself.

A Panel is like a Canvas, but it's also a Container, so it can hold other user interface components. In the same way, a lightweight container is a simple extension of
the AWT Container class.

Enabling and Disabling Components

Standard AWT components can be turned on and off by calling the enable() and
disable() methods. When a component like a Button or TextField is disabled, it
becomes "ghosted" or "greyed-out" and doesn't respond to user input.

For example, let's see how to create a component that can be used only once. This
requires getting ahead of the story; I won't explain some aspects of this example
until later. Earlier, I said that a Button generates an ActionEvent when it is
pressed. This event is delivered to the listeners' actionPerformed() method. The
code below disables whatever component generated the event:

```
public boolean void actionPerformed(ActionEvent e ) {
    ...
    ((Component)e.getSource()).disable();
}
```

This code calls getSource() to find out which component generated the event. We
cast the result to Component because we don't necessarily know what kind of component we're dealing with; it might not be a button, because other kinds of components can generate action events. Once we know which component generated
the event, we disable it.

You can also disable an entire container. Disabling a Panel, for instance, disables
all the components it contains. Unfortunately, disabling components and containers is handled by the AWT toolkit at a low level. It is currently not possible to notify
custom (pure Java) components when their native containers are disabled. This
flaw should be corrected in a future release.

Focus, Please

In order to receive keyboard events, a component has to have keyboard *focus*. The
component with the focus is simply the currently selected input component. It
receives all keyboard event information until the focus changes. A component can
ask for focus with the Component's requestFocus() method. Text components like
TextField and TextArea do this automatically whenever you click the mouse in
their area. A component can find out when it gains or loses focus through the
FocusListener interface (see Tables 13-1 and 13-2 later in this chapter). If you
want to create your own text-oriented component, you could implement this
behavior yourself. For instance, you might request focus when the mouse is clicked
in your component's area. After receiving focus, you could change the cursor or
do something else to highlight the component.

Many user interfaces are designed so that the focus automatically jumps to the "next available" component when the user presses the Tab key. This behavior is particularly common in forms; users often expect to be able to tab to the next text entry field. AWT handles automatic focus traversal for you when it is applicable. You can get control over the behavior through the `transferFocus()` and `isFocus-Traversable()` methods of `Component`. `transferFocus()` passes the focus to the next appropriate component. You can use `transferFocus()` to control the order of tabbing between components by overriding it in the container and implementing your own policy. `isFocusTraversable()` returns a `boolean` value specifying whether the component should be considered eligible for receiving a transfer focus. Your components can override this method to determine whether they can be "tabbed to."

Other Component Methods

The `Component` class is very large; it has to provide the base level functionality for all of the various kinds of Java GUI objects. We don't have room to document every method of the component class here, but we'll flesh out our discussion by covering some more of the important ones:

`Container getParent()`

> Return the container that holds this component.

`String getName() / void setName(String name)`

> Get or assign the `String` name of this component. Naming a component is useful for debugging. The name shows up when you do a `toString()`.

`setVisible(boolean visible)`

> Make the component visible or invisible, within its container. If you change the component's visibility, remember to call `validate()` on the container; this causes the layout manager to lay out the container again.

`Color getForeground() / void setForeground(Color c)`
`Color getBackground() / void setBackground(Color c)`

> Get and set the foreground and background colors for this component. The foreground color of any component is the default color used for drawing. For example, it is the color used for text in a text field; it is also the default drawing color for the `Graphics` object passed to the component's `paint()` method. The background color is used to fill the component's area when it is cleared by the default implementation of `update()`.

`Font getFont() / void setFont(Font f)`

> Get or set the `Font` for this component. (Fonts are discussed in Chapter 16.) You can set the `Font` on text components like `TextField` and `TextArea`. For `Canvases`, `Panels`, and lightweight components, this will also be the default font used for drawing text on the `Graphics` context passed to `paint()`.

`FontMetrics getFontMetrics(Font font)`

> Find out the characteristics of a font when rendered on this component. `FontMetrics` allow you to find out the dimensions of text when rendered in that font.

`Dimension getSize() / void setSize(int width, int height)`

> Get and set the current size of the component. Remember to call `validate()` on the component's container if you change its size. There are other methods in `Component` to set its location, but normally this is the job of a layout manager.

`Cursor getCursor() / void setCursor(Cursor cursor)`

> Get or set the type of cursor (mouse pointer) used when the mouse is over this component's area. For example:

```
Component myComponent = ...;
Cursor crossHairs = Cursor.getPredefinedCursor( Cursor.CROSSHAIR_CURSOR );
myComponent.setCursor( crossHairs );
```

Containers

Now that you understand components a little better, our discussion of containers should be easy. A container is a kind of component that holds and manages other AWT components. If you look back to Figure 13-1, you can see the part of the `java.awt` class hierarchy that descends from `Container`.

Three of the most useful `Container` types are `Frame`, `Panel`, and `Applet`. A `Frame` is a top-level window on your display. `Frame` is derived from `Window`, which is pretty much the same but lacks a border. A `Panel` is a generic container element used to group components inside of `Frames` and other `Panels`. The `Applet` class is a kind of `Panel` that provides the foundation for applets that run inside Web browsers. As a `Panel`, an `Applet` has the ability to contain other user interface components. All these classes are subclasses of the `Container` class. You can also use the `Container` class directly, like a `Panel`, to hold components inside of another container. This is called a *lightweight container* and is closely related to lightweight components.

Because a `Container` is a kind of `Component`, it has all of the methods of the `Component` class, including the graphical and event-related methods we're discussing in this chapter. But a container also maintains a list of "child" components, which are the components it manages, and therefore has methods for dealing with those components. By themselves, most components aren't very useful until they are added to a container and displayed. The `add()` method of the `Container` class adds a component to the container. Thereafter, this component can be displayed in the container's area and positioned by its layout manager. You can also remove a component from a container with the `remove()` method.

Layout Managers

A *layout manager* is an object that controls the placement and sizing of components within the display area of a container. A layout manager is like a window manager in a display system; it controls where the components go and how big they are. Every container has a default layout manager, but you can easily install a new one by calling the container's `setLayout()` method.

AWT comes with a few layout managers that implement common layout schemes. The default layout manager for a `Panel` is a `FlowLayout`, which tries to place objects at their preferred size from left to right and top to bottom in the container. The default for a `Frame` is a `BorderLayout`, which places a limited number of objects at named locations like "North," "South," and "Center." Another layout manager, the `GridLayout`, arranges components in a rectangular grid. The most general (and difficult to use) layout manager is `GridBagLayout`, which lets you do the kinds of things you can do with HTML tables. We'll get into the details of all of these layout managers in Chapter 15.

As I mentioned earlier, you normally call `add()` to add a component to a container. There is an overloaded version of `add()` that you may need, depending on what layout manager you're using. You'll often use the version of `add()` that takes a single `Component` as an argument. However, if you're using a layout manager that uses "constraints," like `BorderLayout` or `GridBagLayout`, you need to specify additional information about where to put the new component. For that you can use the version that takes a constraint object:

```
add( Component component, Object constraint);
```

For example, to add a component to the top of a `BorderLayout`, you might say:

```
add( newComponent, "North");
```

In this case, the constraint object is the string "North." The `GridBagLayout` uses a much more complex constraint object to specify positioning.

Insets

Insets specify a container's margins; the space specified by the container's insets won't be used by a layout manager. Insets are described by an Insets object, which has four int fields: top, bottom, left, and right. You normally don't need to worry about the insets; the container will set them automatically, taking into account extras like the menu bar that may appear at the top of a frame. However, you should modify the insets if you're doing something like adding a decorative border (for example, a set of "index tabs" at the top of a container) that reduces the space available for components. To change the insets, you override the component's getInsets() method, which returns an Insets object. For example:

```
//reserve 50 pixels at the top, 5 at the sides and 10 at the bottom
public Insets getInsets() {
    return new Insets (50,5,10,5);
}
```

Z-Ordering (Stacking Components)

In most layout schemes, components are not allowed to overlap, but they can. If they do, the order in which components were added to a container matters. When components overlap they are "stacked" in the order in which they were added: the first component added to the container is on top; the last is on the bottom. To give you more control over stacking, two additional forms of the add() method take an additional integer argument that lets you specify the component's exact position in the container's stacking order.

validate() and layout()

A layout manager arranges the components in a container only when asked to. Several things can mess up a container after it's initially laid out:

• Changing its size

• Resizing or moving one of its child components

• Adding, showing, removing, or hiding a child component

Any of these actions cause the container to be marked invalid. Saying that a container is invalid simply means it needs to have its child components readjusted by its layout manager. This is accomplished by calling the Container's validate() method. validate() calls the Container's doLayout() method, which asks the layout manager to do its job. In addition, validate() also notes that the Container has been fixed (i.e., it's valid again) and looks at each child component of the container, recursively validating any containers that are also messed up.

So if you have an applet that contains a small Panel—say a keypad holding some buttons—and you change the size of the Panel by calling its resize() method, you should also call validate() on the applet. The applet's layout manager may then reposition or resize the keypad within the applet. It also automatically calls validate() for the keypad, so that it can rearrange its buttons to fit inside its new area.

There are two things you should note. First, all components, not just containers, maintain a notion of when they are valid or invalid. But most components (e.g., buttons) don't do anything special when they're validated. If you have a custom component that wants to be notified when it is resized, it might be best to make it a container (perhaps a lightweight container) and do your work in the doLayout() method.

Next, child containers are validated only if they are invalid. That means that if you have an invalid component nested inside a valid component and you validate a container above them both, the invalid component may never be reached. However, the invalidate() method that marks a container as dirty automatically marks parent containers as well, all the way up the container hierarchy. So that situation should never happen.

Component Peers and addNotify()

A component gets its peer when it's added to a container. Containers are associated with display devices through Toolkit objects, and thus control the process of peer creation. This means that you can't ask certain questions about a component before it's placed in a container. For example, you can't find out about a component's size or its default font until the component knows where it's being displayed (until it has its peer).

You probably also shouldn't be able to ask a component with no peer about other resources controlled by the peer, such as off-screen graphics areas and font metrics. Java's developers apparently thought this restriction too onerous, so container-less components are associated with the "default" toolkit that can answer some of these kinds of inquiries. In practice, the default toolkit is usually able to provide the right answer, because with current implementations of Java, the default toolkit is probably the only toolkit available. This approach may cause problems in the future, if Java's developers add the ability for different containers to have different toolkits.

The same issue (the existence of a component's peer) also comes up when you are making your own kinds of components and need access to some of these peer resources before you can complete the setup. For example, suppose that you want to set the size or some other feature of your component based on the default font used. You can't complete this setup in your constructor because the peer doesn't exist yet. The solution to all of these problems is proper use of the addNotify() method. As its name implies, addNotify() can be used to get notification when the peer is created. You can override it to do your own work, as long as you remember to call super.addNotify() to complete the peer creation. For example:

```
class FancyLabel  {
    FancyLabel() {
        // No peer yet...
    }
    public void addNotify() {
        super.addNotify();  // complete the peer creation
        // Complete setup based on Fonts
        // and other peer resources.
    }
}
```

Managing Components

There are a few additional tools of the Container class that we should mention:

Component[] getComponents()

Returns the container's components in an array.

void list(PrintWriter out, int indent)

Generates a list of the components in this container and writes them to the specified PrintWriter.

Component getComponentAt(int x, int y)

Tells you what component is at the specified coordinates in the container's coordinate system.

Listening for Components

Finally, an important tool to be aware of is the ContainerListener interface. It lets you receive an event whenever a component is added to or removed from a container. (It lets you hear the tiny cries of the component as it is imprisoned in its container or torn away.) You can use the ContainerListener interface to automate the process of setting up components when they are added to your container. For instance, your container might need to register other kinds of event listeners with its components to track the mouse or handle certain kinds of actions.

Windows and Frames

Windows and frames are the top-level containers for Java components. A `Window` is simply a plain, graphical screen that displays in your windowing system. Windows have no frills; they are mainly suitable for making "splash" screens and dialogs—things that limit the user's control. `Frame`, on the other hand, is a subclass of `Window` that has a border and can hold a menu bar. Frames are under the control of your window manager, so you can drag a frame around on the screen and resize it, using the ordinary controls for your environment. Figure 13-5 shows a `Frame` on the left and a `Window` on the right.

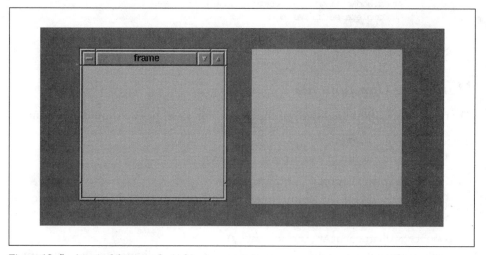

Figure 13–5: A typical frame and window

All other components and containers in Java must be held, at some level, inside of a `Window` or `Frame`. Applets, as we've mentioned a few times, are a kind of `Panel`. Even applets must be housed in a Java frame or window, though normally you don't see an applet's parent frame because it is part of (or simply is) the browser or *appletviewer* displaying the applet.

A `Frame` is the only `Component` that can be displayed without being added or attached to another `Container`. After creating a `Frame`, you can call the `show()` method to display it. Let's create a standalone equivalent (see Figure 13-6) of our `HelloWeb` applet from Chapter 2.

```
class HelloWebApp {
    public static void main( String [] args ) {
        Frame myFrame = new Frame("The Title");
        myFrame.add("Center", new Label("Hello Web!", Label.CENTER) );
        myFrame.pack();
```

Figure 13–6: Standalone equivalent of the HelloWeb applet

```
        myFrame.show();
    }
}
```

Here we've got our minimal, graphical, standalone Java application. The Frame constructor can take a String argument that supplies a title, displayed in the Frame's title bar. (Another approach would be to create the Frame with no title and call setTitle() to supply the title later.) After creating the Frame, we add our Label to it and then call pack(), which prepares the Frame for display. pack() does a couple of things, but its most important effect in this case is that it sets the size of the Frame to the smallest size required to hold all of its components. Specifically, pack() calls:

```
    setSize( preferredSize() );
```

Next, we call show() to get the Frame onto the screen. The show() method returns immediately, without blocking. Fortunately, our application does not exit while the Frame is showing. To get rid of a Frame, call the dispose() method. If you want to hide the Frame temporarily, call setVisible(false). You can check to see if a Frame is showing with the isShowing() method.

In this example, we let pack() set the size of the Frame for us before we show() it. If we hadn't, the Frame would have come up at an undefined size. If we instead want the Frame to be a specific size (not just hugging its child components) we could simply call setSize() instead of pack().

```
    ...
    myFrame.setSize( 300, 300 );
    myFrame.show();
```

Other Methods for Controlling Frames

The setLocation() method of the Component class can be used on a Frame or Window to set its position on the screen. The x and y coordinates are considered relative to the screen's origin (the top left corner).

You can use the toFront() and toBack() methods, respectively, to pull a Frame or Window to the front of other windows or push it to the background. By default, a user is allowed to resize a Frame, but you can prevent resizing by calling setResizable(false) before showing the Frame.

On most systems, frames can be "iconified"; that is, they can be represented by a little icon image. You can get and set a frame's icon image by calling getIconImage() and setIconImage(). As you can with all components, you set the cursor by calling the setCursor() method.

Using Windows

Windows and frames have a slightly convoluted relationship. We said earlier that Frame is a subclass of Window. However, if you look, you'll see that to create a Window you have to have a Frame available to serve as its parent. The Window constructor takes a Frame as an argument:

```
Window myWindow = new Window( myFrame );
```

The rationale for this limitation is long and boring. Suffice it to say that it will probably go away in the future.

Prepacking Windows and Frames

Earlier we said that calling pack() on a Frame sets the frame's size to the preferred size of its layout. However, the pack() method is not simply equivalent to a call to setSize(). pack() is often called before any of the frame's components have their peers. Therefore, calling pack() forces the container to choose its Toolkit and to create the peers of any components that have been added to it. After that is done, the layout manager can reliably determine its preferred size.

For a large frame with lots of components, packing the frame is a convenient way to do this setup work in advance, before the frame is displayed. Whether this is useful depends on whether you'd rather have your application start up faster or pop up its frames faster once it is running.

AWT Performance and Lightweight Components

Java's developers initially decided to implement the standard AWT components with a "mostly native" toolkit. As we described earlier, that means that most of the important functionality of these classes is delegated to peer objects, which live in the native operating system. Using native peers allows Java to take on the look and feel of the local operating environment. Macintosh users see Mac applications, PC users see Windows' windows, and UNIX users can have their Motif motif; warm fuzzy feelings abound. Java's chameleon-like ability to blend into the native environment is considered by many to be an integral part of platform independence. However, there are a few important downsides to this arrangement.

First, as we mentioned earlier, using native peer implementations makes it much more difficult (if not impossible) to subclass these components to specialize or modify their behavior. Most of their behavior comes from the native peer, and therefore can't be overridden or extended easily. As it turns out, this is not a terrible problem because of the ease with which we can make our own components in Java. It is also true that a sophisticated new component, like an HTML viewer, would benefit little in deriving from a more primitive text-viewing component like TextArea.

Next, porting the native code makes it much more difficult to bring Java to a new platform. For the user, this can only mean one thing—bugs. Quite simply, while the Java language itself has been stable, the cross platform behavior of the AWT has been an Achilles' heel. Although the situation is steadily improving, the lack of large, commercial quality Java applications until relatively recently testifies to the difficulties involved. At this time, new development has been saturated with Java for well over a year (a decade in Net time), and very few real applications are with us.

Finally, we come to a somewhat counterintuitive problem with the use of native peers. In most current implementations of Java, the native peers are quite "heavy" and consume a lot of resources. You might expect that relying on native code would be much more efficient than creating the components in Java. However, it can take a long time to instantiate a large number of GUI elements when each requires the creation of a native peer from the toolkit. And in some cases you may find that once the native peers are created, they don't perform as well as the pure Java equivalents that you can create yourself.

An extreme example would be a spreadsheet that uses an AWT TextField for each cell. Creating hundreds of TextFieldPeer objects would be something between slow and impossible. While simply saying "don't do that" might be a valid answer, this begs the question: how do you create large applications with complex GUIs? Java would not be a very interesting environment if it was limited only to simple tasks. One solution, taken by development environments like Sun's JavaWorkshop, is to use wrapper classes for the standard AWT components; the wrapper controls when peer objects are created. Another attack on the problem has been to create lightweight components that are written entirely in Java, and therefore don't require native code.

Using Lightweight Components and Containers

A lightweight component is simply a component that is implemented entirely in Java. You implement all of its appearance by drawing in the paint() and update() methods; you implement its behavior by catching user events (usually at a low level) and possibly generating new events. Lightweight components can be used to create new kinds of gadgets, in the same way you might use a Canvas or a Panel. But they avoid some of the performance penalties inherent in the use of peers, and, perhaps more importantly, they provide more flexibility in their appearance. A lightweight component can have a transparent background, allowing its container to "show through" its own area. It is also more reasonable to have another component or container overlap or draw into a lightweight component's area.

You create a lightweight component by subclassing the Component and Container classes directly. That is, instead of writing:

```
class myCanvas extends Canvas { ... }
```

you write:

```
class myCanvas extends Container { ... } // lightweight
```

That's often all you need do to create a lightweight component. When the lightweight component is put into a container, it doesn't get a native peer. Instead, it gets a LightweightPeer that serves as a placeholder and identifies the component as lightweight and in need of special help. The container then takes over the responsibilities that would otherwise be handled by a native peer: namely, low-level delivery of events and paint requests. The container receives mouse movement events, key strokes, paint requests, etc., for the lightweight component. It then sorts out the events that fall within the component's bounds and dispatches them to it. Similarly, it translates paint requests that overlap the lightweight component's area and forwards them to it.

Figure 13-7 shows a component receiving a paint() request via its container. This makes it easy to see how a lightweight component can have a transparent background. The component is actually drawing directly onto its container's graphics context. Conversely, anything that the container drew on its background is visible in the lightweight component. For an ordinary container, this will simply be the container's background color. But you can do much cooler things too. (See the PictureButton example at the end of Chapter 14.) All of the normal rules still apply; your lightweight component's paint() method should render the component's entire image (assume that the container has obliterated it), but your update() method can assume that whatever drawing it has done previously is still intact.

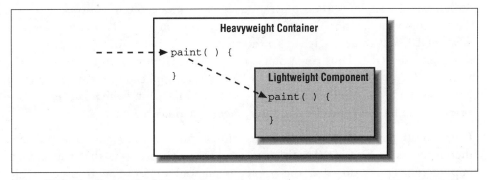

Figure 13–7: Sending a paint() request to a component

Just as you can create a lightweight component by subclassing Component, you can create a lightweight container by subclassing Container. A lightweight container can hold any components, including other lightweight components and containers. When lightweight containers contain other lightweight components, event handling and paint requests are managed by the first "regular" container in the container hierarchy. (There has to be one somewhere, if you think about it.) This brings us to the cardinal rule of subclassing containers, which is: "Always call super.paint() if you override a container's paint() method." If you don't, the container won't be able to manage lightweight components properly.

To summarize, lightweight components are very flexible, pure Java components that are managed by their container and have a transparent background by default. Lightweight components do not rely on native peers from the AWT toolkit to provide their implementations, and so they cannot readily take on the look and feel of the local platform. In a sense, a lightweight component is just a convenient way to package an extension to a container's painting and event handling methods. But, again, all of this happens automatically, behind the scenes; you can create and use lightweight components as you would any other kind of component.

Applets

If you've been waiting for a more detailed discussion of the applet class, here it is. An Applet is something like a Panel with a mission. It is a GUI container that has some extra structure to allow it to be used in an "alien" environment like a Web browser or *appletviewer*. Applets also have a life cycle that lets them act more like an application than a static component. Although applets tend to be relatively simple, there's no inherent restriction on their complexity. There's no reason you couldn't write an air traffic control system (well, let's be less ambitious—a word processor) as an applet.

Structurally, an applet is a sort of wrapper for your Java code. In contrast to a standalone graphical Java application, which starts up from a main() method and creates a GUI, an applet is itself a Component that expects to be dropped into someone else's GUI. Thus, an applet can't run by itself; it runs in the context of a Web browser or *appletviewer*. Instead of having your application create a Frame to hold your GUI, you stuff your application inside an Applet (which is itself a Container), and let someone else add the applet to their GUI.

Pragmatically, an applet is an intruder into someone else's environment, and therefore has to be treated with suspicion. The Web browsers that run applets impose restrictions on what the applet is allowed to do. The restrictions are enforced by a security manager, which the applet is not allowed to change. The browser also provides an "applet context," which is additional support that helps the applet live within its restrictions.

Aside from that top level structure and the security restrictions, there is no difference between an applet and an application. If your application can live within the restrictions imposed by a browser's security manager, you can easily structure it to function as an applet and a standalone application. (We'll show an example of an Applet that can also be run as a standalone below.) Conversely, if you can supply all of the things that an applet requires from its environment, you can use applets within your stand-alone applications and within other applets (though this requires a bit of work).

As we said a moment ago, an Applet expects to be embedded in GUI (perhaps a document) and used in a viewing environment that provides it with special resources. In all other respects, however, applets are just ordinary Panel objects. As Figure 13-8 shows, an applet is a kind of Panel. Like any other Panel, an Applet can contain user interface components and use all the basic drawing and event-handling capabilities of the Component class. We draw on an Applet by overriding its paint() method; we respond to events in the Applet's display area by providing the appropriate event listeners. Applets have additional structure that helps them interact with the viewer environment.

Applet Control

The Applet class contains four methods an applet can override to guide it through its life cycle. The init(), start(), stop(), and destroy() methods are called by the *appletviewer* or a Web browser, to direct the applet's behavior. init() is called once, after the applet is created. The init() method is where you perform basic setup like parsing parameters, building a user interface, and loading resources. Given what we've said about objects, you might expect the Applet's constructor would be the right place for such initialization. However, the constructor is meant to be called by the applet's environment, for simple creation of the applet. This

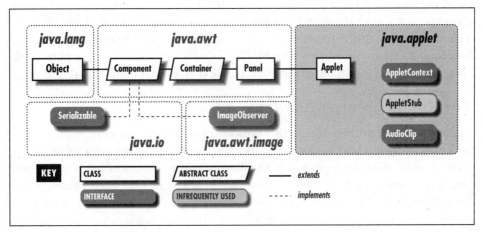

Figure 13–8: The java.applet package

might happen before the applet has access to certain resources, like information about its environment. Therefore, an applet doesn't normally do any work in its constructor; it relies on the default constructor for the Applet class and does its initialization in the init() method.

The start() method is called whenever the applet becomes visible; it shouldn't be a surprise then that the stop() method is called whenever the applet becomes invisible. init() is only called once in the life of an applet, but start() and stop() can be called any number of times (but always in the logical sequence). For example, start() is called when the applet is displayed, such as when it scrolls onto the screen; stop() is called if the applet scrolls off the screen or the viewer leaves the document. start() tells the applet it should be active. The applet may want to create threads, animate, or otherwise perform useful (or annoying) activity. stop() is called to let the applet know it should go dormant. Applets should cease CPU-intensive or wasteful activity when they are stopped and resume it when (and if) they are restarted. However, there's no requirement that an invisible applet stop computing; in some applications, it may be useful for the applet to continue running in the background. Just be considerate of your user, who doesn't want an invisible applet dragging down system performance. And for the users: be aware of the tools that will develop to let you monitor and squash rogue applets in your Web browser.

Finally, the destroy() method is called to give the applet a last chance to clean up before it's removed—some time after the call to stop(). For example, an applet might want to close down suspended communications channels or remove graphics frames. Exactly when destroy() is called depends on the browser; Netscape Navigator calls destroy() just prior to deleting the applet from its cache. This means that although an applet can cling to life after being told to stop(), how long it can go on is unpredictable. If you want to maintain your applet as the user progresses through other activities, consider putting it in an HTML frame.

The Applet Security Sandbox

Applets are quarantined within the browser by an applet SecurityManager. The SecurityManager is part of the application that runs the applet—for example, the Web browser or applet viewer. It is installed before the browser loads any applets and implements the basic restrictions that let you run untrusted applets safely. Remember, aside from basic language robustness, there are no inherent security restrictions on a standalone Java application. It is the browser's responsibility to install a special security manager and limit what applets are allowed to do.

Most browsers impose the following restrictions on untrusted applets:

- Untrusted applets cannot read or write files on the local host.

- Untrusted applets can only open network connections (sockets) to the server from which they originated.

- Untrusted applets cannot start other processes on the local host.

- Untrusted applets cannot have native methods.

The motivation for these restrictions should be fairly obvious: you clearly wouldn't want a program coming from some random Internet site to access your files or run arbitrary programs. Although untrusted applets cannot directly read and write files on the client side or talk to arbitrary hosts on the network, applets can work with servers to store data and communicate. For example, an applet can use Java's RMI (Remote Method Invocation) facility to do processing on its server. An applet can communicate with other applets on the Net by proxy through its server.

Trusted applets

The latest version of Java makes it possible to sign archive files that contain applets. Because a signature identifies the applet's origin unambiguously, we can now distinguish between "trusted" applets (i.e., applets that come from a site or person you trust not to do anything harmful) and run of the mill "untrusted" applets. In Web browsers that support signing, trusted applets can be granted permission to "go outside" of the applet security sandbox. Trusted applets can be allowed to do most of the things that standalone Java applications can do: read and write files, open network connections to arbitrary machines, and interact with the local operating system by starting processes. Trusted applets still can't have native methods, but including native methods in an applet would make it unportable, and would therefore be a bad idea.

Chapter 3 discussed how to package your applet's class files and resources into a JAR file and sign it with your digital signature. Currently, HotJava is the only browser that supports signing, but Netscape Navigator, Internet Explorer, and others will probably catch up soon.

Getting Applet Resources

An applet needs to communicate with its applet viewer. For example, it needs to get its parameters from the HTML document in which it appears. An applet may also need to load images, audio clips, and other items. It may also want to ask the viewer about other applets on the same HTML page in order to communicate with them. To get resources from the applet viewer environment, applets use the `AppletStub` and `AppletContext` interfaces. Unless you're writing a browser or some other application that loads and runs applets, you won't have to implement these interfaces, but you do use them within your applet.

Applet parameters

An applet gets its parameters from the parameter tags placed inside the `<applet>` tag in the HTML document. For example, the code below reads the "sheep" parameter from its HTML page:

```
String imageName = getParameter( "imageName" );
try {
    int numberOfSheep = Integer.parseInt(getParameter( "sheep" ));
} catch ( NumberFormatException e ) { // use default }
```

A friendly applet will provide information about the parameters it accepts through its `getParameterInfo()` method. `getParameterInfo()` returns an array of string arrays, listing and describing the applet's parameters. For each parameter, three strings are provided: the parameter name, its possible values or value types, and a verbose description. For example:

```
public String [][] getParameterInfo() {
    String [][] appletInfo =
        {"logo",    "url", "Main logo image"}
        {"timer", "int",    "Time to wait before becoming annoying"},
        {"flashing", "constant | intermittant",  "Flag for how to flash"},
```

```
        return appletInfo;
    }
```

Applet resources

An applet can find where it lives by calling the getDocumentBase() and getCode-
Base() methods. getDocumentBase() returns the base URL of the document in
which the applet appears; getCodeBase() returns the base URL of the Applet's
class files. An applet can use these to construct relative URLs from which to load
other resources like images, sounds, and other data. The getImage() method takes
a URL and asks for an image from the viewer environment. The image may be
pulled from a cache or loaded asynchronously when later used. The getAudio-
Clip() method, similarly, retrieves sound clips.

The following example uses getCodeBase() to construct a URL and load a properties configuration file, located at the same location as the applet's class file:

```
    Properties props = new Properties();
    try {
        URL url = new URL(getCodeBase(), "appletConfig.props");
        props.load( url.openStream() );
    } catch ( IOException e ) { // failed }
```

A better way to load resources is by calling the getResource() and getResource-
AsStream() methods of the Class class, which search the applet's JAR files (if any)
as well as its codebase. The following code loads the properties file appletCon-
fig.props:

```
    Properties props = new Properties();
    try {
        props.load( getClass().getResourceAsStream("appletConfig.props") );
    } catch ( IOException e ) { // failed }
```

Driving the browser

The status line is a blurb of text that usually appears somewhere in the viewer's display, indicating a current activity. An applet can request that some text be placed
in the status line with the showStatus() method. (The browser isn't required to do
anything in response to this call, but most browsers will oblige you.)

An applet can also ask the browser to show a new document. To do this, the applet
makes a call to the showDocument(url) method of the AppletContext. You can get
a reference to the AppletContext with the applet's getAppletContext() method.
showDocument() can take an additional String argument to tell the browser where
to display the new URL:

```
    getAppletContext().showDocument( url, name );
```

The name argument can be the name of an existing labeled HTML frame; the document referenced by the URL will be displayed in that frame. You can use this method to create an applet that "drives" the browser to new locations dynamically, but stays active on the screen in a separate frame. If the named frame doesn't exist, the browser will create a new top-level window to hold it. Alternatively, name can have one of the following special values:

self
> Show in the current frame

_parent
> Show in the parent of our frame

_top
> Show in outermost (top-level) frame

_blank
> Show in a new top-level browser window.

Both showStatus() and showDocument() requests may be ignored by a cold-hearted viewer or Web browser

Inter-applet communication

Applets that are embedded in documents loaded from the same location on a Web site can use a simple mechanism to locate one another (rendezvous). Once an applet has a reference to another applet, it can communicate with it, just as with any other object, by invoking methods and sending events. The getApplet() method of the applet context looks for an applet by name:

```
Applet clock = getAppletContext().getApplet("theClock");
```

You give an applet a name within your HTML document using the name attribute of the <APPLET> tag. Alternatively, you can use the getApplets() method to enumerate all of the available applets in the pages.

The tricky thing with applet communications is that applets run inside of the security sandbox. An untrusted applet can only "see" objects that were loaded by the same class loader. That means that only applets that share a class loader can communicate. Currently, the only reliable criterion for when applets share a class loader is when they share a common base URL. For example, all of the applets contained in Web pages loaded from the base URL of *http://foo.bar.com/mypages/* should share a class loader and should be able to see each other. This would include documents like *mypages/foo.html* and *mypages/bar.html*, but not *mypages/morestuff/foo.html*.

When applets do share a class loader, other techniques are possible too. As with any other class, you can call static methods in applets by name. So you could use static methods in one of your applets as a "registry" to coordinate your activities. In the future, applets which are also Java Beans will be able to use the more general communications mechanisms that are part of the upcoming Java Beans specifications. There are also proposals that would allow you to have more control over when applets share a class loader and how their life cycles are managed.

Applets versus standalone applications

The following list summarizes the methods of the applet API:

```
// from the AppletStub
boolean isActive();
URL getDocumentBase();
URL getCodeBase();
String getParameter(String name);
AppletContext getAppletContext();
void appletResize(int width, int height);

// from the AppletContext
AudioClip getAudioClip(URL url);
Image getImage(URL url);
Applet getApplet(String name);
Enumeration getApplets();
void showDocument(URL url);
public void showDocument(URL url, String target);
void showStatus(String status);
```

These are the methods that are provided by the applet viewer environment. If your applet doesn't happen to use any of them or if you can provide alternatives to handle special cases (such as loading images), your applet could be made able to function as a standalone application as well as an applet. For example, our HelloWeb applet from Chapter 2 was very simple. We can easily give it a main() method to allow it to be run as a standalone application:

```
public class HelloWeb extends Applet {

    public void paint( java.awt.Graphics gc ) {
        gc.drawString( "Hello Web!", 125, 95 );
    }

    public static void main( String [] args ) {
        Frame theFrame = new Frame();
        Applet helloWeb = new HelloWeb();
        theFrame.add("Center", helloWeb);
        theFrame.setSize(200,200);
        helloWeb.init();
        helloWeb.start();
```

```
        theFrame.show();
    }
}
```

Here we get to play "appletviewer" for a change. We have created an instance of `HelloWeb` using its constructor—something we don't normally do—and added it to our own `Frame`. We call its `init()` method to give the applet a chance to wake up and then call its `start()` method. In this example, `HelloWeb` doesn't implement these, `init()` and `start()`, so we're calling methods inherited from the `Applet` class. This is the procedure that an applet viewer would use to run an applet. (If we wanted to go further, we could implement our own `AppletContext` and `AppletStub`, and set them in the `Applet` before startup.)

Trying to make your applets into applications as well often doesn't make sense and is not always this trivial. We show this example only to get you thinking about the real differences between applets and applications. It is probably best to think in terms of the applet API until you have a need to go outside it. Remember that trusted applets can do almost all of the things that applications can. It may be wiser to make an applet that requires trusted permissions than an application.

Events

We've spent a lot of time discussing the different kinds of objects in AWT—components, containers, and a few special containers like applets. But we've neglected communications between different objects. A few times, we've mentioned events, and we have even used them in the occasional program, but we have deferred a discussion of events until later. Now is the time to pay that debt.

AWT objects communicate by sending events. The way we talk about "firing" events and "handling" them makes it sound as if they are part of some special Java language feature. But they aren't. An event is simply an ordinary Java object that is delivered to its receiver by invoking an ordinary Java method. Everything else, however interesting, is purely convention. The entire Java event mechanism is really just a set of conventions for the kinds of descriptive objects that should be delivered; these conventions prescribe when, how, and to whom events should be delivered.

Events are sent from a single source object to one or more listeners (or *receivers*). A listener implements specific event-handling methods that enable it to receive a type of event. It then registers itself with a source of that kind of event. Sometimes an *adapter* object may be interposed between the event source and the listener, but a connection is always established before any events are delivered.

An event object is a subclass of `java.util.EventObject` that holds information about something that's happened to its source. The `EventObject` class serves mainly to identify event objects; the only information it contains is a reference to the event source (the object that sent the event). Components do not normally send or receive `EventObjects` as such; they work with subclasses that provide more specific information. `AWTEvent` is a subclass of `EventObject` that is used within AWT; further subclasses of `AWTEvent` provide information about specific event types.

For example, events of type `ActionEvent` are fired by buttons when they are pushed. `ActionEvents` are also sent when a menu item is selected or when a user presses Enter in a `TextField`. Similarly, `MouseEvents` are generated when you operate your mouse within a component's area. You can gather the general meaning of these two events from their names; they are relatively self-descriptive. `ActionEvents` correspond to a decisive "action" that a user has taken with the component—like pressing a button or pressing Enter. An `ActionEvent` thus carries the name of an action to be performed (the *action command*) by the program. `MouseEvents` describe the state of the mouse, and therefore carry information like the x and y coordinates and the state of your mouse buttons at the time the `MouseEvent` was created. You might hear someone say that `ActionEvent` is at a "higher semantic level" than `MouseEvent`, which means that `ActionEvent` is an interpretation of something that happened and is, therefore, conceptually more powerful than the `MouseEvent`, which carries raw data. An `ActionEvent` lets us know that a component has done its job, while a `MouseEvent` simply confers a lot of information about the mouse at a given time. You could figure out that somebody clicked on a `Button` by examining mouse events, but it is simpler to work with action events. The precise meaning of an event, however, can depend on the context in which it is received.

Event Receivers and Listener Interfaces

An event is delivered by passing it as an argument to an event-handler method in the receiving object. `ActionEvents`, for example, are always delivered to a method called `actionPerformed()` in the receiver:

```
// Receiver
public void actionPerformed( ActionEvent e ) {
        ...
}
```

For each type of event, there is a corresponding listener interface that describes the methods it must provide to receive those events. In this case, any object that receives `ActionEvents` must implement the `ActionListener` interface:

```
    public interface ActionListener extends java.util.EventListener {
        public void actionPerformed( ActionEvent e );
}
// Receiver implements ActionListener
```

All listener interfaces are subinterfaces of java.util.EventListener, but EventListener is simply an empty interface. It exists only to help the compiler identify listener interfaces.

Listener interfaces are required for a number of reasons. First, they help to identify objects that are capable of receiving a given type of event. This way we can give the event-handler methods friendly, descriptive names and still make it easy for documentation, tools, and humans to recognize them in a class. Next, listener interfaces are useful because several methods can be specified for an event receiver. For example, the FocusListener interface contains two methods:

```
    abstract void focusGained( FocusEvent e );
    abstract void focusLost( FocusEvent e );
```

Athough these methods both take a FocusEvent as an argument, they correspond to different meanings as to why the event was fired; in this case, whether the FocusEvent means that focus was received or lost. You could figure out what happened by inspecting the event; all AWTEvents contain a constant specifying the event's subtype. By requiring two methods, the FocusListener interface saves you the effort: if focusGained() is called, you know the event type was FOCUS_GAINED. Similarly, the MouseListener interface defines five methods for receiving mouse events (and MouseMotionListener defines two more), each of which gives you some additional information about why the event occurred. In general, the listener interfaces group sets of related event-handler methods; the method called in any given situation provides a context for the information in the event object.

There can be more than one listener interface for dealing with a particular kind of event. For example, the MouseListener interface describes methods for receiving MouseEvents when the mouse enters or exits an area, or a mouse button is pressed or released. MouseMotionListener is an entirely separate interface that describes methods to get mouse events when the mouse is moved (no buttons pressed) or dragged (buttons pressed). By separating mouse events into these two categories, Java lets you be a little more selective about the circumstances under which you want to receive MouseEvents. You can register as a listener for mouse events without receiving mouse motion events; since mouse motion events are extremely common, you don't want to handle them if you don't need to.

Finally, two simple patterns govern the naming of AWT event listener interfaces and handler methods:

- Event-handler methods are public methods that return type void and take a single event object (a subclass of java.util.EventObject as an argument).[*]

- Listener interfaces are subclasses of java.util.EventListener that are named with the suffix "Listener"—for example, FooListener.

These may seem pretty obvious, but they are important because they are our first hint of a *design pattern* governing how to build components that work with events.

Event Sources

The previous section described the machinery that an event receiver uses to accept events. In this section we'll describe how the receiver tells an event source to start sending it events as they occur.

To receive events, an eligible listener must register itself with an event source. It does this by calling an "add listener" method in the event source and passing a reference (a callback) to itself. For example, the AWT Button class is a source of ActionEvents. In order to receive these events, our code might do something like the following:

```
// source of ActionEvents
Button theButton = new Button("Belly");

// receiver of ActionEvents
class TheReceiver implements ActionListener {
    setupReceiver() {
        ...
        theButton.addActionListener( this );
    }
    public void actionPerformed( ActionEvent e ) {
        // Belly Button pushed...
    }
```

The receiver makes a call to addActionListener() to complete its setup and become eligible to receive ActionEvents from the button when they occur. It passes the reference this, to add itself as the ActionListener.

To manage its listeners, an ActionEvent source (like the Button) always implements two methods:

```
// ActionEvent source
public void addActionListener(ActionListener listener) {
    ...
}
```

---

[*] This rule is not complete. JavaBeans allows event-handler methods to take additional arguments when absolutely necessary and also to throw checked exceptions.

```
    public void removeActionListener(ActionListener listener) {
       ...
  }
```

The removeActionListener() method complements addActionListener() and does what you'd expect: it removes the listener from the list so that it will not receive future events from that source.

Now, you may be expecting an EventSource interface listing these two methods, but there isn't one. There are no event source interfaces in the current conventions. If you are analyzing a class and trying to determine what events it generates, you have to look for the add and remove methods. For example, the presence of the addActionListener() and removeActionListener() methods define the object as a source of ActionEvents. If you happen to be a human being, you can simply look at the documentation; but if the documentation isn't available, or if you're writing a program that needs to analyze a class (a process called "reflection"), you can look for this design pattern:

- A source of events for the FooListener interface must implement a pair of add/remove methods:

  - addFooListener(FooListener listener)

  - removeFooListener(FooListener listener)

- If an event source can support only one event listener (unicast delivery), the add listener method can throw the checked exception java.util.TooManyListenersException.

So what do all the naming patterns up to this point accomplish? Well, for one thing they make it possible for automated tools and integrated development environments to divine what are sources and what are sinks of particular events. Tools that work with Java Beans will use the Java reflection and introspection APIs to search for these kinds of design patterns and identify the events that can be fired and received by a component.

It also means that event hookups are strongly typed, just like the rest of Java. So it's not easy to accidentally hook up the wrong kind of components; for example, you can't register to receive ItemEvents from a Button, because a button doesn't have an addItemListener() method. Java knows at compile-time what types of events can be delivered to whom.

Event Delivery

AWT events are multicast; every event is associated with a single source but can be delivered to any number of receivers. Events are registered and distributed using an observer/observable model. When an event listener registers itself with an event source, the event source adds the listener to a list. When an event is fired, it is delivered individually to each listener on the list (Figure 13-9).

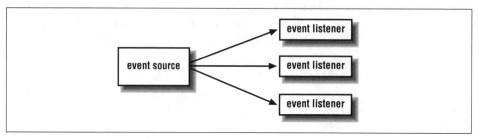

Figure 13–9: Event delivery

There are no guarantees about the order in which events will be delivered. Neither are there any guarantees about what happens if you register yourself more than once with an event source; you may or may not get the event more than once. Similarly, you should assume that every listener receives the same event data. Events are immutable; they can't be changed by their listeners. There's one important exception to this rule, which we'll discuss later.

To be complete we could say that event delivery is synchronous with respect to the event source, but that follows from the fact that the event delivery is really just the invocation of a normal Java method. The source of the event calls the handler method of each listener. However, listeners shouldn't assume that all of the events will be sent in the same thread. An event source could decide to send out events to all of the listeners in parallel.

How exactly an event source maintains its set of listeners, constructs, and fires the events is up to it. Often it is sufficient to use a `Vector` to hold the list. We'll show the code for a component that uses a custom event in Chapter 14. For efficiency, AWT components all use the `java.awt.AWTEventMulticaster` object, which maintains a linked tree of the listeners for the component. You can use that too, if you are firing standard AWT events. We'll describe the event multicaster in Chapter 14 as well.

AWTEvents

All of the events used by AWT GUI components are subclasses of `java.awt.AWTEvent`. `AWTEvent` holds some common information that is used by AWT to identify and process events. You can use or subclass any of the `AWTEvent` types for use in your own components. Figure 13-10 shows the event hierarchy.

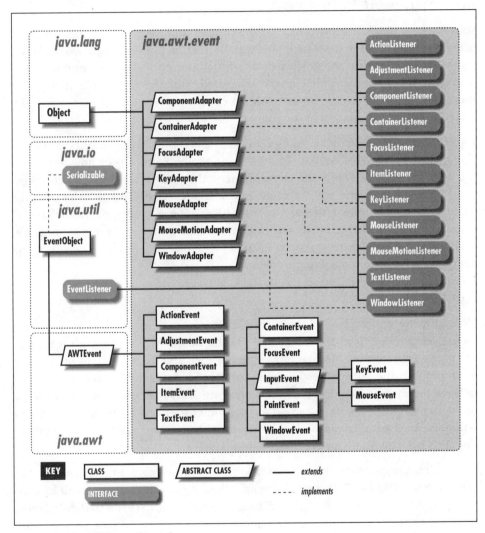

Figure 13–10: AWT event hierarchy

ComponentEvent is the base class for events that can be fired by any AWT component. This includes events that provide notification when a component changes its
dimensions or visibility, as well as the other event types for mouse operation and
key presses. ContainerEvents are fired by AWT containers when components are
added or removed.

java.awt.event.InputEvent

MouseEvents, which track the state of the mouse, and KeyEvents, which are fired
when the user uses the keyboard, are types of java.awt.event.InputEvent. Input
events from the mouse and keyboard are a little bit special. They are normally produced by the native Java machinery associated with the peers. When the user
touches a key or moves the mouse within a component's area, the events are generated with that component as the source.

Input events and some other AWT events are placed on a special event queue that
is managed by the AWT toolkit. This gives the toolkit control over how the events
are delivered. First, under some circumstances, the toolkit can decide to compress
a sequence of the same type of event into a single event. This is done to make
some event types more efficient—in particular, mouse events and some special
internal events used to control repainting. Perhaps more important to us, input
events are delivered with a special arrangement that lets listeners decide if the
component itself should act on the event.

Consuming Events

Normally, the native peer of a standard AWT component operates by receiving
InputEvents telling it about the mouse and keyboard. When you push a Button,
the native ButtonPeer object receives a MouseEvent and does its job in native land
to accomplish the button-pressing behavior. But for InputEvents, the Toolkit first
delivers the event to any listeners registered with the component and gives those
listeners a chance to mark the event as "consumed," effectively telling the peer to
ignore it. An InputEvent is marked "consumed" by calling the consume() method.
(Yes, this is a case where an event is not immutable.)

So we could stop our Button from working by registering a listener with it that
catches "mouse button depressed" events. When it got one, we could call its con-
sume() method to tell the ButtonPeer to ignore that event. This is particularly useful if you happen to be building a development environment in Java, and you want
to "turn off" components while the user arranges them.

In a trusted application you can, if necessary, get access to the AWT event queue.
The toolkit uses an instance of java.awt.EventQueue. With it you can peek at
pending AWT events or even push in new ones.

Mouse and Key Modifiers on InputEvents

InputEvents come with a set of flags for special modifiers. These let you detect if the Shift or Alt key was held down during a mouse button or key press, or if the second or third mouse buttons were pressed. The following are the flag values contained in java.awt.event.InputEvent:

- SHIFT_MASK

- CTRL_MASK

- META_MASK

- ALT_MASK

- BUTTON1_MASK

- BUTTON2_MASK

- BUTTON3_MASK

To check for these masks, you can simply do a boolean AND of the modifiers, returned by the InputEvent's getModifiers() method and the flag or flags you're interested in:

```
public void mousePressed (MouseEvent e) {
    int mods = e.getModifiers();
    if ((mods & InputEvent.SHIFT_MASK) != 0)


        { // Shifted Mouse Button press }
}
```

The three BUTTON flags can be used to detect which mouse button was pressed on a two- or three-button mouse. If you use these, you run the risk that your program won't work on platforms without multibutton mice. Currently, BUTTON2_MASK is equivalent to ALT_MASK, and BUTTON3_MASK is equivalent to META_MASK. This means that pushing the second mouse button is equivalent to pressing the first (or only) button with the Alt key depressed, and the third button is equivalent to the first with the Meta key depressed. However, if you really want to guarantee portability, you should limit yourself to a single button, possibly in combination with keyboard modifiers, rather than relying on the button masks.

Key events provide one other situation in which events aren't immutable. You can change the character that the user typed by calling setKeyChar(), setKeyCode(), or `setKeyModifiers()`. A user's keystroke isn't displayed until the `KeyEvent` is delivered to the peer. Therefore, by changing the character in the `KeyEvent`, you can change the character displayed on the screen. This is a good way to implement a field that displays only uppercase characters, regardless of what the user types.

AWT Event Summary

Tables 13-1 and 13-2 summarize the AWT events, which components fire them, and the methods of the listener interfaces that receive them.

Table 13–1: AWT Component and Container Events

Event	Fired by	Listener Interface	Handler Method
ComponentEvent	All components	ComponentListener	componentResized() componentMoved() componentShown() componentHidden()
FocusEvent	All components	FocusListener	focusGained() focusLost
KeyEvent	All components	KeyListener	keyTyped() keyPressed() keyReleased()
MouseEvent	All components	MouseListener MouseMotionListener	mouseClicked() mousePressed() mouseReleased() mouseEntered() mouseExited() mouseDragged() mouseMoved()
ContainerEvent	All containers	ContainerListener	componentAdded() componentRemoved()

Table 13–2: Component-Specific AWT Events

Event	Fired by	Listener Interface	Handler Method
ActionEvent	TextField MenuItem List Button	ActionListener	actionPerformed()
ItemEvent	List Checkbox Choice	ItemListener	itemStateChanged()

Table 13–2: Component-Specific AWT Events (continued)

Event	Fired by	Listener Interface	Handler Method
	`CheckboxMenuItem`		
`AdjustmentEvent`	`ScrollPane` `Scrollbar`	`AdjustmentListener`	`adjustmentValue-` `Changed()`
`TextEvent`	`TextArea` `TextField`	`TextListener`	`textValueChanged()`

`WindowEvent`	`Frame`
	`Dialog`
		`WindowListener`	`windowOpened()`
			`windowClosing()`
			`windowClosed()`
			`windowIconified()`
			`windowDeiconified()`
			`windowActivated()`
			`windowDeactivated()`

Adapter Classes

It's not usually ideal to have your application components implement a listener interface and receive events directly. Sometimes it's not even possible. Being an event receiver forces you to modify or subclass your objects to implement the appropriate event listener interfaces and add the code necessary to handle the events. Since we are talking about AWT events here, a more subtle issue is that you are, of necessity, building GUI logic into parts of your application that shouldn't have to know anything about the GUI. Let's look at an example.

In Figure 13-11 we have drawn the plans for our Vegomatic food processor. Here we have made our Vegomatic object implement the `ActionListener` interface so that it can receive events directly from the three `Button` components: Chop, Puree, and Frappe. The problem is that our Vegomatic object now has to know more than how to mangle food. It also has to be aware that it will be driven by three controls—specifically, buttons that send action commands—and be aware of which methods in itself it should invoke for those commands. Our boxes labeling the GUI and application code overlap in an unwholesome way. If the marketing people should later want to add or remove buttons or perhaps just change the names, we have to be careful. We may have to modify the logic in our Vegomatic object. All is not well.

An alternative is to place an adapter class between our event source and receiver. An adapter is a simple object whose sole purpose is to map an incoming event to an outgoing method.

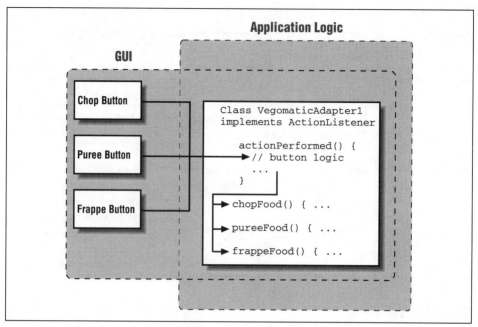

Figure 13–11: Implementing the ActionListener interface directly

Figure 13-12 shows a better design that uses three adapter classes, one for each button. The implementation of the first adapter might look like:

```
class VegomaticAdapter1 implements actionListener {
    Vegotmatic vegomatic;
    VegomaticAdapter1 ( Vegotmatic vegomatic ) {
        this.vegomatic = vegomatic;
    }
    public void actionPerformed( ActionEvent e ) {
        vegomatic.chopFood();
    }
}
```

So somewhere in the code where we build our GUI, we could register our listener like so:

```
// building GUI for our Vegomatic
Vegomatic theVegomatic = ...;
Button chopButton = ...;
```

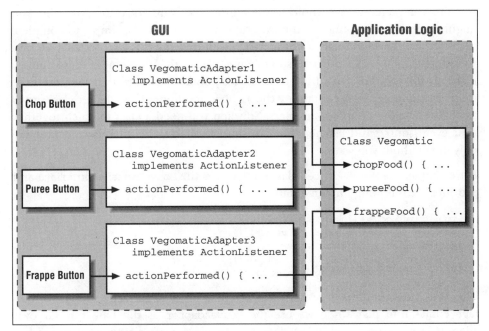

Figure 13–12: A design using adapter classes

```
// make the hookup
chopButton.addActionListener( new VegomaticAdapter1(theVegomatic) );
```

We have completely separated the messiness of our GUI from the application code. However, we have added three new classes to our application, none of which does very much. Is that good? That depends on your vantage point.

Under different circumstances, our buttons may have been able to share a common adapter class that was simply instantiated with different parameters. Various trade-offs can be made between size, efficiency, and elegance of code. Adapter classes will often be generated automatically by development tools. The way we have named our adapter classes VegomaticAdapter1, VegomaticAdapter2, and VegomaticAdapter3 hints at this. More often, when hand coding, you'll use an inner class. At the other extreme, we can forsake Java's strong typing and use the reflection API to create a completely dynamic hookup between an event source and listener.

AWT dummy adapters

Many listener interfaces contain more than one event-handler method. Unfortunately, this means that to register yourself as interested in any one of those events, you must implement the whole listener interface. And to accomplish this you might find yourself typing in dummy "stubbed out" methods, simply to complete the interface. There is really nothing wrong with this, but it is a bit tedious. To save you some trouble, AWT provides some helper classes that implement these dummy methods for you. For each listener interface containing more than one method, there is an adapter class containing the stubbed methods. The adapter class serves as a base class for your own adapters. So when you need a class to patch together your event source and listener, you can simply subclass the adapter and override only the methods you want.

For example, the MouseAdapter class implements the MouseListener interface and provides the following implementation:

```
public void mouseClicked(MouseEvent e) {};
public void mousePressed(MouseEvent e) {};
public void mouseReleased(MouseEvent e) {};
public void mouseEntered(MouseEvent e) {};
public void mouseExited(MouseEvent e) {};
```

This isn't a tremendous time saver; it's simply a bit of sugar. The primary advantage comes into play when we use the MouseAdapter as the base for our own adapter in an anonymous inner class. For example, suppose we want to catch a mousePressed() event in some component and blow up a building. We can use the following to make the hookup:

```
someComponent.addMouseListener( new MouseAdapter() {
    public void MousePressed(MouseEvent e) {
        building.blowUp();
    }
} );
```

We've taken artistic liberties with the formatting, but I think it's very readable. Writing adapters is common enough that it's nice to avoid typing those extra few lines and perhaps stave off the onset of carpal tunnel syndrome for a few more hours. Remember that any time you use an inner class, the compiler is generating a class for you, so the messiness you've saved in your source still exists in the output classes.

Old Style and New Style Event Processing

Although Java is still a youngster, it has a bit of a legacy. Versions of Java before 1.1 used a different style of event delivery. Back in the old days (a few months ago), event types were limited, and an event was delivered only to the Component that generated it or one of its parent containers. The old style component event-handler methods (now deprecated) returned a `boolean` value declaring whether or not they had handled the event:

```
boolean handleEvent( Event e ) {
    . . .
}
```

If the method returns `false`, the event is automatically redelivered to the component's container to give it a chance. If the container does not handle it, it is passed on to its parent container, and so on. In this way, events were propagated up the containment hierarchy until they were either consumed or passed over to the component peer, just as current `InputEvents` are ultimately interpreted using the peer if no registered event listeners have consumed them.

Although this style of event delivery was convenient for some simple applications, it is not very flexible. Events could be handled only by components, which meant that you always had to subclass a `Component` or `Container` type to handle events. This was a degenerate use of inheritance (i.e., bad design) that led to the creation of lots of unnecessary classes.

We could, alternatively, receive the events for many embedded components in a single parent container, but that would often lead to very convoluted logic in the container's event-handling methods. It is also very costly to run every single AWT event through a gauntlet of (often empty) tests as it traverses its way up the tree of containers. This is why Java now provides the more dynamic and general event source/listener model that we have described in this chapter. The old style events and event-handler methods are, however, still with us.

Java is not allowed to simply change and break an established API. Instead, older ways of doing things are simply deprecated in favor of the new ones. This means that code using the old style event handler methods will still work; you may see old style code around for a long time. The problem with relying on old style event delivery, however, is that the old and new ways of doing things cannot be mixed.

By default, Java is obligated to perform the old behavior—offering events to the component and each of its parent containers. However, Java turns off the old style delivery whenever it thinks that we have elected to use the new style. Java determines whether a `Component` should receive old style or new style events based on whether any event listeners are registered, or whether new style events have been explicitly enabled. When an AWT event listener is registered with a `Component`, new style events are implicitly turned on (a flag is set). Additionally, a mask is set telling the component the types of AWT events it should process. The mask allows components to be more selective about which events they process.

processEvent()

When new style events are enabled, all events are first routed to the dis-patchEvent() method of the Component class. The dispatchEvent() method examines the component's event mask and decides whether the event should be processed or ignored. Events that have been enabled are sent to the process-Event() method, which simply looks at the event's type and delegates it to a helper processing method named for its type. The helper processing method finally dis-patches the event to the set of registered listeners for its type.

This process closely parallels the way in which old style events are processed and the way in which events are first directed to a single handleEvent() method that dispatches them to more specific handler methods in the Component class. The dif-ferences are that new style events are not delivered unless someone is listening for them, and the listener registration mechanism means that we don't have to sub-class the component in order to override its event-handler methods and insert our own code.

Enabling new style events explicitly

Still, if you are subclassing a Component or you really want to process all events in a single method, you should be aware that it is possible to emulate the old style event handling and override your component's event processing methods. You simply have to call the Component's enableEvents() method with the appropriate mask value to turn on processing for the given type of event. You can then override the corresponding method and insert your code. The mask values, listed in Table 13-3, are found in the java.awt.AWTEvent class.

Table 13–3: AWTEvent Masks

java.awt.AWTEvent mask	Method
COMPONENT_EVENT_MASK	processComponentEvent()
FOCUS_EVENT_MASK	processFocusEvent()
KEY_EVENT_MASK	processKeyEvent()
MOUSE_EVENT_MASK	processMouseEvent()
MOUSE_MOTION_EVENT_MASK	processMouseMotionEvent()

For example:

```
public void init() {
    ...
    enableEvent( AWTEvent.KEY_EVENT_MASK ):
}
public void processKeyEvent(KeyEvent e) {
    if ( e.getID() == KeyEvent.KEY_TYPED )
        // do work
```

```
        super.processKeyEvent(e);
    }
```

If you do this, it is very important that you remember to make a call to super.process . . . Event() in order to allow normal event delegation to continue. Of course, by emulating old style event handling, we're giving up the virtues of the new style; this code is a lot less flexible than the code we could write with the new event model. As we've seen, the user interface is hopelessly tangled with the actual work your program does. A compromise solution would be to have your subclass declare that it implements the appropriate listener interface and register itself, as we have done in the simpler examples in this book:

```
class MyApplet implements KeyListener ...
    public void init() {
        addKeyListener( this ):
        ...
    }
    public void keyTyped(KeyEvent e) {
        // do work
    }
```

14

Creating GUI Components

The previous chapter discussed a number of concepts, including how Java's user interface facility is put together and how the larger pieces work. You should understand what components and containers are, how you use them to create a display, what events are, how components use them to communicate with the rest of your application, and what layout managers are. In other words, we've covered a lot of material that's "good for you."

Now that we're through with the general concepts and background, we'll get to the fun stuff: how to do things with AWT. We will cover all the components that the AWT package supplies, how to use these components in applets and applications, and how to build your own components. We will have lots of code and lots of pretty examples to look at.

Buttons and Labels

We'll start with the simplest components: buttons and labels. Frankly, there isn't much to say about them. If you've seen one button, you've seen them all; and you've already seen buttons in the applets in Chapter 2 (HelloWeb3 and HelloWeb4). A button generates an ActionEvent when the user presses it. To receive these events, your program registers an ActionListener, which must implement the actionPerformed() method. The argument passed to actionPerformed() is the event itself.

There's one more thing worth saying about buttons, which applies to any component that generates an action event. Java lets us specify an "action command" for buttons (and other components, like menu items, that can generate action events). The action command is less interesting than it sounds. It is just a String that serves to identify the component that sent the event. By default, the action command of a Button is the same as the text of its label; it is included in action events, so you can use it to figure out which button an event came from. To get the action command from an action event, call the event's getActionCommand() method. The following code checks whether the user pressed the Yes button:

```
public void actionPerformed(ActionEvent e){
    if (e.getActionCommand().equals("Yes") {
        //the user pressed "Yes"; do something
        ...
    }
}
```

You can change the action command by calling the button's setActionCommand() method. The code below changes button b's action command to "confirm":

```
myButton.setActionCommand("confirm");
```

It's a good idea to get used to setting action commands explicitly because they prevent your code from breaking when you or some other developer "internationalizes" it. If you rely on the button's label, your code will stop working as soon as that label changes; a French user might see the label "Oui" rather than "Yes." By setting the action command, you eliminate one source of bugs; for example, the button myButton in the previous example will always generate the action command "confirm," regardless of what its label says.

There's even less to be said about Label components. They're just text strings housed in a component. There aren't any special events associated with labels; about all you can do is specify the text's alignment, which controls the position of the text within the area that the label occupies when displayed. The following code creates some labels with different alignments:

```
Label l1 = new Label("Lions"); //label with default alignment (CENTER)
Label l2 = new Label("Tigers", LEFT); //left aligned label
Label l3 = new Label (); //label with no text, default alignment
l3.setText("and Bears"); //assigning text to l3
l3.setAlignment(RIGHT); //setting l3's alignment
```

Now we've built three labels, using all three constructors and several of the class's methods. To display the labels, you only have to add them to a container by calling the container's add() method.

The other characteristics you might like to set on labels, like changing their font or color, are accomplished using the methods of the Component class. For example, you can call setFont() and setColor() on a label, as with any other component.

Given that labels are so simple, why do we need them at all? Why not just call drawString() whenever we need text? Remember that a Label is a Component. That's important; it means that labels have the normal complement of methods for setting fonts and colors that we mentioned above, as well as the ability to be managed sensibly by a layout manager. Therefore, they're much more flexible.

Speaking of layouts—if you use the setText() method to change the text of your label, its preferred size will probably change. So you should remember to call validate() on its container, to lay things out again:[*]

```
label.setText(...);
label.invalidate();
validate();   // on the container holding the label
```

Text Components

AWT gives us two basic text components: TextArea is a multiline text editor with vertical and horizontal scrollbars; TextField is a simple, single line text editor. Both TextField and TextArea derive from the TextComponent class, which provides the functionality they have in common. This includes methods for setting and retrieving the displayed text, specifying whether the text is "editable" or read-only, manipulating the cursor position in the display, and manipulating the selected text.

Both TextAreas and TextFields send TextEvents to listeners when their text is modified. In order to receive these events, you must implement the java.awt.TextListener interface and register by calling the component's addTextListener() method. In addition, TextField components generate an ActionEvent whenever the user presses the Return key within the field. To get these events, implement the ActionListener interface, and call addActionListener() to register.

The next sections contain a couple of simple applets that show you how to work with text areas and fields.

---

* At least as of Java 1.1, labels aren't very smart. Simply validating the container isn't enough. We had to explicitly invalidate the label first.

A TextEntryBox

Our first example, TextEntryBox, creates a TextArea and ties it to a TextField, as you can see in Figure 14-1. When the user hits Return in the TextField, we receive an ActionEvent and add the line to the TextArea's display. Try it out. You may have to click your mouse in the TextField to give it focus before typing in it. If you fill up the display with lines, you can test drive the scrollbar:

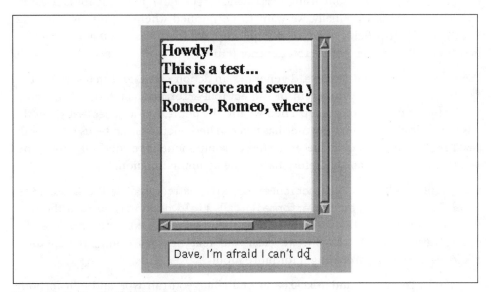

Figure 14–1: The TextEntryBox applet

```
import java.awt.*;
import java.awt.event.*;
public class TextEntryBox extends java.applet.Applet
implements ActionListener {
    TextArea area;
    TextField field;

    public void init() {
        setLayout( new BorderLayout() );
        add( "Center", area = new TextArea() );
        area.setFont( new Font("TimesRoman",Font.BOLD,18) );
        area.setText("Howdy!\n");
        add( "South", field = new TextField() );
        field.addActionListener ( this );
    }
    public void actionPerformed(ActionEvent e) {
        area.append( field.getText() + '\n' );
```

```
        field.setText("");
    }
}
```

TextEntryBox is exceedingly simple; we've done a few things to make it more interesting. First, we set the applet's layout manager to BorderLayout. We use Border-Layout to position the TextArea above the TextField; the text area goes in the "North" region of the layout, and the text field is in the "South" region. We give the text area a bigger font using Component's setFont() method; fonts are discussed in Chapter 16. Finally, we want to be notified whenever the user presses Return in the text field, so we register our applet (this) as a listener for action events by calling field.addActionListener(this).

Pressing Return in the TextField generates an action event, and that's where the fun begins. We handle the event in the actionPerformed() method of our container, the TextEntryBox applet. Then we use the getText() and setText() methods to manipulate the text the user has typed. These methods can be used for both TextField and TextArea, because these components are derived from the TextComponent class, and therefore have some common functionality.

Our event handler is called actionPerformed(), as required by the ActionListener interface. First, actionPerformed() calls field.getText() to read the text that the user typed into our TextField. It then adds this text to the TextArea by calling area.append(). Finally, we clear the text field by calling the method field.setText(""), preparing it for more input.

By default, TextField and TextArea are editable; you can type and edit in both text components. They can be changed to output-only areas with the setEditable() method. Both text components also support *selections*. A selection is a subset of text that is highlighted for copying and pasting in your windowing system. You select text by dragging the mouse over it; you can then copy and paste it into other text windows. You can get the selected text explicitly with getSelected-Text().

TextWatcher Applet

Our next example is a TextWatcher that consists of two linked text areas; Figure 14-2 shows what the applet looks like. Anything the user types into either area is reflected in both. It demonstrates how to handle a TextEvent, which is generated whenever the text changes in a TextComponent. It also demonstrates how to use an adapter class, which is a more realistic way of setting up event listeners. Registering the applet as a listener is okay for simple programs, but the technique shown here will serve you better in more complex situations:

```java
import java.awt.*;
import java.awt.event.*;
public class TextWatcher extends java.applet.Applet {
    TextArea area1, area2;

    public void init() {
        setLayout( new GridLayout(2,1) );
        add( area1 = new TextArea() );
        add( area2 = new TextArea() );
        area1.addTextListener ( new TextSyncAdapter( area2 ));
        area2.addTextListener ( new TextSyncAdapter( area1 ));
    }
    class TextSyncAdapter implements TextListener {
        TextArea targetArea;
        TextSyncAdapter( TextArea targetArea ) {
            this.targetArea = targetArea;
        }
        public void textValueChanged(TextEvent e) {
            TextArea sourceArea = (TextArea)e.getSource();
            if ( ! targetArea.getText().equals( sourceArea.getText() ) )
                targetArea.setText( sourceArea.getText() );
        }
    }
}
```

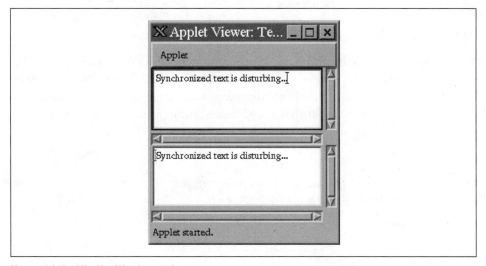

Figure 14–2: The TextWatcher applet

Setting up the display is simple. We use a GridLayout and add two text areas to the layout. Then we add our listeners for text events, which are generated whenever the text in a TextComponent is changed. There is one listener for each text area; both are TextSyncAdapter objects. One listens to events from area1 and modifies the text in area2; the other listens to events from area2 and modifies the text in area1.

All the real work is done by the `TextSyncAdapter`. This is an inner class; its definition is contained within `TextWatcher` and can't be referenced by classes outside of our `TextWatcher`. The adapter implements the `TextListener` interface, and therefore includes a `textValueChanged()` method.

`textValueChanged()` is the heart of the listener. First, it extracts the source area from the incoming event; this is the area that generated the event. The area whose text the listener is changing (the target area) was stored by the constructor. Then it tests whether the texts in both areas are the same. If they aren't, it calls the target area's `setText()` method to set its text equal to the source area's.

The one mysterious feature of this method is the test for equality. Why is it necessary? Why can't we just say "the text in one area changed, so set the text in the other"? A `TextEvent` is generated whenever a `TextComponent` is modified for any reason; this includes changes caused by software, not just changes that occur when a user types. So think about what happens when the user types into `area1`. Typing generates a `TextEvent`, which causes the adapter to change the text in `area2`. This generates another `TextEvent`, which, if we didn't do any testing, would cause us to change `area1` again, which would generate another `TextEvent`, ad infinitum. By checking whether the texts in our two areas are equivalent, we prevent an infinite loop in which text events ping-pong back and forth between the two areas.

Managing Text Yourself

Text areas and text fields do the work of handling keystrokes for you, but they're certainly not your only options for dealing with keyboard input. Any `Component` can register `KeyListeners` to receive `KeyEvents` that occur when their component has focus. Here's an example that shows how you might use these to make your own text gadgets; Figure 14-3 shows what `KeyWatcher` looks like.

```
import java.awt.*;
import java.awt.event.*;
public class KeyWatcher extends java.applet.Applet {
    StringBuffer text = new StringBuffer();
    public void init () {
        setFont( new Font("TimesRoman",Font.BOLD,18) );
        addKeyListener ( new KeyAdapter() {
            public void keyPressed( KeyEvent e ) {
                System.out.println(e);
                type( e.getKeyCode(), e.getKeyChar() );
            }
        } );
        requestFocus();
    }
    public void type(int code, char ch ) {
        switch ( code ) {
            case ( KeyEvent.VK_BACK_SPACE ):
                if (text.length() > 0)
```

```
                    text.setLength( text.length() - 1 );
                break;
            case ( KeyEvent.VK_ENTER ):
                    System.out.println( text );   // Process line
                    text.setLength( 0 );
                break;
            default:
                if ( (ch >= ' ') && (ch <= '~') )
                    text.append( ch );
            }
        repaint();
    }

    public void paint(Graphics g) {
        g.drawString(text.toString() + "_", 20, 20);
    }
}
```

Figure 14–3: The KeyWatcher applet

Fundamentally, all we are doing is collecting text in a StringBuffer and using the drawString() method to display it on the screen. As you'd expect, paint() is responsible for managing the display.

In this applet, we're interested in receiving KeyEvents, which occur whenever the user presses any key. To get these events, the applet calls its own addKeyListener() method. The KeyListener itself is an anonymous class. It doesn't have a name and can't be used anywhere else. We create this class by getting a new KeyAdapter() and overriding its keyPressed() method. (Remember that KeyAdapter contains do-nothing implementations of the methods in the KeyListener interface.) All keyPressed() does is call our private method type() with two arguments: the key code of the key that was pressed, and the logical character represented by the keystroke.

type() shows you how to deal with keystrokes. Each key event is identified with a code, which identifies the actual key typed, and a character, which identifies what the user meant to type. This sounds confusing, but it isn't. Basically, there is a constant for each key on the keyboard: VK_ENTER for the Enter (Return) key, VK_A for the letter A, and so on. However, the physical keystroke isn't usually the same as what the user types: the uppercase character *A* is made up of two keystrokes (the A key and the Shift key), while lowercase *a* is made up of one.

Therefore, you can expect events for both physical keystrokes and typed characters. The int constant VK_UNDEFINED is used for the physical key code when the event doesn't correspond to a single keystroke. The char constant CHAR_UNDEFINED indicates that the event corresponds to a physical keystroke but not a typed character.

The type() method is called with both the key constant and the character as arguments. The way we use them is relatively simple and would need more work for an industrial strength program. Simply, if the physical key is VK_BACK_SPACE, we delete the last character from the StringBuffer we're building. If it's VK_ENTER, we clear the StringBuffer. If the physical key has any other value, we look at the character the user typed. If this is a printable character, we add it to the StringBuffer. Anything else we ignore. Once we've handled the event, we call repaint() to update the screen. Using key codes to handle operations like backspace or enter is easier and less bug-prone than working with odd Control key combinations.

A final note on our anonymous adapter class: in essence our adapter is letting us write a "callback," by calling type() whenever keyPressed() is called. That's one important use for adapters: to map methods in the various listener interfaces into the methods that make sense for your class. Unlike C or C++, Java won't let us pass a method pointer as an argument, but it will let us create an anonymous class that calls our method and passes an instance of that class.

Lists

A List is a step up on the evolutionary chain. Lists let the user choose from a group of alternatives. They can be configured to force the user to choose a single selection or to allow multiple choices. Usually, only a small group of choices are displayed at a time; a built-in scrollbar lets you move to the choices that aren't visible.

A List generates two kinds of events. If the user single-clicks on a selection, the List generates an ItemEvent. If the user double-clicks, a List generates an ActionEvent. Therefore, a List can register both ItemListeners and ActionListeners. In either case, the listener can use the event to figure out what the user selected.

The applet below, SearchableListApplet shown in Figure 14-4, contains a List and a text field. Several of the items in the list aren't visible, because the list is too long for the space we've allotted for it (enough to display three items). When you type the name of an item into the text field, the applet displays the item you want and selects it. Of course, you could do this with a scrollbar, but then we wouldn't have the opportunity to demonstrate how to work with lists.

```java
import java.awt.*;
import java.awt.event.*;
public class SearchableListApplet extends java.applet.Applet {
    public void init() {
        String [] items = { "One", "Two", "Three", "Four", "Five", "Six" };
        add( new SearchableList( items ) );
    }
}
class SearchableList extends Container implements ActionListener {
    List list;
    TextField field;
    SearchableList( String [] items ) {
        list = new List( 3 );   // Let some scroll for this example
        for(int i=0; i< items.length; i++)
            list.addItem( items[i] );
        field = new TextField();
        field.addActionListener( this );
        setLayout( new BorderLayout() );
        add("Center", list);
        add("South", field);
    }
    public void actionPerformed( ActionEvent e ) {
        String search = field.getText();
        for (int i=0; i< list.getItemCount(); i++)
            if ( list.getItem( i ).equals( search ) ) {
                list.select( i );
                list.makeVisible( i );  // Scroll it into view
                break;
            }
        field.setText(""); // clear the text field
    }
}
```

We create the List and the TextField in a new class, SearchableList; the applet itself only displays the SearchableList. SearchableList itself is a new kind of animal; it is a lightweight component that subclasses Container directly. In the constructor for SearchableList, we create our List by calling its constructor, setting it to display at most three components. We then call the addItem() method to add the possible selections to the list; these are the numbers "One" through "Six," passed to us in an array.

We then create our TextField and register ourselves (i.e., SearchableList) as an ActionListener for the field's events. Finally, we set the layout for SearchableList

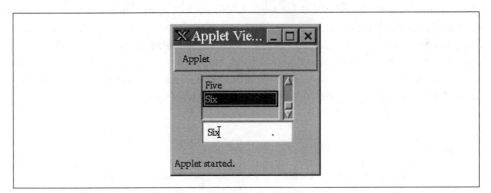

Figure 14–4: The SearchableListApplet

to a border layout, put List in the center of the layout, and TextField at the bottom.

The actionPerformed() method is called whenever the user presses Return in our TextField. In this method, we call getText() to extract the text the user typed. Then we loop through all the items in the list to see if there's a match. getItem-Count() tells us the number of items in the list; getItem() gives us the text associated with any particular item. When we find a match, we call select() to make the matching item the selected item, and we call makeVisible() to make sure that this item is displayed.

By default, List only allows a single selection. We've done nothing in this example to allow multiple selections, so whenever a user chooses an item, the previous selection is automatically dropped. If you want a list that supports multiple selections, call setMultipleMode(true). In this case, you must use the deselect() method to clear the user's selections.

Menus and Choices

A Menu is a standard, pull-down menu with a fixed name. Menus can hold other menus as submenu items, letting you implement complex menu structures. Menus come with several restrictions; they must be attached to a menu bar, and the menu bar can be attached only to a Frame (or another menu). You can't stick Menu at an arbitrary position within a container. A top-level Menu has a name that is always visible in the menu bar. (An important exception to these rules is PopupMenu, which we'll describe in the next section.)

A Choice is an item that lets you choose from a selection of alternatives. If this sounds like a menu, you're right. Choices are free-spirited relatives of menus. A Choice item can be positioned anywhere, in any kind of container. It looks something like a button, with the current selection as its label. When you press the mouse button on a choice, it unfurls to show possible selections.

Both menus and choices send action events when an item is selected. We'll create a little example that illustrates choices and menus and demonstrates how to work with the events they generate. Since Menu has to be placed in the menu bar of Frame, we'll take this opportunity to show off a Frame object as well. DinnerMenu pops up a window containing a **Food** choice and a menu of **Utensils**, as shown in Figure 14-5. DinnerMenu prints a message for each selection; choosing **Quit** from the menu removes the window. Give it a try.

```java
import java.awt.*;
import java.awt.event.*;
import java.util.EventListener;
public class DinnerMenu extends java.applet.Applet {
    public void init() {
        new DinnerFrame().show();
    }
}
class DinnerFrame extends Frame implements ActionListener, ItemListener {
    DinnerFrame() {
        setTitle("Dinner Helper");
        setLayout( new FlowLayout() );
        add( new Label("Food") );
        Choice c = new Choice ();
        c.addItem("Chinese");
        c.addItem("Italian");
        c.addItem("American");
        c.addItemListener( this );
        add( c );
        Menu menu = new Menu("Utensils");
        menu.add( makeMenuItem("Fork") );
        menu.add( makeMenuItem("Knife") );
        menu.add( makeMenuItem("Spoon") );
        Menu subMenu = new Menu("Hybrid");
        subMenu.add( makeMenuItem("Spork") );
        subMenu.add( makeMenuItem("Spife") );
        subMenu.add( makeMenuItem("Knork") );
        menu.add( subMenu);
        menu.add( makeMenuItem("Quit") );
        MenuBar menuBar = new MenuBar();
        menuBar.add(menu);
        setMenuBar(menuBar);
        pack();
    }
    public void itemStateChanged(ItemEvent e) {
        System.out.println( "Choice set to: " + e.getItem() );
    }
```

```
    public void actionPerformed(ActionEvent e) {
        String command = e.getActionCommand();
        if ( command.equals( "Quit" ) )
            dispose();
        else
            System.out.println( "Menu selected: " + e.getActionCommand() );
    }
    private MenuItem makeMenuItem( String name ) {
        MenuItem m = new MenuItem( name );
        m.addActionListener( this );
        return m;
    }
}
```

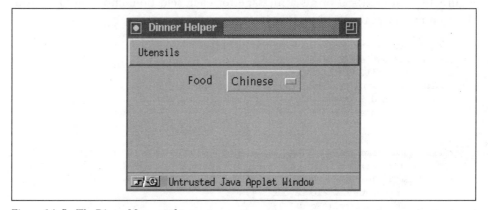

Figure 14–5: The DinnerMenu applet

Yes, I know. **Quit** doesn't belong in the **Utensils** menu. If it's driving you crazy, you can go back and add a **File** menu as an exercise when we're through.

So what do we have? Well, we've created a new kind of component called `Dinner-Frame` that implements our palette of dinner options. We do our setup work in the `DinnerFrame` constructor. `DinnerFrame` sets the name on its titlebar with `setTitle()`. The constructor also handles a few other miscellaneous details, such as setting the layout manager that places things side by side in the display area and later, resizing itself by calling `pack()`.

We make an instance of `Choice` and add three options to it with its `addItem()` method. `Choice` options are simple `String` objects. When one is picked, we get an action event with an argument that specifies the selected option name. We can also examine the currently selected item at any time with the `Choice`'s `getSelected-Item()` method. A `Choice` generates an `ItemEvent` when a user makes a selection, so we register the `DinnerFrame` as an `ItemEvent` listener by calling addItemListener(). (This means we must also implement the ItemListener interface and provide an itemStateChanged() method.) As with any component, we display the Choice by adding it to our applet's layout with add().

The Menu has a few more moving parts. A Menu holds MenuItem objects. A simple MenuItem just has a String as a label. It sends this as an argument in an action event when it's selected. We can set its font with setFont(). We can also turn it on or off with setEnabled(); this method controls whether the MenuItem is available. A Menu object is itself a kind of MenuItem, and this allows us to use a menu as a submenu in another menu.

We construct Menu with its name and call its add() method to give it three new MenuItem objects. To create the menu items, we call our own makeMenuItem() helper method. Next, we repeat this process to make a new Menu object, subMenu, and add it as the fourth option. Its name appears as the menu item along with a little arrow, indicating it's a submenu. When it's selected, the subMenu menu pops up to the side, and we can select from it. Finally, we add one last simple menu item to serve as a **Quit** option.

We use a private method, makeMenuItem(), to create our menu items for us. This method is convenient because, with menus, every item generates its own events. Therefore, we must register an ActionListener for every selection on the menu. Rather than write lots of code, we use a helper method to register our DinnerFrame (this) as the listener for every item. It should be no surprise then, that Dinner-Frame must implement ActionListener and provide an actionPerformed() method.

Now we have the menu; to use it, we have to insert it in a menu bar. A MenuBar holds Menu objects. We create MenuBar and set it as the menu bar for DinnerFrame with the Frame.setMenuBar() method. We can then add our menu to it with menuBar.add():

```
MenuBar menuBar = new MenuBar();
menuBar.add(menu);
setMenuBar(menuBar);
```

Suppose our applet didn't have its own frame? Where could we put our menu? Ideally, you'd like the applet to be able to add a menu to the top-level menu bar of the Web browser or applet viewer. Unfortunately, as of Java 1.1, there is no standard for doing so. (There are obvious security considerations in allowing an applet to modify its viewer.) There has been talk of adding this ability as part of Java Beans, but so far, it's not possible.

One final note about the DinnerMenu example. As we said in the previous chapter, any time you use Frame, and thus create a new top-level window, you should add code to destroy your frame whenever the user closes the window with her native window manager. To do so, you register your frame as a WindowListener, implement the WindowListener interface, and provide a windowClosing() method that calls dispose(). By calling dispose(), we indicate the window is no longer needed, so that it can release its window system resources.

PopupMenu

One of the new components in Java 1.1 is PopupMenu: a menu that automatically appears when you press the appropriate mouse button inside of a component. Which button you press depends on the platform you're using; fortunately, you don't have to care.

The care and feeding of PopupMenu is basically the same as any other menu. You use a different constructor (PopupMenu()) to create it, but otherwise, you build a menu and add elements to it the same way. The big difference is that you don't need to attach it to MenuBar, and consequently don't need to worry about putting MenuBar in a Frame. Instead, you call add() to add the PopupMenu to any component.

The PopupColorMenu applet contains three buttons. You can use a PopupMenu to set the color of each button or the applet itself, depending on where you press the mouse. (Setting the color of the applet also sets the buttons' colors.) Figure 14-6 shows the applet in action; the user is preparing to change the color of the rightmost button.

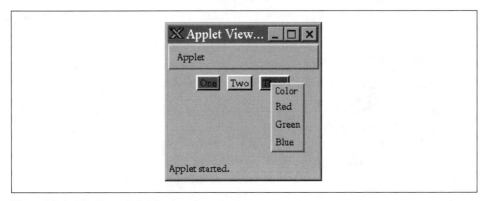

Figure 14–6: The PopupColorMenu applet

```
import java.awt.*;
import java.awt.event.*;
public class PopUpColorMenu extends java.applet.Applet
implements ActionListener {
    PopupMenu colorMenu;
    Component selectedComponent;
    public void init() {
        add( new Button("One") );
        add( new Button("Two") );
        add( new Button("Three") );

        colorMenu = new PopupMenu("Color");
        colorMenu.add( makeMenuItem("Red") );
        colorMenu.add( makeMenuItem("Green") );
        colorMenu.add( makeMenuItem("Blue") );
        addMouseListener( new MouseAdapter() {
            public void mousePressed(MouseEvent e) {
                if ( e.isPopupTrigger() ) {
                    selectedComponent = getComponentAt( e.getX(), e.getY() );
                    colorMenu.show(e.getComponent(), e.getX(), e.getY());
                }
            }
        } );
        add(colorMenu);
    }
    public void actionPerformed(ActionEvent e) {
        String color = e.getActionCommand();
        if ( color.equals("Red") )
            selectedComponent.setBackground( Color.red );
        else if ( color.equals("Green") )
            selectedComponent.setBackground( Color.green );
        else if ( color.equals("Blue") )
            selectedComponent.setBackground( Color.blue );
    }
    private MenuItem makeMenuItem(String label) {
        MenuItem item = new MenuItem(label);
        item.addActionListener( this );
        return item;
    }
}
```

Because the popup menu is triggered by mouse events, we need to register a
MouseListener. In our call to addMouseListener(), we create an anonymous inner
class based on the MouseAdapter. In this class, we override the mousePressed()
method to display the popup menu when we get an appropriate event. How do we
know what an "appropriate event" is? Fortunately, we don't need to worry about
the specifics of our user's platform; we just need to call the event's isPopupTrig-
ger() method. If this method returns true, we know the user has done whatever
normally displays a popup menu on his system.

Once we know that the user wants to raise a popup menu, we figure out which component the mouse is over by calling getComponentAt(), with the coordinates of the mouse click (given by e.getX() and e.getY()). Then we display the popup menu by calling its show() method, again with the mouse coordinates as arguments.

If we wanted to provide different menus for different types of components or the background, we could add a test within the check for the popup trigger:

```
if ( e.isPopupTrigger() ) {
    selectedComponent = getComponentAt( e.getX(), e.getY() );

    if ( selectedComponent instanceof Button )
        colorMenu.show(e.getComponent(),
                           e.getX(), e.getY());
    else if ( selectedComponent instanceof Applet )
            // show a menu for the background
    else if ( selectedComponent instanceof someOtherComponent )
            // show another menu
}
```

The only thing left is to handle the action events from the popup menu items. As in our earlier example, we use a helper method called makeMenuItem() to register the applet as an action listener for every item we add. The applet implements ActionListener and has the required actionPerformed() method. This method reads the action command from the event, which is equal to the selected menu item's label by default. It then sets the background color of the selected component appropriately.

Checkbox and CheckboxGroup

A Checkbox is a labeled toggle button. A group of such toggle buttons can be made mutually exclusive by tethering them together with a CheckboxGroup object. By now you're probably well into the swing of things and could easily master the Checkbox on your own. We'll throw out an example to illustrate a different way of dealing with the state of components and to show off a few more things about containers.

A Checkbox sends item events when it's pushed, just like a List, a Menu, or a Choice. In our last example, we caught the action events from our choice and menu selections and worked with them when they happened. For something like a checkbox, we might want to be lazy and check on the state of the buttons only at some later time, such as when the user commits an action. It's like filling out a form; you can change your choices until you submit the form.

The following applet, DriveThrough, lets us check off selections on a fast food menu, as shown in Figure 14-7. DriveThrough prints the results when we press the **Place Order** button. Therefore, we can ignore all the item events generated by our checkboxes and listen only for the action events generated by the button.

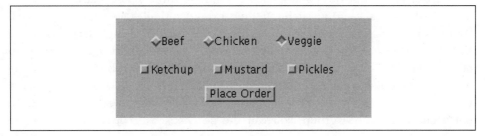

Figure 14–7: The DriveThrough applet

```java
import java.awt.*;
import java.awt.event.*;
public class OrderForm extends java.applet.Applet implements ActionListener {
    Panel condimentsPanel = new Panel();
    CheckboxGroup entreeGroup = new CheckboxGroup();
    public void init() {
        condimentsPanel.add( new Checkbox("Ketchup"));
        condimentsPanel.add( new Checkbox("Mustard"));
        condimentsPanel.add( new Checkbox("Pickles"));
        Checkbox c;
        Panel entreePanel = new Panel();
        entreePanel.add( c = new Checkbox("Beef") );
        c.setCheckboxGroup( entreeGroup );
        entreePanel.add( c = new Checkbox("Chicken") );
        c.setCheckboxGroup( entreeGroup );
        entreePanel.add( c = new Checkbox("Veggie") );
        c.setCheckboxGroup( entreeGroup );
        entreeGroup.setCurrent( c );
        Panel orderPanel = new Panel();
        Button orderButton = new Button("Place Order");
        orderButton.addActionListener( this );
        orderPanel.add( orderButton );
        setLayout( new GridLayout(3, 1) );
        add( entreePanel );
        add( condimentsPanel );
        add( orderPanel );
    }
    public void actionPerformed(ActionEvent e) {
        takeOrder();
    }
    void takeOrder() {
        Checkbox c = entreeGroup.getCurrent();
            System.out.println( c.getLabel() + " sandwich" );
        Component [] components = condimentsPanel.getComponents();
        for (int i=0; i< components.length; i++)
```

```
            if ( (c = (Checkbox)components[i]).getState() )
                System.out.println( "With " + c.getLabel() );
        System.out.println("Thank you, drive through...");
    }
}
```

DriveThrough lays out two panels, each containing three checkboxes. The check-boxes in the entreePanel are tied together through a single CheckboxGroup object. We call their setCheckboxGroup() methods to put them in a single CheckboxGroup that makes the checkboxes mutually exclusive. The CheckboxGroup object is an odd animal. One expects it to be a container or a component, but it isn't; it's simply a helper object that coordinates the functionality of the Checkbox objects. Because a CheckboxGroup isn't a container, it doesn't have an add() method. To put a checkbox into a group, you call the setCheckboxGroup() method of the Checkbox class.

Once a set of checkboxes has been placed in a checkbox group, only one of the boxes may be checked at a time. In this applet, the checkbox group forces you to choose a beef, chicken, or veggie entree, but not more than one. The condiment choices, however, aren't in a checkbox group, so you can request ketchup, mustard, and pickles on your chicken sandwich.

When the **Place Order** button is pushed, we receive an ActionEvent via our actionPerformed() method. At this point, we gather the information in the check-boxes and print it. actionPerformed() simply calls our takeOrder() method, which reads the checkboxes. We could have saved references to the checkboxes in a number of ways; this example demonstrates two. First, we find out which entree was selected. To do so, we call the CheckboxGroup's getCurrent() method. getCurrent() returns the selected Checkbox; we use getLabel() to extract the name of the entree.

To find out which condiments were selected, we use a more complicated proce-dure. The problem is that condiments aren't mutually exclusive, so we don't have the convenience of a CheckboxGroup. Instead, we ask the condiments Panel for a list of its components. The getComponent() method returns an array of references to the container's child components. We'll use this to loop over the components and print the results. We cast each element of the array back to Checkbox and call its getState() method to see if the checkbox is on or off. Remember that if we were dealing with different types of components, we could determine what kind of component we had with the instanceof operator.

ScrollPane and Scrollbars

One of the big advantages of Java 1.1 is the addition of a ScrollPane container. Previously, unless you were working with a text component, you had to manage scrolling yourself. It wasn't terribly difficult, but it was a pain: you had to create Scrollbar objects, attach them to whatever you were scrolling, and redisplay everything with new positions whenever the user made an adjustment. ScrollPane does it all for you. About the only time you absolutely need a Scrollbar is when you want to create a "volume control-type" object. For example, you might want to create a paint mixer that blends different amounts of red, blue, and green, depending on some scrollbar settings.

The unifying theme behind both ScrollPane and Scrollbar is the Adjustable interface, which defines the responsibilities of scrollable objects. An object that implements Adjustable lets you modify an integer value through some fixed range. When a user changes the value, the object generates an AdjustmentEvent; as you might expect, to get an AdjustmentEvent, you must implement AdjustmentListener and register by calling addAdjustmentListener(). Scrollbars implement Adjustable, and ScrollPane can return Adjustable objects for each of its scrollbars.[*]

In this section, we'll demonstrate both the ScrollPane and Scrollbar classes. We'll start with a ScrollPane.

Working with ScrollPane

Technically, ScrollPane is a Container, but it's a funny one. It has its own layout manager, which can't be changed. It can only accommodate one component at a time. This seems like a big limitation, but it isn't. If you want to put a lot of stuff in a ScrollPane, just put your components into a Panel, with whatever layout manager you like, and put that panel into the ScrollPane.

When you create a ScrollPane, you can specify the conditions under which its scrollbars will be displayed. This is called the *scrollbar display policy*; you can specify the policy by using one of the three constants below as an argument to the ScrollPane constructor:

SCROLLBARS_AS_NEEDED
Displays scrollbars only if the object in the ScrollPane doesn't fit.

---

* There may be a bug in the Adjustable objects you get from ScrollPane. Although you can read their settings, you can't change them; methods like setMinimum() and setMaximum() (which should set the object's minimum and maximum values) throw an AWTError.

SCROLLBARS_ALWAYS

Always displays scrollbars, regardless of the object's size.

SCROLLBARS_NEVER

Never displays scrollbars, even if the object is too big. If you use this policy, you
should provide some other way for the user to manipulate ScrollPane.

By default, the policy is SCROLLBARS_AS_NEEDED.

Here's an applet that uses a ScrollPane to display a large image. As you'll see, the
applet itself is very simple; all we do is get the image, set the applet's layout manager, create a ScrollPane, put the image in our pane, and add the ScrollPane to
the applet. To make the program slightly cleaner, we create an ImageComponent
component to hold the image, rather than placing the image directly into the
ScrollPane. Here's the applet itself:

```
import java.awt.*;
public class ScrollPaneApplet extends java.applet.Applet {
    public void init() {
        Image image = getImage( getClass().getResource(getParameter("image")) );
        setLayout( new BorderLayout() );
        ScrollPane scrollPane = new ScrollPane();
        scrollPane.add( new ImageComponent(image) );
        add( "Center", scrollPane );
    }
}
```

And here's the ImageComponent. It waits for the image to load, using a Media-
Tracker, and sets its size to the size of the image. It also provides a paint()
method to draw the image. This takes a single call to drawImage(). The first argument is the image itself; the next two are the coordinates of the image relative to
the ImageComponent; and the last is a reference to the ImageComponent itself
(this), which serves as an image observer. (We'll discuss image observers in Chapter 17; for the time being, take this on faith.)

```
import java.awt.*;
class ImageComponent extends Component {
    Image image;
    Dimension size;
    ImageComponent ( Image image ) {
        this.image = image;
        MediaTracker mt = new MediaTracker(this);
        mt.addImage( image, 0 );
        try { mt.waitForAll(); } catch (InterruptedException e) { /* error */ };
        size = new Dimension ( image.getWidth(null), image.getHeight(null) );
        setSize( size );
    }
    public void update( Graphics g ) {
        paint(g);
    }
    public void paint( Graphics g ) {
```

```
        g.drawImage( image, 0, 0, this );
    }
    public Dimension getPreferredSize() {
        return size;
    }
}
```

ImageComponent also supplies an update() method that calls paint(). As we'll see later, the default version of update() automatically clears the screen, which wastes time if we already know that our image will cover the entire screen. Therefore, we override update() so that it doesn't bother clearing the screen first. Finally, Image-Component provides a getPreferredSize() method, overriding the method it inherits from Component. This method simply returns the image's size, which is a Dimension object. When you're using ScrollPane, it's important for the object you're scrolling to provide a reliable indication of its size, particularly if the object is a lightweight component. Figure 14-8 shows the ScrollPaneApplet with the ImageComponent.

Figure 14–8: The ScrollPaneApplet

Using Scrollbars

Our next example is basically the same as the previous one, except that it doesn't use the ScrollPane; it implements its own scroller using scrollbars. With Java 1.1, you don't have to write code like this, but it does show how much work the ScrollPane saves and also demonstrates how to use scrollbars in other situations.

Our applet is called ComponentScrollerApplet; it uses a home-grown scrollpane called ComponentScroller. In appearance, it is identical to the ScrollPaneApplet (Figure 14-8). The component that we scroll is the ImageComponent we developed in the previous example.

Now let's dive into the code for ComponentScrollerApplet:

```java
import java.awt.*;
import java.awt.event.*;
public class ComponentScrollerApplet extends java.applet.Applet {
    public void init() {
        Image image = getImage( getClass().getResource(getParameter("image")) );
        ImageComponent canvas = new ImageComponent( image );
        setLayout( new BorderLayout() );
        add( "Center", new ComponentScroller(canvas) );
    }
}
class ComponentScroller extends Container {
    Scrollbar horizontal, vertical;
    Panel scrollarea = new Panel();
    Component component;
    int orgX, orgY;
    ComponentScroller( Component comp ) {
        scrollarea.setLayout( null );    // We'll handle the layout
        scrollarea.add( component = comp );
        horizontal = new Scrollbar( Scrollbar.HORIZONTAL );
        horizontal.setMaximum( component.getSize().width );
        horizontal.addAdjustmentListener( new AdjustmentListener() {
            public void adjustmentValueChanged(AdjustmentEvent e) {
                component.setLocation( orgX = -e.getValue(), orgY );
            }
        } );
        vertical = new Scrollbar( Scrollbar.VERTICAL );
        vertical.setMaximum( component.getSize().height);
        vertical.addAdjustmentListener( new AdjustmentListener() {
            public void adjustmentValueChanged(AdjustmentEvent e) {
                component.setLocation( orgX, orgY = -e.getValue() );
            }
        } );
        setLayout( new BorderLayout() );
        add( "Center", scrollarea );
        add( "South", horizontal );
        add( "East", vertical );
    }
    public void doLayout() {
        super.doLayout();
        horizontal.setVisibleAmount( scrollarea.getSize().width );
        vertical.setVisibleAmount( scrollarea.getSize().height );
    }
}
```

What do our new components do? Let's start at the top and work our way down. The applet itself is very simple; it does all of its work in init(). First it sets its layout manager to BorderLayout. Then it acquires an Image object with a call to getImage(). Finally, the applet creates an ImageComponent to hold our image, creates a ComponentScroller to hold the ImageComponent, and adds the scroller to the "Center" region of the layout. I chose BorderLayout because it resizes its central component to fill the entire area available.

Next comes the ComponentScroller itself. ComponentScroller takes a reference to our ImageComponent in its constructor. It adds the component it will be scrolling to a Panel with no layout manager. It then creates horizontal and vertical Scrollbar objects (HORIZONTAL and VERTICAL are constants of the Scrollbar class, used to specify a scrollbar's direction), sets their maximum values using the height and width of the Panel, and registers an AdjustmentListener for each scrollbar. The AdjustmentListener is an anonymous inner class that implements the adjust-mentValueChanged() method. This method is called whenever the user moves the scrollbar. It extracts the new scrollbar setting from an AdjustmentEvent and uses this to move the component we're scrolling to its new location. We have a separate listener for each scrollbar, so we don't have to figure out which scrollbar generated the event. The listener for the horizontal scrollbar adjusts the component's x coordinate (orgX) and leaves its y coordinate unchanged; likewise, the listener for the vertical scrollbar adjusts the component's y coordinate. By adjusting the location of the ImageComponent, we control how much of the image is displayed; anything that falls outside of the scroller's Panel (scrollarea) isn't displayed.

The ComponentScroller overrides the doLayout() method of the Container class. This gives us an opportunity to change the size of the scrollbar "handles" whenever the scroller is resized. To do so, we call super.doLayout() first, to make sure that the container gets arranged properly; although we're overriding this method, we need to make sure that it does its work. Then we call the setVisibleAmount() method of each scrollbar with the new width and height of the scrolling area.

So in review, we call setMaximum() to set the vertical scrollbar's maximum value to the image's height; we call setVisibleAmount() to tell the vertical scrollbar how much area we have available, and it sets the size of its "handle" accordingly. For example, if the image is 200 pixels high and the visible amount is 100 pixels, the scrollbar sets its handle to be roughly half its length. We do similar things to the horizontal scrollbar. As a result, the handles grow or shrink as we change the size of the viewing area and indicate how much of the image is visible.

The setMaximum() and setVisibleAmount() are both part of the Adjustable inter-face, which scrollbars implement. Other methods of this interface are listed in Table 14-1.

Table 14–1: Methods of the Adjustable Interface

Method	Description
getOrientation()	Tells you whether the scrollbar is HORIZONTAL or VERTICAL. There is no setOrientation() method in the interface, but the Scrollbar class does support setOrientation().

Table 14–1: Methods of the Adjustable Interface (continued)

Method	Description
getVisibleAmount() and setVisibleAmount()	Lets you control the size of the scrollbar's handle (slider). As we saw earlier, this is a convenient way to give the user a feel for the size of the object you're scrolling.
getValue() and setValue()	Lets you retrieve or change the scrollbar's current setting.
getMinimum() and setMinimum()	Lets you control the scrollbar's minimum value.
getMaximum() and setMaximum()	Lets you control the scrollbar's maximum value.
getUnitIncrement() and setUnitIncrement()	Lets you control the amount the scrollbar will move if the user clicks on the scrollbar's arrows; in many environments, this means the user wants to move up or down one line.
getBlockIncrement() and setBlockIncrement()	Lets you control the amount the scrollbar will move if the user clicks between an arrow and the slider; in many environments, this means the user wants to move up or down one page.
addAdjustmentListener() and removeAdjustmentListener()	Adds or removes listeners for the scrollbar's events.

It's worth asking why we put our image in a Canvas, which we then put into a Panel, which we put into another Panel, which we put into the applet. Surely there's a more efficient way. Yes there is, but we wanted to make as many reusable components as possible. With this design, you can use ImageComponent wherever you need to display an image and check that it is loaded first; you can use ComponentScroller wherever you need to scroll any kind of component, not just an image or a Canvas. Making reusable components is one of the major advantages of object-oriented design; it's something you should always keep in mind.

Dialogs

A Dialog is another standard feature of user interfaces. In Java, a Dialog is a kind of Window, which means that it's really a container into which you put other components. A Dialog can be either *modal* or *nonmodal*. A modal dialog seizes the attention of the user by staying in the foreground and grabbing all input until it is satisfied. A nonmodal dialog isn't quite so insistent; you're allowed to do other things before dealing with the dialog. Dialog objects are useful for popup messages and queries or important user-driven decisions.

Most of the components we've seen so far have some special kinds of events associated with them. A Dialog doesn't have any special events. Of course, this doesn't mean that a dialog doesn't generate events. Since a dialog is a Window, it can generate any event that a Window can. However, there aren't any special events, like action events or item events, to worry about. When you're dealing with a Dialog, your primary concern will be events generated by the components that you put into the Dialog.

We'll do a quick example of a Dialog window and then take a look at FileDialog, a subclass of Dialog that provides an easy-to-use file-selector component. Our example will be a modal dialog that asks a simple question.

A Simple Query Dialog

The heart of this example is a class called ModalYesNoDialog that implements a simple form with a question and two buttons. Figure 14-9 shows the dialog.

Figure 14–9: The YesNo dialog

```
import java.awt.*;
import java.awt.event.*;
class ModalYesNoDialog extends Dialog implements ActionListener {
    private boolean isYes = false;
    ModalYesNoDialog( Frame frame, String question ) {
        super(frame, true /* modal */);
        Label label = new Label(question);
        label.setFont( new Font("Dialog",Font.PLAIN,20) );
        add( "Center", label );
        Panel yn = new Panel();
        Button button = new Button("Yes");
        button.addActionListener( this );
        yn.add( button );
        button = new Button("No");
        button.addActionListener( this );
        yn.add( button );
        add("South", yn);
        pack();
    }
    synchronized public boolean answer() {
        return isYes;
    }
```

```
        synchronized public void actionPerformed ( ActionEvent e ) {
            isYes = e.getActionCommand().equals("Yes");
            dispose();
        }
        public static void main(String[] s) {
            Frame f = new Frame();
            f.add( "Center", new Label("I'm the application") );
            f.add( "South", new Button("Can you press me?") );
            f.pack();
            f.show();
            ModalYesNoDialog query = new ModalYesNoDialog( f, "Do you love me?");
            query.show();
            if ( query.answer() == true )
                System.out.println("She loves me...");
            else
                System.out.println("She loves me not...");
        }
    }
```

To create the Dialog, our class's constructor calls its superclass's constructor
(super()), which is Dialog(). When we create the dialog, we must supply a parent
Frame; we also specify that the Dialog is modal.

The rest of the constructor—for that matter, the rest of the class—doesn't have
any surprises. We use a Label to display the question; we add a pair of buttons,
labeled "Yes" and "No," for the user to give her answer. We provide an answer()
method so we can ask the dialog which button the user pushed; and we provide an
actionPerformed() method to receive the button events.

The rest of our program is an application that uses the ModalYesNoDialog. It creates a Frame, creates the ModalYesNoDialog, displays the dialog by calling its
show() method, and reads the answer.

We used an application rather than an applet to demonstrate the Dialog because
dialogs are somewhat unwieldy in applets. You need to have a Frame to serve as the
dialog's parent, and most applets don't need frames. However, there's a simple
workaround. There's no reason an applet can't use an invisible frame: just create a
Frame, call its pack() method, but never call its show() method. The Frame won't
be displayed but will be able to serve as the parent to a dialog box.

Now let's talk briefly about nonmodal dialogs. The most obvious change is in the
constructor. Now you call:

```
    new Dialog(myFrame, false);
```

But there are a few other issues to think about. Using a nonmodal dialog is slightly
more complex because it's asynchronous: the program doesn't wait until the user
responds. Therefore, you might want to modify the answer() method so that it
calls wait() to wait until the user replies. The code would look like this:

```
    // add a new boolean for the answer() method
    private boolean isAnswered = false;
    // add a wait() in the answer() method
    synchronized public boolean answer() {
        while ( !isAnswered )
            try { wait(); } catch (InterruptedException e) { /* error */ }
        return isYes;
    }
```

If you do this, you also need to modify actionPerformed() to call notifyAll() and terminate the wait():

```
        // add a notify() in the actionPeformed() method
        synchronized public void actionPerformed ( ActionEvent e ) {
            isYes = e.getActionCommand().equals("Yes");
            isAnswered = true;
            notifyAll();
            dispose();
        }
    }
```

File Selection Dialog

A FileDialog is a standard file-selection box. As with other AWT components, most of FileDialog is implemented in the native part of the AWT toolkit, so it looks and acts like a standard file selector on your platform.

Selecting files all day can be pretty boring without a greater purpose, so we'll exercise the FileDialog in a mini-editor application. Editor provides a text area in which we can load and work with files. (The FileDialog created by Editor is shown in Figure 14-10.) We'll stop just shy of the capability to save and let you fill in the blanks (with a few caveats):

```
import java.awt.*;
import java.awt.event.*;
import java.io.*;
class Editor extends Frame implements ActionListener {
    TextArea textArea = new TextArea();
    Editor() {
        super("Editor");
        setLayout( new BorderLayout() );
        add("Center", textArea);
        Menu menu = new Menu ("File");
        menu.add ( makeMenuItem ("Load") );
        menu.add ( makeMenuItem ("Save") );
        menu.add ( makeMenuItem ("Quit") );
        MenuBar menuBar = new MenuBar();
        menuBar.add ( menu );
        setMenuBar( menuBar );
        pack();
    }
    public void actionPerformed( ActionEvent e ) {
```

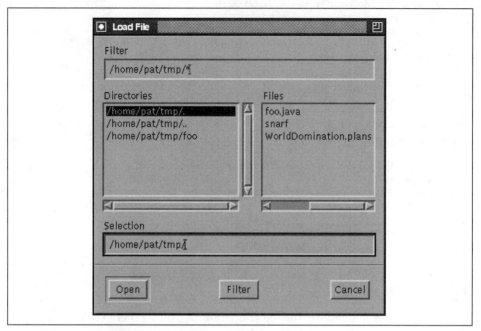

Figure 14–10: A FileDialog

```
        String command = e.getActionCommand();
        if ( command.equals("Quit") )
            dispose();
        else if ( command.equals("Load") )
            loadFile();
        else if ( command.equals("Save") )
            saveFile();
    }
    private void loadFile () {
        FileDialog fd = new FileDialog( this, "Load File", FileDialog.LOAD );
        fd.show();
        String file = fd.getFile();
        if ( file == null ) // Cancel
            return;
        try {
            FileInputStream fis = new FileInputStream ( fd.getFile() );
            byte [] data = new byte [ fis.available() ];
            fis.read( data );
            textArea.setText( new String( data ) );
        } catch ( IOException e ) {
            textArea.setText( "Could not load file..." );
        }
    }
    private void saveFile() {
        FileDialog fd = new FileDialog( this, "Save File", FileDialog.SAVE );
        fd.show();
        // Save file data...
```

```
        }
        private MenuItem makeMenuItem( String name ) {
            MenuItem m = new MenuItem( name );
            m.addActionListener( this );
            return m;
        }
        public static void main(String[] s) {
            new Editor().show();
        }
    }
```

Editor is a Frame that lays itself out with a TextArea and a pull-down menu. From
the pull-down **File** menu, we can opt to **Load, Save,** or **Quit**. The action() method
catches the events associated with these menu selections and takes the appropriate
action.

The interesting parts of Editor are the private methods loadFile() and save-
File(). loadFile() creates a new FileDialog with three parameters: a parent
frame (just as in the previous Dialog example), a title, and a directive. This parameter should be one of the FileDialog class's static identifiers LOAD or SAVE, which
tell the dialog whether to load or save a file.

A FileDialog does its work when the show() method is called. Unlike most components, its show() method blocks the caller until it completes its job; the file
selector then disappears. After that, we can retrieve the designated filename with
the FileDialog's getFile() method. In loadFile(), we use a fragment of code
from Chapter 10 to get the contents of the named file. We then add the contents
to the TextArea with setText(). You can use loadFile() as a road map for the
unfinished saveFile() method, but it would be prudent to add the standard safety
precautions. For example, you could use the previous YesNo example to prompt
the user before overwriting an existing file.

Creating Custom Components

In the previous sections, we've worked with many different user interface objects
and made a lot of new classes that are sort of like components. Our new classes do
one particular thing well; a number of them can be added to applets or other containers just like the standard AWT components; and several of them are
lightweight components that use system resources efficiently because they don't
rely on a peer.

But these new classes still aren't really components. If you think about it, all our
classes have been fairly self-contained; they know everything about what to do and
don't rely on other parts of the program to do much processing. Therefore, they

are overly specialized. Our menu example created a `DinnerFrame` class that had a menu of dinner options, but it included all the processing needed to handle the user's selections. If we wanted to process the selections differently, we'd have to modify the class. That's not what we want; we'd like to separate registering the user's choices from processing those choices. In contrast, true components don't do any processing. They let the user take some action and then inform some other part of the program, which processes the action.

So we need a way for our new classes to communicate with other parts of the program. Since we want our new classes to be components, they should communicate the way components communicate: that is, by generating events and sending those events to listeners. So far, we've written a lot of code that listened for events but haven't seen any examples that generated events.

Generating events sounds like it ought to be difficult, but it isn't. You can either create new kinds of events by subclassing `AWTEvent`, or use one of the standard event types. In either case, you need to register listeners for your events and provide a means to deliver events to your listeners. If you are using the standard events, AWT provides an `AWTEventMulticaster` class that handles most of the machinery. We'll focus on that option in this section; at the end, we'll make some comments on how you might manage events on your own.

The `AWTEventMulticaster` is one of those things that looks a lot more complicated than it is. It is confusing, but most of the confusion occurs because it's hard to believe it's so simple. Its job is to maintain a linked list of event listeners and to propagate events to all the listeners on that linked list. So we can use a multicaster to register (and unregister) event listeners and to send any events we generate to all registered listeners.

The best way to show you how to use the multicaster is through an example. The following example creates a new component called `PictureButton`. `PictureButton` looks at least somewhat button-like and responds to mouse clicks (`MOUSE_RELEASED` events) by generating action events. (Figure 14-11 shows a `PictureButton` in both depressed and raised modes.) The `PictureButtonApplet` is passed the events in its `actionPerformed()` method, just as with any other button, and prints a message each time it's pressed:

```
import java.awt.*;
import java.awt.event.*;
public class PictureButtonApplet extends java.applet.Applet
                              implements ActionListener {
    Image image;
    public void init() {
        image = getImage( getClass().getResource(getParameter("image")) );
        PictureButton pictureButton = new PictureButton( image );
        add ( pictureButton );
```

Figure 14–11: The PictureButton

```
            pictureButton.setActionCommand("Aaargh!");
            pictureButton.addActionListener( this );
        }

        public void actionPerformed( ActionEvent e ) {
            System.out.println( e );
        }
    }
    class PictureButton extends Component {
        private Image image;
        boolean pressed = false;
        ActionListener actionListener;
        String actionCommand;
        PictureButton(Image image) {
            this.image = image;
            MediaTracker mt = new MediaTracker(this);
            mt.addImage( image, 0 );
            try { mt.waitForAll(); } catch (InterruptedException e) { /* error */ };
            setSize( image.getWidth(null), image.getHeight(null) );
            enableEvents( AWTEvent.MOUSE_EVENT_MASK );
        }
        public void paint( Graphics g ) {
            g.setColor(Color.white);
            int width = getSize().width, height = getSize().height;
            int offset = pressed ? -2 : 0;   // fake depth
            g.drawImage( image, offset, offset, width, height, this );
            g.draw3DRect(0, 0, width-1, height-1, !pressed);
            g.draw3DRect(1, 1, width-3, height-3, !pressed);
        }
        public Dimension getPreferredSize() {
            return getSize();
        }
        public void processEvent( AWTEvent e ) {
            if ( e.getID() == MouseEvent.MOUSE_PRESSED ) {
                pressed = true;
                repaint();
            } else
            if ( e.getID() == MouseEvent.MOUSE_RELEASED ) {
```

```
                    pressed = false;
                    repaint();
                    fireEvent();
                }
                super.processEvent(e);
            }
        public void setActionCommand( String actionCommand ) {
            this.actionCommand = actionCommand;
        }
        public void addActionListener(ActionListener l) {
            actionListener = AWTEventMulticaster.add(actionListener, l);
        }
        public void removeActionListener(ActionListener l) {
            actionListener = AWTEventMulticaster.remove(actionListener, l);
        }
        private void fireEvent() {
            if (actionListener != null) {
                ActionEvent event = new ActionEvent( this,
                            ActionEvent.ACTION_PERFORMED, actionCommand );
                actionListener.actionPerformed( event );
            }
        }
    }
}
```

Before diving into the event multicaster, here are a few notes about the applet and the PictureButton. The applet is an ActionListener because it is looking for events coming from the button. Therefore, it registers itself as a listener and contains an actionPerformed() method. The PictureButton doesn't have a label, so the applet explicitly sets the button's action command by calling setActionCommand().

The button itself is concerned mostly with being pretty. It uses a media tracker to make sure that the image has loaded before displaying itself. The paint() method, which we won't discuss in detail, is devoted to making the button appear "pressed" (i.e., recessed) when the mouse is pressed. The getPreferredSize() method lets layout managers size the button appropriately.

Now we'll start with the button's machinery. The button needs to receive mouse events. It could register as a mouse listener, but in this case, it seems more appropriate to override processEvent(). processEvent() receives all incoming events. It first checks whether we have a MOUSE_PRESSED event; if so, it tells the button to repaint itself in its "pressed" mode. If the event is a MOUSE_RELEASED event, it tells the button to paint itself in its "unpressed" mode and calls the private fireEvent() method, which sends an action event to all listeners. Finally, processEvent() calls super.processEvent() to make sure normal event processing occurs; this is a good practice whenever you override a method that performs a significant task.

However, processEvent() doesn't receive events if they aren't generated; and normally, events aren't generated if there are no listeners. Therefore, the button's constructor calls enableEvents() with the argument MOUSE_EVENT_MASK to turn on mouse event processing.

Now we're ready to talk about how to generate events. The picture button has addActionListener() and removeActionListener() methods for registering listeners. These just call the static methods add() and remove() of the AWTEventMulticaster class. Here's the addActionListener() method:

```
public void addActionListener(ActionListener l) {
    actionListener = AWTEventMulticaster.add(actionListener, l);
}
```

If you look back to see how the instance variable actionListener is declared, you'll see that it is an ActionListener. No big surprise—except that this code doesn't appear to make sense. It's saying "add an action listener to an action listener and store the result back in the original action listener."

There are a couple of tricks here. First, an AWTEventMulticaster implements all of the listener interfaces. Therefore, a multicaster can appear wherever an Action-Listener (or any other listener) is required. In this case, the actionListener object will be a multicaster—perhaps not what you expected, and certainly not what's being passed in the argument l. Now the code is starting to make sense: earlier, I said that multicasters maintained linked lists of listeners. So this method really adds l to the linked list of action listeners that a multicaster is managing, and saves the new list.

But that begs the question: where does the multicaster come from? The linked list has to start somewhere. This is where the second trick comes in. add() is a static method, so we don't need a multicaster to call it. But we still need some way to start the linked list. The class's constructor is never called—in fact, it's protected, so you can't call it. The answer lies in the add() method, which creates an AWTEventMulticaster when you need it—that is, as soon as you add the second listener to the list. The arguments to add() may be null; one of them probably is null when you register your first action listener.

Removing action listeners works the same way. We use the AWTEventMulticaster's remove() method. After the last listener is taken off the linked list, remove() returns null.

With this machinery in place, sending an event to all registered listeners is very simple. You just create an event by calling its constructor, and then call the appropriate method in the listener interface to deliver it. The AWTEventMulticaster

makes sure that the event gets to all the listeners. In this example, we create an
ActionEvent and deliver the event to the listeners' actionPerformed() methods by
calling actionListener.actionPerformed(event).

The code to generate other kinds of events is almost exactly the same. Remember
the multicaster implements all the listener interfaces and has overloaded add()
and remove() methods for every standard listener type. Therefore, it can be used
for any kind of AWTEvent. It shouldn't be hard to adapt this example to other situations.

What if you want to generate your own event type by subclassing AWTEvent? To
make things concrete, let's say you want to create an ExplosionEvent that you generate whenever your monitor catches fire. In this case, you should define your own
ExplosionListener interface and (possibly) your own ExplosionAdapter class. You
can't use the AWTEventMulticaster unless your new event is a subclass of a standard event; extending the multicaster to support new event types probably isn't
worth the effort. It's easier to write an addExplosionListener() method that maintains a Vector of listeners and to deliver events by calling the appropriate method
of each listener in the Vector. We'll demonstrate this approach in the next section, where we implement another new component: a Dial.

A Dial Component

The standard AWT classes don't have a component that's similar to an old fash-
ioned dial—for example, the volume control on your radio. Such a component is
something of a rarity; I don't remember seeing one used recently. But that's all the
more reason to build one. In this section, we implement a Dial class. We also
define a new event type, DialEvent, and a new listener interface, DialListener.
The dial can be used just like any other Java component. It is built entirely in Java
and, therefore, is a lightweight component; it extends Component directly and
doesn't have a native peer.

We will create the new event type used in this example mainly as an exercise. It
might make more sense for our dial to use the standard AdjustmentEvent (and
probably to implement the Adjustable interface as well). However, this gives us a
chance to show how to handle event listeners without using the AWT event multicaster. There are many situations in which defining a new event type is the appropriate solution.

Figure 14-12 shows what the dial looks like; it is followed by the code.

```
import java.awt.*;
import java.awt.event.*;
import java.util.*;

public interface DialListener extends EventListener {
```

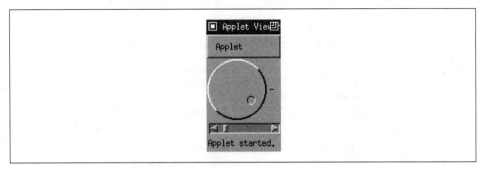

Figure 14–12: The Dial component

```
    void dialAdjusted( DialEvent e );
}

public class DialEvent extends EventObject {
        int value;

        DialEvent( Dial source, int value ) {
                super( source );
                this.value = value;
        }
        public int getValue() {
                return value;
        }
}

public class Dial extends Component {
        int minValue = 0, value, maxValue = 100, radius;
        Vector dialListeners;

        public Dial() {
                enableEvents( AWTEvent.MOUSE_MOTION_EVENT_MASK );
        }
        public Dial( int maxValue ) {
                this();
                this.maxValue = maxValue;
        }

        public void paint( Graphics g ) {
                int tick = 10;
                radius = getSize().width/2 - tick;
                g.drawLine(radius*2+tick/2, radius, radius*2+tick, radius);
                draw3DCircle( g, 0, 0, radius, true );
                draw3DCircle( g, 1, 1, radius-1, true );
                int knobRadius = radius/7;
                double th = value*(2*Math.PI)/(maxValue-minValue);
                int x = (int)(Math.cos(th)*(radius-knobRadius*3)),
                        y = (int)(Math.sin(th)*(radius-knobRadius*3));
                draw3DCircle( g, x+radius-knobRadius, y+radius-knobRadius,
                        knobRadius, false );
```

```java
        }


        private void draw3DCircle( Graphics g, int x, int y,
                                   int radius, boolean raised ) {
                g.setColor( raised ? Color.white : Color.black );
                g.drawArc( x, y, radius*2, radius*2, 45, 180);
                g.setColor( raised ? Color.black : Color.white);
                g.drawArc( x, y, radius*2, radius*2, 225, 180);
        }


        public void processEvent( AWTEvent e ) {
                if ( e.getID() == MouseEvent.MOUSE_DRAGGED ) {
                        int y=((MouseEvent)e).getY();
                        int x=((MouseEvent)e).getX();
                        double th = Math.atan( (1.0*y-radius)/(x-radius) );
                        int value=((int)(th/(2*Math.PI)*(maxValue-minValue)));
                        if ( x < radius )
                                setValue( value + maxValue/2 );
                        else if ( y < radius )
                                setValue( value + maxValue );
                        else
                                setValue( value );
                        fireEvent();
                }
                super.processEvent( e );
        }


        public Dimension getPreferredSize() {
                return new Dimension( 100, 100 );
        }

public void setValue(int value) {
                this.value = value;
                repaint();
        }
public int getValue()   { return value; }
public void setMinimum(int minValue )   { this.minValue = this.minValue; }
public int getMinimum()   { return minValue; }
public void setMaximum(int maxValue )   { this.maxValue = maxValue; }
public int getMaximum()   { return maxValue; }

        public void addDialListener(DialListener listener) {
                if ( dialListeners == null )
                        dialListeners = new Vector();
                dialListeners.addElement( listener );
        }
        public void removeDialListener(DialListener listener) {
                if ( dialListeners != null )
                        dialListeners.removeElement( listener );
        }
        private void fireEvent() {
                if ( dialListeners == null )
                        return;
```

```
                    DialEvent event = new DialEvent(this, value);
                    for (Enumeration e = dialListeners.elements();
                                     e.hasMoreElements(); )
                          ((DialListener)e.nextElement()).dialAdjusted( event );
         }
    }

    public class DialApplet extends java.applet.Applet
                        implements DialListener, AdjustmentListener {
        final int max = 100;
        Scrollbar scrollbar = new Scrollbar( Scrollbar.HORIZONTAL, 0, 1, 0, max );
        Dial dial = new Dial( max );
        public void init() {
            setLayout( new BorderLayout() );
            dial.addDialListener( this );
            add( "Center", dial );
            scrollbar.addAdjustmentListener( this );
            add( "South", scrollbar );
        }
        public void dialAdjusted( DialEvent e ) {
            scrollbar.setValue( e.getValue() );
        }
        public void adjustmentValueChanged( AdjustmentEvent e ) {
            dial.setValue( e.getValue() );
        }
    }
```

Let's start from the top. We'll focus on the event handling and leave you to figure out the trigonometry on your own. The DialListener interface contains a single method, dialAdjusted(), which is called when a DialEvent occurs. The DialListener interface extends java.util.EventListener, which defines no methods, but serves as a flag that implementers of the interface are a type of event receiver. The DialEvent itself is simple. It carries one item of data: the dial's new value. It has a single "get" method that returns this value. Note that our event is not a subtype of java.awt.AWTEvent, but of the more general event base class java.util.EventObject. If we had wanted to, we could have subclassed a standard AWT event and specialized it.

The constructor for the Dial class stores the dial's maximum value; its minimum defaults to 0. It then enables mouse motion events, which the Dial needs to tell how it is being manipulated.

paint(), draw3DCircle(), and processEvent() do a lot of trigonometry to figure out how to display the dial. draw3DCircle() is a private helper method that draws a circle that appears either raised or depressed; we use this to make the dial look three dimensional. processEvent() is called whenever any event occurs within the component's area. We only expect to receive mouse motion events, because these are the only events we enabled. processEvent() first checks the AWT event's ID; if it is MOUSE_DRAGGED, the user has changed the dial's setting. We respond by computing a new value for the dial, repainting the dial in its new position, and firing a DialEvent. Any other events (in particular, MOUSE_MOVED) are ignored. However, we call the superclass's processEvent() method to make sure that any other processing needed for this event occurs.

The next group of methods provide ways to retrieve or change the dial's current setting and the minimum and maximum values. They are similar to the methods in the Adjustable interface; again, you could argue that Dial really ought to implement Adjustable. But the important thing to notice here is the pattern of "getter" and "setter" methods for all of the important values used by the Dial. We will talk more about this in Chapter 18 when we discuss JavaBeans.

Finally, we reach the methods that work with listeners. addDialListener() adds a new listener to a Vector of listeners by calling addElement(). If the vector doesn't already exist, addDialListener() creates it. removeDialListener() simply takes a listener off the list so that it won't receive any further events. fireEvent() is a private method that creates a DialEvent and sends it to every listener. It does so by converting the Vector into an Enumeration and running through every element in the list by calling nextElement() until hasMoreElements() returns false. To send the event to a listener, it calls the listener's dialAdjusted() method. Note that nextElement() returns an Object; we must cast this object to DialListener before we can deliver the event.

To show how the applet is used, I included a simple applet called DialApplet. This applet places a Dial and a Scrollbar in a border layout. Any change to either the dial or the scrollbar is reflected by the other. The applet implements both Dial-Listener and AdjustmentListener and therefore has both dialAdjusted() and adjustmentValueChanged() methods. Although this isn't a good argument for creating new event types, it's worth noticing that the logic of the listener methods is much simpler than it would have been if the dial generated its own adjustment events. You could achieve the same benefit without creating new events by simply defining additional event listener interfaces. Remember that event receivers are strongly typed, and their types are determined by the listener interfaces that they implement.

15

Layout Managers

A layout manager arranges the child components of a container, as shown in Figure 15-1. It positions and sets the size of components within the container's display area according to a particular layout scheme. The layout manager's job is to fit the components into the available area while maintaining the proper spatial relationships between the components. AWT comes with a few standard layout managers that will collectively handle most situations; you can make your own layout managers if you have special requirements.

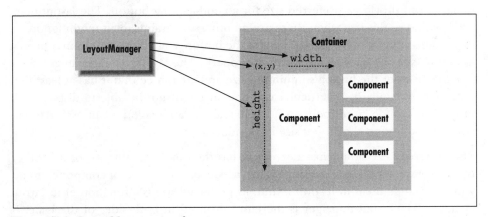

Figure 15–1: LayoutManager at work

Every container has a default layout manager; therefore, when you make a new container, it comes with a LayoutManager object of the appropriate type. You can install a new layout manager at any time with the setLayout() method. We set the layout manager of a container to a BorderLayout:

```
setLayout ( new BorderLayout() );
```

Notice that we call the BorderLayout constructor, but we don't even save a reference to the layout manager. This is typical; once you have installed a layout manager, it does its work behind the scenes, interacting with the container. You rarely call the layout manager's methods directly, so you don't usually need a reference (a notable exception is CardLayout). However, you do need to know what the layout manager is going to do with your components as you work with them.

The LayoutManager is consulted whenever a container's doLayout() method is called (usually when it is validated) to reorganize the contents. It does its job by calling the setLocation() and setBounds() methods of the individual child components to arrange them in the container's display area. A container is laid out the first time it is displayed, and thereafter whenever the container's validate() method is called. Containers that are a subclass of the Window class (which include Frame) are automatically validated whenever they are packed or resized. Calling pack() sets the window's size so it is as small as possible while holding all its components at their preferred sizes.

Every component determines three important pieces of information used by the layout manager in placing and sizing it: a minimum size, a maximum size, and a preferred size. These are reported by the getMinimumSize(), getMaximumSize(), and getPreferredSize() methods of Component, respectively. For example, a plain Button object can normally be sized to any proportions. However, the button's designer can provide a preferred size for a good-looking button. The layout manager might use this size when there are no other constraints, or it might ignore it, depending on its scheme. Now if we give the button a label, the button may need a minimum size in order to display itself properly. The layout manager might show more respect for the button's minimum size and guarantee that it has at least that much space. Similarly, a particular component might not be able to display itself properly if it is too large (perhaps it has to scale up an image); it can use getMaximumSize() to report the largest size it considers acceptable.[*]

The preferred size of a Container object has the same meaning as for any other type of component. However, since a Container may hold its own components and want to arrange them in its own layout, its preferred size is a function of its layout manager. The layout manager is therefore involved in both sides of the issue. It asks the components in its container for their preferred (or minimum) sizes in order to arrange them. Based on those values, it calculates the preferred size that is reported by its own container to that container's parent.

---

[*] Unfortunately, the current set of layout managers doesn't do anything with the maximum size. This may change in a future release.

When a layout manager is called to arrange its components, it is working within a fixed area. It usually begins by looking at its container's dimensions, and the preferred or minimum sizes of the child components. It then doles out screen area and sets the sizes of components according to its scheme. You can override the getMinimumSize(), getMaximumSize(), and getPreferredSize() methods of a component, but you should do this only if you are actually specializing the component, and it has new needs. If you find yourself fighting with a layout manager because it's changing the size of one of your components, you are probably using the wrong kind of layout manager or not composing your user interface properly. Remember that it's possible to use a number of Panel objects in a given display, where each one has its own LayoutManager. Try breaking down the problem: place related components in their own Panel and then arrange the panels in the container. When that becomes too complicated, you can choose to use a constraint-based layout manager like GridBagLayout, which we'll discuss later in this chapter.

FlowLayout

FlowLayout is a simple layout manager that tries to arrange components with their preferred sizes, from left to right and top to bottom in the display. A FlowLayout can have a specified justification of LEFT, CENTER, or RIGHT, and a fixed horizontal and vertical padding. By default, a flow layout uses CENTER justification, meaning that all components are centered within the area allotted to them. FlowLayout is the default for Panel components like Applet.

The following applet adds five buttons using the default FlowLayout; the result is shown in Figure 15-2.

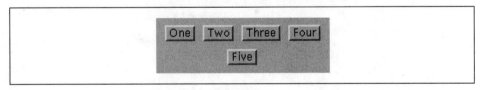

Figure 15–2: A flow layout

```
import java.awt.*;

public class Flow extends java.applet.Applet {
    public void init() {
        // Default for Applet is FlowLayout
        add( new Button("One") );
        add( new Button("Two") );
        add( new Button("Three") );
        add( new Button("Four") );
```

```
                add( new Button("Five") );
        }
    }
```

If the applet is small enough, some of the buttons spill over to a second or third row.

GridLayout

GridLayout arranges components into regularly spaced rows and columns. The components are arbitrarily resized to fit in the resulting areas; their minimum and preferred sizes are consequently ignored. GridLayout is most useful for arranging very regular, identically sized objects and for allocating space for Panels to hold other layouts in each region of the container.

GridLayout takes the number of rows and columns in its constructor. If you subsequently give it too many objects to manage, it adds extra columns to make the objects fit. You can also set the number of rows or columns to zero, which means that you don't care how many elements the layout manager packs in that dimension. For example, GridLayout(2,0) requests a layout with two rows and an unlimited number of columns; if you put ten components into this layout, you'll get two rows of five columns each.

The following applet sets a GridLayout with three rows and two columns as its layout manager; the results are shown in Figure 15-3.

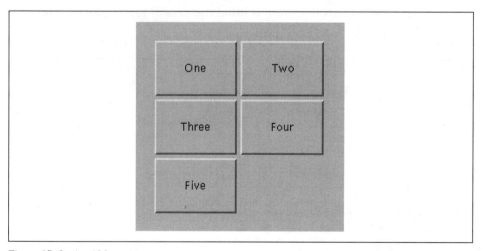

Figure 15–3: A grid layout

```
import java.awt.*;

public class Grid extends java.applet.Applet {
    public void init() {
        setLayout( new GridLayout( 3, 2 ));
        add( new Button("One") );
        add( new Button("Two") );
        add( new Button("Three") );
        add( new Button("Four") );
        add( new Button("Five") );
    }
}
```

The five buttons are laid out, in order, from left to right, top to bottom, with one empty spot.

BorderLayout

BorderLayout is a little more interesting. It tries to arrange objects in one of five geographical locations: "North," "South," "East," "West," and "Center," possibly with some padding between. BorderLayout is the default layout for Window and Frame objects. Because each component is associated with a direction, BorderLayout can manage at most five components; it squashes or stretches those components to fit its constraints. As we'll see in the second example, this means that you often want to have BorderLayout manage sets of components in their own panels.

When we add a component to a border layout, we need to specify both the component and the position at which to add it. To do so, we use an overloaded version of the add() method that takes an additional argument as a constraint. This additional argument is passed to the layout manager when the new component is added. In this case it specifies the name of a position within the BorderLayout. Otherwise the LayoutManager is not consulted until it's asked to lay out the components.

The following applet sets a BorderLayout layout and adds our five buttons again, named for their locations; the result is shown in Figure 15-4.

```
import java.awt.*;

public class Border extends java.applet.Applet {
    public void init() {
        setLayout( new java.awt.BorderLayout() );
        add( new Button("North"), "North" );
        add( new Button("East"), "East" );
        add( new Button("South"), "South" );
        add( new Button("West"), "West" );
        add( new Button("Center"), "Center" );
    }
}
```

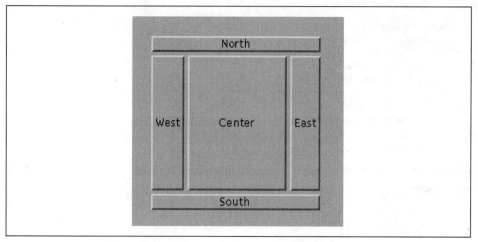

Figure 15–4: A border layout

So, how exactly is the area divided up? Well, the objects at "North" and "South" get their preferred height and are expanded to fill the full area horizontally. "East" and "West" components, on the other hand, get their preferred width, and are expanded to fill the remaining area between "North" and "South" vertically. Finally, the "Center" object takes all of the rest of the space. As you can see in Figure 15-4, our buttons get distorted into interesting shapes.

What if we don't want `BorderLayout` messing with the sizes of our components? One option would be to put each button in its own `Panel`. The default layout for a `Panel` is `FlowLayout`, which respects the preferred size of components. The preferred sizes of the panels are effectively the preferred sizes of the buttons, but if the panels are stretched, they won't pull their buttons with them. `Border2` illustrates this approach as shown in Figure 15-5.

```
import java.awt.*;

public class Border2 extends java.applet.Applet {
    public void init() {
        setLayout( new BorderLayout() );
        Panel p = new Panel();
        p.add(new Button("East") );
        add( p, "East" );
        p = new Panel();
        p.add(new Button("West") );
        add( p, "West" ;
        p = new Panel();
        p.add(new Button("North") );
        add( p, "North" );
        p = new Panel();
        p.add(new Button("South") );
```

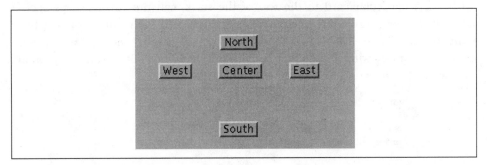

Figure 15–5: Another border layout

```
        add(p, "South" );
        p = new Panel();
        p.add(new Button("Center") );
        add( p, "Center" );
    }
}
```

In this example, we create a number of panels, put our buttons inside the panels, and put the panels into the applet, which has the BorderLayout manager. Now, the Panel for the "Center" button soaks up the extra space that comes from the BorderLayout. Each Panel's FlowLayout centers the button in the panel and uses the button's preferred size. In this case, it's all a bit awkward. (This is one of the problems that getMaximumSize() will eventually solve.) We'll see how we could accomplish this more directly using GridBagLayout shortly.

Finally, this version of the applet has a lot of unused space. If we wanted, we could get rid of the extra space by resizing the applet:

```
    setSize( getPreferredSize() );
```

CardLayout

CardLayout is a special layout manager for creating the effect of a stack of cards. Instead of arranging all of the container's components, it displays only one at a time. You would use this kind of layout to implement a hypercard stack or a Windows-style set of configuration screens. When you add a component to the layout, you use the two-argument version of add(); the extra argument is an arbitrary string that serves as the card's name:

```
    add("netconfigscreen", myComponent);
```

To bring a particular card to the top of the stack, call the CardLayout's show() method with two arguments: the parent Container and the name of the card you want to show. There are also methods like first(), last(), next(), and previous() for working with the stack of cards. These methods take a single argument: the parent Container. Here's a simple example:

```
import java.awt.*;

public class main extends java.applet.Applet {
        CardLayout cards = new CardLayout();

        public void init() {
                setLayout( cards );
                add( new Button("one"), "one" );
                add( new Button("two"), "two" );
                add( new Button("three"), "three" );
        }

        public boolean action( Event e, Object arg) {
                cards.next( this );
                return true;
        }
}
```

We add three buttons to the layout and cycle through them as they are pressed. In a more realistic example, we would build a group of panels, each of which might implement some part of a complex user interface, and add those panels to the layout. Each panel would have its own layout manager. The panels would be resized to fill the entire area available (i.e., the area of the Container they are in), and their individual layout managers would arrange their internal components.

GridBagLayout

GridBagLayout is a very flexible layout manager that allows you to position components relative to one another using constraints. With GridBagLayout (and a fair amount of effort), you can create almost any imaginable layout. Components are arranged at logical coordinates on a abstract grid. We'll call them "logical" coordinates because they really designate positions in the space of rows and columns formed by the set of components. Rows and columns of the grid stretch to different sizes, based on the sizes and constraints of the components they hold.

A row or column in a GridBagLayout expands to accommodate the dimensions and constraints of the largest component in its ranks. Individual components may span more than one row or column. Components that aren't as large as their grid cell can be anchored within their cell. They can also be set to fill or expand their area in either dimension. Extra area in the grid rows and columns can be parceled out according to the weight constraints of the components. Therefore, you can control how various components will grow and stretch when a window is resized.

GridBagLayout is much easier to use in a graphical, WYSIWYG GUI builder environment. That's because working with GridBag is kind of like messing with the "rabbit ears" antennae on your television. It's not particularly difficult to get the results that you want through trial and error, but writing out hard and fast rules for how to go about it is difficult. In short, GridBagLayout is complex and has some quirks. It is also simply a bit ugly both in model and implementation. Remember that you can do a lot with nested panels and by composing simpler layout managers within one another. If you look back through this chapter, you'll see many examples of composite layouts; it's up to you to determine how far you should go before making the break from simpler layout managers to a more complex "do it all in one" layout manager like GridBagLayout.

GridBagConstraints

Having said that GridBagLayout is complex and a bit ugly, I'm going to contradict myself and say that it's surprisingly simple. There is only one constructor with no arguments (GridBagLayout()), and there aren't a lot of fancy methods to control how the display works.

The appearance of a grid bag layout is controlled by sets of GridBagConstraints, and that's where things get hairy. Each component managed by a GridBagLayout is associated with a GridBagConstraints object. GridBagConstraints holds the following variables, which we'll describe in detail shortly:

int gridx, gridy
> Controls the position of the component on the layout's grid.

int weightx, weighty
> Controls how additional space in the row or column is allotted to the component.

int fill
> Controls whether the component expands to fill the space allocated to it.

int gridheight, gridwidth
> Controls the number of rows or columns the component occupies.

int anchor
> Controls the position of the component if there is extra room within the space allocated for it.

int ipadx, ipady
   Controls padding between the component and the borders of its area.

Insets insets
   Controls padding between the component and neighboring components.

To make a set of constraints for a component or components, you simply create a new instance of GridBagConstraints and set these public variables to the appropriate values. There are no pretty constructors, and there's not much else to the class at all.

The easiest way to associate a set of constraints with a component is to use the version of add() that takes a layout object as an argument, in addition to the component itself. This puts the component in the container and associates your GridBagConstraints object with it:

```
Component component = new Label("constrain me, please...");
GridBagConstraints constraints = new GridBagConstraints;
constraints.gridx = x;
constraints.gridy = y;
...
add( component, constraints );
```

You can also add a component to a GridBagLayout by using the single argument add() method, and then later calling the layout's setConstraints() method directly, to pass it the GridBagConstraints object for that component:

```
add( component );
...
myGridBagLayout.setConstraints( component, constraints );
```

In either case, the set of constraints is copied when it is applied to the component. Therefore, you're free to create a single set of GridBagConstraints, modify it as needed, and apply it as needed to different objects. You might find it helpful to create a helper method that sets the constraints appropriately, then adds the method with its constraints to the layout. That's the approach we'll take in our examples; our helper method is called addGB(), and it takes a component plus a pair of coordinates as arguments. These coordinates become the gridx and gridy values for the constraints. We could expand upon this later and overload addGB() to take more parameters for other constraints that we often change from component to component.

Grid Coordinates

One of the biggest surprises in the GridBagLayout is that there's no way to specify the size of the grid. There doesn't have to be. The grid size is determined implicitly by the constraints of all the objects; the layout manager picks dimensions large enough so that everything fits. Thus, if you put one component in a layout and set its gridx and gridy constraints to 25, the layout manager creates a 25 x 25 grid, with rows and columns both numbered from 0 to 24. If you add a second component with a gridx of 30 and a gridy of 13, the grid's dimensions change to 30 x 25. You don't have to worry about setting up an appropriate number of rows and columns. The layout manager does it automatically, as you add components.

With this knowledge, we're ready to create some simple displays. We'll start by arranging a group of components in a cross shape. We maintain explicit x and y local variables, setting them as we add the components to our grid. This is partly for clarity, but it can be a handy technique when you want to add a number of components in a row or column. You can simply increment gridx or gridy before adding each component. This is a simple and problem-free way to achieve relative placement. (Later, we'll describe GridBagConstraints's RELATIVE constant, which does relative placement automatically.) Here's our first layout (see Figure 15-6).

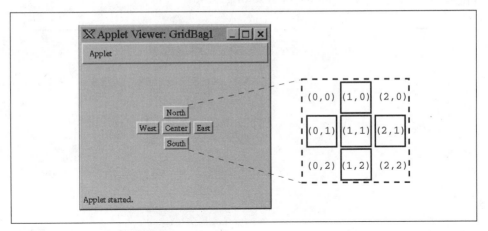

Figure 15–6: A simple GridBag layout

```
import java.awt.*;
public class GridBag1 extends java.applet.Applet {
    GridBagConstraints constraints = new GridBagConstraints();
    void addGB( Component component, int x, int y ) {
        constraints.gridx = x;
                constraints.gridy = y;
        add ( component, constraints );
    }

    public void init() {
        setLayout( new GridBagLayout() );
        int x, y;  // for clarity
        addGB( new Button("North"),  x=1,y=0 );
```

```
        addGB( new Button("West"),   x=0,y=1 );
        addGB( new Button("Center"), x=1,y=1 );
        addGB( new Button("East"),   x=2,y=1 );
        addGB( new Button("South"),  x=1,y=2 );
    }
}
```

You probably noticed that the buttons in this example are "clumped" together in the center of their display area. Each button is displayed at its preferred size, without stretching the button to fill the available space. This is how the layout manager behaves when the "weight" constraints are left unset. We'll talk more about weights in the next two sections.

Fill

Let's make the buttons expand to fill the entire applet. To do so, we must take two steps: we must set the fill constraint for each button to the value BOTH, and we must set the weightx and weighty values to a nonzero value, as shown in the applet below. Figure 15-7 shows the resulting layout.

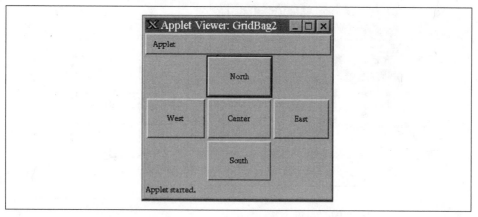

Figure 15–7: Using fill to make buttons fill the available space

```
        public void init() {
            setLayout( new GridBagLayout() );
            constraints.weightx = 1.0;
            constraints.weighty = 1.0;
            constraints.fill = GridBagConstraints.BOTH;
            int x, y;  // for clarity
            addGB( new Button("North"),  x=1,y=0 );
            addGB( new Button("West"),   x=0,y=1 );
            addGB( new Button("Center"), x=1,y=1 );
            addGB( new Button("East"),   x=2,y=1 );
            addGB( new Button("South"),  x=1,y=2 );
        }
```

BOTH is one of the constants of the GridBagConstraints class; it tells the component to fill the available space in both directions. Here is a list of the constants that you can use to set the fill field:

HORIZONTAL

Fill the available horizontal space.

VERTICAL

Fill the available vertical space.

BOTH

Fill the available space in both directions.

NONE

Don't fill the available space; display the component at its preferred size.

We set the weight constraints to 1.0; in this example it doesn't matter what they are, provided that each component has the same nonzero weight. fill doesn't happen if the component weights in the direction you're filling are 0, which is the default value.

Spanning Rows and Columns

One of the most important features of GridBaglayout is that it lets you create arrangements in which components span two or more rows or columns. To do so, you set the gridwidth and gridheight variables of the GridBagConstraints. Here's an applet that creates such a display; button one spans two columns vertically, and button four spans two horizontally (see Figure 15-8):

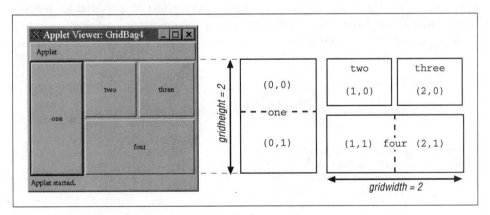

Figure 15–8: Making components span rows and columns

```
public void init() {
    setLayout( new GridBagLayout() );
    constraints.weightx = 1.0;
```

```
      constraints.weighty = 1.0;
      constraints.fill = GridBagConstraints.BOTH;
      int x, y;  // for clarity
      constraints.gridheight = 2; // Span two rows
      addGB( new Button("one"),   x=0, y=0 );
      constraints.gridheight = 1; // set it back
      addGB( new Button("two"),   x=1, y=0 );
      addGB( new Button("three"), x=2, y=0 );
      constraints.gridwidth = 2; // Span two columns
      addGB( new Button("four"),  x=1, y=1 );
      constraints.gridwidth = 1; // set it back
  }
```

The size of each element is controlled by the gridwidth and gridheight values of its constraints. For button one, we set gridheight to 2. Therefore, it is two cells high; its gridx and gridy positions are both zero, so it occupies cell (0,0) and the cell directly below it, (0,1). Likewise, button four has a gridwidth of 2 and a gridheight of 1, so it occupies two cells horizontally. We place this button in cell (1,1), so it occupies that cell and its neighbor, (2,1).

In this example, we set the fill to BOTH and weightx and weighty to 1 for all components. By doing so, we told each button to occupy all the space available. Strictly speaking, this isn't necessary. However, it makes it easier to see exactly how much space each button occupies.

Weighting

The weightx and weighty variables of a GridBagConstraints object determine how "extra" space in the container is distributed among the columns or rows in the layout. As long as you keep things simple, the effect these variables have is fairly intuitive: the larger the weight, the greater the amount of space allocated to the component. Figure 15-9 shows what happens if we vary the weightx constraint from 0.1 to 1.0 as we place three buttons in a row.

```
  public void init() {
      setLayout( new GridBagLayout() );
      constraints.fill = GridBagConstraints.BOTH;
      constraints.weighty = 1.0;
      int x, y; // for clarity
      constraints.weightx = 0.1;
      addGB( new Button("one"),   x=0, y=0 );
      constraints.weightx = 0.5;
      addGB( new Button("two"),    ++x, y );
      constraints.weightx = 1.0;
      addGB( new Button("three"), ++x, y );
  }
```

The specific values of the weights are not meaningful; it is only their proportions

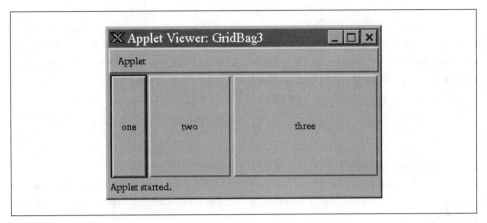

Figure 15–9: Using weight to control component size

relative to one another that matter. After the preferred sizes of the components (including padding and insets—see below) are determined, any extra space is dolled out in proportion to the component's weights. So, for example, if each of our three components had the same weight each would receive a third of the extra space. To make this more obvious, you may prefer to have your weights in a row or column add to 1 when possible. Components with a weight of 0 receive no extra space.

The situation is a bit more complicated when there are multiple rows or columns and when there is even the possibility of components spanning more than one cell. In the general case, GridBagLayout calculates an effective overall weight for each for each row and each column and then distributes the extra space to them proportionally. Note that our single row example above is just a special case where the columns each have one component. The gory details of the calculations follow.

Calculating the weights of rows and columns

For a given row or column, GridBagLayout first considers the weights of all of the components contained strictly within that rank—ignoring those that span more than one cell. The greatest individual weight becomes the overall weight of the row or column. Intuitively this means that GridBagLayout is trying to accomodate the needs of the weightiest component in that rank. Next, GridBagLayout considers the components that occupy more than one cell. Here things get a little weird. GridbagLayout wants to evaluate them like the others, to see if they affect the determination of the largest weight in a row or column. However, because these components occupy more than one cell, GridBagLayout divides their weight among the ranks (rows or columns) that they span. GridBagLayout tries to calculate an effective weight for the portion of the component that occupies each of its rows or columns. It does this by trying to divide the weight of the component among the ranks in the same proportions that the length (or height) of the component will be shared by the ranks. But how does it know what the proportions will be before the whole grid is determined? That's what it's trying to calculate after all. It simply guesses based on the row or column weights already determined. GridbagLayout uses the weights determined by the first round of calculations to split up the weight of the component over the ranks that it occupies. For each row or column, it then considers that fraction of the weight to be the component's weight for that rank. That weight then contends for the "heaviest weight" in the row or column, possibly changing the overall weight of that row or column, as we described earlier.

Anchoring

If a component is smaller than the space available for it, it is centered by default. But centering isn't the only possibility. The anchor constraint tells a grid bag layout how to position a component within its space. Possible values are: GridBagConstraints.CENTER, NORTH, NORTHEAST, EAST, SOUTHEAST, SOUTH, SOUTHWEST, WEST, and NORTHWEST. For example, an anchor of GridBagConstraints.NORTH centers a component at the top of its display area; SOUTHEAST places a component at the bottom left of its area.

Padding and Insets

Another way to control the behavior of a component in a grid bag layout is to use padding and insets. Padding is determined by the ipadx and ipady fields of GridBagConstraints. They specify additional horizontal and vertical space that is added to the component when it is placed in its cell. In Figure 15-10, the West button is larger because we have set the ipadx and ipady values of its constraints to 25. Therefore, the layout manager gets the button's preferred size and adds 25 pixels in each direction to determine the button's actual size. The sizes of the other buttons are unchanged because their padding is set to 0 (the default), but their spacing is different. The West button is unnaturally tall, which means that the middle row of the layout must be taller than the others.

```
public void init() {
    setLayout( new GridBagLayout() );
    int x, y;  // for clarity
    addGB( new Button("North"),   x=1,y=0 );
    constraints.ipadx = 25;   // set padding
    constraints.ipady = 25;
    addGB( new Button("West"),    x=0,y=1 );
    constraints.ipadx = 0;    // set padding back
```

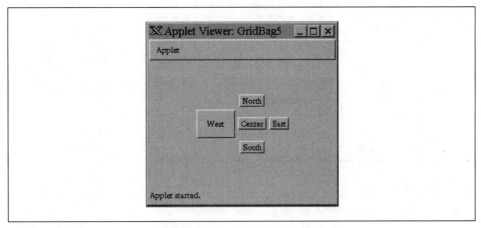

Figure 15–10: Layout using padding and insets

```
        constraints.ipady = 0;
        addGB( new Button("Center"), x=1,y=1 );
        addGB( new Button("East"),   x=2,y=1 );
        addGB( new Button("South"),  x=1,y=2 );
    }
```

Notice that the horizontal padding, ipadx, is added on both the left and right sides of the button. Therefore, the button grows horizontally by twice the value of ipadx. Likewise, the vertical padding, ipady, is added on both the top and the bottom.

Insets add space between the edges of the component and its cell. They are stored in the insets field of GridBagConstraints, which is an Insets object. An Insets object has four fields, to specify the margins on the top, bottom, left, and right of the component. The relationship between insets and padding can be confusing. As shown in Figure 15-11, padding is added to the component itself, increasing its size. Insets are external to the component and represent the margin between the component and its cell.

Padding and weighting have an odd interaction with each other. If you use padding, it is best to use the default weightx and weighty values for each component.

Relative Positioning

In all of our grid bag layouts so far, we have specified the gridx and gridy coordinates of each component explicitly using its constraints. Another alternative is *relative positioning.*

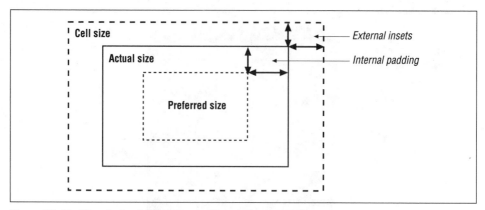

Figure 15–11: The relationship between padding and insets

Conceptually, relative positioning is simple: we simply say "put this component to the left of (or below) the previous component." To do so, set gridx or gridy to the constant GridBagConstraints.RELATIVE. Unfortunately, it's not as simple as this. Here are a couple of warnings:

- To place a component to the right of the previous one, set gridx to RELATIVE *and* use the same value for gridy as you used for the previous component.

- Similarly, to place a component below the previous one, set gridy to RELATIVE *and* leave gridx unchanged.

- Setting both gridx and gridy to RELATIVE places all the components in one row, not in a diagonal line, as you would expect. (This is the default.)

In other words, if gridx or gridy is RELATIVE, you had better leave the other value unchanged. RELATIVE makes it easy to arrange a lot of components in a row or a column. That's what it was intended for; if you try to do something else, you're fighting against the layout manager, not working with it.

GridBagLayout allows another kind of relative positioning, in which you specify where, in a row or a column, the component should be placed. To do so, you use the gridwidth and gridheight fields of GridBagConstraints. Setting either of these to the constant REMAINDER says that the component should be the last item in its row or column, and therefore should occupy all the remaining space. Setting either gridwidth or gridheight to RELATIVE says that it should be the second to the last item in its row or column. Obviously, you can use these constants to create constraints that can't possibly be met; for example, you can say that two components must be the last component in a row. In these cases, the layout manager tries to do something reasonable—but it will almost certainly do something you don't want. Again, relative placement works well as long as you don't try to twist it into doing something it wasn't designed for.

Composite Layouts

Sometimes things don't fall neatly into little boxes. This is true of layouts as well as life. For example, if you want to use some of GridBagLayout's weighting features for part of your GUI, you could create separate layouts for different parts of the GUI and combine them with yet another layout. That's how we'll build the pocket calculator interface in Figure 15-12. We will use three grid bag layouts: one for the first row of buttons (C, %, +), one for the last (0, ., =), and one for the applet itself. The master layout (the applet's) manages the text field we use for the display, the panels containing the first and last rows of buttons, and the twelve buttons in the middle.*

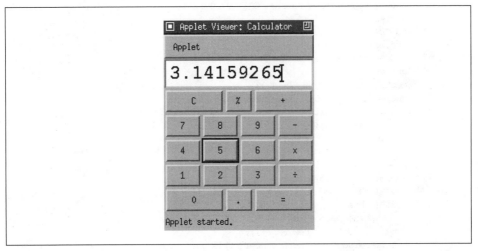

Figure 15–12: The Calculator applet

Here's the code for the Calculator applet. It implements only the user interface (i.e., the keyboard); it collects everything you type in the display field, until you press C (clear). Figuring out how to connect the GUI to some other code that would perform the operations is up to you. One strategy would be to send an event to the object that does the computation whenever the user presses the equals sign. That object could read the contents of the text field, parse it, do the computation, and display the results.

```
import java.awt.*;
import java.awt.event.*;
public class Calculator extends java.applet.Applet
                    implements ContainerListener, ActionListener {
```

---

* If you're curious, this calculator is based on the ELORG-801, which I found in an online "calculator museum"; see *http://www.geocities.com/CapeCanaveral/6747/elorg801.jpg*.

```java
GridBagConstraints gbc = new GridBagConstraints(); {
    gbc.weightx = 1.0;  gbc.weighty = 1.0;
    gbc.fill = GridBagConstraints.BOTH;
}
TextField theDisplay = new TextField();
public void init() {
    setFont( new Font("Monospaced", Font.BOLD, 24) );
    addContainerListener( this );
    gbc.gridwidth=4;
    addGB( this, theDisplay, 0, 0 );
    // make the top row
    Panel topRow = new Panel();
    topRow.addContainerListener( this );
    gbc.gridwidth = 1;
    gbc.weightx = 1.0;
    addGB( topRow, new Button("C"), 0, 0 );
    gbc.weightx = 0.33;
    addGB( topRow, new Button("%"), 1, 0 );
    gbc.weightx = 1.0;
    addGB( topRow, new Button("+"), 2, 0 );
    gbc.gridwidth = 4;
    addGB( this, topRow, 0, 1 );
    gbc.weightx = 1.0;  gbc.gridwidth = 1;
    // make the digits
    for(int j=0; j<3; j++)
        for(int i=0; i<3; i++)
            addGB( this, new Button( "" + ((2-j)*3+i+1) ), i, j+2 );
    // -, x, and divide
    addGB( this, new Button("-"), 3, 2 );
    addGB( this, new Button("x"), 3, 3 );
    addGB( this, new Button("\u00F7"), 3, 4 );
    // make the bottom row
    Panel bottomRow = new Panel();
    bottomRow.addContainerListener( this );
    gbc.weightx = 1.0;
    addGB( bottomRow, new Button("0"), 0, 0 );
    gbc.weightx = 0.33;
    addGB( bottomRow, new Button("."), 1, 0 );
    gbc.weightx = 1.0;
    addGB( bottomRow, new Button("="), 2, 0 );
    gbc.gridwidth = 4;
    addGB( this, bottomRow, 0, 5 );
}
private void addGB( Container cont, Component comp, int x, int y  ) {
    if ( ! (cont.getLayout() instanceof GridBagLayout) )
        cont.setLayout( new GridBagLayout() );
    gbc.gridx = x;  gbc.gridy = y;
    cont.add( comp, gbc );
}
public void componentAdded( ContainerEvent e ) {
    Component comp = e.getChild();
    if ( comp instanceof Button )
        ((Button)comp).addActionListener( this );
}
```

```
            public void componentRemoved( ContainerEvent e ) { }
            public void actionPerformed( ActionEvent e ) {
                if ( e.getActionCommand().equals("C") )
                    theDisplay.setText( "" );
                else
                    theDisplay.setText( theDisplay.getText() + e.getActionCommand() );
            }
        }
```

Once again, we use an addGB() helper method to add components with their constraints to the layout. Before discussing how to build the display, let's look at
addGB(). We said earlier that three layout managers are in our user interface: one
for the applet itself, one for the panel containing the first row of buttons (topRow),
and one for the panel containing the bottom row of buttons (bottomRow). We use
addGB() for all three layouts; its first argument specifies the container to add the
component to. Thus, when the first argument is this, we're adding an object to
the applet itself. When the first argument is topRow, we're adding a button to the
first row of buttons. addGB() first checks the container's layout manager, and sets it
to GridBagLayout if it isn't already set properly. It sets the object's position by modifying a set of constraints, gbc, and then uses these constraints to add the object to
the container.

We use a single set of constraints throughout the applet, modifying fields as we see
fit. The constraints are created and initialized at the beginning of the applet, using
a nonstatic initializer block. Before calling addGB(), we set any fields of gbc for
which the defaults are inappropriate. Thus, for the display itself, we set the grid
width to 4, and add the display directly to the applet (this). The add() method,
which is called by addGB(), makes a copy of the constraints, so we're free to reuse
gbc throughout the applet.

The first row of buttons (and the last) are the motivation for the composite layout.
Using a single GridBagLayout, it's very difficult (or impossible) to create buttons
that aren't aligned with the grid; that is, you can't say "I want the C button to have
a width of 1.5." Therefore, topRow has its own layout manager, with three horizontal cells, allowing each button in the row to have a width of 1. To control the size of
the buttons, we set the weightx variables so that the clear and plus buttons take up
more space than the percent button. We then add the topRow as a whole to the
applet, with a width of 4. The bottom row is built similarly.

To build the buttons for the digits 1 through 9, we use a doubly nested loop.
There's nothing particularly interesting about this loop, except that it's probably a
bit too clever for good taste. The minus, multiply, and divide buttons are also simple: we create a button with the appropriate label and use addGB() to place it in
the applet. It's worth noting that we used a Unicode constant to request a real
division sign, rather than wimping out and using a slash.

That's it for the user interface; what's left is event handling. Each button generates action events; we need to register listeners for these events. We'll make the applet the listener for all the buttons. To register the applet as a listener, we'll be clever. Whenever a component is added to a container, the container generates a ContainerEvent. Therefore, we can write componentAdded() and componentRemoved() methods, declare that the applet is a ContainerListener, and use componentAdded() to register listeners for our buttons. This means that the applet must register as a ContainerListener for itself, and for the two panels, topRow and bottomRow. Our componentAdded() method is very simple. It calls getChild() to find out what component caused the event (i.e., what component was added). If that component is a button, it registers the applet as an ActionListener for that button.

actionPerformed() is called whenever the user presses any button. It clears the display if the user pressed the C button; otherwise, it appends the button's action command (in this case, its label) to the display.

Combining layout managers is an extremely useful trick. Granted, this applet verges on overkill. You won't often need to create a composite layout using multiple grid bags. Composite layouts are most common with BorderLayout; you'll frequently use different layout managers for each of a border layout's regions. For example, the "Center" region might be a ScrollPane, which has its own special-purpose layout manager; the "East" and "South" regions might be panels managed by grid layouts or flow layouts, as appropriate.

Nonstandard Layout Managers

We've covered the basic layout managers; with them, you should be able to create just about any user interface you like.

But that's not all, folks. If you want to experiment with layout managers that are undocumented, may change, and may not be available locally on all platforms, look in the sun.awt classes. You'll find a HorizBagLayout, a VerticalBagLayout, an OrientableFlowLayout, and a VariableGridLayout. Furthermore, public domain layout managers of all descriptions are beginning to appear on the Net; keep your eye on Gamelan and the other Java archives.

Absolute Positioning?

It's possible to set the layout manager to null: no layout control. You might do this to position an object on the display at some absolute coordinates. This is almost never the right approach. Components might have different minimum sizes on different platforms, and your interface would not be very portable.

The following applet doesn't use a layout manager and works with absolute coordinates instead:

```java
import java.awt.*;

public class MoveButton extends java.applet.Applet {
    Button button = new Button("I Move");

    public void init() {
        setLayout( null );
        add( button );
        button.setSize( button.getPreferredSize() );
        button.move( 20, 20);
    }

    public boolean mouseDown( Event e, int x, int y ) {
        button.move( x, y );
        return ( true );
    }

}
```

Click in the applet area, outside of the button, to move the button to a new location. If you are running the example in an external viewer, try resizing the window and note that the button stays at a fixed position relative to the display origin.

16

In this chapter:
- *Basic Drawing*
- *Colors*
- *Fonts*
- *Images*
- *Drawing Techniques*

Drawing with AWT

If you've read the last few chapters, you've probably picked up the basics of how graphical operations are performed in Java. Up to this point, we have done some simple drawing and even displayed an image or two. In this chapter, we will finally give graphics programming its due and go into depth about drawing techniques and the tools for working with images in Java. In the next chapter, we'll explore image-processing tools in more detail, and we'll look at the classes that let you generate images pixel by pixel on the fly.

Basic Drawing

The classes you'll use for drawing come from the java.awt package, as shown in Figure 16-1.*

An instance of the java.awt.Graphics class is called a *graphics context*. It represents a drawable surface such as a component's display area or an off-screen image buffer. A graphics context provides methods for performing all basic drawing operations on its area, including the painting of image data. We call the Graphics object a graphics context because it also holds contextual information about the drawing area. This information includes the drawing area's clipping region, painting color, transfer mode, and text font. If you consider the drawing area to be a painter's canvas, you might think of a graphics context as an easel that holds a set of tools and marks off the work area.

There are four ways you normally acquire a Graphics object. Roughly, from most common to least, they are as follows:

---

* The current set of drawing tools has many limitations. In the near future, JavaSoft will be releasing packages for advanced 2D graphics, which will have much greater capabilities. A 3D package is also planned.

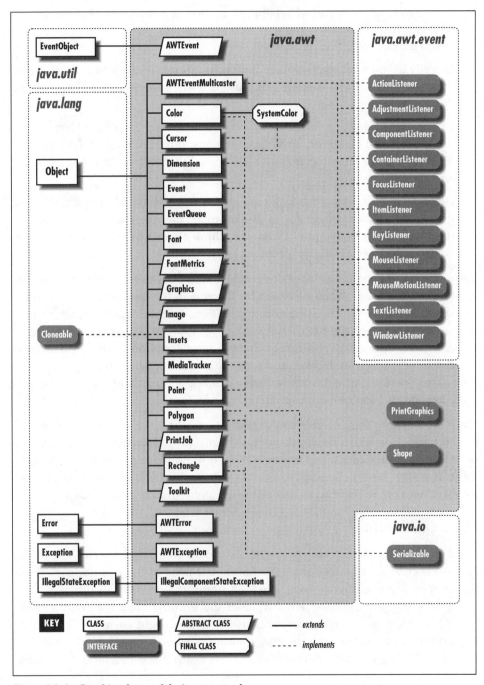

Figure 16–1: Graphics classes of the java.awt package

- From AWT, as the result of a painting request. In this case, AWT acquires a new graphics context for the appropriate area and passes it to your component's `paint()` or `update()` method.

- Directly from an off-screen image buffer. In this case, we ask the image buffer for a graphics context directly. We'll use this when we discuss techniques like double buffering.

- By copying an existing `Graphics` object. Duplicating a graphics object can be useful for more elaborate drawing operations; different copies of a `Graphics` object draw into the same area on the screen, but can have different attributes and clipping regions.

- Directly from an on-screen component. It's possible to ask a component to give you a `Graphics` object for its display area. However, this is almost always a mistake; if you feel tempted to do this, think about why you're trying to circumvent the normal `paint()`/`repaint()` mechanism.

Each time a component's `update()` or `paint()` method is called, AWT provides the component with a new `Graphics` object for drawing in the display area. This means that attributes we set during one painting session, such as drawing color or clipping region, are reset the next time `paint()` or `update()` is called. (Each call to `paint()` starts with a tidy new easel.) For the most common attributes, like foreground color, background color, and font, we can set defaults in the component itself. Thereafter, the graphics contexts for painting in that component come with those properties initialized appropriately.

If we are working in a component's `update()` method, we can assume our on-screen artwork is still intact, and we need only to make whatever changes are needed to bring the display up to date. One way to optimize drawing operations in this case is by setting a clipping region, as we'll see shortly. If our `paint()` method is called, however, we have to assume the worst and redraw the entire display.

Drawing Methods

Methods of the `Graphics` class operate in a standard coordinate system. The origin of a newly created graphics context is the top left pixel of the component's drawing area, as shown in Figure 16-2, which illustrates the default coordinate system. The point (0,0) is at the top left corner of the drawing area; the point (width, height) is just outside the drawing area at the bottom right corner. The point at the bottom right corner within the drawing area has coordinates (width-1, height-1). This gives you a drawing area that is width pixels wide and height pixels high.

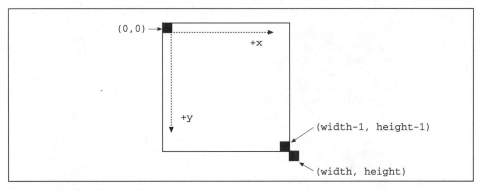

Figure 16–2: Graphics coordinate system

The coordinate system can be translated (shifted) with the `translate()` method to specify a new point as the origin. The drawable area of the graphics context can be limited to a region with the `setClip()` method.

The basic drawing and painting methods should seem familiar to you if you've done any graphics programming. The following applet, `TestPattern`, exercises most of the simple shape drawing commands; it's shown in Figure 16-3.

Figure 16–3: The TestPattern applet

```
import java.awt.*;
import java.awt.event.*;
public class TestPattern extends java.applet.Applet {
    int theta = 45;
    public void paint( Graphics g ) {
        int Width = size().width;
```

```
        int Height = size().height;
        int width = Width/2;
        int height = Height/2;
        int x = (Width - width)/2;
        int y = (Height- height)/2;
        int [] polyx =  { 0, Width/2, Width, Width/2 };
        int [] polyy =  { Height/2, 0, Height/2, Height };
        Polygon poly = new Polygon( polyx, polyy, 4 );

        g.setColor( Color.black );
        g.fillRect( 0, 0, size().width, size().height );
        g.setColor( Color.yellow );
        g.fillPolygon( poly );
        g.setColor( Color.red );
        g.fillRect( x, y, width, height );
        g.setColor( Color.green );
        g.fillOval( x, y, width, height );
        g.setColor( Color.blue );
        int delta = 90;
        g.fillArc( x, y, width, height, theta, delta );
        g.setColor( Color.white );
        g.drawLine( x, y, x+width, x+height );
    }
    public void init() {
        addMouseListener( new MouseAdapter() {
            public void mousePressed( MouseEvent e ) {
                theta = (theta + 10) % 360;
                repaint();
            }
        } );
    }
}
```

TestPattern draws a number of simple shapes and responds to mouse clicks by rotating the filled arc and repainting. Compile it and give it a try. If you click repeatedly on the applet, you may notice that everything flashes when it repaints. TestPattern is not very intelligent about redrawing; we'll examine some better algorithms in the upcoming section on drawing techniques.

With the exception of fillArc() and fillPolygon(), each method takes a simple x, y coordinate for the top left corner of the shape and a width and height for its size. We have picked values that draw the shapes centered, at half the width and height of the applet.

The most interesting shape we have drawn is the Polygon, a yellow diamond. A Polygon object is specified by two arrays that contain the x and y coordinates of each vertex. In our example, the coordinates of the points in the polygon are (polyx[0], polyy[0]), (polyx[1], polyy[1]), and so on. There are simple drawing methods in the Graphics class that take two arrays and draw or fill the polygon, but we chose to create a `Polygon` object and draw it instead. The reason is that the `Polygon` object has some useful utility methods that we might want to use later. A `Polygon` can, for instance, give you its bounding box and tell you if a given point lies within its area.

AWT also provides a `Shape` interface, which is implemented by different kinds of 2D objects. Currently, it is implemented only by the `Rectangle` and `Polygon` classes, but it may be a sign of things to come, particularly when JavaSoft releases the extended 2D drawing package. The `setClip()` method of the `Graphics` class takes a `Shape` as an argument, but for the time being, it works only if that `Shape` is a `Rectangle`.

The `fillArc()` method requires six integer arguments. The first four specify the bounding box for an oval—just like the `fillOval()` method. The final two arguments specify what portion of the oval we want to draw, as a starting angle and an offset. Both the starting angle and the offset are specified in degrees. Zero degrees is at three o'clock; a positive angle is clockwise. For example, to draw the right half of a circle, you might call:

```
g.fillArc(0, 0, radius * 2, radius * 2, -90, 180);
```

Table 16-1 shows the shape-drawing methods of the `Graphics` class. As you can see, for each of the `fill()` methods in the example, there is a corresponding `draw()` method that renders the shape as an unfilled line drawing.

Table 16–1: Shape-Drawing Methods in the Graphics Class

Method	Description
draw3DRect()	Draws a highlighted, 3D rectangle
drawArc()	Draws an arc
drawLine()	Draws a line
drawOval()	Draws an oval
drawPolygon()	Draws a polygon, connecting endpoints
drawPolyline()	Draws a line connecting a polygon's points
drawRect()	Draws a rectangle
drawRoundRect()	Draws a rounded-corner rectangle
fill3DRect()	Draws a filled, highlighted, 3D rectangle
fillArc()	Draws a filled arc
fillOval()	Draws a filled oval
fillPolygon()	Draws a filled polygon
fillRect()	Draws a filled rectangle
fillRoundRect()	Draws a filled, rounded-corner rectangle

draw3DRect() automatically chooses colors by "darkening" the current color. So you should set the color to something other than black, which is the default (maybe gray or white); if you don't, you'll just get black on both sides. For an example, see the PictureButton in Chapter 14.

A few important drawing methods are missing from Table 16-1: for example, the drawString() method, which draws text, and the drawImage() method, which draws an image. We'll discuss these methods in detail in later sections.

Colors

The TestPattern applet fills its shapes with a number of colors, using the set-Color() method of the Graphics object. setColor() sets the current color in the graphics context, so we set it to a different color before each drawing operation. But where do these color values come from?

The java.awt.Color class handles color in Java. A Color object describes a single color. You can create an arbitrary Color by specifying the red, green, and blue values, either as integers between 0 and 255 or as floating-point values between 0.0 and 1.0. You can also use getColor() to look up a named color in the system properties table, as described in Chapter 9. getColor() takes a String color property name, retrieves the integer value from the Properties list, and returns the Color object that corresponds to that color.

The Color class also defines a number of static final color values; these are what we used in the TestPattern example. These constants, such as Color.black and Color.red, provide a convenient set of basic colors for your drawings.

Desktop Colors

The Color class I just described makes it easy to construct a particular color; however, that's not always what you want to do. Sometimes you want to match a preexisting color scheme. This is particularly important when you are designing a user interface; you might want your components to have the same colors as other components on that platform, and to change automatically if the user redefines his or her color scheme.

That's what the SystemColor class is for. A system color represents the color used by the local windowing system in a certain context. The SystemColor class holds lots of predefined system colors, just like the Color class holds some predefined basic colors. For example, the field activeCaption represents the color used for the background to the title of an active window; activeCaptionText represents the color used for the title itself. menu represents the background color of menu selection; menuText represents the color of a menu item's text when it is not selected; textHighlightText is the color used when the item is selected; and so on. You could use the window value to set the color of a Window to match the other Windows on the user's screen—whether or not they're generated by Java programs.

```
myWindow.setBackground( SystemColor.window );
```

Because the SystemColor class is a subclass of Color, you can use it wherever you would use a Color. However, the SystemColor constants are tricky. They are constants as far as you, the programmer, are concerned; your code is not allowed to modify them. However, they can be modified at run-time by the toolkit. If the user changes his color scheme, the system colors are automatically updated to follow suit; as a result, anything displayed with system colors will also change color the next time it is redrawn. For example, the window myWindow would automatically change its background color to the new background color.

The SystemColor class has one noticeable shortcoming. You can't compare a system color to a Color directly; the Color.equals() method doesn't return reliable results. For example, if you want to find out whether the window background color is red, you can't call:

```
Color.red.equals(SystemColor.window);
```

Instead, you should use getRGB() to find the color components of both objects and compare them, rather than comparing the objects themselves.

Fonts

Text fonts in Java are represented by instances of the java.awt.Font class. A Font object is constructed from a font name, style identifier, and a point size. We can create a Font at any time, but it's meaningful only when applied to a particular component on a given display device. Here are a couple of fonts:

```
Font smallFont = new Font("Monospaced", Font.PLAIN, 10);
Font bigFont = new Font("Serif", Font.BOLD, 18);
```

The font name is a symbolic name for the font family. The following font names should be available on all platforms.[*]

---

[*] The names Helvetica, TimesRoman, Courier, Symbol, and ZapfDingbats are supported in Java 1.1 for backwards compatibility but shouldn't be used; they may be removed in a future version. Symbols and ZapfDingbats, which used to be available as Font names have now taken their proper place as ranges in the Unicode character table: 2200–22ff and 2700–27ff, respectively.

- Serif (for example, TimesRoman)

- SansSerif (for example, Helvetica)

- Monospaced (for example, Courier)

- Dialog

- DialogInput

The font you specify is mapped to an actual font on the local platform. Java's *fonts.properties* files map the font names to the available fonts, covering as much of the Unicode character set as possible. If you request a font that doesn't exist, you get the default font.

You can also use the static method Font.getFont() to look up a font name in the system properties list. getFont() takes a String font property name, retrieves the font name from the Properties table, and returns the Font object that corresponds to that font. You can use this mechanism, as with Colors, to define fonts with properties from outside your application.

The Font class defines three static style identifiers: PLAIN, BOLD, and ITALIC. You can use these values on all fonts. The point size determines the size of the font on a display. If a given point size isn't available, Font substitutes a default size.*

You can retrieve information about an existing Font with a number of routines. The getName(), getSize(), and getStyle() methods retrieve the symbolic name, point size, and style, respectively. You can use the getFamily() method to find out the platform-specific font family to which the font actually maps.

Finally, to actually use a Font object, you can simply specify it as an argument to the setFont() method of a Component or Graphics object. Subsequent text-drawing commands like drawString() for that component or in that graphics context use the specified font.

Font Metrics

To get detailed size and spacing information for text rendered in a font, we can ask for a java.awt.FontMetrics object. Different systems will have different real fonts available; the available fonts may not match the font you request. Thus, a FontMetrics object presents information about a particular font on a particular system, not general information about a font. For example, if you ask for the metrics of a nine-point Monospaced font, what you get isn't some abstract truth about Monospaced fonts; you get the metrics of the font that the particular system uses for

---

* There is no straightforward way to determine if a given Font is available at a given point size in the current release of Java. Fonts are one of Java's weak points. Sun has promised better Font handling (and perhaps true, portable Fonts) as part of the 2D graphics package.

nine-point `Monospaced`—which may not be exactly nine point or even `Monospaced`.

Use the `getFontMetrics()` method for a `Component` to retrieve the `FontMetrics` for a `Font` as it would appear for that component:

```
public void init() {
    ...
    // Get the metrics for a particular font on this component
    FontMetrics smallFont = myLabel.getFontMetrics( smallFont );
    ...
}
```

The `Graphics` object also has a `getFontMetrics()` method that gets the `FontMetrics` information for the current font in the graphics context.

```
public void paint( Graphics g ) {
    // Get the metrics for the current font
    FontMetrics fm = g.getFontMetrics();
    ...
}
```

The following applet, `FontShow`, displays a word and draws reference lines showing certain characteristics of its font, as shown in Figure 16-4. Clicking in the applet toggles the point size between a small and a large value.

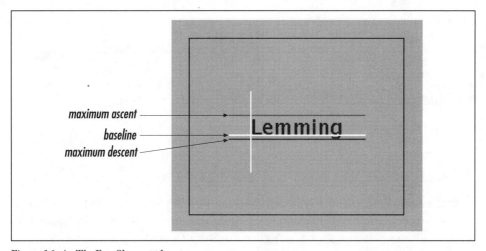

Figure 16–4: The FontShow applet

```
import java.awt.*;
import java.awt.event.*;
public class FontShow extends java.applet.Applet {
    static final int LPAD=25;    // Frilly line padding
    boolean bigFont = true;
    public void init() {
        addMouseListener( new MouseAdapter() {
```

```
        public void mouseClicked(MouseEvent e) {
            bigFont = !bigFont;
            repaint();
        }
    } );
}
public void paint( Graphics g ) {
    String message = getParameter( "word" );
    g.drawRect(0, 0, getSize().width-1, getSize().height-1);
    if ( bigFont )
        g.setFont( new Font("Dialog",Font.PLAIN,24) );
    else
        g.setFont( new Font("Dialog",Font.PLAIN,12) );
    FontMetrics metrics = g.getFontMetrics();
    int fontAscent = metrics.getMaxAscent ();
    int fontDescent = metrics.getMaxDescent();
    int messWidth = metrics.stringWidth ( message );
    // Center text
    int startX = getSize().width/2 - messWidth/2;
    int startY = getSize().height/2 - fontDescent/2 + fontAscent/2;
    g.drawString(message, startX, startY);
    g.setColor( Color.white );  // Base lines
    g.drawLine( startX-LPAD, startY, startX+messWidth+LPAD, startY );
    g.drawLine( startX, startY+ LPAD, startX, startY-fontAscent-LPAD );
    g.setColor( Color.green );  // Ascent line
    g.drawLine( startX-LPAD, startY-fontAscent,
                startX+messWidth+LPAD, startY-fontAscent );
    g.setColor( Color.red );    // Descent line
    g.drawLine( startX-LPAD, startY+fontDescent,
                startX+messWidth+LPAD, startY+fontDescent );
}
}
```

Compile FontShow and run it with an applet tag like the following:

```
<applet height=200 width=250 code=FontShow>
    <param name="word" value="Lemming">
</applet>
```

The word parameter specifies the text to be displayed.

FontShow may look a bit complicated, but there's really not much to it. The bulk of the code is in paint(), which simply sets the font, draws our word, and adds a few lines to illustrate some of the font's characteristics (metrics). For fun we also catch mouse clicks (in the mouseClicked() method) and alternate the font size by setting the bigFont variable and repainting.

By default, text is rendered above and to the right of the coordinates specified in the drawString() method. If you think of that starting point as the origin of a coordinate system, we'll call the axes the *baselines* of the font. FontShow draws these lines in white. The greatest height the characters stretch above the baseline is called the *ascent* and is shown by a green line. Some fonts also have parts of letters that fall below the baseline. The farthest distance any character reaches below the baseline is called the *descent.* FontShow illustrates this with a red line.

We ask for the ascent and descent of our font with the FontMetrics getMaxAscent() and getMaxDescent() methods. We also ask for the width of our string (when rendered in this font) with the stringWidth() method. We use this information to center the word in the display area. To center the word vertically, we average the influence of the ascent and descent. Table 16-2 provides a short list of methods that return useful font metrics.

Table 16–2: Font Metric Methods

Method	Description
getFont()	Font object these metrics describe
getAscent()	Height above baseline
getDescent()	Depth below baseline
getLeading()	Standard vertical spacing between lines
getHeight()	Total line height (ascent + descent + leading)
charWidth(char ch)	Width of a character
stringWidth(String str)	Width of a string
getWidths()	The widths of the first 256 characters in this font; returns int[]
getMaxAdvance()	Maximum character width of any character

Leading space is the padding between lines of text. The getHeight() method reports the total height of a line of text, including the leading space.

Images

So far, we've worked with methods for drawing simple shapes and displaying text. For more complex graphics, we'll be working with images. AWT has a powerful set of tools for generating and displaying image data that address the problems of working in a distributed and multithreaded application environment. We'll start with the basics of the java.awt.Image class and see how to get an image into an Applet and draw it on a display. This job isn't quite as simple as it sounds; the browser might have to retrieve the image from a networked source when we ask for it. Fortunately, if we're just interested in getting the image on the screen whenever it's ready, we can let AWT handle the details for us. Later in this chapter, we'll discuss how to manage image loading ourselves, as well as how to create raw image data and feed it efficiently to the rest of an application.

The Image Class

The `java.awt.Image` class represents a view of an image. The view is created from an image source that produces pixel data. Images can be from a static source, such as GIF or JPEG data, or a dynamic one, such as a video stream or a graphics engine. The `Image` class in Java 1.1 also handles GIF89a animations, so that you can work with simple animations as easily as static images.

An applet can ask its viewer to retrieve an image by calling the `getImage()` method. The location of the image to be retrieved is given as a URL, either absolute or fetched from the applet's resources:

```
public class MyApplet extends java.applet.Applet {
    public void init() {
        try {
            // absolute URL
            URL monaURL = new URL(
                "http://myserver/images/mona_lisa.gif");
            Image monaImage = getImage( monaURL );

            // applet resource URL
            URL daffyURL = getClass().getResource("cartoons/images/daffy.gif");
            Image daffyDuckImage = getImage( daffyURL );
        }
        catch ( MalformedURLException e ) { // unintelligable url }
```

We usually want to package an applet's images with the applet itself, so using `getResource()` is preferred; it looks for the image in the applet's JAR file (if there is one), before looking elsewhere in the server's filesystem.

For a standalone application where we don't have the applet's `getImage()` method available, we can pass our image URLs to the AWT toolkit:

```
Image dukeImage = getToolkit().getImage( url );
```

As with the previous example, this works just as well for URLs that we construct or those returned by `getResource()`.

Once we have an `Image` object, we can draw it into a graphics context with the `drawImage()` method of the `Graphics` class. The simplest form of `drawImage()` takes four parameters: the `Image` object, the x, y coordinates at which to draw it, and a reference to a special *image observer* object.

Image Observers

Images in AWT are processed asynchronously, which means Java performs image operations like loading and scaling on its own time. For example, the `getImage()`

method always returns immediately, even if the image data has to be retrieved over the network from Mars and isn't available yet. In fact, if it's a new image, Java won't even begin to fetch it until we try to use it. The advantage of this technique is that Java can do the work of a powerful, multithreaded image-processing environment for us. However, it also introduces several problems. If Java is loading an image for us, how do we know when it's completely loaded? What if we want to work with the image as it arrives? What if we need to know properties of the image (like its dimensions) before we can start working with it? What if there's an error in loading the image?

These problems are handled by image observers—designated objects that implement the `ImageObserver` interface. All operations that draw or examine `Image` objects return immediately, but they take an image-observer object as a parameter. The `ImageObserver` monitors the image's status and can make that information available to the rest of the application. When image data is loaded from its source, an image observer is notified of its progress, including when new pixels are available, when a complete frame of the image is ready, and if there is an error during loading. The image observer also receives attribute information about the image, such as its dimensions and properties, as soon as they are known.

The `drawImage()` method, like other image operations, takes a reference to an `ImageObserver` object as a parameter. `drawImage()` returns a `boolean` value specifying whether or not the image was painted in its entirety. If the image data has not yet been loaded or is only partially available, `drawImage()` paints whatever fraction of the image it can and returns. The image-observer object, however, is registered as being interested in information about the image. It's then called repeatedly as more pixel information is available and again when the entire image is complete. The image observer can do whatever it wants with this information. Most often it calls `repaint()` to prompt the applet to draw the image again with the updated data; as you should recall, a call to `repaint()` initiates a call to `paint()` to be scheduled. In this way an applet can redraw the image as it arrives, for a progressive loading effect. Alternatively, it could wait until the entire image is loaded before displaying it.

We'll discuss creating image observers a bit later. For now, we can avoid the issue by using a prefabricated image observer. It just so happens that the `Component` class implements the `ImageObserver` interface and provides some simple repainting behavior for us. This means that every component can serve as its own default image observer; we simply pass a reference to our applet (or other component) as the image-observer parameter of a `drawImage()` call. Hence the mysterious `this` we've occasionally seen when working with graphics:

```
class MyApplet extends java.applet.Applet {
    ...
   public void paint( Graphics g ) {
       drawImage( monaImage, x, y, this );
       ...
```

Our applet serves as the image observer and calls repaint() for us to redraw the image as necessary. If the image arrives slowly, our applet is notified repeatedly, as new chunks become available. As a result, the image appears gradually, as it's loaded. The awt.image.incrementaldraw and awt.image.redrawrate system properties control this behavior. redrawrate limits how often repaint() is called; the default value is every 100 milliseconds. incrementaldraw specifies whether or not drawing is delayed until the entire image has arrived. By default, this property is set to true; set it to false to turn off incremental redrawing.

Scaling and Size

Another version of drawImage() renders a scaled version of the image:

```
drawImage( monaImage, x, y, x2, y2, this );
```

This draws the entire image within the rectangle formed by the points x, y and x2, y2, scaling as necessary. (Cool, eh?) drawImage() behaves the same as before; the image is processed by the component as it arrives, and the image observer is notified as more pixel data and the completed image are available. Several other overloaded versions of drawImage() provide more complex options: you can scale, crop, and perform some simple transpositions.

If you want to actually make a scaled copy of an image (as opposed to simply painting one at draw-time), you can call getScaledInstance(). Here's how:

```
Image scaledDaffy = daffyImage.getScaledInstance(100,200,SCALE_AREA_AVERAGING);
```

This method scales the original image to the given size; in this case, 100 by 200 pixels. It returns a new Image that you can draw like any other image. SCALE_AREA_AVERAGING is a constant that tells getScaledImage() what scaling algorithm to use. The algorithm used here tries to do a decent job of scaling, at the expense of time. Some alternatives that take less time are SCALE_REPLICATE, which scales by replicating scan lines and columns (which is fast, but probably not pretty). You can also specify either SCALE_FAST or SCALE_SMOOTH and let the implementation choose an appropriate algorithm that optimizes for time or quality. If you don't have specific requirements, you should use SCALE_DEFAULT, which, ideally, would be set by a preference in the user's environment.

Scaling an image before calling `drawImage()` can improve performance, because the image loading and scaling can take place before the image is actually needed. Of course, the same amount of work is required, but in most situations, prescaling will make the program appear faster because it takes place while other things are going on; the user doesn't have to wait as long for the image to display.

The `Image getHeight()` and `getWidth()` methods retrieve the dimensions of an image. Since this information may not be available until the image data is completely loaded, both methods also take an `ImageObserver` object as a parameter. If the dimensions aren't yet available, they return values of –1 and notify the observer when the true value is known. We'll see how to deal with these and other problems a bit later. For now, we'll use `Component` as an image observer to get by, and move on to some general painting techniques.

Drawing Techniques

Having learned to walk, let's try a jog. In this section, we'll look at some techniques for doing fast and flicker-free drawing and painting. If you're interested in animation or smooth updating, you should read on.[*]

Drawing operations take time, and time spent drawing leads to delays and imperfect results. Our goal is to minimize the amount of drawing work we do and, as much as possible, to do that work away from the eyes of the user. You'll remember that our `TestPattern` applet had a blinking problem. It blinked because `TestPattern` performs several, large, area-filling operations each time its `paint()` method is called. On a very slow system, you might even be able to see each shape being drawn in succession. `TestPattern` could be easily fixed by drawing into an off-screen buffer and then copying the completed buffer to the display. To see how to eliminate flicker and blinking problems, we'll look at an applet that needs even more help.

`TerribleFlicker` illustrates some of the problems of updating a display. Like many animations, it has two parts: a constant background and a changing object in the foreground. In this case, the background is a checkerboard pattern and the object is a small, scaled image we can drag around on top of it, as shown in Figure 16-5. Our first version of `TerribleFlicker` lives up to its name and does a very poor job of updating.

```
import java.awt.*;
import java.awt.event.*;
public class TerribleFlicker extends java.applet.Applet
                    implements MouseMotionListener {
```

---

[*] At this point, you still have to build your own animation software. JavaSoft will be releasing an animation package as part of the Java Media APIs.

Figure 16–5: The TerribleFlicker applet

```
int grid = 10;
int currentX, currentY;
Image img;
int imgWidth = 60, imgHeight = 60;
public void init() {
    img = getImage( getClass().getResource(getParameter("img")) );
    addMouseMotionListener( this );
}
public void mouseDragged( MouseEvent e ) {
    currentX = e.getX(); currentY = e.getY();
    repaint();
}
public void mouseMoved( MouseEvent e ) { }; // ignore Mouse motion
public void paint( Graphics g ) {
    int w = getSize().width/grid;
    int h = getSize().height/grid;
    boolean black = false;
    for ( int y = 0; y <= grid; y++ )
        for ( int x = 0; x <= grid; x++ ) {
            g.setColor( (black = !black) ? Color.black : Color.white );
            g.fillRect( x * w, y * h, w, h );
        }
        g.drawImage( img, currentX, currentY, imgWidth, imgHeight, this );
}
}
```

Try dragging the image; you'll notice both the background and foreground flicker as they are repeatedly redrawn. What is TerribleFlicker doing, and what is it doing wrong?

As the mouse is dragged, TerribleFlicker keeps track of its position in two instance variables, currentX and currentY. On each call to mouseDragged(), the coordinates are updated, and `repaint()` is called to ask that the display be updated. When `paint()` is called, it looks at some parameters, draws the checkerboard pattern to fill the applet's area, and finally paints a small version of the image at the latest coordinates.

Our first, and biggest, problem is that we are updating, but we have neglected to implement the applet's `update()` method with a good strategy. Because we haven't overridden `update()`, we are getting the default implementation of the `Component` `update()` method, which looks something like this:

```
// Default implementation of applet update
public void update( Graphics g ) {
    setColor ( backgroundColor );
    fillRect( 0, 0, getSize().width, getSize().height );
    paint ( g );
}
```

This method simply clears the display to the background color and calls our `paint()` method. This is almost never the best strategy, but is the only appropriate default for `update()`, which doesn't know how much of the screen we're really going to paint.

Our applet paints its own background, in its entirety, so we can provide a simpler version of `update()` that doesn't bother to clear the display:

```
// add to TerribleFlicker
public void update( Graphics g ) {
    paint( g );
}
```

This applet works better because we have eliminated one large, unnecessary, and (in fact) annoying graphics operation. However, although we have eliminated a `fillRect()` call, we're still doing a lot of wasted drawing. Most of the background stays the same each time it's drawn. You might think of trying to make `paint()` smarter, so that it wouldn't redraw these areas, but remember that `paint()` has to be able to draw the entire scene because it might be called in situations when the display isn't intact. The solution is to have `update()` help out by restricting the area `paint()` can draw.

Clipping

The `setClip()` method of the `Graphics` class restricts the drawing area of a graphics context to a smaller region. A graphics context normally has an effective clipping region that limits drawing to the entire display area of the component. We can specify a smaller clipping region with `setClip()`.

How is the drawing area restricted? Well, foremost, drawing operations that fall outside of the clipping region are not displayed. If a drawing operation overlaps the clipping region, we see only the part that's inside. A second effect is that, in a good implementation, the graphics context can recognize drawing operations that fall completely outside the clipping region and ignore them altogether. Eliminating unnecessary operations can save time if we're doing something complex, like filling a bunch of polygons. This doesn't save the time our application spends calling the drawing methods, but the overhead of calling these kinds of drawing methods is usually negligible compared to the time it takes to execute them. (If we were generating an image pixel by pixel, this would not be the case, as the calculations would be the major time sink, not the drawing.)

So we can save time in our applet by having our update method set a clipping region that results in only the affected portion of the display being redrawn. We can pick the smallest rectangular area that includes both the old image position and the new image position, as shown in Figure 16-6. This is the only portion of the display that really needs to change; everything else stays the same.

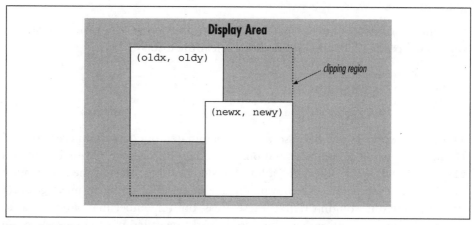

Figure 16–6: Determining the clipping region

A smarter update() could save even more time by redrawing only those regions that have changed. However, the simple clipping strategy we've implemented here can be applied to many kinds of drawing, and gives quite good performance, particularly if the area being changed is small.

One important thing to note is that, in addition to looking at the new position, our updating operation now has to remember the last position at which the image was drawn. Let's fix our applet so it will use a clipping region. To keep this short and emphasize the changes, we'll take some liberties with design and make our next example a subclass of TerribleFlicker. Let's call it ClippedFlicker:

```
public class ClippedFlicker extends TerribleFlicker {
    int nextX, nextY;

    public void mouseDragged( MouseEvent e ) {
        nextX = e.getX(); nextY = e.getY();
        repaint();
    }
    void clipToAffectedArea( Graphics g, int oldx, int oldy, int newx,
                                  int newy, int width, int height) {
        int x = Math.min( oldx, newx );
        int y = Math.min( oldy, newy );
        int w = ( Math.max( oldx, newx ) + width ) - x;
        int h = ( Math.max( oldy, newy ) + height ) - y;
        g.setClip( x, y, w, h );
    }
    public void update( Graphics g ) {
        int lastX = currentX, lastY = currentY;
        currentX = nextX; currentY = nextY;
        clipToAffectedArea( g, lastX, lastY, currentX, currentY,
                            imgWidth, imgHeight );
        paint( g );
    }
}
```

You should find that `ClippedFlicker` is significantly faster, though it still flickers. We'll make one more change in the next section to eliminate that.

So, what have we changed? First, we've overridden `mouseDragged()` so that instead of setting the current coordinates of the image, it sets another pair of coordinates called `nextX` and `nextY`. These are the coordinates at which we'll display the image the next time we draw it.

`update()` now has the added responsibility of taking the next position and making it the current position, by setting the `currentX` and `currentY` variables. This effectively decouples `mouseDragged()` from our painting routines. We'll discuss why this is advantageous in a bit. `update()` then uses the current and next coordinates to set a clipping region on the `Graphics` object before handing it off to `paint()`.

We have created a new, `private` method to help it do this. `clipToAffectedArea()` takes as arguments the new and old coordinates and the width and height of the image. It determines the bounding rectangle as shown in Figure 16-6, then calls `setClip()` to set the clipping region. As a result, when `paint()` is called, it draws only the affected area of the screen.

So, what's the deal with `nextX` and `nextY`? By making `update()` keep track of the next, current, and last coordinates separately, we accomplish two things. First, we always have an accurate view of where the last image was drawn, and second, we have decoupled where the next image will be drawn from `mouseDragged()`.

It's important to decouple painting from mouseDragged() because there isn't necessarily a one-to-one correspondence between calls to repaint() and subsequent calls by AWT to our update() method. This isn't a defect; it's a feature that allows AWT to schedule and consolidate painting requests. Our concern is that our paint() method may be called at arbitrary times while the mouse coordinates are changing. This is not necessarily bad. If we are trying to position our object, we probably don't want the display to be redrawn for every intermediate position of the mouse. It would slow down the dragging unnecessarily.

If we were concerned about getting every single change in the mouse's position, we would have two options. We could either do some work in the mouseDragged() method itself, or put our events into some kind of queue. We'll see an example of the first solution in our DoodlePad example a bit later. The latter solution would mean circumventing AWT's own event-scheduling capabilities and replacing them with our own, and we don't want to take on that responsibility.

Double Buffering

Now let's get to the most powerful technique in our toolbox: *double buffering*. Double buffering is a technique that fixes our flickering problems completely. It's easy to do and gives us almost flawless updates. We'll combine it with our clipping technique for better performance, but in general you can use double buffering with or without clipping.

Double buffering our display means drawing into an off-screen buffer and then copying our completed work to the display in a single painting operation, as shown in Figure 16-7. It takes the same amount of time to draw a frame, but double buffering instantaneously updates our display when it's ready.

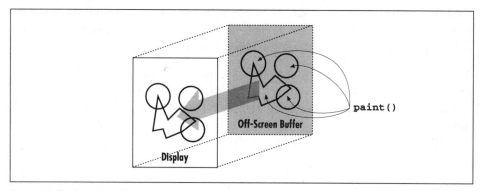

Figure 16–7: Double buffering

We can get this effect by changing just a few lines of our `ClippedFlicker` applet. Modify `update()` to look like the following and add the new `offScreenImage` instance variable as shown:

```
...
public class DoubleBufferedClipped extends ClippedFlicker {
    Image offScreenImage;
    Graphics offScreenGC;
    public void update( Graphics g ) {
        if ( offScreenImage == null ) {
            offScreenImage = createImage( getSize().width, getSize().height );
            offScreenGC = img.getGraphics();
        }
        int lastX = currentX, lastY = currentY;
        currentX = nextX; currentY = nextY;
        clipToAffectedArea( offScreenGC, lastX, lastY, currentX, currentY,
                            imgWidth, imgHeight );
        clipToAffectedArea( g, lastX, lastY, currentX, currentY,
                            imgWidth, imgHeight );
        paint( offScreenGC );
        g.drawImage(offScreenImage, 0, 0, this);
    }
}
...
```

Now, when you drag the image, you shouldn't see any flickering. The update rate should be about the same as in the previous example (or marginally slower), but the image should move from position to position without noticeable repainting.

So, what have we done this time? Well, the new instance variable, `offScreenImage`, is our off-screen buffer. It is a drawable `Image` object. We can get an off-screen `Image` for a component with the `createImage()` method. `createImage()` is similar to `getImage()`, except that it produces an empty image area of the specified size. We can then use the off-screen image like our standard display area by asking it for a graphics context with the `Image getGraphics()` method. After we've drawn into the off-screen image, we can copy that image back onto the screen with `drawImage()`.

The biggest change to the code is that we now pass `paint()` the graphics context of our off-screen buffer, rather than that of the on-screen display. `paint()` is now drawing on `offScreenImage`; it's our job to copy the image to the display when it's done. This might seem a little suspicious to you, as we are now using `paint()` in two capacities. AWT calls `paint()` whenever it's necessary to repaint our entire applet and passes it an on-screen graphics context. When we update ourselves, however, we call `paint()` to do its work on our off-screen area and then copy that image onto the screen from within `update()`.

Note that we're still clipping. In fact, we're clipping both the on-screen and off-screen buffers. Off-screen clipping has the same benefits we described earlier: AWT should be able to ignore wasted drawing operations. On-screen clipping minimizes the area of the image that gets drawn back to the display. If your display is fast, you might not even notice the savings, but it's an easy optimization, so we'll take advantage of it.

We create the off-screen buffer in update() because it's a convenient and safe place to do so. Our image observer probably won't be called, since drawImage() isn't doing anything nasty like scaling, and the image itself is always available.

The dispose() method of the Graphics class allows us to deallocate a graphics context explicitly when we are through with it. This is simply an optimization. If we were creating new graphics contexts frequently (say, in each paint()), we could help the system get rid of them. This might provide some performance improvement when doing heavy drawing. We could allow garbage collection to reclaim the unused objects; however, the garbage collection process might be hampered if we are doing intense calculations or lots of repainting.

Off-Screen Drawing

In addition to serving as buffers for double buffering, off-screen images are useful for saving complex, hard-to-produce, background information. We'll look at a simple example: the "doodle pad." DoodlePad is a simple drawing tool that lets us scribble by dragging the mouse, as shown in Figure 16-8. It draws into an off-screen image; its paint() method simply copies the image to the display area.

```java
import java.awt.*;
import java.awt.event.*;
public class DoodlePad extends java.applet.Applet implements ActionListener {
    DrawPad dp;
    public void init() {
        setLayout( new BorderLayout() );
        add( "Center", dp = new DrawPad() );
        Panel p = new Panel();
        Button clearButton = new Button("Clear");
        clearButton.addActionListener( this );
        p.add( clearButton );
        add( "South", p );
    }
    public void actionPerformed( ActionEvent e ) {
        dp.clear();
    }
}
class DrawPad extends Canvas {
    Image drawImg;
    Graphics drawGr;
    int xpos, ypos, oxpos, oypos;
    DrawPad() {
```

Figure 16–8: The DoodlePad applet

```
        setBackground( Color.white );
        enableEvents( AWTEvent.MOUSE_EVENT_MASK
            | AWTEvent.MOUSE_MOTION_EVENT_MASK );
    }
    public void processEvent( AWTEvent e ) {
        int x = ((MouseEvent)e).getX(), y = ((MouseEvent)e).getY();
        if ( e.getID() == MouseEvent.MOUSE_DRAGGED ) {
            xpos = x; ypos = y;
            if ( drawGr != null )
                drawGr.drawLine( oxpos, oypos, oxpos=xpos, oypos=ypos );
            repaint();
        } else
        if ( e.getID() == MouseEvent.MOUSE_PRESSED ) {
            oxpos = x; oypos = y;
        }
        super.processEvent(e);
    }
    public void update( Graphics g ) {
        paint(g);
    }
    public void paint( Graphics g ) {
        if ( drawImg == null ) {
            drawImg = createImage( getSize().width, getSize().height );
            drawGr = drawImg.getGraphics();
        }
        g.drawImage(drawImg, 0, 0, null);
    }
```

```
    public void clear() {
        drawGr.clearRect(0, 0, getSize().width, getSize().height);
        repaint();
    }
}
```

Give it a try. Draw a nice moose, or a sunset. I just drew a lovely cartoon of Bill Gates. If you make a mistake, hit the **Clear** button and start over.

The parts should be familiar by now. We have made a type of Canvas called Draw-Pad. The new DrawPad component handles mouse events by enabling both simple mouse events (mouse clicks) and mouse motion events (mouse drags), and then overriding the processEvent() method to handle these events. By doing so, we are simulating the old (Java 1.0) event-handling model; in this situation, it's a little more convenient than implementing all the methods of the MouseListener and MouseMotionListener interfaces. The processEvent() method handles MOUSE_DRAGGED movement events by drawing lines into an off-screen image and calling repaint() to update the display. DrawPad's paint() method simply does a drawImage() to copy the off-screen drawing area to the display. In this way, Draw-Pad saves our sketch information.

What is unusual about DrawPad is that it does some drawing outside of paint() or update(). In our clipping example, we talked about decoupling update() and mouseDragged(); we were willing to discard some mouse movements in order to save some updates. In this case, we want to let the user scribble with the mouse, so we should respond to every mouse movement. Therefore, we do our work in processEvent() itself. As a rule, we should be careful about doing heavy work in event-handling methods because we don't want to interfere with other tasks the AWT thread is performing. In this case, our line-drawing option should not be a burden, and our primary concern is getting as close a coupling as possible between the mouse movement events and the sketch on the screen.

In addition to drawing a line as the user drags the mouse, the part processEvent() that handles MOUSE_DRAGGED() events maintains a set of old coordinates, to be used as a starting point for the next line segment. The part of processEvent() that handles MOUSE_PRESSED events resets the old coordinates to the current mouse position whenever the user picks up and moves to a new location. Finally, DrawPad provides a clear() method that clears the off-screen buffer and calls repaint() to update the display. The DoodlePad applet ties the clear() method to an appropriately labeled button through its actionPerformed() method.

What if we wanted to do something with the image after the user has finished scribbling on it? Well, as we'll see in the next chapter, we could get the pixel data for the image from its ImageProducer object and work with that. It wouldn't be hard to create a save facility that stores the pixel data and reproduces it later. Think about how you might go about creating a networked "bathroom wall" where people could scribble on your Web pages.

17

Working with Images

Image Processing

Up to this point, we've confined ourselves to working with the high-level drawing commands of the Graphics class and using images in a hands-off mode. In this section, we'll clear up some of the mystery surrounding images and see how they are produced and used. The classes in the java.awt.image package handle image processing; Figure 17-1 shows the classes in this package.

First, we'll return to our discussion about image observers and see how we can get more control over image data as it's processed asynchronously by AWT components. Then we'll open the hood and have a look at image production. If you're interested in creating sophisticated graphics, such as rendered images or video streams, this will teach you about the foundations of image construction in Java.[*]

Objects that work with image data fall into one of three categories: image-data producers, image-data consumers, and image-status observers. Image producers implement the ImageProducer interface. They create pixel data and distribute it to one or more consumers. Image consumers implement a corresponding ImageConsumer interface. They eat the pixel data and do something useful with it, such as display it on screen or analyze its contents. Image observers, as I mentioned earlier, implement the ImageObserver interface. They are effectively nosy neighbors of image consumers that watch as the image data arrives.

Image producers generate the information that defines each pixel of an image. A pixel has both a color and a transparency; the transparency specifies how pixels underneath the image show through. Image producers maintain a list of

---

[*] You will also want to pay attention to the forthcoming Java Media API. Java Media will support plug-and-play streaming media.

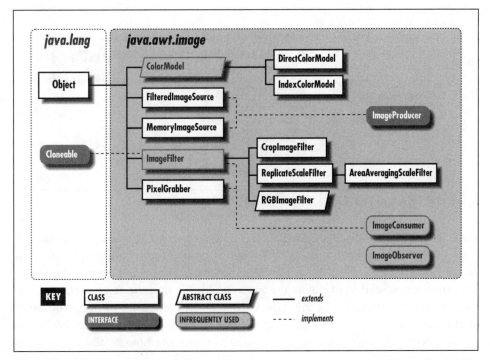

Figure 17–1: The java.awt.image package

registered consumers for the image and send them this pixel data in one or more passes, as the pixels are generated. Image producers give the consumers other kinds of information as well, such as the image's dimensions. The producer also notifies the consumer when it has reached a boundary of the image. For a static image, such as GIF or JPEG data, the producer signals when the entire image is complete, and production is finished. For a video source or animation, the image producer could generate a continuous stream of pixel data and mark the end of each frame.

An image producer delivers pixel data and other image-attribute information by invoking methods in its consumers, as shown in Figure 17-2. This diagram illustrates an image producer sending pixel data to three consumers by invoking their setPixels() methods.

Each consumer represents a view of the image. A given consumer might prepare the image for display on a particular medium, or it might simply serve as a filter and pass the image data to another consumer down the line.

Figure 17-2 also shows an image observer, watching the status of one of the consumers. The observer is notified as new portions of the image and new attributes are ready. Its job is to track this information and let another part of the application

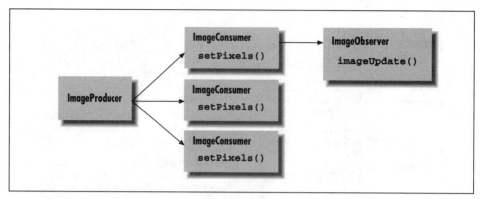

Figure 17–2: Image observers, producers, and consumers

know its status. As I discussed earlier, the image observer is essentially a callback that is notified asynchronously as the image is built. The default `Component` class image observer that we used in our previous examples called `repaint()` for us each time a new section of the image was available, so that the screen was updated more or less continuously as the data arrived. A different kind of image observer might wait for the entire image before telling the application to display it; yet another observer might update a loading meter showing how far the image loading had progressed.

Implementing an ImageObserver

To be an image observer, you have to implement the single method, `imageUpdate()`, defined by the `java.awt.image.ImageObserver` interface:

```
public boolean imageUpdate(Image image, int flags, int x, int y,
                      int width, int height)
```

`imageUpdate()` is called by the consumer, as needed, to pass the observer information about the construction of its view of the image. Essentially, any time the image changes, the consumer tells the observer so that the observer can perform any necessary actions, like repainting. `image` holds a reference to the `Image` object the consumer is processing. `flags` is an integer whose bits specify what information about the image is now available. The values of the flags are defined as `static` identifiers in the `ImageObserver` interface, as shown in Table 17-1.

Table 17–1: ImageObserver Information Flags

Flag	Description
HEIGHT	The height of the image is ready.
WIDTH	The width of the image is ready.
FRAMEBITS	A frame is complete.
SOMEBITS	An arbitrary number of pixels have arrived.
ALLBITS	The image is complete.
ABORT	The image loading has been aborted.
ERROR	An error occurred during image processing; attempts to display the image will fail.

The flags determine which of the other parameters, x, y, width, and height, hold valid data and what that data means. To test whether a particular flag in the flags integer is set, we have to resort to some binary shenanigans. The following class, MyObserver, implements the ImageObserver interface and prints its information as it's called:

```
import java.awt.*;
import java.awt.image.*;

class MyObserver implements ImageObserver {

    public boolean imageUpdate( Image image, int flags, int x, int y,
                                int width, int height) {

        if ( (flags & HEIGHT) !=0 )
            System.out.println("Image height = " + height );

        if ( (flags & WIDTH ) !=0 )
            System.out.println("Image width = " + width );

        if ( (flags & FRAMEBITS) != 0 )
            System.out.println("Another frame finished.");

        if ( (flags & SOMEBITS) != 0 )
            System.out.println("Image section :"
                        + new Rectangle( x, y, width, height ) );

        if ( (flags & ALLBITS) != 0 ) {
            System.out.println("Image finished!");
            return false;
        }

        if ( (flags & ABORT) != 0 ) {
            System.out.println("Image load aborted...");
            return false;
        }
```

```
            return true;
        }
    }
```

The `imageUpdate()` method of `MyObserver` is called by the consumer periodically, and prints simple status messages about the construction of the image. Notice that `width` and `height` play a dual role. If `SOMEBITS` is set, they represent the size of the chunk of the image that has just been delivered. If `HEIGHT` or `WIDTH` is set, however, they represent the overall image dimensions. Just for amusement, we have used the `java.awt.Rectangle` class to help us print the bounds of a rectangular region.

`imageUpdate()` returns a `boolean` value indicating whether or not it's interested in future updates. If the image is finished or aborted, `imageUpdate()` returns `false` to indicate it isn't interested in further updates. Otherwise, it returns `true`.

The following example uses `MyObserver` to print information about an image as AWT loads it:

```
import java.awt.*;

public class ObserveImage extends java.applet.Applet {
    Image img;
    public void init() {
        img = getImage( getClass().getResource(getParameter("img")) );
        MyObserver mo = new MyObserver();
        img.getWidth( mo );
        img.getHeight( mo );
        prepareImage( img, mo );
    }
}
```

After requesting the `Image` object with `getImage()`, we perform three operations on it to kick-start the loading process. `getWidth()` and `getHeight()` ask for the image's width and height. If the image hasn't been loaded yet, or its size can't be determined until loading is finished, our observer will be called when the data is ready. `prepareImage()` asks that the image be readied for display on the component. It's a general mechanism for getting AWT started loading, converting, and possibly scaling the image. If the image hasn't been otherwise prepared or displayed, this happens asynchronously, and our image observer will be notified as the data is constructed.

You may be wondering where the image consumer is, since we never see a call to `imageUpdate()`. That's a good question, but for now I'd like you to take it on faith that the consumer exists. As you'll see later, image consumers are rather mysterious objects that tend to hide beneath the surface of image-processing applications. In this case, the consumer is hiding deep inside the implementation of `Applet`.

You should be able to see how we could implement all sorts of sophisticated image loading and tracking schemes. The two most obvious strategies, however, are to draw an image progressively, as it's constructed, or to wait until it's complete and draw it in its entirety. We have already seen that the Component class implements the first scheme. Another class, java.awt.MediaTracker, is a general utility that tracks the loading of a number of images or other media types for us. We'll look at it next.

Using a MediaTracker

java.awt.MediaTracker is a utility class that simplifies life if we have to wait for one or more images to be loaded before they're displayed. A MediaTracker monitors the preparation of an image or a group of images and lets us check on them periodically, or wait until they are completed. MediaTracker uses the ImageObserver interface internally to receive image updates.

The following applet, LoadMe, uses a MediaTracker to wait while an image is prepared. It shows a "Loading . . . " message while it's waiting. (If you are retrieving the image from a local disk or very fast network, this message might go by quickly, so pay attention.)

```java
import java.awt.*;
public class TrackImage extends java.applet.Applet implements Runnable {
    Image img;
    final int MAIN_IMAGE = 0;
    MediaTracker tracker;
    boolean show = false;
    Thread runme;
    String message = "Loading...";
    public void init() {
        img = getImage( getClass().getResource(getParameter("img")) );
        tracker = new MediaTracker(this);
        tracker.addImage( img, MAIN_IMAGE );
    }
    public void start() {
        if ( !tracker.checkID( MAIN_IMAGE ) ) {
            runme = new Thread( this );
            runme.start();
        }
    }
    public void stop() {
        runme.stop();
        runme = null;
    }
    public void run() {
        repaint();
        try {
            tracker.waitForID( MAIN_IMAGE );
        } catch( InterruptedException e) { }
```

```
            if ( tracker.isErrorID( MAIN_IMAGE ) )
                message= "Error";
            else
                show = true;
            repaint();
    }
    public void paint( Graphics g ) {
        if ( show )
            g.drawImage( img, 0, 0, this );
        else {
            g.drawRect( 0, 0, getSize().width-1, getSize().height-1 );
            g.drawString( message, 20, 20 );
        }
    }
}
```

From its `init()` method, `LoadMe` requests its image and creates a `MediaTracker` to
manage it. Later, after the applet is started, `LoadMe` fires up a thread to wait while
the image is loaded. Note that we don't do this in `init()` because it would be rude
to do anything time-consuming there; it would take up time in an AWT thread that
we don't own. In this case, waiting in `init()` would be especially bad because
`paint()` would never get called and our "loading" message wouldn't be displayed;
the applet would just hang until the image loaded. It's often better to create a new
thread for initialization and display a startup message in the interim.

When we construct a `MediaTracker`, we give it a reference to our component
(`this`). After creating a `MediaTracker`, we assign it images to manage. Each image
is associated with an integer identifier we'll use later for checking on its status.
Multiple images can be associated with the same identifier, letting us manage them
as a group. The value of the identifier is also used to prioritize loading when waiting on multiple sets of images; lower IDs have higher priority. In this case, we want
to manage only a single image, so we created one identifier called `MAIN_IMAGE` and
passed it as the ID for our image in the call to `addImage()`.

In our applet's `start()` method, we call the `MediaTracker`'s `checkID()` routine
with the ID of the image to see if it's already been loaded. If it hasn't, the applet
fires up a new thread to fetch it. The thread executes the `run()` method, which
simply calls the `MediaTracker` `waitforID()` routine and blocks on the image, waiting for it to finish loading. The `show` flag tells `paint()` whether to display our status message or the actual image. We do a `repaint()` immediately upon entering
`run()` to display the "Loading..." status, and again upon exiting to change the
display. We test for errors during image preparation with `isErrorID()` and change
the status message if we find one.

This may seem like a lot of work to go through, just to put up a status message while loading a single image. MediaTracker is more valuable when we are working with many images that have to be available before we can begin parts of our application. It saves us from implementing a custom ImageObserver for every application. In the future, MediaTracker should also be able to track the status of audio clips and other kinds of media (as its name suggests).

Producing Image Data

What if we want to make our own image data? To be an image producer, we have to implement the five methods defined in the ImageProducer interface:

- addConsumer()
- startProduction()
- isConsumer()
- removeConsumer()
- requestTopDownLeftRightResend()

Four methods of ImageProducer simply deal with the process of registering consumers. addConsumer() takes an ImageConsumer as an argument and adds it to the list of consumers. Our producer can then start sending image data to the consumer whenever it's ready. startProduction() is identical to addConsumer(), except that it asks the producer to start sending data as soon as possible. The difference might be that a given producer would send the current frame of data or initiate construction of a frame immediately, rather than waiting until its next cycle. isConsumer() tests whether a particular consumer is already registered, and removeConsumer() removes a consumer from the list. We'll see shortly that we can perform these kinds of operations easily with a Vector.

An ImageProducer also needs to know how to use the ImageConsumer interface of its clients. The final method of the ImageProducer interface, requestTopDownLeft-RightResend(), asks that the image data be resent to the consumer, in order, from beginning to end. In general, a producer can generate pixel data and send it to the consumer in any order that it likes. The setPixels() method of the ImageConsumer interface takes parameters telling the consumer what part of the image is being delivered on each call. A call to requestTopDownLeftRightResend() asks the producer to send the pixel data again, in order. A consumer might do this so that it can use a higher quality conversion algorithm that relies on receiving the pixel data in sequence. It's important to note that the producer is allowed to ignore this request; it doesn't have to be able to send the data in sequence.

Color Models

Everybody wants to work with color in their application, but using color raises problems. The most important problem is simply how to represent a color. There are many different ways to encode color information: red, green, blue (RGB) values; hue, saturation, value (HSV); hue, lightness, saturation (HLS); and more. In addition, you can provide full color information for each pixel, or you can just specify an index into a color table (palette) for each pixel. The way you represent a color is called a *color model*. AWT provides tools for two broad groups of color models: *direct* and *indexed*.

As you might expect, you need to specify a color model in order to generate pixel data; the abstract class java.awt.image.ColorModel represents a color model. A ColorModel is one of the arguments to the setPixels() method an image producer calls to deliver pixels to a consumer. What you probably wouldn't expect is that you can use a different color model every time you call setPixels(). Exactly why you'd do this is another matter. Most of the time, you'll want to work with a single color model; that model will probably be the default direct color model. But the additional flexibility is there if you need it.

By default, the core AWT components use a direct color model called ARGB. The A stands for "alpha," which is the historical name for transparency. RGB refers to the red, green, and blue color components that are combined to produce a single, composite color. In the default ARGB model, each pixel is represented by a 32-bit integer that is interpreted as four 8-bit fields; in order, the fields represent the transparency (A), red, green, and blue components of the color, as shown in Figure 17-3.

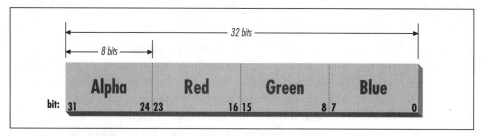

Figure 17–3: ARGB color encoding

To create an instance of the default ARGB model, call the static getRGBdefault() method in ColorModel. This method returns a DirectColorModel object; DirectColorModel is a subclass of ColorModel. You can also create other direct color models by calling a DirectColorModel constructor, but you shouldn't need to unless you have a fairly exotic application.

In an indexed color model, each pixel is represented by a smaller amount of information: an index into a table of real color values. For some applications, generating data with an indexed model may be more convenient. If you have an 8-bit display or smaller, using an indexed model may be more efficient, since your hardware is internally using an indexed color model of some form.

While AWT provides IndexedColorModel objects, we won't cover them in this book. It's sufficient to work with the DirectColorModel. Even if you have an 8-bit display, the Java implementation on your platform should accommodate the hardware you have and, if necessary, dither colors to fit your display. Java also produces transparency on systems that don't natively support it by dithering colors.

Creating an Image

Let's take a look at producing some image data. A picture may be worth a thousand words, but fortunately, we can generate a picture in significantly fewer than a thousand words of Java. If we just want to render image frames byte by byte, we can use a utility class that acts as an ImageProducer for us.

java.awt.image.MemoryImageSource is a simple utility class that implements the ImageProducer interface; we give it pixel data in an array and it sends that data to an image consumer. A MemoryImageSource can be constructed for a given color model, with various options to specify the type and positioning of its data. We'll use the simplest form, which assumes an ARGB color model.

The following applet, ColorPan, creates an image from an array of integers holding ARGB pixel values:

```java
import java.awt.*;
import java.awt.image.*;
public class ColorPan extends java.applet.Applet {
    Image img;
    int width, height;
    int [] pixData;
    public void init() {
        width = getSize().width;
        height = getSize().height;
        pixData = new int [width * height];
        int i=0;
        for (int y = 0; y < height; y++) {
            int red = (y * 255) / (height - 1);
            for (int x = 0; x < width; x++) {
                int green = (x * 255) / (width - 1);
                int blue = 128;
                int alpha = 255;
                pixData[i++] = (alpha << 24) | (red << 16) |
                               (green << 8 ) | blue;
            }
        }
```

```
        }
        public void paint( Graphics g ) {
            if ( img == null )
                img = createImage( new MemoryImageSource(width, height,
                                              pixData, 0, width));
            g.drawImage( img, 0, 0, this );
        }
    }
```

Give it a try. The size of the image is determined by the size of the applet when it starts up. You should get a very colorful box that pans from deep blue at the upper left corner to bright yellow at the bottom right, with green and red at the other extremes.

We create the pixel data for our image in the init() method and then use MemoryImageSource to create and display the image in paint(). The variable pixData is a one-dimensional array of integers that holds 32-bit ARGB pixel values. In init() we loop over every pixel in the image and assign it an ARGB value. The alpha (transparency) component is always 255, which means the image is opaque. The blue component is always 128, half its maximum intensity. The red component varies from 0 to 255 along the y axis; likewise, the green component varies from 0 to 255 along the x axis. The line below combines these components into an ARGB value:

```
    pixData[i++] = (alpha << 24) | (red << 16) | (green << 8 ) | blue;
```

The bitwise left-shift operator (<<) should be familiar to C programmers. It simply shoves the bits over by the specified number of positions. The alpha value takes the top byte of the integer, followed by the red, green, and blue values.

When we construct the MemoryImageSource as a producer for this data, we give it five parameters: the width and height of the image to construct (in pixels), the pixData array, an offset into that array, and the width of each scan line (in pixels). We'll start with the first element (offset 0) of pixData; the width of each scan line and the width of the image are the same. The array pixData has width * height elements, which means it has one element for each pixel.

We create the actual image once, in paint(), using the createImage() method that our applet inherits from Component. In the double-buffering and off-screen drawing examples, we used createImage() to give us an empty off-screen image buffer. Here we use createImage() to generate an image from a specified Image-Producer. createImage() creates the Image object and receives pixel data from the producer to construct the image. Note that there's nothing particularly special about MemoryImageSource; we could use any object that implements the image-producer interface inside of createImage(), including one we wrote ourselves. Once we have the image, we can draw it on the display with the familiar drawImage() method.

Updating a MemoryImageSource

MemoryImageSource can also be used to generate a sequence of images or to update an image dynamically. In Java 1.1, this is probably the easiest way to build your own low-level animation software. This example simulates the static on a television screen. It generates successive frames of random black and white pixels and displays each frame when it is complete. Figure 17-4 shows one frame of random static, followed by the code:

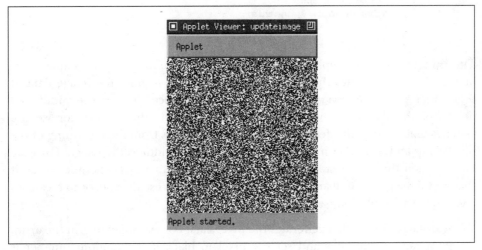

Figure 17–4: A frame of random static

```
import java.awt.*;
import java.awt.image.*;
public class StaticGenerator
        extends java.applet.Applet
        implements Runnable {
    int arrayLength, pixels[];
    MemoryImageSource source;
    Image image;
    int width, height;
    public void init() {
        width = getSize().width; height = getSize().height;
        arrayLength = width * height;
        pixels = new int [arrayLength];
        source = new MemoryImageSource(width, height, pixels, 0, width);
        source.setAnimated(true);
        image = createImage(source);
        new Thread(this).start();
    }
    public void run() {
        while (true) {
            try {
                Thread.sleep(1000/24);
```

```
            } catch( InterruptedException e ) { /* die */ }
            for (int x = 0; x < width; x++)
                for (int y = 0; y < height; y++)  {
                    boolean rand = Math.random() > 0.5;
                    pixels[y*width+x] =
                        rand ? Color.black.getRGB() : Color.white.getRGB();
                }
            // Push out the new data
            source.newPixels(0, 0, width, height);
        }
    }
    public void paint( Graphics g ) {
        g.drawImage(image, 0, 0, this);
    }
}
```

The init() method sets up the MemoryImageSource that produces the sequence of images. It first computes the size of the array needed to hold the image data. It then creates a MemoryImageSource object that produces images the width and height of the display, using the default color model (the constructor we use assumes that we want the default). We start taking pixels from the beginning of the pixel array, and scan lines in the array have the same width as the image. Once we have created the MemoryImageSource, we call its setAnimated() method to tell it that we will be generating an image sequence. Then we use the source to create an Image that will display our sequence.

We next start a thread that generates the pixel data. For every element in the array, we get a random number and set the pixel to black if the random number is greater than 0.5. Because pixels is an int array, we can't assign Color objects to it directly; we use getRGB() to extract the color components from the black and white Color constants. When we have filled the entire array with data, we call the newPixels() method, which delivers the new data to the image.

That's about all there is. We provide a very uninteresting paint() method that just calls drawImage() to put the current state of the image on the screen. Whenever paint() is called, we see the latest collection of static. The image observer, which is the Applet itself, schedules a call to paint() whenever anything interesting has happened to the image. It's worth noting how simple it is to create this animation. Once we have the MemoryImageSource, we use it to create an image that we treat like any other image. The code that generates the image sequence can be arbitrarily complex—certainly in any reasonable example, it would be more complex than our (admittedly cheesy) static. But that complexity never infects the simple task of getting the image on the screen and updating it.

Image Producers and Consumers

In this section we'll create an image producer that generates a stream of image frames rather than just a static image. Unfortunately, it would take too many lines of code to generate anything really interesting, so we'll stick with a simple modification of our ColorPan example. After all, figuring out what to display is your job; I'm primarily concerned with giving you the necessary tools. After this, you should have the needed tools to implement more interesting applications.

A word of advice: if you find yourself writing image producers, you're probably making your life excessively difficult. Most situations can be handled by the dynamic MemoryImageSource technique that we just demonstrated. Before going to the trouble of writing an image producer, convince yourself that there isn't a simpler solution. Even if you never write an image producer yourself, it's good (like Motherhood and Apple Pie) to understand how Java's image-rendering tools work.

Image Consumers

First, we have to know a little more about the image consumers we'll be feeding. An image consumer implements the seven methods that are defined in the Image-Consumer interface. Two of these methods are overloaded versions of the setPix-els() method that accept the actual pixel data for a region of the image. They are identical except that one takes the pixel data as an array of integers, and the other uses an array of bytes. (An array of bytes is natural when you're using an indexed color model because each pixel is specified by an index into a color array.) A call to setPixels() looks something like:

```
setPixels(x, y, width, height, colorModel, pixels, offset, scanLength);
```

pixels is the one-dimensional array of bytes or integers that holds the pixel data. Often, you deliver only part of the image with each call to setPixels(). The x, y, width, and height values define the rectangle of the image for which pixels are being delivered. x and y specify the upper left-hand corner of the chunk you're delivering, relative to the upper left-hand corner of the image as a whole. width specifies the width in pixels of the chunk; height specifies the number of scan lines in the chunk. offset specifies the point in pixels at which the data being delivered in this call to setPixels() starts. Finally, scanLength indicates the width of the entire image, which is not necessarily the same as width. The pixels array must be large enough to accommodate width*length+offset elements; if it's larger, any leftover data is ignored.

We haven't said anything yet about the colorModel argument to setPixels(). In our previous example, we drew our image using the default ARGB color model for pixel values; the version of the `MemoryImageSource` constructor that we used supplied the default color model for us. In this example, we also stick with the default model, but this time we have to specify it explicitly. The remaining five methods of the `ImageConsumer` interface accept general attributes and framing information about the image:

- `setHints()`
- `setDimensions()`
- `setProperties()`
- `setColorModel()`
- `imageComplete()`

Before delivering any data to a consumer, the producer should call the consumer's `setHints()` method to pass it information about how pixels will be delivered. Hints are specified in the form of flags defined in the `ImageConsumer` interface. The flags are described in Table 17-2. The consumer uses these hints to optimize the way it builds the image; it's also free to ignore them.

Table 17–2: ImageConsumer setHints() Flags

Flag	Description
RANDOMPIXELORDER	The pixels are delivered in random order
TOPDOWNLEFTRIGHT	The pixels are delivered from top to bottom, left to right
COMPLETESCANLINES	Each call to `setPixels()` delivers one or more complete scan lines
SINGLEPASS	Each pixel is delivered only once
SINGLEFRAME	The pixels define a single, static image

`setDimensions()` is called to pass the width and height of the image when they are known.

`setProperties()` is used to pass a hashtable of image properties, stored by name. This method isn't particularly useful without some prior agreement between the producer and consumer about what properties are meaningful. For example, image formats such as GIF and TIFF can include additional information about the image. These image attributes could be delivered to the consumer in the hashtable.

`setColorModel()` is called to tell the consumer which color model will be used to process most of the pixel data. However, remember that each call to `setPixels()` also specifies a `ColorModel` for its group of pixels. The color model specified in `setColorModel()` is really only a hint that the consumer can use for optimization. You're not required to use this color model to deliver all (or for that matter, any) of the pixels in the image.

The producer calls the consumer's `imageComplete()` method when it has completely delivered the image or a frame of an image sequence. If the consumer doesn't wish to receive further frames of the image, it should unregister itself from the producer at this point. The producer passes a status flag formed from the flags shown in Table 17-3.

Table 17–3: ImageConsumer imageComplete() Flags

Flag	Description
STATICIMAGEDONE	A single static image is complete
SINGLEFRAMEDONE	One frame of an image sequence is complete
IMAGEERROR	An error occurred while generating the image

As you can see, the `ImageProducer` and `ImageConsumer` interfaces provide a very flexible mechanism for distributing image data. Now let's look at a simple producer.

A Sequence of Images

The following class, `ImageSequence`, shows how to implement an `ImageProducer` that generates a sequence of images. The images are a lot like the `ColorPan` image we generated a few pages back, except that the blue component of each pixel changes with every frame. This image producer doesn't do anything you couldn't do with a `MemoryImageSource`. It reads ARGB data from an array and consults the object that creates the array to give it an opportunity to update the data between each frame.

This is a complex example, so before diving into the code, let's take a broad look at the pieces. The `ImageSequence` class is an image producer; it generates data and sends it to image consumers to be displayed. To make our design more modular, we define an interface called `FrameARGBData` that describes how our rendering code provides each frame of ARGB pixel data to our producer. To do the computation and provide the raw bits, we create a class called `ColorPanCycle` that implements `FrameARGBData`. This means that `ImageSequence` doesn't care specifically where the data comes from; if we wanted to draw different images, we could just drop in another class, provided that the new class implements `FrameARGBData`. Finally, we create an applet called `UpdatingImage` that includes two image consumers to display the data.

Here's the `ImageSequence` class:

```
import java.awt.image.*;
import java.util.*;
public class ImageSequence extends Thread implements ImageProducer {
    int width, height, delay;
```

```
ColorModel model = ColorModel.getRGBdefault();
FrameARGBData frameData;
private Vector consumers = new Vector();
public void run() {
    while ( frameData != null ) {
        frameData.nextFrame();
        sendFrame();
        try {
            sleep( delay );
        } catch ( InterruptedException e ) {}
    }
}
public ImageSequence(FrameARGBData src, int maxFPS ) {
    frameData = src;
    width = frameData.size().width;
    height = frameData.size().height;
    delay = 1000/maxFPS;
    setPriority( MIN_PRIORITY + 1 );
}
public synchronized void addConsumer(ImageConsumer c) {
    if ( isConsumer( c ) )
        return;
    consumers.addElement( c );
    c.setHints(ImageConsumer.TOPDOWNLEFTRIGHT |
            ImageConsumer.SINGLEPASS );
    c.setDimensions( width, height );
    c.setProperties( new Hashtable() );
    c.setColorModel( model );
}
public synchronized boolean isConsumer(ImageConsumer c) {
    return ( consumers.contains( c ) );
}
public synchronized void removeConsumer(ImageConsumer c) {
    consumers.removeElement( c );
}
public void startProduction(ImageConsumer ic) {
    addConsumer(ic);
}
public void requestTopDownLeftRightResend(ImageConsumer ic) { }
private void sendFrame() {
    for ( Enumeration e = consumers.elements(); e.hasMoreElements();  ) {
        ImageConsumer c = (ImageConsumer)e.nextElement();
        c.setPixels(0, 0, width, height, model, frameData.getPixels(),
                    0, width);
        c.imageComplete(ImageConsumer.SINGLEFRAMEDONE);
    }
}
}
```

The bulk of the code in ImageSequence creates the skeleton we need for implementing the ImageProducer interface. ImageSequence is actually a simple subclass

of Thread whose run() method loops, generating and sending a frame of data on each iteration. The ImageSequence constructor takes two items: a FrameARGBData object that updates the array of pixel data for each frame, and an integer that specifies the maximum number of frames per second to generate. We give the thread a low priority (MIN_PRIORITY+1) so that it can't run away with all of our CPU time.

Our FrameARGBData object implements the following interface:

```
interface FrameARGBData {
    java.awt.Dimension size();
    int [] getPixels();
    void nextFrame();
}
```

In ImageSequence's run() method, we call nextFrame() to compute the array of pixels for each frame. After computing the pixels, we call our own sendFrame() method to deliver the data to the consumers. sendFrame() calls getPixels() to retrieve the updated array of pixel data from the FrameARGBData object. sendFrame() then sends the new data to all of the consumers by invoking each of their setPixels() methods and signaling the end of the frame with imageComplete(). Note that sendFrame() can handle multiple consumers; it iterates through a Vector of image consumers. In a more realistic implementation, we would also check for errors and notify the consumers if any occurred.

The business of managing the Vector of consumers is handled by addConsumer() and the other methods in the ImageProducer interface. addConsumer() adds an item to consumers. A Vector is a perfect tool for this task, since it's an automatically extendable array, with methods for finding out how many elements it has, whether or not a given element is already a member, and so on.

addConsumer() also gives the consumer hints about how the data will be delivered by calling setHints(). This image provider always works from top to bottom and left to right, and makes only one pass through the data. addConsumer() next gives the consumer an empty hashtable of image properties. Finally, it reports that most of the pixels will use the default ARGB color model (we initialized the variable model to ColorModel.getRGBDefault()). In this example, we always start sending image data on the next frame, so startProduction() simply calls addConsumer().

We've discussed the mechanism for communications between the consumer and producer, but I haven't yet told you where the data comes from. We have a FrameARGBData interface that defines how to retrieve the data, but we don't yet have an object that implements the interface. The following class, ColorPanCycle, implements FrameARGBData; we'll use it to generate our pixels:

```
import java.awt.*;
class ColorPanCycle implements FrameARGBData {
    int frame = 0, width, height;
```

```java
    private int [] pixels;
    ColorPanCycle ( int w, int h ) {
        width = w;
        height = h;
        pixels = new int [ width * height ];
        nextFrame();
    }
    public synchronized int [] getPixels() {
        return pixels;
    }
    public synchronized void nextFrame() {
        int index = 0;
        for (int y = 0; y < height; y++) {
            for (int x = 0; x < width; x++) {
                int red = (y * 255) / (height - 1);
                int green = (x * 255) / (width - 1);
                int blue = (frame * 10) & 0xff;
                pixels[index++] =
                    (255 << 24) | (red << 16) | (green << 8) | blue;
            }
        }
        frame++;
    }
    public Dimension size() {
        return new Dimension ( width, height );
    }
}
```

ColorPanCycle is like our previous ColorPan example, except that it adjusts each pixel's blue component each time nextFrame() is called. This should produce a color cycling effect; as time goes on, the image becomes more blue.

Now let's put the pieces together by writing an applet that displays a sequence of changing images: UpdatingImage. In fact, we'll do better than displaying one sequence. To prove that ImageSequence really can deal with multiple consumers, UpdatingImage creates two components that display different views of the image. Once the mechanism has been set up, it's surprising how little code you need to add additional displays.

```java
import java.awt.*;
import java.awt.image.*;
public class UpdatingImage extends java.applet.Applet {
    ImageSequence seq;
    public void init() {
        seq = new ImageSequence( new ColorPanCycle(100, 100), 10);
        setLayout( null );
        add( new ImageCanvas( seq, 50, 50 ) );
        add( new ImageCanvas( seq, 100, 100 ) );
        seq.start();
    }
    public void stop() {
        if ( seq != null ) {
```

```
                    seq.stop();
                    seq = null;
            }
        }
    }
    class ImageCanvas extends Canvas {
        Image img;
        ImageProducer source;
        ImageCanvas ( ImageProducer p, int w, int h ) {
            source = p;
            setSize( w, h );
        }
        public void update( Graphics g ) {
            paint(g);
        }
        public void paint( Graphics g ) {
            if ( img == null )
                img = createImage( source );
            g.drawImage( img, 0, 0, getSize().width, getSize().height, this );
        }
    }
```

UpdatingImage constructs a new ImageSequence producer with an instance of our
ColorPanCycle object as its frame source. It then creates two ImageCanvas components that create and display the two views of our animation. ImageCanvas is a subclass of Canvas; it takes an ImageProducer and a width and height in its constructor
and creates and displays an appropriately scaled version of the image in its paint()
method. UpdatingImage places the smaller view on top of the larger one for a sort
of "picture in picture" effect.

If you've followed the example to this point, you're probably wondering where in
the heck is the image consumer. After all, we spent a lot of time writing methods in
ImageSequence for the consumer to call. If you look back at the code, you'll see
that an ImageSequence object gets passed to the ImageCanvas constructor, and that
this object is used as an argument to createImage(). But nobody appears to call
addConsumer(). And the image producer calls setPixels() and other consumer
methods; but it always digs a consumer out of its Vector of registered consumers,
so we never see where these consumers come from.

In UpdatingImage, the image consumer is behind the scenes, hidden deep inside
the Canvas—in fact, inside the Canvas' peer. The call to createImage() tells its
component (i.e., our canvas) to become an image consumer. Something deep
inside the component is calling addConsumer() behind our backs and registering a
mysterious consumer, and that consumer is the one the producer uses in calls to
setPixels() and other methods. We haven't implemented any ImageConsumer
objects in this book because, as you might imagine, most image consumers are

implemented in native code, since they need to display things on the screen. There are others though; the `java.awt.image.PixelGrabber` class is a consumer that returns the pixel data as a byte array. You might use it to save an image. You can make your own consumer do anything you like with pixel data from a producer. But in reality, you rarely need to write an image consumer yourself. Let them stay hidden; take it on faith that they exist.

Now for the next question: How does the screen get updated? Even though we are updating the consumer with new data, the new image will not appear on the display unless the applet repaints it periodically. By now, this part of the machinery should be familiar: what we need is an image observer. Remember that all components are image observers (i.e., the class `Component` implements `ImageObserver`). The call to `drawImage()` specifies our `ImageCanvas` as its image observer. The default `Component` class-image-observer functionality then repaints our image whenever new pixel data arrives.

In this example, we haven't bothered to stop and start our applet properly; it continues running and wasting CPU time even when it's invisible. There are two strategies for stopping and restarting our thread. We can destroy the thread and create a new one, which would require recreating our `ImageCanvas` objects, or we could suspend and resume the active thread. Neither option is particularly difficult.

Filtering Image Data

As I said earlier, you rarely need to write an image consumer. However, there is one kind of image consumer that's worth knowing about. In this final section on images, we'll build a simple image filter. An image filter is simply a class that performs some work on image data before passing the data to another consumer.

The `ColorSep` applet acquires an image; uses an image filter to separate the image into red, green, and blue components; and displays the three resulting images. With this applet and a few million dollars, you could build your own color separation plant.

```
import java.awt.*;
import java.awt.image.*;
public class ColorSep extends java.applet.Applet {
    Image img, redImg, greenImg, blueImg;
    public void init() {
        img = getImage( getClass().getResource( getParameter("img")) );
        redImg = createImage(new FilteredImageSource(img.getSource(),
                                  new ColorMaskFilter( Color.red )));
        greenImg = createImage(new FilteredImageSource(img.getSource(),
                                  new ColorMaskFilter( Color.green )));
        blueImg = createImage(new FilteredImageSource(img.getSource(),
                                  new ColorMaskFilter( Color.blue )));
    }
```

```
        public void paint( Graphics g ) {
            int width = getSize().width, height = getSize().height;
            g.drawImage( redImg, 0, 0, width/3, height, this );
            g.drawImage( greenImg, width/3, 0, width/3, height, this );
            g.drawImage( blueImg, 2*width/3, 0, width/3, height, this );
        }
    }
    class ColorMaskFilter extends RGBImageFilter {
        Color color;
        ColorMaskFilter( Color mask ) {
            color = mask;
            canFilterIndexColorModel = true;
        }
        public int filterRGB(int x, int y, int pixel ) {
            return
                255 << 24 |
                (((pixel & 0xff0000) >> 16) * color.getRed()/255) << 16 |
                (((pixel & 0xff00) >> 8) * color.getGreen()/255) << 8 |
                (pixel & 0xff) * color.getBlue()/255 ;
        }
    }
```

The `FilteredImageSource` and `RGBImageFilter` classes form the basis for building and using image filters. A `FilteredImageSource` is an image producer (like `MemoryImageSource`) that is constructed from an image and an `ImageFilter` object. It fetches pixel data from the image and feeds it through the image filter before passing the data along. Because `FilteredImageSource` is an image producer, we can use it in our calls to `createImage()`.

But where's the consumer? `FilteredImageSource` obviously consumes image data as well as producing it. The image consumer is still mostly hidden, but is peeking out from under its rock. Our class `ColorMaskFilter` extends `RGBImageFilter`, which in turn extends `ImageFilter`. And `ImageFilter` is (finally!) an image consumer. Of course, we still don't see the calls to `addConsumer()`, and we don't see an implementation of `setPixels()`; they're hidden in the `ImageFilter` sources and inherited by `ColorMaskFilter`.

So what does `ColorMaskFilter` actually do? Not much. `ColorMaskFilter` is a simple subclass of `RGBImageFilter` that implements one method, `filterRGB()`, through which all of the pixel data are fed. Its constructor saves a mask value we use for filtering. The `filterRGB()` method accepts a pixel value, along with its x and y coordinates, and returns the filtered version of the pixel. In `ColorMaskFilter`, we simply multiply the color components by the mask color to get the proper effect. A more complex filter, however, might use the coordinates to change its behavior based on the pixel's position.

One final detail: the constructor for ColorMaskFilter sets the flag canFilterIndexColorModel. This flag is inherited from RGBImageFilter. It means our filter doesn't depend on the pixel's position. In turn, this means it can filter the colors in a color table. If we were using an indexed color model, filtering the color table would be much faster than filtering the individual pixels.

Working with Audio

So you've read all the material on drawing and image processing, and you're wondering what in the world audio has to do with images. Well, not much actually, except that true multimedia presentations often combine image techniques such as animation with sound. So we're going to spend a few minutes here talking about audio, for lack of a better place to discuss it.

As we write this, the good people at Sun are hard at work developing the API that Java applets will use for playing audio. A future release of Java will have support for real-time and continuous audio streams, sound management, mixing, synchronization, and filtering. Unfortunately, at the moment, we can tell you only about the basics.

java.applet.AudioClip defines an interface for objects that can play sound. An object that implements AudioClip can be told to play() its sound data, stop() playing the sound, or loop() continually.

An applet can call its getAudioClip() method to retrieve sounds over the network. This method takes an absolute or relative URL to specify where the audio file is located. The viewer may take the sound from a cache or retrieve it over the network. The following applet, NoisyButton, gives a simple example:

```
import java.awt.*;
import java.awt.event.*;
public class NoisyButton extends java.applet.Applet implements ActionListener {
    java.applet.AudioClip sound;
    public void init() {
        sound = getAudioClip( getClass().getResource(getParameter("sound")) );
        Button button = new Button("Play Sound");
        button.addActionListener( this );
        add ( button );
    }
    public void actionPerformed( ActionEvent e ) {
        if ( sound != null )
            sound.play();
    }
}
```

NoisyButton retrieves an AudioClip from the server; we use getParameter() to supply the name of the sound and getResource() to locate it. (The applet tag that displays NoisyButton must include a parameter tag for sound.) When the button is pushed, we simply call the play() method of the AudioClip to start things. After that it will play to completion unless we call the stop() method to interrupt it. Unfortunately, this is about the extent of what we can do with sound right now. If you want to experiment, there are a few additional methods in the sun.audio classes. Stay tuned for a bigger and better audio API as part of the upcoming Java Media package.

18

Java Beans

JavaBeans[*] is one of the most interesting new directions in Java. As a whole, it is a component architecture for Java. It is a set of rules for writing highly reusable software elements that can be linked together in a "plug and play" fashion to build applications. To build an application, you may not even need to write code; eventually, when libraries of Beans are widespread, it will be possible to create applications entirely by connecting prefabricated modules using a graphical development tool.

JavaBeans is a rich topic, and I can't give it more than a brief overview here. If this overview whets your appetite, look for *Developing Java Beans* by Rob Englander (O'Reilly & Associates).

What's a Bean?

So, what exactly is or are Java Beans? As I said earlier, JavaBeans defines a set of rules; Java Beans are ordinary Java objects that play by these rules. That is, Java Beans are Java objects that conform to the JavaBeans API and design patterns so that they can be recognized and manipulated within visual application builder environments. Beans live and work in the Java VM, as do all Java objects. They communicate with their neighbors using events and other normal method invocations.

For examples of Beans, we have to look no further than the `java.awt` package. All of the familar AWT components, like `Button`, `TextArea`, `Scrollpane`, etc., are not only suggestive of things suitable to be Beans, but are, in fact, Beans! Much of what

---

[*] "JavaBeans" refers to the component architecture; "Java Beans" refers to components that use this architecture.

you learned in Chapter 13 about AWT concepts has prepared you for understanding Beans. Although the AWT components are relatively simple, Beans can also be large and complex application components, like spreadsheets or document editors. We'll talk more about what exactly makes a Bean a Bean in a moment. For now, I want to give you a better sense of how they are used.

I said that Java Beans are objects intended to be manipulated visually, within a graphical application builder. By that I mean that they will generally be chosen from a palette of tools and manipulated graphically in an application builder's workspace. In this sense Beans are somewhat like widgets used in a traditional GUI builder; user interface components can be assembled to make application "screens." But in traditional GUI builders, the result is usually just some automatically generated code that provides a skeleton on which you hang the meat of your application. GUI builders generally build GUIs, not entire applications.

In contrast, Java Beans can be not only simple UI components like buttons and sliders but more complex and abstract components as well. It is easy to get the impression that Beans are, themselves, always graphical objects (like the AWT components that we mentioned). But Java Beans can implement any part of an application, including "invisible" parts that perform calculations, storage, and communications. We would like to be able to snap together a substantial application using prefabricated Beans, without ever writing a line of code! Three characteristics of the JavaBeans architecture make this possible:

Design patterns

The first important characteristic of a Java Bean is simply a layer of standardization. Design patterns (i.e., coding conventions) let tools and humans recognize the basic features of a Bean and manipulate it without knowing how it is implemented. We might say that Beans are "self-documenting." By examining a Bean, we tell what events it can fire and receive; we can also learn about its properties (the equivalent of its public variables) and its methods. Beans can also, optionally, provide very explicit information about their features tailored specifically for builder tools.

Reflection

Reflection is an important new feature of the Java language. (It's discussed in Chapter 7.) Reflection makes it possible for Java code to inspect and manipulate Java objects at run-time. In the context of JavaBeans, reflection lets a development tool analyze a Bean's capabilities, change the values of its variables, and invoke its methods. Essentially, reflection allows Java objects that meet at run-time to do all of the things that could be done if they had been put together at compile-time. Even if a Bean doesn't come bundled with any "built-in" documentation, we can still gather information about its capabilities and properties by directly inspecting the class, using reflection.

Object serialization

Finally, the Java Serialization API allows us to "freeze dry" (JavaSoft prefers the word "pickle") a living, breathing application or application component and revive it later. This is a very important step; it makes it possible to piece together applications without extensive code generation. Rather than customizing and compiling large amounts of Java code to build our application on startup, we can simply paste together Beans, configure them, tweak their appearance, and then save them. Later, the Beans can be restored with all of their state and all of their interconnections intact. This makes possible a fundamentally different way of thinking about the design process. It is easy to use serialized objects from handwritten Java code as well, so we can freely mix "freeze dried" Beans with plain old Bean classes and other Java code.

How Big Is a Bean?

Our examples of Beans have ranged from simple buttons to spreadsheets. Obviously, a button Bean would be much less complex than a spreadsheet and would be used at a different level of the application's design. At what level are Beans intended to be used? The JavaBeans architecture is supposed to scale well from small to large; simple Beans can be used to build larger Beans. A small Bean may consist of a single class; a large Bean may have many. In the near future, Java Beans should also be able to team up at run-time to form groups that act like a single, virtual Bean.

Simple Beans are little more than ordinary Java objects. In fact, any Java class that has a default (empty) constructor could be considered a Bean. A Bean should also be serializable, although the JavaBeans specification doesn't strictly require that. These two criteria ensure that we can create an instance of the Bean dynamically, and that we can later save the Bean, as part of a group or composition of Beans. There are no other requirements. Beans are not required to inherit from a base Bean class, and they don't have to implement any special interface. In this sense, most well-behaved Java objects could already be considered Beans.

A more useful Bean would want to send and receive events or expose its properties to the world. To do so, it follows the appropriate design patterns for naming the relevant methods, so that these features can be automatically recognized. Most nontrivial Beans will also provide information about themselves in the form of a BeanInfo class. A BeanInfo class implements the BeanInfo interface, which holds methods that can describe a Bean's features. Normally, this "bean info" is supplied by a separate class that is named for and packaged with the Bean.

The BeanBox

We can't have a meaningful discussion of Beans without spending a little time talking about the builder environments in which they will be used. In this book we will talk about the BeanBox container that comes with JavaSoft's Bean Development Kit (BDK).[*] BeanBox is by no means a real application builder environment. Its job is to provide a simple reference platform in which you can test your Beans. BeanBox reads basic Bean information, creates instances of Beans, and allows the most basic hookup of events and properties. It also comes with some interesting test Beans. Aside from that, it offers little. Its main advantage is that it is free (including source code) and universally available because it is written in pure Java. I'll use the BeanBox fairly extensively in this chapter to demonstrate how Beans work. But keep in mind that the BeanBox isn't a real development environment, and that real development tools will do a lot more.

Running the BeanBox

Follow JavaSoft's directions for installing the BDK and running the BeanBox. Figure 18-1 shows the Bean palette, BeanBox work area, and a properties sheet (or customizer window). The properties sheet or customizer changes its contents based on the Bean selected in the work area.

To add a Bean to the BeanBox, drag it from the palette, and drop it into the work area. (If that doesn't work, try clicking on the Bean in the palette and then clicking in the work area.) Once placed in the BeanBox, a Bean can be selected by clicking on it or just outside of it. You can move the Bean within the BeanBox and reshape it by dragging its corners.

Properties and Customizers

Properties represent the "state" or "data" content of a Bean. They are features that can be manipulated externally to configure the Bean. For a Bean that's a GUI component, you would expect its properties to include its color, label, and other features of its basic appearance. Properties are similar to an object's public variables. Like a variable, a property can be a primitive type (like a number or boolean) or it can be a complex object type (like a `String` or a collection of spreadsheet data). Unlike variables, properties are implemented using methods, so that a Bean can take action when a property changes. By sending an event when a property changes, a Bean can notify other interested Beans of the change. (See the section "Bound Properties" later in this chapter.)

---

[*] The BDK is available from *http://splash.javasoft.com/beans.* However, the basic Beans API and support classes are incorporated into Java 1.1; the BDK primarily provides tools like the BeanBox.

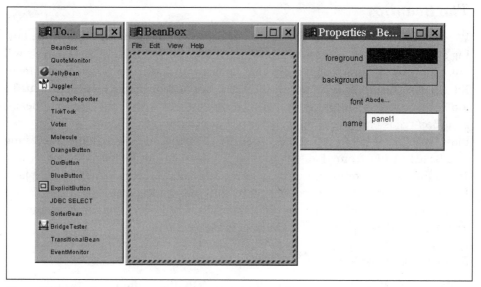

Figure 18–1: The Bean palette, a BeanBox, and a properties sheet

Let's pull a Bean into the BeanBox and take a look at its properties. Drag a Juggler Bean (one of JavaSoft's test Beans) into the workspace; the animation should start, and Duke should begin juggling his coffee beans as soon as you put him in the BeanBox, as shown in Figure 18-2. Don't worry, we'll have him under our control soon enough.

When the Juggler Bean was first loaded by the BeanBox, it was inspected to discover its properties. When we select a juggler, the BeanBox displays these properties in the properties sheet and allows us to modify them. As you can see in the figure, the juggler has five properties. "Foreground" and "background" are colors; their current values are displayed in the corresponding box. "Font" is the font that would be used if juggler were displaying any text; an example of the font is shown. The "name" is a simple string that identifies the component (don't worry about the value of name just yet).

These four basic properties will become familiar to you; many GUI Beans inherit them from the AWT's Component class. For Juggler, these four properties don't do much. Since Juggler just displays images and doesn't do any drawing, the foreground and background colors and font won't have any visible effect. In fact, these really shouldn't be listed in the properties sheet at all. We'll show how to hide them in our own Beans later.

Now turn your attention to the property called "animationRate". This is a more useful feature. It is an integer property that controls the interval in milliseconds between displaying the juggler's frames. Try changing its value. The juggler

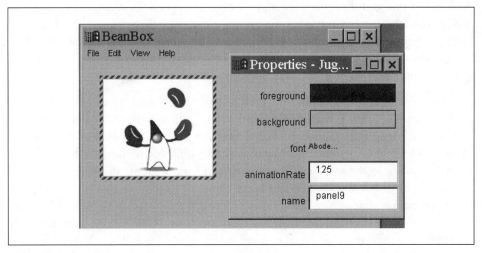

Figure 18–2: Juggling Beans

changes speed as you type. Good Beans give you immediate feedback on changes to their properties.

Notice that the property sheet understands and provides a way to display and edit each of the different property types. For the foreground and background properties, the sheet displays the color; if you click on it, a color selection dialog pops up. Similarly, if you click on the "font" property, you get a font dialog. For integer and string values, you can type a new value into the field. The BeanBox understands and can edit the most useful basic Java types.

Since the types of properties are open ended, BeanBox can't possibly anticipate them all. Beans with more complex property types can supply a property editor; if it needs even more control over how its properties are displayed, a Bean can provide a *customizer*. A customizer allows a Bean to provide its own GUI for editing its properties. The Molecule Bean that we'll play with in the next section uses a custom property editor that lets us choose the type of molecule.

Events Hookups and Adapters

Beans use events to communicate. As we described in Chapter 13, events are not limited to GUI or AWT components but can be used for signaling and passing information in more general applications. An event is simply a notification; information describing the event and other data are wrapped up in a subclass of Event-Object and passed to the receiving object by a method invocation. Event sources register listeners who want to receive the events when they occur. Event receivers implement the appropriate listener interface containing the method needed to receive the events.

Sometimes it is useful to place an adapter object between an event source and a listener. The adapter can translate the event into some other action, like a call to a different method or an update of some data. One of the jobs of the BeanBox is to let us hook up event sources to event listeners. Another job is to provide or produce adapters that allow us to hook up events in more complex ways.

But before we get into details, let's look at Figure 18-3 and try to get our Juggler under control. Grab a button Bean—the one called ExplicitButton—from the palette, and drop it in the workspace. Using the properties sheet, edit its label to "Start". Now while the **Start** button is selected, pull down the **Edit** menu of the BeanBox. Choose the submenu **Events**. You will see a menu showing the listener interfaces to which the button can send events. The names may not match the interface names that you're familiar with, but the relationship between the menu and the interfaces should be clear. (The button provides "friendly" names for the interfaces, rather than using the unadorned interface names. You also see a "bound property change" event category; that's another kind of listener defined by JavaBeans, which we'll discuss soon.) Select the **Button push** submenu (which corresponds to the ActionListener interface), and you'll see the actual event types that can be sent. In this case, there's only one: "action performed". Choose that. Recall that buttons and other AWT components generate ActionEvents when they are used; you have just chosen an event source. You should see a red line that looks like a rubber band stretching from the button. Drag the line over to the Juggler, and click on it. A dialog will appear, prompting you to choose a method to which to "hook" this event.

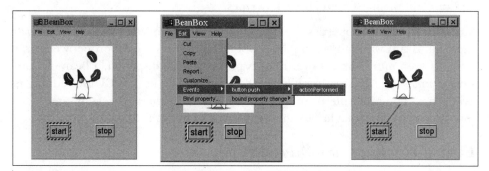

Figure 18–3: Connecting events to Beans

What does it mean to hook an event to a method? If you remember our discussion of AWT, you know that event sources signal event listeners through a very specific method, namely one defined by a listener interface. Furthermore, all the methods that can handle an ActionEvent accept an ActionEvent as an argument. Some of the methods the target dialog presents surely don't take `ActionEvents` as arguments. And if you take a peek at the Juggler source code, you will see that it doesn't even implement an appropriate listener interface. How can we direct events to it at all?

The answer is that the BeanBox automatically makes an adapter class for us, giving us the option of delivering an event to any method that could possibly make sense. That includes any method that could accept the `ActionEvent` object as an argument, including methods that take as an argument the type `Object`. More importantly, it includes methods that take no arguments at all. In that case, the BeanBox creates an adapter that throws away the `ActionEvent` and invokes the target method whenever the event is fired.

The Juggler methods we're interested in are `startJuggling()` and `stopJuggling()`. Select **startJuggling** to complete the hookup of our **Start** button. The BeanBox briefly displays a message saying that it is creating and compiling the necessary adapter class. Follow the same procedure to create a **Stop** button, and hook it to **stopJuggling**. Finally, the Juggler will do our bidding. You should be able to start and stop him with the buttons. Choose the **Save** option from the menu to save the state of the BeanBox; we'll use the controllable Juggler later in another example.

Let's look at one more interesting example, shown in Figure 18-4, before moving on. Grab a Molecule Bean, and place it in the BeanBox. By dragging the mouse within the image you can rotate the model in three dimensions. Try changing the type of molecule using the properties sheet—ethane is fun. Now let's see what we can do with our molecule. Grab a TickTock Bean from the palette. TickTock is a timer. Every so many seconds, TickTock fires a `PropertyChangeEvent`, which is an event defined by JavaBeans that notifies Beans of a change to another Bean's properties. The timer is controlled by an integer property called "interval," which determines the number of seconds between events. TickTock is an "invisible" Bean; it is not derived from an AWT `Component` and doesn't have a graphical appearance, just as an internal timer in an application wouldn't normally have a presence on the screen. BeanBox represents invisible Beans by a simple dashed border and a label containing its name.

Grab the `PropertyChangeEvent` from the **Events** submenu, and click on our Molecule as the target for the event. Hook the event to the `rotateOnX()` method. Now the Molecule should turn on its own, every time it receives an event from the timer (which is controlled by the "interval" property). Try changing the interval. You could also hook TickTock to the Molecule's `rotateOnY()` method, or you could use a different instance of TickTock and cause it to turn at different rates in each dimension by setting different intervals. There is no end to the fun.

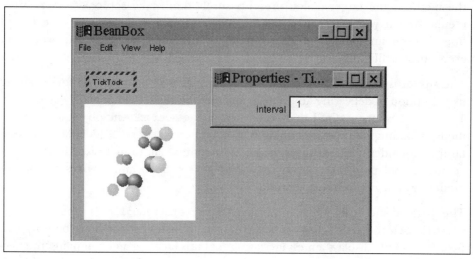

Figure 18–4: The Molecule Bean and the timer

Bound Properties

By using a combination of events and smart adapters, we can connect Beans in many interesting ways. We can even "bind" two Beans together so that if a property changes in the first Bean, the corresponding property is automatically changed in the second Bean. In this scenario, the Beans don't necessarily have to be of the same type, but, to make sense, the properties do.

Grab two JellyBean Beans from the palette, and drop them in the BeanBox, as shown in Figure 18-5. You'll notice that a JellyBean has the four simple properties of an AWT component, plus an integer property called "price in cents". Select the **Bind Property** option under the **Edit** menu. (Yes, this is new, it wasn't there with our other Beans.) A dialog appears, asking which property we would like to bind. Choose "price in cents". Now drag the rubber band over to the second JellyBean. Another dialog appears, asking to which property you would like to bind this value. In this case, there is only one appropriate property: the corresponding "price in cents". However, if a JellyBean had other integer properties, the dialog would list more options. After you choose the price property, BeanBox will say that it is creating and compiling an adapter. When the hookup is complete, go back to the first Bean, and try changing its price. Switch to the second, and you'll see that its price has changed as well. The second Bean's property has been bound to the first.

How does this work? It's only slightly more complicated than our previous example in which we hooked an event to an arbitary method. In that case the BeanBox generated an adapter that received the event and, in turn, invoked the method.

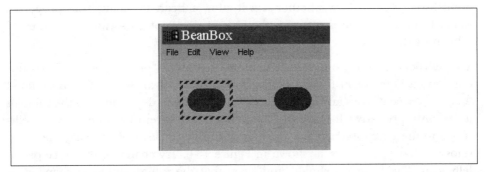

Figure 18–5: Binding properties

Bound properties rely on the fact that the source Bean promises to fire a `Proper-tyChangeEvent` whenever one of its properties changes. The JellyBean supports this feature, and that is why the **Bind propery** option appears in the menu for it. BeanBox uses the feature by generating an adapter that listens for the `Property-ChangeEvent` and updates the property value in the target. Whenver the adapter receives the event, it finds the new value and sets it in the target Bean. Try binding the price property in the other direction as well, so that you can change the value in either Bean, and the changes are propagated in both directions. (Some simple logic in the Beans prevents loops from happening here.)

If you look under the **Events** submenu for one of the JellyBeans you'll see the `PropertyChangeEvent` that we described. You can use this event like any other event; for example, you could go ahead and hook it up to a method. Try setting things up so that your Molecule rotates when you change the price of the Jelly-Bean. A more appropriate use for `PropertyChangeEvent` would be to connect it to the `reportChange()` method of a ChangeReporter test Bean. The ChangeReporter will then display a message describing each change event it receives.

The JellyBean only has type of `PropertyChangeEvent`. How does the recipient know which property has changed? Well, for a simple Bean, a `Property-ChangeEvent` is fired whenever any bound property changes; information in the event describes which property changed. A sophisticated Bean could provide a sep-arate type of `PropertyChangeEvent` for each bindable property.

Constrained Properties

In the previous section, we discussed how Beans fire `PropertyChangeEvents` to notify other Beans (and adapters) that a property has changed. In that scenario, the object that receives the event is simply a passive listener, as far as the event's source is concerned. JavaBeans also supports *constrained properties*, in which the event listener gets to say whether it will allow a Bean to change the property's value. If the new value is rejected, the change does not go forward, and the old value is used.

The JellyBean supports one constrainable property: the "price in cents". To try this out, grab a Voter Bean from the palette. The Voter Bean listens for constrained PropertyChangeEvents and votes "yes" or "no" on them, depending on the value of its "vetoAll" property. Hook up the "vetoableChange" event from one of your Jelly-Beans to the vetoableChange() method of the Voter Bean. By default, the Voter vetos all change requests, as shown in Figure 18-6. Try changing the price of the JellyBean. The BeanBox should notify you that the value cannot be changed. If you set the "vetoAll" property to "yes," you will be free to change the price again.

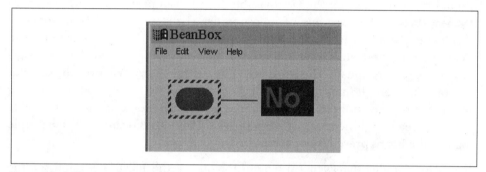

Figure 18–6: Vetoing all change requests

How are constrained properties implemented? Normally, PropertyChangeEvents are delivered to a propertyChange() method in the listener. Constrained proper-ties are implemented by delivering PropertyChangeEvents to a separate listener method called vetoableChange(). The vetoableChange() method throws a PropertyVetoException if it doesn't like a proposed change.

Beans can handle the process of proposing changes in two ways. The first is to use a "two phase commit" style, in which the Bean first issues a vetoable change. If the change passes (i.e., none of the listeners throw a PropertyVetoException), the Bean issues a regular property change. The Bean takes no action until the second (regular) property change arrives. The second strategy is to allow Beans to act on the vetoable change; if the change is rejected by a listener, the Bean sends out a followup vetoable change to restore the property's original value. In this scenario, it would be legitimate to ignore a crazy listener that wouldn't take the old value back.

Keep in mind that binding properties and constraining properties are two separate issues. We can have either one without the other. How popular builder environments will choose to represent the two features remains to be seen. While the BeanBox does a good job of binding properties for us, it does not currently shield us from the details of hooking up constrained properties. In a real builder environment, the two processes would presumably be made to look more similar.

Building Beans

Now that you have the feel from the user's perspective, let's build some Beans. In this section we will become the Magic Beans company. We will create some Beans, package them for distribution, and use them in the BeanBox to build a very simple application.

The first thing to note is that absolutely anything can be a Bean. Even the class below is a Bean, albeit an invisible one:

```
public class Trivial implements java.io.Serializable {}
```

Of course, this Bean isn't very useful: it doesn't have any properties, and it doesn't do anything. But it's a Bean, nonetheless. It's important to realize that JavaBeans really doesn't give a hard and fast definition for what a Bean is required to be. In practice though, we'll want Beans that are a little more useful.

Creating a Component with Bindable Properties

We created a nifty `Dial` component in Chapter 14. What would it take to turn it into a Bean? Well, surprise, it is already a Bean! As I said, there are very few requirements placed on Beans. Furthermore, the `Dial` has a number of properties that it exposes in the way prescribed by JavaBeans. A "get" method retrieves the value of a property; for example, `getValue()` retrieves the dial's current value. Likewise, a "set" method (`setValue()`) modifies the dial's value. The dial has two other properties, which also have "get" and "set" methods: "minimum" and "maximum." This is all the `Dial` needs to do to inform a tool like BeanBox what properties it has and how to work with them. In addition, `Dial` is a lightweight component, and if you look, you'll see that the `Component` class follows the same rules for its important properties (for example, its font).

Now we know that `Dial` is already a Bean; in order to use it, we have to put it in our magicbeans package and store it in a JAR file that can be loaded by the Bean-Box. This is easy. Create a directory called *magicbeans* to hold our Beans, add a package statement to each class, put the source (*.java*) files into the *magicbeans* directory, and compile them to create class files.

Next, we need to create a manifest that tells the BeanBox which of the classes in the JAR file are Beans and which are support files or unrelated. At this point, we only have one Bean, *Dial.class*, so we create the following file called *magicbeans.manifest*:

```
Name: magicbeans/Dial.class
Java-Bean: True
```

The `Name:` label identifies the class file as it will appear in the JAR: `magicbeans/Dial.class`. Fields appearing after the name and before an empty line apply to that item. (See the section on JARs and manifest files in Chapter 3 for more details.) We have added the attribute `Java-Bean: True`, which flags this class as a Bean to tools that read the manifest. We will add an entry like this for each Bean in our package. We don't need to flag support classes (like `DialEvent` and `DialListener`) as Beans, because we won't want to manipulate them directly with the BeanBox; in fact, we don't need to mention them in the manifest at all. The *jar* utility will add appropriate entries for them automatically.

To create the JAR file, including our manifest information, give the following command:

```
% jar cvmf magicbeans.manifest magicbeans.jar magicbeans/*.class
```

Now we can load our JAR into the BeanBox using the **Load JAR** option under the **File** menu. Use the **File** dialog to locate our JAR and select it. An entry for `Dial` should appear in the Bean palette. We have loaded our first Bean! Drop an instance of Dial Bean into the BeanBox.

As Figure 18-7 shows, the dial's properties ("value," "minimum," and "maximum") are on the properties sheet and can be modified by the BeanBox. We're almost there. But these properties are not very useful to other Beans unless we can notify them when the dial's value changes. We need to make "value" a bound property by firing `PropertyChangeEvents` when the value changes. As you'll recall, our Bean already fires special `DialEvents` when we change the value, so it won't be hard to add `PropertyChangeEvents`.

Add the following code to the `Dial` class:

```
package magicbeans;

import java.beans.*;

public class Dial extends Component {
    ...

    private PropertyChangeSupport propChanges = new PropertyChangeSupport(this);

    public void addPropertyChangeListener(PropertyChangeListener listener) {
```

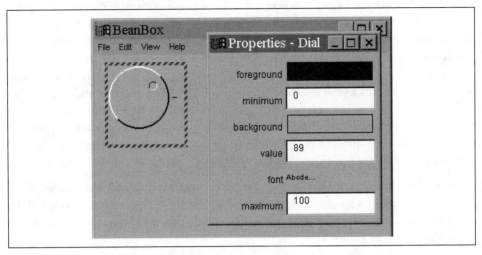

Figure 18–7: The Dial component, as a Bean

```
        propChanges.addPropertyChangeListener(listener);
    }
    public void removePropertyChangeListener(PropertyChangeListener listener) {
        propChanges.removePropertyChangeListener(listener);
    }
}
```

And insert the `firePropertyChange` statement below as the first line of the `Dial`'s `fireEvent()` method:

```
    private void fireEvent() {
        propChanges.firePropertyChange( "value", null, new Integer(value));
            . . .
    }
```

That's all it takes to make `Dial` a source of `PropertyChangeEvents`. We use the `java.beans.PropertyChangeSupport` class, which does all the work for us (registering listeners, unregistering listeners, and sending the actual events); you can pretty much copy the code above into any Beans you create. `PropertyChangeSupport` is analogous to the `AWTEventMulticaster` that we used to help us fire AWT events in Chapter 14. We have added the necessary `addListener()` and `removeListener()` methods so that `Dial` can register objects that want to receive `Property-ChangeEvents`. In these methods, we simply delegate the calls to the `Property-ChangeSupport` object and let it keep track of them for us. To fire an event, we use `propChanges`'s `firePropertyChange()` method.

The firePropertyChange() method takes three arguments: the name of the property and the old and new values. In our case we don't keep track of the old value, so we are allowed to set that parameter to null. It may seem superfluous to send both the old and new values, but there is one bonus when we do: the firePropertyChange() method doesn't generate an event if the value has not actually changed. This saves us the trouble of implementing this logic over and over (and it is important logic to prevent looping and other bad behavior). The arguments to firePropertyChange() are objects, so we have to wrap up properties of primitive types in their appropriate wrapper objects. In this case, we use an Integer because the "value" property has an int value.

Now we're ready to put the Dial to use. Recompile and re-JAR the classes. Next, reload the Juggler example that we asked you to save in the first section of this chapter. (Did you save it?) Add an instance of our new magic Dial Bean to the scenario, as shown in Figure 18-8.

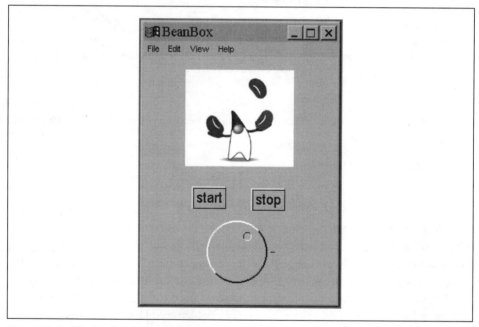

Figure 18–8: The juggler with a dialable animation rate

Let's try to bind the "value" property of the Dial to the "animationRate" of the Juggler. The **Bind Property** option should now be available under the **Edit** menu because the BeanBox recognizes that we are a source of PropertyChangeEvents. When you complete the hookup, you should be able to vary the speed of the juggler by turning the dial. Try changing the "maximum" and "minimum" values of the dial to change the range.

Design patterns for properties

I said earlier that tools like BeanBox found out about a Bean's properties by looking at its "get" and "set" methods. The easiest way to make properties visible is to follow these simple design patterns:

```
public propertyType getPropertyName()
public void setPropertyName( propertyType arg )
public boolean is PropertyName()
```

The last method is used only for properties with `boolean` values and is optional.

So it turns out that the appropriate "set" and "get" methods for these features of our Bean are already in the `Dial` class, either directly or inherited from `java.awt.Component`:

```
// Inherited from Component
public Color getForeground()
public void setForeground(Color c)

public Color getBackground()
public void setBackground(Color c)

public Font getFont()
public void setFont(Font f)

public String getName()
public void setName(String name)

// Part of the Dial itself
public int getValue()
public void setValue(int v)

public int getMinimum()
public void setMinimum(int m)

public int getMaximum()
public void setMaximum(int m)
```

One of the biggest changes between Versions 1.0 and 1.1 of Java was rewriting AWT in terms of these design patterns. For our Dial Bean, BeanBox uses the reflection API to find out about its methods (both its own and the methods it inherits); it then uses the design patterns to figure out what properties are available. When we use the properties sheet to change a value, the BeanBox dynamically invokes the correct "set" method to change the value.

But wait—if you look further at the `Component` class, you'll notice that other methods match the design pattern. For example, what about the `setCursor()` and `getCursor()` pair? Well, BeanBox doesn't know how to display or edit a cursor, so it simply ignores those properties in the properties sheet.

One more thought: BeanBox automatically pulls the property's name from the name of its accessor methods; it then "decapitalizes" the name for display on the properties sheet. For example, the "font" property is not listed as "Font". Later, I'll show how to provide a BeanInfo class that overrides the way these properties are displayed, letting you provide your own property names.

Finally, JavaBeans allows read-only and write-only properties, which are implemented by simply leaving out the "getter" or "setter" as desired.

A (Slightly) More Realistic Example

Now that we have one nifty Bean for the Magic Beans products list, let's try to round out the set before we start advertising. Our goal is to build the Beans we need to make a very simple form. The application performs a simple calculation after you enter data. You could see this as an extremely primitive spreadsheet.

A Bean for displaying text

One thing that we will need in almost any application is a plain old text label. Fortunately, the AWT's `Label` class gives us a head start. We'll package it up as a Bean as follows:

```
package magicbeans;

import java.awt.*;

public class TextLabel extends Label {

    public void setText( String s ) {
        super.setText( s );
        updateSize();
    }
    public void setFont( Font f ) {
        super.setFont( f );
        updateSize();
    }

    private void updateSize() {
        Container parent = getParent();
        if ( parent != null ) {
            invalidate();
            parent.validate();
        }
    }

    public void update( java.awt.Graphics g ) { }
}
```

Pretty much all of the contents of this class are refinements to make the `TextLabel` work a little more smoothly in a builder environment like BeanBox. Technically, we could have gotten by with a trivial subclass of Label, but it would have lacked the immediate feedback that we like when changing properties. In TextLabel, we override the two "set" methods that might change the preferred size of the Label: setText() and setFont(). Our new methods call our private updateSize() method to explicitly invalidate the Label and validate its parent container, causing it to lay out the Label again.[*] We have also overridden the AWT update() method, to prevent an accidental repaint() from messing up our component.[†]

Go ahead, repackage and try out the label in the BeanBox. Don't forget to add *TextLabel.class* to the manifest and to specify that it is a Bean. Once you have the TextLabel in the BeanBox, it should automatically grow to accommodate changes in text and font. Notice the property called "alignment" (which it inherited from the AWT Label class); try changing its value to 1, 2, or 3, and see what happens.

A Bean for validating numeric data

Another component that we're sure to need in a form is a text field that accepts numeric data. Let's build a text entry Bean that accepts and validates numbers and makes the values available as a property. You should recognize almost all of the parts of the NumericField Bean:

```
package magicbeans;

import java.awt.*;
import java.awt.event.ActionEvent;
import java.beans.*;

public class NumericField extends TextField {
    private double value;
    private PropertyChangeSupport propChanges = new PropertyChangeSupport(this);

    public NumericField() {
        enableEvents( AWTEvent.ACTION_EVENT_MASK );
    }

    public void processActionEvent(ActionEvent e) {
        try {
            setValue( new Double( getText() ).doubleValue() );
        } catch ( NumberFormatException ex ) {
            select(0, getText().length());
        }
        super.processActionEvent(e);
    }
```

---

[*] A proper implementation of Label should probably invalidate itself when its preferred size changes.

[†] Heavyweight AWT components like Label, Button, etc., do not expect to have an explicit update scheduled via repaint(). As you'll recall, the default implementation of update() wipes the area to the background color, whether or not the component has a peer. For a lightweight component, this behavior is undesirable.

```
        public double getValue() {
            return value;
        }
        public void setValue( double newValue ) {
            double oldValue = value;
            setText( "" + newValue );
            propChanges.firePropertyChange("value",
                new Double(oldValue), new Double(newValue));
        }

        public void setColumns( int cols ) {
            super.setColumns( cols );
            Container parent = getParent();
            if ( parent != null ) {
                invalidate();
                parent.validate();
            }
        }

        public void addPropertyChangeListener(PropertyChangeListener listener) {
            propChanges.addPropertyChangeListener(listener);
        }
        public void removePropertyChangeListener(PropertyChangeListener listener) {
            propChanges.removePropertyChangeListener(listener);
        }

        public void update( Graphics g ) { }
    }
```

NumericField extends the AWT's TextField component; it's fairly similar to our TextLabel. The heart of NumericField is in the processActionEvent() method. You'll recall that a TextField generates ActionEvents whenever the user presses Return to enter the data. We catch those events and try to parse the user's entry as a number, giving it a Double value. If we succeed, we update the "value" property using our setValue() method. setValue() then fires a PropertyChangeEvent to notify any interested Beans. This means that NumericField lets us bind its "value" property. If the text doesn't parse properly as a number, we give feedback to the user by selecting (highlighting) the text.

As with our TextLabel, we override a method that might affect the NumericField's size—setColumns()—and add code to validate our container whenever the number of columns changes. You should be able to change the "columns" property of the NumericField and to adjust its size dynamically. (We'll let you paste in the bit of code to handle setFont() if you want.)

Verify the operation of NumericField by placing two of them in the BeanBox and binding the "value" property of one to the other. You should be able to enter a new floating point value and see the change reflected in the other.

An invisible multiplier

Finally, let's try our hand at an invisible Bean: one that performs a calculation rather than providing part of a user interface. Multiplier is a simple invisible Bean that multiplies the values of two of its properties (A and B) to produce the value of a third read-only property (C). Here's the code:

```
package magicbeans;

import java.beans.*;

public class Multiplier implements java.io.Serializable {
    private double a, b, c;

    synchronized public void setA( double val ) {
        a = val;
        multiply();
    }
    synchronized public double getA() {
        return a;
    }
    synchronized public void setB( double val ) {
        b = val;
        multiply();
    }
    synchronized public double getB() {
        return b;
    }
    synchronized public double getC() {
        return c;
    }
    private void multiply() {
        double oldC = c;
        c = a * b;
        propChanges.firePropertyChange("c", new Double(oldC), new Double(c));
    }

    private PropertyChangeSupport propChanges = new PropertyChangeSupport(this);

    public void addPropertyChangeListener(PropertyChangeListener listener) {
        propChanges.addPropertyChangeListener(listener);
    }
    public void removePropertyChangeListener(PropertyChangeListener listener) {
        propChanges.removePropertyChangeListener(listener);
    }
}
```

The code is straightforward. Whenever the value of property A or B changes, we call multiply(), which multiplies their values and fires a PropertyChangeEvent. So Multiplier supports binding of any of its properties.

Putting them together

Finally, let's demonstrate that we can put our Beans together in a useful way. Arrange three TextLabels, three NumericFields, and a Multiplier into the scene in Figure 18-9.

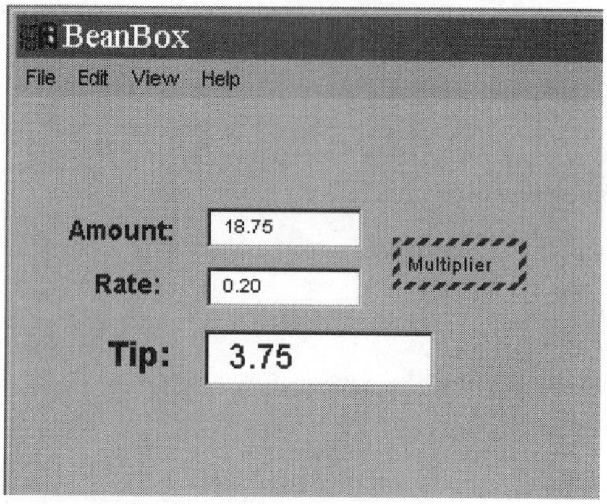

Figure 18–9: TextLabels, NumericFields, and a Multiplier

Bind the values of the first two NumericFields to the A and B properties of the Multiplier; bind the C value to the third NumericField. Now we have a simple calculator. You could use this as a tip calculator, but it's important to realize that much more is possible. Try some other arrangements. Can you build a calculator that squares a number? Can you see how you might build a simple spreadsheet?

Before moving on, save this work so that you can reuse it later. This time, use the BeanBox's **Serialize component** option to serialize the BeanBox container itself. To select the top-level BeanBox, click on the background of the workspace. The dashed line should appear around the entire BeanBox. Then use the **Serialize component** option to save your work. By serializing the BeanBox container, we save all of the Beans it contains and all of their interconnections. In a section later in this chapter, we'll show you how to put these to use.

Customizing with BeanInfo

So far, everything the BeanBox has known about our Beans has been determined by low-level reflection—that is, looking at the methods of our classes. The java.beans.Introspector class analyzes and describes a Bean to any tool that wants to know about it. The introspection process works only if we follow design patterns that restrict what we call our methods; furthermore, it gives us little

control over exactly what properties and events appear in the BeanBox menus. We
have been forced to live with all of the stuff that we inherit from the base AWT
components, for example. We can change all that by creating BeanInfo classes for
our Beans. A BeanInfo class lets us provide explicit information about our properties, methods, and events; we can even use it to customize the text that appears in
the BeanBox's menus.

Technically, a BeanInfo class is required to implement the BeanInfo interface.
However, that's a complicated proposition, particularly since in most situations,
the introspector's default behavior is reasonable. So instead of implementing
BeanInfo, we extend SimpleBeanInfo, which is a utility that implements all of
BeanInfo's methods. We can override specific methods to provide the information
we want; when we don't override a method, we'll get the introspector's default
behavior.

In the next few sections, we'll develop a DialBeanInfo class that provides explicit
information about our Dial Bean.

Properties info

We'll start out by describing the Dial's properties. To do so, we must implement
the getPropertyDescriptors() method. This method simply returns an array of
PropertyDescriptor objects—one for every property we want the development
tool to know about.

To create a PropertyDescriptor, we call its constructor with two arguments: the
property's name and the class. In the following code, we create descriptors for the
Dial's "value," "minimum," and "maximum" properties. Then we call a few methods of the PropertyDescriptor class to provide additional information about each
property. In this example, we call the setBound() method to state that "minimum"
and "maximum" are not bound properties but that "value" is a bound property.
Our code also is prepared to catch an IntrospectionException, which can occur
if something goes wrong while creating the property descriptors.

```
package magicbeans;

import java.beans.*;

public class DialBeanInfo extends SimpleBeanInfo {

    public PropertyDescriptor[] getPropertyDescriptors() {
        try {
            PropertyDescriptor value =
                new PropertyDescriptor("value", Dial.class);
            PropertyDescriptor minimum =
                new PropertyDescriptor("minimum", Dial.class);
            PropertyDescriptor maximum =
```

```
                    new PropertyDescriptor("maximum", Dial.class);

            value.setBound(true);
            minimum.setBound(false);
            maximum.setBound(false);

            return new PropertyDescriptor [] { value, minimum, maximum };
        } catch (IntrospectionException e) {
            return null;
        }
    }
```

Perhaps the most interesting thing about DialBeanInfo is that, by providing explicit information for our properties, we automatically hide any other properties that introspection might find. In other words, if you don't provide any property information, a development tool like BeanBox will find out about all sorts of properties, including properties inherited from the superclass: when we loaded the Dial into the BeanBox, we saw a number of properties inherited from Component. If you compile DialBeanInfo, package it with the Dial, and load the resulting JAR file into the BeanBox, you'll see that the Component properties no longer appear in the properties sheet.

Of course, a PropertyDescriptor can provide a lot of other information about a property: it can provide the names of the accessor methods, if you decide not to use the design patterns; whether the property is constrained; and a class to use as a property editor, if the standard property editors aren't sufficient.

Events info

The Dial defines its own event: the DialEvent. We'd like to tell development tools about this event, so that we can build applications using it. The process for telling the world about our event is similar to what we did previously: we add a method to the DialBeanInfo class called getEventSetDescriptors(), which returns an array of EventSetDescriptors.

There's just one minor complication: events are described in terms of their listener interfaces, not in terms of the event classes themselves. So our getEventSetDescriptors() method creates a descriptor for the DialListener interface. We also have to tell the world that we generate PropertyChangeEvents, so we create a descriptor for the PropertyChangeListener. Here's the code to add to the DialBeanInfo class:

```
public class DialBeanInfo extends SimpleBeanInfo {
    ...

    public EventSetDescriptor[] getEventSetDescriptors() {
        try {
            EventSetDescriptor dial = new EventSetDescriptor( Dial.class,
```

```
            "dialAdjusted", DialListener.class, "dialAdjusted");
        dial.setDisplayName("Dial Adjusted");

        EventSetDescriptor changed = new EventSetDescriptor( Dial.class,
            "propertyChange", PropertyChangeListener.class,
            "propertyChange" );
        changed.setDisplayName("Bound property change");

        return new EventSetDescriptor [] { dial, changed };
    } catch (IntrospectionException e) {
        return null;
    }
}
```

In this method, we create two EventSetDescriptor objects: dial and changed. The constructor for an EventSetDescriptor takes four arguments: the class that generates the event, the name of the event set (i.e., the name that will be displayed by default by a development tool), the listener class, and the name of the method to which the event can be delivered. (Other constructors let you deal with listener interfaces that have several methods.) After creating these objects, we call the set-DisplayName() method to provide a more friendly name to be displayed by development tools like the BeanBox.

Just as the property descriptors we supply hid the properties that were discovered by reflection, the EventSetDescriptors hide events that are inherited from the Component class. Therefore, when you recompile DialBeanInfo, package it in a JAR, and load it into the BeanBox, you'll no longer see mouse events, action events, and all the other AWT events. You will see only the two events that we have explicitly described: our own DialEvent and a PropertyChangeEvent.

Again, once you have an EventSetDescriptor, you can provide other kinds of information about the event. In particular, you can state that the event is "unicast," which means that it can only have one listener.

Supplying icons

Some of the Beans that come with the BeanBox are displayed on the palette with a cute icon. This makes it easier for a nontechnical user to identify which Bean he or she wants. Icon images are supplied using the BeanInfo object we have been developing. To supply an icon, implement the getIcon() method. You may supply as many as four icons: they may be either 16 x 16 or 32 x 32, and either color or monochrome. Here's the getIcon() method for DialBeanInfo:

```
public class DialBeanInfo extends SimpleBeanInfo {
    ...

    public java.awt.Image getIcon(int iconKind) {

        if (iconKind == BeanInfo.ICON_COLOR_16x16) {
```

```
            return loadImage("DialIconColor16.gif");
        } else
        if (iconKind == BeanInfo.ICON_COLOR_32x32) {
            return loadImage("DialIconColor32.gif");
        } else
        if (iconKind == BeanInfo.ICON_MONO_16x16) {
            return loadImage("DialIconMono16.gif");
        } else
        if (iconKind == BeanInfo.ICON_MONO_32x32) {
            return loadImage("DialIconMono32.gif");
        }
        return null;
    }
```

This method is called with a constant indicating what kind of icon is being requested; for example, `BeanInfo.ICON_COLOR_16x16` requests a 16 x 16 color image. If an appropriate icon is available, it loads the image and returns an `Image` object. If the icon isn't available, it returns `null`. For convenience, you can package the images in the same JAR file as the Bean and its BeanInfo class.

While we haven't used them, you can also use a `BeanInfo` object to provide information about other public methods of your Bean, "indexed properties" (i.e., array-valued properties), and other features.

Creating customizers and property editors

JavaBeans also lets you provide a customizer for your Beans. Customizers are objects that do advanced customization for a Bean as a whole; they let you provide your own GUI for tweaking your Bean. (The Select Bean uses a customizer rather than the standard properties sheet.) I won't show you how to write a customizer; it's not too difficult, but it's beyond the scope of this chapter. Suffice it to say that a customizer must implement the `java.beans.Customizer` interface, and should extend `Component` so that it can be displayed.

A property editor isn't quite as fancy as a customizer. Property editors are a way of giving the properties sheet additional capabilities. For example, you would supply a property editor to let you edit a property type that is specific to your Bean. You could provide a property editor that would let you edit an object's price in dollars and cents. We've already seen a couple of property editors: the editor used for `Color`-valued properties is fundamentally no different from a property editor you might write yourself. In addition, the Molecule Bean used a property editor to specify its moleculeName property.

Again, describing how to write a property editor is beyond the scope of this chapter. Briefly, a property editor must implement the `PropertyEditor` interface; it usually does so by extending the `PropertyEditorSupport` class, which provides default implementations for most of the methods.

Hand-Coding with Beans

So far, we've seen how to create and use Beans within a Bean application builder environment. That is the primary role of a Java Bean in development. But Beans are not limited to being used by automated tools. There's no reason we can't use Beans in handwritten code. You might use a builder to assemble Beans for the user interface of your application and then load that serialized Bean collection in your own code. We'll give an example of that in a moment.

Bean Instantiation and Type Management

Beans are an abstraction over simple Java classes. They add, by convention, features that are not part of the Java language. Over the course of the next year, the JavaBeans specification will evolve to give Beans even greater capabilities. The goal is to allow groups of Beans to work together as an aggregate or a sort of "virtual Bean."

To enable us to treat a collection of Beans as a single type within the Java language, we have to use some special tools. Specifically, when working with Beans, we need replacements for three basic Java operations: creating an object with new, checking the type of an object with the instanceof operator, and casting a type with a cast expression. In place of these, use the corresponding static methods of the java.beans.Beans class, shown in Table 18-1.

Table 18–1: Methods of the java.beans.Beans Class

Operator	Equivalent
new	Beans.instantiate(classloader, name)
instanceof	Beans.isInstanceOf(object, class)
explicit cast	Beans.getInstanceOf(object, class)

Beans.instantiate() is the new operation for Beans. It takes a classloader and the name of a Bean class or serialized Bean as arguments. Its advantage over the new operator is that it can also load Beans from a serialized class. If you use intantiate(), you don't have to specify in advance whether you will provide the Bean as a class or as a serialized object.

Beans.isInstanceOf() and Beans.getInstanceOf() do the jobs of checking a Bean's type and casting it to a new type. In the future these methods will be used to let Beans take control of this behavior, providing different "views" of themselves.

Working with Serialized Beans

Remember the tip calculator we developed a few sections back? I asked you to serialize the BeanBox container and save it. As I mentioned earlier, BeanBox is a Bean itself. We can therefore pull the serialized BeanBox along with all of our previous work into another application and use it just as we had left it. We'll assume that you saved the serialized BeanBox in a file called *tipcalc.ser*.

Compile the following small application:

```java
import java.awt.*;
import java.beans.*;

public class MyApplication extends Frame {

    public MyApplication() {
        super("Tip Calculator");
        try {
            Object bean = Beans.instantiate(
                getClass().getClassLoader(), "tipcalc" );

            if ( Beans.isInstanceOf(bean, Component.class) ) {
                Component comp =
                    (Component)Beans.getInstanceOf(bean, Component.class);
                add("Center", comp);
            } else
                System.out.println("Bean is not a Component...");

        } catch ( java.io.IOException e1 ) {
                        // Error loading the serialized object
        } catch ( ClassNotFoundException e2 ) {
                        // Can't find the class that goes with the object
        }
        pack();
    }

    public static void main(String [] args) {
        new MyApplication().show();
    }
}
```

Run this program, making sure that the BeanBox classes and our *magicbeans.jar* file are in your class path. You should see the restored BeanBox, just as you left it, as shown in Figure 18-10.

Here we use `Beans.instantiate()` to load our serialized Bean by name. Then we check to see if it is a GUI component using `Beans.isInstanceOf()`. (It is because the BeanBox itself is a subclass of `java.awt.Panel`.) Finally, we cast the instantiated object to a `Component` with `Beans.getInstanceOf()` and add it to our application's `Frame`. Notice that we still need a static Java cast to turn the `Object` returned by `getInstanceOf()` into a `Component`. This cast may seem gratuitous; in the future,

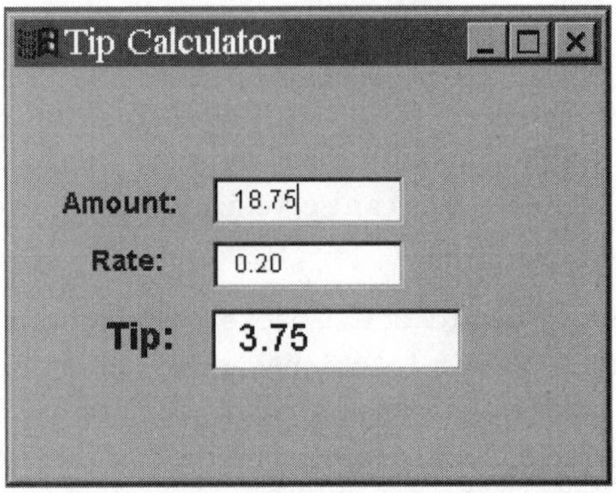

Figure 18–10: The restored BeanBox

an aggregate Bean consisting of several simple Beans could use this feature to present an object with the desired behavior.

One important question remains: how does `instantiate()` find a Bean using the name "tipcalc"? First, it appends the extension *.ser* to form the filename *tipcalc.ser*. If it can find this file anywhere along the class path, it loads it as a serialized Bean. It also needs the serialized Bean's original *.class* file; the name of that file is included in the serialized object and usually doesn't have any relation to the name of the serialized object. (In this case, `instantiate()` would look for *BeanBox.class* and the classes for the components in the BeanBox.)

If the *.ser* file doesn't exist, `instantiate()` appends *.class* to the name (in this case, yielding *tipcalc.class*) and looks for a class file. In this case, `instantiate()` instantiates the Bean like any other object—that is, with the new operator.

Putting Reflection to Work

I've discussed reflection largely in terms of how design tools use it to analyze your classes. But it would be a shame to end this discussion without showing you how to use reflection for your own purposes. It's a powerful tool that lets you do many things that wouldn't be possible otherwise. In this section, we'll build a dynamic event adapter that can be configured at run-time.

In Chapter 13 we saw how adapter classes could be built to connect event firings to arbitrary methods in our code, allowing us to cleanly separate GUI and logic in our applications. In this chapter, I have described how the BeanBox interposes adapters between Beans to do this for us. I have also described how the BeanBox uses adapters to bind and constrain properties between Beans.

One of the primary motivations behind the new AWT event model was to reduce the need to subclass components to perform simple hookups. But if we start relying heavily on special adapter classes, we can quickly end up with as many adapters as objects. Anonymous inner classes let us hide the existence of these classes, but they're still there. A potential solution for large or specialized applications is to create generic event adapters that can serve a number of event sources and sinks simultaneously.

The following example, `DynamicActionAdapter`, is a generic adapter for `Action-Events`. A single instance of `DynamicActionAdapter` can be used to hook up a number of `ActionEvent` sources. `DyanicActionAdapter` uses reflection so that each event source can be directed to an arbitrary method of the target object.

Here's the code:

```java
import java.awt.*;
import java.awt.event.*;
import java.util.Hashtable;
import java.lang.reflect.Method;

class DynamicActionAdapter implements ActionListener {
    Hashtable actions = new Hashtable();

    public void hookup( Object sourceObject, Object targetObject,
                        String targetMethod ) {
        actions.put( sourceObject, new Target( targetObject, targetMethod ) );
        invokeReflectedMethod( sourceObject, "addActionListener",
            new Object [] { this }, new Class [] { ActionListener.class } );
    }

    public void actionPerformed(ActionEvent e) {
        Target target = (Target)actions.get( e.getSource() );
        if ( target == null )
            throw new RuntimeException("unknown source");
        invokeReflectedMethod( target.object, target.methodName, null, null );
    }

    private void invokeReflectedMethod(
        Object target, String methodName, Object [] args, Class [] argTypes ) {

        try {
            Method method = target.getClass().getMethod( methodName, argTypes );
            method.invoke( target, args );
        } catch ( Exception e ) {
            throw new RuntimeException("invocation problem: "+e);
        }
    }

    class Target {
        Object object;
        String methodName;
```

```
            Target( Object object, String methodName ) {
                this.object = object;
                this.methodName = methodName;
            }
        }
    }
```

Once we have an instance of DynamicActionAdapter, we can use its hookup() method to connect an ActionEvent source to some method of a target object. The target object doesn't have to be an ActionListener—or any other particular kind of object. The following applet, DynamicTest, uses an instance of our adapter to connect a button to its own launchTheMissiles() method:

```
public class DynamicHookupTest extends java.applet.Applet {
    DynamicActionAdapter actionAdapter = new DynamicActionAdapter();

    public void init() {
        Button launchButton = new Button("Launch!");
        actionAdapter.hookup( launchButton, this, "launchTheMissiles" );
        add( launchButton );
    }

    public void launchTheMissiles() {
        System.out.println("Fire...");
    }
}
```

Here we simply call the dynamic adapter's hookup() method, passing it the ActionEvent source, the target object, and a string with the name of the method to invoke when the event arrives.

As for the code, it's pretty straightforward. DynamicActionAdapter implements the ActionListener interface. When hookup() is called, it registers itself with the event source, using reflection to invoke the source's addActionListener() method. It stores information about the target object and method in a Target object, using an inner class. This object is stored in a Hashtable called actions.

When an action event arrives, the dynamic adapter looks up the target for the event source in the Hashtable. It then uses reflection to look up the requested method in the target object and invoke that method. Our adapter can only invoke a method that takes no arguments. If the method doesn't exist, the adapter throws a RuntimeException.

The heart of the adapter is the invokeReflectedMethod() method. This is a private method that uses reflection to look up and invoke an arbitrary method in an arbitrary class. First, it calls the target's getClass() method to get the target's Class object. It uses this object to call getMethod(), which returns a Method object. Once we have a Method, we can call invoke() to invoke the method.

The dynamic adapter is important because it has almost no built-in knowledge. It doesn't know what object will be the event source; it doesn't even know what kind of object will be the event source. Likewise, it doesn't know what object will receive the event, or what method it should call to deliver the event. All this information is provided at run-time, in the call to hookup(). We use reflection to look up and invoke the event source's addActionListener() method, and to look up and invoke the target's event handler. All this is done on the fly. Therefore, you can use this adapter in almost any situation requiring an ActionEvent.

Safety Implications

If the target's event-handling method isn't found, the adapter throws a RuntimeException. Therein lies the problem with this technique. By using reflection to locate and invoke methods, we abandon Java's strong typing and head off in the direction of scripting languages. We add power at the expense of safety.

Compile-Time versus Run-Time Hookups

Our dynamic event adapter is limited to handling ActionEvents. What if we want to build something like the BeanBox, that can hook up arbitrary event sources to arbitrary destinations? Can we build an adapter that can listen to any kind of event?

The short answer is "no," not without the ability to compile Java code on the fly. Event listener registration is statically typed. Your adapter simply has to be of the correct type to register itself as a listener for any given type of event. But this isn't good enough for a tool like the BeanBox, which may need to deal with events (like our DialEvent) that aren't part of the Java specification and that it has never seen before. The BeanBox solves this problem by doing just what we suggested: generating and compiling Java code on the fly. This is what's happening when you see the message that the BeanBox is "generating and compiling an adapter class." One of the sample Beans, the EventMonitor, also generates adapters on the fly so it can register itself as a listener for all types of events coming from a Bean. If you really need to deal with arbitrary event types or you have some other reason for generating Java code at run-time, look at the EventMonitor Bean and the *sunw.demo.encapsulatedevents* package. This will give you some ideas about generating the code and invoking the compiler.

Glossary

abstract

The abstract keyword is used to declare abstract methods and classes. An abstract method has no implementation defined; it is declared with arguments and a return type as usual, but the body enclosed in curly braces is replaced with a semicolon. The implementation of an abstract method is provided by a subclass of the class in which it is defined. If an abstract method appears in a class, the class is also abstract.

API (Application Programming Interface)

An API consists of the functions and variables programmers use in their applications. The Java API consists of all public and protected methods of all public classes in the java.applet, java.awt, java.awt.image, java.awt.peer, java.io, java.lang, java.net, and java.util packages.

applet

An embedded Java application that runs in the context of an applet viewer, such as a Web browser.

<APPLET> tag

HTML tag that specifies an applet run within a Web document.

appletviewer

Sun's application that implements the additional structure needed to run and display Java applets.

application

A Java program that runs standalone; i.e., it doesn't require an applet viewer.

AWT (Abstract Window Toolkit)

Java's platform-independent windowing, graphics, and user interface toolkit.

`boolean`

A primitive Java data type that contains a truth value. The two possible values of a `boolean` variable are `true` and `false`.

`byte`

A primitive Java data type that's an 8-bit two's-complement signed number (in all implementations).

callback

A behavior that is defined by one object and then later invoked by another object when a particular event occurs.

cast

A technique that explicitly converts one data type to another.

`catch`

The `catch` statement introduces an exception-handling block of code following a `try` statement. The `catch` keyword is followed by an exception type and argument name in parentheses and a block of code within curly braces.

certificate

An electronic document used to verify the identity of a person, group, or organization. Certificates attest to the identity of a person or group and contain that organization's public key. A certificate is signed by a certificate authority.

certificate authority (CA)

An organization that is entrusted to issue certificates, taking whatever steps are necessary to verify the identity for which it is issuing the certificate.

`char`

A primitive Java data type; a variable of type `char` holds a single 16-bit Unicode character.

class

a) An encapsulated collection of data and methods to operate on the data. A class may be instantiated to produce an object that's an instance of the class.

b) The `class` keyword is used to declare a class, thereby defining a new object type. Its syntax is similar to the `struct` keyword in C.

class loader

An object in the Java security model that is responsible for loading Java binary classes from the network into the local interpreter. A class loader keeps its classes in a separate namespace, so that loaded classes cannot interact with system classes and breach system security.

class method

A method declared `static`. Methods of this type are not passed implicit `this` references and may refer only to class variables and invoke other class methods of the current class. A class method may be invoked through the class name, rather than through an instance of the class.

class path

The directory path specifying the location of compiled Java class files on the local system.

class variable

A variable declared `static`. Variables of this type are associated with the class, rather than with a particular instance of the class. There is only one copy of a static variable, regardless of the number of instances of the class that are created.

client

The application that initiates a conversation as part of a networked client/server application. See **server**.

compilation unit

The source code for a Java class. A compilation unit normally contains a single class definition and, in most current development environments, is simply a file with a *.java* extension.

compiler

A program that translates source code into executable code.

component

Any of the GUI primitives implemented in the `java.awt` package as subclasses of `Component`. The classes `Button`, `Choice`, and `TextField` (among many others) are components.

component architecture

A component architecture is a methodology for building parts of an application. It is a way to build reusable objects that can be easily assembled to form applications.

composition

Using objects as part of another, more complex object. When you compose a new object, you create complex behavior by delegating tasks to the internal objects. Composition is different from inheritance, which defines a new object by changing or refining the behavior of an old object. See **inheritance**.

constructor

A method that is invoked automatically when a new instance of a class is created. Constructors are used to initialize the variables of the newly created object. The constructor method has the same name as the class.

container

One of the `java.awt` classes that "contain" GUI components. Components in a container appear within the boundaries of the container. The classes `Dialog`, `Frame`, `Panel`, and `Window` are containers.

content handler

A class that is called to parse a particular type of data and converts it to an appropriate object.

datagram

A packet of data sent to a receiving computer without warning, error checking, or other control information.

data hiding

See **encapsulation**.

`double`

A Java primitive data type; a `double` value is a 64-bit (double-precision) floating-point number.

encapsulation

An object-oriented programming technique that makes an object's data private or protected (i.e., hidden) and allows programmers to access and manipulate that data only through method calls. Done well, encapsulation reduces bugs and promotes reusability and modularity of classes. This technique is also known as *data hiding*.

event

A user's action, such as a mouse click or key press.

event model

The overall design of the mechanism for sending and receiving events. The Java event model changed between the 1.0 and 1.1 releases in order to allow more explicit control over how and when events are delivered from sources to listeners.

exception

A signal that some unexpected condition has occurred in the program. In Java, exceptions are objects that are subclasses of Exception or Error (which themselves are subclasses of Throwable). Exceptions in Java are "raised" with the throw keyword and received with the catch keyword. See throw, throws, and catch.

extends

The extends keyword is used in a class declaration to specify the superclass of the class being defined. The class being defined has access to all the public and protected variables and methods of the superclass (or, if the class being defined is in the same package, it has access to all non-private variables and methods). If a class definition omits the extends clause, its superclass is taken to be java.lang.Object.

final

The final keyword is a modifier that may be applied to classes, methods, and variables. It has a similar, but not identical, meaning in each case. When final is applied to a class, it means that the class may never be subclassed. java.lang.System is an example of a final class. When final is applied to a variable, the variable is a constant; i.e., it can't be modified.

finalize

finalize is not actually a Java keyword, but a reserved method name. The finalize() method is called when an object is no longer being used (i.e., when there are no further references to it), but before the object's memory is actually reclaimed by the system. A finalizer should perform cleanup tasks and free system resources not handled by Java's garbage-collection system.

`finally`

This keyword introduces the `finally` block of a `try/catch/finally` construct. `catch` and `finally` blocks provide exception handling and routine cleanup for code in a `try` block. The `finally` block is optional, and appears after the `try` block, and after zero or more `catch` blocks. The code in a `finally` block is executed once, regardless of how the code in the `try` block executes. In normal execution, control reaches the end of the `try` block and proceeds to the `finally` block, which generally performs any necessary cleanup.

`float`

A Java primitive data type; a `float` value is a 32-bit (single-precision) floating-point number represented in IEEE 754 format.

garbage collection

The process of reclaiming the memory of objects no longer in use. An object is no longer in use when there are no references to it from other objects in the system and no references in any local variables on the method call stack.

GC

An abbreviation for garbage collection or garbage collector (or occasionally "graphics context").

graphics context

A drawable surface represented by the `java.awt.Graphics` class. A graphics context contains contextual information about the drawing area and provides methods for performing drawing operations in it.

GUI (graphical user interface)

A GUI is a user interface constructed from graphical push buttons, text fields, pull-down menus, dialog boxes, and other standard interface components. In Java, GUIs are implemented with the classes in the `java.awt` package.

hashcode

An arbitrary-looking identifying number used as a kind of signature for an object. A hashcode stores an object in a hashtable. See **hashtable**.

hashtable

An object that is like a dictionary or an associative array. A hashtable stores and retrieves elements using key values called hashcodes. See **hashcode**.

hostname

The name given to an individual computer attached to the Internet.

HotJava

A WWW browser written in Java that is capable of downloading and running Java applets.

ImageConsumer

An interface for receiving image data from an image source. Image consumers are usually implemented by the awt.peer interface, so they are largely invisible to programmers.

ImageObserver

An interface in the java.awt.image package that receives information about the status of an image being constructed by a particular ImageConsumer.

ImageProducer

An interface in the java.awt.image package that represents an image source (i.e., a source of pixel data).

implements

The implements keyword is used in class declarations to indicate that the class implements the named interface or interfaces. The implements clause is optional in class declarations; if it appears, it must follow the extends clause (if any). If an implements clause appears in the declaration of a non-abstract class, every method from each specified interface must be implemented by the class or by one of its superclasses.

import

The import statement makes Java classes available to the current class under an abbreviated name. (Java classes are always available by their fully qualified name, assuming the appropriate class file can be found relative to the CLASS-PATH environment variable and that the class file is readable. import doesn't make the class available; it just saves typing and makes your code more legible.) Any number of import statements may appear in a Java program. They must appear, however, after the optional package statement at the top of the file, and before the first class or interface definition in the file.

inheritance

An important feature of object-oriented programming that involves defining a new object by changing or refining the behavior of an existing object. That is, an object implicitly contains all the non-private variables of its superclass and can invoke all the non-private methods of its superclass. Java supports single inheritance of classes and multiple inheritance of interfaces.

inner class

A class definition that is nested within another class. An inner class functions within the lexical scope of another class.

instance

An object. When a class is instantiated to produce an object, we say the object is an instance of the class.

instance method

A non-static method of a class. Such a method is passed an implicit this reference to the object that invoked it. See also **class method** and static.

instanceof

instanceof is a Java operator that returns true if the object on its left-hand side is an instance of the class (or implements the interface) specified on its right-hand side. instanceof returns false if the object is not an instance of the specified class or does not implement the specified interface. It also returns false if the specified object is null.

instance variable

A non-static variable of a class. Copies of such variables occur in every instance of the created class. See also **class variable** and static.

int

A primitive Java data type that's a 32-bit two's-complement signed number (in all implementations).

interface

The interface keyword is used to declare an interface. More generally, an interface defines a list of methods that enables a class to implement the interface itself.

internationalization

The process of making an application accessible to people who speak a variety of languages. Sometimes abbreviated I18N.

interpreter

The module that decodes and executes Java bytecode.

introspection

The process by which a Java Bean provides additional information about itself, supplementing information learned by reflection.

ISO 8859-1

An 8-bit character encoding standardized by the ISO. This encoding is also known as Latin-1 and contains characters from the Latin alphabet suitable for English and most languages of western Europe.

ISO 10646

A 4-byte character encoding that includes all of the world's national standard character encodings. Also known as UCS. The 2-byte Unicode character set maps to the range 0x00000000 to 0x0000FFFF of ISO 10646.

Java WorkShop

Sun's Web browser-based tool written in Java for the development of Java applications.

JavaBeans

A component architecture for Java. It is a way to build interoperable Java objects that can be manipulated easily in a visual application builder environment.

Java Beans

Individual Java Beans are Java classes that are built using certain design patterns and naming conventions.

JavaScript

A language, developed by Netscape, for creating dynamic Web pages. From a programmer's point of view, it's unrelated to Java, although some of its capabilities are similar. Internally, there may be a relationship, but even that is unclear.

JDBC

The standard Java API for talking to an SQL (structural query language) database.

JDK (Java Development Kit)

A package of software distributed by Sun Microsystems for Java developers. It includes the Java interpreter, Java classes, and Java development tools: compiler, debugger, disassembler, appletviewer, stub file generator, and documentation generator.

layout manager

An object that controls the arrangement of components within the display area of a container. The java.awt package contains a number of layout managers that provide different layout styles.

Latin-1

A nickname for ISO8859-1.

lightweight component

A Java component that has no native peer in the AWT.

local variable

A variable that is declared inside a single method. A local variable can be seen only by code within that method.

long

A primitive Java data type that's a 64-bit two's-complement signed number (in all implementations).

message digest

A long number computed from a message, used to determine whether the message's contents have been changed in any way. A change to a message's contents will change its message digest. It is almost impossible to create two similar messages with the same digest.

method

The object-oriented programming term for a function or procedure.

method overloading

Providing definitions of more than one method with the same name but with different argument lists or return values. When an overloaded method is called, the compiler determines which one is intended by examining the supplied argument types.

method overriding

Defining a method that exactly matches (i.e., same name, same argument types, and same return type) a method defined in a superclass. When an overridden method is invoked, the interpreter uses "dynamic method lookup" to determine which method definition is applicable to the current object.

modifier

A keyword placed before a class, variable, or method that alters the item's accessibility, behavior, or semantics. See abstract, final, native, private, private protected, protected, public, static, and synchronized.

Model/View/Controller (MVC) framework

A user-interface design that originated in Smalltalk. In MVC, the data for a display item is called the "model." A "view" displays a particular representation of the model, and a "controller" provides user interaction with both. Java incorporates many MVC concepts.

NaN (not-a-number)

This is a special value of the double and float data types that represents an undefined result of a mathematical operation, such as zero divided by zero.

native

native is a modifier that may be applied to method declarations. It indicates that the method is implemented (elsewhere) in C, or in some other platform-dependent fashion. A native method should have a semicolon instead of a body. A native method cannot be abstract, but all other method modifiers may be used with native methods.

native method

A method that is implemented in a native language on a host platform, rather than being implemented in Java. Native methods provide access to such resources as the network, the windowing system, and the host filesystem.

new

new is a unary operator that creates a new object or array (or raises an OutOfMemoryException if there is not enough memory available).

> null is a special value that indicates a variable doesn't refer to any object. The value null may be assigned to any class or interface variable. It cannot be cast to any integral type, and should not be considered equal to zero, as in C.

object

> An instance of a class. A class models a group of things; an object models a particular member of that group.

<OBJECT> **tag**

> A proposed HTML tag that may replace the widely used but nonstandard <APPLET> tag.

package

> The package statement specifies which package the code in the file is part of. Java code that is part of a particular package has access to all classes (public and non-public) in the package, and all non-private methods and fields in all those classes. When Java code is part of a named package, the compiled class file must be placed at the appropriate position in the CLASSPATH directory hierarchy before it can be accessed by the Java interpreter or other utilities. If the package statement is omitted from a file, the code in that file is part of an unnamed default package. This is convenient for small test programs, or during development because it means the code can be interpreted from the current directory.

<PARAM> **tag**

> HTML tag used within <applet> ... </applet> to specify a named parameter and string value to an applet within a Web page.

peer

> The actual implementation of a GUI component on a specific platform. Peer components reside within a Toolkit object. See Toolkit.

primitive type

> One of the Java data types: boolean, char, byte, short, int, long, float, double. Primitive types are manipulated, assigned, and passed to methods "by value" (i.e., the actual bytes of the data are copied). See also **reference type**.

private

> The private keyword is a visibility modifier that can be applied to method and field variables of classes. A private field is not visible outside its class definition.

protected

> The protected keyword is a visibility modifier that can be applied to method and field variables of classes. A protected field is visible only within its class, within subclasses, or within the package of which its class is a part. Note that subclasses in different packages can access only protected fields within themselves or within other objects that are subclasses; they cannot access protected fields within instances of the superclass.

protocol handler

> Software that describes and enables the use of a new protocol. A protocol handler consists of two classes: a StreamHandler and a URLConnection.

public

> The public keyword is a visibility modifier that can be applied to classes and interfaces and to the method and field variables of classes and interfaces. A public class or interface is visible everywhere. A non-public class or interface is visible only within its package. A public method or variable is visible everywhere its class is visible. When none of the private, protected, or public modifiers are specified, a field is visible only within the package of which its class is a part.

public key cryptography

> A cryptographic system that requires two keys, a public key and a private key. The private key can be used to decrypt messages encrypted with the corresponding public key, and vice versa. The public key can be made available to the public without compromising cryptographic security.

reference type

> Any object or array. Reference types are manipulated, assigned, and passed to methods "by reference." In other words, the underlying value is not copied; only a reference to it is. See also **primitive type**.

reflection

> The ability of a programming language to interact with structures of the language itself. Reflection in Java allows a Java program to examine class files at run-time to find out about their methods and variables, and to invoke methods or modify variables dynamically.

Remote Method Invocation (RMI)

> RMI is a native Java distributed object system. With RMI you can pass references to objects on remote hosts and invoke methods in them just as if they were local objects.

root

> The base of a hierarchy, such as a root class, whose descendants are subclasses. The `java.lang.Object` class serves as the root of the Java class hierarchy.

`SecurityManager`

> The Java class that defines the methods the system calls to check whether a certain operation is permitted in the current environment.

serialize

> To serialize means to put in order or make sequential. A serialized object is an object that has been packaged so that it can be stored or transmitted over the network. Serialized methods are methods that have been synchronized so that only one may be executing at a given time.

server

> The application that accepts a request for a conversation as part of a networked client/server application. See **client**.

shadow

> To declare a variable with the same name as a variable defined in a superclass. We say the variable "shadows" the superclass's variable. Use the super keyword to refer to the shadowed variable, or refer to it by casting the object to the type of the superclass.

signature

> A combination of a message's message digest, encrypted with the signer's private key, and the signer's certificate, attesting to the signer's identity. Someone receiving a signed message can get the signer's public key from the certificate, decrypt the encrypted message digest, and compare that result with the message digest computed from the signed message. If the two message digests agree, the recipient knows that the message has not been modified and that the signer is who he or she claims to be.

signed class

> A Java class (or Java archive) that has a signature attached. The signature allows the recipient to verify the class's origin and that it is unmodified. The recipient can therefore grant the class greater run-time privileges.

`short`

> A primitive Java data type that's a 16-bit two's-complement signed number (in all implementations).

socket

An interface that listens for connections from clients on a data port and connects the client data stream with the receiving application.

static

The static keyword is a modifier applied to method and variable declarations within a class. A static variable is also known as a class variable as opposed to non-static instance variables. While each instance of a class has a full set of its own instance variables, there is only one copy of each static class variable, regardless of the number of instances of the class (perhaps zero) that are created. static variables may be accessed by class name or through an instance. Non-static variables can be accessed only through an instance.

stream

A flow of data, or a channel of communication. All fundamental I/O in Java is based on streams.

String

A class used to represent textual information. The String class includes many methods for operating on string objects. Java overloads the + operator for string concatenation.

subclass

A class that extends another. The subclass inherits the public and protected methods and variables of its superclass. See extends.

super

The keyword super refers to the same value as this: the instance of the class for which the current method (these keywords are valid only within non-static methods) was invoked. While the type of this is the type of the class in which the method appears, the type of super is the type of the superclass of the class in which the method appears. super is usually used to refer to superclass variables shadowed by variables in the current class. Using super in this way is equivalent to casting this to the type of the superclass.

superclass

A class extended by some other class. The superclass's public and protected methods and variables are available to the subclass. See extends.

synchronized

The synchronized keyword is used in two related ways in Java: as a modifier and as a statement. First, it is a modifier applied to class or instance methods. It indicates that the method modifies the internal state of the class or the internal state of an instance of the class in a way that is not thread-safe. Before running a synchronized class method, Java obtains a lock on the class, to ensure that no other threads can modify the class concurrently. Before running a synchronized instance method, Java obtains a lock on the instance that invoked the method, ensuring that no other threads can modify the object at the same time.

Java also supports a synchronized statement that serves to specify a "critical section" of code. The synchronized keyword is followed by an expression in parentheses, and a statement or block of statements. The expression must evaluate to an object or array. Java obtains a lock on the specified object or array before executing the statements.

TCP

Transmission Control Protocol. A connection-oriented, reliable protocol. One of the protocols on which the Internet is based.

this

Within an instance method or constructor of a class, this refers to "this object"—the instance currently being operated on. It is useful to refer to an instance variable of the class that has been shadowed by a local variable or method argument. It is also useful to pass the current object as an argument to static methods or methods of other classes.

There is one additional use of this: when it appears as the first statement in a constructor method, it refers to one of the other constructors of the class.

thread

A single, independent stream of execution within a program. Since Java is a "multithreaded" programming language, more than one thread may be running within the Java interpreter at a time. Threads in Java are represented and controlled through the Thread object.

throw

The throw statement signals that an exceptional condition has occurred by throwing a specified exception object. This statement stops program execution and resumes it at the nearest containing catch statement that can handle the specified exception object. Note that the throw keyword must be followed by an exception object, not an exception class.

throws

The throws keyword is used in a method declaration to list the exceptions the method can throw. Any exceptions a method can raise that are not subclasses of Error or RuntimeException must either be caught within the method or declared in the method's throws clause.

Toolkit

The property of the Java API that defines the look and feel of the user interface on a specific platform.

try

The try keyword indicates a block of code to which subsequent catch and finally clauses apply. The try statement itself performs no special action. See the entries for catch and finally for more information on the try/catch/finally construct.

UCS (universal character set)

A synonym for ISO10646.

UDP

User Datagram Protocol. A connectionless unreliable protocol. UDP describes a network data connection based on datagrams with little packet control.

Unicode

A 16-bit character encoding that includes all of the world's commonly used alphabets and ideographic character sets in a "unified" form (i.e., a form from which duplications among national standards have been removed). ASCII and Latin-1 characters may be trivially mapped to Unicode characters. Java uses Unicode for its char and String types.

UTF-8 (UCS transformation format 8-bit form)

An encoding for Unicode characters (and more generally, UCS characters) commonly used for transmission and storage. It is a multibyte format in which different characters require different numbers of bytes to be represented.

vector

A dynamic array of elements.

verifier

A theorem prover that steps through the Java byte-code before it is run and makes sure that it is well-behaved. The byte-code verifier is the first line of defense in Java's security model.

Index

Symbols

& (ampersand)
    AND operator, 111
    dereference operator in C, 111
    && (conditional AND) operator, 111
    &= (assignment) operator, 111
* (asterisk)
    for importing classes, 174
    multiplication operator, 110
    reference operator in C, 111
    *= (assignment) operator, 111
@ (at sign) in doc comments, 99
\ (backslash) in paths, 284
! (bang)
    logical complement operator, 110
    not operator, 63
    != (inequality) operator, 111
| (vertical bar)
    OR operator, 111
    |= (assignment) operator, 111
    || (conditional OR) operator, 111
[] (index) operator, 124
^ (XOR) operator, 111
^= (assignment) operator, 111
, (comma) operator in C, 108, 111
{} curly braces
    for code blocks, 107
    for creating arrays, 55, 126
– (hyphen)
    in class names, 343
    subtraction operator, 111
    unary minus operator, 110

−− (decrement) operator, 110
−= (assignment) operator, 111
. (dot) notation, 112, 135
= (equal sign)
    assignment operator, 111
    equality operator, 111
    == (identity) operator, 53, 235
> (greater than) operator, 111
>= (greater than or equal) operator, 111
>> (rightwise shift) operator, 111
>>= (assignment) operator, 111
>>> (rightwise shift) operator, 111
>>>= (assignment) operator, 111
< (less than) operator, 111
<= (less than or equal) operator, 111
<< (leftwise shift) operator, 111, 508
<<= (assignment) operator, 111
( ) parentheses, 110
% (remainder) operator, 110
%= (assignment) operator, 111
+ (plus)
    addition operator, 111
    string concatenation operator, 9, 106,
        111, 233, 240
    unary plus operator, 110
    += (assignment) operator, 111
    ++ (increment) operator, 110
?: (conditional ternary) operator, 111
/ (slash)
    division operator, 110
    in paths, 284
    /= (assignment) operator, 111

About the Authors

Patrick Niemeyer (*pat@pat.net*) became involved with Oak while working at Southwestern Bell Technology Resources and experimenting with executable content in the TkWWW Web browser. He is currently an independent consultant in the areas of networking and distributed applications. Most recently, Pat has developed components of the network and application architecture at Edward Jones, Inc.

Joshua Peck (*jbpeck@icon-stl.net*) has worked as a World Wide Web designer and information systems consultant. He currently works as a senior systems analyst in the Advanced Technology Development Group at Maritz Performance Improvement Company. Josh holds a degree in engineering from Washington University in St. Louis.

Colophon

Our look is the result of reader comments, our own experimentation, and feedback from distribution channels. Distinctive covers complement our distinctive approach to technical topics, breathing personality and life into potentially dry subjects.

The cover of *Exploring Java* features a suitcase covered in luggage labels. Labels such as these were popular during the "Golden Age of Travel," a time that can roughly be placed between the 1880s and 1950s. The labels, which were given out by hotels, ocean-liners, railroads, and, after World War I, airlines, served two purposes. For the companies that gave them away, they were a portable and inexpensive way to advertise themselves around the world. For the travelers who affixed the labels to their luggage, they were also a form of advertisement; the colorful and exotic-looking labels told all who saw them that the person carrying that suitcase was well-traveled and adventurous and, of course, wealthy. With the introduction of the jet engine in the 1950s, traveling became less expensive and more convenient, and, therefore, more accessible to all. As being well-traveled became less a mark of distinction and as the world began to seem a smaller and smaller place, luggage labels became obsolete.

Edie Freedman designed the cover of this book, using an image from the CMCD PhotoCD Collection that she manipulated in Adobe Photoshop. The cover layout was produced with Quark XPress 3.3 using the Bodoni Black font from URW Software.

The inside layout was designed by Nancy Priest.

Whenever possible, our books use RepKover™, a durable and flexible lay-flat binding. If the page count exceeds RepKover's limit, perfect binding is used.

Text was prepared by Erik Ray in SGML DocBook 2.4 DTD. The print version of this book was created by translating the SGML source into a set of gtroff macros using a filter developed at ORA by Norman Walsh. Steve Talbott designed and wrote the underlying macro set on the basis of the GNU troff -gs macros; Lenny Muellner adapted them to SGML and implemented the book design. The GNU groff text formatter version 1.09 was used to generate PostScript output. The heading font is Bodoni BT; the text font is New Baskerville. The illustrations that appear in the book were created in Macromedia Freehand 5.0 by Chris Reilley and Rob Romano. This colophon was written by Clairemarie Fisher O'Leary.

 # More Titles from O'Reilly

Java Programming

Java in a Nutshell, DELUXE EDITION

By David Flanagan, et al.
1st Edition June 1997
628 pages, includes CD-ROM and book
ISBN 1-56592-304-9

Java in a Nutshell, Deluxe Edition, is a Java programmer's dream come true in one small package. The heart of this Deluxe Edition is the Java Reference Library on CD-ROM, which brings together five volumes for Java developers and programmers, linking related info across books. It includes: *Exploring Java, 2nd Edition*; *Java Language Reference, 2nd Edition*; *Java Fundamental Classes Reference*; *Java AWT Reference*; and *Java in a Nutshell, 2nd Edition*, included both on the CD-ROM and in a companion desktop edition. *Java in a Nutshell, Deluxe Edition*, is an indispensable resource for anyone doing serious programming with Java 1.1.

The Java Reference Library alone is also available by subscription on the World Wide Web. Please see http://www.oreilly.com/catalog/javarlw/ for details. The electronic text on the Web and on the CD is fully searchable and includes a complete index to all five volumes as well as the sample code found in the print volumes. A web browser that supports HTML 3.2, Java, and Javascript, such as Netscape 3.0 or Internet Explorer 3.0, is required. (The CD-ROM is readable on all UNIX and Windows platforms. However, current implementations of the Java Virtual Machine for the Mac do not support the Java search applet in the CD-ROM.)

Java Cryptography

By Jonathan B. Knudsen
1st Edition May 1998
362 pages, ISBN 1-56592-402-9

Java Cryptography teaches you how to write secure programs using Java's cryptographic tools. It includes thorough discussions of the java.security package and the Java Cryptography Extensions (JCE),showing you how to use security providers and even implement your own provider. It discusses authentication, key management, public and private key encryption, and includes a secure talk application that encrypts all data sent over the network. If you work with sensitive data, you'll find this book indispensable.

Java Security

By Scott Oaks
1st Edition May 1998
474 pages, ISBN 1-56592-403-7

This essential Java 1.2 book covers Java's security mechanisms and teaches you how to work with them. It discusses class loaders, security managers, access lists, digital signatures, and authentication and shows how to use these to create and enforce your own security policy.

Java Virtual Machine

By Jon Meyer & Troy Downing
1st Edition March 1997
452 pages, includes diskette
ISBN 1-56592-194-1

This book is a comprehensive programming guide for the Java Virtual Machine (JVM). It gives readers a strong overview and reference of the JVM so that they may create their own implementations of the JVM or write their own compilers that create Java object code. A Java assembler is provided with the book, so the examples can all be compiled and executed.

Developing Java Beans

By Robert Englander
1st Edition June 1997
316 pages, ISBN 1-56592-289-1

Developing Java Beans is a complete introduction to Java's component architecture. It describes how to write Beans, which are software components that can be used in visual programming environments. This book discusses event adapters, serialization, introspection, property editors, and customizers, and shows how to use Beans within ActiveX controls.

Java Programming

Java Examples in a Nutshell

By David Flanagan
1st Edition September 1997
414 pages, ISBN 1-56592-371-5

From the author of *Java in a Nutshell*, this companion book is chock full of practical real-world programming examples to help novice Java programmers and experts alike explore what's possible with Java 1.1. If you learn best by example, this is the book for you.

Java Threads

By Scott Oaks and Henry Wong
1st Edition January 1997
268 pages, ISBN 1-56592-216-6

With this book, you'll learn how to take full advantage of Java's thread facilities: where to use threads to increase efficiency, how to use them effectively, and how to avoid common mistakes like deadlock and race conditions. Covers Java 1.1.

Java Language Reference, Second Edition

By Mark Grand
2nd Edition July 1997
492 pages, ISBN 1-56592-326-X

This book helps you understand the subtle nuances of Java—from the definition of data types to the syntax of expressions and control structures—so you can ensure your programs run exactly as expected. The second edition covers the new language features that have been added in Java 1.1, such as inner classes, class literals, and instance initializers.

Java Fundamental Classes Reference

By Mark Grand & Jonathan Knudsen
1st Edition May 1997
1114 pages, ISBN 1-56592-241-7

The *Java Fundamental Classes Reference* provides complete reference documentation on the core Java 1.1 classes that comprise the *java.lang, java.io, java.net, java.util, java.text, java.math, java.lang.reflect*, and *java.util.zip* packages. Part of O'Reilly's Java documentation series, this edition describes Version 1.1 of the Java Development Kit. It includes easy-to-use reference material and provides lots of sample code to help you learn by example.

Netscape IFC in a Nutshell

By Dean Petrich with David Flanagan
1st Edition August 1997
370 pages, ISBN 1-56592-343-X

This desktop quick reference and programmer's guide is all the documentation programmers need to start creating highly customizable graphical user interfaces with the Internet Foundation Classes (IFC), Version 1.1. The IFC is a Java class library freely available from Netscape. It is also bundled with Communicator, making it the preferred development environment for the Navigator 4.0 web browser. Master the IFC now for a head start on the forthcoming Java Foundation Classes (JFC).

Java Programming

Java Network Programming

By Elliotte Rusty Harold
1st Edition February 1997
442 pages, ISBN 1-56592-227-1

The network is the soul of Java. Most of what is new and exciting about Java centers around the potential for new kinds of dynamic, networked applications. *Java Network Programming* teaches you to work with Sockets, write network clients and servers, and gives you an advanced look at the new areas like multicasting, using the server API, and RMI. Covers Java 1.1.

Java in a Nutshell, Second Edition

By David Flanagan
2nd Edition May 1997
628 pages, ISBN 1-56592-262-X

This second edition of the bestselling Java book describes all the classes in the Java 1.1 API, with the exception of the still-evolving Enterprise APIs. And it still has all the great features that have made this the Java book most often recommended on the Internet: practical real-world examples and compact reference information. It's the only quick reference you'll need.

Java Native Methods

By Alligator Descartes
1st Edition November 1998 (est.)
300 pages (est.), ISBN 1-56592-345-6

Although Java offers the promise of platform-independent programming, there are situations where you may still need to use native C or C++code compiled for a particular platform. Maybe you have to tie some legacy code into a Java application. Or maybe you want to implement some computer-intensive methods for a performance-critical application in native code. *Java Native Methods* tells you everything you need to know to get your native code working with Java, using either Sun's Java Native Interface (JNI) or Microsoft's Raw Native Interface (RNI).

Database Programming with JDBC and Java

By George Reese
1st Edition June 1997
240 pages, ISBN 1-56592-270-0

Database Programming with JDBC and Java describes the standard Java interfaces that make portable, object-oriented access to relational databases possible and offers a robust model for writing applications that are easy to maintain. It introduces the JDBC and RMI packages and includes a set of patterns that separate the functions of the Java application and facilitate the growth and maintenance of your application.

Java AWT Reference

By John Zukowski
1st Edition April 1997
1074 pages, ISBN 1-56592-240-9

The *Java AWT Reference* provides complete reference documentation on the Abstract Window Toolkit (AWT), a large collection of classes for building graphical user interfaces in Java. Part of O'Reilly's Java documentation series, this edition describes both Version 1.0.2 and Version 1.1 of the Java Development Kit, includes easy-to-use reference material on every AWT class, and provides lots of sample code.

Java Distributed Computing

By Jim Farley
1st Edition January 1998
384 pages, ISBN 1-56592-206-9

Java Distributed Computing offers a general introduction to distributed computing, meaning programs that run on two or more systems. It focuses primarily on how to structure and write distributed applications and, therefore, discusses issues like designing protocols, security, working with databases, and dealing with low bandwidth situations.

Web Programming

Web Client Programming with Perl

By Clinton Wong
1st Edition March 1997
228 pages, ISBN 1-56592-214-X

Web Client Programming with Perl shows
you how to extend scripting skills to the
Web. This book teaches you the basics of
how browsers communicate with servers
and how to write your own customized
web clients to automate common tasks.
It is intended for those who are motivated to develop software
that offers a more flexible and dynamic response than a standard
web browser.

HTML: The Definitive Guide, 2nd Edition

By Chuck Musciano & Bill Kennedy
2nd Edition May 1997
552 pages, ISBN 1-56592-235-2

This complete guide is chock full of
examples, sample code, and practical,
hands-on advice to help you create truly
effective web pages and master advanced
features. Learn how to insert images and
other multimedia elements, create useful
links and searchable documents, use Netscape extensions, design
great forms, and lots more. The second edition covers the most
up-to-date version of the HTML standard (HTML version 3.2),
Netscape 4.0 and Internet Explorer 3.0, plus all the common
extensions.

Dynamic HTML: The Definitive Reference

By Danny Goodman
1st Edition July 1998
1088 pages, ISBN 1-56592-494-0

Dynamic HTML: The Definitive Reference
is an indispensable compendium for Web
content developers. It contains complete
reference material for all of the HTML tags,
CSS style attributes, browser document
objects, and JavaScript objects supported
by the various standards and the latest versions of Netscape
Navigator and Microsoft Internet Explorer.

Frontier: The Definitive Guide

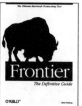

By Matt Neuburg
1st Edition February 1998
618 pages, 1-56592-383-9

This definitive guide is the first book devoted
exclusively to teaching and documenting
Userland Frontier, a powerful scripting
environment for web site management
and system level scripting. Packed with
examples, advice, tricks, and tips, Frontier:
The Definitive Guide teaches you Frontier from the ground up. Learn
how to automate repetitive processes, control remote computers
across a network, beef up your web site by generating hundreds of
related web pages automatically, and more. Covers Frontier 4.2.3
for the Macintosh.

WebMaster in a Nutshell

By Stephen Spainhour & Valerie Quercia
1st Edition October 1996
374 pages, ISBN 1-56592-229-8

Web content providers and administrators
have many sources for information, both in
print and online. WebMaster in a Nutshell
puts it all together in one slim volume for
easy desktop access. This quick reference
covers HTML, CGI, JavaScript, Perl, HTTP,
and server configuration.

Information Architecture
for the World Wide Web

By Louis Rosenfeld & Peter Morville
1st Edition January 1998
226 pages, ISBN 1-56592-282-4

Learn how to merge aesthetics and
mechanics to design web sites that "work."
This book shows how to apply principles
of architecture and library science to
design cohesive web sites and intranets
that are easy to use, manage, and expand.
Covers building complex sites, hierarchy design and organization,
and techniques to make your site easier to search. For webmas-
ters, designers, and administrators.

Web Programming

CGI Programming on the World Wide Web

By Shishir Gundavaram
1st Edition March 1996
450 pages, ISBN 1-56592-168-2

This book offers a comprehensive explanation of CGI and related techniques for people who hold on to the dream of providing their own information servers on the Web. It starts at the beginning, explaining the value of CGI and how it works, then moves swiftly into the subtle details of programming.

JavaScript: The Definitive Guide, 3rd Edition

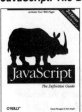

By David Flanagan & Dan Shafer
3rd Edition June 1998
800 pages, ISBN 1-56592-392-8

This third edition of the definitive reference to JavaScript covers the latest version of the language, JavaScript 1.2, as supported by Netscape Navigator 4.0. JavaScript, which is being standardized under the name ECMAScript, is a scripting language that can be embedded directly in HTML to give web pages programming-language capabilities.

Learning VBScript

By Paul Lomax
1st Edition July 1997
616 pages, includes CD-ROM
ISBN 1-56592-247-6

This definitive guide shows web developers how to take full advantage of client-side scripting with the VBScript language. In addition to basic language features, it covers the Internet Explorer object model and discusses techniques for client-side scripting, like adding ActiveX controls to a web page or validating data before sending to the server. Includes CD-ROM with over 170 code samples.

WebMaster in a Nutshell, Deluxe Edition

By O'Reilly & Associates, Inc.
1st Edition September 1997
374 pages, includes CD-ROM & book
ISBN 1-56592-305-7

The Deluxe Edition of *WebMaster in a Nutshell* is a complete library for web programmers. It features the Web Developer's Library, a CD-ROM containing the electronic text of five popular O'Reilly titles: *HTML: The Definitive Guide*, 2nd Edition; *JavaScript: The Definitive Guide*, 2nd Edition; *CGI Programming on the World Wide Web*; *Programming Perl*, 2nd Edition—the classic "camel book"; and *WebMaster in a Nutshell*, which is also included in a companion desktop edition.

Web Authoring and Design

Designing for the Web: Getting Started in a New Medium

By Jennifer Niederst
with Edie Freedman
1st Edition April 1996
180 pages, ISBN 1-56592-165-8

Designing for the Web gives you the basics you need to hit the ground running. Although geared toward designers, it covers information and techniques useful to anyone who wants to put graphics online. It explains how to work with HTML documents from a designer's point of view, outlines special problems with presenting information online, and walks through incorporating images into web pages, with emphasis on resolution and improving efficiency.

O'REILLY™

TO ORDER: *800-998-9938* • *order@oreilly.com* • *http://www.oreilly.com/*
OUR PRODUCTS ARE AVAILABLE AT A BOOKSTORE OR SOFTWARE STORE NEAR YOU.
FOR INFORMATION: *800-998-9938* • *707-829-0515* • *info@oreilly.com*

Web Authoring and Design

Designing with JavaScript

By Nick Heinle
1st Edition September 1997
256 pages, Includes CD-ROM
ISBN 1-56592-300-6

Written by the author of the "JavaScript Tip of the Week" web site, this new Web Review Studio book focuses on the most useful and applicable scripts for making truly interactive, engaging web sites. You'll not only have quick access to the scripts you need, you'll finally understand why the scripts work, how to alter the scripts to get the effects you want, and, ultimately, how to write your own groundbreaking scripts from scratch.

GIF Animation Studio

By Richard Koman
1st Edition October 1996
184 pages, Includes CD-ROM
ISBN 1-56592-230-1

GIF animation is bringing the Web to life—without plug-ins, Java programming, or expensive authoring tools. This book details the major GIF animation programs, profiles work by leading designers (including John Hersey, Razorfish, Henrik Drescher, and Erik Josowitz), and documents advanced animation techniques. A CD-ROM includes freeware and shareware authoring programs, demo versions of commercial software, and the actual animation files described in the book. GIF Animation Studio is the first release in the new Web Review Studio series.

Shockwave Studio

By Bob Schmitt
1st Edition March 1997
200 pages, Includes CD-ROM
ISBN 1-56592-231-X

This book, the second title in the new Web Review Studio series, shows how to create compelling and functional Shockwave movies for web sites. The author focuses on actual Shockwave movies, showing how the movies were created. The book takes users from creating simple time-based Shockwave animations through writing complex logical operations that take full advantage of Director's power. The CD-ROM includes a demo version of Director and other software sample files.

Photoshop for the Web

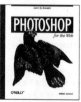

By Mikkel Aaland
1st Edition April 1998
238 pages, ISBN 1-56592-350-2

Photoshop for the Web shows you how to use the world's most popular imaging software to create Web graphics and images that look great and download blazingly fast. The book is crammed full of step-by-step examples and real-world solutions from some of the country's hottest Web producers, including HotWired, c\net, Discovery Online, Second Story, SFGate, and more than 20 others.

Designing with Animation

By J. Scott Hamlin
1st Edition December 1998 (est.)
250 pages (est.), ISBN 1-56592-441-X

Designing with Animation treats the subject of Web animation with a level of sophistication that both meets the needs of today's demanding professionals and pushes the envelope for amateur animators. Topics include GIF animation, advanced animation techniques, seamless integration of animation, creative interactive animation with Java, JavaScript, and Macromedia Flash, vector-based and 3D animation, adding sound to animation, and animation techniques with Photoshop.

Web Navigation: Designing the User Experience

By Jennifer Fleming
1st Edition September 1998 (est.)
300 pages (est.), Includes CD-ROM
ISBN 1-56592-351-0

Web Navigation: Designing the User Experience offers the first in-depth look at designing web site navigation. Through case studies and designer interviews, a variety of approaches to navigation issues are explored. The book focuses on designing by purpose, with chapters on entertainment, shopping, identity, learning, information, and community sites. The accompanying CD-ROM includes a tour of selected sites, a "netography," and trial versions of popular software tools.

How to stay in touch with O'Reilly

1. Visit Our Award-Winning Web Site
http://www.oreilly.com/

★ "Top 100 Sites on the Web" — *PC Magazine*
★ "Top 5% Web sites" — *Point Communications*
★ "3-Star site" — *The McKinley Group*

Our web site contains a library of comprehensive product information (including book excerpts and tables of contents), downloadable software, background articles, interviews with technology leaders, links to relevant sites, book cover art, and more. File us in your Bookmarks or Hotlist!

2. Join Our Email Mailing Lists
New Product Releases
To receive automatic email with brief descriptions of all new O'Reilly products as they are released, send email to:
listproc@online.oreilly.com
Put the following information in the first line of your message (*not* in the Subject field):
subscribe oreilly-news

O'Reilly Events
If you'd also like us to send information about trade show events, special promotions, and other O'Reilly events, send email to:
listproc@online.oreilly.com
Put the following information in the first line of your message (*not* in the Subject field):
subscribe oreilly-events

3. Get Examples from Our Books via FTP

There are two ways to access an archive of example files from our books:

Regular FTP
- ftp to:
  ftp.oreilly.com
  (login: anonymous
  password: your email address)
- Point your web browser to:
  ftp://ftp.oreilly.com/

FTPMAIL
- Send an email message to:
  ftpmail@online.oreilly.com
  (Write "help" in the message body)

4. Contact Us via Email
order@oreilly.com
To place a book or software order online. Good for North American and international customers.

subscriptions@oreilly.com
To place an order for any of our newsletters or periodicals.

books@oreilly.com
General questions about any of our books.

software@oreilly.com
For general questions and product information about our software. Check out O'Reilly Software Online at **http://software.oreilly.com/** for software and technical support information. Registered O'Reilly software users send your questions to: **website-support@oreilly.com**

cs@oreilly.com
For answers to problems regarding your order or our products.

booktech@oreilly.com
For book content technical questions or corrections.

proposals@oreilly.com
To submit new book or software proposals to our editors and product managers.

international@oreilly.com
For information about our international distributors or translation queries. For a list of our distributors outside of North America check out:
http://www.oreilly.com/www/order/country.html

O'Reilly & Associates, Inc.
101 Morris Street, Sebastopol, CA 95472 USA
TEL 707-829-0515 or 800-998-9938
(6am to 5pm PST)
FAX 707-829-0104

Titles from O'Reilly

WEB

Advanced Perl Programming
Apache: The Definitive Guide
Building Your Own Web Conferences
Building Your Own Website™
CGI Programming
  for the World Wide Web
Designing for the Web
Designing Sound for the Web
Designing with Animation
Designing with JavaScript
Dynamic HTML:
  The Definitive Reference
Frontier: The Definitive Guide
Gif Animation Studio
HTML: The Definitive Guide,
  2nd Edition
Information Architecture
  for the World Wide Web
JavaScript: The Definitive Guide,
  3nd Edition
Mastering Regular Expressions
Netscape IFC in a Nutshell
Photoshop for the Web
Shockwave Studio
WebMaster in a Nutshell
WebMaster in a Nutshell,
  Deluxe Edition
Web Navigation:
  Designing the User Experience
Web Security & Commerce

PERL

Learning Perl, 2nd Edition
Learning Perl for Win32 Systems
Perl5 Desktop Reference
Perl Cookbook
Perl in a Nutshell
Perl Resource Kit—UNIX Edition
Perl Resource Kit—Win32 Edition
Programming Perl, 2nd Edition
Web Client Programming with Perl

JAVA SERIES

Database Programming with
  JDBC and Java
Developing Java Beans
Exploring Java, 2nd Edition
Java AWT Reference
Java Cryptography
Java Distributed Computing
Java Examples in a Nutshell
Java Fundamental Classes Reference
Java in a Nutshell, 2nd Edition
Java in a Nutshell, Deluxe Edition
Java Language Reference, 2nd Edition
Java Native Methods
Java Network Programming
Java Security
Java Threads
Java Virtual Machine

SYSTEM ADMINISTRATION

Building Internet Firewalls
Computer Crime:
  A Crimefighter's Handbook
Computer Security Basics
DNS and BIND, 2nd Edition
Essential System Administration,
  2nd Edition
Essential WindowsNT
  System Administration
Getting Connected:
  The Internet at 56K and Up
High Performance Computing,
  2nd Edition
Linux Network Administrator's Guide
Managing Internet Information
  Services, 2nd Edition
Managing IP Networks
  with Cisco Routers
Managing Mailing Lists
Managing NFS and NIS
Managing the WinNT Registry
Managing Usenet
MCSE: The Core Exams in a Nutshell
MCSE: The Electives in a Nutshell
Networking Personal Computers
  with TCP/IP
PalmPilot: The Ultimate Guide
Practical UNIX & Internet Security,
  2nd Edition
PGP: Pretty Good Privacy
Protecting Networks with SATAN
sendmail, 2nd Edition
sendmail Desktop Reference
System Performance Tuning
TCP/IP Network Administration,
  2nd Edition
termcap & terminfo
Using & Managing PPP
Using & Managing UUCP
Virtual Private Networks
Volume 8: X Window System
  Administrator's Guide
Web Security & Commerce
WindowsNT Backup & Restore
WindowsNT Desktop Reference
WindowsNT in a Nutshell
WindowsNT Server 4.0
  for Netware Administrators
WindowsNT SNMP
WindowsNT User Administration

GRAPHICS & MULTIMEDIA

Director in a Nutshell
Photoshop in a Nutshell
QuarkXPress in a Nutshell

UNIX

Exploring Expect
Learning VBScript
Learning GNU Emacs, 2nd Edition
Learning the bash Shell, 2nd Edition
Learning the Korn Shell
Learning the UNIX Operating System,
  4th Edition
Learning the vi Editor, 5th Edition
Linux Device Drivers
Linux in a Nutshell
Linux Multimedia Guide
Running Linux, 2nd Edition
SCO UNIX in a Nutshell
sed & awk, 2nd Edition
Tcl/Tk Tools
UNIX in a Nutshell, Deluxe Edition
UNIX in a Nutshell, System V Edition
UNIX Power Tools, 2nd Edition
Using csh & tsch
What You Need To Know:
  When You Can't Find Your
  UNIX System Administrator
Writing GNU Emacs Extensions

WINDOWS

Access Database Design
  and Programming
Developing Windows Error Messages
Inside the Windows 95 File System
Inside the Windows 95 Registry
VB/VBA in a Nutshell: The Languages
Win32 Multithreaded Programming
Windows95 in a Nutshell
Windows NT File System Internals
Windows NT in a Nutshell

USING THE INTERNET

AOL in a Nutshell
Bandits on the Information
  Superhighway
Internet in a Nutshell
Smileys
The Whole Internet for Windows95
The Whole Internet:
  The Next Generation
The Whole Internet
  User's Guide & Catalog

ANNOYANCES

Excel97 Annoyances
Office97 Annoyances
Outlook Annoyances
Windows97 Annoyances
Word97 Annoyances

SONGLINE GUIDES

NetLaw	NetResearch
NetLearning	NetSuccess
NetLessons	NetTravel

PROGRAMMING

Advanced Oracle PL/SQL
  Programming with Packages
Applying RCS and SCCS
BE Developer's Guide
BE Advanced Topics
C++: The Core Language
Checking C Programs with lint
Encyclopedia of Graphics File
  Formats, 2nd Edition
Guide to Writing DCE Applications
lex & yacc, 2nd Edition
Managing Projects with make
Mastering Oracle Power Objects
Oracle8 Design Tips
Oracle Built-in Packages
Oracle Design
Oracle Performance Tuning,
  2nd Edition
Oracle PL/SQL Programming,
  2nd Edition
Oracle Scripts
Porting UNIX Software
POSIX Programmer's Guide
POSIX.4: Programming
  for the Real World
Power Programming with RPC
Practical C Programming, 3rd Edition
Practical C++ Programming
Programming Python
Programming with curses
Programming with GNU Software
Pthreads Programming
Software Portability with imake,
  2nd Edition
Understanding DCE
UNIX Systems Programming for SVR4

X PROGRAMMING

Vol. 0: X Protocol Reference Manual
Vol. 1: Xlib Programming Manual
Vol. 2: Xlib Reference Manual
Vol. 3M: X Window System User's
  Guide, Motif Edition
Vol. 4M: X Toolkit Intrinsics
  Programming Manual,
  Motif Edition
Vol. 5: X Toolkit Intrinsics Reference
  Manual
Vol. 6A: Motif Programming Manual
Vol. 6B: Motif Reference Manual
Vol. 8 : X Window System
  Administrator's Guide

SOFTWARE

Building Your Own WebSite™
Building Your Own Web Conference
WebBoard™ 3.0
WebSite Professional™ 2.0
PolyForm™

O'REILLY™

International Distributors

UK, EUROPE, MIDDLE EAST AND NORTHERN AFRICA (EXCEPT FRANCE, GERMANY, SWITZERLAND, & AUSTRIA)

INQUIRIES

International Thomson Publishing Europe
Berkshire House
168-173 High Holborn
London WC1V 7AA
United Kingdom
Telephone: 44-171-497-1422
Fax: 44-171-497-1426
Email: itpint@itps.co.uk

ORDERS

International Thomson Publishing Services, Ltd.
Cheriton House, North Way
Andover, Hampshire SP10 5BE
United Kingdom
Telephone: 44-264-342-832 (UK)
Telephone: 44-264-342-806 (outside UK)
Fax: 44-264-364418 (UK)
Fax: 44-264-342761 (outside UK)
UK & Eire orders: itpuk@itps.co.uk
International orders: itpint@itps.co.uk

FRANCE

Editions Eyrolles
61 bd Saint-Germain
75240 Paris Cedex 05
France
Fax: 33-01-44-41-11-44

FRENCH LANGUAGE BOOKS

All countries except Canada
Telephone: 33-01-44-41-46-16
Email: geodif@eyrolles.com
English language books
Telephone: 33-01-44-41-11-87
Email: distribution@eyrolles.com

GERMANY, SWITZERLAND, AND AUSTRIA

INQUIRIES

O'Reilly Verlag
Balthasarstr. 81
D-50670 Köln
Germany
Telephone: 49-221-97-31-60-0
Fax: 49-221-97-31-60-8
Email: anfragen@oreilly.de

ORDERS

International Thomson Publishing
Königswinterer Straße 418
53227 Bonn, Germany
Telephone: 49-228-97024 0
Fax: 49-228-441342
Email: order@oreilly.de

JAPAN

O'Reilly Japan, Inc.
Kiyoshige Building 2F
12-Banchi, Sanei-cho
Shinjuku-ku
Tokyo 160-0008 Japan
Telephone: 81-3-3356-5227
Fax: 81-3-3356-5261
Email: kenji@oreilly.com

INDIA

Computer Bookshop (India) PVT. Ltd.
190 Dr. D.N. Road, Fort
Bombay 400 001 India
Telephone: 91-22-207-0989
Fax: 91-22-262-3551
Email: cbsbom@giasbm01.vsnl.net.in

HONG KONG

City Discount Subscription Service Ltd.
Unit D, 3rd Floor, Yan's Tower
27 Wong Chuk Hang Road
Aberdeen, Hong Kong
Telephone: 852-2580-3539
Fax: 852-2580-6463
Email: citydis@ppn.com.hk

KOREA

Hanbit Media, Inc.
Sonyoung Bldg. 202
Yeksam-dong 736-36
Kangnam-ku
Seoul, Korea
Telephone: 822-554-9610
Fax: 822-556-0363
Email: hant93@chollian.dacom.co.kr

SINGAPORE, MALAYSIA, AND THAILAND

Addison Wesley Longman Singapore PTE Ltd.
25 First Lok Yang Road
Singapore 629734
Telephone: 65-268-2666
Fax: 65-268-7023
Email: daniel@longman.com.sg

PHILIPPINES

Mutual Books, Inc.
429-D Shaw Boulevard
Mandaluyong City, Metro
Manila, Philippines
Telephone: 632-725-7538
Fax: 632-721-3056
Email: mbikikog@mnl.sequel.net

CHINA

Ron's DataCom Co., Ltd.
79 Dongwu Avenue
Dongxihu District
Wuhan 430040
China
Telephone: 86-27-83892568
Fax: 86-27-83222108
Email: hongfeng@public.wh.hb.cn

ALL OTHER ASIAN COUNTRIES

O'Reilly & Associates, Inc.
101 Morris Street
Sebastopol, CA 95472 USA
Telephone: 707-829-0515
Fax: 707-829-0104
Email: order@oreilly.com

AUSTRALIA

WoodsLane Pty. Ltd.
7/5 Vuko Place, Warriewood NSW 2102
P.O. Box 935
Mona Vale NSW 2103
Australia
Telephone: 61-2-9970-5111
Fax: 61-2-9970-5002
Email: info@woodslane.com.au

NEW ZEALAND

Woodslane New Zealand Ltd.
21 Cooks Street (P.O. Box 575)
Waganui, New Zealand
Telephone: 64-6-347-6543
Fax: 64-6-345-4840
Email: info@woodslane.com.au

THE AMERICAS

McGraw-Hill Interamericana Editores, S.A. de C.V.
Cedro No. 512
Col. Atlampa 06450
Mexico, D.F.
Telephone: 52-5-541-3155
Fax: 52-5-541-4913
Email: mcgraw-hill@infosel.net.mx

SOUTH AFRICA

International Thomson Publishing South Africa
Building 18, Constantia Park
138 Sixteenth Road
P.O. Box 2459
Halfway House, 1685 South Africa
Telephone: 27-11-805-4819
Fax: 27-11-805-3648

O'REILLY™

O'REILLY™

O'Reilly & Associates, Inc.
101 Morris Street
Sebastopol, CA 95472-9902
1-800-998-9938

Visit us online at:
http://www.ora.com/
orders@ora.com

O'REILLY WOULD LIKE TO HEAR FROM YOU

Which book did this card come from?

_____

Where did you buy this book?
- ❏ Bookstore   ❏ Computer Store
- ❏ Direct from O'Reilly   ❏ Class/seminar
- ❏ Bundled with hardware/software
- ❏ Other _____

What operating system do you use?
- ❏ UNIX   ❏ Macintosh
- ❏ Windows NT   ❏ PC(Windows/DOS)
- ❏ Other _____

What is your job description?
- ❏ System Administrator   ❏ Programmer
- ❏ Network Administrator   ❏ Educator/Teacher
- ❏ Web Developer
- ❏ Other _____

❏ Please send me O'Reilly's catalog, containing a complete listing of O'Reilly books and software.

Name _____   Company/Organization _____

Address _____

City _____   State _____   Zip/Postal Code _____   Country _____

Telephone _____   Internet or other email address (specify network) _____

Nineteenth century wood engraving
of a bear from the O'Reilly &
Associates Nutshell Handbook®
Using & Managing UUCP.

POST CARD

BUSINESS REPLY MAIL

FIRST CLASS MAIL   PERMIT NO. 80   SEBASTOPOL, CA

Postage will be paid by addressee

O'Reilly & Associates, Inc.
101 Morris Street
Sebastopol, CA 95472-9902